Language and State

A Theory of the Progress of Civilization

Second Edition

Xing Yu

 FriesenPress

One Printers Way
Altona, MB R0G 0B0
Canada

www.friesenpress.com

Copyright © 2022 by Xing Yu
Second Edition — 2022

ISBN
978-1-03-912517-9 (Hardcover)
978-1-03-912516-2 (Paperback)
978-1-03-912518-6 (eBook)

1. LANGUAGE ARTS & DISCIPLINES, LINGUISTICS, SOCIOLINGUISTICS

Distributed to the trade by The Ingram Book Company

To All Those Who Seek the Progress of Civilization

Table of Contents

Prologue

This monograph is a study of the correlation between language and state. It is an attempt to study the fundamental role played by language first and then to study how language creates a condition for the genesis and growth of the state. On one hand, language is defined as a system composed of signs created by humans for communication and it is considered a basic element of the evolution from the primitive society to the civilized one and a basis for the growth of the state. On the other hand, the state is defined as a community which comprises a group of people, a territory and a government with sovereignty and it is considered the result of the evolution of human society due to the role played by language. This is because using language, spoken or written, is only significant of creating a basic condition for setting up a long-term evolution from the tribe to the state. My reasoning is that, since the dissolution of tribes or communal families in favor of the state, humans have become isolated as individuals outside their core families characteristic of monogamy. Under these circumstances, what connects all is language. Thus, language is to the state what kinship is to the tribe. In the beginning, humans are tribal people. They perform communication by way of behavioral display. For example, they smile or bow or wave their hands, all forms of communication. They may even dance, another form of communication. I consider such behavior non-verbal behavior, and such behavior is the original medium. By "medium," I mean any being or form that creates a condition for communication. As behavior is the medium in communication over short distances, such a limited method of communication only enables humans to form a small community. Kinship is the essential linkage in such an environment. The birth of language is a revolution. Language enables humans to create various media. Media further play a part in extending the distance of mutual communication. Thus, spoken, or written, communication extends the distance of communication. In terms of spoken communication, people function as media in the process of communication because such a process of communication is often in the form of human-chain linguistic communication. In terms of written communication, people use materials. They used to use clay tablet, papyrus, and parchment. Today they still use stone, metal object and paper. They are media. The use of media extends the time span and the reach of communication. Humans communicate over a long stretch of time and on a large scale. The exploitation of media in communication results in a long-term increase in the size of their community, leading inevitably to the formation of the state and the dissolution of the tribe. Thus, interpreting the role of language in the formation and growth of the state may allow us to give a true systematic description of the formation and growth of the state, a job that may further enable us to create a new theory about the state.

Interpreting the origin of the society, the philosophers of the past mention the role of language in the formation of the society in their writings. They hold that language enables people to exchange feelings, to impart thoughts or ideas, and even to chronicle history. They insist that humans form their society because of language. For example, Aristotle points out that language is the peculiarity of humans. He writes that "a human being is more of a political animal than is any bee or than are any of those animals that live in herds." He indicates that humans can exchange feelings and present their views about justice and injustice due to the use of language.[1] Thomas Hobbes also mentions language that plays a role in the formation of the society. He writes that:

> [T]he most notable and profitable invention of all other, was that of Speech, consisting of *Names* or *Appellations*, and their Connexion; whereby men register their Thoughts; recall them when they are past; and also declare them one to another for mutuall utility and conversation; without which, there had been amongst men, neither Commonwealth, nor Society, nor Contract, nor Peace, no more than amongst Lyons, Bears, and Wolves.[2]

They may conceive of the role of language in the formation of the society instead of the state. They only believe that humans associate together due to their shared use of language. Yet it is arguable that humans may also associate together to form a society like some social animals even if they have neither written nor spoken language. Their view cannot give clarity to the origin of the state. This view may merely show that language serves as a foundation for humans to form their society, not their state. I cannot completely agree with them. To me, studying the role of language needs studying the role of media since using language in communication necessitates the creation of an array of media. The creation of media extends the distance of linguistic communication. Thus language, together with media, extends the time span and the reach of communication. Then humans build a permanent and large community. This leads to the formation of the state and the dissolution of the tribes. A quantitative change leads to a qualitative change. In the past kinship was the basic element of the unity of the tribe which was a small community. Today language is one basic element of the unity of the state which is a large community if we interpret language in the sense of something that language gives origin to all kinds of media except the original medium—namely, behavior—and media further underlie the genesis and growth of the state.

We can reinterpret the theories of the origin of the state, advanced by the philosophers of the past. The interpretations, given by them, may be neither complete nor accurate. If we interpret the origin and growth of the state from a new perspective, we may see the state in a more systematic and accurate way.

The key is that in their interpretations of language the philosophers of the past failed to behold the role of media in support of the application of language. If they devoted their attention to the role of media in linguistic communication and found that it was the extension of the distance of linguistic communication that led to the formation of the state, they would probably be aware of the role of language in support of the growth of the state. This is because language has irreversibly changed the condition of human communication since humans began to speak. Media rely on language. Media attach themselves to language. Language may be viewed differently if the role of media is also studied. Language not only facilitates humans to communicate with each other, but also necessitates the creation of media that extend the distance of linguistic communication. Then humans associate together on a large scale. This culminates in the dissolution of the original community formed on the basis of kinship and the birth of the new community formed on the basis of linguistic communication. Thus, if we study the role of language in the creation of media, we may be able to invent a new theory about the genesis and growth of the state and this theory may give an interpretation better than the views offered by the philosophers of the past. We can compare this newly-proposed view with the related views offered by the philosophers of the past to give a systematic interpretation. This interpretation should be more reasonable and more accurate.

First, the study of the genesis and growth of the state, at the angle of the role of language mentioned by us, is more systematic than the view of the formation of the state adduced by Aristotle. This view may enable us to see the formation of the state more completely. Specifically, in his book *Politics* Aristotle says that the state grows naturally. Describing the city that serves as a basis for the formation of the state in ancient Greece, Aristotle states that:

> The first communities are the two natural ones of (i) husband and wife for generation and (ii) master and slave for survival. These two together form the household. Households exist for the needs of the day. Villages spring from households, above all through the generation of children and grandchildren, and exist for needs beyond the day.[3]

He continues that "[w]hen the community made up of several villages is complete, it is then a city, possessing the limit of every self-sufficiency."[4] Aristotle implies that the city is the cluster of many villages and each village is a cluster of many households. Smaller communities merge to become a larger community. Thus the city grows by nature. Though we can see the city as growing by nature, we can interpret this phenomenon, described by Aristotle, to reveal the role of language mentioned by us to examine his theory in depth. Why does the community grow in size gradually? Why are people willing to form a larger community regardless of the original smaller communities built on the basis of kinship? Will people always form a larger community along with an increase in population? An interpretation of such a situation accentuates that humans create media in their mutual communication. Then media enable them to extend the distance of communication. Extending the distance of communication further enables them to communicate over a long span of time and on a large scale. People, from different tribes, are enabled to communicate with each other. Then they have their common memory of the community; they exchange goods and services; and they share traditional ideas. They may even embrace the same religious belief. They come to have common interest. They form a new community, leaving the original tribes dissolved. A piece of evidence is that the household is composed of a master and a slave or some slaves as discussed by Aristotle. He implies that the slave is a tool. He directly mentions that "the slave is a living possession."[5] The linkage between a master and a slave should not be kinship. Though this slave is the property of a family, the formation of such a family reveals the dissolution of the tribe. A new community must have emerged. This new community was formed by citizens (and their dependents) and slaves. This is the reason for the emergence of villages, towns and cities. That is why animals are usually unable to form a permanent and large community. For example, a group of lions or wolves may form a community, but this community may be dissolved at any time and is always small. As humans are able to use language, communicating over a long span of time and on a large scale, thousands of people, or even millions of people, may form a permanent and large community such as a state.

We may further prove the role of language in the formation of the state this way. We may further indicate that linguistic communication leads to the expansion of the community and the expansion of the community erodes and loosens the organization of the tribe. Then humans, from different tribes, begin to cooperate and unite, and then they form their community in which kinship is no longer an important element of the formation of the community. Kinship attenuates. The attenuation of kinship results in the gradual dissolution of the tribe. Humans form the families characteristic of monogamy because there is no longer the original tribe that conditions group marriage. Polygyny and polyandry have also been extinct. The reason is that outside the tribe people are usually only able to form the families of monogamy as now people no longer unite on the basis of kinship. The original community, formed because of kinship, ends and a new community grows on the basis of linguistic communication. Households of monogamy become the basic economic units. The city emerges along with the formation of households of monogamy. Aristotle insists that a man cannot survive if he is not part of the city.[6] He alludes to the fact that families take shape within the city. Obviously, he believes that the city, instead of tribe, is the chief community of Greeks in which Greeks build their families. This indicates that language is a medium in support of human communication. It extends the time and reach of communication. Then people dissolve their tribes and form their state.

I believe that while Aristotle gave his interpretation of the formation of the state, he only interpreted the formation of the city-state. Though his view is not totally groundless, his explanation seems over-simplified. How can we interpret the formation of ancient empires? How can we interpret the formation of kingdoms in medieval times? Were those states formed in a natural way? While Aristotle presents his view, he emphasizes that people depend on each other in production and living. He means, I argue, that as families depend on each other in production and living, they congregate. Then families congregate to form a village and villages congregate to form a city. People, however, may not always form their states this way. In view of the emergence of some empires in history, we see that sometimes a group of people conquered a region and then a state took form. In other words, humans built various types of states in history. They not only built city-states, but also established some other types of states such as feudal kingdoms and empires. How can we interpret the formation of a kingdom or an empire in history? How can we interpret the formation of a territorial state? How do we interpret the formation of a state formed by immigrants in modern times? If we find an approach to interpret the origin of a kingdom or an empire or an immigration state, how do we interpret the formation of city-states in ancient Greece? Since written language is a prerequisite for the formation of a civilized society, language should play a role in the formation of the state. We need to study in depth how humans associate together and then build their society and the state. Describing the course of the growth of the state only may not adequately clarify how a state takes form. The formation of a state may not be so simple. But pinpointing the role of language should be a better approach for us to have an insight into the formation of the state throughout history because Aristotle's view may not enable us to clearly see the formation of all kinds of states.

In presenting a view about the origin of the state from the perspective of language, I prefer not to view the formation and the growth of the state from the angle of the natural formation of the state only. Needless to say, along with an increase in population, people form a large community. Scholars may argue, for example, that a tribe may evolve to be an ethnic group of people and an ethnic group of people may evolve to be a nation along with an increase in population. Then humans form nation-states. However, not all states may come into existence this way, as noted earlier. How can we interpret the formation of some states on the basis of national fusion following the migration of a group of people from one region to another in history? How can we interpret the formation of some states that absorbed different ethnic groups of people in history? How can we interpret the origin of some states which were empires in the past? I do not deny that some states take form naturally in history, but I also insist that some other states may take form in a different way. In this aspect scholars may overlook the role of language in the growth of the state. If we argue that a batch of families form a village and a batch of villages form a town and a batch of towns form a city and a city becomes a state, we will ask how people build kingdoms, empires and some other nation-states formed by different ethnic groups of people. Is there an approach for us to interpret the formation of various types of states that emerged in history? I pinpoint the role of language in the formation and growth of the state. In other words, in some cases a state takes form naturally, but language also plays a role in the formation of the state. In some other cases, a state takes form for a special reason. In these cases, language definitely plays a role in the formation of the state. The reason is that language serves as a basis for the creation of a wide range of media and media extend the reach of linguistic communication across and between communities. People form a large community. If scholars argue that a state takes form naturally, I argue that it is because language plays a role.

I mean that while humans use language in communication, they have to create and use a variety of media. These media constitute the social fabric. Then we see that while humans communicate using language, they interact with language and language interacts with media and media just mean the formation of the society and the state. Then humans interact with the society and the state. Sometimes it seems that a state takes form by nature, but it is actually the extension of the distance of linguistic communication that results in the formation of the state. In some other cases, a state does not take form by nature, but language invariably plays a part in the formation of that state. For example, a number of villages may form a town and a number of towns may form a city. How do these villages form a town and how do these towns form a city? People have to communicate with one another. People have to use language. Then all villages and all towns can communicate with each other. But we can view this case conversely. If humans did not use language, they would not build a large community because they were unable to create and use media. Then they would not form a state. So my view is that the formation of the state in a seemingly natural way involves the role played by language. Scholars cannot satisfactorily interpret the origin of the state without pinpointing the role of language.

Second, the theory of social contract may enlighten us to think of the role of language, but this theory overlooks the fact that people make a contract because they use language. The social contract theory is the theory that stresses the obligations undertaken by ordinary people and the sovereign, or the government, as well as the rights had by ordinary people and the sovereign or the state in the formation of the state. The social contract theory of the state is identical with the interpretation of the genesis of the state from the perspective of language in the respect that humans have to use language in making a social contract. A contract means the formation of common interest between parties. Language itself denotes the possibility of generating common interest because without common interest people will not communicate, or keep on communicating, with each other by using language. But the shortcoming of the theory of social contract is that the use of language is antecedent to the making of a social contract and hence the interpretation, from the angle of contract, may not be a final theoretical solution though the theory of social contract may support the description of the role of language in the formation of the state. The key is that the philosophers of early modern times interpreted the origin of the state by relying on the theory of natural law created by some philosophers of the Roman and Greek world of ancient times. For instance, the philosophers of Stoics discuss the law of nature. Thus, they argue that humans are in the state of nature in the beginning. Each of them is responsible for his own safety and security as well as well-being. All are subject to the law of nature. Then Hobbes, a philosopher emerging in late medieval times or in early modern times, insists in his book *Leviathan* that as humans are often in a state of war of every man against every man, they cede part of their freedoms and rights to the sovereign in exchange for the protection of themselves by the sovereign. He believes that people are unable to establish order and organize the state unless they cede some of their rights to the sovereign and let the sovereign establish order and organize the state. [7]

John Locke believes that people cooperate with each other in the outset. But he also believes that the government takes form because people make a social contract. In the book *Second Treatise of Government*, Locke argues that the individual places some of his rights present in the state of nature in trusteeship with the sovereign (government) in return for the protection of certain natural individual rights. [8] Locke mentions that an original compact is entered into to make one body politic under one government. [9]

Hobbes and Locke are followed by Jean Jacques Rousseau in the building of a theoretical edifice of social contract as Rousseau opines that "the social order is a sacred right which is the basis of all other rights. Nevertheless, this right does not come from nature and must therefore be founded on conventions."[10] He offers his theory of social contract on the grounds that "Since no man has a natural authority over his fellow, and force creates no right, we must conclude that conventions form the basis of all legitimate authority among men."[11] The result is that, according to Rousseau,

> [E]ach man, in giving himself to all, gives himself to nobody; and as there is no associate over whom he does not acquire the same right as he yields others over himself, he gains an equivalent for everything he loses, and an increase of force for the preservation of what he has.[12]

Undoubtedly, the past philosophers only engage in hypothetical reasoning. The state of nature is described to offer their views about what the state ought to be. Their arguments may be even assumptive. Rousseau makes the following comment that:

> Every one of them, in short, constantly dwelling on wants, avidity, oppression, desires and pride, has transferred to the state of nature ideas which were acquired in society; so that,

in speaking of the savage, they described the social man. It has not even entered into the heads of most of our writers to doubt whether the state of nature ever existed; but it is clear from the Holy scriptures that the first man, having received his understanding and commandments immediately from God, was not himself in such as state; and that, if we give such credit to the writings of Moses as every Christian philosopher ought to give, we must deny that, even before the deluge, men were ever in the pure state of nature; unless, indeed, they fell back into it from some very extraordinary circumstances; a paradox which it would be very embarrassing to defend, and quite impossible to prove.[13]

He stresses that the inquiry must not be considered to be historical truths, but only as mere conditional and hypothetical reasoning.[14]

Why do the past philosophers engage in hypothetical reasoning this way? I venture to argue that they overlook the role of language in the genesis and growth of the state though the reasoning, based on the view of the law of nature, can follow the logic. If language is assumed to underlie the genesis and growth of the state, we may find out the secret of the genesis and growth of the state. Though the study of the role of language in the genesis and growth of the state is not historical either, it may create a more solid foundation in our study of the genesis and growth of the state. The grounds, offered by us, are simple. Humans must have already commenced to use language for their mutual communication if they are aware of the existence of such a contract for no contract is made without using language. Such a contract cannot exist among those who do not perform linguistic communication with each other.

If we argue that the state is formed by those who are originally stateless, we can also believe that the theory of social contract can be viewed as part of the formation of the state set in motion by language. This view can be revised to advance the argument that humans first use language and then make a social contract. Even the interpretation of the state of nature cannot deny the existence of linguistic communication. Thus we can believe that, due to the extension of the distance of linguistic communication, this linguistic communication must, in theory, be performed freely by anyone with all others. All interact with all. So the state is formed in the process of linguistic communication.

Therefore, the theory of social contract, coupled with the interpretation of the state of nature, may be revised to create a theory of the genesis and growth of the state from the perspective of language. The genesis and growth of the state can be viewed from the perspective of the role of language in the dissolution of the tribe and the formation of the state. For example, Hobbes writes that:

> The Children of Israel, were a Common-wealth in the Wildernesse; but wanted the commodities of the Earth, till they were masters of the Land of Promise; which afterward was divided amongst them, not by their own discretion, but by the discretion of *Eleazar* the Priest, and *Joshua* their Generall: who when there were twelve Tribes, making them thirteen by subdivision of the Tribe of Joseph; made never-theless but twelve portions of the Land; and ordained for the Tribe of Levi no land; but assigned them the Tenth part of the whole fruits; which division was therefore Arbitrary.[15]

His description clearly shows that prior to the growth of the civilized society in which there is a state, humans remained tribal people. When people were the members of the tribe, they were actually organized. They were not isolated individual people without the assistance given by all others whenever they needed assistance. Each of them was not isolated because each was connected with all others by kinship. Particularly, the situation might not be that each was totally responsible for his own security. Each and the other might cooperate with each other. They might not be in the state of war though a tribe might be often in the state of war against another one. In other words, tribes, as communities, might often be in the state of war between each other, but each individual within the tribe might not be in the state of war because kinship meant love and mutual assistance between one another. The relationship between one tribe and another may be character-ized by war while the relationship between one person and another within the tribe may be characterized by peace. The tribe was governed by the tribal chief and was not in the state of disorder. There was the order within the tribe. Customs, as unwritten laws in some cases, might be obeyed by the members of the tribe. The reason that humans depart from tribes to form a state is that they use language. In the meantime, language enables people to communicate on a large scale. People are thus enabled to dissolve tribes and hence to form a larger community along with an increase in population. For instance, in ancient times, Hebrews built their state on the basis of the union of different tribes.

That is, as humans use language, language underlies the formation of their own common interest. If they bear obligations required by all others in order to gain rights given by all others because they now form a community on the basis of linguistic communication, there should be, at least, a tacit contract. If they admit that they actually gain certain rights given by all others because they bear obligations expected by all others, there is a de facto contract. Thus, one can give an interpretation of the role of language because people should make a social contract in a process of linguistic communication. In a word, when people perform linguistic communication with each other, they give undertakings to each other this way or that way. They may form their state and dissolve their tribes. Thus history tells us that in ancient Greece tribes existed long after or at least upon the formation of the city-states. Narrating the life of Theseus (legendary), a Grecian noble man, Plutarch writes that after the death of his father Aegeus, forming in his mind a great and wonderful design, he gathered all the inhabitants of Attica into one town and made them one people of one city, whereas in the past they lived dispersed and were not easy to assemble upon any affair for the common interest. The related background is that differences and even wars often occurred between them. Then he, by his persuasions, appeased those differences and wars, going from township to township, and from tribe to tribe. [16].Likewise, in Rome there were also tribes though we believe that the state, such as the Roman Republic, was formed at that time. Narrating the life of Romulus (8th century B.C.), a Roman noble man, Plutarch also notes that the city doubled in number and one hundred of the Sabines were elected senators and the legions were increased to six thousand foot and six hundred horse. Then they divided the people into three tribes: the first, from Romulus, named Ramnenses; the second from Tatius, Tatienses; the third Luceres, from the *lucus* or grove where the Asylum stood to which many fled for sanctuary. And they were just three and the very name of *tribe* and *tribune* seemed to show this fact. That is, each tribe contained ten *curie* or brotherhood.[17]

Then I argue that philosophers, advocating the theory of social contract, believe that all must make an agreement to confer all their power and strength upon one man or entity. This cannot happen unless humans are able to use language. People think that it is so even though they have never acted to make such an agreement. This is imagined by those philosophers. Their explanation is characteristic of being hypothetical in reasoning or even assumptive. Yet they imply, or mean, that the power of the state is given by the people. The state, according to their view, is formed because the people make a contract among themselves and make a contract with the power holder of the state. This means that, in the formation of a state, there is already a contract made by all; there is a contract made by the ruled and the ruler and the sovereign rules the state according to the related contract. Such an interpretation is not repugnant to the interpretation of the role of language in the genesis of the state. This is because we can believe that humans must use language in the making of a social contract. But we can revise the related presentation to argue that language comes into use before humans make a contract. Humans first start using language for their mutual interaction, and such mutual interaction leads to the formation of a new community. They cooperate with each other in production and living. Then they may conceptualize the obligations and rights in their cooperation. Then it is arguable that people have already made a contract or two to authorize an individual or an entity to govern the community. This complex process may lead to the birth of the state.

Third, this view may also help us review the theories of some other philosophers, or thinkers, who do not concur with the philosophers advocating the theory of social contract. Among these philosophers or thinkers, some philosophers, or thinkers, uphold the view that people form the state through the use of force or conquest. They accentuate the role played by the military leader of a social group in the formation of the state. They do not believe that any social contract is made in the building of the state. They believe that the formation of the state is not the volition of ordinary people, but the will of a strong man. They seem to believe that the formation of the government can be equated with the formation of the state. In other words, the formation of the state is the matter of those who hold power. In their view, in the formation of the state, people, residing passively within it, cannot leave this state freely. Thus the state is imposed on those ordinary people. For example, David Hume writes that:

> Almost all the governments, which exist at present, or of which there remains any record in story, have been founded originally, either on usurpation or conquest, or both, without any pretence of a fair consent, or voluntary subjection of the people. When an artful and bold man is placed at the head of an army or faction, it is often easy for him, by employing, sometimes violence, sometimes false pretences, to establish his dominion over a people a hundred times more numerous than his partizans.[18]

He asserts that the theory of social contract disagrees with the facts, saying that everywhere rulers assert their independent right of sovereignty from conquest or succession[19]

Franz Oppenheimer, a German sociologist, largely agrees to Hume's conclusion though his relevant analysis differs from Hume's in detail. He insists that:

> The State, completely in its genesis, essentially and almost completely during the first stages of its existence, is a social institution, forced by a victorious group of men on a defeated group, with the sole purpose of regulating the dominion of the victorious group over the vanquished, and securing itself against revolt from within and attacks from abroad.[20]

Although the theory of conquest sheds light on the origin of the state in a certain aspect, an analysis of the role of language, given from the perspective of linguistic communication, may expose one of the major omissions of this view. This omission is that the formation of a government cannot be equated with the formation of the state though the formation of the government is essential for the formation of the state. The formation of the government is one necessary condition for the formation of the state, but cannot represent all the necessary conditions for the formation of the state. The role of language should be stressed for the presentation of an overall view of the formation of the state. My analysis starts here: In the formation of the state, people, forming the state, should be able to communicate with each other, using language, so that a great many people, in a large community, can communicate with each other in order to maintain the unity of the state. If, in the outset, the victorious group, using one language, conquers another defeated group using another language, the two languages may amalgamate into one later. Describing the combination of the victorious group of people and the defeated group, Oppenheimer mentions that:

> We saw in the second stage . . . how the net of psychical relations becomes ever tighter and closer enmeshed, as the economic amalgamation advances. The two dialects become one language; or one of the two, often of an entirely different stock from the other, becomes extinct. This, in some cases, is the language of the victors, but more frequently that of the vanquished.[21]

People, who communicate with each other by using language, also build the common memory of the community, embrace the common religious belief, adhere to the same custom and mores, put into practice common cultural ideas, and know that they belong to the same group. If we argue that conquest is against the will of the conquered people and the conquerors solely intend to exploit the conquered people in the outset, the conquerors may gradually recognize the value of the conquered people. People may understand each other gradually. They may be aware of the formation of the common interest between the two sides. For example, the state may be formed due to the fact that the nomads conquer the peasants. The nomads become the conquerors while the peasants become the conquered people. Yet, they may rely on each other later because the nomads, as the conquerors, need tributes given by the peasants as the conquered people while the conquered people, the peasants, need the protection of the conquerors, the nomads. Nevertheless, as the birth of language antedates conquest, language can be the key to the philosophical interpretation of the totality of the state.

That is, Hume's and Oppenheimer's views may be considered single-faceted if we view the role played by language in the growth of the state. My reasoning is that this theory of conquest or, in some sense, subjugation cannot deny that language appears long before the appearance of the state. When humans were still tribal people, they commenced to use language in their mutual communication. Language should be a factor in the extension of the distance of linguistic communication and the expansion of the human community and hence a factor in the final formation of the state. Thus initial conquest may be a step precipitating the formation of the state. In the formation of the state, people, forming the state, should have already had their mores, religion, art, literature, history, philosophy and law, etc. Even if we accept the view of conquest and believe that the mores, religion, art, literature, history, philosophy and law, had by the victors, differ from those had by the vanquished, those cultural or social constructs may amalgamate. For example, as Oppenheimer writes, "Both cults amalgamate into one religion, in which the tribal god of the conquerors is adored as the principal divinity, while the old gods of the vanquished become either his servants, or, as demons or devils, his adversaries."[22] Thus those cultural or social forms are also the factors conditioning the genesis of the state. The initial effort, made by the conqueror, is merely an element functioning in the formation of the state. In other words, in early times, people, forming small communities in different areas, may not be strongly motivated to form a large community. They may be temporarily under the governance of the society though such a society may not be stable or perpetual. It is the conqueror that conquers the conquered people builds the large community called the state and becomes the ruler of the state. People may be forced by the conqueror to form a state in a period of time only.

This comment is identical with the related historical narratives in which the state is ruled by a despot in the outset. Though in ancient Greek cities people established democracy, the establishment of a despotic system should antedate that of a democracy. Yet we can also believe that in late medieval times or early modern times what was witnessed by people was largely the replacement of despotic states by democratic states in Europe. In North America democracy was built when new nation-states were born. In other regions outside Europe and North America peoples did not start building democracy at that time, but they also begin to build democracy in modern times. Studying the long-term growth of the state may enable us to see that the conqueror of the state, objectively, functions as a medium that precipitates the formation of the state in history. To put it differently, linguistic communication results in the formation of the common interest of all from different tribes and hence results in the dissolution of the tribes and the formation of the state. But an individual person, acting as a conqueror, may hasten the formation of the state. Discussing representative government, John Stuart Mill writes that:

> [K]ingly government, free from the control (though perhaps strengthened by the support) of representative institutions, is the most suitable form of polity for the earliest stages of any community, not excepting a city-community like those of ancient Greece: where, accordingly, the government of kings, under some real but no ostensible or constitutional control by public opinion, did historically precede by an unknown and probably great duration all free institutions, and gave place at last, during a considerable lapse of time, to oligarchies of a few families.[23]

He believes that in the beginning, the government was quite despotic.[24] Yet, we can assert that a kingly government functions in ancient times on behalf of the representative government established in modern times because we can hold that the pre-modern state is inherited by the modern state. This is because in history people cannot build the state at one fell swoop. The conqueror becomes a medium. Despotism creates a condition for the later growth of the state that adopts democracy. Despotism stems from conquest. Conquest is aimed at interest. Interest is available in a large community. If people do not use language in mutual communication and hence fail to form a large community, there should not be an abundance of the property owned by the community. Thus the potential conqueror may not conquer them. This is because the conqueror usually conquers the people of a region in an attempt to seize a great deal of property including land. Nevertheless, though conquest is aimed at interest, after the conquest, the conqueror also needs ruling legitimacy in order to rule the state for a long time and the conqueror does not gain certain ruling legitimacy until he becomes the ruler. The initial conquest may be only part of a long process of the formation of the state in which language plays an essential role. I present one piece of evidence in support of my argument. That is, feudal states evolve to be nation-states, and nation-states establish democracy. Thus, I argue that the initial conquest may serve as a medium in the process of the formation, or the growth, of the state. For example, France that used to be a kingdom in the Middle Ages grew to be a nation-state in early modern times. In the transition from a kingdom to a nation-state, the kings of France, including Louis XIV, sometimes launched the war of conquest and expanded the territory of, and increased the population of, France. French people later inherited the state growing large historically due to the role played by language after France had become a republic. Thus, any ruler of the Middle Ages in the history of France is only a medium in the formation of the state. He is a historic medium. This is because, at that time, it proved impossible for ordinary people to form a large state. The commitment of the ruler in the expansion of the state created a condition for the formation of the modern state later. But the entire growth of the state proves that the state always grows due to the role played by language and culture derived from that language.

That means that it is language that is fundamentally significant for the formation of the state. Initial conquest is a temporary phenomenon in the formation of the state. The state takes form finally because of the use of language instead of initial conquest. In narrating the history of Germany, Karl Marx and Frederick Engels note an important phenomenon. In writing that barbarians from Germany took the Roman Empire, they do not forget to mention that "the conquerors very soon took over language, culture and manners from the conquered."[25] Obviously, they noticed the role of language in the formation and building of the state. In Chinese history, Mongolians conquered China in the thirteenth century and Manchurians conquered China in the seventeenth century. But the Han Chinese, the main ethnic group, assimilated part of Mongolians and all Manchurians. It is true that the conquerors expanded the territory of China, but all those assimilated ethnic groups of people learned the Chinese language, namely, Mandarin. It is language, together with the culture developed on the basis of this language, that determines the final formation of the state. When the Japanese army invaded China from 1931 to 1945, many Japanese military officers, staying in China, spoke pidgin Mandarin, communicating with the native Chinese people. The language of a small population gave way to the language of a large population when two different nations interacted directly. In addition, the traditional Chinese culture is more advanced than the Japanese traditional culture because in history the Japanese culture was influenced by the Chinese culture. Thus, I believe that if we suppose that the Japanese army eventually conquered China and Japan annexed China, the final result, shown in the following several hundred years, might be that Japanese were assimilated by Chinese. Then Japan might become part of China. The rulers of Japan in the 1930s believed the theory of initial conquest. This view is single-faceted. That is, language gives origin to the state.

As such, it is arguable that the view of initial conquest may be a facet of the entire process of state formation, but not all facets of state formation. The view of initial conquest can be revised. In order to describe the origin of the state, we need to have a broad field of vision. We can perhaps prove the role of language in the genesis and growth of the state. We can take into consideration a long process of state formation underlain by language. Thus the view of the role of language, in the genesis and growth of the state, should have a unique value.

Fourth, thinkers, or philosophers, or other scholars, sometimes ascribe the origin of the state to the necessity of self-defense of people. This view is in conformity with the view of social contract in a certain aspect because this view stresses that people unite to build a state in order to ensure the security of the community. In other words, people may cede part of their rights to the state for them to be protected by the state. Thus Hobbes admits that this is one of several reasons for the establishment of the government, as mentioned earlier. This view also confirms indirectly its possible relevance to war. It holds that a war precipitates the formation of the state. It may agree to the view that initial conquest results in the formation of some other states. The related philosophers, however, focus on the necessity of the union of people in order to guard against foreign invasion and take the union of people as the reason for the formation of the state. Some of them emphasize, in particular, that self-defense is the sole origin of the state under certain circumstances. They pinpoint the external threat as a special reason for the formation of the state. They insist that people form their state under external pressure. They argue, in particular, that dispersed families, threatened by the invasion or intrusion of herdsmen or external groups of people, unite to increase their own strength of defense to bar herdsmen or others because herdsmen or others do not regard invasion as forbidden. The union of the local people results in the building of a state. They imply that the common need of all culminates in the union of all and hence the building of the state. The external pressure is the cause. The state is built within a region. In this regard, Immanuel Kant is among a few prominent philosophers particularly holding this view. In the essay entitled *Speculative Beginning of Human History* (1786), he writes that:

> When subsistence depends on the earth's cultivation and planting (especially trees), permanent housing is required, and its defense against all intrusions requires a number of men who will support one another. Consequently, men who adopt this form of life can no longer remain in scattered families, but must instead come together and found villages (improperly called towns) in order to protect their property against wild hunters or hordes of wandering herdsmen. The primary needs of life required by a *different way of living* could not be *exchanged* for one another. Culture and the beginning of art, of entertainment, as well as of industrious-ness must have sprung from this; but above all, some form of civil constitution and of public justice began, at first, to be sure, only in regard to the grossest brutality, revenge for which was no longer sought by the single individual, as it was in the state of savage, but rather by a lawful power that preserved the whole, i.e., became a form of government, and was controlled by no other power.[26]

In later times some other scholars further confirm that the consolidation of defense, needed for the security of all, is the origin of the state. Their descriptions are that a war compels the ruler of the state to recruit soldiers, to increase the levies of taxes and to strengthen administration. All measures, taken for the purpose of defense, lead to the building of the state. As defense is built against possible invasion, they regard a war between one state and another as a cause of the formation and growth of the state. For example, some scholars accentuate the role of a war in the building of nation-state in ancient China, in early modern Europe and in the United States of early modern times.[27] They believe that the outbreak of a war hastens the pace of state building. Their basic view is that the defense of the community leads to the ruler's exertion of his effort in state building for survival. Is this view plausible? My view is that self-defense only necessitates the union of people and merely reflects a course of state building instead of the origin of the state though the related descriptions and researches can be used to support the philosophical view about the origin of the state advanced on the basis of analyzing the role of language in state formation. If humans did not speak, they would not be able to extend the distance of their mutual communication. They would remain within the tribe. If they needed self-defense at that time, they would make an effort to build the tribe instead of a state because people would not be able to form a large community such as a state without language. Yet we can also believe that, as humans speak and write, they are enabled to communicate over a long time and on a large scale. Many people begin to communicate with one another. They unite for self-defense. Then they no longer strengthen the building of the tribe but the building of the state. Therefore, it is arguable that language bolsters the formation of a large community. Civilization germinates because humans extend the distance of linguistic communication. Extending the distance of linguistic communication is the sole basis for the long-time cooperation and the union of a great many people. Strengthening the defense of the community has been merely a process of strengthening the building of the state in the formation and the growth of the state since the birth of language. The only one plausible interpretation of the genesis and growth of the state should be given in view of language. As people, from different areas, unite, their original heterogeneous cultures may amalgamate into one homogeneous culture. They may have the same memory of history as gradually as time goes on. They may gradually uphold the same religious belief. They may often exchange feelings. They may cooperate in production. They may jointly engage in some large public engineering projects. They may jointly engage in some social undertakings. Then some may come forward to form a government. Forming a government is a step toward the formation of the state.

While we offer a view about the origin of the state, such a view should be able to interpret the origin of all types of the state. If we advance a view about the origin of some types of the state only, we have to think about why sometimes humans form their state in some other way around. Is the view about the origin of the state presented from the perspective of defense or war plausible? How do we interpret the formation of the United States, or modern Italy, or modern Germany as a nation? How do we interpret the formation of many states in Africa and Asia after World War Two? Were those states not formed in the state of peace? How should we understand the birth of some states in the state of peace in this world? Accentuating the role played by language in the origin of the state is, I argue, a better interpretation of the formation of the state. This view can interpret the origin of all types of the state successfully. A war may not lead to the formation of the state if people do not use language. A war may lead to the formation of the state in some cases if people have already built a large community. Yet such a war should be deemed as a medium that precipitates the building of the state that originally takes form after humans begin their mutual interaction realized by using language on a large scale. Tribes were also often at war. Prior to the arrival of Europeans in North America, the tribes of Indigenous people were at war from time to time. A war might not lead to the formation of a state because a state has to be a large community. To form a large community, people have to communicate in writing. Written language is a basis for the formation of a state. This point of view is in line with the common sense that the birth of script symbolizes the beginning of human civilization. A state emerges in the civilized society. So even though sometimes a war seemingly leads to the formation of a state, this war only hastens the formation of the state because the process of forming a state should begin at the time when people begin to use written language. If we see that sometimes a war leads to the formation of the state and sometimes a war does not lead to the formation of the state, the interpretation of the role of war in the formation of the state should be problematic. People may doubt the accuracy of such an interpretation.

In other words, a war often breaks out in the course of the formation of the state rather than before it. The formation of a state often needs a long period of time. This period of time starts when humans begin to communicate using language. Despite that sometimes a war breaks out before the final formation of the state in a certain region, what underlies the formation of the state is language rather than a conflict between a group of people and another. A conflict, such as a war, even sometimes destroys a state or states.

For instance, the First Emperor unified China in 221 BC through a series of wars, putting an end to the Period of Warring States in Chinese history. Yet these wars were also the reason for the disappearance of many other kingdoms. If scholars can argue that war is also the reason for the disappearance of many states, it is not plausible to assert the state always takes form through a war. If scholars assert that some states emerge through a war and some other states disappear due to a war, war should not be a constant condition for the formation of the state. Is there a constant condition for the formation of the state? Scholars are likely to give diversified interpretations of the origin of the state. The interpretation of the role of war in the formation of the state is one of them. I believe that people need to have a clear understanding of the evolution from the primitive society to the civilized one. An interpretation of the role of language in the formation of the state can give clarity to the understanding of the formation of the state. Therefore, if we can accept the interpretation of the role of language in the formation of the state, we should regard war merely as a medium that precipitates the formation of the state on some occasions. The interpretation of the role of war in the formation of the state is not totally groundless, but such an interpretation is not the best. The interpretation of the role of language in the formation of the state is the best. Such an interpretation is the most systematic and complete. Such an interpretation is also reliable.

In short, the state normally comes into existence for the internal reason. If there is an external reason for the formation of the state, this external reason should not substitute for the internal reason. If one argues that the state takes form only through a war, others may question if the state is to be dissolved when people are at peace. The interpretation of the role of war in the formation of the state accentuates external pressure. One has to explain why a state grows steadily when people are at peace. Does peace affect the formation of the state? If one admits that peace does not affect the formation of the state, he still has to explain why the state can endure at peace? If a state exists no matter whether it is at peace or at war, there should be another reason for the formation of the state. I pinpoint the role of language.

Fifth, the theory, arguing that the formation of the state is due to the appearance of private property and the emergence of social classes, may be another theory needing to be discussed here. This theory holds that both the formation of families and the dissolution of tribes pertain to the appearance of private property. The appearance of private property is a condition for the development of the division of labor and social classes emerge from the division of labor. On the basis of analyzing the arguments offered by some other scholars, including Lewis Henry Morgan, Frederick Engels argues that originally humans lived in a state of sexual promiscuity.[28] Group marriage appeared later. Then humans experienced the periods of polyandry and polygyny before the appearance of monogamy. He mentions language. When describing the lower stage of Savagery, he writes that:

> Man still lived in his original habitat, in tropical or sub-tropical forests, and was partially at least a tree-dweller, for otherwise his survival among huge beasts of prey cannot be explained. Fruits, nuts and roots served him for food. The development of articulate speech is the main result of this period.[29]

Thus we can believe that humans began to extend the distance of mutual communication at that time. This was the time the human community began to expand. Thus in the beginning the tribe or gens was just a big family. Children might have several fathers and mothers. At that time, people formed pairing families, as called by Morgan. In pairing families there was no doubt about whom to call father, mother, son, daughter, brother and sister. But these names were used differently. In the Sandwich Islands, Hawaii, in the first half of the nineteenth century, there existed the form of family in which the fathers and mothers, brothers and sisters, sons and daughters, uncles and aunts, nephews and nieces were exactly what was required by the American ancient Indian system of consanguinity. According to this system, all children of brothers and sisters were, without exception, brothers and sisters of one another and were considered to be the common children not only of their mother and her sisters or of their father and his brothers, but of all the brothers and sisters of both their parents without distinction.[30] By contrast, the form of family of Iroquois was a later one. The Iroquois called not only his own children his sons and daughters, but also the children of his brothers, and they called him father. The children of his sisters, however, he called his nephews and nieces, and they called him their uncle. The Iroquois woman, on the other hand, called her sisters' children, as well as her own, her sons and daughters, and they called her mother. But her brothers' children she called her nephews and nieces, and she was known as their aunt. Similarly, the children of brothers called one another brother and sister, and so do the children of sisters. A woman's own children and the children of her brother, on the other hand, called one another cousins.[31] When people trace back the origin of the family, they may find that humans lived in polygamy and their wives in polyandry, and their common children were therefore considered common to them all. This situation changed gradually later. This means that the system of primitives underwent a long series of changes before they finally ended in monogamy, as indicated by Engels.[32]

Why does the family evolve this way? My view is that language extends the distance of mutual communication of people and extends the reach of their activities. The community grows in size as a result. An increase in the population and area of the community loosens kinship ties until the dissolution of kinship. In the meantime, as people interact with more other people, it becomes difficult, or impossible, for group marriage or polygamy to continue. People may often interact with strangers for business, for example. They and others do not live together day and night. As living space expands greatly, a person cannot keep close relationship with many other people. A man cannot get married with many women at the same time. Monogamy finally appears. The formation of the state is along with the formation of monogamy, but this does not mean that the formation of monogamy leads to the formation of the state. Extending the reach of linguistic communication leads to the formation of the state. Likewise, extending the reach of linguistic communication leads to the formation of monogamy.

If people perform spoken communication only, spoken language hampers the steady growth of the community because spoken language, as a dialect, is used on a small scale. Among the Northern American Indians an originally homogeneous tribe spread over a huge continent. Language changed until they not only became unintelligible to other tribes but also lost almost every trace of their original identity.[33] In the meantime, people find that, when a tribe grew in population and area to a certain extent, it broke up into several tribes. The distance of spoken communication set a limit to the size of the community and humans did not form the large community, namely, the state until they began to perform written communication for the reason that people used written language on a very large scale. Thus written language is a condition for the formation of the state.

In the meantime, private property appeared. Private property appeared along with the enhancement of people's ability of production. Engels gives his interpretation. He seems to believe that private property originated from the exploitation of domesticated animals and slaves. He accepts Morgan's criteria that the difference between Savage and Barbarism is that in the period of Savage humans gathered food while in the period of Barbarism they produced food.[34] He mentions that, after humans learned to domesticate some animals, they began to use those animals as tools of labor. Later they started to use some other people as the tools of labor. People, captured in a war, became slaves. Thus he writes that "Once it had passed into the private possession of families and there rapidly begun to augment, this wealth dealt a severe blow to the society founded on pairing marriage and the matriarchal gens."[35]

Plainly, his view differs from the interpretation of Immanuel Kant. Kant holds that when property was secure, men started to produce food.[36] My view is that people establish private property while developing productive forces or people develop productive forces while establishing private property. Each of them may be a condition for the appearance of the other. But both productive forces and private property system cannot be a decisive condition for the formation of the state if the community cannot grow in size. People's egoism is the reason for the formation of private property. This egoism should not stem from the existence of private property. Egoism stems from the nature of humans. Nature orders humans to be egoist because otherwise nature will not ensure people's survival. The consciousness of kinship, however, suppresses people's egoism. For example, the father may be very altruist toward his son. Likewise, the mother helps her daughter without considering her own interest. This means that after humans commence to speak and write, they extend the distance of linguistic communication. Extending the distance of linguistic communication leads to the expansion of the community and the expansion of the community leads to the formation of the state. Kinship no longer plays a role in the formation of the community. Thus as kinship is no longer the crucial element of the formation of the community, no consciousness of kinship checks egoism outside the family of monogamy. Egoism becomes prevalent. Engels mentions that when humans were on the lower stage of Savage, the period of time when they gathered food, they began to speak. That time should be the beginning of the expansion of the human community. So we can believe that private property originates from language because since humans started to use language, egoistic action has become the action of keeping private property. If one argues that private property appears as a result of food production and hence the appearance of surplus food, this does not necessarily result in the appearance of private property. If humans did not begin to use language, their community must be no larger than the original tribe. Within the tribe all were connected with all by kinship. Even though there was a lot of surplus food, the consciousness of kinship would remind people of keeping common property.

This amounts to the fact that if language is, fundamentally speaking, a reason for the appearance of private property, it may also be the reason for the appearance of social classes. Since humans commenced to communicate using language, the community has grown large and becomes complex. People may engage in large-scale production. They realize the division of labor in production. The development of the division of labor magnifies the variation of competence from one person to another. The opportunities of giving play to one's competence increase substantially. Engels, discussing the origin of social classes, shows this picture. He states that:

> The first division of labor is that between man and woman for the propagation of children.' And today I can add: The first class opposition that appears in history coincides with the development of antagonism between man and woman in monogamous marriage, and the first class oppression coincides with that of the female sex by the male. Monogamous marriage was a great historical step forward; nevertheless, together with slavery and private wealth, it opens the period that has lasted until today in which every step forward is also relatively a step backward, in which prosperity and development for some is won through the misery and frustration of others.[37]

He ascribes the emergence of social classes to the progress of the division of labor. He points out that the first great social division of labor led to the appearance of masters and slaves.[38] The second great social division of labor led to the separation of handicraft from agriculture.[39] The third great social division of labor led to the appearance of merchants that were no longer concerned with production, but only with the exchange of the products.[40] Yet, if humans did not extend the distance of linguistic communication and hence did not expand their community, social classes might not appear because the emergence of social classes originates from the division of labor that appears in a large community. One can find the relevance of extending the distance of linguistic communication to the emergence of social classes. That is, social classes appear following the formation of the state. This does not mean that the irreconcilable contradiction of social classes leads to the formation of the state. When humans communicate using language, they create a condition for the formation of their common interest. Social classes originate from the division of labor and the division of labor stems from the variation of competence from one person to another. The variation of the competence of people will not disappear. What humans can do is to let themselves to show their diversified competences so that the disadvantageous position of one person in one aspect can be compensated by the advantageous position of that person in another aspect. The state exists not because of the oppression of one class by the other, but because of the formation of the common interest of people within the state. Exploitation exists indeed. But it is usually committed on individual basis. The members of the ruling class never unite to form a monolithic organization completely on the basis of the class, or on behalf of this class, throughout the state though some power holders may govern the state in the interest of their own that is objectively in line with the interest of others in the same class. The so-called oppression of one class by another in the state was imagined because the state is inherently not a natural tool used by one class to oppress the other. The exploitation and oppression of one class by another may appear in the society, but this problem can be solved by the state when a reasonable political system is established and a reasonable policy is made. If there is the discourse created by the writers or thinkers on behalf of the bourgeoisie in the state in history because they belong to the times of capitalism, those writers, or thinkers, advocate democracy and equality of all. A step forward for one class may not mean a step backward for another class. Industrialization benefits all albeit to a varying extent. The state does not specifically belong to a certain social class. As Engels states, the absolute monarchy of the 18th century balanced the nobility and the bourgeoisie against one another. The Bonapartism of the First and particularly of the Second French Empire played off the proletariat against the bourgeoisie and the bourgeoisie against the proletariat. In the German Empire of the Bismarckian nation, the capitalists and the workers were balanced against one another.[41] The state is not, in a fundamental sense, formed as a result of the initiative of a ruling class. The formation of the state antedates the emergence of any social class. It is also likely for social classes to emerge along with the formation of the state. My view, in this aspect, is that if humans did not use language, they would still stay in the tribe. No private property would appear because egoism was checked by the consciousness of kinship that was a basic element of the unity of the tribe. No exchange of goods and services would appear. In the meantime, people would not have any lasting common memory of the community and would not have their ripe common culture. They would not build their state.

In summary, the view this monograph is going to present may serve as the one in contrast to the views of the genesis of the state adduced by the past philosophers. Each of the theories of the genesis of the state usually addresses its subject matter in only one aspect. If scholars regard the state as being formed naturally, one may find that sometimes people proactively build the state. If scholars describe the state as originating from the making of a social contract, one may find that sometimes people build a despotic state as a result of initial conquest. If scholars regard the state as being formed in the outset due to initial conquest, one may sometimes find a case that people build a state on voluntary basis. If scholars consider the state to be formed because people, forming the state, intend to strengthen their defense against the invasion of foreigners, one may also find a case that people form themselves into the state in the state of peace. If one interprets the state as a ruling apparatus amid class struggle, one may also find that people may form the state on the basis of the cooperation of all. These arguments are inconsistent with each other to a varying extent. We cannot piece together all of these arguments in order to adduce a comprehensive theory of the genesis of the state.

Unlike the traditional hypothetical or assumptive views about the genesis of the state, the view of the role of language in the genesis and growth of the state is neither hypothetical nor assumptive. Specific facts can prove this view. One can present this view in almost all aspects of the genesis and growth of the state. One can offer this view by way of showing that humans are social animals. They must interact with each other. In their mutual interaction, language extends the distance of communication. They change the mode of their mutual interaction as a result because now they interact on a very large scale. This paves a way for the formation and growth of the state. Then we can demonstrate that language is a medium in the realization of mutual interaction between one another on a large scale. Language leads to the disappearance of immediacy between one another in the tribe. I mean direct blood relationship by the word "immediacy." Language is an extension of humans. Then it further becomes a proto-medium that conditions the creation of a variety of other media. These media further lay a foundation for the construction of a new community in which humans interact with each other more and more by way of those media. Humans build their new community, namely, the state, on a new basis. They develop the new modes of their mutual interaction to build their state, to support the organization of their state and to rationalize their state. Then language conditions the formation of the state and underlies the dissolution of the tribe, resulting in a critical progress from the primitive society to the civilized one. In short, humans do not form their state freely, but in linguistic communication. Please allow me to try to present my view systematically in the main body of this monograph as follows.

Notes

1. Aristotle writes that "It is clear, then, that a human being is more of a political animal than is any bee or than are any of those animals that live in herds. For nature, as we say, makes nothing in vain, and humans are the only animals who possess reasoned speech. Voice, of course, serves to indicate what is painful and pleasant; that is why it is also found in the other animals, because their nature has reached

the point where they can perceive what is painful and pleasant and express these to each other. But speech serves to make plain what is advantageous and harmful and so also what is just and unjust. For it is a peculiarity of humans, in contrast to the other animals, to have perception of good and bad, just and unjust, and the like; and community in these things makes ahousehold and a city. Please see: Aristotle, *The Politics of Aristotle*, translated by Peter L. Phillips Simpson (Chapel Hill: The University of North Carolina Press, 1997), 11.

2. Thomas Hobbes, *Leviathan*, edited with an introduction by C. B. Macpherson (New York: Penguin Books, 1985), 100.

3. Aristotle, *The Politics of Aristotle*, 9. He believes that a household should include a house, a wife and an ox if the household is poor because an ox can replace a slave. See: Aristotle, *The Politics of Aristotle*, 10.

4. Ibid.,11.

5. Ibid.,14.

6. Aristotle writes that "[T]he city is by nature prior to the household and to each one of us taken singly. For the whole is necessarily prior to the part. For instance, there will be neither foot nor hand when the whole body has been destroyed (except equivocally, as when one speaks of a foot or hand made of stone), for such a foot or hand will have been ruined. Everything is defined by its work and by its power, so that a foot and hand in such a condition should no longer be said to be the same thing (except equivocally). It is clear, then, that the city exists by nature and that it has priority over the individual. For if no individual is self-sufficient when isolated, he will be like all other parts in relation to their whole." See: Ibid., 11–12.

7. Hobbes writes that the only way to erect a common power, as may be able to defend them from the invasion of foreigners and the injuries of one another, and thereby to secure them in such a way, as that by their own industry and by the fruits of the earth, they may nourish themselves and live contentedly, is to confer all their power and strength upon one man, or upon one assembly of men, that may reduce all their wills, by plurality of voices, unto one will. See: Hobbes, *Leviathan*, 227.

8. Locke writes that "Men being, as has been said, by nature, all free, equal, and independent, no one can be put out of this estate, and subjected to the political power of another, without his own consent. The only way whereby any one divests himself of his natural liberty, and puts on the *bonds of civil society*, is by agreeing with other men to join and unite into a community for their comfortable, safe, and peaceable living one amongst another, in a secure enjoyment of their properties, and a greater security against any, that are not of it. This any number of men may do, because it injures not the freedom of the rest; they are left as they were in the liberty of the state of nature. When any number of men have so *consented to make one community or government*, they are thereby presently incorporated, and make one body politic, wherein the *majority* have a right to act and conclude the rest." See: John Locke, *Second Treatise of Government*, edited by C.B. Macpherson (Indianapolis, Indiana: Hackett Publishing Company, Inc., 1980), 52.

9. Ibid.

10. Jean Jacques Rousseau, *Social Contract* (Chicago: Encyclopaedia Britannica, Inc., 1952), 387.

11. Ibid., 389.

12. Ibid., 391.

13. Jean Jacques Rousseau, *A Dissertation on the Origin and Foundation of the Inequality of Mankind* (Chicago: Encyclopaedia Britannica, Inc., 1952),333.

14. Ibid., 334.

15. Hobbes, *Leviathan*, 296–297.

16. Plutarch, *The Lives of the Noble Grecians and Romans*, the Dryden Translation (Chicago: Encyclopaedia Britannica, Inc., 1952), 9.

17. Ibid., 24–25.

18. Please see: Jerry Z. Muller (ed.), *Conservatism: An Anthology of Social and Political Thought from David Hume to the Present* (Princeton: Princeton University Press, 1997), 55.

19. See: Ibid., 54.

20. Franz Oppenheimer, *The State* (Montréal, Canada: Black Rose Books, 2007), 8.

21. Ibid., 48–49.

22. Ibid., 49.

23. John Stuart Mill, *Representative Government* (Chicago: Encyclopaedia Britannica, Inc., 1952), 353.

24. Mill writes that "To enable it to do this, the constitution of the government must be nearly, or quite, despotic. A constitution in any degree popular, dependent on the voluntary surrender by the different members of the community of their individual freedom of action, would fail to enforce the first lesson which the pupils, in this stage of their progress, require. Accordingly, the civilisation of such tribes, when not the result of juxtaposition with others already civilised, is almost always the work of an absolute ruler, deriving his power either from religion or military prowess; very often from foreign arms." Please see: Ibid., 339.

25. Karl Marx and Frederick Engels, *The Germany Ideology*, edited by C. J. Arthur (New York: International Publishers, 1970), 90.

26. Immanuel Kant, *Perpetual Peace and Other Essays on Politics, History, and Morals* (Annapolis: Hackett Publishing Company, 1983), 56.

27. Please see: Victoria Tin-bor Hui, *War and State Formation in Ancient China and Early Modern Europe* (Cambridge: Cambridge University Press, 2005); Charles Tilly, *Coercion, Capital, and European States, AD 990–1990* (Cambridge, Massachusetts: Basil Blackwell, Inc., 1990); Bruce D. Porter, *War and the Rise of the State* (New York: The Free Press, 2002); and other related books.

28. See: Frederick Engels, *The Origin of the Family, Private Property and the State* (New York: International Publishers, 1972), 75.

29. See: Ibid., 87.

30. Ibid., 95.

31. Ibid., 94.

32. Ibid., 96.

33. See: Ibid., 158.

34. See: Ibid., 13.

35. Ibid., 118–119.

36. Kant writes that "Among all the animals, the *horse* was the first that man learned to tame and to domesticate in the process of populating

the earth and the *first instrument of war* (for the elephant belongs
to a later period, to luxury of already established nations). The art
of cultivating certain kinds of grasses, called *grains*, whose original
characteristics are no longer known, as well as the propagation and
refinement of various *fruits* by transplanting and grafting (in Europe
perhaps only two species, the crab apple and the wild pear), could arise
only under conditions provided by already established nations, where
property was secure, and it could occur only after men had already
undergone the transition from the lawless freedom of hunting, fishing,
and herding to the life of *agriculture*. See: Kant, *Perpetual Peace and
Other Essays on Politics, History, and Morals*, 122.

37. Engels, *The Origin of the Family, Private Property and the State*, 129.
38. Ibid., 220.
39. Ibid., 222.
40. Ibid., 224–225.
41. Ibid., 231.

Part One
Language and State Communication

Introduction

First of all, we need to prove that the essence of language is a condition for the development of media. People cannot fully understand language without an interpretation of media. Thus an interpretation of the state can be given from the perspective of an interrelationship between language and media. Media are created or used as required by language. Media extend the time span and the reach of people's mutual interaction. If one interacts with the other, language should be used in a period of time and on a certain scale because media are also used. Then language plays a role in the formation of the state.

In other words, an interpretation of the genesis and growth of the state, given from the perspective of language, is perhaps a philosophical interpretation of the genesis of the state because language is the factor leading to the dissolution of the tribe and hence the factor leading to the formation of the state though the state is seemingly formed before the dissolution of tribes. This is because whenever one communicates with the other, he may use language. Whenever he uses language, he uses a medium. Using a medium extends the distance of linguistic communication. Extending the distance of linguistic communication invariably leads to extending the time and the reach of linguistic communication. Then, people form a large community. They build a state.

In other words, as now people can communicate over long distances, many of them can communicate with one another. Media assist them in communicating over a long time and on a large scale, leading to the dissolution of the original community formed on the basis of the immediacy of kinship between one another. Besides, language is a special medium. There is an interaction between language and media. Many people come to be aware of the formation of certain common interest in their community. They help each other in their neighborhood. They exchange goods and services to give what is needed by each. They comply with the same custom and mores. They keep the common memory of the community. They embrace the same religious belief. They exchange feelings among themselves. They form their society. As the society needs to be governed, they set up their government. They perform all these activities in the background given rise to by linguistic communication. Then people build their state, a community in which language and the media utilized by language intermediate mutual interactions between one another. They extend the distance of linguistic communication, resulting in a change of the structure of the community mentioned in the prologue. Kinship gradually fails to function along with the disappearance of tribes. Then it follows that people make the progress of civilization step by step along with the disappearance of immediacy between one another. Language plays a pivotal role in the development of various media, and then, language, powered by media, supports the growth of the community and finally contributes to the birth of the state. In sum, every human community undergoes this process in the formation of the state throughout the world. Language is a foundation for the building of the state. Please allow me to substantiate this view from Chapter One to Chapter four of this manuscript as follows first.

Chapter One

Humans

1. Power Holders

Humans were originally tribal people. Their original community was the tribe. The tribe was a small community. Since they began to communicate using language, they have created media in support of linguistic communication. Then, extending the distance of linguistic communication leads to the dissolution of the tribe. In view of the growth of the state, extending the distance of linguistic communication is also the key. My reasoning is that whenever people use language, they find a chance to create or use a medium. The creation or the use of this medium results in the extension of the distance of linguistic communication. Humans who perform linguistic communication are actually also such media. Linguistic communication, performed by them, is usually boosted by them. They may function as auxiliary boosters. They can be active in support of such communication because their communication leads to the formation of their common interest. They need to cooperate. Their common interest is a basis. They always communicate with each other. They take initiative to strengthen their mutual communication. In the meantime, they are suitable for such communication. For example, each individual person receives information and saves it in his brain. This person uses it and may send it out. He is the first person who sends out a piece of information in some cases, but he may also be a person who passes on a piece of information to another person. He extends the distance of communication whenever he moves from one place to another. Humans function to extend the distance of communication by themselves. Their community grows in size. They break immediacy between one another. Kinship ties, as the ties of people, are replaced by linguistic communication. As humans live on earth generation by generation, they surely tell their experience to their future generations. They may know something about their ancestors. They perform linguistic communication between one generation and another. Thus humans perform human-chain linguistic communication, extending the time of linguistic communication. The so-called human-chain linguistic communication is the linguistic communication performed by the first person with the third person through a second person who passes on information in the middle. They communicate over a long stretch of time. In terms of such communication that goes on in an area, there is a similar situation. They communicate on a large scale. A person, in this process of linguistic communication, may never be an end of this process of linguistic communication. Humans, able to move from one place to another in order to build their community, are mobile media. They function as media. Since humans started to use language, they have actually come to be used by language as media, too. They and language interact with each other. They are the user of language. Language is also what uses them as a medium. Then human-chain linguistic communication plays a role in increasing the size of the human community. The community grows larger than a tribe. Tribes disappear gradually. States finally emerge. In the beginning humans built small states such as city-states. City-states might see a slave-owning system. If kingdoms emerged, the kingdoms often saw a feudal system. These states were often small, too. As these states were small, humans might temporarily rely on a method of building the society to build the state. Personal relationship was important. But they could not rely on such a method to build a large state. To build a large state, they had to build an administrative system.

In China, the Shang Dynasty (1600-1046BC) saw slavery. The state was small. During the Zhou Dynasty (1046-256BC) and the Warring States Period (475-221BC) slavery declined and the slave system shifted to a feudal system. People built the state on the basis of the feudal system. Such a state was usually small in size. The ruler relied on a personal relationship and kinship ties to build the state. The Zhou kings feoffed land to their fellow warriors and relatives. Such a feudal system allocated a piece of land as a region to an individual and established him as the ruler of a region. These regional rulers eventually rebelled against the Zhou kings and set up their own kingdoms. These kingdoms might be small in size. In the early period of Eastern Zhou that followed the period of Western Zhou, city-states were based on lineage.[1] During the Warring States Period, the feudal system continued, but it was hard for those states to grow in size. The reason is that the feudal system relied on an unreliable personal relationship in the building of the state. If humans wanted to build a large state, some kind of administrative structure would naturally develop.[2] Various administrative units had to be set up. Officials would be appointed on the basis of merit. The officials of those administrative units should perform human-chain linguistic communication. The Chinese Empire that grew in history is just a case in point. The Chinese Empire was initially established by Qin Shihuangdi (First Emperor) in 221 BC. In the building of this empire, the state recruited bureaucratic elite from all over the realm, a practice vigorously advocated by Li Si, the chief minister under Qin Shihuangdi, and established *Junxian* system, i.e. the division of the country into administrative units, i.e. commanderies and subordinate districts in the background that the empire was not bound to one particular nation or the people of a common territorial identity or an ethnic origin.[3]

In other words, building the state underwent a change. The method of organizing the state substituted for the method of organizing the society. The reason is that human-chain linguistic communication that functioned in the organization of the society failed to support the organization of the state when such communication was needed to go on over long distances. Some new chains replaced old ones. The evolution of pre-modern state to modern state in Europe also reflects this trend. This is a process gone through by the state in its formation and growth. Specifically, many historical events concern the replacement of those old links of the chain of linguistic communication in the growth of the state. This is in relation to the development of administrative system of the state. If a state is small, the power holder may rule the state directly. If a state is large, the power holder may rule the whole state indirectly. The power holder may delegate his power to his representatives and authorize them to govern various different areas. One example is that tribal areas existed in England in early history. Later petty kingdoms, including Powys, Dumnonia and Elmet, emerged. As those kingdoms were small, human-chain linguistic communication did not develop within the regime. By the time of the Norman conquest, the kingdom was divided into shires. Yet as each fiefdom was governed by the feudal lords, the traditional Anglo-Saxon shire system became less important. Though the state grew large, people realized human-chain linguistic communication through a personal relationship between the sovereign and the lords and this personal relationship was also the method used in the organization of a society in history. That is, what defined this personal relationship might not be the law of the state, but personal contracts. Lords governed the areas—fiefs—controlled by them. Each lord governed an area as entrusted in some sense. It was a phenomenon across Europe at that time. As Harold J. Berman writes,

> It was a basic principle of justice throughout the West that every lord had the right to hold court, that is, to preside over his vassals—or over his tenants, whether or not they were vassals—in court proceedings. This principle was an expression of the merger of military-economic and political relations: the military-economic enterprise of administering a fief was at the same time the political enterprise of governing the community of people who were attached to the fief.[4]

Along with the growth of the state, the state was required to be organized in the method of organizing the state. When the method of organizing the state superseded the method of organizing the society, the old links of the chain were no longer able to support the building of the regime and people created the new links of the chain. So in medieval Europe, the sovereign found gradually that lords might not always function as the links of the chain. King John of England found it difficult to control barons. Philip the First of France lost all authority over his barons.[5]

In other countries, cities gained their autonomy or independence. Adam Smith writes that:

> In countries, such as Italy and Switzerland, in which, on account either of their distance from the principal seat of government, of the natural strength of the country itself, or of some other reason, the sovereign came to lose the

whole of his authority, the cities generally became independent republics, and conquered all the nobility in their
neighbourhood, obliging them to pull down their castles in
the country and to live, like other peaceable inhabitants, in
the city.[6]

This situation is followed by the creation of the new links of the chain
for the direct interaction between the sovereign and the masses. People performed long-distance linguistic communication. This actually means that linguistic communication, performed by the ruler with the masses, becomes the
linguistic communication that goes on in the organization of the state. This
linguistic communication no longer functions on the basis of personal relationship. Administrative system develops because the ruler appoints his representatives to govern different local areas. In ancient England, for instance,
the ruler set up counties. By the time of the Norman conquest, shires also
became counties. Boroughs were also set up. During the 13th century the
English Parliament became the de facto governing body for the country. In
1297, it decreed that the representatives to the House of Commons would be
allocated on the basis of the administrative units of counties and boroughs.
In the 1540s the regime instituted the office of Lord Lieutenant in each
county and such Lord Lieutenants replaced feudal lords as the Crown's direct
representatives in the county. From the 16th century onward, the regime
increasingly used the county as a unit of local government. As cities grew,
the regime also allowed for the cities to set up their local governments. An
administrative system took shape. In modern times a country often consists
of regions or provinces, cities or towns or districts or counties, and so on.
Today a state almost always has a central government in the capital and many
local governments in other cities or areas. As the officials of the government
need to communicate with one another when necessary, human-chain linguistic communication goes on throughout the administrative system.

In sum, the human-chain linguistic communication, performed by the
ruler with the lords in organizing the state in the principle of organizing
the society, evolved to be the human-chain linguistic communication performed by the administrative personnel of various levels. Now administrative personnel perform human-chain linguistic communication between the
different levels of the administrative body. For example, the officials of the

administrative body may orally, or in writing, pass on a command from the higher level to the lower level or they may orally, or in writing, pass on a report from the lower level to the higher level. If a courier is engaged, an official of the national government may get in touch with an official of the provincial government and an official of the provincial government may get in touch with an official of the government of a county. Officials may also submit a report to the official of the higher level and level by level in the same way. Besides, officials may hold a meeting to pass on the directive of the government of the higher level to the government of the lower level or to submit a report of the government of the lower level to the government of the higher level.

That is, the development of the administrative system is part of the building of the state. In the outset, people, under the governance of the state, do not perform frequent linguistic communication because they are not well organized in economic and cultural aspects. Officials, working for the regime, become media crucially in support of the linguistic communication that goes on throughout the state. In other words, after the formation of a state, the regime, in charge of governing the state, requires the internal division of labor in governing the state. The state ruler, in control of the regime, is unable to govern the state by himself only. He usually sets up a team of bureaucrats in charge of governing the state. He fields officials to take charge of the work of the government bodies of different levels. This is due to the variation of the circumstances of different regions. Some officials are assigned the task of governing the local areas while some other officials are assigned the task of governing the whole state. The officials of the lower level are the representatives of the officials of the higher level. Certain human-chain linguistic communication goes on in the system of bureaucracy. As the officials of different levels can realize such human-chain linguistic communication, the power holder of the state sets up an administrative system covering the entire state. People see a hierarchy of administrative units in each state. The emergence of many great states in the world shows this trend.

This indicates that along with the growth of the state, people have to build an administrative system that ensures the human-chain linguistic communication that effectively sustains the operation of a government that has various local branches governing different areas within the state. Human-chain linguistic communication particularly develops within the administrative system. The power holder of the state can delegate his power to his agents in governing the state. In describing the administrative structure of ancient China, E. N. Gladden writes that:

> Ultimate responsibility for everything that happened anywhere in the Empire rested with the Emperor, who delegated a measure of that responsibility to his immediate subordinates, who in their turn delegated strands of their responsibilities throughout the ranks of officialdom. The chain of delegation reached down to the heads of households.[7]

The chain of delegation mentioned by Gladden should be based on the chain of linguistic communication formed by humans, namely, officials of various levels and their assistants.

In the history of France the development of an administrative system followed the same logic. Joseph R. Sprayer writes that:

> [W]hile the French government was willing to tolerate a wide degree of diversity in local practices, there had to be some uniformity in such matters as taxation, some way of reconciling conflicting local interests, some means of asserting the ultimate authority of the king. Thus France had to develop a many-layered administrative structure. Local officials were supervised by provincial officials who were supervised by regional officials who were supervised by councils, courts, and chambers sitting in Paris. There was a constant flow of orders, rebukes, judicial decisions, and requests for information running from central to local authorities, and an equally constant flow of protests, appeals, excuses, and explanations running the other way.[8]

This means that people who communicate using language are bound to develop various media in support of linguistic communication. Humans that function as media in the formation of human-chain linguistic communication are the media that appear when people perform linguistic communication to build a regime. That is, officials themselves function as media in support of the related linguistic communication. In view of the organization of the state throughout history, it normally involves intermediaries, representatives and messengers who are typically supposed to perform such human-chain linguistic communication to issue orders, or instructions, and to submit reports because people have broken immediacy between one another. Jack Goody, an English social anthropologist, writes that:

> In societies of the smallest scale internal communication can be maintained by direct face-to-face contact between, say, a lineage and its elders. But for a state, even a simple one, the increase in scale, the intervention of spatial distance, the inclusion of larger numbers of individuals in the organization, mean that communication between its members requires the use of intermediaries, representatives, messengers and the like.[9]

The evolution of such links of the chain demonstrates a long-time historical process of establishing such links of the chain fitting in with the regime in charge of building the state. The building of the state includes the building of the regime. The building of the regime includes the creation of the communicative links of the chain of power holders in governing all the regions within the state.

In modern times the situation remains largely unchanged. The officials of each level function as the links of the chain in linguistic communication performed either by the officials of the higher level with the officials of the lower level or by the officials of the lower level with the officials of the higher level. One case in point is also the case of China. Before the Communist Party of China took power in China in 1949, the underground organizations of the Communist Party of China functioned in the region under the control of the Nationalist Party of China, the ruling party of the Republic of China, founded in 1912. As all activities were often performed underground, the instructions of the leaders of the Communist Party of China were often passed on from the higher level to the lower level through oral human-chain linguistic communication though people also performed written human-chain linguistic communication. Since the Communist Party of China took power in China in 1949, the administrative system has been continuing to rely on human-chain linguistic communication. The officials of the government of the

Communist Party of China often pass on the instructions of the government through human-chain linguistic communication, oral or written. Meetings are regularly held to pass on the instructions of the higher level to the lower level. As people stress vertical leadership, such human-chain linguistic communication is a guarantee for the functioning of the administrative system. Perhaps one case, experienced by me during my childhood in China, can be used to illustrate this situation. When I was a boy, China was in the period of the so-called Cultural Revolution launched by Mao Zedong, the supreme power holder of China from 1949 to 1976. During the Cultural Revolution, the internal linguistic communication system, based on the human links of the chains formed by officials, was down due to turmoil or disorder. Then the heads of the so-called revolutionary factions, mobilized by Mao to upset the original government system, used to function as officials and they functioned as the links of the chains of linguistic communication that passed on the directives of Mao because Mao directly participated in the activities of mass mobilization due to the fact that the original normal administrative system collapsed in that political campaign. Mao needed to communicate directly with the masses. He often issued the so-called "supreme instructions" to the masses and the masses were required to listen to the reading of the supreme instructions immediately. Then the so-called Revolutionary Committee of each province, each city and each county was responsible for passing on the so-called supreme instructions of the "great leader." Such links of the chains of communication reached the grassroots. Sometimes a supreme instruction was transmitted to the masses in the evening. In order to notify all to come to the factory, or the school, or any work unit of the government, to listen to the reading of the supreme instruction, each worker of the factory or each student of the school or each cadre of the government body was arranged for to pass on the notice from door to door so that all could come to get together to listen to the reading of the supreme instruction. People performed human-chain linguistic communication to organize themselves. I was a school student at that time. The students were organized just this way. People often performed such human-chain linguistic communication orally.

In terms of written human-chain linguistic communication, I argue that formal human-chain linguistic communication within the system of bureaucracy should also often be written. Written communication, performed within the system of bureaucracy, may be supported by human-chain linguistic communication. One example is that officials within the government may perform written human-chain linguistic communication though sometimes direct written communication can replace human-chain linguistic communication due to the use of material media as alternatives. This means that sometimes written communication also needs to be boosted by humans themselves. When people establish the administrative system, they need such communication. Goody tells us that in the early 1930s the British colonial government in a certain African country called Gold Coast decided upon a policy of Indirect Rule, which meant setting up a subordinate level of administration based on indigenous customs and known as Native Authorities. This proposal entailed a flurry of literate activity on the part of administrators who were called upon to report (in writing) upon local practice. Then it meant not only recognizing some form of chiefship (even where this did not exist in pre-colonial times) but handing over some responsibilities of a judicial, fiscal and administrative kind. Such responsibilities were necessarily seen as involving the maintenance of similar records, since only in this way could one report to higher authority and ultimately to the British Government.[10]

If people build democracy, another kind of human-chain linguistic communication develops in the opposite direction. Such human-chain linguistic communication is the one that suits the operation of the modern state. As Bertrand Russell narrated, in antiquity the representative system was unknown. Citizens, assembled in the market place, voted on each issue. As the state was confined to a single city, each citizen had a sense of real power and responsibility. He could understand most of the issues according to his own experience. But democracy could not extend over a wider area without an elected legislature. When Roman citizenship was granted to the inhabitants of other parts of Italy, the new citizens could not, in practice, acquire any share of political power, since this could only be exercised by those who were actually in Rome. The practice of choosing representatives in modern world overcame the geographic difficulty.[11] Representatives function as the links of the chains in the process of linguistic communication performed by the citizens with the power holders as a result. People perform this linguistic communication in the opposite direction.

This means that as the practice of democracy requires election, such election becomes a process of linguistic communication performed by a collective being composed of the electorate with themselves. When the state grows large and is no longer geographically confined to a city, people find that they are no longer able to perform linguistic communication to elect government officials in the traditional way. As voters, as a collective being, are slow to act, it is, obviously, inconvenient for them to express their opinions frequently. Then people perform linguistic communication in the process of election with the election candidates some of whom later become representatives elected by the electorate. Representatives become the links of the chains of linguistic communication performed on a large scale and are thus authorized by the electorate to express their opinions on the governance of the state. Representatives become the standardized links of the chains in the process of linguistic communication performed by the voters with the authorities or the state. If each riding has one representative, this representative should be one standardized link of the chain in the linguistic communication performed by the voters in this riding with the authority such as the council of the city or the parliament of the province or the parliament of the state. Normally, voters do not directly perform linguistic communication with the authorities of the state now and they communicate with the authorities of the state in the process of human-chain linguistic communication. So each link of the chain in the human-chain linguistic communication supports the modern representative democracy that runs across the state.

Political parties can also be deemed as the links of the chains together with the representatives. Political parties can be deemed as the organizations that create a condition for the organization of the representatives in performing linguistic communication with the authorities. This is because as each riding at least generates one representative, many representatives will emerge across the state. The organization of a modern state requires effective linguistic communication performed by the representatives with the authorities of the state across the state. Representatives need to coordinate their action in order to express clearly their opinions on the governance of the state. Then opinions, expressed by various representatives, need to be consolidated in order that they express a clear and general opinion to the authorities of the state. Political parties naturally become the links of the chains in linguistic communication. They help voters to save time and energy in expressing their opinions in election because a small portion of people can represent a large portion of people. Then they make themselves special media used by the voters to express their opinions in election. Then political parties become the special links of the chains in linguistic communication. In the meantime, as each political party becomes a link of the chain in the process of linguistic communication in support of the interaction between the citizens and the state, it exercises its influence in politics. As linguistic communication, performed by the electorate with the authorities of the state, is crucial under democracy, each political party has the potential of controlling the functioning of the apparatus of the state. If one political party is formally authorized to represent the electorate, it may hold the state power. Thus human-chain linguistic communication plays a role in the formation of the government in the state that puts representative democracy into practice.

A state leader is, in some sense, also a link of the chain in human-chain linguistic communication that underpins the building of the state because the state leader represents the people forming the state. This is because we cannot find another person who is suitable to represent the whole people of the state and sometimes the people of a state indeed require one person to represent them in expressing their opinion or will. Then the state leader is selected in the process of human-chain linguistic communication. Voters first elect their representatives. The representatives then, in some sense, elect one political party holding state power. Then this political party elects one person to be the state leader to represent the state. As the state is formed by the people, this state leader normally also becomes the representative of the people of the whole state. The state leader emerges in the process of human-chain linguistic communication. Usually, the process of human-chain linguistic communication in this case is the longest in comparison with the process of human-chain linguistic communication that generates a ruling party or a representative. Whenever the state leader functions to express the will of the people of the whole state, he relies on the operation of a process of human-chain linguistic communication. Thus I argue that, originally, humans engage in linguistic communication in order to organize their society either in the form of human-chain linguistic communication or otherwise. Yet since the birth of the state humans have extended the distance of human-chain linguistic communication in support of the formation of the state built in the principle of modern representative democracy. If humans were unable to function as the links of the chain in linguistic communication, people would not establish such a political system of the state.

Similarly, if we look into the function of those who are in charge of carrying out a law in the formation of the state, we also see that they also work in the process of human-chain linguistic communication. In early times people already made a certain law in the governance of the state. This law was usually unwritten. This law might be a customary law. This law was handed down in the process of spoken communication. This process of spoken communication is human-chain linguistic communication. Each that hands down the law functions as a link of the chain in a long process of human linguistic communication. If we accept the view, adduced by Lewis H. Morgan, that the time of the existence of the primitive society is much longer than the time of the existence of the civilized society in the process of evolution of human society, we can also surely believe that human-chain linguistic communication, performed to hand down an unwritten law, has at least run for a very long period of time. Yet as humans are born one generation after another and humans are able to learn to use language, people perform such linguistic communication year in, year out. Thus humans are able to make a law in governing their community. In the primitive society humans may already use a law to govern their tribe. In the civilized society humans may use such a law to govern their state. If they still insist on using an unwritten law, they should perform human-chain linguistic communication orally to hand down the law. The judges usually function as the links of the chain. The judges are in charge of carrying out the law. This law is often the case law or customary law in nature. The judgment, made by the preceding judge, is a reference used by a following judge. Then judges hand down the unwritten law. For example, in ancient Greece judges used to award judgments according to the law handed down through spoken human-chain linguistic communication. In modern times people still use unwritten laws in the states in which common law is prevalent. In the United Kingdom, people carry out common law. The common law is normally handed down through spoken human-chain linguistic communication. If a state adopts the legal system consisting mainly of written laws, there may also be a process of human-chain linguistic communication in the operation of a law. People may memorize the law by virtue of spoken communication. In Jewish tradition, the Mishna is the oral law while the Mikra is the written law. These two laws are memorized together. Though the written form of law is more easily memorized, oral law is used as a supplement. Therefore Jack Goody writes that:

> In Jewish tradition, the Mishna is the oral law, as opposite to the Mikra, the written law. The oral law was delivered by God to Moses with the Pentateuth, but as an oral supplement. It now exists in written form but is learned verbatim, so that it is in a sense preserved orally in memory (and if necessary transmitted by word of mouth). The word *Mishna* is in fact derived from the verb meaning 'to teach,' especially 'to teach by means of oral repetition.' [12]

Generally speaking, judges are invariably in the process of human-chain linguistic communication performed to memorize the law. If the lawmakers, forming the legislative branch, make a law, this law represents a process of one-way long-distance linguistic communication performed by the lawmakers with the citizens. Yet as this process of linguistic communication is one way and of long distance, the lawmakers are usually prevented from conducting any dialogue with the citizens. Then it follows that in applying a law, people need such a dialogue, namely, a process of two-way linguistic communication. Judges are appointed to help conduct such a dialogue. Judges are actually, or in some sense, the representatives of the lawmakers though they are in charge of applying laws in each specific case. Even though today the written law realizes the direct long-distance linguistic communication between the lawmakers and the citizens, people may still need human-chain linguistic communication. In early times humans formed tribes. They might not need judges. Peoples, living in the German or Greek or Roman tribes in ancient times, used to hold assemblies to hear a case and to deliver a judgment. Ordinary people themselves used to be the judges. Yet since the formation of the states, their communities have grown large. Then in each state the government appoints judges to take charge of judicial judgment. Judges function as the links of the chain in human-chain linguistic communication.

Such human-chain linguistic communication underpins the building of the state.

2. Businessmen

Businessmen and businesswomen (hereinafter referred to as "businessmen") emerged in the transition from the primitive society to the civilized one. In the primitive society each was connected with all others by kinship. If each member of the tribe needed the assistance from any other member of the tribe, such assistance might be received without the need of using language. For example, the son got a help from the father without using language. There was no private property. People might occasionally realize the division of labor in production in the line of gender or age. But they did not exchange goods and services. Later, humans commenced to perform linguistic communication. They extended communication distance. They communicated over a long time and on a large scale. They gradually formed a large community. Then they came to have their private property. They began to exchange goods and services. They realized the division of labor widely. The result is that language put an end to immediacy between one another, but it constructed intermediacy between one another. It began to play a role in the exchange of goods and services. Its role highlighted the construction of a new human society. By contrast, without language, the society, formed by humans, should be like the one of animals. In that society animals do not exchange anything. As Smith writes,

> Nobody ever saw a dog make a fair and deliberate exchange of one bone for another with another dog. Nobody ever saw one animal by its gestures and natural cries signify to another, this is mine and that yours; I am willing to give this for that. When an animal wants to obtain something either of a man or of another animal, it has no other means of persuasion but to gain the favour of those whose service it requires. A puppy fawns upon its dam, and a spaniel endeavours by a thousand attractions to engage the attention of its master who is at dinner, when it wants to be fed by him.[13]

While humans exchange goods and services, they need to use language to indicate the intention of exchange and to talk about the price of the exchange. They may also perform human-chain linguistic communication through the exchange of goods and services. Economic growth depends on the incessant exchange of goods and services. It is possible for a person to sell one product to the second person and for a second person to sell the same product to the third person or for the third person to buy one product from the second person and for the second person to buy the same product from the first person. Selling and buying involves human-chain linguistic communication. Selling and buying creates value embedded in a product or a service. People perform such communication in their economic activities. The economy of commodity germinates and grows.

The growth of the economy of commodity, first of all, changes the method of using various resources. Tribal people might use various resources for their own livelihood. They might not need to use language. If they communicated with one another within the tribe, they might even not be required to use language. Yet since their departure from the tribe, people, using language, have been exchanging goods and services. They commercialize production. The commercialization of production includes the commercialized use of various resources. They perform human-chain linguistic communication to realize sale and purchase. Various businessmen emerge. As they are involved in different sectors or industries, they engage in different kinds of business. They exploit various resources.

Some of them sell land. They are land owners. They perform human-chain linguistic communication in order to make profits from the land they own. Then it follows that the first owner of a piece of land may sell it to the second owner, and then the second owner of this piece of land may sell it to the third owner, and so on and so forth. The sale of this piece of land many times is realized in human-chain linguistic communication. The sale of this piece of land many times, in order that this piece of land is developed to produce agricultural products or to make industrial products, should be significant for the acquirement of profits or for the growth of economy because each time the sale of this piece of land is usually supposed to bring about profits. Otherwise it will not be sold. Obviously, this phenomenon cannot appear in a human community such as a herd in which people use no language.

In the tribe of the primitive society, in which language may be used, land is not used for commercial purpose either. Land has the value of use, but it does not have any value of market. Thus people in the tribe do not sell land. Thus people commit no act involving human-chain linguistic communication. Thus the commercialized use of land is a primary way for humans to perform economic activities in the civilized society. Human-chain linguistic communication should play a role therein.

In the meantime, we sometimes see that some people especially operate a forest farm. They are involved in the business of logging. They may be called the timber-men. As timber will be sold, they are involved in human-chain linguistic communication. In other words, after the commercialization of timber, some people produce timber while some other people consume timber. Without the human-chain linguistic communication performed by those who produce timber and those who consume timber, the business of developing the resources of timber cannot develop. Human-chain communication creates a condition for business operation. Thus we see that, although a forest may belong to a tribe in the primitive society, the forest plays a very limited role in the growth of the community. The forest may not be meaningfully used. Yet since humans started to use language and since humans formed their civilized society, they have commercialized the cultivation of trees and the production of timber. The industry of logging appears. Then trees play a role in the economic growth of the state.

Fishermen may play the same role. While humans were still tribal people, fish in the rivers might belong to their tribe. However, fish might not play any role in the economic growth of the tribe. Fish did not contribute to the growth of the tribe because it was not a commodity. Yet since humans started to use language, they have been performing human-chain linguistic communication. They, as producers, may catch fish from the river and other people, as consumers, may buy fish. There may appear a process of human-chain linguistic communication that goes on to realize the production and consumption of a lot of fish. Fish may become a staple. There may appear a group of people who manage fisheries and there may also appear another group of people who especially sell fish. Fishery may become a sector of economy. If we postulate that all businessmen spearhead the formation of an economic community, I argue that fishery also boosts the growth of the economic community, which boosts the growth of the state.

Businessmen, especially involved in the business of trading furs, may also make such a natural resource an important commodity. While humans were tribal people, furs were never used to make profits. They were consumed. But they were only consumed within the tribe. The tribe was a small community. Yet as people who perform linguistic communication can function as media in civilized society, they are prone to perform human-chain linguistic communication. They expand their community. This community grows large in population and area. The growth of the community paves a way for them to build a market. Then it is possible for them to hunt wild animals, process furs, and sell them on the market. The development of human-chain linguistic communication creates a condition for the development of such a business. A special economic sector emerges.

In short, without human-chain linguistic communication, humans cannot commercialize the related natural resources.

People, especially committed to the production of certain products, may even perform widely human-chain linguistic communication. Products may be touched by different hands. There is a special process of producing them and there is also a special process of selling them. People, producing or selling them, rely deeply on the process of human-chain linguistic communication. Some businessmen are especially involved in the process of human-chain linguistic communication. Their business is to make deals with many people. They need to perform human-chain linguistic communication. In the meantime, as they engage in their business in a certain economic sector, the work, done by them, becomes a special occupation. As a result, they also perform special human-chain linguistic communication in order to realize the goal of their business.

In this regard, the owners of property are typical. After people produce the property, the owners of the property may sell it to make profits. If this property is a house, they may sell it many times. They are involved in a process of human-chain linguistic communication. Without human-chain linguistic communication, the owners cannot sell it time and again and hence will not get profits. Thus the owner of a house, in some sense, functions as a link of the chain in human-chain linguistic communication. This situation is also at variance with the situation of any tribe of the primitive society. In some sense primitives have dwellings, but they do not sell them. The case is different in the civilized society. In this society, performing human-chain linguistic communication creates a condition for humans to sell real estate in order to make profits. Needless to say, tribal people might use language. But before extending the distance of linguistic communication, people, as the members of the tribe, did not sell their dwellings if any because they had no private property within the tribe. By contrast, within the state, people have private property and perform human-chain linguistic communication to sell and buy real estate. Then people become the sellers and buyers of real estate. They perform human-chain linguistic communication.

Businessmen, involved in the production of industrial products, may also be in the process of human-chain linguistic communication in relation to them. They engage in production. People may process products on several different stages in production. A product may be manufactured by using another product. Different producers cooperate with each other. For example, a textile factory produces fabrics. Another garment factory uses these fabrics to make clothes. Likewise, we may see that a plant produces steel materials. Another factory uses these steel materials to make automobiles. In addition, a factory may manufacture semi-conductors. Another factory may use semi-conductors to make radios or television sets. A series of factories may participate in the production of one product. All manufacturers may be involved in a process of human-chain linguistic communication. If a number of manufacturers do not perform human-chain linguistic communication, they will not make a wide variety of industrial products. Whenever people convert a product into another form, there is a process of human-chain linguistic communication. Business develops because of the extension of human-chain linguistic communication.

Vendors may also extend human-chain linguistic communication within the system of the sales of goods. There are several levels of wholesale of certain products and the distribution of those products relies on human-chain linguistic communication that goes on between the different levels of distribution realized by the vendors of different levels. The wholesaler of the first level sells a batch of products to the wholesalers of the second level and the wholesalers of the second level sell this batch of products to the wholesalers of the third level. Human-chain linguistic communication makes such commercial activity possible. The system of sales comprises several levels of wholesalers. Then a retailer sells the products. The retailer is also a link of the chain in the sales. Relying on such human-chain linguistic communication the manufacturer sells its products across the state.

Self-employed people, selling their products or providing their services, also conduct human-chain linguistic communication. They sell goods and provide services. They make a living or make profits. They realize their goal by offering their personal skills. So we see the following situation: The first man works as a mason; the second man works as a smith; the third man works as a baker; the fourth man works as a shoemaker; the fifth man works as a tailor; the sixth man works as a brewer; and the seventh man works as a carpenter. Then all of them supply and purchase goods or services. As the goods, produced by them by using the working skill, are offered by each, goods are circulated. On one hand each sells his goods and on the other each buys the goods sold by others. People also buy and provide services. They realize the exchange of goods and services among them by way of human-chain linguistic communication. All function as the links of the chain in linguistic communication performed to build an economic community and support the growth of the economy of the state.

We can also demonstrate this situation if we look into the role played by currency, a result of repetitive human-chain linguistic communication that assists people in the exchange of goods and services. The history of currency indicates this situation. In early times the chief commodities, exchanged by pastoral tribes, were cattle. Cattle became the commodities by which all other commodities were valued. Cattle acquired a money function.[14] In the meantime, upon every exchange, people used language. They indicated the value of the exchanged cattle by using language. Human-chain linguistic communication extended. Later, humans exchanged goods by using gold or silver as a means of exchange. Though people did not use the scales to weigh them on certain occasions, people, exchanging goods, estimated the weight of gold or silver. Their estimation was based on the imagination of the exchange of equal values indicated by using language. People might imagine the graduation shown on the beam of the scales indicating the weight of gold or silver. That graduation was language. Later, people made coin or bill. Coin, or bill, indicated a certain amount of money or a certain value. Language gradually played a prominent role. As linguistic communication went on with the person who held this bill, or coin, in the exchange of goods and services, this linguistic communication should be a process of human-chain linguistic communication that was part of a network of human-chain linguistic communication. Bills, or coins, used as currencies, further highlighted the role played by language on the basis of which people constructed a network of multiple processes of human-chain linguistic communication on the market. The processes of human-chain linguistic communication that paralleled and crossed each other formed a network of human-chain linguistic communication, leading to the growth of a market, which served as an economic basis for the building of the state. Then people further built a financial market.

In other words, all those who engage in their business need to use currency. The act of using currency invariably involves a process of human-chain linguistic communication. A ten dollar bill, for example, is used by a person who makes payment to another person in the exchange of goods and services, and this bill is usually used by countless producers or vendors or consumers one by one. The use of this bill is subject to the incessant exchange of different goods and services. This bill is transferred from the hand of one person to that of the other. This bill functions in human-chain linguistic communication. People can hardly realize the division of labor without such human-chain linguistic communication. As such, Adams Smith says that after the end of barter, money has become the common means of commerce. Every commodity is more frequently exchanged for money than for any other commodity. The butcher carries his beef or mutton to the market, where he exchanges them for money because he no longer frequently carries them to the baker or the brewer to exchange them for bread or for beer, and then he exchanges that money for bread or for beer. He also points out that the quantity of money the butcher gets for them regulates the quantity of bread and beer which he can afterwards buy. It is more natural for him to estimate their value by the quantity of money than by that of bread and beer. That is, the butcher tends to estimate that his meat is worth threepence or fourpence a pound than that it is worth three or four pounds of bread or three or four quarts of small beer. Then the exchangeable value of every commodity is more frequently estimated by the quantity of money than by the quantity either of labor or of any other commodity which can be had in exchange for it.[15]

Some people are especially involved in the saving and distribution of money of the state in order that people can efficiently use money for production and consumption. Bankers establish banks to attract those who have extra money to deposit money into the banks and then provide the money to the borrowers who need money. Banks provide loans to producers or service providers or ordinary consumers. Money flows to the places where it is most urgently needed. People, thus, perform human-chain linguistic communication to let money flow to those places. Then they allocate funding efficiently for production and consumption. This boosts the economy of a state.

Those who establish and manage stock markets also intend to make the efficient use of the idle funds in support of the production and consumption within the state. There is a process of linguistic communication performed by the lenders and those who manage the stock market. There is also a process of linguistic communication between the stock market managers and the borrowers. The stock market managers usually establish companies. Those companies help borrowers to seek lenders and help lenders to seek borrowers. People allocate funding efficiently this way.

Those bond market operators do the similar work. As companies sometimes run out of their own funds and need to borrow funds from the potential investors in the society and many investors who have extra personal funds and intent to invest to make more money are willing to lend their funds, some businessmen establish companies to build the bond market to enhance efficiency in the use of funding in the state. They function as the links of the chain in the process of linguistic communication. They enhance the circulation of funds in the economy. As they accelerate the circulation of funds, they invigorate the economy. They bolster the growth of the economy of the state.

The fund managers also do the similar work. They establish companies that manage the funds used in the investment in various economic sectors. As citizens may have funding that can be used for investment, they put their money into the funds managed by the fund managing companies. The fund managing companies build a portfolio of investment in order to minimize the risk of investment and maximize the return of the investment. They are also involved in the process of human-chain linguistic communication.

Insurance is also part of the financial sector because insurers operate their insurance business in order to make profits by using the money provided by those who subscribe insurance. Insurers are also involved in the process of human-chain linguistic communication. That is, those who seek insurance usually pay premiums in order to purchase a policy. The result is that the money, provided by a portion of people, is used to give protection to another portion of people. Thus insurance becomes a business. Insurers, thus, are able to help people to use some money to seek guarantee and to eschew loss. Insurers are the links of the chain in the process of linguistic communication performed by all those who give guarantee with all those who seek guarantee. Without such links of the chain, the business of insurance will not flourish. Without insurance, people may not use funding efficiently and people may not have their property and lives effectively protected.

Communication is also what is needed by businessmen. Communication is an undertaking. This undertaking facilitates the service of providing market information. As this undertaking accelerates the circulation of information, it is a medium. This medium generates the various processes of human-chain linguistic communication. Human links of the chain in linguistic communication are also media. People extend the distance of linguistic communication as a result. Thus one businessman conveys the related information to the other. People usually provide postal service in a process of human-chain linguistic communication. Specifically, each city has a general post office. Individual businessmen may subcontract the postal service in different areas. Postmen deliver mails. They are involved in human-chain linguistic communication. They read the address of each mail. Then each mail is delivered to the right address. Telegraph service may be provided by each telegraph office in each region. There is a network of telegraph within the state. Telephone service is also provided by the telephone companies. All telephone companies jointly build a nationwide telephone service network. One office is connected with another office. Thus there is a process of human-chain linguistic communication in the operation of this telegraph service or telephone service across the state.

A network of the transportation of land route, water route and air route may also take shape. The growth of this network can also reflect the development of a network of human-chain linguistic communication. People consider the geographic position, the terrain, the industrial technologies, and the special products of each area as all factors in the development of transportation in order to boost commerce and economic prosperity. Businessmen, involved in the development of transportation, are actually media in support of the building of a network of transportation that bolsters the construction of the national economy. Transportation is also a medium. Such a network of transportation serves to build the network of human-chain linguistic communication widely. For example, a city, located at the mouth of a long river running through the country, may attract more human, material and financial resources because it is easy to build a network of human-chain linguistic communication in support of the economic activities. People may build a network of transportation, functioning around such a city as an economic hub, in support of the formation of national economy. This also includes the fact that people construct roads, or highways, or railways, leading to those places where it is easy or appropriate to develop the transportation system. In the meantime, people install other facilities of transportation facilitating the exchange of goods and services between those different areas. It becomes easy for people in different areas to exchange goods and services. Through human-chain linguistic communication, human, material and financial resources and products flow across the state.

Cities, built by businessmen involved in the development of cities, may also give rise to the development of human-chain linguistic communication. As urbanites reside at one location, they actively exchange goods and services. Then businessmen blossom in the cities first. They are always involved in human-chain linguistic communication. They include businessmen in the sector of real estate development, the sector of logistics, the catering sector, the clothing manufacturing sector and other sectors. For example, businessmen in the sector of real estate development survive and develop because people always need residential premises. Restaurants survive and develop because they serve different customers. They provide goods and services on the market. All are involved in close human-chain linguistic communication. The operation of the economy of the city depends on the circulation of goods provided in human- chain linguistic communication as well as services provided in the city. Cities are actually media. Thus business is chiefly operated in the cities. Each city is a place where it is convenient for people to perform human-chain communication for business purpose. There is a distance between one human link of the chain and another. If people strengthen the connections between the two human links of the chain, they will enhance the efficacy of linguistic communication and hence the exchange of goods and services. The downtown of each city is the area where commerce is concentrated. It is not accidental that the exchange of goods and services develops first in the urban area. Therefore commerce usually runs in the urban area. The more the people who communicate with one another frequently in a certain area for commerce, the more the people who perform human-chain linguistic communication. Resources, products and wealth circulate within the city. The city-states that grew in ancient Greece may shed light on this situation. At that time people normally formed themselves into the state on the basis of the formation of a city. They tended not to form a state if they lived in the rural area. Commerce played a role. So in the outset only in the cities did the common interest of people basically take shape. Thus in the growth of city-states in Greece kings depended on the cities. It was said that throughout the Hellenistic period the royal administration recruited leading functionaries from the urban upper class. The cities controlled most economic activities and substantially contributed to the general prosperity and the royal budget.[16] In medieval times commerce also first developed in the cities in Italy and Germany. Some cities were autonomous because they differed from rural areas. Cities became prosperous because of the development of commerce. Some cities were states. When nation-states grew in early modern times, big cities also played a prominent role. They became the political or economic or financial centers of the state. The urban area played a larger role in state formation than the rural area did. So, capital, human resources, technologies and raw materials all flew chiefly to the cities other than to the rural areas. Urbanization means a special progress made in the economic domain.

In short, the exchange of goods and services prompts the exploitation of natural resources and gives play to the expertise or skills of businessmen. The provision of financial service enhances efficiency in the utilization of funding. Likewise, the development of communication, transportation and cities reduces the cost of transaction. All of those activities depend on the development of human-chain linguistic communication.

3. Culture Workers

People, involved in creating or showing cultural works, contribute to the development of culture. I discussed culture in the previous manuscript *Language and State: An Inquiry into the Progress of Civilization*, and I accentuated that various cultural forms of expression are actually the media of language in human communication. Yet if we study the relationship between culture and humans, we also need to stress that humans, involved in handing down or creating any culture or demonstrating it, are also special media in the growth of the state. They are the important links of the chains in human linguistic communication that enable humans to create, demonstrate, promote and hand down culture. As humans can learn culture and population may increase, those who are especially involved in developing culture function as the links of the chains in the process of linguistic communication in the promotion of culture and the growth of the cultural community that further supports the growth of the state. If people perform linguistic communication for their daily life, linguistic communication performed by them may not be human-chain linguistic communication. If people perform linguistic communication to spread culture, linguistic communication performed by them is usually human-chain linguistic communication because linguistic communication, performed by them to spread culture, is usually, in some sense, endless. Any culture, created in a certain human community, is bound to be shared. Therefore, humans keep on performing linguistic communication to spread culture. Thus people preserve, spread and hand down culture. As such, those who especially engage in the spread of culture are media which serve all who share that culture.

At least, those who engage in the cause of education may be the links of the chains of linguistic communication. They spread culture. They impart knowledge. They impart the knowledge of science and literature. They also impart the knowledge of language. The knowledge of language is part of culture. Though a teacher may not teach spoken language, he usually teaches script. Script is taught by teachers to the pupils and students. Pupils and students, going to school, learn how to read and write under the guidance of a teacher. Children do not need a teacher to teach them how to comprehend and speak a language, but they often need a teacher to teach them how to read and write script. More difficult than speaking, writing requires complicated skills. Pupils and students need a textbook and memorize how to read and write script. The vocabulary of words or characters in writing is usually much larger than that of spoken words or characters. In order to expedite the process of learning how to read and write script, pupils and students need the assistance of a teacher. Pupils, or students, usually use a textbook. However, they often read the text aloud. When they read the text aloud, the teacher can test whether or not they have understood the text. They may sometimes have to ask one question. When discussing teaching in class in India, Goody writes that "the process of reading aloud means that the pupil can ask questions and hence improve his opportunities for learning."[17]

Students may also need to learn rhetoric because the knowledge of rhetoric is part of the knowledge of language. Script is only constituted by signs. When script is used to write a presentation, the skill of rhetoric is required. In some sense, the rhetoric is the skill used to give a presentation. A presentation relies on the utilization of rhetoric. We seldom see that a student studies rhetoric himself at home. The knowledge of rhetoric is complex. It is not easy for a student to learn it well through self-study. He may ask questions when learning the knowledge of rhetoric. The knowledge is often imparted in a dialogue conducted between a student and a teacher. This situation is the same as the case that pupils learn to read and write script, as just mentioned earlier. That is, a student learns rhetoric in the school. An experienced teacher teaches the skill of rhetoric to him. The teacher teaches the knowledge of rhetoric to him systematically. Thus he can learn such a skill smoothly because a teacher guides him.

Likewise, a teacher teaches students how to write a composition in the school. When a student writes a composition, he has to master the skill of writing script. He needs the knowledge of rhetoric. In the meantime, the teacher will check if a composition, written by a student, meets the requirement. The teacher may make a comment. The student gets the teacher's comment. Based on this comment, the student improves his skill of writing a composition. He can learn the knowledge of writing a composition from a textbook or other reference books for sure, but learning how to write a composition in the school is usually indispensable. In other words, learning knowledge may often need to be customized. The method of learning knowledge, or skill, varies from person to person. A student may get into a particular difficulty in learning how to write a composition. Thus, he needs a special advice from the teacher.

Thus, the knowledge of language is often taught by a teacher in a school. Particularly, in modern times the teachers of educational establishment are often responsible for such a task. There is a teaching program formulated by people according to experience. Qualified teachers are employed to teach the students. Thus teachers cannot be totally replaced by books. They are culture workers. If the creator of script is assumed to teach all others to read and write the script in the beginning, we can also believe that now teachers teach children to read and write the script on behalf of the creator of the script. The knowledge of rhetoric is originally created by someone. Teachers, passing on the knowledge of rhetoric, perform human-chain linguistic communication. Usually, a teacher who teaches how to write a composition learns the related skill from his teacher. He performs human-chain linguistic communication. Thus the teachers of each generation perform human-chain linguistic communication when passing on the skills of writing.

In terms of a teacher passing on knowledge to students, I argue that people perform human-chain linguistic communication because students may become teachers in future. Sometimes people need to pass on knowledge to students face-to-face. Passing on knowledge face-to-face, they usually perform spoken communication. Even though people may use books to pass on knowledge, teaching in class is still essential. Teachers even control the process of imparting knowledge. For example, a teacher may draft a courseware. He explains the content of this courseware in class. Though he also performs written communication because he writes something on the blackboard from time to time, he controls the progress of passing on knowledge in class. Oral interpretation is important. Thus, a teacher can help the students to master the knowledge of language. Students can learn the knowledge of language most efficiently.

It is true that language is an important part of culture had by one nation. People usually impart the knowledge of language and the skill of using language through human-chain linguistic communication. Education involves a process of human-chain linguistic communication performed by culture workers actively. As culture workers engage in education, education becomes an impetus to the continuation and extension of linguistic communication, particularly human-chain linguistic communication. As communication may create a condition for the formation of the common interest of all, people cooperate with each other in the process of linguistic communication. First of all, the person who sends out information in this process of linguistic communication sets up this process of linguistic communication. Then the person who receives information in this process of linguistic communication finds it necessary to enter this process of linguistic communication. He acknowledges the validity of this process of linguistic communication. The role, played by the person sending out information and the role, played by the person receiving the information, are both critical. Both of them need this process of linguistic communication. This is the process in which the person, sending out information, and the person, receiving information, can boost the said human-chain linguistic communication, so that people can extend such linguistic communication incessantly.

People may also propagate moral ideas. Those who proactively propagate moral ideas are often the links of the chains of linguistic communication that disseminates those moral ideas. Ethicists may actively research morality and propagate moral ideas. They may write articles and books disseminating moral ideas in the society. They may also give lectures to disseminate moral ideas. As ethicists of each generation disseminate moral ideas, they are the links of the chains of linguistic communication that disseminates moral ideas. A teacher, a priest, a government official, or an elder of the local community, may also propagate a moral idea on behalf of the ethicist. For example, in Chinese society people disseminate the Confucian moral idea generation by generation. Many kinds of people, such as a teacher or an elder, may teach that moral idea on behalf of Confucius. People may also teach morality in writing. Some books may disseminate a moral idea on behalf of an ethicist. For example, a novel may disseminate a moral idea on behalf of an ethicist when it tells a story. In the meantime, people often need to support the dissemination of the moral idea in the middle of the process of linguistic communication that disseminates the moral idea. We cannot ascertain who invents the moral idea in the society, but we can ascertain that there are always some people who disseminate the moral idea. Some people may strengthen linguistic communication to disseminate a moral idea in the middle of the process of linguistic communication. People, performing linguistic communication to disseminate the moral idea, may set an example of morality. If no one acts to boost the discourse of morality in a process of linguistic communication that disseminates such morality, people may not disseminate morality effectively. Ordinary people may not be able to come up with any moral idea. One reason is that when one propagates a moral idea, he should have the systematic knowledge of ethics. To have such systematic knowledge of ethics, he needs to study ethics in a college or university. Those who especially study ethics in a college or university are not many. If one does not have the systematic knowledge of ethics, he is unable to communicate on a large scale. A moral idea is often disseminated in writing indeed. But, usually, not all read the books of propagating a moral idea within the state. Only a small number of people advocate morality. People are led to obey morality. People usually disseminate a moral idea, advanced by a small number of people in the outset, in their mutual interaction. If people propagate a moral idea in the form of book, the propagation may not be so effective. The moral idea is highlighted in human-chain linguistic communication. People hand down the moral idea through human-chain linguistic communication mainly.

Folklorists, or other scholars who study folk customs or traditional culture, may also propagate customs or tradition that functions in support of the operation of the society. They write books. But they also found academies, libraries and museums to explain and propagate various customs and traditions adhered to by people within the society. Ordinary people obey these customs and traditions. Ordinary people may learn how to obey such customs and traditions. However, inheriting customs and traditions often entails support given by folklorists as well as other scholars. People directly obey those customs and traditions. For example, when two people meet each other on a formal occasion, they may shake hands to greet each other. When a man shows respects to another man, he may bow. Body language, used by a nation, may reflect a culture. They perform behavioral communication and linguistic communication concurrently. As all may perform such communication, all obey a rule. People formulate such a rule according to the advice of those folklorists and other related people. Ordinary people obey such customs and traditions and they put into practice such customs and traditions. Thus, the method of giving gifts may be special within the society and the state. This is because such customs are part of the culture especially created within a specific state. The behavior, displayed by people, and the gifts, presented by people, in their mutual interaction, may be the symbols set by a specific culture of folk custom. People perform linguistic communication at the same time. Likewise, traditional festivals are usually part of the culture of folk society. People celebrate these festivals in a traditional way. The method of celebrating these festivals usually remains unchanged over time because it is defined by the folklorists as well as other experts and scholars. This is the custom formed as required by a paradigm of culture. For example, Europeans celebrate Christmas Day and Easter Day. People in India and some other countries celebrate the Festival of Lights. Chinese and Koreans celebrate the Spring Festival and Dragon Boat Festival. In the meantime, folklorists as well as other experts and scholars perform linguistic communication to interpret their behavior from time to time. As some folklorists and some other experts as well as scholars invigorate the ideas that may strengthen, or highlight, the customs and the tradition from time to time, people show and inherit the folk customs and the folk tradition generation by generation.

Sociologists also propagate social norms and social systems. Ordinary people are unable to do so. As sociologists have knowledge, they are influential. They are media. Monogamy comes into existence in the progress of human civilization. Knowledgeable people propagated it in ancient times. In modern times sociologists interpret monogamy. They propagate the idea of monogamy. It may be influenced by the traditional culture. In some industrialized states today a portion of people request the same sex marriage. Another portion of people oppose it. Jurists, ethicists and sociologists argue about the rationality of the same sex marriage. They, instead of others, propagate a social norm or a social system. In a traditional society, male chauvinism may be prevalent in a society because of cultural tradition. It is often directly, or indirectly, encouraged by the traditional social norm or social system formed in medieval times. In modern times, feminism, which opposes the hegemony of male within the family as well as in the society, is committed to the dissemination of the idea of equality between female and male and the idea of equality between male and female comes to be prevalent. In some states people encourage and exalt filial piety. Filial piety may be part of culture because it is part of the social norm formed in a cultural background. The style of clothes and the custom of diet are also sometimes influenced by a cultural idea. A wedding is held when a man and a woman get married. The ceremony of wedding may be heavily influenced by a culture. When a person dies, people hold a funeral. People may hold the ceremony of the funeral in a method influenced by culture. People may hand down these social norms and social practice in written communication. Some books may describe these social norms and social practice in detail and systematically. These social norms and social practice may be studied by scholars. However, without the support from the sociologists or some other experts of each generation, those social norms and social practice may not be able to continue as expected. In fact, social norms and social practice evolve over time. Sociologists propagate the social norms and social practice, traditional or modern. These social norms and social practice may be part of culture.

Humans also produce cultural products, which not only instill a cultural idea into the minds of people but also propagate a spirit. They spread high culture in a particular form. These cultural products are usually produced and promoted by professionals who excel in producing and promoting a special cultural product. Unlike ordinary people, they are cultural talents. They are especially involved in the production and promotion of high quality cultural products. They are media. They are also the links of the chains in the related linguistic communication. They offer the various forms of culture.

For example, people exchange feelings with each other for the purpose of consolidating the unity of the society and the state, and they often adopt the aesthetic form of expression. Such an aesthetic form of expression is often a cultural form. Thus it follows that those who spread culture function as the links of the chains in human-chain linguistic communication. Any aesthetic form of expression can potentially function this way. As long as people convey a certain message in a certain aesthetic form of expression, people, involved in spreading it, will be part of the process of human-chain linguistic communication. A process of linguistic communication is sometimes set to show a cultural work to other people or share it with other people. Such a process of linguistic communication is very likely to be a process of human-chain linguistic communication. The reason is that people enjoy a cultural work time and again.

Telling a story is a process of presenting a cultural work. It is also a typical and very commonly seen process of performing human-chain linguistic communication. For example, in some sense, telling a story is the inchoate form of literature that appears in the civilized society. The man who tells the story to others is just a link of the chain or a medium. For example, in antiquity people performed spoken communication, spreading a culture given the fact that writing was not extant or people did not often write. If one told a story to the other, he might activate a process of spreading a culture in the spoken form of human-chain linguistic communication. David Diringer writes that:

> Story-telling is . . . one of the oldest cultural manifestations of man. From very early times, before the dawn of recorded history, man endeavoured to educate himself and his children, and told them of his and his father's adventures, of the lives and struggles of their gods and witches. His community was, of course, very much smaller than even many present-day villages. The feeling of community would be shared by all who would gather together in a convenient place of assembly, for instance, around a camp fire, where they would listen to the gifted story-teller relating the ancient traditions. The story-teller may have been a gifted singer who could recite his story in simple verse, and all would join in. Probably the story-teller or bard, growing old, would find a likely successor and pass on to him his store of stories, ballads or songs. Thus, for instance, Polynesian story-tellers trained their own memories and that of their sons so that they were able to hand down to posterity by word of mouth their people's history, especially their valuable migration traditions.[18]

When a person reads aloud one poem, written by a famous poet, to a group of people, people communicate with each other. They perform human-chain linguistic communication. Homeric Epics narrated the deeds of ancient Greek people. Before people noted down the *Iliad* and *Odyssey* in writing, they handed down them orally for years generation by generation. Homeric Epics might be even created by several different poets. Martyn

Lyons believes that Homer's *Iliad*, which emerged around 700BCE, was created due to a long tradition of oral composition by various authors. He indicates that "Homer" himself was probably a number of different poets. Some of the works may have been recited from memory, other portions improvised in the course of performance. Far from being the creation of a single genius, the *Iliad* inherited the creative efforts of generations, and that heritage was renewed and transformed by a series of individual poets.[19] People spread them crucially through human-chain spoken communication and handed them down through it in ancient times. The *Book of Odes* (*Shih Ching*), one of the most famous Chinese classics, contains some 300 lyrical and historical poems, many of which treat of warfare and marital fidelity, agriculture and hunting or feasting. This book shows the finest picture of the social conditions of the eighth and seventh centuries B.C. People sung of their courtship and marriage, women of their errant lovers, soldiers of their misery and others together with popular myths and legends. This form of literature is like Hebrew Psalms and the Song of Solomon, as said by Diringer and L.G. Goodrich.[20] The content of this book was usually, or often, transmitted among people orally from one person to another in ancient times though their form of writing such as book might be occasionally available.

A drama may also involve a process of human-chain linguistic communication. Dramas are written by playwrights. Playwrights perform linguistic communication with the masses through dramas. Yet as dramas need actors and actresses to help them to show themselves, we can consider actors and actresses the links of the human chain through which playwrights communicate with the masses. As people may appreciate dramas over the long term, the actors and actresses of different times give dramatic performances time and again. In the meantime, as a great many people may appreciate dramas, actors and actresses go to many places to give a dramatic performance. Thus playwrights communicate over a long time and on a large scale. People spread a cultural form represented by dramas. It supports the building of a cultural community. For example, the performances of dramas, created by William Shakespeare, have been given over centuries and in many places in the United Kingdom. When actors and actresses give the performance of the drama *Hamlet*, a work of Shakespeare, for example, they function as the links of the chain in a process of human-chain linguistic communication activated by Shakespeare in the beginning. Thus Shakespeare contributes to the growth of culture in the United Kingdom. This depends on the nature of language. As language allows for humans to perform human-chain linguistic communication, they preserve and develop their culture.

When people chorus in the theatre, they also function as the links of the chain of linguistic communication activated by the song writer and the composer in the beginning. Songs are created by the song writers and the composers. But without singers, people cannot spread the songs among the masses. If a song is pleasant to hear because the melody of this song is beautiful, singers may love to sing it. Human-chain linguistic communication will make this song famous. Similarly, music is also a medium in support of the process of human-chain linguistic communication. After a composer writes a piece of music, this piece of music is often performed by a musician or a group of musicians. This piece of music is usually performed many times. If this piece of music is a masterpiece, it may be performed many years and in many places. Think of classical music. As every piece of music has a title, language interprets it. People may also introduce each piece of music. Without human-chain linguistic communication, people may not know a master piece of music. Musicians, performing a piece of music in a concert, perform human-chain linguistic communication with plenty of music lovers.

Similarly, an opera is a performance given by actors and actresses. These actors and actresses are also singers on the basis of a libretto. They sing the songs. The songs are created by the song writer or the song writers. Each song writer performs linguistic communication with the audience. A composer helps the song writer. In the meantime, the playwright writes the story. All of them communicate with the audience through actors and actresses. Thus people perform human-chain linguistic communication. Thus many people appreciate operas over the long term and across the state. This is the way used by humans to preserve and develop operas.

In some sense, all the dramatists, song writers and artists create their works on behalf of the people because those works are needed by the people for the exchange of feelings among themselves. They are also the links of the chain of linguistic communication. That is, people may need to strengthen linguistic communication over long distances. Thus sometimes some people may further function to reiterate, or present time and again, the themes presented in the process of linguistic communication by showing the related works. They often fulfill this task in a cultural form. As culture brings a value to people, they are tempted to take initiative to perform linguistic communication in the cultural forms of expression and people are likely to enter the related process of linguistic communication. Then people exchange their feelings on a large scale. Then people within the state may unite because they share the same culture. In a word, the building of the state includes the building of a corresponding cultural community that ensures the cultural homogeneity that underlies the formation of the state.

History of humans, a cultural work, is also handed down through human-chain linguistic communication. Historians are responsible for this task. Although I have mentioned in my previous manuscript that history is almost the longest process of human linguistic communication performed by each nation within the state, the related linguistic communication, performed by historians with the masses, may go on through human-chain linguistic communication. In a process of communication, people may perform long-distance direct linguistic communication and human-chain linguistic communication simultaneously. People often make history serve the contemporary need. History is not a form of expression that simply chronicles the facts of history. People write history not only to memorize the historical facts but also to disseminate their ideas. As their ideas play a role in the formation of a cultural community and in support of the building of the state, they may revise the ideas, intended to be disseminated in the historical presentation, to support the building of the state in the best way. People may revise history along with the passage of time. When they hand down history generation by generation, they need the historians of each generation to update the presentation of history. As Judith N. Shklar observes, "each age writes history anew to serve its own purposes."[21] If people compile a chronicle, they may not update it. But all true history needs update. Benedetto Croce writes that "all true history is contemporary history."[22] Sometimes people change their philosophical view or their values, and then they need to re-evaluate a certain historical event or a certain historical figure. Or sometimes people change their social idea. In order to promote a new social idea, they may find that they need to adjust the presentation of a certain piece of history. In addition, the presentation of a piece of history may not be complete. Sometimes people discover new historical facts. Then they adjust the presentation of a certain piece of history. If new historical materials are found or discovered, people will add them to the related history. If people forget a piece of history, a historian may even rediscover it. This means that a historian may recover a lost link of the chain. Thus historians narrate and interpret history generation by generation. Then people hand down history through human-chain linguistic communication activated by historians of different periods of time though humans also hand down history in writing directly. In the meantime, people keep on researching historical facts. They accumulate historical materials. They broaden and deepen their knowledge of a piece of history. Their knowledge of a piece of history may become complete along with the passage of time. Their knowledge of a piece of history may become rational or scientific. Thus the role of history also relies on the support of human-chain linguistic communication though history is usually underpinned by the written form of presentation.

Politics also influences the compilation of history because historiography is a program in support of the formation of a state and a state is usually formed first of all in the process of politics. Particularly, the compilation of contemporary or modern history often concerns people's idea of governing the state. As politics changes frequently in the state, people may compile the presentation of history to satisfy the requirement of politics. Thus there is the process of human-chain linguistic communication involving the presentation of history. This is particularly so in the state in which historiography is under the strict control of the government. If the government strictly controls historiography, it may restrict the freedom of academic activities. The presentation of a certain piece of history may be required to meet the regulations formulated by the authorities. Yet as the policy of the state may vary from time to time, there is the possibility that people revise a certain piece of history due to a change of the related policy. After the disintegration of the former Soviet Union, a political change took place in the East European countries. People re-compiled the modern history of each of those countries in Eastern Europe to a varying extent. Thus people perform human-chain linguistic communication when revising their history.

Philosophy can be construed as part of culture, too. Yet philosophy is usually created by a group of people who are called philosophers. Though philosophers usually perform written communication and hence basically long-distance direct linguistic communication, they are not prevented from entering the human-chain linguistic communication. As people create and enrich philosophical ideas over the long term, a philosopher may come up with a philosophical idea under the influence of another philosopher. For example, before a man becomes a philosopher, he is a student. He learns philosophy from a philosopher or several. There is a process of human-chain linguistic communication when a student learns philosophy in the university. The lectures, given by the philosophers of the preceding generation, symbolize the process in which people perform human-chain linguistic communication. Besides, students read the works of the philosophers of the preceding generations for reference. Some philosophical ideas may become obsolete. Then the philosophers of the upcoming generation may update those philosophical ideas. As new philosophers keep on emerging, people deepen the research of philosophy. They may amend the existing philosophical ideas because they keep on deepening their understanding of a philosophical issue. Philosophers, writing philosophical books, perform direct linguistic communication with the readers indeed. Yet they themselves are, in some sense, just the links of the chain in linguistic communication that passes on the knowledge and thought of philosophy. If it is difficult for ordinary people to understand a philosophical book full of obscurities, some people may perform the task of popularizing the philosophical idea created in that book. They give an interpretation. An interpretation activates a new process of linguistic communication as the extension of linguistic communication initiated by that philosopher. They create a process of human-chain linguistic communication. This means that sometimes people find it difficult to understand a philosophical idea. Failure to understand it impedes the extension of human-chain linguistic communication. A new process of linguistic communication boosts the popularization of this philosophical idea. People often disseminate philosophical ideas that become a major source of the values upheld by people across the state. They do so particularly in the extended process of linguistic communication reinforced by those who popularize philosophical ideas. Thus philosophy powerfully supports the building of the state.

In addition, priests are committed to the dissemination of a religious dogma sanctioned by the church or the temple. One can regard priests as the links of the chain of linguistic communication activated by those who compiled, or wrote, the bible. They promote a cultural product. Though a bible performs long-distance direct linguistic communication with religious believers, such linguistic communication often needs support given by human-chain linguistic communication. For example, some people wrote the Old Testament and the New Testament. Then people can regard those who disseminate the Old Testament and the New Testament as the links of the chain of linguistic communication because we can believe that they extend the process of linguistic communication performed by the Bible compilers. The Bible cannot propagate itself among the masses. Thus the Bible always needs clergymen to help it. Thus clergymen keep on disseminating the religious dogma over the long term. Clergymen even travel a long way to disseminate the religious dogma in unfamiliar areas. Henri-Jean Martin writes that:

> Communication in the vast area of religion can be seen schematically: On one side there was God; on the other, the mass of the faithful. Between them stood the cleric, an initiate of a sacred language and an intercessor endowed with supernatural powers. Dogma—that is, the set of verities that were the objects of faith—issued from Revelation. It included both explicit and implicit truths. The theologians' mission was to clarify dogma under the supervision of the hierarchy, which drew conclusions from their findings.[23]

This situation happens because of the need of religious service in the growing human community. People propagate religious belief in a larger and larger area, and then extend the distance of human-chain linguistic communication step by step. Thus, the Bible compilers cannot always perform the related linguistic communication directly with the masses but in human-chain linguistic communication. In each section of the process of the related linguistic communication, certain priests reinforce the related linguistic communication. Even written communication, performed by the religious literature, needs support from human-chain linguistic communication. As such, Rex Ahdar and Ian Leigh write that:

The decades after the resurrection of Christ witnessed an exponential growth in the church from a few hundred believers in Jerusalem to a plethora of fledgling local churches along the trade routes across Asia and throughout the Roman Empire.[24]

The spread of religion relies on human-chain linguistic communication that functions on those trade routes.

The Reformation in France in the early modern history more specifically shows this case. As Martin writes,

> Lutheran writings arrived in Paris through Basel, and they were immediately condemned by the Faculty of Theology and the Parlement. The booksellers of Basel responded by organizing barely clandestine relay stations that passed books from Lyons to Chalon-sur-Saône and from Paris to Nantes. At the same time the first bases for an underground struggle appeared outside France, first in Strasbourg from where Latin editions of Lutheran pamphlets were dispatched throughout France.[25]

In short, if humans spread culture, they extend the processes of human-chain linguistic communication. For example, in the Middle Ages, the circulation of books relied absolutely on the support of human-chain linguistic communication. Martin writes that:

> At the end of the Middle Ages an author often wrote with his own hand the presentation copy of a work he offered to a protector, and copyists, usually working on commission, grouped together in small, specialized workshops to reproduce texts for university professors, humanists, or pious laymen. The majority of the manuscripts in circulation, however, were collections of notes or copies that students, churchmen, or men of letters made for their own use, which subsequently passed from hand to hand.[26]

Since the development of printing, human-chain linguistic communication has still been in need in some cases. Different presses may print the same book over time. People perform written human-chain linguistic communication. That is, spoken and written human-chain linguistic communication continues because in every section of the process of linguistic communication people still need to boost the whole process of linguistic communication in the middle. For example, teachers may interpret the knowledge disseminated by an original work in the classrooms of the university or other books may give an interpretation to popularize the knowledge created by an original work. People use books to pass on their knowledge and books may also use people to pass on knowledge.

In sum, people build culture in the various processes of human-chain linguistic communication that spreads it. Culture is a special foundation stone for the formation of the state.

Notes

1. Dingxin Zhao, *The Confucian-Legalist State: A New Theory of Chinese History* (Oxford: Oxford University Press, 2015), 91.
2. Adrew Eisenberg, *Weberian Patrimonialism and Imperial Chinese History* in Theory and Society (1998) 27, 85; cited from Diongxin Zhao, Ibid. 64.
3. See Zhu Weizheng, *Interlude: Kingship and Empire*, in Fritz-Heiner Mutschler and Achim Mittag, ed., *Conceiving the Empire China and Rome Compared* (Oxford: Oxford University Press, 2008), 35–36.
4. Harold J. Berman, *Law and Revolution: The Formation of Western Legal Tradition* (Cambridge, Massachusetts: Harvard University Press, 1983), 307.
5. Adams Smith, *The Wealth of Nations*, with an Introduction by D.D. Raphael (New York: Alfred A. Knopf, 1991), 355.
6. Ibid., 356.
7. E. N. Gladden, *A History of Public Administration, Vol.2: From the Eleventh Century to the Present Day* (London: Frank Cass and Company Limited, 1972), 212.
8. Joseph R. Sprayer, *On the Medieval Origins of the Modern State* (Princeton, New Jersey: Princeton University Press, 1970), 52.

9. Jack Goody, *The Logic of Writing and Organization of Society* (Cambridge: Cambridge University Press, 1986), 106.

10. Ibid., 114.

11. Bertrand Russell, *Power* (New York: W.W. Norton & Company, Inc., 1938), 194.

12. See: Jack Goody, *The Power of the Written Tradition* (Washington: Smithsonian Institution Press, 2000), 33.

13. Smith, *The Wealth of Nations*, 12.

14. Please see: Frederick Engels, *The Origin of the Family, Private Property and the State* (New York: International Publishers, 1972), 219.

15. Smith, *The Wealth of Nations*, 27–28.

16. See Albrecht Dihle, *City and Empire*, in Mutschler and Mittag (ed.), *Conceiving the Empire China and Rome Compared* (Oxford: Oxford University Press, 2008), 14.

17. Jack Goody, *The Interface between the Written and the Oral* (Cambridge: Cambridge University Press, 1987), 119.

18. David Diringer, *The Book Before Printing: Ancient, Medieval and Oriental* (New York: Dover Publications, Inc., 1982), 15.

19. Martyn Lyons, *Books: A Living History* (Los Angeles: The J. Paul Getty Museum, 2011), 25.

20. Diringer, *The Book Before Printing: Ancient, Medieval and Oriental*, 383.

21. Judith N. Shklar, *Political Thought and Political Thinkers*, edited by Stanley Hoffmann (Chicago: The University of Chicago Press, 1998), 206.

22. Benedetto Croce, *History, Its Theory and Practice*, translated by Douglas Ainslie (New York: Russell & Russell, 1960), 12.

23. Henri-Jean Martin, *The History and Power of Writing*, translated by Lydia G. Gochrane (Chicago: The University of Chicago Press, 1994), 172.

24. Rex Ahdar and Ian Leigh, *Religious Freedom in the Liberal State* (Oxford: Oxford University Press, 2005), 12.

25. Martin, *The History and Power of Writing*, 254.

26. Ibid., 186.

Chapter Two

Materials

1. Geological Materials

Writing is a crucial progress in the history of human communication. Writing means the act that an individual person writes script on the surface of a material. Then a material may become a substitute for a human being in the process of linguistic communication. It may become a medium in support of linguistic communication. Then one can regard it as a link of the chain in human linguistic communication. One can consider it to be the link of the chain in place of the links of the chain formed by humans. As spoken human-chain linguistic communication is usually ephemeral, such communication cannot go on all the time. This restricts the role played by language in the formation of human community. Therefore, humans make use of many kinds of materials. These materials can be detached from human bodies. And then, using them, humans communicate over a long time and on a large scale. The time span of such communication may be longer than the time span of spoken communication and the reach of such communication may be longer than the reach of spoken communication. Thus, such materials may give another special role to language in the formation of the state. As materials can be durable, or can be large in size, or can be supplied anywhere, or can be carried over long distances because they are light, humans further extend the time of human communication and further extend the reach of human communication. Thus language plays a key role in the growth of the state. These materials are thus very special as language functions together with them. Stone is one of such materials. Please allow me to discuss the role played by stone first.

Stone   When we look into the role played by materials used as media in communication, we can first scrutinize the role played by stone because part of the earliest script created by humans often appears first on stone. This indicates that stone should be a special material significant in the formation of the state in early times. There must be a point of time that separates the civilized times from the primitive times. Stone may be one of the first media used by humans to perform linguistic communication that marks the beginning of the civilized society. Stone should also play a role in the formation of the state though it could not play a role in the formation of a tribe. Before humans created script, stone was usually not used for linguistic communication. Stone originally belonged to the natural world and did not belong to the human world. So I argue that stone did not play any role in the formation of any tribe. But stone plays a role in the formation of a state. In other words, since humans used no script in the tribe, stone should, normally, not be used for any communication in a tribe. Humans might use stone as a tool or a weapon when they formed a tribe, but they never, or seldom, used it as a medium for communication at that time. In this sense stone becomes part of linguistic communication in the state only. Humans not only use stone for defense such as the building of barricade or for construction such as the building of houses, but also use it for linguistic communication after the formation of the state. We should study the relationship between stone and the state.

What is the significance of stone? Stone is itself a kind of hard material. People can supply it everywhere and can supply a large quantity of stone. Stone material can be of large size. People can place stone material outdoors because it can resist erosion caused by rain or wind. As language is carried by all who use it, stone available everywhere is often used to perform linguistic communication that goes on over a long time and on a large scale. People can use it in support of communication that extends over a long time and reaches any far-flung place. As stone is usually the durable material, people can use it over the long term. As it can be used over the long term, it becomes valuable if people use language for communication that goes on for long. In the meantime, as a piece of stone can be large, one can use it to perform communication that reaches many people in a large area. Besides, people may supply a great deal of stone material. Then people may use it to perform the same linguistic communication everywhere under the condition that people need to perform such linguistic communication all the time and everywhere in the public. Such linguistic communication, supported by stone as a medium, can be the linguistic communication that underpins the operation of the state just because a state is expected to subsist over the long term and is expected to function in a large area. The state is unlike the tribe in this respect. Time is not so meaningful for a tribe and space needed by a tribe is not so significant. But it is so for the state. The state, to subsist over the long term and to function on a large scale, needs support from language. Language, in turn, needs the support of various media. Stone is one of such media.

First, stone functions as a medium in support of the linguistic communication performed by the power holder of the state with the common people in order to realize the mutual interaction between the ruler and the ruled throughout history. For example, the power holder of the state performed communication with the common people in governing the state through stone rather than other media in Mesopotamia, Greece and the Roman Empire. People used stone to show the presence of the ruler. By using stone, they performed communication to demonstrate the achievements of the ruler or the state in various civilizations in history. In this way they exalted the ruler. They demonstrated the authority of the ruler. They used the selected stone on purpose for the masses to remember the ruler forever. Describing writing in Mesopotamia, Diringer says that:

> Stone was sometimes the main material used . . . for immortalizing the work of a ruler. Sometimes the hardest volcanic rocks were employed for the purpose; sometimes softer stones, especially alabaster and marble, and even stones of comparatively rarity, such as lapis lazuli, were employed.[1]

In the history of the expansion of the Roman Empire, people also used stele inscriptions to demonstrate the monumental achievements of the ruler in order to strengthen the authority of the state. According to the information provided by Christian Witschel, after Caius Caesar had died in the small town of Limyra on the southern coast of Asia Minor, a *kenotaphion* was built for him at the place of his death. There the monumental inscription of about 30m length gave an abridged version of Caius' most memorable deeds in fighting for the empire on its eastern frontier.[2]

In the formation, or the building, of the state, the ruler needs to communicate with all commoners throughout the state. He needs to use a medium. He may use stone as a medium. Maybe stone can support the process of linguistic communication to demonstrate the sovereignty of the state. In Chinese history, the First Emperor used such a method to demonstrate the sovereignty of the state. As some historical books, such as *Shi Ji,* indicate, shortly after completing his final conquest and establishing the unified empire in 221 BC, the Qin First Emperor began to tour the newly conquered eastern regions. He erected a series of stele inscriptions on the top of venerated mountains. The following chronology is provided by *Shi Ji* : 219 BC on Mt. Yi, Mt. Tai and Mt. Langye; 218 BC on Mt. Zhifu and on its 'eastern vista' (Zhifu *Dongguan*); 215 BC at the 'gate' of Jieshi (Jieshi Men); and December 211 or January 210 BC on Mt. Kuaiji. In the First Emperor's 'Basic Annals' in *Shi Ji,* the brief entry on the first inscription, placed on Mt. Yi in 219 BC, reads as follows:

> In his twenty-eighth year, the First August (Emperor) went eastward and proceeded through the commanderies and counties. He ascended Mt. Yi in Zou County and erected a stone. He conducted a discussion with the classicists (rusheng) from Lu and had them carve the stone to eulogize the virtuous power of Qin. They discussed the matters of the *Feng* and *Shan* sacrifices and of the *wang* sacrifices to the mountains and rivers. [3]

Second, stone may support linguistic communication that promulgates laws or decrees. In Near East, people used stone for this purpose. Narrating Hammurabi's Code of Laws in the eighteenth century B.C., Diringer states that:

> This code of laws, one of the oldest in the world, was inscribed by order of Hammurabi on a block of black diorite nearly eight feet in height and set up in Babylon, but at a later time, an Elamite conqueror took this pillar away as

a trophy to his capital, Susa, where it was discovered in the de Morgan excavations during the winter of 1901-2. The laws are written in Semitic Babylonian (or Akkadian).[4]

Also as Harold A. Innis writes, since the fifth century, "Stonecutting had been used in the publication of laws and in the making of records, as Greek epigraphy attests."[5] Some of the laws made by Draco and Solon were inscribed on the surface of stone.

In some cities in ancient Greece, the state protected the stones on which people inscribed decrees or laws. If the letters were made illegible there would be a sacred fine as defined by a treaty between Elis and Heraia which was inscribed at Olympia c. 500.[6] In other words, the authorities must promulgate laws to the public. By using stones, the authorities perform public communication in order to publicize the laws.

Third, people use stone to record history. In the ancient state formed by Israelites, the description of ancient Israelites in the past appeared on stones. Perhaps they used stones to chronicle their history. We can construe stones as media in support of a process of linguistic communication that strengthens people's historical memory. This bolsters the formation of the state if people enhance their sense of historical belonging this way. Thus stones used to play directly a role in the growth of the state. Thus, Thomas Hobbes narrates that:

> That the Book of *Jushua* was also written long after the time of *Joshua*, may be gathered out of many places of the Book it self. *Joshua* had set up twelve stones in the middest of *Jordan*, for a monument of their passage; of which the Writer saith thus, *They are there unto this day*; for *unto this day*, is a phrase that signifieth a time past, beyond the memory of man.[7]

Fourth, in some states or in a certain period of time in some states religion underpins the formation of the state. Then people may use stone as a medium in support of a religious discourse that supports the formation of a related state. Leo Deuel recorded the search of European scholars for the lost manuscripts and records in the nineteenth and twentieth centuries in Egypt and elsewhere in the world. According to Deuel, the findings of such search are that inscriptions carved on stone constitute the oldest actual remains of Egyptian literature from Old Kingdom. He writes in detail that:

These inscriptions are by no means limited in length on account of their physical rendering. Indeed, when collected and edited, they make up two formidable volumes of a total of more than a thousand pages. The collection goes by the name of the Pyramid Texts, since the pieces were copied from the walls of chambers of some six pyramids of the Fifth and Sixth Dynasties (c. 2450-2250 B.C.). But, like much else in the Egyptian language, particularly anything of a religious or literary nature, they probably date back to the beginning of the Old Kingdom (c. 2800 B.C.), if not to proto-and pre-Dynastic days. Some of the formulas found on the walls of pyramids reflect a much cruder age, as for example the 'cannibalistic" hymn of Unas, which describes the lassoning of the gods.[8]

Fifth, people also inscribe or carve the thought of philosophers on stone. Thus stone may assist in disseminating philosophy within the state and make a contribution to the cause of creating a philosophical system in the development of the spirit of the state. For example, according to Martyn Lyons, Confucian writings were initially transmitted by the Han rulers to their subjects via large carved stone slabs. The earliest slabs still legible date from 175CE, when the reigning emperor ordered stone copies of the *Five Classics* and the *Analects of Confucius*. The "library" took eight years to complete and covered nearly fifty slabs of stone, each 1.75 meters high, with over 200,000 characters in all.[9]

The use of stone for communication is very special in the state indeed. As not all are able to use a stone tablet as a medium to communicate with all others in a public place, the person, able to use the stone tablet to communicate with all others, must have a certain privilege. Stone, as a medium, functions as an agent entrusted by the power holder, or the ruler, to show and propagate his authority, or the history, the law, the religion and the philosophy of the state. Thus we can surely understand that using this privilege strengthens the said linguistic communication between the ruler and common people or between the state and common people. This linguistic communication strengthens the authority of the ruler and the spirit of the state. This linguistic communication bolsters the cohesion of the state. Since the supply of stone is ample stone is often used by the ruler to strengthen linguistic communication performed by him, or by the state, with the masses. A piece of stone especially symbolizes a process of communication between the ruler or the state and the masses.

Clay Similar to stone, clay did not play any role in the formation of any tribe in terms of time and space, but it used to play a role in the formation of the state in terms of time and space because clay could be a material used to make clay tablets on which humans wrote, or inscribed, script. This is significant for the building of the state. Specifically, after they created script, people created various media to extend the process of linguistic communication in support of the growth of their new community, which grew to be a state. This is because the utilization of certain media extended the distance of linguistic communication. These materials functioned as media. Media enabled them to realize long-distance linguistic communication. Long-distance linguistic communication might be the long-time linguistic communication. Clay tablet is an example. As Henri-Jean Martin writes,

> The clay tablet was a heavy and relatively cumbersome medium, but cuneiform writing permitted a large number of signs to be crowded onto a small surface. This means that above all the cuneiform clay tablet was an aid to memorization.[10]

Memorization can mean a course of extending the distance of linguistic communication. Humans could use clay tablets over the long term. Martin writes that "The peoples of the Middle East used a good many other materials, but the clay tablet guaranteed them a degree of durability even though clay deteriorates over the very long term."[11] This long-distance linguistic communication might also become the communication that reached far-flung places. Thus, people might use clay tablets to communicate on a large scale. That is, they extended the reach of communication. Then clay played a role in the formation of the state.

First, using clay tablets in linguistic communication, humans created a condition for the making of written law. Then they drafted laws on the basis of the study of the social relations of people. Criminal law and civil law appeared. As written communication developed, scribes were trained. Some of them became judges. The development of the legal system underpinned the building of the state.

Second, clay might play a role in the formation of an economic community in support of the formation of the state. When humans engaged in their business, they performed accounting and made business contracts. Clay tablets were used to record accounts and to make contracts. Clay tablets might also be used to record some other business information or business activities. Innis writes that:

> Writing was invented in Sumer to keep tallies and to make lists and, hence was an outgrowth of mathematics. The earliest clay tablets include large numbers of legal contracts, deeds of sale, and land transfer, and reflect a secular and utilitarian interest.[12]

Third, as humans used clay tablets in support of written communication, they chronicled history. As the formation of a state is often impossible without a history shared by all, the role, played by clay tablet in those ancient states, should be very special. Yet as clay tablet was the main material used to perform written communication at a certain place in ancient times, the historical role, played by it in this respect, is also evident.

Fourth, clay tablets might also play a role in the development of literature and art which was important in the development of people's spiritual world in support of the building of the ancient state. In Mesopotamia clay tablets were used to write down Sumerian literature as well as hymns to the gods. Clay tablets might also be used to record the deeds of the ancient rulers in a certain aesthetic form of expression. For example, the clay tablets from the scholarly library of King Ashurbanipal of Nineveh (668-c.630BCE) were used to present the Assyrian version of the epic of *Gilgamesh*. The story of *Gilgamesh* tells of a mythical king of the Sumerian city of Uruk and his exploits in search of immortality.[13]

So historians write that in Mesopotamia people who had already learned how to make and paint pottery found it natural to use clay to make writing tablets.[14] Goody writes in detail that:

> The earliest elaborated system of writing is the cuneiform (wedge-shaped) orthography which appeared at the end of

the fourth millennium BC. This script was used to write down the language of the Sumerian people who inhabited the lower part of Mesopotamia, 'the land between the two rivers' of the Tigris and Euphrates where they flowed in to the Persian Gulf, and was later taken over by another people of this area, the Akkadians. It was written on moistened clay tablets on which the scribe stamped the triangular end of a reed to produce various combinations of the basic impression.[15]

In short, as Diringer writes,

> The inscribed clay tablets, countless in number and infinitely various in size, shape and contents, far outweigh in importance all other kinds of cuneiform inscriptions in existence. Cuneiform writing on clay tablets was used, indeed, for many centuries, throughout the whole of ancient western Asia for correspondence, promulgating decrees, recording history, codifying laws, compiling religious literature, and for all the needs of a thriving and highly developed society. In Mesopotamia it was the main and permanent medium of communication and of the transmission of thought for nearly three thousand years.[16]

Metal objects Script, engraved on metal objects such as bronze objects, is especially used by humans to extend the distance of linguistic communication because they are durable materials. They are hard and cannot be easily worn or damaged. So since humans learned to extract metal from ore, they have commenced to make metal objects. They may use metal objects for many purposes. But one of the purposes is to support linguistic communication because since humans learned to use language, they have been motivated to extend the distance of communication in order to seek cooperation with more and more people so as to reap more benefits derived from such cooperation. They need to strengthen such linguistic communication. They exert their effort to communicate over a long time and on a large scale until the formation of the state and the dissolution of the tribes. In this process humans design metal objects to fulfill a task of communicating over a long time and on a large scale, a task that cannot be usually fulfilled by other materials such as stone, or clay tablet, for the same purpose. Thus linguistic communication performed by using metal objects must go on over a long time and on a large scale and must be very important. At least, such linguistic communication must be performed by an important figure, or god, or the authorities, with the masses or other people. Such linguistic communication must be performed over long distances. Such linguistic communication is usually not performed by an individual person, or a family, or a social organization, with any other individual person or family or social organization. Such linguistic communication must be performed by the state, or must be needed by the state, or must be performed as approved by the state. Thus such linguistic communication must be vital to the formation and building of the state. That is, it was impossible for metal objects to play a role in the formation of a tribe, but it is possible for them to play a role in the formation of a state. This is because the formation of the state is due to linguistic communication while the formation of a tribe is due to the functioning of kinship. To put it differently, if the tribe was also formed due to linguistic communication performed by all members of the tribe in order to keep the formation of the tribe, it was not crucial because a tribe was, first of all, formed on the basis of kinship, a natural basis. Linguistic communication must especially play a role in the formation and building of the state. In this regard metal objects may play a special part because sometimes the state needs a process of communication that goes on over a long time and on a large scale. As a result, we find that sometimes certain courses of communication that goes on over a long time and on a large scale need to be especially set up by using a metal object in support of the formation of the state. Therefore, we find that sometimes such linguistic communication is performed by an important figure or a god or a secular authority. There may be chiefly three purposes of such linguistic communication performed by people through a metal object.

First, linguistic communication, performed by using a metal object, can be the linguistic communication performed to promulgate a law. As a law is supposed to function over the long term and is authoritative and sacrosanct, a metal object, such as a bronze object, can reflect the spirit of this law. This is because a bronze object is a special material. If linguistic communication is not important, people will not use such a material. It is not easy to engrave script on the surface of such a material. By using such a material, one sends a message to all seeing it to imply that the related linguistic communication is special or important. Besides, such a metal object is hard and durable. People can use it over the long term. A law is also in operation over the long term. By engraving a law on a piece of bronze, people present that law on that metal object. They buttress the authority of the law. Thus they make bronze tables, or bronze tripods, or some other similar utensils, for this purpose. The bronze tables are especially designed and used for the important linguistic communication performed by a law as required by the operation of the state. Diringer writes that:

> Among the Greeks, the Romans and other Italic peoples, the laws penal, civil, religious and ceremonial were often engraved on tables of bronze or of other metals. It is said that more than three thousand tables of bronze or brass kept in the Roman Capitol perished by a fire in the reign of Vespasian; these tables are supposed to have contained proclamations, laws and treaties of alliance.[17]

The well-known Twelve Tables of the Roman times are the laws engraved on twelve bronze tables. The bronze tripods are also used to perform such linguistic communication as script is often engraved on them.

Second, linguistic communication, performed by using a metal object, can be the linguistic communication performed for economic activities. Thus people make coins from either gold or silver or copper or iron. This means that currency needs to be used time and again in order to perform linguistic communication authorizing the exchange of goods or services at any time and at any place as sanctioned or endorsed by the authorities when people engage in such exchange. The related background is that the exchange of goods and services is the basis of the development of an economic community in support of the formation of the state. Goods and services are exchanged constantly and everywhere within the state. Coins are durable. They can be used time and again. Such metal objects are usually manufactured. The same metal objects can be cast. A large quantity of the same kind of metal objects can be made. They are light when only the small size of them is required.

Then they can be preserved and can be carried away. Then they can be the means of exchange. Describing currency, Aristotle writes that:

> [P]eople came to an agreement of that sort, namely for the purpose of exchange, to give and take from each other something which, being itself something useful, was easily adaptable to the needs of life—such as iron, silver, and anything else of the sort. At first this was determined simply by size and weight, but eventually they stamped it with a mark so as to release themselves from measuring it, since the mark stood as an indication of how much there was.[18]

That means that the state relies on the support of a related economic community and the operation of such an economic community relies on the exchange of goods and services and the exchange of goods and services needs the use of such currency. The state needs the functioning of such currency in economic life. When currency needs to be made from a material that can be used time and again by different people in the same way for the purpose of exchanging goods and services in the process in which the value of the currency does not vary with different people or with different places of transaction as sanctioned or endorsed by the state, people design, make and use coins. Metal materials play a role in this regard. So narrating his theory of economics, Smith writes that originally in all countries a legal tender of payment could be made only in the coin of that metal, which was peculiarly considered as the standard or measure of value. He indicates that in England gold was not considered as a legal tender for a long time after it was coined into money. The proportion between the values of gold and silver money was not fixed by any public law or promulgation, but was left to be settled by the market. If a debtor offered payment in gold, the creditor might either reject such payment or accept of it at such a valuation of the gold he and his debtor could agree upon. Copper was not a legal tender at that time except in the change of the smaller silver coins.[19] He also explains that as time went on and as people became gradually more familiar with the use of the different metals in coin and then better acquainted with the proportion between their respective values, it was found, in most countries, "convenient to ascertain this proportion, and to declare by a public law that a guinea, for example, of such a weight and fineness should exchange for one-and-twenty shillings or be a legal tender for a debt of that amount."[20]

Third, linguistic communication, performed by using a metal object, can be the linguistic communication performed to demonstrate a certain figure to propagate values, or an idea, in the state. For example, people make bronze statues of important figures such as a hero or a ruler or a general or an important politician or a poet or a writer or a scientist or a philosopher or a historian or a jurist or an artist or a theologian. They do not make the bronze statue of any ordinary person because an ordinary person is unable to communicate over a long time and on a large scale. An ordinary person usually performs linguistic communication for routine social intercourse such as linguistic communication performed with a neighbor or a friend or a relative. Linguistic communication, performed by an ordinary person, is not significant for the building of the state as an ordinary person is unable to take initiative to perform linguistic communication over the long term and across the state. In contrast, an important figure is able to perform such linguistic communication. Thus a bronze statue may play a role in support of such linguistic communication in the formation of the state in a certain aspect. So in Europe people often make the bronze statue of a great figure such as a philosopher, a theologian, a writer, an artist, a jurist, a poet, a scientist or a historian because the contribution made by each of them in history is always memorized by ordinary people. People may engrave their names on the bronze statues. They may briefly engrave their deed. They may disseminate a humanistic thought that way. They may also install the bronze statue of an ancient ruler of the state. They may engrave his name and deed on the bronze statue. In China the bronze statues of some important political figures are made because the building of the state in China is especially supported by the culture of officialdom. No matter whether it is in a European state or in China, people often use a special material, as a medium, in support of a process of linguistic communication needed to underpin the building of the state.

The role, played by metal objects in the formation of the state, is evident if we think of the importance of the linguistic communication that goes on through those media.

2. Materials from Animals

If humans were unable to develop various materials to be used as media in support of linguistic communication, written language might never appear. Written language creates a form of language used to apply a certain material in communication. If humans perform linguistic communication for simple social intercourse, they may use spoken language only. Spoken communication may suffice for humans to realize social intercourse in daily life. Yet as humans, forming their state, have increased substantially the size of the community, they have to make an extra effort to communicate with one another to maintain the unity of this community. They need to communicate over a long time and on a large scale. Then they use various media. Materials, taken from the bodies of the animals, may also be used. So we see that in a primitive society animals did not directly play any role in the formation of the tribe. In a civilized society animals may directly play a role in the formation of the state because written communication needs support from the media made by using various materials, including those taken from the bodies of some animals, albeit usually in a historical period. That is, materials, taken from the bodies of the animals, are no longer used today for linguistic communication, but they were used in the past and they played a role in the formation and growth of the state in history. They played a role in the progress of human civilization. Please allow me to discuss them in detail.

Tortoise Shell, Bone, Ivory and Silk   Oracle bones, discussed by scholars, often include the pieces of tortoise shell. Scholars conduct researches on these oracle bones. They may also include the shoulder blades of sheep, cattle, deer, reindeer, saiga, caribou, seal, wild boar, pig, hare, dog, lynx, fox, beaver, camel and porcupine.[21] They are most often the pieces of ox scapulae or turtle plastrons. They were in use in many areas in the world. They were used in ancient times. It is said that they were used in the areas like the south part of Arabian peninsula, Central Asia, Mongolia, Siberia, Manchuria, South and West China, Japan, the Arctic and Labrador.[22] In order to have the supply of these materials taken from the bodies of animals, some animals might be reared. For example, the turtle shells of all sizes, large or small, of ancient times, found in the Hsiao-t'un village in China, suggests that turtles were reared in ancient China.[23] They were especially used in ancient China, mainly during the late Shang Dynasty (1766-1122BC) for some specific purposes in relation to the building of the state. As Steven Roger Fischer writes,

> The earliest Chinese writing comprises divinatory oracles on ox scapulae (shoulder blades) and turtle plastrons (the under part of the shell or armour) dating from perhaps as early as 1400BC during the formation of the Shang Dynasty, China's first attested civilization. A cache of 21 such 'oracle bones' was discovered as recently as 1971 near modern Anyang on Henan's northern border. Many scholars assume from the conventionalized appearance of China's earliest inscriptions that Chinese writing must have experienced a protracted local development.[24]

As far as the role of these materials in relation to the organization of the state are concerned, they played a role in the following aspects.

First, people inscribed decrees or laws on oracle bones. They promulgated decrees or laws for the purpose of governing the state. As a decree or law involved a process of linguistic communication, this linguistic communication was performed by the ruler with all across the state. As linguistic communication could rely on a certain material, the time of linguistic communication was extended substantially, and linguistic communication could even become perpetual.

Second, oracle bones were used to record the royal genealogy of the Shang Dynasty. The purpose of recording the royal genealogy of the ruling family was to establish the order of the state. It confirmed the authoritativeness of the ruling family and described the tradition in the governance of the state. In the meantime, the written communication underpinned by oracle bones ensured the continuity of the ruling family. In some sense, they played a part in the consolidation of the state.

Third, people used oracle bones for divination. They carved questions onto the bone or shell in oracle bone script, using a sharp tool. Intense heat was applied with a metal rod until the bone or shell cracked. Then the diviner interpreted the pattern of the crack and wrote prognostication upon the piece. This means that divination disseminated the idea of god or heaven.

This idea of god or heaven was used to persuade the commoners to subordinate themselves to the providence. The idea of god or heaven was used to support the formation of the state as at that time divination actually served the ruler. At that time political questions were religious questions.[25]

Fourth, people chronicle history, as one of the spiritual resources, in support of the formation of the state. One piece of evidence is that people recorded the warfare of early times. For example, according to David N. Keightley, the Shang general appeared in the inscriptions on oracle bones in period I of Shang dynasty. Divinations about "the three hundred archers," or "the many archers," were recorded in period I.[26] Military campaign was recorded. Since the history of war was part of history, oracle bones supported a discourse of history that further supported the formation of the state at least in the respect of spirit. In addition, sacrifices, agriculture and administration were chronicled. These contents may also become the contents of history.

So we see that oracle bones were not used for the social intercourse of commoners in their daily life. They were chiefly used by the ruler for the building and the governance of the state. As it was more difficult for ancients to cut inscriptions on oracle bones in pristine times than for moderns to write on a piece of paper, linguistic communication performed on oracle bones should have been very important. The most important task at that time was to build the state. If people did not intend to build the state, they would not make such a great effort to cut inscriptions on oracle bones. As Keightley writes,

> [T]he gathering of the plastrons and scapulas, the making of the cracks, and the carving of the inscriptions required much effort; that effort alone indicates how greatly pyromancy must have been valued. Shang divination records, like the ritual bronzes, were the product of intense mental effort, attention to cultic detail, and concentration of economic and bureaucratic resources.[27]

Thus he rightly concludes that:

> The bone records, therefore, are not simply a discarded priestly archive. They are religious-political records of decision-making, incarnation, reassurance, and communication at the highest level of theocratic government. If a topic does

appear in the bones, we are justified in thinking that it was a topic of central concern to the Shang kings and—since there are likely to have been few atheists in a Bronze Age theocracy—to the Shang state as a whole.[28]

Evidently, oracle bones extended the distance of linguistic communication. This means that oracle bones extended the time of communication and extended the reach of communication. This situation underpinned the formation of the state. The state was built in such a process of linguistic communication.

Ivory might also be used as a material of written communication for rare occasions in pre-modern times when other convenient writing materials were often unavailable. So the role of ivory, as a rare material in the development of written communication, should be mentioned briefly here, too. This material was sometimes used in Asia, Europe and America in history. Usually ivory was used in the areas inhabited by elephants. However, trade might result in the transportation of ivory from one place to another. For example, it was found that in ancient times ivory was used as writing material for linguistic communication in Europe. As ivory was a rare material for writing at that time, people usually used it for important linguistic communication. Such linguistic communication was also needed by people in the building of the state because linguistic communication for the building of the state was the most important. There are two cases bearing testimony to this situation.

First, according to the existing historical literature, ivory, used as writing material, supported chiefly the linguistic communication significant for the building of the state from ancient to medieval times. In ancient Rome, people used ivory, as a writing material, to promulgate or record the decrees or laws. This is because the state was a large community in which written communication was often performed by people in their mutual interaction. Spoken communication often proved insufficient in support of the building of the state. Particularly, the authorities of the state needed to issue decrees or promulgate laws. The authorities of the state had to communicate with ordinary people on a very large scale in order to organize the state. Thus, as the most important task of the building of the state involved the governance of the state, ivory, the most precious writing material, was used for this purpose in pre-modern times when writing materials were often in shortage. Thus, according to Isaac Disraeli, "The Romans used ivory to write the edicts of the senate on, with a black color."[29] Written edicts enhanced the authority of the government of the Romans.

Second, ivory table-books were often used by Europeans and Americans as memoranda from ancient to early modern times. Ordinary people might use ivory table-books. But the elites of the state more often used ivory table-books. When power holders or politicians used ivory table-books as memoranda, such table-books supported the governance, or the organization, of the state because they needed to note down important affairs on them. So we see that ivory table-books had been in use since the Roman Times. For example, Disraeli mentions that in ancient Rome, "Table-books of ivory" were "used for memoranda, written with black-lead pencils."[30] If table-books were widely used by people, we can suppose that ivory, as a medium, played a role in support of written communication indeed at that time. The use of table-book did not discontinue later. In medieval times, Shakespeare penned that Hamlet used an ivory table-book to note down important events happening within the court. In America, Thomas Jefferson carried an ivory table-book to keep his daily accounts and Benjamin Franklin used one to record his plan for self-examination.[31]

The woven cloth of silk was another material used by humans for written communication. It was chiefly used in ancient times. It was used in Rome, but it was chiefly used in China. Such material was made of silk. The silk was produced from silkworm cocoons made by silkworms. Silk is one of the sources of raw materials made by Chinese to produce costumes. Chinese have been using such a method to produce some costumes since ancient times. Yet silk cloth was also used by ancient Chinese as a material for writing when suitable writing materials were rare. As writing materials were rare, silk was also of importance. Ancient Chinese used silk cloth to write letters because silk cloth was light and it was convenient to carry silk cloth. Such letters extended the distance of linguistic communication. These letters became part of the linguistic communication in support of the formation of the state because keeping the unity of any other community, such as a tribe or a small society, did not need such a method of communication.

It might support chiefly the formation of the state in two ways.

First, such a writing material might enable officials to extend the distance of communication and allow them to communicate with one another on a large scale. Then they could expand the administrative system along with an increase in the size of the state. The result is that authorities set up local governments under the control of the central government. An administrative system emerged, covering all the regions within the state. The woven cloth of silk could serve as a writing material for the need of such linguistic communication. It could indirectly enhance the efficacy of mutual communication between different officials, or different government branches, located in different regions. Thus the use of silk cloth satisfied the need of clerks and bureaucrats who actually lived by the written word and were more interested in getting things written down quickly and accurately.[32] In this case we can believe that silk cloth supported the administration of the state in ancient China.

Second, using such a writing material, people made books, and books could disseminate the knowledge of history, literature and religion, etc. For example, some rare books were made of silk cloth in the period of Han Dynasty (206BC-220AD). As, comparatively speaking, silk was costly, silk books were dear indeed. As indicated by S. J. Edgren, "The important silk books discovered in the early Han tomb at Mawangdui clearly were luxury products."[33] Also as Amalia E. Gnanadesikan writes,

> The innovation of using woven cloth, usually silk, as a writing surface and the invention of the camel's-hair brush spurred the further development of book making as well as art of calligraphy. Cloth made for a porous, smooth surface that could be made in large enough strips to make a scroll.[34]

The preciousness of silk books was in relation to the importance of linguistic communication. Such linguistic communication was usually required by the formation of the state. It was usually required in the respect of the construction of the spirit. As a result, the contents of silk books were mainly of history or religion or literature. These books had played a role in the construction of the spirit of the state for hundreds of years before paper came into use widely in place of any other materials in the production of books. In other words, people disseminated knowledge and thought by virtue of such writing material at that time. They needed such knowledge and thought particularly in the organization of the state at that time. They needed to have the common memory, or to uphold the same religious belief, or to embrace the same cultural idea in order to unite and then to form the state.

Vellum Materials, made by using animal skins, were other materials used by humans for their linguistic communication in pre-modern times. The Greek word for "book", *diphthéra*, means "skin." This means that animal hides were used for writing.[35] Vellum was one of those materials.

The term vellum derives from the French for "calf." Vellum is a translucent material produced from the skin of a young animal, particularly from that of a calf though since Roman times the term may also refer to the skin of any other animal.

In the outset, people happened to find that vellum, taken from a cattle, could be used as a material for writing. Later, they deliberately raised cattle in order to take vellum from the bodies of cattle and used vellum as a writing material. As Engels writes, in Asia men found animals which could be tamed and, when once tamed, bred. The wild buffalo cow had to be hunted; the tame buffalo cow gave a calf yearly and milk as well. A number of the most advanced tribes—the Aryans, Semites, perhaps already also the Turanians—now made their chief work first the taming of cattle, later their breeding and tending. The pastoral tribes produced not only more necessities of life than the other barbarians, but different ones. They possessed the advantage over them of having not only milk, milk products and greater supplies of meat, but also skins, wool, goat hair, and spun and woven fabrics, which became more common as the amount of raw material increased.[36] Then people came to use the skin of calf as a writing material. The method of using vellum as a writing material must later be spread to Europe and Africa as well. Then vellum played a role in the growth of the state because the state depended on a writing system. For example, in early Greek vellum manuscripts, uncial was the ordinary hand. Uncial used "majuscules" or large, upper-case letters composed of curves instead of the angular capitals of monumental texts. Uncial writing in early Greek manuscripts of great eloquence and strength flourished once vellum was used as a main material of writing.[37]

During the fourth century, the vellum codex, a manuscript volume of individual sheets bound together, began to be widely used. With vellum, one could write on both sides of a sheet, thus doubling writing capacity. The first reference to the codex had appeared in six epigrams of the poet Martial (AD 40-103) written as labels for six codices holding the works of Homer, Virgil, Cicero, Livy, Ovid and Martial himself—the earliest known 'books' in the modern sense.[38] Henri-Jean Martin, a French historian, asserts that "The appearance of the codex—the work presented on pages written on both sides rather than on one side of a continuous scroll—was undoubtedly the most important revolution in the book in the Common Era."[39]

Vellum used to make the following contributions in history.

First, people recorded laws on vellum. Laws came to be in the form of written communication that reached many people in the state. All obeyed these laws. As a result, vellum directly played a role in the building of the state.

Second, people wrote land records on vellum. They made important business documents with vellum. Vellum played a role in the building of an economic community in support of the growth of the state.

Third, vellum supported the growth of religion, which might be a spiritual support given to the state. For example, Johannes Gutenberg made about 45 copies of his Bible on vellum (thereby using 7,650 calfskins).[40] And approximately a quarter of the 180 copy edition of Johannes Gutenberg's first Bible printed in 1455 with movable type was printed on vellum, presumably because his market expected this for a high quality book. In addition, some Gandharan Buddhist texts were written on vellum. All Sifrei Torah were written on vellum.

Fourth, vellum might be used to support the development of art. In medieval times, vellum was used as one of the materials of painting.[41] Vellum was more widely used for paintings before canvas became popular in about 1500. Art might serve as a special form to disseminate a spirit that supported the operation of the state.

All of these circumstances show that after humans domesticated certain animals, these animals can make contributions to humans. Some of them can help humans to farm land. Some of them can help humans to transport goods. The skin of the domesticated animals might also be processed and used as a kind of material of written communication. Thus, Vellum in this case played a role in the building of the state in pre-modern times.

Parchment   Parchment is a thin material made from hide. It is usually manufactured from sheep skin or goat skin. Its most common usage is as a writing material for documents, notes or the pages of a book, codices or manuscripts. Parchment is different from vellum. Finer-quality parchment is not called vellum. The word vellum is derived from the Latin *vitulinum*, exclusively meaning calfskin. Yet like vellum, parchment is another kind of hide which is taken from the body of an animal. Thus we can say that animals did not play any role in the formation of a tribe in the respect of the social, but animals used to play a role in the formation of the state since people used parchment in support of written communication critical for the growth of the state in history.

The function of parchment is that the skins of certain animals used to be the media in support of certain written communication. If we presume that stone only enables humans to inscribe large font script such as a series of characters or words in order to communicate with many people outdoors in the public, the skins of certain animals enabled people to write down small-font script in order to communicate with many people indoors in any place where people might have privacy. Such skins might be parchment. In a very small community, people may not need to perform written communication because people can perform spoken communication with one another. By performing written communication, people gradually extend the distance of communication. The community grows large. People may need to develop more media. Thus people came to use the skin of sheep or goats, raised by people, as the material of writing. In the meantime, I argue that in a small community, the supply of parchment was very limited. But in a large community, humans could increase the supply of parchment. Then the parchment could be used as a medium of written communication in the operation of the state. Even the business of supplying parchment flourished. According to David Diringer, in the early second century B.C. parchment was employed at an outpost such as Dura Europos, and it may be assumed as certain that in more central places it was employed at least in the late third century B.C. The story concerning the invention of parchment by Eumenes II, King of Pergamum, may contain the truth that Pergamum was a particularly important emporium for trade in parchment and a great centre for its manufacture, probably with the aid of some new appliances by which the Pergamum product, i.e. the "parchment", became famous.[42] Later, parchment began to be popular around the fourth century AD, along with the codex. The first known codices date to the first century AD.[43]

Unlike the case that parchment was not widely used in India, Southeast Asia or East Asia because people there refrained from writing texts on the skin of butchered animals for religious reason or already had other writing materials, Europeans used parchment as writing material from ancient to medieval times. In Western Europe, the Middle Ages have even been hailed as the "Age of Parchment."[44]

Thus parchment played a role in the growth of the state in Europe and some other areas at least in the following four aspects.

First, using parchment, people wrote the law in order to narrate the law in detail and accurately in medieval times. If we assume that stone was often the material on which a law was written in ancient times, parchment was a typical material on which a law was written in medieval times. This is because elaborated laws were needed in the governance of the society along with the growth of the state in medieval times. Communication realized by parchment was very special. It was often used by the state. Commoners were unable to use parchment in communication between each other. They seldom used it to write a letter because it was dear. But it was used by the state to write the law because the law was essential and important in the operation of the state. Besides, parchment was durable. It could be used for a long period of time. The law also functioned over a long period of time. Therefore, using parchment, people copied the code. It was not used to write an ordinary letter. And by using the income of tax, the state could purchase parchment and then write a law on it. In the meantime we see that along with the growth of the state, people increased the output of agriculture. They increased the supply of parchment accordingly. Then, by applying the law, the government enhanced efficiency in governing the state.

Second, the use of parchment enhanced efficiency in communication within the system of administration in medieval times. Using parchment as a medium of communication, officials transmitted a large amount of information to one another. A large amount of information was sometimes required as administration became professionalized. Using parchment as a medium of communication, officials were also able to perform confidential communication. The work of administration often needed internal communication to coordinate every part of administration and to carry out administrative orders issued from the top level to the grassroots level. Such communication was often not permitted to be revealed to the public. Using parchment, officials could sign documents. Parchment even created a condition for the use of seals because parchment was a suitable material to bear the imprint of a seal. The application of parchment buttressed the operation of administration and enhanced the technical standard of administration. Particularly, the affixation of the seals of the power holder to parchment led to the direct communication and the continuation of the rule of the power holder throughout the administrative system.[45] The ubiquitous rule of the state could be ensured. The state became omnipresent.

Third, due to the use of parchment, people could make certificates and contracts. Thus parchment might support the growth of economy. As economy was also a basis for the growth of the state, parchment also played a role in this respect. For example, chirograph or indenture was used when business document or contract was made after parchment had come widely into use. As E.N. Gladden describes, chirograph seemed to be introduced during the tenth century and came widely into use during the following period. He writes that:

> Originally, it consisted of a threefold text covering an agreement between two parties. The three identical texts on the same parchment were divided by the word CYROGRAPHUM through which the *chirograph* was cut and, in its later form, indented, in such a way that a part of the word remained on each piece, thus enabling them to be easily matched up later as proof of identity. One piece was given to each of the parties, while the other remained in a neutral place, possibly an abbey or royal treasury.[46]

That means that as people engaged in trade, they needed to make sure that the two parties were willing to close a transaction in good faith. In order to make sure that both parties intended to close such a transaction in good faith, they made a contract. A contract often represented a written language solution between two strangers. This written language solution depended on the use of a writing material. Parchment served as such a writing material at that time.

Fourth, by using parchment, people made religious books such as the Bible in support of the growth of religion. The background of that time is that ordinary people could not afford to use parchment for their daily communication, but the religious organization might be able to use it because the church might be able to use contributions given by the churchgoers for the undertaking of religion. For example, according to Henri-Jean Martin, in early Middle Ages it took two hundred skins to make the Souvigny Bible, which contains 392 large-format leaves measuring roughly 560X390mm.[47] And according to Diringer, in 332 the Emperor Constantine ordered "fifty copies of the Sacred Scripture . . . to be written on prepared parchment in a legible manner, and in a convenient, portable form . . ." for the churches in Byzantium, which became his new capital, Constantinople.[48] Innis states that parchment contributed to the development of a powerful ecclesiastical organization in Western Europe.[49] In ancient times Koran was also written on parchment. Then the church or temple was able to spread religion. As religion was part of the resources of building the state, the church or temple might be thus able to play a role in support of the formation and growth of the state. The result is that people, communicating by using language, extended the distance of communication. People formed themselves into a large community. Then the large community increased the supply of parchment. The supply of parchment underpinned the development of the religious undertaking. Then religion underpinned the formation of the state in some cases.

In short, parchment did not play any role in the formation of a tribe, but sometimes it played a role in the formation of the state.

3. Materials from Plants

Like certain animals, nearly all plants are necessary companions of humans after the appearance of humans on earth. A large portion of food, such as the food made of wheat and rice, is produced by humans using part of plants as raw materials. In the meantime, like certain animals, plants have never played a role in the formation of any tribe in the primitive society, but they may play a role in the formation of the state in the civilized society. Particularly, certain materials from plants are processed by people to produce the media of writing. Papyrus was part of such materials. Although papyrus has been out of use today, it played a role in the formation of the state in history. Please allow me to discuss papyrus first.

Papyrus Papyrus was used by people in ancient Near East or Europe. Papyrus, especially produced in ancient Egypt, was such a material. Papyrus, made from a kind of plant growing in the Nile River delta, was light. It was easy for people to carry papyrus in comparison with stone or clay tablet. In addition, it was easier to write script on the surface of papyrus than to inscribe script on the surface of a stone or to write script on a clay tablet. Particularly, in the place where it was difficult to find a clay tablet or to carry it, people might use papyrus. So describing the Semitic peoples, Innis writes that:

> Semitic peoples in contact with Egyptians at some time before 1500BC apparently invented an alphabet which was developed in Palestine and perfected on the Phoenician coast. Papyrus and alphabet prevailed over clay in regions in which the latter was difficult to find and to which it was difficult to transport.[50]

The use of papyrus underlay the growth of the state. For example, in ancient Greece people did not have adequate feasible materials in support of the written communication over a long term. Alfonse Dain Writes that:

> The average Greek wrote on anything at hand, and first on pottery fragments —*ostraca*. We have all seen the picture in our schoolbooks of the sherd on which an ordinary Athenian had written the name of Themistocles to vote for his ostracism. In a later age, in the time of Ptolemy, an ode of Sappho was written on a pottery fragment. . . . The ordinary person in Greece used quite perishable materials for his private purpose, materials that have left only very few authentic fragments. They wrote on waxed tablets, bits of leather or pieces of skin—one document was written on snakeskin.

They used thin plates of lead and later sheets of gold and silver; lead was preferred for formulaic incantations.[51]

But along with the large-scale introduction of papyrus into Greece after the fourth century as a result of the Ptolemies' support of exportation, certain form of written communication, such as book, appeared particularly in the fifth century.[52] When written communication developed substantially, larger states would appear. In comparison, city-states whose formation heavily relied on spoken communication declined to give way to the growth of larger states. Romans also attained benefits from the use of papyrus. In Rome, despite the overwhelming importance of eloquence and spoken communication in the formation of the state, people performed written communication widely by using papyrus. Written communication supported the rise of the Roman Empire.

So papyrus, used by people in ancient times in Egypt or in Near East or in Europe, played a role in support of the building of the state, particularly the building of kingdoms and empires in a certain period of time in human history. Such a role was played by it in several important ways.

First, the use of papyrus boosted the development of written communication. Written communication could enhance efficiency in administration. Enhancing efficiency in administration bolstered the building of the state. Describing such a situation in ancient Egypt, Innis writes that:

> With the increased use of papyrus and the simplification of hieroglyphic script into hieratic characters—in response to the demands of a quicker, cursive hand and the growth of writing and reading—administration became more efficient. Scribes and officials charged with the collection and administration of revenues, rents, and tributes from the peasants became members of an organized civil service, and prepared accounts intelligible to their colleagues and to an earthly god, their supreme master.[53]

Second, with papyrus ancients made written law. Written law buttressed the authority of the state in some sense. It was unlike unwritten law. Written law could bring clarity to the tenet of a law and the capacity of the lawmaker. Unwritten law actually highlighted the self-governance of the society because unwritten law was usually made by some unknown people on behalf of the folk society. By contrast, written law directly represented the authority of the state. This happened in ancient Greece and Rome.

Third, papyrus boosted the development of literature. In ancient Greece oral tradition prevailed although script had already been in use. As the media of materials were rare, the underdevelopment of media checked the development of literature. Oral tradition still remained prevalent. Yet after papyrus came widely into use, writing developed quickly, resulting in the quick development of literature. Commenting on the literature of ancient Greece, Innis writes that:

> The appearance of a large number of short personal lyrics in the late seventh and sixth centuries has been held to coincide with the spread of writing and an increase in the use of papyrus. The position of professional minstrels was weakened as literature was propagated and perpetuated by the increase in writing.[54]

As literature was an important part of the building of a cultural community and the cultural community was one of the bases in support of the building of the state, papyrus played a role in the building of the state.

Fourth, papyrus was also an important medium used by people to chronicle history or to create their philosophy. Papyrus was used to make books in Egypt, Greece and Rome. Thucydides (c. 460-400 BCE), Plato (c.428-c.347 BCE) and Cicero (106-43 BCE) all wrote on papyrus.[55] Papyrus indirectly played a role in this regard so as to support the growth of the state. As people keep on making progress in the building of a state, they rely on thoughts contributed by historians, philosophers and others. Thoughts often need to be saved on certain materials though thoughts can also be handed down through human-chain linguistic communication. In ancient times some thoughts of historians, philosophers and others were saved on papyrus.

So Leo Deuel insists that papyrus, made from papyrus plant, is as evocative of the ancient land of the Nile as its pyramids. Its share in the shaping of Egyptian civilization is immeasurable. Moreover, papyrus reached other Near Eastern countries, and classical Greece and Rome, through Egypt and was adopted as their principal writing material after it had already been in use along the Nile for millennia. Even to the Mesopotamians, whose favorite medium was clay tablets, papyrus was by no means unknown.[56]

Bamboo and Wooden Slips   In early times in China people used a variety of materials as the media of writing. Inscriptions appeared on bones or tortoise shells as early as the Shang Dynasty period, as mentioned earlier. The woven cloth of silk was also used as a writing material shortly later in ancient China. However, bamboo and wooden slips trumped bones, tortoise shells and silk as the media of writing mainly because a large amount of bamboo and wooden slips could be supplied. This was another kind of writing material. It was used chiefly in China. Thus during the Shang Dynasty period those who mastered the art of writing only numbered several hundreds. They were of the higher order of the society. At that period of time script was mainly inscribed on bones, tortoise shells and some other objects. Thus, a limited supply of bones, tortoise shells and other objects restricted written communication to a small number of people in the society. The woven cloth of silk was expensive though Chinese began to use it as a writing material in later times in ancient history. The use of bamboo and wooden slips greatly extended the reach of communication in support of the growth of the state because the supply of a large amount of bamboo and wooden slips enabled much more people to engage in written communication. The reason is that all people needed to keep on communicating with all in the growth of the state. The authorities of the state also needed to communicate with all this way. Bamboo and wooden slips played a role.

First, by using bamboo and wooden slips, officials issued imperial edicts or decrees, or they promulgated laws. They were bound together to become a volume. Imperial edicts, or decrees, or laws, were thus issued or promulgated to all in the kingdom or the empire. These bamboo and wooden slips facilitated the governance of the state in ancient times. As imperial edicts, or decrees, or laws, needed to be known to common people, bamboo and wooden slips extended the reach of linguistic communication performed by the authorities with the common people. This situation bolstered the interaction between the regime and the common people. For example, some bamboo slips unearthed are such documents of the government of ancient times in China. In 1930 and 1972 many bamboo slips of Juyan were unearthed in today's Jinta County, Gansu Province and Ejina County of Inner Mongolian

Autonomous Region. Some bamboo slips were government documents of East Han Dynasty. In particular, bamboo and wooden slips were, in some sense, the "mass media" of ancient times if we compare bamboo slips with bones and tortoise shells used earlier, or the woven cloth of silk used shortly later, by literate people.

Second, people create history through historiography. Historiography relied on the use of bamboo and wooden slips in history. Part of the Chinese history is handed down by bamboo and wooden slips. The *Bamboo Annals* (*Zhushu Jinian*), also called the *Jizhong Annals*, is a chronicle of ancient China. It begins at the earliest legendary times (the Yellow Emperor) and extends to 299BC, focusing on the history of the State of Wei in the Warring States period. It covers a similar period to Sima Qian's *Records of the Grand Historian* (91BC). As the original text was interred with King Xiang of Wei (died 296BC) and re-discovered in 281AD (Western Jin Dynasty) in the Jizhong discovery, the chronicle survived the burning of books by Qin First Emperor. They were written on bamboo slips. The slips were arranged in order and transcribed by court scholars. It was identified as the state chronicle of Wei by the scholars in later times though the original recovered slips had disappeared ever since. Though the original chronicle cannot be found now, what is certain is that bamboo slips were indeed used by ancients to record their chronicles. And the bamboo and wooden slips, through which people narrated the chronicles, clearly show that bamboo and wooden slips play a role in narrating part of Chinese ancient history and history is one of the resources used by people to build their state. That is, there is no history for a tribe, but there is usually a piece of history for a state. As a result, we can assert for sure that bamboo or wood played a role in the growth of the state in a certain period of time given that bamboo and wooden slips used to support historiography in the past.

Third, bamboo and wooden slips bolstered the spread of culture to the great masses of the people. Cultural idea is a kind of idea that may support the formation of the state because culture is a basis for the formation of a society and the society is a basis for the formation of the state. *The Book of Songs* (China's earliest collection of poetry), discovered in the grave of Marquis Ruyin of the Western Han (206BC–25AD) in Fuyang, Anhui Province in 1970s, was written on bamboo slips. A religious or ethical idea may be an idea in favor of the formation of a community under the influence of a certain belief and hence the building of a certain state that relies on the support of that belief for internal unity. For example, the Confucian classic *The Book of Rites,* found from Han tombs in Wuwei, Gansu Province in 1990s, was written on wooden slips. These ideas were effectively and widely disseminated in written communication. Bamboo and wooden slips bolstered written communication in the time when other better media had not been developed yet. So in the Spring and Autumn Period and the Warring States period (770-221 BC) in China people disseminated the thoughts of Confucius and Laozi widely. The classics, spreading their thoughts, were bamboo and wooden books. A hundred schools of thought contended when people used bamboo and wooden slips widely in those periods of time.

Paper Chinese started to make paper based on the substance made of various fibers in ancient times. In early modern times peoples across the world commenced to make paper from the pulp of woods. As there is a large amount of supply of the raw materials for making paper, paper plays a significant role in the formation of the state because the formation of the state relies on linguistic communication that goes on across the state. When ancient Egyptians developed papyrus for linguistic communication, papyrus was only used by people in a certain region and some other adjacent regions because people could only produce papyrus in a certain region. The supply of papyrus to a few regions only restricted its use. In the meantime, bamboo, used as a writing material, also had some shortcomings. Bamboo was comparatively heavy and awkward. When bamboo was used to make a book, this book was a large bundle. The amount of bamboo supplied by the market would not be as large as the amount of the pulp of woods supplied by the market today. Paper can be produced from the materials found by people all over the world. Thus paper is more widely used in modern times. In addition, paper is the most desirable material in support of linguistic communication as it is cheap and it can be easily preserved and carried. Paper is very significant for the formation of the state.

First, since paper came widely into use, people have often been writing letters to each other. They form a large community, and the large community extends the distance between one person and another. Yet as they need to keep on interacting with one another, they need to keep in touch. Then they write letters with paper. That is, people need to write script on the surface of a certain material and such script needs to be carried to another place. They need to move from one place to another. Any material may function to carry the script. But paper should be the most desirable material in most cases. The first reason is that paper is cheap and a large amount of paper can be produced and supplied. The second reason is that paper is light. It can be carried by any person easily. It can be small in size if it is only used to carry the script to perform the linguistic communication between two individual persons. The third reason is that it is easy to write script on a piece of paper. It is the material on which it is convenient for people to write script. Paper supports the growth of the state, particularly the growth of a nation-state. Although we know that family members and friends, far from each other, often write letters with paper to communicate with each other and hence to keep emotional ties with each other, the use of paper is particularly significant for the building of the state because paper can be widely used by the bureaucrats of the government to write letters or to make documents. The growth of the state particularly relies on the use of paper. People often need to perform linguistic communication over long distances within the state. If we assume that a society is also formed, such a society may be small in size. People usually organize the state on a large scale. The reason is that a society can be large or small. The state, however, is usually large as compared with a society. A village can be a society. This village, however, cannot become a state. Thus, I postulate that the government, in charge of organizing the state, acts on a large scale. This case requires the internal coordination of the government. The power holder of the government needs to keep on communicating with the bureaucrats of various levels. The power holder needs to communicate with the bureaucrats over long distances. The bureaucrats of various levels within the government may also need to communicate with each other over long distances because the government has local branches. They often write letters to each other. They sometimes write letters to which they affix their own signatures. They also circulate documents. Paper is widely used. Thus paper supports the operation of the government on a large scale significant for the formation of the state.

Second, by using paper, people make contracts. In ancient Egypt people wrote contracts on papyrus. But due to the limited supply of papyrus particularly in Europe in ancient times it was mainly the material used by people to make codes, religious documents and books. In a greater part of medieval times, papyrus was unavailable in Europe. Without papyrus, people found it difficult to make contracts when they engaged in their business. The background is that businessmen cooperated in the operation of business and they needed to make promises to each other. They usually made promises to each other orally. Oral promise might not be reliable. Henry Maine writes, when describing the contract law of ancient Europe, that when ancients make a promise, the promise is "accompanied with a solemn ceremonial. Not only are the formalities of equal importance with the promise itself, but they are, if anything, of greater importance." [57] This case tells us that when paper was not in use, people were unable to make a written contract. They held a rite to stress their promises. Yet since paper came into use widely, promises, made by people, have often become contracts or some other documents such as agreements or covenants. This is because contracts are more reliable. Here we find that paper plays an important role. Those rites, held to accentuate promises, can be obviated. People can strengthen linguistic communication for a special purpose particularly in economic domain. People, therefore, strengthen cooperation in the domain of economic life. This bolsters the formation of the state more or less because the formation of the state always depends on the economic growth and the economic growth depends on the economic cooperation between one another throughout the state.

Third, people can use paper as a kind of material to manufacture bills. Bills are the means of exchange. Bills represent a portion of money circulated within a certain state. As bills are light, it is easy or convenient to carry them. Though bills are not as durable as coins because paper, used to produce bills, is not as durable as a metal object used to manufacture coins, the users of currency tend to take good care of bills when they hold them because bills are authorized by the state to allow for the holder of bills to purchase a good or a service needed by the holder of the bills at any time and at any place. Thus paper plays a role in the growth of the economy of a state, in some sense, just like metal objects in this respect. Thus paper plays a role in the formation of the state indirectly as the formation of the state relies on the formation of an economic community built by people in their economic life just like some metal objects. So describing gold and silver as the currency used in England, Smith writes that:

> Buying and selling was transacted by means of money in England then as well as now. The quantity of circulating money must have borne the same proportion to the number and value of purchases and sales usually transacted at that time, which it does to those transacted at present; or rather it must have borne a greater proportion, because there was then no paper, which now occupies a great part of the employment of gold and silver.[58]

This means that when paper is in use, it is sometimes used to manufacture bills. Bills are circulated across the state. Bills support the operation of the economic community in support of the formation of the state.

Fourth, the physical nature of paper dictates that it is easier for people to affix script to it. It is the very reason that printing can develop. Thus it particularly assists the men of letters, who are especially capable of performing written communication by creating their works, in communicating with ordinary people across the state. They are theologians, philosophers, writers, artists, historians, and others. They disseminate belief, knowledge, values, experience, thoughts and others. In a state that grows in size, all need to communicate with all potentially in order to ensure the formation of the state. Ordinary people are usually unable to communicate with each other very effectively. The men of letters are media used by ordinary people to help them to ensure the formation of the state. Thus, at least, literate culture becomes an element of the formation of the state. For example, the flourishing of literate culture has especially supported the growth of the state in China since the invention of printing in ancient times. As Edgren writes that:

> That the invention of printing took place at all in China in the early Tang Dynasty has to be seen as the direct result of the availability of paper, which existed as part of a widespread literate culture. Once high-quality paper was available for manuscript production, then impressions could be taken from inked seals and small wooden pictorial stamps, and ink-squeeze rubbings of text could be made from stone

inscriptions. These simple means of duplicating word and image evolved into the use of carved wooden blocks (xylography) to print multiple copies of complete texts.[59]

Paper also plays a role in the growth of the state, particularly, the nation-state in the West. The use of paper creates a condition for the invention of modern printing. In early modern Europe the spread of the works of the men of letters and the development of printing went hand in hand. The men of letters relied on presses to promote their works. Accordingly, the growth of presses buttressed the cause of the men of letters that underpinned the development of culture. The development of culture further underpinned the growth of the nation-state. For example, in the period from fifteenth to eighteenth century, presses directly engaged scholars, translators, editors and compilers. As Elisabeth Eisenstein writes,

> During this interval, printers served as patrons for authors, acted as their own authors, and sought patronage, privileges, and favors from official quarters as well. This was the era when men of letters and learning were likely to be familiar with print technology and commercial trade routes.[60]

To put it another way, if there were no language, there would be no script. If there were no script, people would not make a special effort to produce paper. If there were no paper, printing would not develop. If printing did not develop, communication performed by the men of letters with ordinary people would be slow and parochial. The men of letters, as a result, would not be powerful enough to support the growth of the state, particularly the nation-state. As a result, in modern times knowledge is gradually popularized as compared with the situation in the medieval time in which knowledge was usually disseminated by a small number of learned people to a small portion of other people learning knowledge. One of the factors that underlie the dissemination of knowledge among all citizens is that the wide use of paper creates a condition for the development of printing and thus the men of letters disseminate knowledge through plenty of books in the growth of the state.

Fifth, the supply of a large amount of cheap paper paves a way for people to manufacture mass media. Due to the birth of mass media, people perform one-to-many linguistic communication efficiently. This is significant for linguistic communication that goes on across the state in support of the formation of the state. The use of paper, together with the development of printing, allows for people to perform one-to-many linguistic communication efficiently across the state. This progress underpins the growth of the mass society. Then in the mass society citizens need to interact with the government or with themselves. They need the coverage of current events. They need to get the news. Newspapers and magazines flourish. In medieval times the messages about state affairs were sent to ordinary people. Ordinary people also spread news to each other, but they did so mainly in the form of spoken communication. For example, churchgoers gossiped when they met. People performed spoken communication in the local area only. Printing spurs the development of written communication that reaches those who are in far-flung corners of the state. News reporters can perform communication with plenty of people directly across the state. In this era, the market supplies a large amount of paper, enabling a few journalists, or a few authors, to communicate with the masses across the state. A mass society takes shape. The mass society further requires the power holders of the state to undertake the responsibility of managing the mass society because now ordinary people, who form the mass society, demand the provision of public services from the authorities. The state has to be governed according to the expectation of the mass society as a result. Then we see that the authorities of the state need to engage in the political mobilization of the masses in order to keep ruling legitimacy at this time. This is because the building of the state especially requires the positive interaction between the authorities and the masses in modern times due to the formation of a mass society.

Paper plays an important role in the growth of modern society and the building of the modern state because paper supports the linguistic communication that goes on in nearly all aspects throughout the state. A decrease in the cost of making communicative media further boosts the required linguistic communication. Analyzing the progress of civilization in the West, Fischer writes that:

> People seldom appreciate paper's impact on Western civilization. Parchment and vellum could never have supported mass literacy, worldwide printing, modern offices, newspapers,

government records, general education and so on. These are the consequences of paper and the printing press.[61]

The role played by paper in the building of a modern state is self-evident. It particularly supports the growth of nation-state in modern times.

Notes

1. David Diringer, *The Book Before Printing: Ancient, Medieval and Oriental* (New York: Dover Publications, Inc., 1982), 82.
2. Christian Witschel, The *Res Gestea Divi Augusti* and the Roman Empire, in Fritz-Heiner Mutschler and Achim Mittag (ed.), *Conceiving the Empire China and Rome Compared* (Oxford: Oxford University Press, 2008), 259.
3. Shi Ji 6/242; cited from Martin Kern, *Announcements from the Mountains: The Stele Inscriptions of the Qin First Emperor*, in Mutschler and Mittag (ed.), *Conceiving the Empire China and Rome Compared*, 217.
4. Diringer, *The Book Before Printing: Ancient, Medieval and Oriental*, 93.
5. Harold A. Innis, *Empire and Communications* (Victoria: Press Porcépic Limited, 1986), 77.
6. Please see: M.T. Mitsos, *Une inscription d' Argos, BCH* 107:243–9; cited from Rosalind Thomas, *Literacy and the City-State in Archaic and Classical Greece*, in Alan K. Bowman and Greg Woolf (ed.), *Literacy and Power in the Ancient World* (Cambridge: Cambridge University Press, 1994), 38.
7. Thomas Hobbes, *Leviathan*, edited with an introduction by C.B Macpherson (New York: Penguin Books, 1985), 418.
8. Leo Deuel, *Testaments of Time: The Search for Lost Manuscripts & Records* (New York: Alfred A. Knopf, 1965), 204–205.
9. Martyn Lyons, *Books: A Living History* (Los Angeles: The J. Paul Getty Museum, 2011), 20.

10. Henri-Jean Martin, *The History and Power of Writing*, translated by Lydia G. Gochrane (Chicago: The University of Chicago Press, 1994), 44.

11. Ibid.

12. Innis, *Empire and Communications*, 1986), 27.

13. See: Lyons, *Books: A Living History*, 17.

14. Martin, *The History and Power of Writing*, 44.

15. Jack Goody, *The Interface between the Written and the Oral* (Cambridge: Cambridge University Press, 1987), 28.

16. Diringer, *The Book Before Printing: Ancient, Medieval and Oriental*, 83.

17. Ibid., 48.

18. Aristotle, *The Politics of Aristotle*, translated by Peter L. Phillips Simpson (Chapel Hill: The University of North Carolina Press, 1997), 24.

19. Adam Smith, *The Wealth of Nations*, with an Introduction by D.D. Raphael (New York: Alfred A. Knopf, 1991), 34–35.

20. Ibid., 35.

21. Please see: David N. Keightley, *Sources of Shang History: The Oracle-Bone Inscriptions of Bronze Age China* (Berkeley: University of California Press, 1978), 5.

22. Ibid.

23. Ibid.,12.

24. Steven Roger Fischer, *A History of Writing* (London: Reaktion Books Ltd, 2001), 168.

25. Keightley, *Sources of Shang History: The Oracle-Bone Inscriptions of Bronze Age China*, 136.

26. Ibid., 180.

27. Ibid., 136–137.

28. Ibid., 136.

29. Isaac Disraeli, *Curiosities of Literature*, Vol. II (Boston: William Veazie, 1858), 184.

30. Ibid.

31. Kevin J. Hayes, *The Road to Monticello: The Life and Mind of Thomas Jefferson* (Oxford: Oxford University Press, 2007), 98.

32. Please see: Amalia E. Gnanadesikan, *The Writing Revolution: Cuneiform to Internet* (Chichester, West Sussex, UK: Wiley-Blackwell, 2009), 62–63.

33. J.S. Edgren, *China*; in Simon Eliot and Jonathan Rose (ed.), *A Companion to the History of the Book* (Malden, MA, USA: Blackwell Publishing, 2007), 99.

34. E. Gnanadesikan, *The Writing Revolution: Cuneiform to Internet*, 69.

35. Deuel, *Testaments of Time: The Search for Lost Manuscripts and Records*, 85.

36. Frederick Engels, *The Origin of the Family, Private Property and the State* (New York: International Publishers, 1972), 218–219.

37. Please see: Fischer, *A History of Writing*, 239.

38. Please see: Ibid., 244.

39. Martin, *The History and Power of Writing*, 59; please also see: Fischer, *A History of Writing*, 244.

40. Gnanadesikan, *The Writing Revolution: Cuneiform to Internet*, 251.

41. Please see: Daniel V. Thompson, *The Materials and Techniques of Medieval Painting* (New York: Dover Publications, Inc., 1956), 27.

42. See: Diringer, *The Book before Printing: Ancient, Medieval and Oriental*, 170; 192.

43. Gnanadesikan, *The Writing Revolution: Cuneiform to Internet*, 241.

44. Fischer, *A History of Writing*, 238.

45. E. N. Gladden observes that " The Great Seal, or seal of majesty, developed, symbolizing authority and facilitating the delegation of power by the formal transference of the seal by the principal to a deputy or agent. The first instance of such in England was the seal of Edward the Confessor. The history of these important seals significantly illustrates the development of administration, through the formulation of procedures designed to facilitate acts of government to deal with new situations. Thus by the transfer to a deputy of the custody of his Great Seal the king could ensure the continuance of his rule in his absence, while the adoption of different seals for different purposes assisted the departmentalization of the Administration; for example, in the emergence of the Exchequer." See: E.N. Gladden, *A History of Public*

Administration, Vol. 2: From the Eleventh Century to the Present Day (London: Frank Cass and Company Limited, 1972), 23.

46. Ibid.

47. Martin, *The History and Power of Writing*, 51.

48. Diringer, *The Book before Printing: Ancient, Medieval and Oriental*, 194–195.

49. Innis, *Empire and Communications*, 123.

50. Ibid., 42.

51. Alphonse Dain, "L'écriture grecque du VIIIe siècle avant notre ère à la fin de la civilization Byzantine," in L'écriture et la phychologie des peuples, 167–180, esp. p. 194, cited from Martin, *The History and Power of Writing*, 47.

52. See: Martin, *The History and Power of Writing*, 48.

53. Innis, *Empire and Communications*, 16.

54. Ibid., 65.

55. Lyons, Books: *A Living History*, 21.

56. Deuel, *Testaments of Time: The Search for Lost Manuscripts and Records*, Ibid., 81.

57. Henry Maine, *Ancient Law* (London: John Murray,1866), 313.

58. Smith, *The Wealth of Nations*, 390.

59. Edgren, *China*, in Eliot and Rose (ed.), *A Companion to the History of the Book*, 103.

60. Elisabeth Eisenstein, *The Printing Revolution in Early Modern Europe* (Cambridge: Cambridge University Press, 1983), 100.

61. Fischer, *A History of Writing*, 264.

Chapter Three

Behavior

1. Behavior as an Example

Behavior was often displayed by humans as the only way of communication that ensured the formation of the community prior to the birth of language. Since the birth of language, however, humans have been displaying the behavior of a certain type as a unique medium in support of linguistic communication in their mutual interaction though language can also serve as a medium in support of behavioral communication. Humans may display such behavior as an example in support of the related linguistic communication. One case in point is that people can no longer always provide all possible information to each other while they extend the distance of communication. Humans, having extended the distance of their linguistic communication, form their state and dissolve their tribes. Then it follows that in the state, a large community, people often need to perform linguistic communication over long distances to ensure the unity of the state. Communicators are often far away from each other and communicators often communicate by using language—a form representing truth without face-to-face contact for visualized verification—to get information. Language may be unable to provide every piece of information needed by all. Information, given by using language, may not always be truer than one expects because people may not always communicate in good faith. As a sufficient interaction, including mutual communication, between one another is essential for the formation of the community, humans may need to display a type of behavior especially in support of linguistic communication. Though people may consider language to be the greatest creature of humans for communication, a person also obtains information from the behavior of another person that serves as a medium of communication and a person may also give information to another person by showing his own behavior as a medium for communication, no matter whether this information is given by a witting or an unwitting behavior.

That is, prior to the birth of language, a behavior served to convey information between two people, or two groups of people. This behavior, serving to convey information, was, in some sense, originally the reaction of a person by instinct in his effort for his interaction with the surrounding world. This behavior played a role of communication without the realization of a person or a group of people. For example, a man might laugh or cry. His behavior of laughing or crying might serve as a process of communication because his behavior could convey a piece of information. Later, he gained more experiences in practice and began displaying his behavior to mean something. Since then, displaying his behavior has gradually led to the formation of a rule of expression when he and other people keep on interacting with one another. Thus, behavior becomes a medium in human communication. Then we see that humans often need to communicate over a long time and on a large scale for mutual interaction in the state. Yet as people may lose some information in communicating over a long time and on a large scale, they sometimes display a behavior as a medium in support of such linguistic communication because a behavior, as a medium, may strengthen such linguistic communication to avoid losing some information. So a person uses this special medium, namely, his behavior, to give expression to his feeling or idea or intention. Then people create a new method of expression to bolster mutual interaction among all. For example, we sometimes see that some Europeans make a gesture when making a speech. The behavior, shown by those Europeans, I believe, is not only used for mutual communication, but also significant for the formation of their mutual interaction in support of linguistic communication in the formation of the society and the state because this shows the inadequacy of linguistic communication on some occasions. Such type of communication has a variety of forms. These forms not only include the behavior of showing emotion, but also even include some artistic forms showing the gestures of body. These forms of communication may include the behavioral communication realized in the course of a dumb show, a dance performance, an acrobatic feat and a gymnastic exhibition, etc. In other words, some performances are given for entertainment. But the actual meaning of them can be considered to be strengthening the mutual interaction of people within a society or a state. They help strengthen linguistic communication that underpins the formation of the society. As the state has to be built on the basis of an existing society, they also help strengthen linguistic communication that underpins the building of the state.

This case is what we often overlook. That is, language alone may not necessarily be the best means of communication under all circumstances and conditions. Though language helps people to convey various complex and crystal-clear information, it excludes gradually, in linguistic communication, the visual and auditory impression people may have from the physical world, and this situation isolates people's subjective world from the objective world. This development results in the fact that people gain the oral or literal capacity in mutual communication between one another, but also incur certain costs at the same time. Specifically, conveying information by using language, people may not get all necessary information because certain information may be merely given through an incomplete linguistic description; some information provided by using language may not be able to reflect the reality such as falsified information provided by a liar; some information may come totally from the imagination of one person's brain; some information provided by using language may be unable to reflect the objective fact correctly and accurately such as the information provided by an exaggerator; and some information may distort the fact after it is cut and tailored by a person for any purpose. Because of this situation, a person, receiving information in linguistic communication, may come to a biased conclusion. People may encounter distrust in mutual linguistic communication. And distrust, given rise to in linguistic communication between one another, may affect cooperation between the two, weaken the cohesion of the community and even lead to the dissolution of the community. This directly or indirectly impairs the unity of the state. Thus in this case a person may shun linguistic communication and turn to performing behavioral communication in an effort to communicate effectively within view and hearing distance. A person performs communication by adopting the communicative method of a small community in a large community. This sort of communication may be conducive to the building of a cooperative relationship, or a trust relationship, between one another. In our daily life, we may often see that when people are unable to communicate effectively with each other, they perform behavioral communication. When two people stand apart over long distances with each unable to make his voice heard by the other, they may make gestures for communication. This reflects the varying applications of different media. However, people often opt for behavioral communication to gain the truthfulness of communication by virtue of the shortest-distance behavioral display against the possible failure of linguistic communication between one another in a large community, particularly, the state.

Despite the fact that language is people's essential means of communication, behavioral communication is often indispensable. Behavior can serve as a special medium. People have to use, at least, one medium in linguistic communication. The behavior of one person can also become a medium in linguistic communication. Such behavior can function as a replacement of linguistic communication when linguistic communication fails. As mentioned earlier, a material can function as a medium for communication in place of a human being. Likewise, behavior can also function as a medium in place of a human being or a material in linguistic communication in some cases. This phenomenon particularly occurs in politics because linguistic communication always functions on a large scale in politics. The distance of linguistic communication between the power holder and the masses is the longest in some sense. Thus, whenever a power holder finds it more effective to display a behavior in communication, he may naturally choose to display a behavior to give expression to his feeling or idea or intention from time to time. Thus, communication, performed by this behavior in support of linguistic communication, also characterizes the mutual interaction of people in support of the operation of the state. That is, he may display his behavior in the public to interact with the citizens. He may display his behavior in the public to show his utter devotion to the operation of the state.

There is an interaction between the citizens and the power holder in the state and this interaction is actually a basis that underpins the unity and the operation of the state. As a precondition for the building of the state, ordinary people entrust the power holder to govern the state. He and the citizenry should have a trust relationship. He may need to let the masses know that he is governing the state. He may need to let the masses know what he supports or opposes. He needs to demonstrate his leadership. So there is the mutual interaction between the power holder and the masses. If a power holder appears in the public, he may send out a signal. If a power holder avoids appearing in the public, he may try to avoid sending out a signal. His behavior may be like that of an ordinary person. For example, a man, swaggering through the street, uses his body and behavior for communication. If a man hides himself, he is trying not to use his body for communication with anybody. However, a behavior, displayed by a power holder of the state, is very special because he is important in political life and he is indispensable in the governance of the state. Please allow me to use a specific example to illustrate this case. If a state leader is suspected of being unable to perform his duties, he may appear in the public to demonstrate his ability to perform his duties. He needs to keep the confidence of the people in him. In the last stage of his presidency, Boris Yeltsin, the Russian president from 1991 to 1999, decreased the chances of making his appearance in the public because of his poor health. His disappearance from the public used to make people suspect his physical unfitness. Many ambitious politicians planned to replace Yeltsin. But Yeltsin refused to give up his power. Then the Presidential Executive Office of Russian Federation arranged for Yeltsin to make a public speech or make public appearance in order to show Yeltsin's "good health status" and ability to perform his duties as the president. For example, on January 13, 1998, Yeltsin rode a snowmobile to demonstrate his physical fitness. Obviously, if Yeltsin failed to appear in the public or to show his physical fitness in person, any linguistic explanation, given to indicate his "good health status," would be ineffective. The more the explanation given by using language, the more the people suspecting Yeltsin's sickness. Only Yeltsin's appearance, demonstrating his physical fitness in the public, could prove his ability to perform his duties for the state. I think that such an event may often occur in a state. The state leader is often irreplaceable. He not only communicates with the citizens by using language, but also does so by displaying his behavior. We cannot imagine that a state leader does not appear in the public. He is expected to appear in the public regularly. If he has failed to appear in the public for a period of time, linguistic communication he performs with the citizens may lose effect. In other words, the people want to see him when he communicates with the people.

In other words, linguistic communication and behavior shown for communication tend to be mutually verified. If one makes the same speech time and again or talks about the same thing many times without the support of any evidence, others may doubt the truthfulness of the related information he gives. The related linguistic communication may lose its function. The failure of the related linguistic communication will prevent one from starting a new process of linguistic communication. He has to get back to the process of the original behavioral communication to make his behavior his medium in order to resume the function of the original linguistic communication. The behavior of making a personal example to convince others, or the behavior of acting as an example shown to others, may be the basic rule for one to show his presence or act or intention. The reason for this is that information conveyed by language is not the motion of the matter itself but the agent of the matter. If information, conveyed by language, is believed to be false, it separates itself from the motion of the matter and hence is unable to be accepted in communication. The communication fails. Even though the true information is transmitted in the following linguistic communication, this information may still be mistaken as being false and hence ignored. Linguistic communication fails. The only way to bear testimony to the truthfulness of the information is to prove it with the behavior displayed by people or the objective fact.

In case of a failure in linguistic communication, one has to prove the truthfulness of the information conveyed in the linguistic communication with the behavior or the fact in order to resume the effectiveness of the linguistic communication. This is a rule for linguistic communication. However, sometimes behavioral language, namely, the expression given through the display of a type of behavior, may not be able to play a role in communication unless linguistic communication fails. The reason is that behavioral language is the form of communication that functions in conjunction with a process of linguistic communication giving an explanation. In terms of the behavioral language of a power holder, his behavioral language relies on the existing semantic environment. It is neither written language nor spoken language, and it relies on the semantic environment in depth in the conveyance of information. If no external observers guessed or might guess the possibility of the deterioration of his health or the possibility of his physical unfitness, Yeltsin's behavior of making a public appearance, especially designed by the Presidential Executive Office of Russian Federation, would be meaningless. In other words, the abovementioned behavior may not be understood unless there is a context or background. This context or background is that it was said that Yeltsin often stopped his work because of illness. Thus some people suspected that Yeltsin was unable to perform his duties as the president. This suspicion occurred in the ambience of linguistic communication. Linguistic communication served as a background for the special behavioral communication. If we replace Boris Yeltsin with Vladimir Putin, the President of Russian Federation succeeding Boris Yeltsin in 1999 or 2000, we see that Putin is in the state of good health and no one once suspects that Putin's state of health deteriorates and Putin is unable to perform his duties. If Putin makes his appearance in the public, his behavior will not have the semantic significance given by Yeltsin's behavior many years ago. Yet as only linguistic communication can give clarity through an interpretation, the related behavior should be a medium in support of linguistic communication.

In the governance of the state, the leader is crucial. No state can run without a leader. Therefore, the leader should appear in the public in order to confirm that he is working or present if necessary. Otherwise the public, or the domestic and foreign observers, will surmise that he is unable to appear for some reasons. During the Cultural Revolution in China, many senior officials of the government were removed from their positions in the power struggle within the Communist Party of China without issuing a bulletin announcing their resignations. Once they stopped appearing in the public, some unofficial sources would announce their removal from their job positions. Even though the regime did not announce formerly their removal, their failure to appear in the public already announced or confirmed their removal on behalf of the regime because if they were still in power, they would always appear in the public. Besides, there were plenty of cases in the past that some senior officials failed to appear in the public and the authorities confirmed their removal from their job positions later. For this reason, observers tended to surmise the likelihood of the removal of an official if he failed to appear in the public. Because this situation may cause misunderstanding, it is a prevailing rule today that a politician must appear in the public on a variety of important occasions as follows: The government holds the ceremony of celebrating some of the most important public holidays or receiving some very distinguished foreign guests; the government holds an important political meeting; the government announces the emergency of the nation-state if any; and the government holds the funeral of an important figure who has passed away such as the former leader of the state. Meanwhile, the power holder, appearing in the public, is focused on by the media. The media report his activities, and the reports given by the media enable the power holder to communicate with the masses by displaying his behavior. If he fails to appear in the public on the occasion on which he should appear, his failure to appear can also serve to communicate with the public. His failure to appear in the public may hint that he is no longer able to perform his job duties. His behavior automatically communicates with the people.

In other words, human linguistic communication may sometimes work ineffectively. In a state a person may express his opinion or view on the matters concerning the governance of the state, hoping to influence the other or others, or persuading the other or others to take certain action, in the mutual interaction of the citizens or the mutual interaction between the citizens and the power holder. But though his words may be heard by the other or others, he may not succeed in influencing the other or others or persuading the other or others to take action. One may set an example in order to persuade the other or others to take action as expected or required. For example, in China the government, under the leadership of Mao Zedong, always instilled a revolutionary ideology into the minds of the people in order to mobilize them from 1950s to 1970s. A state leader might call on the citizens to do volunteer work for the state. He might do some volunteer work in person in order to set an example for the citizens. He might also live simply in order to encourage the people to live simply because the way of living simply could help the state to save economic resources at that time when the country was caught up in poverty. Linguistic communication sometimes does not prove very effective. Thus a person may think of taking direct action in place of words so as to make the behavior attached to the action a medium for special communication. The action, directly taken by one as an example, is the action expected to be taken by all others. Such action is intended to prove the truthfulness of linguistic communication.

This means that a behavior may play a role as a medium in the linguistic communication that goes on between the power holder and the masses. The power holder often displays a behavior in support of his discourse. For example, the power holder may display a certain behavior to strengthen linguistic communication. A power holder may reiterate his view and stance after he gives expression to the same. Reiteration means the repetition of the words uttered or written in the past. A power holder often reiterates the decree or law of the state. That a power holder makes a statement about that decree or law for the first time is the pure linguistic communication. His reiteration of that decree or law does not vary from the statement he has made for the first time. The public hears both of the two statements. However, he still wants to reiterate that decree or law. Evidently, he thinks it necessary to reiterate that decree or law. Apart from the fact that reiteration may confirm the validity of the statement made in the past under new circumstances, in view of human communicative behavior, the second time language-based presentation is the behavioral communication in support of the linguistic communication performed for the first time, whereas the first time language-based communication is the pure linguistic communication. A person who reiterates his statement made earlier utilizes the behavior of repeating the same content to provide new information to the other or others so as to stress the importance or validity of the content in question. Reiteration is the behavior of linguistic communication of a complex structure. The similar linguistic phenomena include it that someone raises his voice, or goes out of his way to speak slowly, in order to have attention from others. If reiteration fails to reach its goal, the related actor may take action unilaterally in another way.

The authorities of any nation-state may be unable to eradicate all social crimes though laws are in place. We can suppose that each of those laws represents a process of linguistic communication, behind which there is even the enforcement irresistible by anyone. However, the related linguistic communication may be unable to prevent people from committing any crime. So the power holder may take action besides linguistic communication. Apart from reiteration, the power holder may warn the potential criminals by showing the behavior of penalizing the existing ones. To penalize criminals more effectively, the power holder tends to take action. However, displaying the behavior in this action to warn the potential criminals is a kind of communicative behavior. It is also a process of alternative linguistic communication. Meanwhile, action is the medium of behavior in linguistic communication. There is a saying in China that "one kills a chicken to warn a herd of monkeys." This means that if one fails to warn "monkeys" by using language, he has to demonstrate the behavior of killing a chicken to scare the monkeys. As language precludes people's direct visual communication, information conveyed this way cannot reach the level of vividness and hence sometimes cannot warn the potential criminals effectively. Showcasing the consequence of refusing to obey the law adds visual impression to the communicative process. So we sometimes find that in a state the authorities cannot eliminate all corruptions of government officials thoroughly because officials' corruption has been so ingrained and habitual and has involved so many people that it can no longer be removed. Then the authorities turn to showing their behavior of penalizing the corruptive officials with a strong hand to bolster the authority of laws. Each behavior of penalty is an alternative course of linguistic communication. Otherwise, the authority of laws will decline and the justice of the state will no longer exist.

Ordinary people also perform communication with themselves or with the authorities by displaying a behavior. Such a behavior is also an integral part of the communication that goes on in the state.

If one finds that he is unable to express his opinion or attitude and to raise his request by using language effectively, he tends to adjust the method of his linguistic communication. He will not reach his goal simply by speaking or writing. He may probably display his behavior in expressing his opinion as well. He and others may even join each other in expressing a certain opinion this way. A demonstration of the masses on the streets is this kind of behavior of linguistic communication. The protest of the masses is a course of linguistic communication indeed, but they also display a behavior. It is the behavior of the masses that functions as a medium of communication because they get together in the course of action. This is the action of linguistic communication of a special form displayed in the public. It is often the behavior of being dissatisfied. The masses may be in conflict with the authorities in expressing their opinion. The masses express their opinion both in linguistic communication and by showing their behavior. The reason is that they, as separate individuals, are unable to build the relation of effective linguistic communication with the authorities. If the authorities are unable to take care of the interest of the masses or ignore their demand, the masses may often choose a confrontation with the authorities in order to communicate therewith. After one suspends pure linguistic communication with another due to the appearance of a dispute, that dispute may lead to the conflict between the two sides. It is similar between the citizens and the authorities. So sometimes citizens wage a demonstration against the policy or a decision made by the authorities because that policy or decision dissatisfies them.

Sometimes one commits a symbolic public act to highlight a speech. In modern times, the national flag is a symbol of the state. Yet sometimes people burn the national flag to send a message in a protest against the government or a foreign state. Some other symbolic public acts may also be committed to realize the similar goal. This is because such kind of speech may be more efficient in communication with the authorities or any other actor because it can be an example of action. For example, in the United States we sometimes hear that someone burns the national flag in order to raise a protest or to show his dissatisfaction. During the Vietnam War, some young men burned draft cards, making a protest against the war policy of the United States government. Such symbolic public act is often regarded as a speech. Nigel Warburton writes that:

> [I]deas can be expressed through symbolic public acts such as destroying a flag or burning a draft card. When such acts are clearly intended to communicate a message, the fact that they don't involve words does not prevent them being examples of speech. If, by law or force, individuals are prevented from communicating their views through such symbolic behavior their freedom of speech is restricted. The United States Supreme Court ruled in 1969 that wearing black armbands in school was protected as a communicative act covered by the First Amendment.[1]

My view is that such a symbolic public act is a behavior that functions as a medium in support of a process of linguistic communication because the related behavior is usually interpreted by someone by using language. The reason that such an act is considered speech is that it conveys a message. In reality, it shows a behavior enhancing the visibility of the related linguistic communication to give stronger effect to the related linguistic communication.

Some types of violent behavior displayed by people are also designed in advance to perform special linguistic communication in which a behavior functions as a medium in support of linguistic communication. Even terrorist attacks are often launched to display the relevant behavior. The statement, made by terrorists, is the interpretation of their terrorist behavior. Without such an interpretation, no one knows the identities of the terrorist attackers and their political demand. On the other hand, a terrorist behavior enhances the effectiveness of the interpretation. A terrorist behavior is by no means the typical behavior of a military attack or the typical behavior of war. The military targets of attacks launched by military forces in a war are usually communication centers, important transportation facilities, arsenals, and armed forces, etc. The targets of attacks launched by terrorists are civilians, commercial facilities, public facilities, transportation systems, and landmark buildings, etc. In the state which is being increasingly urbanized today, an attack on a densely populated area will cause a surprising and tremendous effect. In terms of the nature of the terrorist behavior, it is the communicative behavior of violence. The behavior of communication and the violent behavior are combined in one course of action. The latter is the medium of the former. The target, attacked by terrorists, is sometimes also a communicative medium of the public. A high-rise building in a special shape may be a symbol of a nation's economic prosperity. Attacking such a high-rise building is communicating with the people of this nation. Another similar case is that if a government building is a symbol of the nation, attacking this building also involves a process of communication with the entire nation. We should denounce any terrorist act. Yet we cannot deny at the same time that certain behavior in connection with such an act is often used to enhance the effect of linguistic communication when linguistic communication fails to function as expected. Even a behavior of terrorists is designed for this purpose though such a behavior cannot be accepted according to any moral standard.

In sum, the related behavioral communication, functioning as a medium in support of the linguistic communication, only appears in the state. Such type of linguistic communication is part of, or in relation to, the formation of the state. All in this state may realize such mutual interaction through the related linguistic communication because people are now organized by the state.

2. Behavior as an Indication of Identity

Each person has an identity in the state. Such an identity is usually not confirmed by language, but by a behavior because the display of a behavior is often the most efficient way of confirming the identity of each in the state. Language may also be used to confirm the identity of each. But sometimes linguistic communication only results in the utterance of empty words. Behavioral communication may be essential. As displaying identity is part of the construction of the state, no one can ignore the role of behavioral communication. If such a process of behavioral communication serves a portion of the people and meets with no resistance from other people, for example, some people may perform such behavioral communication as a discourse. Then people display their identity. Displaying their identity this way contributes to the formation of the state.

Behavioral communication, performed to support a social hierarchy in pre-modern times, might be a method in support of the formation of a state in which people established the social or political order on the basis of such a social hierarchy. In medieval Europe, the ruling power rested on the feudal hierarchy, which was manifested not only by the feudal economic, judicial and patriarchal systems, but also by the behavior of the upper class aimed at maintaining the feudal hierarchy beneficial to the upper class. At that time, people, from the upper class, would not associate together with other people from the lower class. The society encouraged the marriage between the male and the female from the same class. The upper class kept the delicate living style as people from the upper class ate nice food and wore sleek clothes. They were sometimes the symbols signifying their higher social status. The social status of businessmen might be low. It was improper for a man from the upper class to do business. Excessive bargaining was not the right behavior of a man from the upper class. Parvenus were not acceptable by the privileged class.

The behavior not identical with the social status was regarded as the behavior disturbing the order of the society and as a challenge posed to the feudal rule. In contrast, people always regarded the "right" behavior as identical with the order of the society and each "correct" act was also a course of affirming the order of the society signified by the relevant behavior. Sometimes a change in the society required people to change their behavior, but the upper class might go out of their way to boycott the change of the out-of-date behavior. They insisted on maintaining the function of the original communication behavior aimed at safeguarding their higher social status. To maintain the old order of the society, some people intentionally displayed a certain type of behavior in line with that social order.

People may also perform such behavioral communication to support the political order of the state. They need to confirm such order time and again for the purpose of keeping order constantly. In the keeping of order, the behavior, displayed for communication, is often more effective than language. Thus people display a behavior, as a medium, to strengthen linguistic communication that underpins the operation of the state. In Europe, people performed behavioral communication to indicate the hierarchy of people in political life from ancient to medieval times. In medieval times, for example, the existence of aristocracy dictated that nobles were part of the ruling group. Nobles, as lords, showed relevant behavior in communication in order to maintain the political order. Nobility might also have their own internal order. They held rituals regularly to confirm the loyalty of the lords to the king. When a lord promised allegiance to the king, they might hold a ritual. Describing the power relationship in the king's government in Europe, John Hirst writes that "The lord gave his allegiance by kneeling down and raising his clasped hands; the king would put his hands around them and the lord would promise to be the king's man, to serve him."[2] As the state was organized in the principle of organizing the society in pre-modern times, the political hierarchy was widespread. The purpose of showing behavior for communication between a lord and the king was to ensure the loyalty of a noble to the king. To put it another way, people organized the state this way at that time. What played a role was behavioral communication in addition to linguistic communication in the building of the state.

In China, social hierarchy was also a basis of the order of the society in ancient or medieval times. Children displayed a certain behavior to pay their respect to their parents. Ordinary people showed their certain behavior to pay respect to officials. For example, an ordinary man might kneel down and then stand up in front of an official when he met that official. There was also the identification between the behavior of people and the social order. In political life, the ruling class particularly stressed the role of behavior in linguistic communication in an attempt to underpin the political order. One case in point is that the political order in ancient China was maintained in various processes of showing a behavior. The feudal state of Chou appearing in about 1030BC adopted a ritual to confirm the allegiance paid by the princes to the king or the ruler. That is, at that time the Chou conquered the Shang people. The king of the Chou was known as the Son of Heaven and bore the title *Wang* or the ruler. All lands outside the domains of the *Wang* were assigned as fiefs to a hierarchy of feudal princes and lords organized into a graded nobility. The difficulties of travel over the long distances that often separated them from the centre tended to enhance their autonomy. Relationship was maintained in accordance with a prescribed ritual through which the princes paid allegiance and homage to the *Wang*.[3] People displayed such a type of behavior in support of the related linguistic communication for about two thousand years in Chinese history. Particularly, after the formation of the Chinese Empire, the rulers reinforced such practice. People not only showed such behavior in the maintenance of social hierarchy but also displayed it in the administrative system. For the governance of the state after the emergence of the empire, such behavior has been mentioned by scholars many times. For example, Charles de Secondat Montesquieu comments in one of his books that:

> The principal object of government which the Chinese legislators had in view was the peace and tranquility of the empire; and subordination appeared to them as the most proper means to maintain it. Filled with this idea, they believed it their duty to inspire a respect for parents, and therefore exerted all their power to effect it. They established an infinite number of rites and ceremonies to do them honour when living, and after their death…A veneration

for their parents was necessarily connected with a suitable respect for all who represented them; such as old men, masters, magistrates, and the sovereign.[4]

As far as the order of the entire state was concerned, the emperor was on the top of the pyramid of a hierarchy maintained by using force. In the meantime, the etiquette of officials was part of this hierarchy. Ministers, or other officials, must kowtow to the emperor when they met the emperor, not to mention the rank and file. When meeting the officials of the higher levels, the officials of the lower levels must kneel down to the officials of the higher levels first. When meeting the officials, the rank and file acted in the same way. It was inadequate for those of the lower levels to manifest loyalty to those of the higher levels or the emperor in words. A sort of behavior must be displayed to bear testimony to their loyalty in advance. The reason is that the logic of power is the strict dominance and obedience. In order to maintain power and dominant status, the ruling class not only required obedience announced by using language but also required the imitation of the behavior of obedience to manifest obedience. The behavior of kowtow and kneeling down was the behavior combining the announcement of obedience by using language and the actual act of obedience because people also spoke at the same time. Behavior supported linguistic communication and linguistic communication supported the feudal order. Some Westerners noted such an event in history as follows:

> When, in the early nineteenth century, Lord Amherst, a British envoy, was sent by Britain to speak with the Chinese emperor, he was tormented with indecision and concern. To kowtow to the emperor would be an act incompatible with the "national dignity" of Britain, in effect, a national disgrace. A fierce argument with the emperor's representative ensued, with Lord Amherst trying to persuade the court to allow him to bow by bending his knee rather than completely prostrating himself on the ground. A compromise was finally reached by which, for this occasion only, Lord Amherst was excused from kowtowing as long as he bowed nine times before the imperial table and, when received by

the emperor, knelt on one knee nine times in succession. Yet this was not the end of it. Enraged by this British affront to his position, the emperor insisted that the envoy kowtow to him, refusing to accept any of the British presents unless this were first done. Lord Amherst, fearing national humiliation, responded that he would kowtow to the emperor only if a Tartar of a rank equal to his did the same before a portrait of the British monarch, or if the emperor issued a decree stating that from that time forward any Chinese ambassador to the British court would kowtow before his British Majesty. When this request was summarily refused, Lord Amherst announced his intention of returning to Britain immediately and, indeed, he left forthwith.[5]

In modern times, people have changed the method of linguistic communication in political life substantially and they have terminated the oppression of the ruling class, but behavioral communication may still function in manifesting the identity of people in maintaining the order of the state though the principle of organizing the state differs substantially. I mean that social hierarchy has largely disappeared due to the formation of the civil society of equality and the grant of civil rights to ordinary people, but the order of power in political life may still depend on the role of behavioral communication in support of the related linguistic communication within the state. The behavioral communication of power holders is still an integral part of the order of the state. When officials hold a meeting, their seats arranged at the meeting may have some communicative functions. When a meeting is held by the government to discuss issues and policies, the official of the highest level usually sits in the center of all other officials because he has the power of final decision-making and his opinion is the most important. That other meeting attendants sit around him may also connote their different levels of positions in this underlying structure of linguistic communication. Sitting in the center signifies the status of power held by the official of the highest level. If a cabinet meeting is held, the president or the prime minister usually sits in the center. If the representatives of more than two independent political parties hold a meeting to discuss some issues, they may hold a roundtable meeting. The roundtable meeting implies that all political parties sending their representatives to attend the meeting have equal status. As the behavior of sitting at a meeting can be used as a medium for communication wittingly or unwittingly, people sometimes design the political behavior of politicians and officials according to the specific requirement of behavioral communication.

The National People's Congress of China holds a plenary meeting every five years to elect the delegates of the People's Congress. After each election, the authorities announce a list of the delegates of the new session of the National People' Congress. The names of the delegates of the new session are printed on written materials according to the sequence of the strokes of the Chinese characters appearing in the names of those elected delegates in order to show that each of the delegates of the National People's Congress has the equal status within the Congress. Though a large portion of the delegates are the officials of the government on the different levels of the bureaucratic system, the presentation of the names of the elected delegates of the National People's Congress of China is designed to show that each delegate has the equal status within the legislature. This means that, theoretically, each delegate of the Congress has the equal right to express his opinion and has the equal right to exercise his right of voting in the legislature. Obviously, the Chinese government will not appoint the leaders and senior officials of the government according to the order of the strokes of the Chinese characters appearing in the names of the delegates.

Political leaders are very clear about the significance of the communication that displays a sort of behavior. If political leaders appear in the public, they always use their behavior associated with their action to show their ranking. The purpose of this behavior is to confirm their power status and the order of the power within the political regime so as to maintain power order. When the leaders reviewed troops or a parade on the Red Square in Moscow in the former Soviet Union, the place of their standing on the reviewing stand symbolized their political status within the regime. In China, the leaders also keep an order of power by appearing in the public according to their ranking. When the Chinese leaders show up to meet the delegates of the National People's Congress in a meeting room, the arrangement is often made in the way that the number one leader, the chairman of the state who is also the general secretary of the Communist Party, shows up first, being followed by the number two leader, the chairman of the standing committee of the National People's Congress, who is further followed by the number three leader, the premier of the State Council and so on and so forth. If the number two leader is absent for a certain reason, then the number one leader is immediately followed by the number three leader when they show up. The positions of their standing or sitting on the occasion of meeting the masses or the delegates of the People's Congress or other organizations are determined according to a rule that signifies their ranking. In the United States, we see the similar picture. When the president, the vice president and other cabinet members show up in the public on a formal occasion, they maintain an order of behavior that symbolizes their ranking. Sometimes the president is the last one who enters the meeting room because the number one leader is supposed to be the last one entering the meeting room. The case is similar in Western Europe. In the last century, Alain Peyrefitte, who acted as a senior administrative official of the French government of the Fifth Republic for years, vividly commented on today's French administrative system by writing that:

> There are various divisions in the immense administrative system. What they are concerned about most is the order of their positions. This is particularly so when their positions function as a symbol to the external world. When a public ceremony is held, decrees are used to define the tiniest details of the presences. Someone played a joke on the unnecessary etiquette of the court of Louis XIV in the past. However, the rigidity of the etiquette of the administration is even more severe at the end of the twentieth century. One decree tells you that chief judge of appellate court should be before the president of a university and after the Large Cross Medal.[6]

There is very often an order of behavior showing the order of power. If this order of behavior falls in disorder, the order of power may be in disorder.

If wearing certain clothes to show a person's social identity is assumed to be a special behavior, wearing those clothes for this purpose is also aimed at creating a medium in support of the related linguistic communication. In ancient slave-owning society or feudal society or traditional society, clothes often reflected the different statuses of social groups in the society. Under normal circumstances, a group of people, wearing one sort of clothes, shoes and caps, were on one certain rung of the social ladder. At that time, the clothes, shoes and caps worn by the ruler differed from those worn by the populace. The clothes, shoes and caps worn by generals were also different from those worn by the soldiers. In the Middle Ages, the kings, nobles, clergymen and peasants wore different clothes, shoes and caps. There were the codes of dress supposed to be obeyed by different social classes. If someone attempted to break a code of dress, he might face punishment. According to Desmond Morris, the men and women of the lower class had the tendency of imitating the men and women of the upper class in living such as trying to buy and wear the costumes worn by the men and women of the upper class in an attempt to enhance their social status. Seeing their position weakened by imitation, the men and women of the upper class reacted harshly. Therefore,

> in England, the law of the Westminster parliament of 1363 was concerned chiefly with regulating the fashion of dress in the different social classes, so important had this subject become. In Renaissance Germany, a woman who dressed above her station was liable to have a heavy wooden collar locked around her neck. In India, strict rules were introduced relating the way you folded your turban to your particular caste. In the England of Henry VIII no woman whose husband could not afford to maintain a light horse for the king's service was allowed to wear velvet bonnets or golden chains. In America, in early New England, a woman was forbidden to wear a silk scarf unless her husband was worth a thousand dollars.[7]

From the eighteenth to the nineteenth century, the development of capitalism in Europe changed the society. Then the new society forced the upper social classes to give up wearing the splendid clothes to symbolize their social status. They wore simple clothes to show their identity. In France, after the revolution, the class distinction, shown by the clothes worn by people, was blurred because the social hierarchy had been smashed. So Paul Johnson narrates that the French Revolution changed clothes fashion. "The French

Revolution had brought about dramatic changes in women's dress, introducing a simplicity that the French believed they had taken from English rustic custom." In terms of the clothes of men, "of all the enduring achievements of the French Revolution, the most important was the replacement of *culottes*, or breeches, by the baggy trousers worn by peasants and working men, the sans-culottes."[8] The clothes worn by people were no longer used to show different social statuses. Then wearing simple clothes indicated the social identity especially in support of the organization of the state. This demonstrates that the clothes, worn by people, were defined by a different political discourse. For example, the power holder might appear in the public, wearing ordinary clothes to win support from the urban populace. At that time, no matter whether the power holder was in France or in other countries, he refrained from wearing the past clothes to indicate his power or social status. The power holder might wear the clothes usually worn by the populace in order to gain support from the masses. As Johnson said, the adoption of simple clothes such as abovementioned trousers by the new French ruling class was "a sign of solidarity with the masses."[9] So in the era when capitalism replaced feudalism, politicians, unlike the nobles in the feudal society who insisted on wearing splendid clothes, chose to wear simple clothes. The newly emerging bourgeoisie communicated with the people in a different way as required by the times.

This change is of historical significance. As long as the style of clothes, in need of being worn, is required by a political or social discourse, clothes continue to function in support of the related linguistic communication. In modern times, for example, people continue to wear certain clothes to display their designed behavior in communication for certain purposes. The styles of clothes, worn by the politicians and the people of a nation-state, are often chosen under the influence of the social values and the political discourse. Under the circumstances that a certain political discourse prevails and dominates public life, the behavior of wearing clothes in support of linguistic communication may be a special manifestation of that political discourse. In China, men tended to wear Chinese tunic suits after the Revolution of 1911 because the Chinese tunic suits, worn by all kinds of men, showed the equality of men in the society. Politicians sometimes wore the Chinese tunic suits in order to show their close relationship with ordinary people.

After the founding of the People's Republic of China in 1949, particularly during the so-called Cultural Revolution from 1966 to 1976, the authorities encouraged the people to wear simple clothes to show the nature of working class. The authorities believed that the simple living style embodied honesty, diligence and justice, and they were the inborn characters of the working people. During the Cultural Revolution, for example, the Red Guards stopped on the streets the pedestrians who wore Hong Kong-style clothes and tore up their clothes because the Red Guards believed that Hong Kong-style clothes "publicized" the bourgeois living style, and this living style represented the exploitation and oppression by the bourgeoisie. Meanwhile, the Chinese leaders called on the people to learn from the People's Liberation Army. Many were proud of wearing military uniforms. In late 1970s, China began to open its door to foreign nation-states and to reform its economic system. Chinese people turned to wearing various styles of clothes, including Western-style clothes. Seeing the change of the clothes worn by Chinese, Westerners believed that Chinese had gained more freedom because they also believed that various different styles of clothes worn by the Chinese people represented the freedom of expression.

In China, Chairman Mao used to wear some special clothes for communication in the public. When the internal struggle of the Communist Party of China raged on during the Cultural Revolution, Mao appeared in the public, wearing the military uniform to bolster his control over the People's Liberation Army. This has become a tradition of the Chinese leaders ever since. Today, special messages are sent out when the Chinese leaders wear military uniforms in the public. According to the rule of exercising political power in China, the leader, acting as the general secretary or the leader of the Communist Party of China, must also be the supreme commander of the People's Liberation Army. Though some Chinese leaders are promoted from the non-military positions, they may wear a military uniform to meet the high-rank military officers in the public in order to highlight their control over the armed forces. According to the principle that defines that "the Party commands the gun," the supreme leader stresses his leadership in national defense by wearing a military uniform in the public.

If we postulate that people can wear clothes, as a medium, in support of a behavior in communication, it is also arguable that people who communicate using language may directly show their behavior. This behavior may also function as a medium. When two different groups of people speak different languages, the different languages spoken by them are often involved in another associated process of communication. The behavior of using a language itself can be a medium. For example, if people who speak the same dialect speak that dialect, their linguistic behavior means nothing in this case. That dialect is only a tool of linguistic communication. But if two people, speaking the same dialect, speak that dialect in the presence of a third person who speaks a different dialect, the dialect, spoken by the first and second person, may send out a message to this third person unwittingly that they have the social status either higher or lower than that of the third person. In other words, if the first and the second person speak to each other by using their dialect, they create a course of communication between them. If a third person, speaking a different dialect, is present, these two people create another course of communication with the third person simultaneously. There appear two courses of communication. The first course is in the nature of linguistic communication, whereas the second course is in the nature of behavioral communication.

This prevailing linguistic phenomenon appears in the mutual interaction of different languages. On one hand, people who speak the same language tell each other by way of behavioral communication that they belong to the same group. On the other hand, each of those who speak different languages tells the other by way of this behavioral communication that they belong to different groups. As people who speak different languages often come from the areas with different historical, cultural and social backgrounds, different languages symbolize different backgrounds of those who use these languages. Some people form the sense of superiority over other people as a result. They may show this sense of superiority while speaking their language. People may find a difference between them in the behavior of this linguistic communication. Thus the boundaries of a social state of mind between different groups of people take form until a group of people gain their self-consciousness. Thus the identities of people take shape. The behavioral communication of speaking language plays a role in this regard. Such a way of communication characterizes the formation of the society and may affect the formation of the state as well.

In other words, there is a correlation between the form of language and the essence of language. So far as different languages are concerned, among them the form of language varies, but the essence of language remains the same. Language is a tool of communication. Its form is its medium. As a result, the form of language buttresses linguistic communication. As linguistic communication enables people to gain the common memory of their community, to embrace the same religious belief, to accept the same customs and mores and to build the same market for the exchange of goods and services, people, using the same language, show the same characters. They realize that they are the same kind of people. They have common interest.

The said behavioral communication underlies the organization of the society or the state. The behavioral communication may even help people to organize the government. Talents who receive good education and have upbringing may be appointed as officials in the governance of the state. For example, within a state, people may receive different educations. Those who receive a good education may be those who have upbringing. In the meantime, well-educated people may speak one standard language and less-educated people may speak a regional language or a dialect. Thus, politicians who speak a standard language may be trusted by the citizens in the governance of the state. Thus politicians who speak a standard language may gain a higher status in political life simply because of the difference of educations received by people. He may be especially trusted in political life because he has received a good education. In ancient Europe, speaking Latin used to be a requirement for a man to become a successful politician. In Rome, Latin was the official language. A man could not become a power holder unless he could speak Latin. Cicero says that the orator who was not a native of Rome, naturally labored under a disadvantage. However skilled he might be, his speaking would lack the authentic urbanitas. The basis of oratory was impeccable Latin pronunciation. He and another historian Quintilian believe that speaking Latin with the skills of a consummate Roman orator was the summit of human ambition.[10]

The behavioral communication may also construct the identity of the occupation of people which is part of the construction of the society. In the heyday of Latin in medieval times speaking and writing Latin might also help those people, religious or secular, build their identity of occupation. As the clergymen of the Roman Catholic Church spoke and wrote Latin, which almost always served as the liturgical language, while the faithful did not, "Latin became the property of a clerical elite."[11] The reason is that clergymen had received formal education, and knew Latin while the faithful did not know it. There was a similar phenomenon in the medical world. Doctors who had learned Latin sometimes uttered Latin words which patients did not know. As Françoise Waquet comments, those Latin words worked on the patients like charms.[12] This meant that "the alliance of Latin and medicine had a long career in the context of power relations. Even doctors known to favour the vernacular used Latin occasionally to proclaim their quality clearly."[13] Latin used by them helped build the identity of their occupation. In the legal world, documents were written in Latin. Those who engaged in legal service used Latin while those others who sought legal service often did not use Latin. Then those who used Latin in the provision of legal service became powerful in the relations between magistrates and accused and between notaries and lawyers and their clients.[14] Likewise, in the world of science Latin helped those who used it to build the identity of their occupation in the same way. For example, scientists, like botanists, often used Latin. Latin helped highlight their professional identity. As Waquet writes:

> The frontier between those who knew Latin and those who did not was of enduring importance in the scientific world. This general remark finds an original illustration in the split that appeared, in botany, between specialists and amateurs after the reform carried out by Linnaeus. This reform, as we have seen, represented a considerable advance for professional naturalists in a discipline that had been threatened with collapse; but at the same time, owing to its Latin nomenclature, it helped to keep amateurs, women in particular, out of the study of plants, or anyway made it more difficult for them.[15]

In the seventeenth and eighteenth century, France became an advanced country in the economic and social development as compared with other nations on the Continent. French culture was also influential in other less-developed countries such as Germany and Russia. People who spoke French were often the members of the upper social class. For example, people were proud of speaking French in and outside the royal court of each principality of Germany or the royal court of Russia at that time. French became the language of high society of some European countries outside France. French represented the culture and society more advanced than other cultures and societies. In some sense, speaking French was a way of showing and maintaining the high social status of the upper social class. So Tim Blanning writes that in German courts, such as Stuttgart in the later seventeenth century French was spoken, as it was later in Russia under Peter and Catherine the Great.[16] Those who aspired to rise socially might also choose to speak a particular language often used by the upper social class because that language symbolized a higher social status. Joan-Lluís Marfany notes that in early modern Catalonia, language became a symbol of class and the ability to speak and write Castilian became necessary to anyone who aspired to rise socially, much like French in Provence or English in Ireland.[17]

The behavior, shown in linguistic communication, may also underlie the dominance of the mainstream culture in the building of the state. The state is built on the basis of a cultural community. Such a cultural community may not be absolutely homogeneous. This means that there may be various sub-communities of local culture. Regional languages or dialects spoken in the local areas may symbolize the existence of those sub-communities of local culture. For example, in the historical transition from a kingdom to a nation-state, France experienced a period of time of cultural consolidation. A mainstream culture, originating from the culture of Paris area, gradually prevailed over other local distinctive cultures in some other areas within France. In the meantime, French emerged finally as the common language formed mainly on the basis of the dialect of Paris area and some of Paris' surrounding areas such as Champagne area. Likewise, in Germany the formation of the mainstream culture, symbolized by the German language in history, was part of the process of the growth of the nation. Speaking or writing German showed the identity of German people. Though there were many regional languages or dialects spoken by people in various different regions, German functioned in support of the growth of the nation and this nation functioned as a foundation for the founding of a nation-state in the years to come. So John E. Joseph describes that:

[T]he "German language," like every national language, is a cultural construct. It dates from the sixteenth century and is generally credited to Martin Luther (1483-1546), who, in translating the Bible, strove to create a form of German that might unite the many dialect groups across what until the late nineteenth century was a patchwork of small and large states.[18]

Likewise, according to Joseph, in the Romance-speaking world during the thousand years from the fall of the Roman Empire to the Renaissance, "language" meant Latin "significantly different from village to village." People spoke a local dialect. Then in 1529 people published Dante's treatise *De Vulgari eloquentia* in which he claimed to discover, not invent, the national language of a nation. The Italian language became a linguistic means to create cultural unity of the Italian peninsula.[19] This means the existence of an inter-relationship between language and culture. Despite the existence of cultural heterogeneity in some cases, the formation of a leading culture in a region may crucially support the formation of the state. The behavior of speaking the related language may become an identity in support of the formation of the state because such a language represents that dominating culture. Particularly, in modern times nation-state invariably takes shape because all people speak the same language and embrace the same culture. In other words, speaking a unified language often means having a unified culture, and having a unified culture means having a condition for the building of a state. Thus, history gradually shows that speaking a language directly becomes a behavior showing the identity of people crucially in support of the formation of the state because this case can confirm that all speak the same language and have the same culture.

If the state is formed by various ethnic groups of people originally speaking different languages, speaking a common language even plays an essential role in the formation of the state. For example, some states are mainly formed by immigrants originally speaking various languages. The gradual prevalence of one common language becomes a foundation for the unity of the state. A new common identity of the citizens takes shape. In the United States the majority of the citizens are the offspring of immigrants. Immigrants usually have different national backgrounds. They speak different languages in the outset. The children of the immigrants, however, learn English in schools and become native English speakers. Thus, gradually, American English is spoken by all. Then speaking American English becomes the common identity of all. Then the common identity of Americans is often the very language used by all. Original national backgrounds gradually become unimportant, but speaking American English becomes important. The behavior of speaking American English supports a process of linguistic communication the goes on throughout the nation-state. The United States is often described by people as a melting pot of different nations. Language plays a special role. Likewise, in Australia native people speak various native languages. Immigrants also speak various languages. However, Australian English augments its influence while the influence of those different native languages and foreign languages comes to be checked because language policy made by the government has strengthened the leading position of Australian English. Now, Australian English, as the common language, is spoken in the schools and universities, in the offices of the government, in the factories and in the shopping centers. Speaking Australian English is a common identity of all. Thus, in most of the states on earth, one common language is often spoken by all the citizens. Whenever this language is spoken, behavioral communication is activated to show the unique character shared by all within the state. The behavior of speaking language highlights the importance of choosing one language as a common language in use throughout the state. Behavioral communication strengthens the unity of the people.

3. Behavior as a Ceremony

People may also standardize or codify behavioral communication in an attempt to realize a special purpose of linguistic communication within the state. This is because a behavior may perform a particular task of communication in place of the original linguistic communication to strengthen the mutual interaction of people when linguistic communication fails to send out the information as expected in so large a community like a state. This is because language is a tool for communication. Language is open to all who have learned to use it. Every one is equal in using language. People, having high social status, use this language and people, having low social status, also use this language. Sometimes people perform linguistic communication for an important matter, whereas at some other times people do not do so. The processes of linguistic communication may vary in significance. For example, linguistic communication, performed on a normal occasion, may be regarded as usual, whereas linguistic communication, performed on a special occasion, may be regarded as special. Linguistic communication, performed on an unofficial occasion, may be considered unofficial, whereas linguistic communication, performed on an official occasion, may be deemed as official. Ordinary linguistic communication may be required for the normal interaction between one another, whereas special linguistic communication may be required for the special interaction between one another. In linguistic communication, language per se may not be able to highlight the special purpose of linguistic communication. Language may not be able to impart certain information. A behavior, displayed in linguistic communication, may help differentiate the process of linguistic communication for a special purpose from that for another generic purpose. A behavior functions as a medium. The combination of linguistic communication and the behavior defined as special thus constitute a ceremony. People, performing linguistic communication, often find it necessary to display a behavior in support of that linguistic communication. In the meantime, they may need to go through some of the processes of such linguistic communication regularly. Ceremony takes shape. So whenever people need special linguistic communication, they may hold a ceremony. Ceremony, in essence, supports the mutual interaction of people and hence the formation of the society. It may also buttress the formation of the state. People often hold a ceremony for important linguistic communication in some sense. People hold some typical ceremonies in the state.

First, people hold a ceremony for the establishment of the government. People often mark the establishment of the government through the procedure of the inauguration of the head of the government. Thus, people hold a ceremony of inauguration upon the formation of a government in any state at least in modern times. As the formation of the state also depends on the formation of the government, simple linguistic communication without a ceremony may not suffice to mark the commencement of the governance of the state of which the government is in charge. The government has to have ruling legitimacy and authority, and the simple process of linguistic communication may not suffice to confirm the legitimacy and authority of the government. A special ceremony is held. In the history of the United States of America power holders used to make an effort to establish a procedure of inauguration of the president in order to confirm the legitimacy and authority of the federal government. When George Washington, the first president, took office, people held a solemn ceremony of inauguration. When such ceremony was held, a triumphant arch was constructed by the workers; a welcoming parade was marched by the militia; and the presidential procession was watched by the on-site audience. When the president passed by, the citizens cheered and greeted him, showing their support to him. A formal inauguration speech was given by the president. A church service was also given. Such a ceremony was designed to bring the republican concept to life, to enliven the relationship between the citizens and the republic, to establish the authority and legitimacy of the government and to strengthen the bond between the government and the citizens. As Sandra Moats writes,

> When George Washington became president on April 30, 1789, the public and Congress had initiated a ceremonial culture before and during the inauguration that included a generous borrowing of monarchical rituals to bring the abstract proceedings to life. Two weeks into his presidency, Washington also found himself tapping into the treasure trove of royal precedents in order to define the president's responsibilities and to illustrate the nascent concept of popular sovereignty.[20]

Though Thomas Jefferson, the third president, retreated into the simplicity of the ceremony when he became the president because he believed that the simplicity of ceremony symbolized the principle of the republican government, no inauguration ceremony has not been held for each following president ever since.

Second, sometimes a body of the government officially commences to function, and the head of the state may attend a ceremony in order to confirm the endorsement or authorization of the state. As the authorization is very important, a ceremony often serves as a procedure to confirm the support given to this body of the government. For example, when the legislative assembly is opened or closed, people may hold a ceremony attended by the head of the state. In the meantime, all the members of the legislative assembly normally attend this ceremony. A formal speech may be made by the head of the state or by the speaker of the legislative assembly. The representatives of different political parties may make a speech of intending to cooperate in the new legislative assembly or a speech of witnessing its close. Such a ceremony may be defined by the constitution or relevant laws in order to confirm the normal operation of the government as long as the constitution requires such a procedure. This procedure is designed to ensure the normal operation of the government. People build and bolster the confidence of all in the normal operation of the government within the state. For example, in the states of constitutional monarchy or the states of some other types, the head of the state often attends the ceremony of opening or closing the legislative assembly to mark the sincere cooperation between the two power centers or the support by one power center to another. A ceremony is held to emphasize such a purpose. Simple speech or articulation does not suffice to fulfill this task. As such, Jeremy Bentham writes that:

> In those Monarchies of Europe which are called Constitutional—in those and in those which have elsewhere sprung from them—it has been customary for the Monarch to open and close the Legislative Assembly by a speech from the throne.[21]

To symbolize the cooperation or support of the head of the state on this occasion, a ceremony is often indispensable.

Third, sometimes a special occasion comes, making citizens reminiscent of the founding of the state such as the anniversary of the founding of the nation-state or the birth date of the founding father of the nation-state or a statutory public holiday, and the state may hold a ceremony to mark that special occasion in order to strengthen the citizens' memory of the history of the state and to propagate the underlying principle of founding the state or to highlight the spirit of the state. Citizens may gather in the public square. The leader of the state may make a speech. A military salute may be given. The national anthem may be played. And the national flag may be hoisted. People do not simply perform linguistic communication to mark this special occasion. They also display their behavior to enliven the relationship between the state and the citizens this way. When people intend to display their patriotic feeling to the state on a special occasion such as the anniversary of founding the nation-state, they also communicate with the state through a symbol. Simple linguistic communication may not suffice to fulfill this task because people need to express their inside mood. People display a special behavior in this case. This behavior becomes a ceremony after it is codified. For example, they may hoist a national flag in support of the intended linguistic communication because they plan to salute the flag and make a speech in front of the flag. National flag is a symbol. Yet if people display a behavior to fly this flag, for example, in the public square in the center of the city, they may hold a ceremony. Many citizens may take part in or observe this ceremony. Ceremony means that people display a behavior as a medium in support of linguistic communication. Thus, discussing the symbolic action of patriotism in the United States, Susan Herbst writes that:

> The flag . . . is powerful in certain contexts because it represents the *entire* nation—the unity that is America: A flag implies universality of belief in country, and all are expected to stand during the moments we pledge our allegiance to it.[22]

The display of a national flag in the public enhances the visibility of linguistic communication people perform with themselves by using that ceremony as a medium. That national flag is also a medium. A ceremony is a procedure of using a series of media in support of people's linguistic communication.

Fourth, sometimes one government body performs linguistic communication for an important work or task in its cooperation with another government body or organization. In this case, people need to corroborate the sincerity of linguistic communication. They need to see the intention of cooperation through the display of a special behavior. As sometimes people pass on falsified information in linguistic communication in real life in the state, the community in the large size, people may especially make an effort to confirm the sincerity of linguistic communication. They do not directly perform linguistic communication. Instead they display a behavior to realize this purpose though they may also perform the related linguistic communication at the same time. A procedure is usually designed and gone through to display such behavior for communication. This procedure may become a ceremony. Especially when two actors interact with each other on an important occasion or for an important business, they may go through such a procedure. If the two government bodies of the same level make a contract, or the central government and a local government make a contract, or the government of one state and the government of another state make a contract, the head of each government body may attend a ceremony of signing the contract in witness of signing this contract to confirm the serious attitude of signing this contract. All personnel, attending the ceremony of signing the contract, may toast a cup of wine. People do not use words to indicate their sincerity because the effect of words is by no means strong at this moment. Behavioral communication often accompanies the process of linguistic communication to augment the power of language on such an occasion. So we see that sometimes the heads of various government bodies attend a ceremony in witness of signing a contract, and their behavior denotes that the personnel in charge of operating government bodies instead of ordinary clerks of the government bodies participate in the procedure of making such a contract in person and they attach importance to such a contract. Upon an occasion of holding a meeting within a government body, a senior official of such a government body may attend the meeting to make a speech as a procedure in order to confirm that such a meeting is approved or attached importance to by this senior official though the meeting may be attended by the junior officials to discuss routine works and to make a normal decision only.

Fifth, sometimes people present their condolence to those who have died in a war, a natural disaster, an airplane crash, a factory accident, and a traffic accident, and so on, and they may choose to express their heartfelt regret and love to those unfortunate people in a special form. They may choose to display a special behavior in a special ceremony in support of linguistic communication they perform with those victims or themselves. They may display yellow ribbons during the day or display candle lights during the night. A procedure, required by this special communication, becomes a ceremony. The procedure is usually gone through by a collective being. This procedure may be arranged by the civil society or the government. For example, in Asian countries earthquakes erupt frequently. When an earthquake hits the densely populated area, it causes many deaths. Then people often hold a ceremony to express their condolence. The related ceremony, held in condolence of those victims, manifests the sympathy of all other people. Such a ceremony bolsters the solidarity of the nation-state. A simple speech, made on this occasion, is usually too cold. An especially designed behavior has to be displayed in support of the process of linguistic communication to send a message of condolence. Through the combination of an act and a speech, people give the greatest effect to the related communication. People cannot omit this way of communication because the related linguistic communication must be supported by a series of media, including a behavior shown in a ceremony, following the formation of the state. They have been in a new environment since they entered the community built on the basis of linguistic communication. They display a sort of behavior in a ceremony in many cases.

In the meantime, we see that an act, such as the act committed in a ceremony, may be especially designed to complete a special course of linguistic communication, and this act may be committed time and again. This act may be defined by a decree or law if the state always needs the related linguistic communication. Then such an act evolves to be a formal procedure. Such a procedure further evolves to be a ceremony or a rite or a ritual, an act committed regularly through a procedure. Thus citizens may attend the ceremony held by the government, for example. Such a ceremony is a special interaction between the behavior and linguistic communication. For example, people may attend a meeting in memory of an important historical event or figure. This meeting is a ceremony. This ceremony is significant of the fact that people use this ceremony as a live medium of communication in support of linguistic communication in the operation of the state. In this course, people perform behavioral communication. Behavioral communication explains linguistic communication. Behavioral communication is a supplement to linguistic communication per se. Although a behavior displayed in communication is never concrete enough to be used to send out a crystal-clear message, it is interpreted by language in the ceremony. Without the interpretation of language, one may not understand what the behavior displayed in the ceremony means. Unlike typical linguistic communication, a ceremony is an integral part of the linguistic communication associated with it in the course of communication realized by the behavior. On the other hand, the behavior is also important in linguistic communication. Without the behavior of the attendants, there is no communication in this context. This behavior is designed to have a fixed form and a procedure according to the specific content or for a specific purpose to be displayed at specific time and on a specific occasion. This ceremony may be hosted regularly or frequently and each ceremony has the same form and procedure.

A ceremony is a method of special communication to strengthen linguistic communication indeed. It differs from language by showing the behavior because a person, involved in linguistic communication, shows a certain behavior strictly defined and regularly shown at a fixed time and place. This special behavior is characteristic of the form of communication more difficult to be performed than linguistic communication, demanding more time and energy, but more effective. It is particularly the case when the masses attend the ceremony of paying homage to the late state leader in his mausoleum or mourning the dead in a memorial hall of the war victims, etc. This means that humans use their behavior to symbolize the action likely to be taken for communication in order to enhance the creditability of the communication. The grand triumphal review of the troops arranged by the state is a ceremony. The purpose of the grand triumphal review of the troops is to display the military forces of the nation-state because the action of soldiers in the grand triumphal review of the troops symbolizes the course of a combat. The message, sent out by way of the march of the soldiers, the formation of lines of the troops, the display of weapons and internal command, is more effective than any written or oral statement made by the authorities expressing its determination to consolidate national defense. The same picture is shown by the ceremony held by the authorities of one local government to welcome or see off the guests of another local government within the state. The authorities often arrange for the masses or various delegates to receive or see off the guests at the airport rather than sending only one representative to the airport. The authorities sometimes also give performance to the guests at the airport to show their welcoming attitude. The ceremony of welcoming or seeing off the guests attended by the masses shows the sincere attitude of the local government because people cannot reach this goal by using language only. Thus, a person, hoping to perform important linguistic communication, often displays his behavior for communication which is more formal, solemn, serious and easily seen in the public. This communication emphasizes the memory of an event and may change the future behavior of the related people. People perform this communication when holding the ceremony of celebrating the founding of a nation-state or a political regime or marking the opening of an important meeting such as the plenary meeting of the political party or commemorating a figure or an event. All in all, people hold ceremonies to combine the present language-based presentation and the action in order to give better effect to communication. Such ceremonies include the inauguration ceremony of the leader, the ceremony of celebrating the national day and the ceremony of showing condolence to the dead of a natural disaster, and so on and so forth.

When people hold a festival, they may also go through a procedure to display their special behavior for communication. This procedure may also be regarded as a ceremony under certain circumstances though the activities of celebrating a festival may not always constitute a ceremony. Needless to say, behavioral communication relies on a process of linguistic communication. That is, without linguistic communication in the course of ceremony, such as a speech made by someone or a written slogan hung on the wall, the ceremony may not be able to express its intention accurately or clearly. We see a group of people celebrating a festival by beating drums and striking gongs. If we are unable to see the slogans in writing or hear the slogans shouted, we may not know what kind of festival they are celebrating. Behavioral communication, however, is also requisite. As now people are in a large community such as a nation-state, they often stay far from each other. They may not fully understand each other. Linguistic communication may fail to convey the adequate information for their mutual interaction. Thus, people often strengthen linguistic communication that goes on among them on some special occasions. Behavioral communication is often an addition to the process of linguistic communication. In this communication, the related behavior provides information in the course of human perception in support of linguistic communication. This behavior tries to unify the fact and its linguistic presentation in one course and make them impossible to separate from each other or to contradict each other. For example, people use a material as a medium for communication such as a national flag hoisted in a ceremony held on a National Day. They hold a ceremony of hoisting the national flag in celebration of the National Day. Though the communication, using a material as a medium, does not always adopt the form of ceremony, many ceremonies use materials as media. This communication is of significance of adding the course of perception to communication and hence enhancing the visibility of the communication as now people often communicate over a long time and on a large scale. Besides, people, celebrating their festivals, also need to exchange feelings. Linguistic communication may not be the best way to exchange feelings. Behavioral communication should be the best way in most cases. For example, people may hold a parade on the streets in celebration of a traditional festival. When people hold a parade, the performers of the parade exchange feelings with the spectators. People may engage in behavioral communication to extend the time and the reach of communication. When people hold a parade in a city, spectators will come from various faraway places and stay there for a long time. Thus, they communicate over a long time and on a large scale with a process of behavioral communication.

The purpose of holding a ceremony is to communicate. No matter whether or not the ceremony is aimed at communicating with the spectators of the ceremony, it is the special communication. It emphasizes the significance of a certain event, or a certain figure, or a certain achievement, or a certain movement or a certain ideal. It highlights the solemn, passionate and sincere attitude of those who hold and attend the ceremony. It is inadequate for them to emphasize their attitude or to clarify their attitude by using language only. One may say that one matter is very important or extremely important. He may use analogy to explain its importance vividly, but the words, chosen by him, are limited. One may have more choices of designed behavior to stress this importance. The behavior of a person offers more forms for him to express his attitude or idea than the words under certain circumstances. A man may express his attitude or idea more effectively and vividly by holding a ceremony than by simply speaking and writing. The reason is that he adds the course of perception to this communication. Of course, in people's daily life, under most circumstances, linguistic communication is more convenient than behavioral communication. If one has learnt language, he will be able to use the programming of language for communication. In contrast, behavioral communication requires designing according to the specific circumstances in order to send out the specific and accurate information. The sender and receiver of the information must use the same code made in the designing

for communication. Yet, behavioral communication shows its unique characteristic at a ceremony: Simple linguistic communication is usually the short-
time communication while behavioral communication may be the long-time
communication as people, invited to attend the ceremony, are involved in the
linguistic communication of the time extended by the ceremony and behavioral communication may be the communication that allows more people
from different regions to communicate with each other at one place as more
people from different regions are invited to attend the ceremony.

People often hold ceremonies in the state. Ceremonies are aimed at serious,
solemn, sincere or warm communication. Otherwise, people do not need
ceremonies for communication. The content or the purpose of the ceremony
is usually sacred because sacredness bolsters communication that goes on for
a long time and on a large scale. Thus as the power holder or the authorities
are in charge of governing the state, no power holder or authorities are not
sacred in philosophical sense. But people cannot experience the sacredness
of a certain object merely through linguistic communication. They need to
experience it by attending a ceremony in support of the related linguistic
communication. If someone tells you that this is a sacred monument, you
can only imagine the sacredness of this monument with the information
provided by using language, but you cannot directly perceive or experience
its sacredness in person. So in the state ceremonies are significant because
ceremonies enable people to experience the sacredness of the power holder
and the authorities with their own eyes and ears. People hold the ceremonies
of celebration or commemoration and other ceremonies on the important
occasions. A ceremony is held when the regime is handed over or a new
state is founded or an important treaty is signed or peace is made. In ancient
times, a king or emperor was enthroned from time to time, and the corona-
tion was held solemnly. In modern times, a new president or chairman of
the state takes power from time to time and people hold an inauguration
ceremony. During the period of revolution, people hold a ceremony of taking
an oath when someone joins the revolution. Prior to the battle, solders may
take an oath of loyalty. When a specific date, in memory of a heroic figure
or in celebration of a historical event, is on, people may hold a ceremony.
People are unable to perform such communication by using oral or written
language only because human nature requires them to perceive the world

through the course of perception rather than the course of linguistic communication. The sacredness of any figure or event or form or being can only be experienced in depth through the course of perception. This is the significance of a ceremony. This is also the logic displayed by the process in which a behavior supports linguistic communication in the operation of the state, a large community. This is also the consequence caused by the fact that people, using language, have broken immediacy between one another and they need to display a behavior in linguistic communication from time to time.

So on many important occasions, people are unable to refuse to hold a ceremony. In comparison with the use of language, a ceremony is the phenomenon of using a special medium. A ceremony is a behavior displayed for communication. People display such a behavior for communication prior to the birth of language. Since the birth of language, people's communication has been basically bifurcated along behavioral and linguistic communication lines. As these two ways of communication may be separated from each other, under certain circumstances, these two kinds of communication may not be in congruence with each other. That is, one is true and the other false. Incongruence or contradiction between one's words and deeds is commonplace in the civilized society. A ceremony is aimed at unifying the words and deeds and guaranteeing that the words will accord with deeds. In the course of a ceremony, people try to connect one sort of action closely with another sort of action he promises to take by dint of behavioral communication so as to make this sort of action a proof of his intention or to highlight it. If a man hopes to express his wishes from the bottom of his heart, he often finds that language is a poor tool for him to express his wishes and it seems to him that he cannot express his wishes thoroughly even by using thousands of words. Thus humans display a special behavior in support of their linguistic communication whenever necessary because now they are in a large community, namely, the state.

Notes

1. Nigel Warburton, *Free Speech: A Very Short Introduction* (Oxford: Oxford University Press, 2009), 5.

2. John Hirst, *The Shortest History of Europe* (Collingwood, Victoria: Black Inc., 2009), 83.

3. E.N. Gladden, *A History of Public Administration Vol. I: From Earliest Times to the Eleventh Century* (London: Frank Cass and Company Limited, 1972), 148.

4. Charles de Secondat, Baron de Montesquieu, *The Spirit of Laws*, translated by Thomas Nugent (Chicago: Encyclopaedia Britannica, Inc., 1952), 140.

5. William W. Rockhill, *Diplomatic Audiences at the Court of China* (London: Luzac. 1905),35-36, cited from David I. Kertzer, *Ritual, Politics and Power*, (New Haven: Yale University Press, 1988), 87–88.

6. Alain Peyrefitte, *Le Mal français,* (Paris: Librairie Plon, 1976), 386. The quotation is originally in French and its English version is translated by the author.

7. Desmond Morris, *The Human Zoo*, (New York: McGraw-Hill Book Company,1969), 65.

8. Paul Johnson, *The Birth of the Modern: World Society 1815–1830* (New York: Harper Collins Publishers, 1991), 457–458.

9. Ibid., 458.

10. Roy Harris, *The Language-Makers* (Ithaca, New York: Cornell University Press, 1980), 124–125.

11. Françoise Waquet, *Latin or the Empire of a Sign: From the Sixteenth to the Twentieth Centuries*, translated by John Howe (London: Verso, 2001), 42.

12. Ibid. 234.

13. Ibid. 234.

14. Ibid. 236

15. Ibid.238.

16. Tim Blanning, *The Culture of Power and the Power of Culture:Old Regime Europe 1660—1789* (Oxford: Oxford University Press, 2002), 55-6; cited from Peter Burke, *Languages and Communities in Early Modern Europe* (Cambridge: Cambridge University Press. 2004), 86.

17. Joan-Lluís Marfany, *La llengua maltractaola: EL castellà i el Català a Catalunya del segle xvi al segle xix* (Barcelona, 2001), 239; 473; cited

from Peter Burke, *Languages and Communities in Early Modern Europe* (Cambridge: Cambridge University Press. 2004), 85.

18. John E. Joseph, *Language and Identity: National, Ethnic, Religious* (New York: Palgrave Macmillan, 2004), 98.

19. Ibid., 99.

20. Sandra Moats, *Celebrating the Republic: Presidential Ceremony and Popular Sovereignty, from Washington to Monroe* (DeKalb: Northern Illinois University Press, 2010), 61–62.

21. Jeremy Bentham, *Securities against Misrule and Other Constitutional Writings for Tripoli and Greece*, edited by Philip Schofield (Oxford: Clarendon Press, 1990), 40.

22. Susan Herbst, *Numbered Voices: How Opinion Polling Has Shaped American Politics* (Chicago: The University of Chicago Press, 1993), 37.

Chapter Four

Consciousness

1. National Consciousness

People usually share consciousness within the state. This case is due to linguistic communication performed by those who propagate the related consciousness to those who embrace the same within the state. On the other hand, consciousness may support the related linguistic communication. We can consider consciousness to be a medium. If and when the related linguistic communication needs support, people create or use a medium. The reason for the appearance of such a phenomenon is that people keep on performing linguistic communication and they extend the distance of linguistic communication at the same time. They perform linguistic communication with one another over long distances. The communication over long distances breaks immediacy between one another. The linkage between one another attenuates. Thus performing linguistic communication over long distances decreases efficiency in linguistic communication steadily. There are some cases indicating a decrease in the efficiency of linguistic communication. The first case is that people, performing linguistic communication over long distances, may stop performing linguistic communication in the middle because they have to make a greater effort to perform linguistic communication over long distances and sometimes they get into difficulties in making a greater effort. For example, sometimes two people, far from each other, have to exchange letters for communication instead of having a conversation. One usually needs to make a greater effort to write a letter than to have a conversation. The second case is that information, conveyed in linguistic communication over long distances, may become inaccurate or unclear. This means that the process of linguistic communication, performed over long distances, may fail to bring accuracy and clarity to the conveyed information. For example, in human-chain linguistic communication performed over long distances, those who function as the links of the chain in the middle may not convey accurate or clear information. Those who function as the links of the chain in the middle of the process of such linguistic communication may not fulfill their task as required. They may not think as expected by the people starting this process of linguistic communication. People may lose some information in the middle, and certain original information may become incomplete in the end. The third case is that an information sender may lose control on the totality of the process of human-chain linguistic communication over long distances, resulting in the fact that people fail to perform linguistic communication timely in the middle or people discontinue linguistic communication in the middle. People often perform linguistic communication over long distances and hence do so on a large scale. Sometimes they fail to perform linguistic communication on a large scale as expected. People, however, share a sort of consciousness across the state. People usually share the consciousness of a certain sort in the same way. In some sense, there is no intermediacy of consciousness between one another. If people share such consciousness, such consciousness may function as a medium boosting linguistic communication that goes on across the state. Consciousness spreads as fast as lightning. It may be very easy for someone to disseminate consciousness to plenty of people across the state. Sometimes people's consciousness spreads without any special effort made by people. The spread of consciousness buttresses linguistic communication that goes on across the state. All have access to such linguistic communication. We can substantiate this view by elaborating the role played by national consciousness in the formation of the state first.

As all belong to the same nation, it is very easy for all to be aware that they are the same kind of people. They will share the same national consciousness very quickly. Then such consciousness may play a role in support of linguistic communication that underpins the formation of the state because people, belonging to the same nation, usually feel close to each other and hence they are tempted to perform linguistic communication with each other more often and more actively. National consciousness may play a role in the formation of the state because it can function as a medium in support of such linguistic communication that further underpins the formation of the state. Whenever and wherever someone propagates national consciousness, such national consciousness will arouse some other people. Thus national consciousness will function to strengthen linguistic communication that goes on across the state. As such, the related linguistic communication will function to underpin the formation of the state. Thus national consciousness also plays a role in the formation of the state. This is precisely because linguistic communication necessitates the design and the use of media to recover the loss of immediacy between one another. National consciousness is a powerful medium because it is usually widely shared. That is, what shows the common character of a group of people such as all of the members of a nation is that all share the same national consciousness without any difference. National consciousness plays a role in the formation of the state. Those who activate a process of linguistic communication to spread national consciousness become even essential in the building of the state.

The appearance of people belonging to a nation such as the color of skin, may not be able to activate the process of spreading national consciousness if all of them are in an isolated community. Yet if they get in touch with another group of people belonging to another nation that shows a different appearance such as the different color of skin, they may feel that people, showing the same appearance, belong to one nation. Thus sometimes the appearance of people is able to arouse national consciousness because each nation can be regarded as a particular group of people defined in terms of nationality in some sense. As people are usually aware that a nation must be, first of all, a group of people defined in terms of nationality, the different appearance of people may, under certain circumstances, arouse national consciousness. As such, people, communicating by using language, have some inborn media at their disposal in constructing their national consciousness. That is, everything may become a medium. People are poised to make use of every medium. A medium facilitates them to communicate. The appearance of people may serve as a medium in this regard.

People who actively perform linguistic communication with each other may also create certain gestures in support of linguistic communication. As people often perform linguistic communication in a large community, they need to develop various forms of expression in support of the related linguistic communication, so that they can perform linguistic communication effectively. Needless to say, they might create many gestures before the birth of language. Since humans started using language, they have begun to use gestures as media in support of linguistic communication. Gestures can serve as the tools of language. As sometimes gestures are those created by a specific nation, gestures, displayed by people belonging to the same nation, may arouse national consciousness. Gestures remind people of the fact that they belong to one nation. For example, the peoples of some East Asian countries bow to show respect to each other, or the peoples of some European countries embrace each other to show their affections, when they meet. Those gestures are often also the forms of etiquette. Etiquette is designed to mean that people respect each other and intend to communicate with each other honestly or in good faith or sincerely. This happens on the occasion of linguistic communication among those who are far from each other or who are strangers or who are aware that they do not belong to a group of people kin to each other. The reason is that after humans extend the distance of linguistic communication, they form a large community. They are no longer close to each other; they are no longer familiar with each other; and they are no longer connected to each other by kinship. They form a state. Then in order to keep on performing linguistic communication for mutual interaction, a basic activity that ensures the unity of the state, people create some forms of communication, such as etiquette, to strengthen the related linguistic communication.

Costumes worn by people, food cooked by people and the custom of diet maintained by people, may also show national characters. They may be in the form of national culture. Whenever people see the costumes worn by people, the styles of costumes, including color and form, often show the national identity of people. Likewise, whenever people see the style of diet demonstrated by people in a local area, the special style may be an indication of a nation. They may be national symbols. A symbol is a simple but exclusive sign that has a connotation interpreted by using language. In the course of sending a message, a symbol is more efficient than a verbal expression. Thus a symbol is a medium. As a symbol is designed to denote a special object, it can be understood by all easily. In terms of the style of costumes and the custom of diet, they take form over the long term. They cannot be changed easily. Thus they emphatically show the national identity of people. Thus they may arouse national consciousness. For example, in Japan kimono and sushi are the symbols of the nation. In France Phrygian cap may be one of the symbols of the nation. In Australia Akubra hat worn by Australians may be the symbol of the Australian nation.

Some artistic forms of expression may show the characteristics of the culture had by a nation. They are intended to be shown. Thus the artistic forms of expression may indicate the national identity of people. They are created in support of the exchange of feelings. Such exchange of feelings further underpins the linguistic communication that goes on across the community. This community evolves to be a nation. All unite as a nation. National consciousness spreads and arouses people. For example, people give a national dance performance to support linguistic communication. That national dance performance arouses national consciousness. In Europe, the dance of each nation is usually unique. Thus we see that Germans always give a German dance performance; Hungarians always give a Hungarian dance performance; and Russians always give a Russian dance performance. A group performance given in the gymnasium may also display a national aesthetic form of expression. This form may arouse national consciousness. In addition, people perform music in support of linguistic communication that reaches all. It is also a special form of the exchange of feelings. It is very attractive. When music is performed, it is attractive to many people far or near. In the meantime, traditional musical instruments used to perform music also bear national character. If I am not wrong, this should be true for the traditional musical instruments of all nations around the world. When Finnish kantele is played by a musician in the public, this musical instrument may arouse national consciousness among the Finnish people. Other traditional musical instruments, such as Norwegian hardanger fiddle or Mongolian horse-head fiddle or Japanese koto or Korean gagageum, may play the same role among the masses of each related nation. As a result, the traditional musical instruments of a nation played by people in the public may arouse national consciousness because they serve, in some sense, as a symbol of the nation.

Famous mountains and rivers, happening to be located within the territory of the state, may become the symbols of the nation if they are unique because they can exclusively represent a nation that possesses those mountains and rivers. So in China the Yellow River and the Yangtze River symbolize the Chinese nation. In Japan Mount Fuji is a symbol of the nation. In Germany the Rhine River is a symbol of the nation. In Australia Uluru is one of the most recognized natural icons. It is, in some sense, a symbol of the nation. In Egypt the River Nile is a symbol of the nation.

Some plants, especially growing in a state, may be adopted to symbolize the nation. Indian lotus symbolizes the Indian nation. Indian Banyan, the national tree, also symbolizes the Indian nation. In China peony may be considered to be the national flower symbolizing the nation. Cherry blossom tree is a national symbol of Japan. Maple leaf symbolizes Canada. King Protea, a kind of flower, may be a symbol of South Africa.

Animals that especially grow within the territory of the state may be adopted to symbolize the nation. Therefore, Red Kangaroo is the national animal of Australia. Beaver is the animal recognized to be a symbol of Canada. Panda always comes from China. Brown bear is sometimes construed as a symbol of Russia. Royal Bengal Tiger is the national mammal of India and Indian Peacock the national bird of India. And Crane, indigenous to Japan, is the national bird chosen to symbolize Japan. Gallic rooster traditionally symbolizes France.

Some buildings, designed in the special shape to display a special artistic style, may play the same role. For example, the Tiananmen Tower, or the Great Wall, often represents China. Moscow Kremlin and Kremlin Palace symbolize, in some sense, Russia. Peace Tower, the Canadian parliament building, is a symbol of Canada. Pyramids are the symbols of Egypt. Sydney Opera House is a symbol of Australia. The Statue of Liberty is a symbol of the United States of America. Those buildings, functioning as the symbols of the nations or the states, show the feelings of the patriotic pride of the related nations.

The characteristics of a nation may also be reflected by a symbol especially made by people. The national flag, designed and flied by each nation, is such a symbol. It often reflects the natural or humanistic characteristics of a nation. The national flag of the United States shows how this nation was formed. The national flag of France may reflect the unique history of the French nation. The national flag of the Republic of Korea may reflect the unique culture of the Korean nation. The national flag of Canada may display the unique natural environment of Canada. A national flag manifests the particularity of a nation.

All in all, people propagate national consciousness. Being propagated, national consciousness plays a role in the formation of the state. The reason that national consciousness can play a role in this context is that it can buttress the linguistic communication that underpins the operation of the state. This means that people, seeing or hearing someone mentioning those symbols, enter subconsciously a process of linguistic communication from time to time. This process of linguistic communication underlies the formation of the state. In some sense, people can embrace national consciousness very quickly even without any interpretation. Thus people will perform the related linguistic communication throughout the state. All will unite.

In some sense, any form of expression, inherently in relation to a nation, may show the identity of the nation because it is special. The specialty of any form of expression demonstrates the special characteristics of people in relation to such a form of expression. The people, defined as a nation, are learned about by the people defined as another nation by virtue of those forms of expression. People can easily see them. They are patent to all. It is easier to see the characteristics of those forms of expression than to see the character of people belonging to that nation. Those forms of expression are media. The reason is that people believe that the uniqueness of the forms of expression defines the character of the nation. People cannot show their own identity unless by virtue of those unique forms of expression. They may create those forms of expression either wittingly or unwittingly. Thus, anything special may symbolize the nation and arouse national consciousness.

People themselves may also become symbols arousing national consciousness. If a person is outstanding among all others because he makes a special contribution to the growth of the nation, he will also be particular or unique. He is an example. He is admired by all other ordinary people. All others may intend to learn from him. Because of this, any person who is outstanding among all others may show the identity of the nation as expected because he is special. Thus I argue that outstanding people who make a great contribution to the nation may play this role. National heroes are those who make a great contribution to the nation. Being reminded of them, ordinary people have a great esteem for them. Thus, national heroes are respected by ordinary people. This is because ordinary people are grateful to national heroes. Then their memory may arouse the national consciousness of the people. This is because humans, forming their states, build or consolidate each state in various processes of linguistic communication in the mutual interaction of all. People need media in support of those processes of linguistic communication. National consciousness is a powerful medium. As the narration of national heroes arouses national consciousness, national heroes play a role in the formation of the state not only because of the heroic act committed by them at their times but also because of the special role played by them at present. They show their perpetual value. So Chinese people remember Yue Fei (1103-1142), a military general who led the defense of the Southern Song Dynasty against invaders from the Jurchen-ruled Jin Dynasty in northern China, Wen Tianxiang (1236-1283), a scholar-general resisting Kublai Khan's invasion and refusing to surrender to the Yuan Dynasty despite being captured and tortured in the last years of the Southern Song Dynasty and Qi Jiguang (1528-1588), a military general, known for his courage and leadership in the fight against Japanese pirates along the east coast of China as well as his reinforcement work on the Great Wall of China and others. People regard them as national heroes. In France all generations of people remember Joan of Arc (1412-1431), a national heroine who led the French army to fight to recover their home land from the English domination in history. In America, people remember Nathan Hale (1755-1776), a soldier of the Continental Army who volunteered for an intelligence-gathering task, and was captured by the British and stated before he was hanged that "I only regret that I have but one life to give for my country" during the American Revolutionary War. They regard him as a national hero.

Political figures that play a role in the struggle for the liberty, or the emancipation, or the independence, or the unification, of the nation are usually remembered by ordinary people. In the meantime, as they make a contribution to the nation, they can also function as media in support of the processes of linguistic communication that underlies the building of the state because mentioning them can arouse national consciousness. This is because people usually believe that they made a contribution to the nation. Then the nation can play a role in the building of the state. This means that as they can function to arouse national consciousness, they are always remembered and mentioned by people. They are buried at certain places after their death. They have their tombs. Then people may regularly pay respect to them in front of their tombs. People may make a speech in memory of them there. This is because national consciousness likely to be aroused is crucial for the building of the state. It is just because people need to strengthen the building of the state that they are of great significance and people keep on paying respect to them. So in nearly all the states built by humans on earth in modern times people memorize those people who made a special contribution to the liberty, or the emancipation, or the independence, or the unification, of the nation. They are respected by people and people keep on propagating their deeds. So in many nation-states in Europe people remember those great figures that made an extraordinary contribution to the independence or the rise of the nation in the past. In Italy Giuseppe Mazzini, Giuseppe Garibaldi and Camillo Benso Cavour are remembered by people because they made a contribution to the unification of Italy. In other regions there are similar cases. In Israel Theodore Herzl is respected by all because he made a great contribution for the liberty of the nation. In India people pay respect to Mohandas Karamchand Gandhi, a political leader of the Indian people who made a great contribution to the independence of the nation.

Thinkers who disseminate a certain nationalist idea may also play a role in this regard. That is, national consciousness may take form gradually. Yet what precipitates the formation of national consciousness may be a series of efforts made by those thinkers in propagating the national idea. As ordinary people are unable to perform linguistic communication over long distances, the spread of national consciousness is usually confined to a local region. It takes a long time to unify national consciousness among plenty of people. Thinkers are usually able to perform linguistic communication over long distances because they are well-known and are able to write books. Thus they are able to perform linguistic communication with all. Besides, ordinary people usually perform short-time linguistic communication while thinkers are able to perform long-time linguistic communication. Thinkers, disseminating the national idea, can constantly communicate with all. Thinkers, constantly communicating with all, assist the nation in the propagation of national consciousness. For example, in early modern times many German thinkers, such as Johann Gottfried Herder, Johann Gottlieb Fichte and many others, disseminated a national idea. The German people read their books which kept on reminding them that they belonged to one nation. After the unification of Germany the German people continued to read those books. Those books kept on arousing national consciousness. Then people remember those German thinkers because they propagated national consciousness. I think that there is a similar situation in China. In ancient times Chinese people did not have strong national consciousness. People witness the very fact that national fusion between Han Chinese and various minorities occurred in history. Yet after China began to stay directly in contact with Western countries in the mid-nineteenth century, some outstanding intellectuals, such as Liang Qichao, Zhang Taiyan, and Lu Xun among others, propagated national consciousness. Although the formation of a nation-state started much earlier, national consciousness did not play any prominent role until China was forced to open its door to the outside world in the nineteenth century. Later, national consciousness played a role in the unity of the nation and in the building of the nation-state. Many national thinkers particularly aroused the national consciousness of the Chinese people at that time. They created a medium in the unity of the nation. Ordinary people remember them in modern times. In other words, the reason that people remember those thinkers is often that people have embraced the national idea propagated by them. The reason that people embrace a certain national idea is that national consciousness is needed to play a role in the building of the state. These circumstances usually appear in modern times.

People may also use language itself to propagate national consciousness under certain circumstances. As a particular language is often used by a particular nation, the unique form of language defines and highlights the character of the nation. As Wilhelm von Humboldt commented, from every language, we can infer backwards to the national character.[1] So Jean Jacques Rousseau used to write that "Speech distinguishes man among the animals; language distinguishes nations from each other; one does not know where a man comes from until he has spoken."[2] Particularly, after the development of printing in early modern times, a vernacular language prevailed gradually within each nation. For example, after the times of Reformation plenty of Martin Luther's books written in German were printed and sold, leading to the wide spread of German. This means that the prevalence of German, a vernacular language, laid a foundation for the end of kingdoms and the feudal states of other types and the birth of a nation-state in the following days because people could use language to propagate national consciousness. Other areas in Europe showed the same trend. Europeans gave up using Latin. Carl Joachim Friedrich writes that:

> In both Italy and Germany the first sweep of nationalism was associated with the birth of a 'universal' vernacular language fashioned by Dante and Luther respectively; in England, France and Spain (as well as other nation-states) the vernacular language crystallized in the course of a more gradual growth. But whichever way it develops, the nation-alism and linguistic self-discovery went hand in hand. Not all linguistic communities are nations, let alone groups inspired by nationalism. Yet nationalism and the building of a nation are greatly aided by linguistic community.[3]

Speaking a unique or particular language can arouse national conscious-ness. Humans usher in an era during which people arouse national conscious-ness because each nation may speak a unique language and the nation-state is to be built. Then, from that time onward humans have entered the times of nation-state. They proactively highlight, or maintain, or strengthen, the particularity of language. People establish a relation of signs. The behavior of speaking a language is the signifier and the nation is the signified. If a certain language defined in this case is especially used by a nation, the behav-ior of using that language usually or often arouses national consciousness. As language is always managed by the state, people may use language in view of the building of the state. If a state does not intend to arouse national consciousness, it may not keep a particular language. So in view of the course of the formation of the state in which national consciousness plays a role, we find that if a national language takes form gradually in a state, this evolution of language is the particularization of language. In France the French lan-guage used to be especially promoted by the state after the French Revolution because French spoken within France was supposed to be used by the French people only. French has been regarded as a means to show the identity of the French people ever since. Speaking French arouses national consciousness. In some other European states, the state defined a regional language originally used by people as the national language in early modern times. People were all encouraged to use the language defined by the state. The language has been particularized ever since. No state intends to use the language which is exactly the same as the one used by another state. The evolution of language shows this case in Hungry, Bulgaria, Ukraine, Latvia, Lithuania, and so on and so forth. In some Asian states, national consciousness is also often aroused in the process of particularizing language and the process of particularizing language is due to the need of the independence of the nation-state. In Japan, Japanese linguistic experts created hiragana and katakana, the two basic components of Japanese writing system in about the tenth century after Chinese characters had been used since about the sixth century. Later, Japanese was created on the basis of Hiragana, Katakana and Kanji, namely, Chinese character. This process of creating a new language is part of the formation of the nation-state. Likewise, in Korea Koreans began to create their own national language in the fifteenth century. This particular language is the particularity of the nation. Similarly, in Vietnam people created and began to use their national language in the early twentieth century. The language, used by Vietnamese today, is distinct from the language used by them in the past. The Vietnamese alphabet in use today is a Latin alphabet. As far as the Turkish language is concerned, we find the case that language was radically reformed to revive an old language in order to particularize language. That is, modern Turkish or Istanbul Turkish is the most widely spoken of the Turkic languages in Western Asia. This language used to be under reform in the first half of the twentieth century. The result of the reform is that Ioanwords of Arabic and Persian origin were replaced with Turkish equivalents. Old Turkish words that had been out of use for centuries were revived. In the meantime, in Israel Hebrew is one of the two official languages. Though various languages are spoken in Israel, 90 percent Jews and over 60 percent Arabs have a good understanding of Hebrew. English is used extensively in the society. Yet, in some sense, the language policy made by the state is particularly intended to set Hebrew as the national language of the Jewish people while the state discourages the use of other Jewish languages, particularly Yiddish. Today, being used widely in government bodies, enterprises, schools and universities, Hebrew functions to symbolize the nation and to arouse national consciousness.

All these cases show that if a state intends to arouse the national consciousness of the people, it will support a particular language. There is a relationship among language, national consciousness and the formation of the state. They constitute a prodigious trinity. They interrelate to one another. If one part is missing, the remaining parts will not function as expected. If people are not going to form a state, language should not play a role of arousing national consciousness as expected. This is mainly because if people are not going to form a state, people may not disseminate national consciousness proactively. Conversely speaking, if people are going to form a state, they may need to arouse national consciousness. If people have already formed the state, they may also need to arouse national consciousness. People may even keep on strengthening national consciousness in the state. In this case the form of language plays a role as a medium in support of the process of linguistic communication at large in the building of the state. That is, the growth of nation-states in modern times in some areas on earth can especially vindicate this judgment. In the building of the state, people often create or adopt a national language under a language policy because the cultivation of national consciousness needs such a language.

This situation is particularly underscored by the interaction of the languages of different nations. In the United Nations the delegates of each nation usually prefer to make a speech in the language of their own country. Delegates usually think that they must use their own languages because using their mother tongues means having their dignity as a nation-state. In the European Union no member country is willing to relinquish its national language though government officials from each state may sometimes communicate with one another in some major working languages for the purpose of internal communication on informal occasions. This means that each nation has its national consciousness. In order to maintain national consciousness, people insist on using their national language on certain formal occasions and they are unwilling to relinquish it. Besides, the people of that nation may feel proud of the fact that some foreigners learn the language of their nation. This is because a language is usually a unique tool used by a nation in the mutual communication of people within the nation. Language is often national. People may think that language not only enables them to communicate with each other more conveniently but also functions as a tool adopted concurrently to underline their national identity and hence arouse their national consciousness. As people are usually proud of their own nation, they are also proud of their own language. Language may represent their national spirit. Language thus is the most convenient tool for them to keep and propagate their national consciousness.

Thus we see that people may highly evaluate the language used by them just because language can arouse national consciousness and national consciousness is important in the building of the state. For example, people may write an essay or a prose to praise the beauty of their own language. People may compose a song or a poem to eulogize their own national language. People may even use a form of art to articulate that they love their own language. In China people created the calligraphy of Chinese characters to demonstrate people's feelings and ideas from the bottom of their hearts. Now people display that calligraphy to show a national spirit from time to time. Thus, by using language, people disseminate national consciousness. This situation may also occur in other states in which writing system is composed of characters.

All the forms, including plants, animals, clothes, performances, musical instruments, outstanding figures and language indicated above, are symbols made, or designated, or used, to arouse national consciousness. The reason that they can function to arouse national consciousness is that they can function as a medium in support of the process of linguistic communication that reaches all within the state. People especially need symbols in their linguistic communication that underpins the unity of the state. Symbols are indispensable in the formation of the state. And the particularity of a symbol lies in the fact that it ensures the visibility of the process of linguistic communication that goes on between the nation and all members of the nation. This symbol often embodies the nation alone. It is powerful. This is because people need to communicate with the nation. The nation cannot show itself unless a symbol represents it. Thus Paul Ricoeur, believing that symbols are the entities that have not evolved to be language, writes that "what asks to be brought to language in symbols, but which never passes over completely into language, is always something powerful, efficacious, forceful."[4] In the background of linguistic communication people use all kinds of media. Thus, those media may arouse national consciousness.

All these cases show that national consciousness, as a medium, supports linguistic communication that reaches all within the state and national consciousness bolsters the building of the state. Language serves as a tool reinforcing the building of the state.

2. Historical Consciousness

Another sort of consciousness is historical consciousness. This sort of consciousness stems from people's knowledge of history. The knowledge of history is disseminated mainly in the processes of linguistic communication. In the meantime, the state takes form in extending the distance of linguistic communication. Historical consciousness can function as a medium in support of the formation of the state because all, forming the state, usually share such historical consciousness. Then we find that there exists the causality between historical knowledge and historical consciousness. There is also the causality between extending the distance of linguistic communication and disseminating historical knowledge. The result is that as history is the history of all, all feel close to each other. All hear the narratives of their history. All know their common origin. All have a sense of belonging. All have the same consciousness. Thus, whenever history functions as a medium, it will underpin the linguistic communication to which all have access because all are aware of it. All unite to form their state. History is, therefore, a spiritual resource for the building of the state. Every form of presenting history may strengthen historical consciousness and function in support of the building of the state. Then people tend to have the same knowledge of their own growth. They understand their own community in the same way. They often view the organization of their community in the same method. They may hold the same idea about how the state should be organized.

Thus my view is that people form their state over a long stretch of time. History plays a certain role. History, in some sense, gives an account of the formation of the state over a long period of time. People often have some memory of the past, including the course of the formation of the state. They have to use language. They have to use language to chronicle history. Then there is the causality between language and history, as noted earlier. People first communicate by using language and then narrate history. The narration of history is a process of spreading historical knowledge and consciousness. There are several basic forms of narrating history. Some of them give particular effect to the spread of historical knowledge and then the spread of historical consciousness.

First, we can regard a history textbook as a basic form of presenting history. As history must be learned by all, history is first learned by students who receive education in schools, colleges and universities. As these education institutions can gather students, the knowledge of history is intensively disseminated to many young people who are growing up. As the related linguistic communication that disseminates history is one-to-many collective linguistic communication, all see or hear the same presentation of history. Then people gain the same knowledge of history and the same historical consciousness. The state usually acknowledges or approves the content of the history textbook and people acquire the related historical consciousness that buttresses the organization of the state. People, gaining the same historical consciousness, always reach a consensus on the evaluation of the building of the state. Such historical consciousness buttresses the legitimacy of the state or the government in charge of governing the state. As the content of the history textbook is the basic knowledge of history, it is also easy for people to gain the same consciousness of history. With the basic narration of history, history becomes a spiritual resource in the building of the state. So in modern times history textbooks are read by the students of the institutions of regular learning in nearly all the states.

Second, history books, written for academic research, constitute another form of presenting history. These books are chiefly written to chronicle history. As history is narrated by history books in detail, the rich knowledge of history is spread particularly among those well-educated people. Those well-educated people may then interpret the content of those history books to less-educated people. Thus people spread the knowledge of history in the society. These books especially strengthen people's common memory. As history ought to be chronicled correctly, people who write these books also try to find out historical truth. Historians who write history books may argue. Their arguments deepen the understanding of history. Some presentations of history, offered by historians, may directly play a role in the construction of the historical consciousness of the state if they can meet the requirement of the state. They usually function to interpret history. If the related interpretation is consonant with the narration of a history textbook, such presentation of history directly participates in the construction of historical consciousness required by the state. If not, the related interpretation may function when the history textbook needs revision. Thus it has been a tradition for historians to keep on writing history books in history. In ancient times historians wrote many well-known history books. Herodotus wrote his *Histories*. Thucydides wrote *The History of the Peloponnesian War*. In early modern times Edward Gibbons wrote *The History of the Decline and Fall of the Roman Empire*. In modern times nation-states emerge. Historians write the books narrating the history of each nation-state. For example, historians may write a book entitled "A History of English People" or "A History of American People." Historical consciousness is disseminated widely within the state.

Third, some cultural forms of describing history may constitute another sort of the presentations of history. These cultural forms are not directly created by historians. They may be offered by poets, writers and artists among others. These cultural forms may be created to help ordinary people to exchange feelings among themselves, to educate people or to provide them with a service for entertainment. But historical knowledge may be spread by them. History, as a subject matter, may function as a medium in support of the spread of culture. Conversely speaking, culture may also function as a medium in the spread of the knowledge of history. As far as history is concerned, such cultural forms absolutely function to spread history though they may not be regarded as the formal presentations of history. When writing is not extant, some cultural forms are the main forms of disseminating history among the people. Almost every nation in the world has its epics. Epics are poems created to disseminate the knowledge of history. One of the most typical examples is Homeric Epics of ancient times. Many famous novels, written by excellent novelists, adopt a piece of history as their subject matter, too. Many plays and films also adopt a piece of history as their subject matter. Given that people who appreciate these cultural products are usually more than those who read history books, the knowledge of history is more widely spread by these cultural forms. History is popularized by these cultural forms to a greater extent. Then the great masses of the people embrace the same or similar historical consciousness. Then such historical consciousness will function as a medium in support of the linguistic communication that reaches all within the state. These cultural forms consolidate the building of the state.

People also interact with history as history is a medium in support of the linguistic communication that bolsters the formation of the state. People learn their history. Then the knowledge of history is instilled into the minds of people. There is an interaction realized by people with history. As there are various forms of such interaction, people come to have their common memory in various ways. There are mainly three ways.

First, sometimes the narration of history results in the interaction between the historical figures and the following generations. In China people worship their ancestors. They regularly hold the related rituals in memory of *Huangdi* and *Yandi*, the ancestors of Chinese nation. They repose their spirit on their ancestors. Thus they have the sense of belonging. In this process they spread historical consciousness because they narrate *Huangdi* and *Yandi* though the detailed description of them is unavailable. This means that people worship their ancestors, and all, participating in the related ceremony, will feel close to each other because at the times of their ancestors people, kin to each other, congregated in a small community. Thinking of that very close blood relationship will make people feel close to each other. They may imagine that they originally belonged to one family. Thus such consciousness is helpful to the building of the state. So currently though China is not unified, people hold the ceremonies of worshipping ancestors in which the Mainlanders and some politicians from Taiwan participate to propagate a historical consciousness in order to build a process of linguistic communication in support of the great cause of the unification of the motherland in the future. Besides, paying respect to the founding fathers of the state may be another kind of behavior generating historical consciousness. This means that people are usually required or supposed to inherit the ideal or the spirit of the founding fathers of the state. So they commemorate the founding fathers of the state in order to continue building their state as expected by their founding fathers. As they commemorate those founding fathers of the state, they propagate a historical consciousness. As a result, people hold related ceremonies regularly in memory of the founding fathers of the state in order to propagate that historical consciousness year in, year out. So we see that American people regularly visit historical monuments, or go to historical memorials, to pay their respect to their founding fathers such as George Washington. In Canada the founding fathers of the nation-state are remembered by Canadian people. They hold relevant ceremonies. They pay respect to those founding fathers, including John A. Macdonald, who played a role in the course leading to Canadian Confederation. In addition, admiring the historical heroes who were originally commoners is also a kind of behavior that may spread the knowledge of history and hence arouse historical consciousness. These historical figures may not be national heroes or founding fathers. They were originally unknown. But they became historical heroes because they committed heroic deeds. These historical heroes may include revolutionary martyrs. These historical heroes may also include some famous philosophers who died because of insisting on their own idea. In some states these historical heroes also include some scientists who insisted on their scientific belief and were hence persecuted in history. These historical heroes may also include some ordinary people who ventured their lives to safeguard the cause of social justice. This is because people are grateful to those historical heroes who either made a great contribution to the building of the state or sacrificed their lives for insisting their own progressive idea in defiance of the oppression of the despotic authorities. Then as people need to memorize them, people narrate and record their deeds. In the meantime, people may pay respect to the statues of historical heroes. People may hold an academic conference in memory of them. Historical consciousness is also aroused this way.

Second, after a historical event comes to an end, people tend to draw on historical experiences and lessons. Then people use historical events memorized by them to propagate a historical consciousness in support of a related discourse that underpins the related linguistic communication in the building of the state. There is an interaction between people and historical events. People not only interact with one another, but also interact with historical events. Therefore, people often hold a ceremony, or host an event, in memory of an important historical event. In this respect we can take the days designated for commemoration as an example. That is, in order to draw on historical experiences and lessons, people often designate the days of the occurrence of some historical events as the days of commemoration. Then on the occasion of each anniversary of each of those days people may especially recollect those historical events in order to memorize in their hearts those historical experiences and lessons. Thus people propagate a historical consciousness. For example, the member states of the Commonwealth of Nations have been observing Remembrance Day in memory of their soldiers who died on their duty in the battlefield each year since World War One. They recall the end of hostility of World War One on November 11, 1918. In the United States people may each year hold a meeting to mark December 7, 1941, the day when Japan attacked the Pearl Harbor. In China people keep on taking various forms to mark July 7, 1937, the day when the Chinese people's war of resistance against Japan's aggression broke out. They also hold ceremonies each year in memory of the victims of the Nanking Massacre which was an episode of mass murder and mass rape committed by the Japanese troops in Nanking, the then capital of the Republic of China, during a period of six weeks starting on December 13, 1937. Their activities arouse strong historical consciousness. In addition, different nation-states may designate a certain day in memory of those who died in the genocides. For example, some states designate some days of each year as holocaust memorial days. In Israel people may hold a meeting, or a mass rally, or a ceremony, to mark the Holocaust and Heroism Remembrance Day on 27 April/May. In some European states, including Bulgaria, France, Germany, Greece, Italy, Netherlands, Poland, Romania, Serbia, Czech Republic and United Kingdom, people also hold meetings to mark holocaust memorial days each year. At least since 2004, twelve states, including Germany, Britain, France, Italy and Scandinavian states, have observed the January 27, the day of the liberation of the Auschwitz Concentration Camp. This means that wars and genocides, breaking out in history, are very important events. To mark the anniversary of an important historical event means to memorize that event and to draw on historical experiences and lessons. Thus people strengthen certain historical consciousness. Particularly, the remembrance of the historical sufferings incurred by people strengthens the related historical consciousness. Such consciousness, as a medium, bolsters the linguistic communication that reaches all within the state. Such consciousness buttresses the solidarity of the state indeed.

Third, due to the fact that history is chronicled by historians and learned by the masses, people gain certain knowledge of some historical remains. The historical remains are usually what have been left by the predecessors living in the past. These historical remains are meaningful because they are actually part of history. They constitute the true evidence of history, and the authorities usually protect them. As a result, historical remains are not only used to pass on historical knowledge to the masses but also interpreted by historians, so that a historical consciousness is spread among the masses. They are often cultural relics. But they are also historical remains. The people and those remains interact. For example, in Europe there are many old castles left by the predecessors living in the Middle Ages. Now many of them become tourist resorts. For example, if you pay a visit to Germany or France or Spain, you may see some old castles there. They narrate history. Besides, some European states still maintain the old city walls or the city gates which have existed since the medieval times. These historical remains narrate history. These historical remains are often, in some sense, part of a dialogue that has been going on between those living in the medieval times and those in the modern times. In addition, the former residences of great philosophers, artists, writers, scientists and theologians are maintained and managed as tourist resorts. When visitors visit those tourist resorts, they gain related historical knowledge. At the same time people may feel proud of the fact that in their countries there are a great number of giants emerging in history. They visit those tourist resorts and receive patriotic education. Thus historical consciousness is aroused to serve patriotic education. Likewise, in China, we find that the situation is similar. Old city walls and bridges are maintained simply because they are part of history. The mausoleums of emperors in history are maintained because they narrate history. In addition, in Chinese history many great poets and writers emerged. Therefore, in China there are many former residences of great poets and writers visited by tourists. Those tourist resorts are usually designated by the government as the bases of patriotic education. In Arab countries some great mosques are tourist resorts. They are also part of history. All those historical remains are media which spread history. They bear testimony to history. Thus people disseminate historical consciousness. They arouse the historical consciousness of all. Thus people keep the same historical discourse. They increase the chances of performing linguistic communication with one another. They are thus determined to unite. Historical remains bolster the consciousness of history which supports the formation of the state over a long span of time.

We can also analyze the structure of the contents of history. If we analyze the structure of the contents of history, we may find that not all past experiences of humans are narrated by historians. Trivial matters are not the subject matters of historical books or some other cultural forms. As history is usually written to draw on the experiences and lessons of human practice, major and important deeds of people are usually chosen as the subject matters of history depicted by historians. This is because people can draw on more experiences and lessons from those major and important deeds of people. As these deeds need to be narrated and studied, they also become media. In other words, as they catch more attention of historians and some other people, they contribute to the flourishing of historiography. Discussing history, Robert F. Berkhofer writes that "Great stories matter greatly to professional historians and the public alike."[5] He further explains that "Great stories matter greatly because they establish the context of the historical context." [6] They crucially buttress the dissemination of historical consciousness. That is, these important deeds of humans enhance the value of history. As a result, writing history, by adopting these deeds of humans as subject matters of historical presentations, bolsters the spread of the knowledge of history. Historical consciousness is spread, too. That is, people narrate history chiefly because of these important human deeds. They are media. As they are media, they support the related linguistic communication. This is the reason that their narration buttresses the building of the state. The following subject matters are especially capable of disseminating the knowledge of history and hence historical consciousness.

First, war is often the subject matter of historical presentations. Peace is usually not the subject matter of historical presentations. Peace is often taken for granted, but war is often viewed as special. People usually do not believe that the state of peace has an impact on their life in all aspects, but the state of war has such an impact. As war is often deemed as a special situation, more lessons may be drawn on from war if one side loses the war, or more experiences may be drawn on from the war if one side wins the war. Therefore, a great war is often the subject matter of some very famous history books. Historians have written their history books about the Peloponnesian war,

Napoleon's war, World War One, and World War Two, to name only a few. Civil wars of many countries are also vehemently narrated by historians. For example, American civil war, waged by Northerners and Southerners in the nineteenth century, is a subject matter of quite a few history books written by American historians. Chinese civil war, waged by the Nationalist Party of China and the Communist Party of China in the twentieth century, is also frequently narrated by Chinese historians. Those wars cause many deaths and damage much property. People suffer a lot from war. Yet war is often a valuable subject matter of history written by humans because it gives them valuable experiences and lessons. Strong historical consciousness is often engendered in the description of a war. Some historians even believe that humans create history through a war. So Arthur Schopenhauer writes that "History shows us the life of nations and can find nothing to relate except wars and insurrections; the years of peace appear here and there only as short pauses, as intervals between the acts." [7]

Second, the history of the state is often focused on by historians who write history. The rise of a state is usually deemed as an important part of history because the state has an important impact on people in all aspects. People are organized by the state and are subject to the governance of the state. Power struggle in the government is sometimes considered an important content of the books of history. The course of the decline of this state is also interesting to historians. This is because historians write history books to help humans to draw on many experiences and lessons from the study of the history of the state. Thus, historians, writing the history of a country, especially describe the rise and decline of the state. If a state is replaced by another one in history, they tend to study the history of each state. They delineate the activities of the rulers and the living conditions of the populace. They try to find out why a state rises and why a state declines. For example, as mentioned earlier, Edward Gibbons wrote the history of Roman Empire. In Great Britain historians write the pre-modern history of the kingdom. History may be divided into various periods in view of the reigns of dynasties. In France history written by historians is sometimes divided into the different periods in view of the reigns of dynasties. Likewise, Chinese historians who write ancient history may write the history of each dynasty. In modern times historians may also write the history of the state. For example, French historians may write the history of the Third Republic or the Fourth Republic. In China historians sometimes especially write the history of the Republic of China or the history of the People's Republic of China. Historians often assert that the best way to write about the history of a nation is to write about the state built by this nation. The state symbolizes the organization of the people. The state is expected to strive for the good of the people. The brilliance of the state is often deemed as the brilliance of history.

Third, many historians take revolution as a major subject matter of history. They believe that it is more meaningful to write about the changing society than to write about the society that remains unchanged. As they usually or often believe that revolution leads to the progress of human society, revolution becomes an important subject matter of modern history. A revolution may sometimes result in a radical change of the society. What is behind a revolution is an idea. Such an idea needs to be evaluated. Then the history of revolution becomes an important part of history. So we see that after the end of English Revolution in the seventeenth century, many English historians wrote the history of English Revolution. After the end of French Revolution, historians kept on writing the books about French Revolution. Books about Russian Revolution in the twentieth century were also published frequently in a period of time in history. In China the most important history books today are the books about Chinese Revolutions. One Chinese Revolution, led by Dr. Sun Yat-Sen, the leader of the Nationalist Party of China, is called the bourgeois revolution and the other, led by Mao Zedong, the leader of the Communist Party of China, is called the proletarian revolution. In China people learn modern history by learning the history of Chinese revolutions. Historical consciousness is often the revolutionary consciousness. So I argue that the history of a revolution is a medium used by people to learn modern history in China. That is, if you learn the modern history of China, the best way for you to realize this objective is to learn the history of each revolution in modern China.

Fourth, the success or failure of social and political reforms initiated by some historical figures is often narrated by historians. Historians are tempted to find out why some reforms succeed or fail. If a reform proves successful in history, historians will be interested in finding out why it succeeded, so that experiences can be drawn on in support of the operation of the state.

If a reform proves unsuccessful in history, historians will also be interested in the research of this reform because people can draw historical lessons. For example, in modern times many states have experienced a process of modernization, which often involves a series of social and political reforms. Historians particularly tend to delineate the process of a social or political reform in the related historical context. So in China historians often write the history of Westernization Movement of 1861-1895, a series of institutional reforms initiated by some statesmen, such as Li Hongzhang, during the late Qing Dynasty after many military defeats and concessions to foreign powers. Some historians confirm that this movement was the inception of China's modernization. Some other historians emphasize that those reforms did not go far enough. In later times there were also some social or political reforms. Among them, the economic reform, advocated by Deng Xiaoping in the late twentieth century, is also studied by historians. Historians usually confirm that Deng changed China's planned economy into the market economy and his reform has led to the long-term growth of Chinese economy since the beginning of 1980s. But his reform is also controversial. Some historians hold that his reform resulted in rampant corruption and he failed to go ahead with the political reform. In European states the narration of social or political reforms shows the similar inclination. For example, Russian historians write the history of reforms under the rule of the Tsar Alexander II following the end of the Crimean War of 1854-1856. Although some historians mention that the emancipation of serfs in Russia in 1861 was a social progress, some other historians point out that his plan of redistribution of land was half-hearted and many reforms were too little and too late. Russian historians also often mention the agrarian reforms initiated by Pyotr Stolypin in order to create a class of prosperous peasants and to modernize Russia between 1906 and 1917. As the reforms are controversial, historians hold different views about Stolypin's reforms. Some historians believe that he largely succeeded because agricultural production increased and land was redistributed among the households in European Russia. In contrast, some other historians insist that Stolypin failed to bring any progress to Russian society. In addition, historians are also interested in narrating the reforms initiated by Mikhail Gorbachev, a statesman of former Soviet Union, who advocated perestroika ("restructuring") and glasnost ("openness") in the late twentieth century.

Some historians praise him because he ended totalitarianism while others insist that his reform did not lead to an effective economic progress.

So the structure of history is, in some sense, the structure of media. The reason is that some practices of humans in history are especially worthy to be mentioned. Not all human deeds are worth mentioning. Thus, as some practices of humans are worth studying because people can draw on useful and valuable experiences and lessons from them, people create their history. Then they gain their strong historical consciousness. As they form their state in various processes of linguistic communication, historical consciousness finally becomes a medium in support of the processes of linguistic communication significant for the building of the state.

3. Social and Political Consciousness

Social and political consciousness, discussed in this context, means an idea or a belief about order, peace, harmony, fairness and justice among others engendered in the mutual interaction of people. It reflects people's wish or hope or ideal in the society or in the state. Whenever some people disseminate this consciousness and some other people embrace it, all often agree to the principle of organizing the society or the state formulated by all on the basis of the consensus of opinion reached by them. Thus they understand and support one another. They usually perform frequent linguistic communication with one another. They feel close to one another. They are tempted to communicate with one another. They tend to see eye to eye with one another on many social or political affairs. Then social and political consciousness may become an invisible medium in support of linguistic communication among all. Then people strengthen their mutual interaction for cooperation. This situation buttresses the unity of the state.

This means that humans, forming their state after the dissolution of tribes, are no longer able to form their community on the basis of kinship. The close relationship, between one another characteristic of immediacy between one another, has disappeared in most cases. They need to form their community in a new way. They must seek order, peace, harmony, fairness and justice on a new basis in order to build a community in which they can reside and live with happiness. Thus to gain happiness, people need to build the society or the state in the principle that they can establish order and realize peace, harmony, fairness and justice. Because of this, people come up with their ideas reflecting their wishes for the establishment of order and the realization of peace, harmony, fairness and justice. Then a consciousness, reflecting such an idea or belief, may develop and spread. Thus all may unite on the basis of such a consciousness. All witness the formation of their common interest. Then people will perform more linguistic communication because they are now motivated to cooperate with one another. They jointly build their state. In the meantime, those who can create an idea or a belief for the people become the creators of social and political consciousness in the operation of the state.

In a state in which some people disseminate religious consciousness to some other people, plenty of people may believe in God. Then God may become a symbol assisting humans in the formation of their community even though not all are religious believers. God can be deemed as an agent in this sense. Thus religious consciousness sometimes plays a role in state formation because the building of the state needs the support of a spirit. As humans depart from their tribes and enter into the new community, they need the sense of safety and need to overcome many difficulties in their own preservation. They may need to eliminate poverty. They may need to avert a war. They thus hope to get a help from a supernatural force. God appears in their mind. Though a religious community does not always necessarily function to support the formation of the state, the religious consciousness, propagated by the religious community, sometimes plays a role in support of the linguistic communication in the formation of the state. The specific situation is that people, sharing a religious belief, may gather to help each other. They have the same religious consciousness. They may intensify linguistic communication among them. They may strengthen their mutual interaction. Then religious consciousness may function as a medium because people, sharing the same religious consciousness, increase their mutual communication and interaction. The increase of mutual communication and interaction among people may also conversely strengthen the spread of religious consciousness. Thus, people form the religious community. Then, as P. Horwitz observes, a religious community affords its members the opportunity to interact and to find a certain sense of identity.[8] The result is that people come to organize the religious community. So Albert Victor Murray writes that:

> The word 'State' has many meanings, but in ordinary speech we mean the Government, acting through its central or local agencies. It is important to realize the local side of government. We somehow never think of the parish council in a village as the 'State' and yet a parish council can be as helpful or as coercive as any government department.[9]

Thus, Jack Goody writes that "The formalization of a pantheon is often connected with the formation of the state, with the incorporation or identification of local gods within a wider national framework."[10]

By the same token, we can further deduce this view: The formation of a religious community is intended to function as a medium as the mission of a church or a temple is to spread a religious idea and belief, and the spread of a religious idea and belief may serve as a condition for the building of the state. This means that many conditions are needed for the formation of the state. All these conditions may not equally function to support the formation of the state. Sometimes some conditions even do not exist. For instance, sometimes people do not have strong national consciousness or historical consciousness. In this case, religious consciousness may especially play a part in the formation of the state particularly in ancient times. Thus sometimes it is crucial to reinforce religious consciousness in the formation of the state. We may find many examples bearing testimony to this argument. One example is that religion played a role in the formation of the state of Hebrews in ancient times before Hebrews had built up their national consciousness or historical consciousness. So some philosophers, including Baruch Spinoza, mention in their works that after departing from Egypt, Hebrews liberated themselves from the oppression of Egyptians. They were no longer bound by the laws of any other nation. They were going to form their own state. They hearkened to Moses, in whom they all placed the greatest confidence and resolved to transfer their rights not to any mortal man, but to God alone. Thus God held the sovereignty over the Hebrews and this state was called the Kingdom of God.[11] It was apparently because of the role played by religious consciousness that Hebrews built smoothly their first state. The religious consciousness especially led all to unite at that time. Thus they performed frequent linguistic communication for cooperation. Such linguistic communication guaranteed that all interacted with all, resulting in the formation of the state.

Similarly, the rise of Islam created a condition for the growth of many Arab states in later times in history. This is also a case showing that if people do not take initiative to form their state because of the absence of strong national or historical consciousness, the propagation of religious consciousness may lay a foundation for the formation of the state. In history, Mohammed added nothing to the material resources of the Arabs, but within a few years of his death, they had acquired a large empire by defeating their most powerful neighbors. The religion, founded by the Prophet, was essential. Then the Prophet even declared war on the Byzantine Empire.[12] In the following historical period Islam continued to play an essential role in the building of the states in Near East. The religion of Islam strengthened the building of the Arab states in a long period of time. Even today we cannot imagine that those states can remain stable if religion fails to give a due support to the state. This situation proves that many Arab people are receptive of religious consciousness. Religious consciousness motivates all to unite. Religious consciousness becomes a medium in support of the linguistic communication that goes on among all. People form themselves into each state particularly on this basis.

In the world of Christianity, there are also plenty of examples showing that religious consciousness sometimes plays a role in support of the formation of the states in history. Sometimes, people give a central role to religious consciousness in the building of the state in the absence of suitable national or historical consciousness. Religious consciousness may substitute for national or historical consciousness in the building of the state in case the state lacks suitable national or historical consciousness. So in early times appeared the situation in which attention was paid by the ruler to the role played by religion in the building of the state. In Britain the state sought support from the Anglican Church. In the Middle Ages the building of the state in Britain was especially marked by the amalgamation of several states built by ancient nations. Welsh national identity emerged among the Celtic Britons after the Roman withdrawal from Britain in the fifth century. Edward I of England completely conquered Wales in late thirteenth century. Though the independence of Wales was restored for a short period of time, the whole of Wales was annexed by England and incorporated within the English legal system under the Laws of Wales Acts 1535-1542. As far as Scotland is concerned, the Kingdom of Scotland emerged as an independent sovereign state in the Early Middle Ages. In 1603 James VI, King of Scotland became King of England. In the meantime he also became King of Ireland. Thus people witnessed the formation of a personal union of three kingdoms. In 1707, Scotland entered into the political union with England. When Ireland was partitioned into Northern Ireland and the Irish Free State (later Republic of Ireland) in 1921, Northern Ireland was declared part of Britain. Before Great Britain grew to be a modern nation-state, unified national consciousness had not yet come into existence. People had not fully built the historical consciousness of the state either because after the amalgamation of various regions it took a long time to construct the historical consciousness of the entire state. Yet, religious consciousness, which usually spread across the borders of the states, might play a role in the building of the state at that time. I mean that the building of the state in Britain started well before the times of nation-state. At that time it was religious consciousness that served chiefly as a sort of social consciousness in support of state building. Thus the state sought support from the Anglican Church. State building in France may demonstrate a similar picture. In the Middle Ages, the Kingdom of France emerged from the western part of Charlemagne's Carolingian Empire known as West Francia. The kingdom was under the rule of the House of Capet in 987. The state was decentralized. The eleventh century marked the apogee of princely power at the expense of the king. Local regions like Normandy, Flanders or Languedoc enjoyed local authority comparable to kingdoms in all but name. After the Hundred Years' War that broke out in 1337, French nationalism gained momentum. Yet before France grew to be a modern nation-state, national or historical consciousness did not play a very prominent role in state formation because the course of the assimilation of culturally heterogeneous regions had not come to an end. Thus in a certain historical period the state apparently relied on support from the Roman Catholic Church in state building. The case of Russia can also be taken as an example. In Russian history the Russian Orthodox Church played the similar role. The fact is that after Russians began to embrace Christianity in the tenth century, the Russian Orthodox Church managed to establish the paradigm of symphonia in Kievan Rus and

Muscovite Russia in a period of time. The head of the state became the head of the church under the principle of Caesaropapism in a period of time and Russian Orthodox Church became part of the state machinery in a period of time. Russian Orthodox Church that propagated soteriological truth successfully established the friendship between God and humans through his grace and won many believers in a long historical period. The spiritual call from the Church to the Russian people became a support given to the unity of the state from time to time. National or historical consciousness might function to support state building. However, religious consciousness also played a special role. The Church especially functioned independently in the spiritual world. Though it gained independence several times in history and its legal independence was recognized again after the establishment of the Russian Federation in late twentieth century, the Church may play a role in state formation under certain circumstances. It is now one of the major symbols of the Russian state.

In addition, though the ruler may build the state through initial conquest, the ruler may not always act against the expectation of the masses in the building of the state if the common interest of all takes shape to a varying extent. This means that after the ruler gains ruling legitimacy, people may become loyal to the ruler. If other conditions for the formation of the state are not fulfilled or sufficient, the consciousness of loyalty to the head of the state may help maintain the unity of the state. As stated by Christian Witschel, in ancient Rome,

> it was quite natural for many inhabitants of the Roman Empire to see the emperor as a sort of godlike ruler; and it was the easiest way to confront such a superhuman being by offering it cultic worship. Right from the beginning of Augustus' sole rule, numerous cults for him sprang up throughout Asia Minor both on a provincial and on a municipal level.[13]

This particularly happened in Galatia. RG (Res Gestae) was inscribed in the temple in Ancyra. It was in all probability the center of this provincial cult.[14]

The king, or queen, or emperor, or empress, of a Western state or an Eastern state also symbolizes the state from medieval to modern times no matter whether he or she is the genuine power holder or a titular power holder. Russell writes that:

> In England, government profits much by the tradition of royalty. Victorian statesmen, even Mr. Gladstone, felt it their duty to the Queen to see it that she was never left without a Prime Minister. The duty of obedience to authority is still felt by many as a duty towards the sovereign. This is a decaying sentiment, but as it decays government becomes less stable, and dictatorships of the right or the left become more possible.[15]

I think that this is the reason why many countries still maintain the polity of constitutional monarchy in modern times. In Europe and Asia today there are still some countries that maintain time-honored constitutional monarchy. Citizens are loyal to the king or the queen.

If the masses no longer accept monarchy, a charismatic leader, regarded by the masses as a state hero, may also be strongly and vehemently supported and followed and then worshipped by the masses for the reason of the formation of the state. The feelings of the masses, originally attached to the monarch, may be then attached to the mass leader. Then this mass leader may successfully build a state. That is, if the masses no longer accept a monarch, they tend to support a mass leader. This mass leader may be very capable of building a powerful state. To put it another way, this mass leader may have saved ordinary people or may have made a great contribution to the revival of the nation. The masses worship him. Under these circumstances the mass leader may play a central role like a monarch in the building of the state albeit at the expense of weakening the construction of the system of political parties and the system of administration. The reason is that the leader is often charismatic, appealing directly to the masses of the grassroots level. Thus there are many historical cases showing that people build the authority of the regime on the basis of the authority of that supreme leader who successfully persuades the masses to support him. In history, the personal cult of Napoleon in France used to serve as an important basis for the building of the state because Napoleon, as the leader of the masses, used to arouse a social and political consciousness among the masses in support of the building of the state under the circumstances of that time. That is, the masses exalt, love and admire the charismatic leader who demonstrates a heroic image. He becomes a savior in the eyes of the masses. He instills his idea into the minds of the masses. The masses embrace the social and political consciousness disseminated by him. The masses unite around him. In the meantime, this mass leader and the masses exchange feelings in the interaction between him and the masses. The related consciousness becomes pervasive. Such consciousness functions as a medium in support of the linguistic communication that goes on between the leader and the masses and among the masses as well.

The masses also often worship a leader of the masses emerging in a revolution. The masses support and follow him vehemently. The reason is that this revolutionary leader achieves prominence and gains authority in the course of revolution. A state is usually built by this revolutionary leader. As a result, this revolutionary leader can directly symbolize the state. He is the founder of the state. He is also the incarnation of the state. The cohesion of the state is chiefly built on the basis of his personal authority among the masses particularly under the condition that the original legal system has been smashed in the revolution and the tradition of the society has been given up by the revolutionary masses. In the meantime the state apparatus is under the sole control of this revolutionary leader. He is the center of the politics of the state. All important officials of the government are appointed by him. He formulates the blueprint of state building. He guides the operation of the government. His leadership is the guarantee of the long-term building of the nation-state because the masses do not submit to any authority but him. Lenin and Mao among others in history are typical examples. The consciousness of worshipping a revolutionary leader is also a social and political consciousness in support of the building of the state. Given that a state is built on the basis of a revolution, the revolutionary leader who becomes the founder of the state is often exalted and admired by the masses. Their consciousness of worshipping the revolutionary leader sometimes becomes a social and political consciousness in support of the related linguistic communication and hence the building of the state.

All of these phenomena occur after the end of the era when the masses worship the monarch. But the masses may continue worshipping the supreme leader of the state in the similar way. This leader may function much like the monarch of the past. This view is not offered by me first. This view is originally offered by Russell. He writes that:

> Monarchy makes social cohesion easy, first, because it is not so difficult to feel loyalty to an individual . . . and secondly, because kingship, in its long history, has accumulated sentiments of veneration which no new institution can inspire. Where hereditary monarchy has been abolished, it has usually been succeeded, after a longer or shorter time, by some other form of one-man rule: tyranny in Greece, the Empire in Rome, Cromwell in England, Napoleons in France, Stalin and Hitler in our own day. Such men inherit a part of the feelings formerly attached to royalty.[16]

What is arguable is that the consciousness of worshipping or adoring the supreme leader of the state lies in the fact that the state is organized by a man. The related consciousness functions as a medium in support of linguistic communication in the formation of the state no matter whether this state is a monarchy or a republic.

Intellectuals may also be the said creators of consciousness. They create ideas and thoughts as entrusted by the society and these ideas and thoughts are embraced by the masses. Then these ideas and thoughts may serve as a basis for the dissemination of social and political consciousness. People feel close to each other because they share the same social and political consciousness. They realize that they are the same kind of people. They are tempted to devote themselves to the same cause. They may perform frequent linguistic communication for close mutual interaction. They tend to associate together. Then such consciousness, in turn, functions as a medium in support of linguistic communication in the formation of the state. Such consciousness also underpins the building of the state.

Such consciousness actually germinates along with the emergence of philosophy or literature or art or law or morality or others. Such consciousness may vary from state to state because of the unbalanced development of philosophy, literature, art, law and others. In some states philosophy flourishes. In some other states the literature and art reach a high level or a time-honored legal system takes shape. As such, the masses have the consciousness in relation to philosophy or literature and art or law. But generally speaking, such consciousness spreads invariably and comes to serve as a basis of building a related social and political consciousness. Though the so-called social and political consciousness consists of many parts, the social and political consciousness, stemming from philosophy, literature and art, law, morality and the like, is an important part. If, over the long term, the religious belief or the consciousness of worshipping the leader of the state does not play a major role in the formation of the state, the said consciousness, stemming from philosophy or literature and art or law or morality or the like, must play such a role instead. A certain social and political consciousness particularly underlies the formation of the state in modern times when God, or a traditional ruler or a mysterious or charismatic power holder no longer serves as a source of spirit. That is, if God loses his influence or religious cause no longer flourishes or if people refrain from engaging in the cult of personality of the state leader or if there are some other similar circumstances in the state, the consciousness, gained by the masses, in support of the formation of the state, may stem from some other sources, including philosophy, morality, law and others. For example, in some states the social and political consciousness, directly stemming from philosophy, plays an extraordinary role in the formation and growth of the state. Some philosophers may be construed as spiritual instructors. The building of the state relies on the support of a philosophical idea. In some other states, the spirit of law is very impressive. The building of the state may also rely on the consciousness directly emanating from the tradition of law that takes form in history. In short, in some states or in a certain period of time in the history of some states, the consciousness, stemming from certain values rather than the religious consciousness or the consciousness of worshipping the ruler or the leader, especially supports the building of the state. In pre-modern times religious consciousness might play an extraordinary role in the growth of the state. In medieval times the consciousness of worshipping the ruler might play a role in state building and in modern times the consciousness of worshipping the ruler or the leader may play a role in state building. But in all times, I believe, consciousness, stemming from philosophy or law or morality or literature and art, may also play the said role over the long term in some other states. Particularly, it plays a prominent role where national or historical consciousness fails to play a role as expected.

If we look at the role of consciousness stemming from philosophy or other forms of culture in support of the formation of the state as a medium described by us in this context in particular, we can find that the formation of each state in the world is also often due to the spread of a certain social and political consciousness that stems from philosophy or law or literature and art or morality. It is unlike national consciousness or historical consciousness. A state may not be formed because of a national or historical consciousness. Then it may be formed because of a social and political consciousness rather than national or historical consciousness. This judgment should be true all around the world. This judgment should not be wrong. No matter whether a state is an Eastern state or a Western state and no matter whether a state is an ancient state or a modern state, this judgment may be true. In short, the state should be mainly formed because of an existing social and political consciousness if the state is not built as supported by a strong national or historical consciousness.

If we have a look at the case of China, a typical Eastern state, we can see that in the long-term growth of this Eastern state in history what supported the growth of the state in China in the respect of consciousness was not national consciousness until the twentieth century. National consciousness played a very tiny role in state formation in China in early history though in modern times the state of China is very strongly buttressed by national consciousness. Historical consciousness plays a role in the formation of the state in China indeed. But my view is that historical consciousness plays a secondary role in the formation of the state in China. The role of philosophy, as a source of social and political consciousness, in the formation of the state, is very special in China. That is, China grew to be a mature state in ancient times not because of nationalism. China became a nation-state without national consciousness in ancient times. Historical consciousness plays a role therein indeed. But this role is not as powerful as the role of the social and political consciousness emanating from philosophy. Though rulers made their greatest effort to build their states in ancient China by force in their conquest, social and political consciousness played a more important role over the long term. During the Period of Warring States, princes built their kingdoms by using coercion. Wars resulted in the formation of various kingdoms. Elites, such as politicians, generals and prestigious well-educated advisers, were very likely to leave their jobs in one kingdom in order to take another job in another kingdom because they were not supposed to be loyal to any specific kingdom due to patriotism. Following the unification of China realized by the Qin First Emperor, the ruler maintained the unity of the empire with an iron hand in a short period of time. Then Confucianism, offered mainly by Confucius to accentuate the role of morality in the building of the society and the state and the importance of keeping social hierarchy, began playing an essential role in the construction of social and political consciousness. Emperor Wu of Han (156-87 BC) endorsed and approved it as the state philosophy and the code of ethics for his empire. As the state orthodox ideology, Confucianism was proactively propagated by the ruling class as Confucian classics were taught to future administrators and ordinary people as well. The related reforms launched by the ruler helped him to build Imperial China because now a strong social and political consciousness could serve as a spiritual basis for such a large state. Though states were replaced one by one in Chinese history, the ruling class built almost each state as supported by Confucianism, except the states occasionally built in the principle advocated by the Legalist school. Today Confucianism is still a social and political thought embraced by many Chinese. Social and political consciousness plays an extraordinary role.

If we have a look at the role of social and political consciousness in the formation of the state in the West, we can also see that this judgment is tenable. The spread of liberalism in the West in early modern times is a case in point. This case is that ordinary people desired to free themselves from the obsolete feudal despotism. Some leading thinkers disseminated liberalism and ordinary people gradually embraced it. Liberalism emphasized the freedoms of people under the governance of the state. It also emphasized the principle that the government should protect the private property. John Locke, an English philosopher, is credited as one of the main liberal thinkers in England in early modern times. As in medieval times religious consciousness might support the building of the states, normally kingdoms, we can argue that in modern times social and political consciousness, stemming from philosophy or others, plainly supports the building of nation-states. It is neither national consciousness nor historical consciousness. It played a prominent role in the formation of the modern state in Britain, France and the United States among other nation-states in early modern times. The United States of America may be the best example that can be used to throw light on this case. If we assume that national or historical consciousness plays a role in the formation of the United States, this role, in my opinion, is not so prominent. In the making of the United States national consciousness plays a minor role because immigrants, coming across the Atlantic Ocean from Europe to settle down in North America, have various different national backgrounds. They come from Great Britain, France, Germany, Italy, Spain, Ireland, the Netherlands, Poland, Austria and many other countries. Unlike Germany or Italy whose nationals keep very strong nationalist consciousness because they are of the same nationality and speak the same language generation after generation, the United States witnesses the fact that its citizens still carry the imprint of their original nations in a period of time in history. It proves unlikely to generate a strong national consciousness within the United States. When North America announced its independence, people, living on this land, seemed no longer to regard Great Britain as their own country. They regarded Great Britain as a foreign country. If people in North America were assumed to have kept strong national consciousness at that time, they should not have separated themselves from Great Britain. The state is described as a melting pot because after each batch of new immigrants steps on the land of the United States they may not embrace the national consciousness of this new country so quickly until a period of time has passed. The historical consciousness of the American people is not comparatively impressive either because the United States of American is, in some sense, still a young nation-state. Its history is still very short. Thus, in my opinion, what plays a prominent role in the formation of the state in North America is the social and political consciousness that excludes the said national or historical consciousness to a certain extent. The social and political consciousness based on the idea of equality and liberty plays an extraordinary role in the growth of the United States. Americans, original residents and newcomers alike, are moved by the Declaration of Independence that proclaims that all are created equal. All citizens have their dignity no matter whether they are rich or poor. Although racial discrimination used to be a major social problem and slave-owning system used to go on in the South, the social and political consciousness based on those ideas of equality and liberty does not fail to play its role in the making of the United States. The formation of such social and political consciousness may be influenced by the special geography of North America or the special social structure that took form naturally in North America. There is, however, no embedded or deep-rooted social hierarchy in North America because no feudal system has ever been established there. All begin to compete on equal footing. In politics despotic thought has never emerged. Thus the social and political consciousness, based mainly on equality, liberty and democracy, is widely embraced by millions of people and hence functions as an important foundation for the building of this great country.

The truth that each state is very often built on the basis of a social and political consciousness can be further indicated by the fact that whenever an existing social and political consciousness is in crisis, another social and political consciousness will fill in the vacuum. In early modern times radical liberalism that developed in France was criticized by some thinkers who advocated the values of gradual social evolution and emphasized the importance of maintaining social order, tradition and morality. Thus conservatism emerged. It, in some sense, intended to repair the shortcomings of liberalism. It accentuated traditional institutions in the context of culture or society. It advocated the continuity of the social or political system. Edmund Burke, an 18th-century thinker who opposed the French Revolution, but supported the American Revolution, is regarded as one of the main theorists of conservatism in Great Britain in the 1790s.

Likewise, in early modern times, liberalism became a basis for the development of liberal capitalism and the development of liberal capitalism resulted in the appearance of wide social issues particularly characteristic of capitalist exploitation of the manufacturing factories motivated to reap profits from the market. Then socialism, an idea that stressed social equality and liberty from class oppression, soon spread in Europe and elsewhere. Henri de Saint-Simon, one of the founders of what would later be called "Utopian Socialism", made the term "socialism" widely known throughout Europe. Then Karl Marx expounded his idea about "socialism" as communism. Then the Bolshevik Revolution in 1917 symbolized the first major attempt made by humans to build a modern state on the basis of the principle of socialism. As a large population belonged to the working class in a certain historical period in many states, socialism used to be influential. Many intellectuals propagated the socialist idea in their own country. Socialist movement throve in almost all countries in Europe in the nineteenth century. It also spread to the states outside Europe in the twentieth century.

We can regard the emergence of conservatism and socialism in the nineteenth century as an attempt made by humans to replace liberalism or to repair the shortcomings of liberalism in Europe. In Western Europe the rise of conservatism in the nineteenth century was a reaction to the growth of liberalism, but it did not oppose all liberal ideas. Later, in the twentieth century, socialism gained momentum. Socialism accepted some of the principles of liberalism, leading to the growth of democratic socialism. As far as Asia is concerned, conservatism was originally the embedded social and political consciousness in the traditional society. Liberalism overwhelmed conservatism because democracy replaced despotism in many Asian countries. Later, the socialist idea became prevalent. And then socialism tended to be combined with traditional social and political consciousness because it failed to function, as an independent medium, in support of the growth and the progress of the state over the long term. One case in point is that in China socialism temporarily replaced Confucianism as a major social and political consciousness in support of the building of the state in the twentieth century. But as the practice of socialism failed in the economic domain, socialism, as a main social and political consciousness in support of the building of the state, has declined. Confucianism may revive because Chinese socialism tends to be combined with Confucianism. It is sometimes called Confucian socialism. Liberalism may also be imported from abroad. At least, economic liberalism characteristic of market economy has been accepted by many today in China. Economic liberalism even becomes a consensus of the Chinese people. It also tends to be combined with economic liberalism characteristic of market economy. It is sometimes called market socialism. The authorities have adjusted social and political consciousness in support of the building of the state. This historical process indicates that without such an applicable social and political consciousness, people may not build the state successfully. The reason is that people will not unite unless they share the same applicable social and political consciousness.

The reason is that all or the majority of the citizens can agree to the idea stemming from this philosophy or some other kind, and then they will maintain a consciousness that leads all to have the same goal and pursue the same cause. Such social and political consciousness ensures the cohesion of the society and the state. One example, showing this situation, is that in social life people may hold different stances toward a social issue because they have different social backgrounds or in political life people may disagree to a specific policy implemented by the government and people may support different political parties, but all may insist on the same principle in the governance of the state and all may have the same social and political consciousness. All may embrace the idea of freedoms and rights of the citizens or the idea of social equality, for example. As all largely have the same social and political consciousness, such social and political consciousness can serve as a basis for the building of the state. Then all citizens see that they have the same interest. They unite. Then they must perform frequent linguistic communication to pursue their common cause. Thus, people witness that they can buttress the unity of the state. So in each of those states people may give different political opinions concerning the governance of the state, but all agree that the major principle in the governance of the state should not be violated. The freedoms and rights of each citizen may be respected as long as these freedoms and rights are exercised according to law in the state in which liberalism prevails, for example. That is, people can be allowed to make their comments that a policy is good or is not good or a policy is fair or is unfair in the states under the domination of liberalism. The government is not the guardian of truth. In some other states under the domination of socialism, the authorities may also implement a scheme of re-distributing income. Thus, sticking to the same principle of governing the state lays the groundwork for the formation of a kind of unified social and political consciousness. Then people, sharing such social and political consciousness, feel close to each other. They tend to realize frequent interaction with each other. They keep on performing linguistic communication with each other for cooperation. So in today's world people usually firmly unite with one another in each state. In history people, upholding different social and political consciousnesses, used to be involved in a civil war. Today a civil war seldom breaks out because, usually, all have the same or similar social and political consciousness. Though different groups of people may eye economic interest, the social and political consciousness proves crucial because if people have the same social and political consciousness concerning the governance of the state, they will be able to resolve the disputes about the distribution of economic interest through a political process under the guidance of that social and political consciousness. As long as people have the similar or the same social and political consciousness, people can ensure the unity of the state ultimately.

As such, I argue that social and political consciousness may stem from a specific source. Such consciousness may originate from the idea advocated by a philosopher or a lawyer or a writer or a politician. Such consciousness may sometimes be or not be supported by the authorities. Such consciousness may stem from tradition, custom, mores, law, literature and art, etc. Such social and political consciousness may also emanate from commerce, agricultural and industrial production or financial activities. Social and political consciousness may often be disseminated through education or mass media or in the form of culture. If such consciousness is embraced by all or the majority in the society or the state, it will function in support of the linguistic communication among all. Then, their action will bolster the cohesion of the state. For example, poets create poems to exchange feelings among all within a nation. Plenty of people recite poems. They memorize poems. They communicate with each other by reading those poems. Those poems may disseminate an idea. Likewise, writers write novels. Novels may disseminate an idea to the great masses of the people. Then it follows that many people near and far may embrace this idea. Operas, dramas, and plays may realize the same goal. Philosophical books that disseminate certain philosophical ideas may function in the similar way. People embrace the similar idea because a well-known philosophy spreads widely. Laws implemented everywhere may keep a spirit that is adhered to and cherished by people. As law is crucial for the realization of justice, people embrace the spirit of law. Social and political consciousness may also spread among merchants because commerce allows for people to communicate with all others on a large scale. Given that this consciousness is instilled into the minds of many people, such consciousness may function, as a medium, in support of the linguistic communication that goes on among all because each accepts this consciousness and each is enlightened and encouraged by this consciousness. Thus people, upholding the same consciousness, become the same sort of people. They unite. They build their state.

Though in modern times all states are described as nation-states, the role, played by national or historical consciousness, may vary from state to state or from time to time. I do not deny that in many cases national or historical consciousness plays an essential or critical role in the formation of the state over the long term. But I should also point out that, in some states or in a certain period of time in some states, it seems that people are prone to strengthen the role of the stated social and political consciousness rather than the stated national or historical consciousness. This is mainly because some states are potentially troubled by their own internal national issues. These states may be formed on the basis of the amalgamation of several nations or ethnic groups. In history some nations or ethnic groups are conquered and then absorbed. As a result, certain ethnic groups of people are strong nationalists. If people emphasize national consciousness, the emphasis may not lead to the strengthening of the solidarity of the people as expected because a certain ethnic group of people are thinking of self-determination. Think of those states in which the states are formed by several different nations or ethnic groups such as the United Kingdom, Spain, Belgium, Canada and some other countries. When people mention history, some stories or narratives may bolster historical consciousness of the people indeed. Yet some other stories or narratives may remind certain ethnic groups of people of their original status of independence. The narration of history may not always work effectively toward the goal of strengthening the solidarity of the people. For example, some people of a certain ethnic group may be reminded by the narrative of a piece of history that their ancestors were absorbed into the country by force. But the role of social and political consciousness in the formation of the state is powerful or effective indeed because certain ideas, as the sources of social and political consciousness, are very constructive and reasonable particularly in some advanced states. The ideas of human rights, liberty, democracy and other humanist ideas, advanced by people since the times of Enlightenment, are almost widely accepted and upheld by the great masses of the people. People in the state may not be always equally aroused by national consciousness or historical consciousness, but they are often equally aroused by the leading social and political consciousness. Though sometimes national or historical consciousness may not play the expected role in state formation, social and political consciousness suffices to lay a solid spiritual foundation for the building of the state. This situation indicates that the so-called consciousness can be divided into different categories. We can divide it into the categories of national, historical, and social and political consciousness. Each consciousness may function independently in some cases or at some time. And in some cases social and political consciousness may have no direct bearing on national or historical consciousness.

In short, we can regard the consciousness of various kinds as a medium in support of the related linguistic communication. As the related linguistic communication underpins the formation of the state, consciousness also supports the formation of the state. It is easy for people to reach a consensus on the rationality of a certain social and political consciousness because people submit to reason amid the competition of different consciousnesses. It is easier for people to embrace a unified social and political consciousness than to perform linguistic communication for mutual interaction within the state because people are the animals of reason. That consciousness is based on reason. In the meantime, people can be educated. People can be persuaded. Consequently, social and political consciousness can function, as a medium, in support of the linguistic communication in the building of the state. People gain such social and political consciousness that will remain in their brains over the long term or permanently. Such consciousness can function as a powerful medium in support of linguistic communication that goes on among all. Sometimes building the processes of linguistic communication that goes on among all encounters difficulties. Social and political consciousness, embraced by all, may bolster the related linguistic communication because people, sharing the same consciousness, tend to perform linguistic communication with each other more frequently.

This means that people unite because they share the same idea. They share the same idea because they have the same consciousness, social and political or otherwise. Amid the interaction between consciousness and linguistic communication consciousness plays a role as a medium. In the meantime, people spread consciousness in the process of linguistic communication. In the process of linguistic communication, consciousness plays a role behind the related process of linguistic communication. Then it follows that consciousness functions as a medium in support of the related linguistic communication because such linguistic communication also needs the support of consciousness. Consciousness ultimately serves as a basis for the formation of the state because it facilitates the related linguistic communication and that linguistic communication is a foundation for the formation and growth of the state.

Notes

1. Wilhelm von Humboldt, *On Language: The Diversity of Human Language-Structure and its Influence on the Mental Development of Mankind, translated by Peter Heath* (Cambridge: Cambridge University Press, 1988), 154.
2. Jean Jacques Rousseau, *On the Origin of Language,* translated by John H. Moran and Alexander Gode (New York: Frederick Ungar Publishing Co., Ltd, 1966), 5.
3. Carl Choachim Friedrich, *Man and His Government, An Empirical Theory of Politics*, (New York: McGraw-Hill Book Company, Inc.,1963), 559.
4. Paul Ricoeur, *Interpretation Theory: Discourse and the Surplus of Meaning* (Fort Worth, Texas: The Texas Christian University Press, 1976), 63.
5. Robert F. Berkhofer, Jr, *Beyond the Great Story: History as Text and Discourse* (Cambridge, Massachusetts: The Belknap Press of Harvard University Press, 1997), 45.
6. Ibid. 172.
7. Arthur Schopenhauer, "Additional Remarks on the Doctrine of the Suffering of the World" in Parerga and Paralipomena, *Short Phislophical Essays*, translated by E.E. J. Payne (Oxford: Oxford University Press, 1974), Vol.2 Chap. XI, Sec. 150; cited from Michael Allen Fox, Understanding Peace: A Comprehensive Introduction (New York: Routledge, 2014), 52.
8. P. Horwitz, *The Sources and Limits of Freedom of Religion in A Liberal Democracy*; Section 2(a) and Beyond (1996) 54 *U Toronto Fac L Rev*

1, 48–9; cited from Rex Ahdar and Ian Leigh, *Religious Freedom in the Liberal State* (Oxford: Oxford University Press, 2005), 54.

9. Albert Victor Murray, *The State and the Church in a Free Society* (London: Cambridge University Press, 1958), 33–34.

10. Jack Goody, *The Logic of Writing and the Organization of Society* (Cambridge: Cambridge University Press, 1986), 31–32.

11. Please see: Baruch Spinoza, *Theological Political Treatise*, translated by Samuel Shirley (Indianapolis: Hackett Publishing Company, 1998), 195–196.

12. Bertrand Russell, *Power* (New York: W.W. Norton & Company, Inc., 1938), 146.

13. Christian Witschel, The *Res Gestea Divi Augusti* and the Roman Empire, in Fritz-Heiner Mutschler and Achim Mittag (ed.), *Conceiving the Empire China and Rome Compared* (Oxford: Oxford University Press, 2008), 252.

14. Ibid., 252–253.

15. Russell, *Power*, 232–233.

16. Ibid., 233–234.

Part Two
Language and State Organization

Introduction

In Part One, we have explored the extension of linguistic communication in the formation of the state. We have discussed how various media play a role in extending linguistic communication that underpins the formation of the state. We have pointed out that various media extend the distance of linguistic communication and media construct the mutual communication between one another on a large scale. Such an evolution underlies the growth of the state. Then I argue that such an evolution results in a change in the linguistic interaction between one another. Immediacy between one another disappears gradually, and humans begin to engage in their new mutual interaction. Such interaction is manifold. Then we see that in the primitive society the mutual interaction of tribal people was simple while in the civilized society the mutual interaction of the members of the state is complex. Language always functions in conjunction with various media. Then I would like to argue that armed with various media, language even enables people to realize a flexible and diverse mutual interaction. Language substitutes widely for behavior in the process of communication and then enables people to impart more information, to bring clarity to complicated thought, to display diversified attitudes, to announce some plans in advance and to forecast any action. Language dominates such an interaction. Language plays a role not only in people's social life but also in their political life. People organize their state in such linguistic communication.

In sum, any physical interaction between one person and another is, in the ultimate sense, like that of animals. People are likely to believe that humans are social or political animals. Humans, however, have distinguished themselves from other animals from the day of starting using language onward. They, later, not only interact with one another physically but also linguistically. In their physical interaction they rely on physical proximity. But in their linguistic interaction they may not need to rely on physical proximity. The role, played by language together with media, makes the community the state. Thus the mode of mutual interaction between one another in their society becomes the mode of mutual interaction shown in their state. Linguistic communication even becomes the constant mutual interaction of humans. This mutual interaction is the basic element of the formation of the state. If we assume that there is a difference between the primitive society and the civilized society, this is the difference. This difference is that humans formed their tribe on the basis of kinship. By contrast, humans form their state on the basis of linguistic communication. In linguistic communication, humans construct their mutual relationship in a new way. A new relationship replaces the old. This results in the formation of the state. The key is that humans, communicating by using language, extend the distance of communication to the far reaches of their community. Then they realize their mutual interaction on a large scale. Realizing their mutual interaction on a large scale, they also diversify their mutual interaction. They gradually engage in various types of mutual interaction. These types of mutual interaction underlie the organization of the state. Looking into these various types of interaction realized by humans in the civilized society ought to be a new way for us to get an insight into the organization of the state. These various types of interaction should be the various ways of organizing the state. We need to know how these types of interaction enable people to organize the state. These types of interaction are searching and providing information, giving and accepting interpretations, expressing and reacting to attitudes, making and accepting promises, and issuing and obeying commands. I am going to delineate them one by one as follows.

Chapter Five

Information

1. Search

First of all, I am going to explicate how people get and provide information. In this section we discuss how people get information. When people get information, they often realize their goal through their search for information. The search, defined by the author, is an effort made by people to learn about new things in the new context. Then searching information is a phenomenon occurring in the interaction between humans and their surrounding world or between one person and another. People realize such an interaction mainly as the members of the state. The search for information means that one commits the act of learning about what he may not know by himself. He usually has to use language. He performs linguistic communication. Tribal people might not need such an interaction. This is because humans formed their community in the outset on the basis of kinship and kinship was an essential element of the formation of the society. They were not necessarily required to use language. Tribal people usually performed mutual communication over short distances as they kept on performing behavioral communication.[1] The community was characterized by immediacy between one another. But since the birth of language, humans have extended the distance of mutual communication, an evolution that breaks immediacy between one another. Extending the distance of communication then allows people to communicate on a large scale. They form a large community. Kinship attenuates. People form their state in which all do not necessarily belong to the same original tribe. A change takes place in the method of communication. That is, in the tribe humans merely communicated with one another by using their sensory organs within their view and hearing distance. They communicated on a small scale. Now they no longer always communicate on such a small scale in the state. They perform linguistic communication on a very large scale. Then a person can communicate with another person who is far away. He is also enabled to receive information from another person who is far away. That all are able to search information on a very large scale lays a foundation for the organization of the state as any interaction realized by all with all may be aimed at the search for information across the state and the organization of the state relies on the circulation of the related information. The reason is that the spread of information increases the size of the community. This is because all need to interact with all. In the mutual interaction between one another, people require the supply of necessary information across the community. Thus, that all search information across the state is an activity that underlies the organization of the state because the organization of the state is sometimes based on the exchange of information among all. All seek such information and interact with all in order that all can know all and all can interact with all. Thus people guarantee the unity of the state.

In other words, we suppose that each member of the tribe received information in person in order to realize satisfactory interactions that maintained the community in the primitive society. All tribal people must interact with one another in order to play a role in the formation of the tribe though researchers may almost neglect this role. Humans are social animals. Their self-preservation depends on a sort of environment in which each of them creates objectively an essential condition for the preservation and growth of all others. Each is connected with all others this way or that way or directly or indirectly. One of the basic methods for each of them to be connected with all others is to perform communication. The distance of communication, performed by all with all, dictates the size of the community because people who do not perform communication regularly or constantly do not form a community. Yet since humans started performing linguistic communication, they have extended the distance of communication and hence increased the size of their community. They have dissolved their tribes and formed their state. Of course, people may still often perform face-to-face communication within each state. But such communication no longer suffices for them to realize all mutual interactions. They often need to realize linguistic interaction with one another. They, forming a large community, may not always be able to perform face-to-face communication due to the disappearance of physical proximity. They begin to perform both spoken and written communication. A person may provide information to another person who is far away. Information tends to be in shortage as people are unable to obtain it within view and hearing distance at any time. Thus, since the formation of the state, each person has often depended on the information provided by another person instead of the first-hand information. Conveying information through a medium is a process in which one provides information to the other.

A person may provide a piece of necessary information to a second person and this second person may further provide this piece of information to a third person. Such human-chain linguistic communication is significant for the organization of the state. In the meantime, one may provide any piece of information through written communication in which one does not keep in touch with the other face-to-face. Human-chain linguistic communication and written communication or direct communication in writing are combined to support the growth of the state.

Given that in the state people convey information by using language, they extend the reach of linguistic communication. Any major event of the state should be known to the citizens even though this event occurs in a place at a good distance off. People no longer depend on their direct experience to learn about this event. No matter whether the information is true or false, if one conveys such information, it may influence the behavior of other people in that state. In other words, in a state people rely on the provision of information and the provision of information is a variable. A person hopes to learn about the events occurring across the state, and his relationship with the state is dynamic. The state is dynamic, so is the reaction of a person to the state. A person is supposed to keep his interaction with all others within the state. He always tries to gain all necessary information about the state. He tends to search for information by dint of linguistic communication such as the description of an event given by another person. In the era when a person lives in a small community, he primarily relies on his direct experience to learn about the surrounding world. After the expansion of their surrounding world, a person more often than ever searches information by using language.

People then change their way of searching information. This is also a way of their mutual interaction. This way of their mutual interaction is also part of the formation of a large community. This community is usually a state. The use of language is essential.

That is, in the process of the development from the tribe, the primitive society, to the state, today's civilized society, a person is increasingly relying on the use of language in general and on writing in particular to learn about the expanded surrounding world. The community grows large and the structure of this community becomes complex. Smooth linguistic communication often depends on the development of media. The development of media allows for all to communicate effectively with all within the state. People gain necessary information within the state in order to interact effectively with all. As a result, people organize the state on the basis of the interaction of all with all.

A person always lives in the environment structured by distance. There is always a distance between him and the state. Information he needs is always in shortage. He needs others to provide information to him so as to shorten the distance between him and the state. A person may need to learn about what others nearby are doing because any activity of others nearby may change his living environment and condition. Every person may need to gain information from any other person. Thus various basic media function to support people's linguistic communication so as to enable them to gain necessary information. Unlike human communication within the tribe, linguistic communication within the state is unbalanced. Communication within the state relies on certain media. These media recover the balance of communication. Thus these media play a crucial role in the creation of certain essential conditions for the linguistic communication needed by people to gain and share information. They include the following three kinds of media.

First, cities are media. Within a state the density of population varies from the urban area to the rural area. The urban area plays an important role in the organization of the state. The urban area creates a condition for people to perform frequent linguistic communication for the purpose of searching and providing needed information. This is because the city is densely populated, whereas the rural area is not. Urbanites reside close to each other. Their houses are adjacent to one another. They construct streets, giving convenience to all who travel within the city. They have more chances of communicating with each other. This is the reason that craftsmen move to the cities and business-men follow them, as already mentioned earlier. The men of letters also cluster in the city. Thus message, knowledge, idea, thought, belief, history, art and technology are more widely spread and shared in the urban area than in the rural area. Thus in terms of linguistic communication that goes on across the state, such linguistic communication goes on mainly in the cities. When cities grow, the state grows. In ancient times, each city was a state in Greece, as already mentioned earlier. In medieval times some cities were also states in the regions of today's Italy and Germany. When a nation-state emerges, the state grows chiefly because of the growth of the cities. If the rural area also develops, it is often due to the radiation of the functions of the cities. So some-times in history the decline of a major city means the decline of a state and the prosperity of a major city means the prosperity of a state. The Renaissance of Italy and some other countries is actually the Renaissance of the cities. So Paul Johnson notes that in the late Middle Ages, wealth was produced in greater quantities than ever and was often concentrated in cities specializing in the new occupations of large-scale commerce and banking, like Venice and Florence. Then wealthy people patronized literature and arts. Sovereigns, popes and princes also joined them to tax the new wealth of their subjects. A number of distinguished scholars also brought many important manuscripts in classical Greek to Italy, escaping from the Turkish rule in the wake of the fall of Constantinople in 1453. They stayed in cities such as Florence. Then the imitation of antiquity became the fashion.[2] This was the Renaissance in literature and scholarship. The Renaissance, the cultural rebirth of some of the literary, philosophical and artistic grandeur of ancient Greece and Rome, revived the city as the center of human activity. The Renaissance paved a way for the growth of those Italian cities in the years to come in the capitalist era. Those cities were either states or the mainstay of each of those states. Hellenic studies also spread to the cities of other states in the West, and humanist spirit also developed there, laying a preliminary foundation for the growth of the European states in early modern times.

Second, the men of letters and other educated people are media. In this case the state appears so much at variance with the tribe. In the tribe the structure of spoken communication, performed by all with all, is basically balanced. In the tribe no one receives any education in a sense we use in the civilized society. Yet along with the formation of the state, education, received by people, varies. Some people are well-educated while others less-educated. People receive varying education for various reasons. Because of this, a change takes place in the structure of linguistic communication that goes on in the state. Such structure is characteristic of unbalance. Well-educated people are able to communicate on a large scale while less-educated people are only able to communicate on a small scale. Well-educated people are able to take initiative to perform linguistic communication across the state, whereas less-educated people are unable to do so. Thus linguistic communication is often performed by the men of letters and other educated people, such as theologians, philosophers, historians, writers, artists, and scientists, rather than other kinds of people across the state. Sometimes the unity of the state is maintained by those who are able to take initiative to perform linguistic communication throughout the state. The reason is that in the organization of the state all need to communicate with all in order to realize their mutual interaction and cooperation. Some less-educated people use spoken language only. Spoken language may be a dialect or a regional language. Such language may not be in use across the state. Some other less-educated people may be able to read limited kinds of books such as textbooks or novels. They can interact with well-educated people. But they are unable to take initiative to perform linguistic communication throughout the state. Well-educated people are able to do so because they are able to write. Writing means taking initiative in using written language. Written language functions on a large scale. Books, written by people, become media for communication across the society. Those who produce cultural products needed by ordinary people are able to take initiative to perform linguistic communication with all. Those cultural products are media used by their creators in linguistic communication throughout the state. Thus, people, unable to create media, are unable to take initiative to perform linguistic communication throughout the state. Thus those who create cultural products, in fact, perform linguistic communication across the state on behalf of all. Such linguistic communication underpins the organization of the state. They are media. Thus, people seek information through those media in the state.

Third, the commercialized processes of production are media. Businesses operate these media. They run in support of linguistic communication that goes on throughout the state. The reason is that linguistic communication must be able to reach the far-flung corners. An individual person is unable to perform such linguistic communication. Businesses can realize this goal. Motivated by profits, entrepreneurs operate media as their business. They may gain those desired profits because the related linguistic communication, performed to supply information, knowledge, idea, belief, and entertainment, is demanded by all. As such demand is massive, entrepreneurs are strongly motivated to found and operate their enterprises. After a writer writes a novel, an entrepreneur operates a publishing house to publish this novel. Without a publishing house, such a writer cannot realize his goal of communicating with all within the state. If a newspaper is to be published, it must be published by an enterprise. A plant is built. Printing equipment is purchased. News reporters and editors are engaged. Some staff members, in charge of distributing newspapers, are recruited. In the meantime, a large number of readers support this business. Thus printing factories usually run for a commercial purpose. Likewise, people found radio stations to supply information to all across the state. Advertisement service is the source of income. It supports the operation of a radio station. The radio station is founded by an enterprise unless it is founded by the government as a non-profit institution. But usually a radio station needs to be operated as a business. The commercialized process of production or operation is one of the important media in support of the linguistic communication that goes on across the state. Entrepreneurs can invest in a business so as to provide a medium able to facilitate linguistic communication for various purposes and they get profits in serving readers and audiences. Both entrepreneurs and consumers cooperate in support of the linguistic communication that goes on throughout the state. Without capitalist business operation one can hardly realize such kind of linguistic communication. Thus capitalist business operation plays a role in the organization of the state that needs multifarious forms of linguistic communication as well as a variety of powerful media in support of those forms of linguistic communication.

Then people extend the reach of linguistic communication. They build and organize the state. The state becomes a large community. The state is large in population and area. This state is a community that highlights the diversity of people. In this community people need to learn different working skills. Different people need to do different jobs as a career. People also need professional knowledge for the governance of the society and the production of spiritual products needed by the society. People need to realize the division of labor. Specifically, since people form a large community, they cannot discover and offer their value unless they do a unique and specific job. Thus, their value becomes the social value. Then, in order to realize this purpose, they need specific or professional or different information. The reason is that people do not seek the same information across the state. They only seek specific or professional or different information across the state. Such information may not be provided in a local area. The more professional the information, the larger the area in which the related information is sought. Like the situation in which the division of labor cannot be realized unless the extent of the market is large, the large community provides the related specific or professional or different information. This is a complex society distinct from a simple society. Assuming that the tribe is a simple society, the state is a complex one. Thus the study of the exchange of information in the state warrants our attention paid particularly to the need of professional information in the organization of the state. We can classify such information into three types as follows.

First, a type of such information is the information sought by people in the domain of governing the community. Since the community, such as a tribe, is small in the beginning and the community grows large gradually, we can believe that the governance of the community is not professional in the outset. Then people professionalize the method of governing their community step by step due to the fact that they need to govern the community that grows large. They need to govern effectively the community that grows large. The governance of the state is unlike the governance of the tribe. People govern the tribe according to common sense. The governance of a tribe is, in some sense, similar to the governance of a big family. The tribes are governed by chiefs prior to the formation of the state. All the tribes are governed according to common sense. The governance of the state, however, needs to be professionalized due to the fact that people need professional knowledge and skill in governing a large community. The state is initially formed due to the formation of a regime. The regime is usually built by the conqueror. The conqueror must gain some knowledge and skill of governing the state. He may engage some advisors to give him some professional advices in governing the state. Historians may write books telling the ruler how to rule the state and the ruler is tempted to read those books. If the ruler engages some assistants, these assistants should also have some knowledge and skill of governing the state. Under democracy, politicians, holding state power, also have certain professional knowledge about the governance of the state. In addition, in the beginning the officials of the regime might not be professionals because these officials were small in number and they were often the retainers of the ruler. The state was organized in the method of organizing the society in the outset because the organization of the state was primarily based on the social intercourse realized by the ruler with his retainers. At that time, services, provided by the state to ordinary people, were very limited. The services of such kind might only be limited to the maintenance of social order and the defense of the state. But in view of the long-term evolution of the state witnessed by us in the West, we find that the state grows large in population and area and nation-state emerges. Then public communication develops, leading to the formation of the mass society. People establish democracy later. Then the authorities come under the pressure to increase services provided to the masses. The result is that the state engages a large number of civil servants. Most of them are not recruited among the retainers or the friends of the power holder of the state. The state recruits them from the labor market. Then a professional standard is formulated to recruit qualified civil servants. The decrees and laws, promulgated by the government, display a professional standard. People turn to governing the state in a professional way. Then the government also shares information with the masses in a professional way. This means that the government cannot govern the state effectively unless the power holders govern the state in a professional way. For example, making a law, the state may invite jurists to give advices. Issuing a decree, the state may invite the experienced advisers of administration to give their opinions. Ordinary people also need to learn some knowledge about the governance of the state and the management of public affairs.

Second, another type of information is the information sought by people in the economic domain. Such information is no longer generic information, but professionalized information. Professionalizing such information accompanies the growth of the community in size from the very beginning. I mean that we can believe that the starting point of this process is the dissolution of tribes. Thanks to an increase in the size of the community in the process of state formation, the division of labor develops. People gradually engage in professional work to make a living. As a result, they need professional information. This is different from the situation faced by tribal people. In the tribe all members of the tribe normally seek and obtain the same information in their mutual interaction and in their production. They usually do the same jobs. If they do not do the same jobs on a rare occasion, they may not always do different jobs. Primitives may do a couple of different jobs, but these jobs are simple. It is simple to learn to do a different job. Their division of labor is the division of labor along age and sex lines only. Thus, all have easy access to information, including simple knowledge, if anyone wants to do a different job. But in the civilized society, people are gradually required to do professional jobs. They are required to get certain professional information. This means that certain information is not needed by all but by a portion of people only. So along with the growth of the state, people increase the size of the community and the population of the community increases, too. In the meantime the supply of professional information increases. An increase in the supply of information is often the steady increase in the supply of professional information. The supply of generic information needed by all may remain unchanged, but the supply of professional information increases greatly. As the community grows by relying on the development of the division of labor, people supply professional information in the various processes of linguistic communication. People perform linguistic communication to supply various types of professional information in support of the growth of the state. Specifically, in the primitive society people may be hunters and gatherers. As hunters they hunt wild animals including beasts. The wild animals, hunted by a tribe, may be of several kinds. But we can believe that since primitives reside in a small area, the wild animals, hunted by them, may be of limited kinds. For example, people, living in a mountainous area, may only hunt bears. In another case we can see that people, residing along a local river, only catch fish from the river. If people are gatherers, their job is simple, too. Information, needed by people, is simple. So within a tribe people supply simple information to each other for production. By contrast, in the state people do complicated jobs. In this large community people engage in diversified production due to the division of labor. Thus, people do not always do the same job. People supply various different kinds of information through linguistic communication. As the goods of a large quantity are made and the services of a large quantity are provided, the supply of information is diversified. People are often in need of a certain kind of information. A mason, for example, builds houses. Therefore, people now do not build houses by themselves. Instead, they engage a mason to build houses for them. The mason should be a professional. He has professional knowledge, but he has acquired this knowledge by learning. This knowledge may be only provided by another mason who is in another place. People build the houses by using knowledge, which is professionalized information, in some sense.

Third, another type of such information is the information sought and provided by people in the cultural domain. Particularly, some information, sought and provided by people, is cultural information. This concerns the exchange of feelings of all in many cases. Tribal people might also exchange feelings in early times. All members of the tribe might keep in touch with one another in the form of exchanging feelings. The exchange of feelings allowed for people to keep emotional ties. At that time people exchanged feelings face-to-face. For example, they might dance, a form of exchanging feelings. In the civilized society the state is the regular community. In the state those who dance in order to exchange feelings become professional dancers. Similarly, people may tell stories and tales to each other in the tribe. In the state some people, telling stories and tales, become novelists and essayists. People might sing songs in the tribe. In the state some people become singers singing songs in the theaters. If we argue that the exchange of feelings in the tribe is a face-to-face interaction, the exchange of feelings in the state may need to develop in more forms. Thus, plays are staged in the theater or in the open. Some people especially engage in writing dramas. Some other people are professional actors and actresses. Some writers and artists of the folk society may also provide their works for the exchange of feelings. But they usually exchange feelings in a local area. They perform linguistic communication over short distances. If they communicate in the aesthetic form of expression, the distance of communication is also short. Professional writers and artists perform long-distance communication. In this regard we see that some sculptors of the folk society may sell their products on the local market. But professional sculptors may offer their works for sale on the national market. They are renowned across the state. Professional sculptors may be celebrities in the state while the sculptors of the folk society may not. If a writer can show a literary work of the higher level or if an artist can show an artistic work of the higher level, he can perform linguistic communication, or show his aesthetic form of expression, on a larger scale. This indicates that people feel the need to provide high level works in order to realize the exchange of feelings on a large scale in the context of long-distance linguistic communication. The works need to be charming, to show the high level of presentation and to propagate a wholesome idea. For example, a work may need to propagate an idea of justice as all hope to see the realization of justice in the state. In this case, such an idea may need to be described by a well-educated man who upholds the humanistic spirit. Such a man should be a professional in a certain domain. I mean that high quality works need to be provided in order to realize the exchange of feelings on a large scale across the state. Thus people share information through the exchange of feelings realized by professionals like writers and artists.

In sum, those professionals help the society to spread information needed by ordinary people because they can take initiative to perform the related linguistic communication or the communication supported by language, and they function as media. This means that in the community that grows in size, people need to use media to support their mutual linguistic communication. Linguistic communication, performed to spread professional information, is a phenomenon occurring in the state. Thus people always need to learn about what is communicated. Searching is an act of getting information through the linguistic communication performed for the formation and the organization of the state.

2. Report

People, communicating by using language, select information. They do not need all information but all necessary information. People also provide information to each other. They provide information needed by all others. Such information is meaningful for the organization of the state. In the meantime, the state is usually organized by the regime. The regime is a sort of organization. An organization is a medium. This medium leads to disequilibrium in the circulation of information in the state. The reason is that an organization has many members affiliated with itself. The members of this organization communicate with one another more frequently. The organization may distribute internal documents to its members or hold a meeting attended by its members. People, outside this organization, do not communicate as frequently as those people within that organization. Thus the government may provide a channel for certain people to communicate with it more often and gather and submit and share more information in the organization of the state. The government is, in some sense, a medium. Then it follows that some other people are especially in charge of organizing the state and collecting certain information. They work for the government. Then the phenomenon of reporting appears. Reporting becomes a formal act of organizing the state. Thus, certain information is especially supposed or required to be submitted to one official or an office of the government. The behavior of submitting such information is reporting defined by us in this context. Reporting means that one submits one report, oral or written. A report is often to be submitted to a person in charge of governing the community. This person is often the power holder particularly under the circumstances described by us here. As the power holder works for the government and the government is a medium, information supplied to him is used for the governance of the state. Thus a report is submitted to the state through him. The report is a form of linguistic communication especially appearing in the state instead of the tribe. In the tribe an affair of the tribe was neither public nor personal. There was no dichotomy between the personal domain and the public domain in the operation of the tribe. So information, required for the operation of the tribe, was usually supplied to all within the tribe. Of course, the tribal chief might get the information first. But the information was likely to spread to all within the tribe because people usually lived together and kept in touch face-to-face. By contrast, there appears the dichotomy between personal affair and public affair in the state. The method of gaining information in social intercourse may not change because people gain information from their surrounding environment directly. They may often communicate with each other face-to-face. The method of their social intercourse may be the same as the method of their mutual interaction in the tribe. But the method of mutual interaction of humans is different in the governance of the state or the management of public affairs in the state. This is because people always need information for governance or management. The state is always in shortage of information because the state is a large community in which the power holders do not always keep in touch with each citizen of the state. The state is organized by the power holders. The power holders are in charge of organizing the state and gathering adequate information for the governance of the state or the management of public affairs within the state. The government is just a medium because power holders are enabled to get more information through and in the government. With information they can make a right decision and take right action. This is because information, needed by an individual person, is usually limited because each needs only limited information for self-preservation provided by others on a small scale. By contrast, the state needs almost limitless information for governance or management and the state may gather such information in all aspects from every corner of the state. The government is set up to gather adequate information for the organization of the state. So in ancient times one of the tasks of the ruler was to gather and keep adequate information concerning the governance of the state or the management of public affairs of the state. Particularly, when the state grew in size, the government also grew in size accordingly. Then, the ruler needed to have adequate information provided by others. Gathering information became one of the important tasks performed by the power holders in the operation of the state. Discussing the building of an administrative system in Sumer, Babylon, Egypt and China in ancient times, E. N. Gladden writes that:

> With the expansion of the basis of government the ruler's need to keep himself informed about what was happening elsewhere led to the appointment of inspectors who went out, often with executive powers, to see that the ruler's commands were being properly executed and to report back. Such inspectors, as the eyes and ears of the ruler, figured in most of these early power systems and theirs was to remain

an important technique of public administration even when other systems of communication became available. Governments needed all the information they could get and every possible means was employed, every traveler being a potential agent of the king.[3]

In medieval times the kings of the states in Europe also needed crucial information provided by their ministers in the governance of the state. Louis XIV, the king of France, was keen to seek as much information as possible. Describing the style of working of this French king, Gladden writes that:

> It was a serious fault for a minister to withhold information or fail to keep him well-informed. Among them Jean Baptiste Colbert (1619-83) was assiduous in his responsibilities as a reporter, as his many detailed but concise reports to the king on proposed reform and changes amply testified.[4]

This means that the state grows in size gradually probably because the ruler conquers more territories or small states merge into a large state. The result is that people extend the reaches of governing the state. People govern the state on a large scale. Accordingly, they need to extend the distance of linguistic communication in submitting reports to the central government or the supreme ruler. The work of gathering adequate information is on the increase along with an increase in the size of the state. Along with an increase in the size of the state, the ruler faces more pressure in building a modern administrative system. This involves a process of building an administrative body, as a medium, in support of the linguistic communication that gathers information. This is because extending the distance of linguistic communication underlies the growth of the state.

In other words, the administrative body needs to be efficient and it needs to act as a medium in the process of the linguistic communication that enables power holders to gather information. As the regime is to organize the state and the state is formed in linguistic communication, the regime also functions in linguistic communication. The officials of the regime should meet the requirement of the administrative body. Officials should be efficient. That is, if those officials cannot work efficiently, the administrative body cannot work, as a medium, in gathering information. If the function of the administrative body is simple, there may not be a branch of the administrative body in charge of gathering information. Thus the administrative body may not be efficient in gathering information. The administrators may not be efficient in this case either. This administrative body is usually small in size. In this case, such an administrative body is inefficient in gathering information. So we see that in medieval times the king relied on the personal loyalty of the lords in the organization of the state. He organized the state in the social intercourse with his retainers or friends. His retainers, or friends, were recruited as the court servants. They were the officials of that time. As these people were recruited on a very small scale, they were recruited because of their personal relationship with the king or the servants of the king. The size of the administrative body was small. As a result, as there was no branch of the administrative body particularly in charge of gathering information, no adequate information was gathered in the organization of the state. In particular, when the state was at war, much information was urgently required. But they were unable to collect enough information for the organization of the state. As Joseph R. Sprayer writes,

> [W]hen the great (and expensive) questions of peace and war, truces and alliances came up, the princes and baronial leaders had to be consulted. Such men were usually not very well informed, nor did they work very hard to repair the gaps in their information. But even if they had been eager to remedy their ignorance, they would have found it difficult to do so. As we have seen, professional bureaucrats with their increasingly rigid routines could not have supplied up-to-date information about internal affairs. No one was charged with collecting information about foreign countries, certainly not the professional bureaucrats, certainly not the aristocratic members of the Council. Thus major policy decisions were made on the basis of very limited knowledge and were often influenced by the personal ambitions or grievances of the great men.[5]

In sum, as Sprayer writes, "Policymakers were ill-informed."[6] This means that in early times, the regime had no special officials in charge of collecting information. Officials could hardly make a well-informed decision. The lack of the supply of adequate information affected the normal operation of the government.

Since the establishment of the modern civil service system, a change has taken place. The state recruits civil servants from the labor market. As a large number of civil servants are usually trained, the government establishes the administrative branch of collecting and treating information. The administrative body works efficiently. It functions as a medium. All matters become smooth. Thus the government repairs the inadequacy of information collected by it. The government establishes a special administrative body to gather, treat and save information needed in the governance of the state or the management of public affairs. If necessary, it will establish more of such administrative bodies. They are very capable of performing long-distance linguistic communication. They strengthen the work of gathering and using information in the government. This is a course of creating a medium in support of the linguistic communication through which officials collect information for the purpose of organizing the state. This means that people establish a modern administrative system, and the government begins to work efficiently. Then people amplify and consolidate the administrative system. First, people establish the statistic bureau of the national government. Then the government takes charge of census. Census means that each citizen submits a report to the government. Personal information is submitted. Information flows to the government from all the places of the state. Second, some offices of archives are set up, and some administrators are especially appointed to the posts supposed to save and preserve related reports submitted by the citizens. Those personnel in the administrative bodies treat and utilize the said information. Ordinary people are not supposed to deal with and keep the related information. Thus information in relation to the organization of the state is largely kept and controlled by the offices of archives. Third, policemen are employed to keep public order. In the meantime, policemen collect related information for the government. The information, collected by the police, is usually in relation to the security of the state. Such information is kept confidential. Ordinary people do not master such information. Such information is also usually given by ordinary people to the police or by the policemen of the grassroots level to the policemen of the upper level. As the related information is collected and kept by the police for the security of the state, such information especially enables the government to enhance its ability of governing the state. The government enhances its ability to keep the normal operation of the state. Fourth, the state establishes the information bureau or intelligence agency to search and save information concerning the security of the state in some special domains. Spies are sent out to gather information needed by the state. The related information is exclusively used by the government instead of ordinary people. The related information may include the information gathered from a foreign state. The administrative bodies have all this abovementioned information in the operation of the state. People strengthen the organization of the state because the government, entrusted by the state, is itself a medium in support of the linguistic communication through which officials collect the related information.

As the government is an organization and an organization is a medium, other conditions that facilitate its work may also become media. Transportation is more important for the state than for ordinary people because without the related information collected from all regions through an efficient transportation system, the state cannot be organized smoothly, but the organization of the society may not be seriously affected. I mean that the society can be deemed as a small community, but the state should be a large one. The society can be fragmented, but the state cannot be fragmented. The society, discussed by us, is a comprehensive community that can be composed of many smaller communities such as regional, or ethnic, or linguistic, communities. Though sometimes the state can mean a society as a whole, the state should differ from the society in some other cases. All regions, forming the state, may be regarded as various communities. These communities can also be deemed as the societies. In this case the state should be different. For example, a society may be defined as a community supported by a community of a dialect. People, in the community of a dialect in a region, form a society. In this sense, there may be countless societies within a state. These societies are formed freely or passively. The state, however, needs to be organized by a regime. The regime is a large organization. Thus the state especially relies on this organization to subsist. The organization of the state especially depends on the development of internal transportation system covering the whole state, so that the reports of supplying information can be effectively submitted to the administrative bodies. For example, information often needs to be delivered by the officials of the governments of the lower level to the officials of the government of the higher level. The delivery of such information relies on transportation. Transportation thus becomes a medium. This situation already occurred in ancient times. Bertrand Russell writes that:

> The most urgent problem for ancient monarchs was that of mobility. In Egypt and Babylonia, this was facilitated by the great rivers; but the Persian rule depended upon roads. Herodotus describes the great royal road from Sardis to Susa, a distance of about 1,500 miles, along which the King's messengers traveled in time of peace, and the King's armies in time of war.[7]

In early modern times nation-states emerged. The emergence of nation-states was also characterized by the fact that roads were widely constructed to facilitate the linguistic communication that went on between the central government and local governments for the delivery of information. In France the network of roads covering the whole state was built in the eighteenth century. In the meantime the government system was centralized because the power of the royal court was greatly strengthened.

The development of other media is also part of the extension of the distance of linguistic communication in this historical process. Along with the construction of roads that facilitate the circulation of information across the state for the purpose of organizing the state, the wide use of light media supports the growth of the state, particularly, the nation-state, in modern times. If the medium, used for linguistic communication, is heavy, it is difficult for people to carry it over long distances and therefore it is difficult for them to communicate over long distances. A medium must be light in order to be carried afar. For example, if stones are used as media in linguistic communication, they are not used in the linguistic communication that goes on across the state or between the two different regions. By contrast, light media are usually used in linguistic communication over long distances. The papyrus was used by Romans in the linguistic communication within the Roman Empire. Roads, leading to everywhere within the empire, were constructed.

They were not only used in the transportation of Roman troops, but also used in the delivery of information between the remote outposts of the Roman troops, or their communities, and the authorities of the Roman Empire. In modern times information, carried across the state for the purpose of organizing the state, is often carried by paper. Paper is light. The production and supply of a large amount of paper accelerates the circulation of information in the organization of the state. The state capitalizes on this development because the administration of the state collects and distributes information within its administrative system throughout the state. Paper enhances the efficiency of the government.

All the cases discussed indicate that information, had by the government, needs to be more than that usually had by ordinary people so as to allow for the government to govern the state effectively. The work of governing the state is more complex than the work of managing a household. Extending the distance of linguistic communication is especially helpful to organizing the state in this respect because an increase in the supply of information results more often than not in an increase of the information to be used by the government. Each household only needs simple information in social intercourse and daily life. The state needs complex information. It is true that the supply of information increases along with the growth of the state. However, the bulk of the increased information is used by the state. Ordinary people are unable to use effectively a large amount of information even though they receive it. Ordinary people only need to use a limited amount of information. Thus, an increase in the supply of information is more meaningful for the government than it is for ordinary people. The value of information, used by the government, is usually also higher than the value of information used by ordinary people. Information, gained by ordinary people, is valuable in a local area while information, gained by the government, may be valuable across the state. As a result, the supply of information across the state, due to the availability of linguistic communication that goes on across the state, especially enhances the ability of the government to organize the state. This is due to the role played by the government in the reinforcement of linguistic communication that goes on throughout the state.

This means that a wide range of information is supplied to the government. This information is especially used by the government. This information is confidential. This information is only available for the inspection conducted by certain officials of the government for the purposes defined by the internal regulations of the government. This information may be originally provided by certain government bodies or other social organizations or individual persons. The information may include the records of the internal talks of the state leaders, the minutes of important meetings held by the government bodies, the financial reports, military situation reports, foreign affair reports, security situation reports, the social investigation reports of some research institutions, some internal statistic reports, all important treaties entered into by the country with all other countries and some historical archives among others. The related information is always kept confidential. Such information consists of various reports submitted through particular channels to the designated government bodies or organs. The related information is especially used by the government, so that people can organize the state as required. If such information or part of it is divulged to the public, the divulgence of the related information will usually cause damage to the interest of the state. To keep the related information confidential and usable by the government is not only in the interest of the government but also in the interest of the state. Thus the government is able to govern the state.

Using such information in governing the state, the government also depends on the cooperation of ordinary people because the supply of information often, or ultimately, relies on the cooperation of ordinary people. For example, the military situation report may be drafted on the basis of the oral reports of many local residents residing on the borders of the state or the security situation report may be written on the basis of an investigation made on the basis of the collaboration of the local residents. And the government needs ordinary people to supply information. Thus, the government encourages ordinary people to submit actively reports to it. Thus the government governs the state more effectively. This is because the government needs that information. One case in point is that the French authorities motivated ordinary people to submit reports to them in history. After the French Revolution, the National Convention established vigilance committees that had covered the whole country with a network of informers. The representatives became very powerful. The Revolution even took away from justice the duty which it had previously performed of defending the individuals against the encroachments of power.[8] Those informers were also media because they were more active in submitting information than others who were less active in submitting information.

Needless to say, people, supporting the government in charge of administration, or concurring with the government's policies, tend to provide more information to the government or government officials in a move to help the government to gain information and carry out effective policies or take effective measures in the governance of the state. They are media used by the government. Karl W. Deutsch indicates that police can be very effective if most people will give them information, but they are powerless where most people will not give information to it. During World War Two, the Gestapo was formidable in Germany, where at least 40 percent of the people were Nazi sympathizers. Despite identical procedures, it was far less effective in France, where only a small minority became active collaborators. Some Frenchmen waited quietly to see who would win, but the great majority gave no support to the Germans.[9]

There is a similar case in China. Before and during World War Two, Japan invaded China and occupied a large part of China, but in the region occupied by Japan the Japanese occupation army and the Chinese puppet government faced difficulties in governance because the majority of Chinese residents were not active in cooperation with the Japanese occupation army and the puppet government. Chinese people refrained from providing the puppet government with the information sought by it. They tried not to provide information to the puppet government even though the Japanese occupation army and the puppet government resorted to all kinds of threats and inducements. They refused to act as media. Therefore, Chinese people engaged in the underground activities of undermining the facilities of transportation and communication widely and the local combatants waged the war of guerrilla widely. Another case in point is that during the civil war in China from 1946 to 1949, the military struggle, between the Nationalist Party of China and the Communist Party of China, became intense. The Communist Party engaged in a lot of clandestine activities in the region controlled by the Nationalist Party. To halt the clandestine activities of the Communist Party in the region controlled by it, the government of the Nationalist Party sought information about the underground organizations of the Communist

Party and its clandestine activities. But as the rural and urban masses were gradually sympathetic with the Communist Party, the effort, made by the Nationalist Party, proved unsuccessful. By contrast, the Communist Party planted successfully many spies, or absorbed successfully many army officers of the Nationalist Party and planted them as spies, in the headquarters of the army of the Nationalist Party, a fact that was considered a cause of the defeat of the army of the Nationalist Party in all major battles. Thus, some people acted as media.

Thus the government needs to keep a large amount of information in the governance of the state and such information is more than that needed by ordinary people. If not, the government may not be able to organize the state successfully. The government needs to control more information in the organization of the state, whereas ordinary people may not need to do so. My reasoning is that though people need information in normal mutual interactions for the purpose of the formation of the state and hence they need to learn about all matters within the state, the control of certain kinds of information may be necessary. To control the circulation of information needed by the government is, in a sense, to govern the state. Thus we sometimes even see such a situation: If a state and another state are at war, the reports of the progress of the war may be cut and given form to in order to keep the confidence of the ordinary people in the rear of the country as well as that of the soldiers fighting at the front line. If an incident of public security, likely to cause social turmoil, happens, the government may restrict the scope of disseminating the information concerning such an incident. If an economic crisis has an impact on the social life of the citizens, the government may release to the public the information selected by it in order to prevent the citizens from feeling uneasy. If there is a reshuffle of the senior officials of the government, the related message may be spread first within the system of administration and then disclosed to the public. This case usually occurs in the state in which there is a mass society. This is usually due to the fact that the government needs to control the usage of information in the organization of the state. This case shows that the control of information by the government in the organization of the state may be or may not be in the interest of all that form the state. If the government is trusted by ordinary people, this usually means that the interest of the people is in line with the interest of the government. The government controls the information for technical purpose only. If the government is not fully trusted by ordinary people, this may mean that the interest of the people is not completely in line with the interest of the government. We cannot ensure that the government always controls information in the interest of all within the state. Particularly, a despotic government, controlling information, may not only organize the state but also keep the power of the power holder. In this case the government may suppress news media providing information to the public. For example, in early modern times, news media sometimes challenged the authority of the government because news media also provided information to the citizens. As news media received various reports from every corner of the state, they were enabled to make comments or even express opinions on the affairs of the state as if they were also the organizers of the state. They sometimes provided to the public the information that the government intended not to provide. News media might provide to the public the information that might not enhance the authority of the government. Thus the government might suppress them. This is because the despotic government usually controlled the circulation of information in the state not only for a technical purpose but also for a political purpose. It was often threatened by independent news media. For example, based on the materials provided by some French scholars, we get to know that Napoleon Bonaparte was quite aware of the power of the press. When he became First Consul, he set about putting the press to his service. By a decree of 27 Nivôse Year VIII (17 January 1800), he winnowed the 73 newspapers published in Paris (not counting scientific and literary journals and advertising gazettes) down to 13. Next, he set up a censorship bureau under Joseph Fouché, the minister of police, and attempted to reestablish prior censorship. When Napoleon became the emperor he went even farther: He had the *journal des débats* seized and renamed it *Le journal de l'empire* (1805), and in 1811 he authorized only four newspapers but confiscated all their property. He also ordered the 170 papers still being published in the provinces to discuss no political questions on their own initiative but to print extracts from *Le Moniteur*, the regime's mouthpiece and a paper that had operated as an official journal of recode since 1799 but that also contained articles of general interest. In 1810 Napoleon reduced the numbers of provincial newspapers to one per département.[10]

The similar historical episode might also occur in some other European countries in early modern times. If a dictator emerged, he almost always controlled the spread of information in the state. As mass media developed, he usually suppressed those mass media that challenged him. This situation also occurred in other regions. In Asia, Latin America and Africa, the regime of a certain country was seized by an armed group from time to time. Those people controlled the capital city first. But along with the development of mass media, controlling some important mass media became a priority. So Jack Goody writes,

> Whereas in the mid nineteenth century a revolt often involved the seizure of the seat of government, the routine of mid-twentieth century Africa centred upon the capture of the media building-the radio station, the television studio and the newspaper office.[11]

The specific situation is that when people formed themselves into a nation-state, the government always needed to get support from the masses through political mobilization. The government needed to use mass media. So after the armed forces overthrew the civilian government, they would soon control all types of news media. But on the whole these events had become rare by the end of the twentieth century. The control of information about public affairs by the government has become difficult or impossible ever since.

The reason is that there has been a trend, since the nineteenth century, that the government controls the information in the organization of the state primarily in the interest of all the citizens, a progress that means the formation of the common interest between the power holder in the government and the masses due to the appearance of diversified media. This results from the development of public communication. Let us discuss public communication as follows.

3. Public Communication

Since the formation of the state in ancient times there has been always a government or regime, which controls the circulation of information in the organization of the state for both technical and political purposes. This situation also often occurs because of the underdevelopment of public communication. Since the formation of the mass society in modern times, however, a change has taken place because ordinary people expect the government to govern the state as expected. As the government is supposed to organize the state as expected, the people need to learn about the affairs of the state in order to evaluate the work of the government. Public communication develops. All need to communicate with all in the state. All sorts of information, except the information especially needed by the government for a technical purpose, need to be shared in order that important affairs of the state can be known to and overseen by all so that people can ensure the formation of the common interest of all. The so-called public communication means the communication likely to be performed by all with all for all purposes concerning the affairs of the state. Like public property that can be used by all and like a public place where everyone can stay, public communication is the communication that can be performed by all with all freely. Public communication depends on extending the distance of linguistic communication. At least a medium is used. Then everyone can have access to it. Some people provide information in public communication while others use it. This is the mutual assistance among people. Information shared by people should be provided without any constraint. To put it another way, though the government also needs information provided by the citizens and it provides information to the citizens, the circulation of information under the control of the government is not enough for the citizens. Citizens need to communicate with one another freely. If a process of linguistic communication is under the control of the regime, information about some affairs of the state may be withheld in the interest of the regime. This is not public communication. Normally, public communication needs to go on across the state. This means that people need to extend the distance of linguistic communication. Such communication is open to all and goes on in the public. Media must play a role in this case.

All of my argument is that citizens need to share the information provided by themselves in the public as long as such information pertains to the interest of the state or the public interest. The common interest cannot take shape unless all can share information concerning public affairs. This means that the authorities need to gain adequate information in governing the state, but information concerning the public good should also be conveyed to all as long as this principle does not affect the organization of the state. The government should not interfere with such linguistic communication that gives information in relation to any public affair. Realizing this goal usually needs the development of media. This situation differs from the situation of ancient times.

In ancient times those who communicated to share information with one another might be citizens only. In ancient Greek city-states the public life of the polis was open to citizens. Citizens were able to communicate with each other, but slaves and women were prohibited from having access to the related process of linguistic communication. This was because of the social inequality between the citizens and all other people. As indicated by Engels, the 90,000 Athenian citizens constituted only a privileged class as against 365,000 slaves who were part of the population. The people's army of the Athenian democracy confronted the slaves as an aristocratic public force and kept them in check.[12] So people witnessed the formation of the common interest within the community of citizens only. Democracy went hand in hand with the rule of men in households and slave economy. In the traditional agricultural society in medieval times people formed the state on the basis of the rule of the ruling class. People performed linguistic communication for public affairs within the ruling class. People witnessed the formation of the common interest of the ruling class. Accordingly, the majority of people were unable to enter the process of linguistic communication that went on across the state. Thus, my argument is that in the outset initial conquest had an impact on the formation of the society. People built the state as a result of the ruler's initiative. Thus, people witnessed the formation of the common interest of the ruling class rather than the formation of the common interest of all. Yet as humans learned to use language, they communicated with each other on a large scale whenever they created media. The development of commerce precipitated urbanization. More people came to cluster in urban areas. Then, in the densely populated area, people resided close to one another. Cities functioned as media facilitating linguistic communication performed by all with all, as already mentioned earlier. The specific situation is that those, belonging to the bourgeoisie that pushed forward the development of commerce, were enabled to perform linguistic communication with one another first. Then as the development of commerce depended on market, many ordinary people were also enabled to enter the process of linguistic communication through the market. This situation spurred public communication. Thus, people performed linguistic communication more often through the market and the market gave rise to the emergence of the city. The related linguistic communication in the city then became the mainstay of public communication that went on throughout the state.

Some cultural forms, having developed since early modern times, also support the development of public communication because all cultural forms are media. Language uses them for its own expansion. This evolution leads to the growth of the civil society. The civil society is the community in which all perform linguistic communication with all without the intervention of the authorities. As a result, we see that coffee houses, salons and reading societies appeared first in early modern times. In France salons might appear early in the era prior to the Revolution. Writers, artists and other intellectuals congregated to discuss books and ideas in the salons in Paris and other cities. Rousseau, Diderot and others used the forum of the salon to develop their theories.[13] In England coffeehouses undertook the same task in the eighteenth century. Steele, Addison and others published excerpts from the coffeehouse conversation in *The Spectator, The Tatler, The Guardian* and other such magazines. Describing the influence of London coffeehouses, Lewis Coser comments that:

> A common opinion cannot be developed before people
> have an occasion to discuss with one another, before they
> have been drawn from the isolation of lonely thought into
> a public world in which individual opinion can be sharp-
> ened and tested in discussion with others. The coffeehouse
> helped to crystallize a common opinion from a multitude of
> individual opinions and to give it form and stability.[14]

In Germany the discussion of public affairs in salons and pubs appeared largely at the same time. According to Ferdinand Tönnies, the progressive spread of freedom to broader and lower social classes resulted from the economic and political emancipation of the bourgeoisie which, at the end of the seventeenth century and during the eighteenth century, brought about the first institutions of the public, which were social places that were "exception-ally important in everyday life for the formation of an opinion of the public: 'the salon' and 'the pub;' both of them sites for meetings of a reflecting, dis-cussing, cleverly chatting, and politicizing 'world'."[15]

Some other cultural forms also mushroomed to meet the need of the development of public communication in early modern times. Theaters were originally attached to the court and palace particularly in Germany, but later they became public. In Great Britain and France ordinary people, including domestic servants, soldiers, apprentices, young clerks, and a lumpenpro-letariat, had been admitted to the Globe Theater and the *Comédie* by the seventeenth century. Though in a long period of time the main floor was the place where those who belonged to the upper stratum of the upper bourgeoi-sie were seated, after revolution theaters became public.[16] In the nineteenth century the emerging middle class also entered the theatre to enjoy dramas in Britain. Richard F. Dietrich writes that Britain's growing middle-class flocked to the theatres for amusement, "thus sparking its physical and institutional development—around fifty theatres were built in London alone between 1800 and 1890."[17] The commercialization of some cultural forms was due to the development of capitalism. Yet if ordinary people did not need the consumption of cultural products, these new forms would not flourish. As those who belonged to the lower classes accounted for the majority of the population, dramas came to be enjoyed and appreciated by the people. Thus, Alexis de Tocqueville writes that "Only in the theater have the upper classes mingled with the middle and lower classes." And "It has always been in the theater that the learned and the educated have had the greatest difficulty in making their tastes prevail over that of the people and preventing themselves from being carried away by them."[18] This indicates that dramas are aimed at communicating with as many people as possible freely. Thus the populariza-tion of some cultural forms bolsters the public communication that reaches the masses.

Another analogous trend is the appearance of concerts attended by the masses. Originally concerts were held in the court or the church. As Jürgen Habermas writes,

> Composers were appointed as court, church, or council
> musicians, and they worked on what was commissioned,

just like writers in the service of patrons and court actors in the service of princes. The average person scarcely had any opportunity to hear music except in church or in noble society.[19]

And later, according to him, "Admission for a payment turned the musical performance into a commodity."[20] Musical halls were operated for a commercial purpose and ordinary people flocked to musical halls to hear music. This situation gave rise to another form of public communication.

Likewise, paintings, shown in the galleries, were originally essentially the paintings for the expert collectors among the nobility. Later, they were forced to work for the market. Painters emancipated themselves from the construction of the guilds, the court and the Church.[21] People might even see a change in the taste of painting. More museums were also built and opened to the public. Art critics made comments as if they were the spokesmen of the public.[22] Thus, ordinary people might be able to appreciate the works of art originally appreciated by nobility only. The related exchange realized in an artistic form met the need of all. It contributed to the development of public communication.

All abovementioned cases demonstrate that the development of cultural forms extends the reach of linguistic communication and extending the reach of linguistic communication bolsters the development of public communication.

The development of news media is also a condition for the development of public communication because news media report public affairs and take journalism as an undertaking. They pay close attention to the public affairs. They are well-informed. They are media used by ordinary people to enter into various processes of public communication. This is totally due to a historical change in the structure of the society. This change is that in the past the working people were largely not required to be literate. Thus they were prevented from entering into the process of written communication that went on across the state. So there was no wide public communication throughout the state. In the meantime, illiterate people usually spoke a dialect or a regional language. Such a dialect or regional language was used on a comparatively small scale. They were unable to use written language because they could not read and write. Yet the emergence of industrialization changed this situation. Prior to industrialization traditional agricultural society did not need a large educated workforce. Education was not a prerequisite for many trades in the agricultural society. Accordingly, the ruling class also believed that the education of ordinary people would result in the shortage of laborers such as servants. As such, according to Carlo M. Cipolla, "The idea that people are born with their 'rank in society' was widespread and according to this idea to educate a labourer was to alter nature and thus an invitation to chaos."[23] Industrialization ushered in a new era. Workers, needed by the factories built in the process of industrialization, needed to master certain skills or technologies, and mass education gradually developed. Thus the development of mass education in turn contributed to the development of public communication. That is, before industrialization, mass education was not available. Along with industrialization, the state pushed ahead with mass education. The specific situation was that in Europe, about 1850, 45-50 per cent of the adult population could not read. If Russia was included, the percentage would go up to about 60%.[24] But from the second half of the nineteenth century onward, the rate of illiteracy in Europe had steadily declined. In France, the rate of illiteracy was about 40-45 per cent around 1850. As late as 1901, the rate declined to 17 per cent.[25] In addition, political development also required a high rate of literacy. In America mass education was mainly public education. Public education developed widely in 1830s and 1840s. The Constitution stipulated that the Congress admit new states to the union only if they had a republican form of government, and by the late nineteenth century the Congress interpreted this provision to mean that new states must have free, nonsectarian public schools.[26] Then the rate of illiteracy fell quickly. Though many immigrants in the United States were the poorest and less educated people in their motherlands, in 1880, the rate of illiteracy among 'native whites' fell to 9 per cent and among 'foreign-born whites' 12 per cent.[27]

In the meantime, literate population grew large and many people began to communicate with one another on a large scale. They hoped to communicate with one another on a large scale easily. Then people developed various media to meet this requirement. Then people would soon communicate on a large scale rather than communicating on a small scale face-to-face. In the outset, they might only perform linguistic communication for social intercourse.

They communicated on a small scale. But later they soon communicated on a large scale not for social intercourse but for the governance of the state or the management of public affairs. They engaged in public communication.

This situation is especially exemplified by the development of newspapers. Newspapers functioned chiefly to report news. As newspapers needed to reach as high readership as possible in order to survive or grow, they supplied various information of public affairs to the citizens. All possible information was supplied. All concerns of the citizens about the public affairs were taken care of. People witnessed the formation of the common interest of all. In the meantime, with citizens being effectively informed, public communication created a condition for the establishment of democracy. Under democracy, citizens were supposed to make an informed decision. They relied on public communication. Therefore, modern democracy emerged first in Europe. The first batch of newspapers also emerged in Europe. So Strasbourg and Wolfenbüttel may have had the first printed newspapers in 1609. Shortly later there were weeklies in Basel, Frankfurt, Vienna, Hamburg, Berlin, Amsterdam and Antwerp.[28] In Britain from the eighteenth to the nineteenth century, people witnessed an extremely fast rise in the number of publications in general and newspapers in particular.[29] Newspapers also appeared in North America almost at the same time. By the early 1800s, as Paul Starr argues, newspapers were more common in America than elsewhere. Even small towns and villages had their own printers and newspapers.[30] In addition, Alexis de Tocqueville, a writer of the nineteenth century, wrote down what he had seen. He says that "There is hardly a hamlet in America without its newspaper."[31] When news was reported by the newspapers, ordinary people might discuss the reported events. Many events were public affairs. Particularly, cheap newspapers, such as those produced by penny presses, ensured high readership, resulting in the creation of a public sphere.[32]

The media of other types that facilitated the development of public communication also developed. Despite that there is a difference between such media and newspaper, such media realized the full coverage of public communication across the state. They depended mainly on the development of electric technology instead of mechanic technology. The application of this new technology accelerated the circulation of information about public affairs of the state. The application of this new technology also enhanced the efficiency of public communication. It became possible for ordinary citizens to communicate with one another thoroughly across the state. People witnessed the formation of the common interest of all, particularly those of lower social classes.

These media include telegraph. In the outset telegraph, invented in France, was initially used for military purpose. Then in many states in Europe and North America telegraph came into use mostly for business. The government might also use it. In the meantime telegraph was also used by journalist institutions for the coverage of major news. For example, in America, during the Civil War where the Union armies advanced, telegraph lines followed, enabling President Lincoln to stay in direct communication with his generals as no other president previously was able to do so in wartime. Then telegraph was used to disseminate news.[33] News was reported across the state within one day or even hours. The cause of news was particularly facilitated by the development of telegraph at that time. The emergence of Reuters and the Associated Press resulted directly from the development of public communication based on the use of telegraph.

The development of radio broadcast contributed another channel for news report in the twentieth century. Radio broadcast did not absolutely rely on written communication. People were not required to be literate in order to enter the related process of public communication. So radio broadcast became another independent form for the growth of public communication. Since then, radio broadcast has not only provided a tool for the state leader to interact directly with the citizens whenever necessary but also disseminated news as needed by different people. Radio stations with different backgrounds can operate. For example, the leader of the state may directly make a speech to the public on some special occasions through radio broadcast. If an international war breaks out, for example, he may make a speech to call on the people to stand up against foreign invasion. On the other hand, if some citizens criticize the government, the related event may also be broadcast by the radio station. All public affairs of the state may be reported by different radio stations to different audiences in different ways. No concern of the citizens about a public affair can be ignored.

The development of television further boosted the development of public communication in the twentieth century. Since then, people have witnessed that audiences not only listen to the broadcast but also watch television. Many important and major events are reported by the television stations in the first instant. As television stations compete for audiences, they report all kinds of public affairs. The broadcast of television serves all. The interest of all must be, in general, taken care of. For example, political advertisements, shown on the screens of television sets, always function to communicate with as many audiences as possible. A policy supported by the government may be supported by a commentator who appears in a program provided in the broadcast of a television station. Yet citizens who criticize that policy may also use television to disseminate their views. As television stations are often operated for business purpose, they strive to serve as many people as possible. Each television station may especially serve a portion of the audiences. People witness the formation of the common interest of all to a varying extent because different television stations engage in the different broadcast.

Those who are especially involved in the management of public affairs are also media. They are professional managers of public affairs. They know the details of public affairs. They are well-informed about related public affairs. As ordinary people are usually not well-informed about public affairs, they often rely on those well-informed to get the information about the public affairs. Politicians and political parties are such media. They contribute to the development of public communication. If politicians and political parties compete against each other lawfully under democracy, they will enhance the circulation of information about public affairs within the state. As noted earlier, the regime may withhold information about some state affairs in its own interest at the expense of the interest of the public. Politicians and political parties, not under the control of the government, however, may reveal to the citizens the information about certain public affairs that the government may conceal. The competition of politicians and political parties shows this case. That is, as they compete, they are independent. As they are independent, communication, performed by them, tends to meet the requirement of different citizens. The related communication should be public communication. For example, political parties in competition seek support from the masses. They must inform the citizens of the public affairs of the state. Though the ruling party in control of the government may sometimes refrain from revealing information about certain public affairs to the public in its own interest, the opposition may reveal the related information to the public. This usually requires the operation of the parliament. There is a historical evolvement in this regard. This historical evolvement is that in the outset, the delegates, invited by the ruler to attend the meeting of the parliament, were those who might not be elected. In Great Britain nobility that attended the meeting of parliament were not elected. In France the nobility that attended the assembly were not elected. In Germany those who attended the meeting of the Imperial Diet might be the lords of manors, not the delegates. As Jürgen Habermas writes,

> When the territorial ruler convened about him ecclesiastic and worldly lords, knights, prelates, and cities (or as in the German Empire until 1806 when the Emperor invited the princes and bishops, Imperial counts, Imperial towns, and abbots to the Imperial Diet), this was not a matter of an assembly of delegates that was someone else's representative. As long as the prince and the estates of his realm 'were' the country and not just its representatives, they could represent it in a specific sense. They represented their lordship not for but 'before' the people.[34]

That is, as the state was usually formed due to initial conquest, linguistic communication only went on between the ruler of the kingdom and the rulers of local areas such as the lords. Linguistic communication was unable to reach all. Thus people only witnessed the formation of the common interest of the ruling class. People performed no public communication. Yet, this situation changed soon because people needed to use various possible media in the development of public communication. Ordinary people requested to have voting rights. They entered the process of election, and independent politicians and political parties emerged. They have been functioning as media since then. As they seek support from the citizens, they should take initiative to reveal the information of important public affairs to the citizens. They buttress public communication.

People, committed to the public good, also emerge in modern times. They establish non-government organizations. They are media, underpinning the development of public communication. They especially promote an undertaking. They often participate in the management of certain public affairs according to an idea or a mission. They pay close attention to some special public affairs. They are very familiar with these public affairs. They usually have professional knowledge of these public affairs. They are well-informed about these public affairs. They often take initiative to reveal the trend of managing certain public affairs to the citizens because they need to seek support from the citizens. These people may be volunteers and these organizations may be formed by volunteers. They may take care of charity, public health, education, environmental protection, the protection of the rights of women or children or animals, and climate change. As citizens are also concerned about these affairs, those people and their non-government organizations underpin the development of public communication. Like politicians and political parties, they may not be controlled by the government. They may disclose the information about the management of certain public affairs of which the government fails, or is unwilling, to inform the citizens.

Among these people and non-government organizations, some people or organizations may show the inclination in support of the government while others may show the tendency of criticizing the government. They may be motivated by an ideology to display a view concerning a public affair. Yet different people and non-government organizations are usually independent, and an individual person or a non-government organization may disclose to the public the information that another person or another non-government organization may refrain from disclosing. The co-existence of these people and non-government organizations with various different backgrounds ensures that the information of any important affair of the state will be finally revealed to the public.

Some academic researchers and academic research institutes that conduct researches on social or economic development or some other subject matters may present some reports in relation to the management of public affairs, too. They are professionals and professional organizations. They are media. Conducting researches may enable them to publish their views in the public. They offer an academic view needed by the state or the society, and they communicate with the public. Their views may reflect the views of ordinary people. If a piece of information about an important public affair is concealed by the government, they may disclose the related information to the public, as required by an ethic standard or a professional code. They may hold the views not in line with the views held by the government. They may make investigations and find out more information about the management of some public affairs. If the government is unwilling to let the public know these public affairs, these researchers or research institutes may reveal these affairs to the public. In particular, those researchers or academic research institutes, not under the direct control of the government, such as those affiliated with private universities or foundations, may actively publish reports on the status quo, or the trend, or the result, of managing many important public affairs to which the great masses of the people pay close attention.

Different researchers and research institutes may show different inclinations. Some display the conservative inclination while others show the liberal inclination. They may compete against each other. They strive to let the public accept their views about the management of public affairs. They may reveal the different kinds of information to the public. If one researcher or research institute refrains from disclosing a certain piece of information to the public, another researcher or research institute may take initiative to disclose this piece of information to the public. There appears a market of information. No one can conceal the important information of a public affair.

All the aforesaid situations show that a great change takes place due to the development of various media. In the outset, people create such media in the linguistic communication people perform on an individual basis. Such media are often in the form of culture. For instance, a poet performs public communication through the poems created by him. Later, people create such media like newspaper and radio broadcast in the linguistic communication to serve the mass society. And finally, people create such media in the linguistic communication in the domain of the management of public affairs. People extend the reach of linguistic communication and diversify the form of linguistic communication. They enhance the efficiency of linguistic communication. More and more people communicate across the state. This is a process of the development of public communication. This also results in the formation of the common interest of the citizens. This is part of the process of the growth of the nation-state.

In short, people form the state on the basis of the formation of the common interest of all. Such a state should be the one in which the amount of information kept by the government is in equivalent to the amount of information kept by ordinary people if possible. If the government intentionally keeps more information and ordinary people have no access to it, the government may use such information in the interest of the power holder at the expense of the interest of the public. However, the steady development of media puts an end to the abovementioned situation. The development of media means extending the distance of linguistic communication. Extending the distance of linguistic communication leads to the formation of the common interest of all. Even the establishment of democracy or the formation of the civil society shows this trend. The development of public communication is an important aspect in the organization of the nation-state. The reason is that extending the distance of linguistic communication leads to the formation of the common interest of more and more people and then the formation of the common interest of all further underlies the organization of a modern state.

Notes

1. For the definition of behavioral communication, please refer to the book *Language and State: An Inquiry into the Progress of Civilization* (Lanham, Maryland: The University Press of America, Inc., 2013), xiv–xv.
2. Paul Johnson, *The Renaissance: A Short History* (New York: Random House, 2000), 15;37; 38.
3. E. N. Gladden, *A History of Public Administration, Vol. I: From Earliest Times to the Eleventh Century* (London: Frank Cass and Company Limited, 1972), 241.
4. E. N. Gladden, *A History of Public Administration, Vol. 2: From the Eleventh Century to the Present Day* (London: Frank Cass and Company Limited, 1972), 148.
5. Joseph R. Sprayer, *On the Medieval Origins of the Modern State* (Princeton, New Jersey: Princeton University Press, 1970), 75.
6. Ibid. 92.
7. Bertrand Russell, *Power* (W.W. Norton & Company, Inc, 1938), 163.

8. Bertrand de Jouvenel, *On Power: Its Nature and the History of Its Growth*, translated by J. F. Huntington (Boston: Beacon Press, 1967), 232.

9. Karl W. Deutsch, *Nationalism and Alternatives* (New York: Alfred A. Knopf, Inc., 1969), 18.

10. See: Henri Welschinger, *La censure sous le premier empire* (Paris: Charavay frères, 1882; Jacques Godechot, "La presse française sous la Révolution et l' Empire," in Bellanger et al., eds., *Histoire générale de la presse française,* I: 403-557, cited from Henri-Jean Martin, *The History and Power of Writing*, translated by Lydia G. Gochrane (Chicago: The University of Chicago Press, 1994), 417–418.

11. Jack Goody, *The Logic of Writing and the Organization of Society* (Cambridge: Cambridge University Press, 1986), 117.

12. Frederick Engels, *The Origin of the Family, Private Property and the State* (New York: International Publishers, 1972), 230.

13. See: Susan Herbst, *Numbered Voices: How Opinion Polling Has Shaped American Politics* (Chicago: The University of Chicago Press, 1993), 53.

14. Lewis Coser, *Men of Ideas* (New York: Free Press, 1970), 20; cited from Herbst, *Numbered Voices: How Opinion Polling Has Shaped American Politics*, 53.

15. Ferdinand Tönnies, *Kritik der Öffentlichen Meinung* (Berlin: Julius Springer, 1922), 202, cited from Slavko Splichal, *Principles of Publicity and Free Press* (Lanham: Rowman & Littlefield Publishers, Inc., 2002), 18.

16. Please see: Jürgen Habermas, *The Structural Transformation of the Public Sphere: An Inquiry into A Category of Bourgeois Society*, translated by Thomas Burger (Cambridge, Massachusetts, The MIT Press, 1991), 38–39.

17. Richard F. Dietrich, *British Drama 1890 to 1950: A Critical History* (Boston: Twayne Publishers, 1989), 2.

18. Alexis de Tocqueville, *Democracy in America*, translated by George Lawrence (New York: Harper Perennial, 1988), 490.

19. Habermas, *The Structural Transformation of the Public Sphere: An Inquiry into A Category of Bourgeois Society*, 39.

20. Ibid.

21. Ibid., 40.

22. Ibid.

23. Carlo M. Cipolla, *Literacy and Development in the West* (Baltimore, Maryland: Penguin Books, 1969), 66.

24. Ibid.

25. Ibid., 94.

26. Paul Starr, *The Creation of the Media: Political Origins of Modern Communications* (New York: Basic Books, 2004), 105.

27. Cipolla, *Literacy and Development in the West*, 99.

28. Michael Stephens, *A History of News* (New York: Viking, 1988), 149–150; cited from Paul Starr, *The Creation of the Media: Political Origins of Modern Communications*, 32.

29. According to Raymond William, the annual titles of publications increased from 370 in 1790 to over 500 in 1820 and to more than 2,600 by the 1850s. After 1815 the more radical "pauper press" began to rise, evading the Stamp Duty then in fore primarily as a political tax by excluding news and publishing only opinion. See: Raymond William, "*The Press and Popular Culture: A Historical Perspective*" in *Newspaper History from the Seventeenth Century to the Present Day*, edited by G. Boyce, J. Curran, and P. Wingate (London: Constable, 1978), 46, cited from Splichal, *Principles of Publicity and Free Press*, 146.

30. Starr, *The Creation of the Media: Political Origins of Modern Communications*, 48.

31. De Tocqueville, *Democracy in America*,185.

32. See: Herbst, *Numbered Voices: How Opinion Polling Has Shaped American Politics*, 73.

33. See: Starr, *The Creation of the Media: Political Origins of Modern Communications*, 177–178.

34. Habermas, *The Structural Transformation of the Public Sphere: An Inquiry into a Category of Bourgeois Society*, 7–8.

Chapter Six

Interpretation

1. Knowledge

Interpretation is another linguistic phenomenon. It pertains to the spread of knowledge. Knowledge is spread among the members of the state. Knowledge was not spread among the members of the tribe. If we postulate that primitives have the ability of understanding, they can more often than not understand common sense. All cognition, acquired by tribal people, is common sense. Common sense usually does not need any interpretation given to the members of the state. Common sense is often what people take for granted. It stems from living experience. That is, people have common sense because they have direct experience. Common sense is similar to the direct experience had by humans. People have common sense because they always engage in production. People have common sense because they always have experience in living. Production and living are the sources of common sense. Simple production and living only rely on common sense. By contrast, knowledge, acquired by the members of the state, often needs to be interpreted because much of knowledge, needed by humans in the state, is not confined to the basic experience of production and living. Of course, summarizing experience is a condition for the creation of knowledge. Knowledge, however, is more complicated and advanced than common sense. Experience is concrete, whereas knowledge may be abstract. Thus, knowledge is often interpreted by those who have a command of knowledge to those who are in need of knowledge. This is because humans, forming their tribe, do not need any interpretation about their tribe. They may not use language. If they use language, they may not use language to interpret their own tribe. But humans, forming their state, need to interpret their state. They do not need to interpret their tribe, but they need to interpret their state because the state is a new community that they cannot understand simply through their direct experience. The understanding of the community is no longer empirically self-evident in the state. The state is a large, complex and advanced community. The state is a special community that people need to use the art of understanding to understand because knowledge, other than the experience acquired through visual observation, is needed to understand the state. Interpretation is a basis of understanding. Thus, humans gain the art of understanding through an interpretation.

Though, traditionally, scholars pay attention to the understanding of the text as studied by hermeneutic philosophers, the understanding of the state also requires an interpretation because a great change has taken place in the human community in the process in which humans depart from their tribes to form their states. If we suppose that a group of people form a tribe, I assert that they do not interpret any text because they do not perform written communication. People, forming the state, interpret the text because now they perform written communication. Yet although hermeneutic philosophers, including Friedrich Schleiermacher (1768-1834) , Wilhelm Dilthey (1833-1911), Martin Heidegger (1889-1976), Hans-Georg Gadamer (1900-2002) among others, focused on the interpretation of the text in order to elucidate the authentic truth behind the text proper, the text is actually a medium used by one to communicate with the other. An interpretation, a course of teaching the art of understanding, is the interpretation given by one to the other. Philosophers of ancient Greece believed that speaking is the translation of thoughts into words.[1] We can also argue that linguistic communication is also the translation of words into thoughts if the thoughts of one become the thoughts of the other. Any type of linguistic communication is performed by one with the other. Therefore, one does not give any interpretation to himself. If one interprets a text, he does not give any interpretation to himself but to another person. An interpretation does not appear between text and mankind but between one person and another. Though interpretation, conceptualized by hermeneutic philosophers, is aimed at finding out the inner sense, interpretation results in the spread of knowledge, enabling people to have the equivalent competence of understanding. That is, the level of knowledge varies from one person to another. The difference of the level of knowledge acquired by humans gives rise to the fact that interpretations are given by people to people in the state. In the meantime, people perform human-chain linguistic communication, and an interpretation may be a link of the chain in linguistic communication. Thus people may give an interpretation one after another. People give interpretations on an increasingly large scale until they give interpretations to all within the state. As Paul Ricoeur writes, "We explain something to someone else in order that he can understand. And what he has understood, he can in turn explain to a third party. Thus understanding and explanation tend to overlap and to pass over into each other."[2] All within the state must be the informed citizens to participate in the building of the state and all need to understand the state in the same way. The organization of the state needs such understanding. Interpretations are given in the organization of the state.

As such, it is significant for people to have the equivalent ability of understanding in the organization of the state. In the meantime, everyone is also often required to interact with all others in the same way. Their harmonious mutual interaction is one aspect of the formation of the state. Thus we see that when an interpretation is given, the level of knowledge had by the interpreter must also be higher than the level of the knowledge had by the one accepting the interpretation. Otherwise no interpretation will be given. Thus an interpretation means the conveyance of knowledge between one another. It is also a process in which people achieve equilibrium in the spread of knowledge among all within the state. An interpretation is normally given to remove obscurity, but to remove obscurity is to spread knowledge among people within the state. If a person finds it difficult to understand a text, it should be an obstacle in the spread of knowledge among people within the state. An interpretation is thus given to remove this obstacle. The interpretation is significant for the interactions between one another in the organization of the state. It is the common sense that the most systematical interpretation is given in schools and universities. Therefore, teaching can be regarded as the cause of an interpretation in essence. Teaching is the act of interpreting knowledge because without an interpretation people cannot understand knowledge. Thus, teaching, a way of imparting knowledge created by humans in the civilized society, is aimed at giving an interpretation though people usually believe that education is designed to disseminate knowledge and to teach working skills. This phenomenon does not occur in the tribe. An interpretation differentiates humans in the state from those in the tribe. The significance of the interpretation is of time and space. Please allow me to substantiate this view as follows.

First, humans, born in the tribe, are naturally the members of the tribe. They are naturally connected with each other through kinship, and kinship dictates the very close relationship between them and the tribe. They are naturally the members of the tribe. The relationship between one another is that of immediacy. Language is not necessarily used to construct such relationship. All are closely connected with each other due to immediacy. However, humans, communicating by using language, extend the distance of communication and break that immediacy. They expand the community to the extent that the community is no longer formed by those who are bound together by the totality of kinship. Yet as a human community often grows in size, the narration of this evolution may become part of history shared within the community. Humans record their own past experience. They chronicle their history. History helps them to find their roots, so that people, sharing the same history, may be aware that they belong to the same community originally formed by their ancestors. The narratives of history bolster the building of the state. Then people interpret history. I mean that history is not only what amounts to historical facts, but also the interpretation of the past. In Chapter Four I have mentioned that historical consciousness may function as a medium in support of the formation of the state. The role of history has been briefly described at that time. However, if we study the phenomenon concerning interpretations, we may find that history plays a role because it is interpreted. People need historical consciousness, but historical consciousness often comes from the interpretation of history. Without an interpretation people may not effectively or completely understand history. People may chronicle history in detail. It may need to be interpreted, so that ordinary people can learn history. The significance of a historical event or figure may need an interpretation as an interpretation allows for people to gain the authentic truth of history. In the meantime, people reconstruct history in the process of an interpretation. History is not merely the description of the place and the date of the occurrence of the event, the course of the event and the outcome or consequence of the event. History is also an interpretation. By giving an interpretation, people spread historical knowledge. They give the related interpretation to all in the linguistic communication that goes on across the state, and all may accept the same interpretation. All may have the same historical memory. Then people have the same knowledge of history in the state. This means that the citizens of the state usually have the same historical knowledge. Historians may have different understandings of a piece of history. Yet ordinary people usually have the same historical knowledge. Ordinary people only have access to the simplified presentation of history. People usually interpret the simplified presentation of history. Ordinary people tend to agree on the simplified presentation of history. Thus, people usually spread such knowledge to all through an interpretation. Such an interpretation is a process of generalizing the understanding of history. People, having the same historical knowledge, tend to understand the process of the growth of the state in the same way. This facilitates the organization of the state.

Second, in the beginning humans had no identity. At that time they formed a tribe, and they were the same kind of people. They knew each other because they associated together due to kinship. The appearance of one individual person was largely the same as that of the other. People of different races did not interact with one another. Then humans started to use language, and they expanded their community until a change took place. Kinship has no longer functioned to ensure the unity of the community since then. As people now form a large community not through kinship, they need to create the identity of all within the community so as to bolster the unity of the community. They interpret that identity. Thus people use language to describe their identity to organize themselves. They construct their identity through an interpretation. In the primitive society people might already use a totem to create their own identity. In the civilized society people build their state. In the meantime their identity is interpreted by using language, so that the state can be formed by those who share the same identity. The creation of identity especially depends on an interpretation. This interpretation is given often through teaching. In other words, people, forming the state, may already have their identity. Yet people may not realize this. Thus an interpretation is necessary. One case in point is that people, residing in a local area, usually stem from an ethnic group. They usually have their own culture. They have their cultural consciousness. Cultural consciousness is spread through formal education such as teaching and learning in the school or in any other way of imparting knowledge through personal contacts. For example, a teacher teaches the students to sing a song or a teacher teaches the students to write a poem. Then people use various forms of culture to create the forms of identity. Then all, sharing the same identity, are supposed to form the same state. This is different from the situation in the tribe. In the tribe people might not need to use any identity to support the formation of the tribe in early times though in later times people might start using a totem to create their identity. Humans, forming their state, invariably have their identity. The reason is that humans communicate using language, and they create various forms of culture. They use those forms of culture to create an identity of the people forming the state. Then such identity supports the formation of the state. In terms of the formation of the tribe, close blood relationship is an element of the formation of the community. In terms of the formation of the state, other means become the essential elements of the formation of the state though people may still have remote blood relationship. The formation of the identity is a way to buttress the formation of the state. Then people give an interpretation. Imparting knowledge, in particular, the knowledge of culture, may also involve the act of giving an interpretation. This interpretation may be the interpretation of identity. People create their own identity for the organization of the state.

Third, people construct the relationship between one another in the state in a new way. They interpret it. The reason is that this relationship is unlike that in the tribe. In the tribe, kinship defines the relationship between one another. People construct such relationship by nature. Kinship determines the role of each. For example, the relationship between two brothers is determined by the role played by each in the construction of the community. By contrast, the relationship between one another in the state is normally no longer determined by kinship. The relationship between one another in the society may be defined by a traditional custom. However, the relationship between one another in the state is usually defined by law. In ancient Greece and Rome, people stipulated the rights of citizens according to law. They conceptualized the relationship between one another among the citizens in the state. In modern times the constitution or the related law stipulates expressly such rights of the citizens in any nation-state. For example, the constitution may stipulate that citizens have voting rights or other rights in relation to the freedom of speech and the freedom of religious belief. The obligations of the citizens may also be expressly stipulated. In the tribe the obligations of each toward the other are not conceptualized. The obligations, undertaken by one toward the other, stem from the natural instinct of people under the influence of kinship. But in the state such obligations are especially stipulated by law. For example, the constitution may require citizens to be obligated to remit taxes and to provide military service to the state. People interpret all those rights and obligations by using language. Through the interpretation of the rights and obligations of the citizens people define and build the relationship between one another and the relationship between citizenry and the state. Laws define what one ought to do and ought not to do by using language. Needless to say, people may sometimes interpret the relationship between one another in the tribe. But such an interpretation is not essential because tribal people invariably obey the consciousness of kinship that determines the relationship between one another by nature. By contrast, the members of the state cannot understand the new relationship between one another without the conceptualization of the rights and obligations of each. Such conceptualization relies on an interpretation. Such an interpretation is often given by the most learned or best-educated people within the state. That is, not all can understand the right relationship between one another in the state built by them. Such an interpretation is required by the organization of the state.

Fourth, people need to interpret the organizational characteristics of the state, but they do not need to interpret the organizational characteristics of the tribe. The simple organizational characteristics of the tribe do not vary substantially from tribe to tribe. Humans form the tribe by nature. Maybe there is a tradition followed by each generation. The organizational characteristics of the tribe may remain unchanged over a long stretch of time. People usually take the organizational characteristics of the tribe for granted. Yet humans often build their states in a different way. A state may have a special organizational characteristic. For example, the institutional setup for the governance of the state may vary. Some states are kingdoms while others are republics. Some states may adopt a unitary system while others a federal system. In pre-modern times the name of a ruling family might be adopted to denote the state in the outset. Yet since then people have gradually found that the name can be used to interpret the state because the state needs an interpretation. Thus, we see that people give interpretations from time to time. They give various interpretations. One interpretation is the interpretation of the nature of the state or the form of the government. For example, there may often be the word "republic" in the name of the state after the long-term evolution of the state. Then people find that the word "republic" interprets the state. Another interpretation is the interpretation of the historical background of the state. For example, the words "united states" may be adopted to mean that the state is formed on the basis of the union of several states. Another interpretation may be the interpretation of the cultural background of the state. For example, "Islamic Republic" may be used in the name. The reason is that the state is a complex community. The organizational characteristics need to be known by all within the state particularly under the circumstances that people are mobilized to participate in politics. For example, if democracy is put into practice, the form of government may be interpreted to facilitate the citizens to participate in politics. Perhaps the party system is also interpreted. The electoral system is also interpreted. People may describe the method of forming the government that rests on support from the parliament. Then they may give the related interpretation.

Fifth, people interpret law. When a law is interpreted, knowledge about law is spread to the masses. This is unlike the situation of the tribe. In the tribe humans may use a custom to rule on a dispute, but this custom is simple. It may not need any interpretation because it is easy for everyone to understand it. Law is different. A law is often made by people who have a good command of knowledge. When this law is applied, it needs to be understood by all. Then people interpret the knowledge of law. As a law usually involves an interpretation of this law behind this law because the knowledge used to make this law is complex, the application of law always requires an interpretation. In some sense, the process of making a judgment by a judge is the process of an interpretation. After a judge of the law court of the lower level makes a judgment, this judgment may not be final. This judgment is sometimes cancelled by a judge of the law court of the higher level after an appeal is lodged. Not surprisingly, the two judges must have given the different interpretations of the same law. Why do judges always give an interpretation of law? My view is that the application of a law needs to be accepted by the principals. The judgment must be reasonable. In the meantime, this law needs to be understood by the principals. The knowledge of law is spread by the judges to the principals through an interpretation. Without the interpretation of a law, the rule of law cannot be put into practice. As law is an important tool in the governance of the state, it is often interpreted by many different people. It is important for the judges to give a related interpretation. The reason is that a law is, in a certain sense, a process of linguistic communication that goes on between the lawmakers and the citizens. As the lawmakers are usually far from the citizens, the former and the latter do not meet. The process of linguistic communication, performed by the lawmakers with the citizens, is of one way. The lawmakers may interpret the law when the law is made. Yet the law needs to be continuously interpreted because the law may be applied to the cases that are not always exactly the same. Thus some others rather than the lawmakers are tempted to interpret the law. For example, sometimes news media interpret a certain law when a comment is made. Officials may interpret the law when necessary. Lawyers may interpret that law. Judges also interpret that law. As judges are supposed to make a judgment, they invariably give an authoritative interpretation of the law. The interpretation of a law shows the importance of using knowledge in the governance of the state. For example, the constitution of the United States is often interpreted by the justices of the supreme court of the federation. Jurists may interpret the constitution of the United States in their own ways. But the interpretation given by the justices should be more authoritative. The role, played by a judge, shows the importance of legal knowledge because someone is especially authorized to interpret it. Interpreting law is an important work in the governance of the state.

The related interpretation is actually a process of linguistic communication performed by those who have a good command of knowledge with those who do not have a good command of knowledge. This is a phenomenon in the state. This does not appear in a tribe. In the tribe the knowledge of people does not vary dramatically from one to another. If an interpretation is ever given, this interpretation is only given by old people to young people. But in the state people who form the state are required to have certain knowledge.

As the knowledge, had by people, varies from one to another, those who have a good command of knowledge give interpretations and hence assume a prominent role in the spread of knowledge. In other words, in the tribe only old people give interpretations to young people, spreading living experience or common sense, but in the state some people other than old people may also give interpretations spreading knowledge. In the tribe the formation of the tribe will not be affected if no interpretation is given. However, in the state the formation of the state will be affected if the interpretation of such a kind is not given. Then some people especially play a role in the formation of the state because they give interpretations.

First, priests or clergymen give interpretations. In some states religion plays an important role in the organization of the state. People within the state are usually the believers of a religion. Then the state may be interpreted while an interpretation of religion is given. Narrating the deeds of Numa Pompilius (8th-7th century B.C.), a man in Roman Times, Plutarch writes that:

> The office of Pontifex Maximus, or chief priest, was to declare and interpret the divine law, or rather, to preside over sacred rites; he not only prescribed rules for public ceremony, but regulated the sacrifices of private persons, not suffering them to vary from established custom, and giving information to every one of what was requisite for purposes of worship or supplication.[3]

Priests played a role. Summarizing the religious interpretation from ancient to late medieval times, Jean Grondin writes that:

> [T]he advent of Christ, which appeared to interrupt Jewish tradition, called special attention to the principles of interpretation. In the early Middle Ages as well, interpretation necessarily assumed a prominent place, since all knowledge depended on interpreting Scripture and the works of the Fathers. When medieval hermeneutics was transformed during the Reformation by the introduction of the rule of *sola scriptura*, hermeneutic reflection acquired renewed energy.[4]

So in history the interpretations of the Bible influence the building of the state. Sometimes a new state is born partly because of the re-interpretation of the Bible. This is because humans do not form their state freely, but often do so according to an idea. Such an idea may be a religious idea. Thus, in history some states take form under the influence of the Church or Temple. Knowledge is sometimes especially imparted by the religious community through interpretations.

Second, teachers give interpretations. Teachers are those who are especially trained or educated. They usually have a good command of knowledge. They usually excel in learning. They give the interpretations of knowledge to the students who go to school. This means that in the tribe there is no teacher. If living experience is handed down to the next generation, it is usually handed down by an elder. But in the state students who need knowledge and teachers who impart knowledge are arranged for to gather in schools. Knowledge is spread. This means that schools are set up to facilitate the spread of knowledge. Students are supposed to master knowledge just like the teachers. Though the knowledge of the same level may not be acquired by all, teachers, as knowledgeable people, are arranged for to impart knowledge to those who need knowledge. Interpretation is the basic way of spreading knowledge. Then people achieve equilibrium in the spread of knowledge in the state, so that all can interact with all in the same way in the formation of the state under the guidance of knowledge. In particular, since the realization of mass education in modern times, youngsters have been required to acquire both scientific knowledge and the knowledge about their state. They are usually required to have national consciousness. They are usually required to acquire historical and geographical knowledge of the state. If people enjoy democracy, they participate in politics. They may have to be further educated to master more knowledge about their state. Sometimes they are even led to gain more knowledge about their nation-state and hence to study in a college or a university. Professors may especially spread deep knowledge about their own state to them. In sum, people, forming their tribe, do not need knowledge. By contrast, people, forming their state, need knowledge. When people formed the state in ancient times, the knowledge, needed by them, was required for the building of a state of ancient times. When people form the state in modern times, the knowledge, needed by them, is required for the building of a modern state. If relevant knowledge is not disseminated through interpretations given to the people, people may not build the state successfully.

Third, scholars give interpretations. Scholars impart, sort out and create knowledge. In summary, scholars produce and disseminate knowledge. They realize their goal in the process of each interpretation. They conduct researches, for example. Conducting researches, they write papers and books. The process of research is the process of preparing giving an interpretation. Knowledge, created by them, must be interpreted by themselves or some others to ordinary people. These scholars include historians, philosophers, jurists, ethicists, sociologists, and economists among others. If they write one book, this book may be read by many ordinary people. Knowledge is acquired by ordinary people. If we assume that teachers interpret knowledge, I argue that they do so in a local area. Scholars interpret knowledge across the state. In other words, knowledge, created or disseminated by the scholars, is very complex, systematic and advanced. Such knowledge is created or disseminated by a few scholars. Such knowledge is needed by all and is interpreted to all. Such an interpretation is given on a large scale. As the state is a large community and a large community is complex, it is formed by people who have knowledge. Mutual interactions realized by people are guided by knowledge. The unity of the state is maintained by people who have knowledge. If people do not master certain knowledge, they may not be the qualified members of this state. Only qualified people are deemed as the qualified members of this state. People are not qualified until they have mastered certain knowledge. For example, they are required to have some historical knowledge of the state. Thus, scholars participate in the building of the state because they impart knowledge to the citizens. Though knowledge may not often be directly interpreted by the scholars to the masses in the school, interpretations are often given by the scholars to spread the knowledge to all in the society.

Fourth, professionals give interpretations. While they give interpretations, they spread knowledge. Such knowledge may be originally spread by scholars. But such knowledge may not be directly spread by scholars. Such knowledge may not be spread by priests or school teachers either. But such interpretations are needed by ordinary people. This knowledge can be professional knowledge. It is sometimes spread by professionals. For example, scientific or technological knowledge may be popularized by an engineer or a technician through interpretations. The knowledge about economy may be spread by an economic analyst through an interpretation. The knowledge about society may be disseminated by a social worker through an interpretation. The knowledge about law may be disseminated by a lawyer through an interpretation. The knowledge about public health policy of the government may be spread by a public health expert through an interpretation. These people who give interpretations may be scholars. But they may not be scholars either. They may be professionals. They have certain applicable knowledge. As they help ordinary people to understand a certain affair within the state, ordinary people enhances their ability to understand the affairs of the state. This means that the formation of a state includes building a community with knowledge. The development of economy and the progress of the state have changed the living conditions of people. The mode of interaction realized by people has also changed. If people do not have certain knowledge, they may not be able to realize effectively interactions with one another. They may not be the qualified members of the state. As a result, people set the goals of the development of all aspects, such as the goal of economic or social development. The knowledge of managing public affairs becomes diversified. People are sometimes required to acquire the related knowledge in order to become the qualified citizens because only qualified citizens can participate in the construction of the state. They need the related interpretations given by professionals. Although they are not necessarily required to master the relevant knowledge systematically, they need such interpretations. The on-going interactions between them and professionals are part of the organization of the state.

Correlatively, people have a different structure of cognition in the state. Unlike tribal people who have the invariable structure of cognition, people in the state have a varying structure of cognition. In the state some people have basic knowledge, whereas some other people have advanced knowledge. Through an interpretation, those who have more knowledge spread knowledge to those who have less knowledge. If we suppose that those who spread knowledge also have a varying structure of knowledge, we can believe that those who have the knowledge of the high level are the fewest in the state, and those who have the knowledge of the elementary level are the most in the state, and those who have the knowledge of the middle level are more than those who have the knowledge of the high level and are fewer than those who have the knowledge of the elementary level. Knowledge may spread from those who have the knowledge of the high level to those who have the knowledge of the middle level first and then spread from those who have the knowledge of the middle level to those who have the knowledge of the elementary level and then spread from those who have the knowledge of the elementary level to those who have no knowledge. Similarly, if we suppose that books are media that spread knowledge, books that provide original knowledge are fewer than the books that popularize the original knowledge. When people interpret the related knowledge, they may interpret that knowledge level by level. Therefore, some books may interpret the original book, and some other books may further interpret the books that interpret the original book. The original book may be one, and the books interpret it may be more than this original book and the books interpret the books that interpret this original book may be more than the books that interpret the original book. Knowledge is interpreted by people level by level. The description of certain knowledge may be simplified level by level, so that it can be understood by more and more people. In schools, colleges and universities, teachers who teach the knowledge of the elementary level are more than those teachers who teach the knowledge of the middle level and the teachers who teach the knowledge of the middle level are more than those who teach the knowledge of the high level. Likewise, students who study for a middle school diploma are more than those who study for a high school diploma, and students who study for a high school diploma are more than those who study for a bachelor degree diploma, and students who study for a bachelor degree diploma are more than those who study for a master degree diploma or a doctoral degree diploma. Educational institutions can also demonstrate this structure of popularizing knowledge. In a nation-state primary schools are more than high schools, and high schools are more than colleges and universities.

This also happens along with an increase in the size of the community. In a large community, people often receive a varying education. For example, in the era before mass education was put into practice, people might receive a varying education. Some people were poor and unable to engage a tutor or go to school. They received less education. Some people might reside in a region where education had not well developed. They might not receive an adequate education. Even though mass education goes on today, education may not develop evenly in all the regions. Education is more flourishing in the urban area than in the rural area. Education is more flourishing in the developed region than in the underdeveloped region. In addition, knowledge, created by people, may not be perfect unless people engage in systematic and deep-going research and thinking. People are unable to engage in such research and thinking except a small number of well-educated people. An increase in the size of the community creates a condition for people to spread knowledge on a large scale. People deepen the division of labor in the large community. A portion of people especially engage in the research and speculation that result in the creation of certain knowledge. People offer the related knowledge. They may be theologians, philosophers, writers, jurists, historians and scientists. These people are often intellectuals. Then people spread knowledge. They spread knowledge level by level. Some people especially engage in the spread of knowledge.

All in all, such interpretations are also needed by the state because the state is formed by people required to participate effectively in the organization of the state. In the formation of a society, the abovementioned knowledge may not be needed. But knowledge is required in the formation of the state. This means that in the society people also give various interpretations. Yet no interpretation is always required to be the same as all other interpretations. The so-called society may be composed of various different parts each of which may function in a different principle or method. Each part of the society may coordinate with any other part of the society, but coordination is not always absolutely required. Thus sometimes one part of the society is in conflict with another part of the society. But in the state interpretations must be given on a large scale or across the state because all are supposed to have the same knowledge and interact with each other in the same way in the organization of the state. The unity of the state is of utmost importance.

The reason is that the organization of the state relies on knowledge. Such knowledge is an element of the formation of various conditions for the building of the state. The formation of the society does not require the interpretation of the society given this way because the society is composed of many small communities that do not require a unified interpretation of the society. The society does not authorize anyone to take charge of organizing the society though the society is formed by all within the society. The society is formed in the mutual interactions of passively existing people. The interpretations given in the society are not unified. By contrast, the state is organized in one principle formulated by people. The organization of the state requires that all, forming the state, understand the state in the same way. Understanding it needs knowledge. Knowledge is disseminated through interpretations level by level. Thus, the interpretations of the state are often given by some people to some other people across the state.

2. Values

People not only form their state with knowledge, but also build their state with a series of values. Values may derive from an idea. An idea cannot always be equated with knowledge. This may give us a hint that values are different from knowledge in nature. Then I argue that humans often come up with an idea in their production and living in a special way. In primitive times, people already had their own traditional idea. They had the notion of the tribe acquired by them in their own mutual interactions realized in the same way generation by generation as if such a notion were acquired by them unwittingly. Their traditional idea or notion of the tribe was usually not in need of any interpretation just like common sense noted earlier. Nobody was in charge of giving such an interpretation in the tribe. Yet since the formation of the state, people have come up with new ideas, notions, views and even worldviews. These ideas, notions, views and worldviews may be combined, systematically sorted out and theoretically enhanced to become an ideology. Then based on this ideology, people come up with their values which reflect their needs, goal and principle or their standard of judging things as good or bad, just or unjust, appropriate or inappropriate and desirable or undesirable. If we assume that people always form their state under the influence of an idea, this idea may enable people to create their values as long as people insist on carrying out this idea over the long term. These values may guide all. All may take collective action as guided by these values.

Specifically, in the formation of their tribe, people were not under the guidance of any values because humans, forming the tribe, did not have any values. They needed no interpretation. They did not propagate any values. Unlike the case that whenever humans form their state, they have a certain idea or a consciousness, the case for the tribe is that the idea or consciousness, had by humans in the tribe, was the idea or consciousness of the lowest level that was nearly tantamount to human social instinct. This idea or consciousness should be required to maintain the community formed by tribal people for self-preservation. This idea or consciousness only satisfied the need of tribal people in their effort for self-preservation. This idea or consciousness could hardly make any progress to reach a higher level because people could not come up with an idea or a consciousness of the higher level without using language. For self-preservation humans always used the same method in the organization of their community. Humans built this community by nature. Yet since humans started to use language in communication, they have gradually turned to building a very large community. Kinship fails to support the building of this large community. Then, the idea or consciousness of kinship no longer suffices to support the formation of the community. People need to have a new idea or consciousness in support of the growth of the large community. People need to have values. Unlike those who formed a tribe as tribal people as guided by the idea of kinship, people, forming themselves into the state, organize themselves under the guidance of some values. Though those values are created by people, people build their state on the basis of their own judgment. Their judgment may be reasonable. Unlike tribal people, people who form the state have more control on the building of their state. They create their own values. Then, values play a role in the formation of the state. For example, people engage in social exchange such as the exchange of goods and services realized through the market in the state. People strengthen such a social exchange as they hold the same values. For instance, people, originally unable to realize face-to-face interaction and cooperation due to the fact they are far from each other, may make an effort to realize interaction and cooperation just because values can play a role as a medium. People usually believe that values are essential for mutual interaction. Values form a foundation for building a trust relationship between one another. Thus, people, holding the same values, tend to realize active interaction and cooperation in a big way even though they are far from each other. This means that people, holding the same values, tend to realize more proactive interaction and effective cooperation over the long term and on a large scale. Other social transactions may also be realized in the way significant for the building of the society on a large scale. As Peter M. Blau writes,

> Common values of various types can be conceived of as media of social transactions that expand the compass of social interaction and the structure of social relations through social space and time. Consensus on social values serves as the basis for extending the range of social transactions beyond the limits of direct social contacts and for perpetuating social structures beyond the life span of human beings.[5]

Thus people may feel close to each other and unite across the state. Then the related values may be used by people in the organization of the state.

The reason is that values are a guide to one's behavior. Values may derive from an idea according to which people form their society. Values may also derive from a spirit that encourages people to jointly build their state. While humans interpret knowledge, they clarify the truth. While humans interpret values, they insist on how they should associate together, how they should realize their personal development, how they should jointly build their society, and how they should govern the state.

Since the state needs these values as a guide or an idea or a spirit, creating these values means organizing the state. As these values may be the sole values guiding the overall building of the state, interpreting these values means, in some sense, using an overall method to organize the state. Then we see that whenever people interpret these values, they interpret the organization of the state. They interpret the totality of organizing the state. They interpret multiple aspects of the building of the state. They interpret every aspect that is part of the organization of the state. Normally, values are what we consider to be abstract and the organization of the state is what we consider to be concrete. People tend to interpret what is concrete in order to interpret what is abstract because it is easier to interpret what is concrete than to interpret what is abstract. In this sense, what is concrete is a medium used by people to interpret what is abstract when they interpret what is abstract. Then it follows inevitably that interpreting the values, people interpret the building of the society and the organization of the state. As one can interpret the building of the society and the organization of the state from numerous perspectives, they give a multiplicity of interpretations. They interpret social norms, social and political systems, and ideas among others. They even interpret all they want to interpret. They interpret mainly the following.

First of all, they interpret morality. Morality has been discussed by us in the preceding text in which I mention ethicists who perform human-chain linguistic communication and disseminate a moral idea. In this section, I would like to point out that people often interpret morality, a cardinal guide to people' behavior in the society. Morality should be a basis for the organization of the state. People establish the order of the state by relying on the strength of morality which takes shape in the society. People propagate political morality which derives from social morality propagated by people in the society. In ancient China Confucius propagated the Confucian idea of morality among ordinary people. Such an idea of morality was sorted out by him on the basis of the thoughts offered by many learned predecessors and was propagated by him and his disciples to many less-educated people male and female, old and young. Confucius hoped that the order of the society and the state could be built in the principle of moral supremacy. In medieval Europe learned people also disseminated the idea of morality to ordinary people. An idea of religious morality was that people should obey the will of God. In modern Europe some learned people propagate the new ideas of morality. All embrace them. For example, all embrace the morality based on a humanitarian idea. So people usually succeed in propagating the same values in relation to morality and all embrace the same idea of morality. People disagree on the settlements of specific disputes very often because they have different interests and they view the things from different perspectives. But it is easy for them to reach a consensus on the reasonableness of values because the reason, had by people, is the same so far as all are educated. The power of reason lies in the fact that a human being is an animal of reason. Values are often reasonable, and people are unable to challenge them. In the propagation of reasonable values, it is difficult for people to ignore them.

People interpret the traditional idea, too because this traditional idea contains values. In a state in which religion plays a powerful role in the growth of the state, a traditional idea may stem from religion. In another state, a traditional idea may stem from the local culture. Besides, in a state a traditional idea may take shape in history. Intellectuals may give the interpretations of that traditional idea. The interpretations of the values may also be given. Values are even created through interpretations. This happens in the state. In a tribe people may not interpret any traditional idea. Yet in the state people often interpret the traditional idea because to a greater extent humans rely on such a traditional idea to organize their state. To put it differently, people, forming a tribe, do not intentionally study any traditional idea, whereas people, forming the state, may do so. People may show respects to totems in the tribe. They stand in awe of totems because they believe that totems are powerful. Yet they have no values concerning totems because they have no philosophy. By contrast, people may have different interests in the state. They are often in different situations. They may view the affairs of the state from different perspectives. However, it is also true that people adhere to a traditional idea over the long term, and they believe that this traditional idea is rational or fair. There may be a sort of philosophy behind this traditional idea. There may be values in this traditional idea. People tend to follow this traditional idea, and interpret the related values. Once people accept and uphold these values because of interpretations, they strengthen their mutual interactions. They may build the state according to this traditional idea.

In modern times people particularly stress economic and social development in nearly all the nation-states, too. Production is the priority of each nation-state. Accordingly, people may interpret the values of work. For example, people highly evaluate work in Europe, North America and some East Asian countries and regions. Both the entrepreneur and the employee are required to work hard for their self-preservation and development. A personal effort is praised and admired. As observed by Max Weber, Protestant ethics underlies the spirit of capitalism. Work is especially highly evaluated by Protestant ethics, a reason for the quick growth of capitalist economy in the state in which Protestantism has prevailed since Reformation. Productive activities are no longer deemed mainly as the effort made for the satisfaction of the need of each family only but especially as the necessity in the operation of enterprises and development of business. The industrious spirit of doing business is exalted. Market exchange is accepted and even encouraged. Many obsolete or out-of-date rules of the Catholic Church are no longer obeyed. A new spirit in line with the creed of Protestantism spreads. In the United States people believe that work is morally right. Material goods are deemed as the just reward of hard work, which is the evidence of God's favor. Thus Alexis de Tocqueville writes that:

> Among democratic peoples where there is no hereditary wealth, every man works for his living, or has worked, or comes from parents who have worked. Everything therefore prompts the assumption that to work is the necessary, natural, and honest condition of all men.[6]

Some analysts also attribute the fast economic growth of some East Asian countries or regions, such as the Republic of Korea, Singapore, Taiwan and Hong Kong, in the 1970s and 1980s to the role of the values of work upheld by the peoples of those countries or regions. People interpret the values of work from time to time. These values are also in relation to the traditional virtue of family thrift, loyalty and self-discipline. People propagate a spirit. This spirit bolsters the economic growth of a state or a region. This spirit also serves as part of a spiritual foundation for the organization of the state or a region.

The worldview is interpreted, too. In some states, the worldview is interpreted according to the belief of Christianity. Secular worldview may also be embraced by many. For example, individualism may be part of this worldview. Individualism may be upheld by many people particularly in the states in which the state protects the personal rights as the civil rights. G. W. F. Hegel writes that:

> Individuality is awareness of one's existence as a unit in sharp distinction from others. It manifests itself here in the state as a relation to other states, each of which is autonomous vis-à-vis the others. This autonomy embodies mind's actual awareness of itself as a unit and hence it is the most fundamental freedom which a people possesses as well as its highest dignity.[7]

These related values may be a reflection of concrete life. For example, in the United States people are seen as separate individuals with individual needs. They stress self-help. They exalt individual's success no matter who he is and from which family he comes. To them, the best in people are selected in competition and free enterprise leads to progress.

People may interpret lifestyle at the same time. The notion of lifestyle can be considered part of the worldview. In particular, in the capitalist era people promote the lifestyle in vogue to highlight the values adhered to by the mainstream society. In the United Kingdom, France and the United States people have been widely discussing technological revolution, mass consumption and mass culture in the public since industrialization and urbanization. Mass media, including newspapers, magazines, movies, radio stations and television stations, present the topics concerning the lifestyle of the advanced states, and propagate the values especially upheld by the mainstream society. The related interpretations are given to all belonging to different social classes. Lifestyle is conceived of being enjoyable by all within the state. That is, lifestyle is witnessed by everyone everyday and it becomes a medium that highlights values.

People may also interpret social system. Some states adopt the capitalist social system, whereas some other states claim that they adopt the socialist social system. Intellectuals, like economists and sociologists as well as politicians, often debate the social system. They compare the advantage and disadvantage of each social system. In the meantime they propagate the values they uphold. In the interpretation of the social system, people often debate heatedly the values concerning freedom or equality. As a social system may have the advantage and disadvantage at the same time, and the social system is very important for the building of the society on the basis of which the state is built, such interpretations are crucial. In the United States people build the whole society on the basis of the system of modern capitalism. The social prosperity of this state much more relies on the vitality of modern capitalism. In the meantime the related interpretation is usually accepted by all or the majority. A related discourse in support of modern capitalism prevails to keep the dominance of the interpretation that functions in support of the organization of the state. The related interpretation, given jointly by news media, politicians and intellectuals daily, proves to be a condition for the organization of the state.

People also interpret the political idea of the state because everyone is supposed to comprehend the political idea of the state. In this case it is widely interpreted by philosophers or writers, politicians and others such as journalists. Thus, once some of them make public a political idea of organizing the state, other people, such as politicians or philosophers or social scientists, may propagate this political idea. Behind this political idea there are often a series of values. People propagate these values. For example, when American people announced independence, the Declaration of Independence, formulated by some politicians, expounded the reason for independence. This reason was presented because they upheld certain values. Despite that the thirteen colonies had been originally the separate or autonomous political entities, they merged to form a unified nation-state partly because they could uphold the same values of founding a state. People, holding the same values, might form one state because the formation of the state relied on the availability of unified values. In fact, these values discussed here were the values embraced by all or at least the vast majority of the American people. People, insisting on this political idea, announced insisting on such values on behalf of all or the vast majority of American people. The Declaration of Independence served as a basis for the building of a new nation-state in North America because values, advocated by it, were accepted and embraced by all or the vast majority. This situation is like the case described by us in Chapter Four, in which it is mentioned that political and social consciousness functions as a medium in support of the linguistic communication that goes on across the state. And the related linguistic communication is a prerequisite for the building of the state. That is, the values, described here, are, in some sense, like political and social consciousness. The shared values may function as media in support of the formation of the state. In the meantime, people give interpretations. Interpretations spur or strengthen the circulation of an idea in the community. The said values may stem from such an idea. Then people uphold these values faithfully and support the organization of the state in the principle formulated according to such values.

Those who draft the constitution may also interpret the constitution as each state normally has a constitution and a constitution often upholds values.

There is a process of linguistic communication performed by the drafters of the constitution with the ordinary citizens. The drafters of the constitution have the knowledge of the constitution, whereas ordinary people may not have adequate knowledge of the constitution. People disseminate values behind the constitution in the interpretation of the constitution. That is, the drafters may summarize and highlight the values reflected by the constitution drafted by them. For example, they may interpret the values of liberty, democracy and human rights. Ordinary citizens are required to understand the spirit of the constitution. In the meantime they are also required to understand the related values. As a result, the values are interpreted after the constitution is drafted and promulgated. People may give different interpretations of the values behind the constitution. For example, some people may say that the constitution reflects the conservative spirit, whereas others may insist that the constitution reflects the liberal spirit. But the interpretation, given by the constitution itself, is authoritative. Mainstream values are propagated in this interpretation. In the United States, for example, the constitution is often interpreted by judges, politicians, scholars and others. Whenever an interpretation is given, the values of democracy, equality and liberty are always propagated through the interpretation. The vitality of the constitution of the United States lies in its insistence on the related values. People may not easily understand the values behind the constitution. As a result, some people interpret such values time and again when they mention the constitution.

People may also interpret the future. To interpret the future often means to propagate an ideal or a series of ideals. In the interpretation of the future, people interpret certain mainstream values. The ideal or a series of ideals are often embedded in the mainstream values. The reason that people keep an ideal or a series of ideals is that people are always or normally preparing for tomorrow. They keep a positive attitude toward the future. Thus the future for them is interpreted, so that values are propagated and those values are expected to function in the organization of the state. In the United States people believe that the future will be better and happier. The so-called American Dream is a national spirit constantly interpreted by some philosophers, thinkers, writers and others since the birth of the United States. It is a set of ideals, the content of which includes the opportunity for personal success with the possibility of an upward social mobility achieved through hard work. In 1930 James Truslow Adams wrote that "The American Dream is that dream of a land in which life should be better and richer and fuller for everyone, with opportunity for each according to ability or achievement" regardless of social class or circumstances of birth.[8] It is in line with the idea of "all men are created equal" proclaimed in the Declaration of Independence of the United States. In later times the dream includes the opportunity for one's children to grow up and receive a good education and have a good career without man-made barriers. In other words, it includes the opportunity to have individual choices without restrictions on anyone because of his or her class, caste, religion, race or ethnicity. The content of the dream also includes the building of a prosperous, powerful country of which all are proud.

By contrast, in some other countries people do not interpret the dream of the nation-state actively and widely. The state fails to propagate the mainstream values in the organization of the state. Jean-Jacques Servan-Schreiber complained that in African society, which exalts the glorious past of ancestors through tales and fables, people do nothing to prepare for the future. The African, anchored in his ancestral culture, is so convinced that the past can only repeat itself that he worries only superficially about the future.[9] This description conversely demonstrates that the future can function as a medium through which people give an interpretation. A different interpretation of the future may guide the state in going in another direction. If people interpret the future as the repetition of the past, the state will tend to be conservative. By contrast, if the future is interpreted as a new one, people may be motivated to make a greater effort for the future.

In short, values are created by people not only by describing the objective world but also by prescribing their idea. Though people make a prescriptive statement when creating these values, they are also created by people on the basis of experience and contemplation. Albeit not being created by making a descriptive statement, values can become a belief. If people keep on interpreting values, these values may become the belief upheld by all. This belief may be a religious belief or a secular one. Yet no matter whether this belief is religious or secular, the belief, upheld by people, always contains some values. As long as people believe that this belief is just, fair, and reasonable, this belief may become powerful. Analyzing power in the state, Russell writes that "The power of a community depends not only upon its numbers and its economic resources and its technical capacity, but also upon its beliefs."[10]

As the state is a complex community, values that guide the organization of the state also rest on the complex thinking of humans. Yet only a small portion of people can engage in complex thinking. People who form the state are different from tribal people. Tribal people invariably engage in simple thinking only. They do not use written language. They do not write books. Their thinking cannot be complex. Among those who form the state, however, their capabilities of thinking vary. Not all can engage in complex thinking. But a small portion of people can engage in complex thinking. Usually, only those people participate in creating the values. Those people are usually learned. Those people may be writers, poets, historians, theologians, artists, philosophers and jurists and so on. They may be writers, poets, historians, theologians, artists, philosopher and jurists by career or otherwise. They offer their ideas to the society when they create their works. They are geniuses. They create their original and unique ideas. These ideas further serve as a basis for people to create the related values. As these values are urgently needed by the society, the masses embrace them. Then these values may form themselves into the mainstream values that guide the organization of the state. Then, people see that a small number of people communicate with a large number of people, spreading values across the state. A small number of people give interpretations to a large number of people.

The reason is that these learned people are those who excel in interpreting values to those who need such interpretations. Those who excel in interpreting values are a small number of people, whereas those who need interpretations are a large number of people. Such interpretations symbolize, in some sense, the organization of the state because such interpretations disseminate values, theorized by a small number of people, to a large number of people and disseminating these values serves as a way of organizing the state. One case in point is that in a civilized society a few learned people interpret morality, law and religion among others. They may also be philosophers, jurists and theologians and so on. For instance, they offer advanced ethics, whereas ordinary people can only present a simple moral idea. The simple moral idea is often similar in different far-flung corners of the society or the state. But such a moral idea is not spread from one location to all other locations. Such a moral idea is presented by people in different places respectively. The standard and content of morality are largely the same or analogous in different areas because people come up with a moral idea by nature in the background of the society or the state which is largely analogous. The reason is that mutual interactions, realized by people in the formation of the society or the state, are largely of the same type. A moral idea, had by ordinary people, originally stems from the common sense. Ordinary people naturally believe that something ought to be or ought not to be. By contrast, advanced ethics is spread across the society or the state because advanced ethics is offered by a few learned people and embraced by plenty of ordinary people. The reason is that the moral idea, offered by learned people, is detailed, or systematic, or profound, or quintessential, or insightful, or convincing, or complete. It is a medium. Thus a few learned people spread their ideas to many others in the form of books. People only present a perfect moral idea in the form of book. Books are also media. Thus this moral idea may become a series of values embraced by many people across the society or the state. For example, the book Nicomachean Ethics by Aristotle discusses happiness in detail. He believes that happiness is the end of life instead of a means. He argues that:

> In speaking of degrees of finality, we mean that a thing pursued as an end in itself is more final than one pursued as a means to something else, and that a thing never chosen as a means to anything else is more final than things chosen both as ends in themselves and as means to that thing; and accordingly a thing chosen always as an end and never as a means we call absolutely final. Now happiness above all else appears to be absolutely final in this sense, since we always choose it for its own sake and never as a means to something else.[11]

Discussing his ethical theory, Benedict Spinoza also states that:

> So each one, from his own affect, judges, *or* evaluates, what is good and what is bad, what is better and what is worse, and finally what is best and what is worst. So the greedy man judges an abundance of money best, and poverty worst. The ambitious man desires nothing so much as esteem and

dreads nothing so much as shame. To the envious nothing is more agreeable than another's unhappiness, and nothing more burdensome than another's happiness. And so, each one, from his own affect, judges a thing good or bad, useful or useless.[12]

Elucidating morality, Kant also believes that morality is a duty for a man. For example, he states that "To be beneficent when we can is a duty."[13] He firmly believes that "if duty is a conception which is to have any import and real legislative authority for our actions, it can only be expressed in categorical and not at all in hypothetical imperatives."[14] He accentuates the purity of morals "for the proper and inestimable worth of an absolutely good will consists just in this, that the principle of action is free from all influence of contingent grounds, which alone experience can furnish."[15] These views about morality are unique, in depth, and reasonable. The presentation of these views cannot be replaced by the presentation of any other views made in the same domain. Thus in the narration of their views, people interpret them at the same time. They give interpretations across the state because their presentations cannot be replaced.

As people normally spread values in linguistic communication, they inevitably take advantage of media. Using media in disseminating values serves as a foundation for the building of the state because empowering values is significant for the building of the state.

First, some learned people are used by some other learned people. Spreading values, learned people may form a hierarchy. Among those learned people, some people are the most learned and some other people are the more learned. The most learned may be those who offer the original ideas. The more learned may be those who help popularize the original ideas offered by the most learned people. In other words, not all people are the most learned people. Values are disseminated from the most learned people to the more learned people and then to the less learned people. The most learned people communicate on the largest scale, but they are the fewest. The more learned people are more than the most learned people, but they do not communicate on the largest scale. That is, if one does not excel in interpreting values, he is usually unable to disseminate values. If one interprets values, he may only interpret them in the local area because he is unable to interpret them systematically and theoretically. If he is able to interpret values most systematically and theoretically because he can present an idea warmly embraced by all others, he is able to interpret the idea on a large scale and even across the state. An idea, created by people, is also improved, summarized and updated. The more advanced or systematic or profound the idea, the larger a scale on which the idea is spread. If an idea trumps any other ideas in terms of the power of interpretation, people from more areas will embrace it. Interpreting this idea is interpreting the related values. Then those who are the most learned people interpret these values to the more learned people and then the more learned people interpret these values to the less learned people.

Second, learned people often found academies and schools. They teach students. As those students may become learned people in future, students assist in spreading the idea. They help spread the values. They also spread the values in linguistic communication. They communicate over long distances. If they cannot communicate with all directly across the state, they may engage in human-chain linguistic communication. In ancient China, Confucius, a well-known philosopher, taught over three thousand disciples. And these disciples also had their disciples. They spread Confucianism on a large scale. Confucianism was a medium that enabled Confucius to communicate with his disciples and enabled his disciples to communicate with their disciples. All of them were well-educated people. They were also media. In other words, the whole society needed the circulation of those values. They were entrusted by the society to spread those values in some sense. And some people might be media used by some other people. For example, the disciples of Confucius were media used by Confucius and the disciples of the disciples of Confucius were media used by the disciples of Confucius. Then these learned people spread Confucianism level by level, presuming that the teacher always spread ideas to his students. That is, the students interpreted the idea of their teacher. People might interpret an idea level by level when they all became teachers. I believe that such a way of spreading values also appeared in Europe and Near East in pre-modern times. In modern times such a way of spreading values continues in schools throughout the world.

Third, people also disseminate values through various forms of association. As people often need cooperation, they associate together. They form social groups. They may even set up various organizations. They disseminate values through those forms of association. Their association serves as a medium in support of their mutual linguistic communication. First, people form families. In some sense, a family is a social cell. In some cases, a family is a social unit. Family members keep on interacting with each other. They disseminate values to each other. For example, parents disseminate values to their children. Second, people gather in their workplace. They work in a factory. This factory is, in some sense, a social organization. The owner of the factory organizes the workers. The owner of the factory communicates with the workers. He may spread values to the workers. The workers may also spread values to each other. All may share certain values at the workplace. Third, trade unions and other professional clubs or associations are also media. People, having joined those organizations, keep on communicating with each other. They hold meetings. The organizers and the members of those organizations spread values from time to time through those organizations. Fourth, political parties are political organizations. They hold activities. Those who organize or join a political party often communicate with all others within this political party. Such a political party disseminates values among all. Fifth, the government is also a political organization. People are governed by the government. They interact with the government. They need the government to provide public services. Thus, the government may propagate values to them.

Different values may also contend. The reason is that since the formation of the state due to extending the distance of linguistic communication people have needed to use a different approach in the organization of the state. People increase the size of the community. Kinship no longer underlies the formation of the community. People begin to have private interest. People have to ensure the fair distribution of the interest of the community though they are also committed to the enhancement of the public interest of the community. Then people offer values to guide the organization of the state to ensure the fair distribution of interest. These values may also have a systematic idea that guides the distribution of interest in the complex society. People need to have such values. People keep on interpreting such values. These values serve as a foundation for the building of the state. Then we see that despite that tribal people hold their idea of kinship by nature, people who form the state have to create their values. People create their values in the form of interpreting them. They interpret those values just like the fact that they interpret knowledge. Yet although humans interpret both knowledge and values, they interpret them in different methods. While humans interpret knowledge, they make a descriptive statement. While humans interpret values, they make a prescriptive statement. As people interpret something that, they think, ought to be when they present their values, they often offer different values. The related background is that the large community becomes complex in structure as compared with the original tribe. In these circumstances, people are in different positions and backgrounds. They may view the same thing from different perspectives. They may have different values. If there are no uniform values that guide the acts of all within the state, people may often be involved in a conflict, and this situation may adversely affect the unity of the state. For example, a person may view an affair of the state from the perspective of liberalism while another person may view this affair from the perspective of conservatism. One may welcome a decision made by the government, whereas the other may oppose this decision made by the government. For instance, a liberalist may support a new lifestyle in vogue while a conservative may oppose this new lifestyle. A person from the lower order of the society may be very concerned about the disparity between the rich and the poor, whereas a person from the upper order of the society may not care about this matter. We even sometimes envision the fact that a revolution exalted by revolutionaries may be regarded by the government as a crime of subverting the government. In a nutshell, as Hans Kelsen writes, "That which is 'good' according to the one norm may be 'bad' according to another."[16] Thus, according to Kelsen, "the norms that are the basis of the value judgments are enacted by human, not superhuman, will."[17] In the meantime, people build a state, and they have to ascertain how to build this state. They may even ask which rights they can have and which obligations they have to undertake in building this state. They have to define their mutual relationship on the basis of equality. They have to define the relationship between them and the state. People usually need to have values that can guide the work of solving these problems. Then different values contend. Then some values figure prominently. They may triumph amid the contention of different values. But if some values triumph over all other values, it is usually due to the fact that these values get endorsed by the fact.

That is, the validity of values lies in the fact that the interpretation of values is in line with the objective fact. Interpreting values means getting these values tested by the objective fact because people always have to interpret values in view of the result of social practice. Assuming that this result of social practice is the objective fact, I argue that the interpretations of these values need to be adjusted if they fail to be identical with the objective fact. Thus people will conduct a review. For example, the moral imperative, expounded by the thinkers and interpreted by other men of letters or intellectuals, must be tested to see if it is objective, appropriate and rational. If one moral standard is not accepted by the mainstream society, the values imbedded in morality and propagated by thinkers, may not function in the state. For example, there may be several moral standards advocated by thinkers. People may disagree on which moral standard should be obeyed. A portion of people may voluntarily obey the moral standard that requires altruism. By contrast, another portion of people may adhere to the moral standard of being neither absolutely altruist nor absolutely egoist. They may uphold the principle that altruism is conditional and egoism should be reasonable. Which moral standard becomes the mainstream moral standard depends on the selection of the majority of the citizens. And the selection of the majority of the citizens means the fact. This means that the values of morality need to be selected by the fact.

The interpretation of the principle of managing public affairs is also tested and hence, in some sense, endorsed by the fact. It is not the fact that is tested by an interpretation. The fact does not compromise with the interpretation. The fact is absolute. Thus an interpretation may change along with the passage of time because the fact varies along with the passage of time. In the period of free capitalism in the nineteenth century the values of laissez-faire policy were interpreted as the normal values in Great Britain. In the bulk of the twentieth century the values, advocated by people according to Keynesianism, were adhered to by the British government in place of the original values of free capitalism embedded in a laissez-faire policy. In the People's Republic of China the Communist government adopted the policy of planned-economy for the management of economic affairs. As this policy had failed from 1950s to 1970s, the government changed it. Then scholars have been interpreting the values of market economy ever since. The change of the values over time is followed by a change in the interpretation of the values because all values must be tested by practice. And the result of this practice can denote the fact. In this process values are often or always interpreted by the fact. They need to be endorsed by the fact. Of course, the fact is historical. A change in history changes the fact. Yet, the fact cannot be changed because of a change in interpretations. The objectivity of the fact cannot be challenged by interpretations. Thus, the fact endorses interpretations.

The interpretations of the social and political system must also be supported by the reality. This reality is the fact. The social and political system may take form by nature. This social and political system may also be designed. No matter whether the social and political system takes form by nature or is designed, since the establishment of such social and political system, it has been always interpreted by the fact. The success of a related social and political system is a basis for the possible success in the interpretation thereof. In the United States people always interpret the social and political system according to the fact. As long as this social and political system is successful, the related interpretations will prevail. In recent years some political scientists suspect that the cooperation between the Congress and the administration led by the president is not smooth because some financial plans, tabled by the administration, cannot be smoothly approved by the Congress. I believe that the interpretations of social and political system are subject to change if the judgment of the social and political system changes. Likewise, the interpretations of the political system given in China may also change. Though the power holder of the ruling party in China insists on maintaining the existing political system, the political system must function effectively and reasonably. Some political scientists advocate political reform because the flaw of the Chinese political system is evident in some aspects. The related interpretations must be tested by the fact. When people interpret the social and political system, they also interpret the related values.

It is evident that primitives do not give any of such interpretations because they have no values in the sense we use. By contrast, people, using written language, may sometimes engage in complex thinking. They create a variety of values. Particular values may arise from them. Then these values sustain the organization of the state. The interpretations of values are helpful to the interpretations of the state. Thus, unlike the case that people engage in the cause of science to interpret the objective world, people interpret values to clarify the subjective world of humans. Able to make a subjective judgment, people organize their state with values. Though values may stem from an ideology, which is often considered biased or the idea especially upheld by a portion of people within the state only, the existence of values indicates the role played by values in the organization of the state. People rely on reason to realize their purpose. Values, upheld by people, may stem from reason. Then the majority of people within the state embrace values and hence these values may finally become the mainstream values of the state. They support the organization of the state. The key is that the interpretations of values function to create or spread values important in the organization of the state due to the fact that without mainstream values the organization of the state will be difficult.

3. Public Affairs

After discussing the interpretations of values, we are going to discuss the interpretations of public affairs managed by the government. Though, as noted earlier, values may guide the management of public affairs and values need an interpretation, such values are often interpreted when people interpret ideas, systems and principles and so on. Public affairs are specific affairs. Interpreting those values may not always succeed when people interpret public affairs because people, sharing the same values, may not understand public affairs in the same way or to the same extent. The reason is that citizens themselves may not always reach an agreement on the management of a specific public affair. Likewise, even though the government and citizens share the same values, they may also understand a public affair differently. The reason is that all sides, sharing the same values, may not reach an agreement when interest is distributed, and the management of public affairs concerns the distribution of interest. People need to additionally reach a consensus to guarantee the fair distribution of interest. If the government is trying to guarantee the fair distribution of interest, it needs to further interpret how it manages each public affair. The reason is that even though citizens and the government share the same values, both the public interest and personal interest exist in the state. As public affairs may concern how the government distributes interest, the government needs to give an interpretation. If we compare a state with a tribe, I argue that no one would give an interpretation to the tribal people in the organization of the tribe. That means that in the tribe every decision, made by the tribal chief, was in the interest of all because there was only the common interest of the tribe. There was no apparent personal interest in the tribe. Though humans in the tribe had the potential idea of private property, this potential idea of private property could not be equated with the real idea of private property in the civilized society. The reason is that in the tribe there was no idea of private property. People, as the members of a tribe, were usually connected with each other through a very close blood relationship. They actually formed the same family, albeit a big one. In this family there was no private property but common property. So people in the tribe tended to cooperate. They were seldom in conflict with each other. Thus, they seldom raised a question about the fair distribution of interest. Yet since the formation of the state, people have no longer kept the sole and monolithic common property. Private property becomes prevalent. Each family has its own private interest though there is also the common interest of the whole state. People may often be in conflict. To distribute the interest fairly, people then present reasons. They give interpretations. They seek cooperation in establishing a system of distributing the interest fairly. If they do not need cooperation, they will not give any interpretation. If one steals the property of another person, he will not interpret his theft. If one defrauds another person, he will never interpret why he defrauds the other. This is because there is no cooperation between the two sides. Yet if one presents a reason for the distribution of interests, this fact may imply that the related two sides have common interest. If an interpretation is given, the person, facing the interpretation, needs to understand the interpretation. Understanding is, in some sense, a process of self-interpretation. The purpose that one interprets something to another is that the interpretation, given by the interpreter, is consonant with the self-interpretation given by the one who faces the interpretation. The two sides have to reach an agreement to make the interpretation successful. Thus, to present a reason, one has to give an interpretation. An interpretation presupposes the formation of the common interest of all albeit often to a varying extent. Conversely, if all have no common interest, no one will give an interpretation.

That is, an interpretation presupposes the formation of the common interest of all within the state, and an interpretation is particularly given to seek people's understanding in the management of public affairs because the management of public affairs directly concerns the distribution of the interest. This is usually a job done by the government. So an interpretation given by the government in the public in the state is often the interpretation of the management of public affairs. Such an interpretation is bound to create a condition for the formation of the common interest of all because such an interpretation is initiated by one side and expected by the other side. Normally, the government gives an interpretation of managing public affairs in the following aspects.

First, the government interprets some public affairs on which people cannot always see eye to eye. The government may set some grandiose programs of social and economic development as the top priorities of the state. Yet people may have different views about those public affairs because they may view related public affairs from different perspectives. For instance, the government tables a program of developing the agriculture of the country as its priority, and some people oppose this program. The reason is that in the era when humans remain the members of the tribe, the tribe manages its affairs without any dispute. But in the era when people become the members of the state, the government manages public affairs which need to be understood by people. If the government tables a great program, people may need to understand it. This program may dictate how the overall interest of the state is distributed among citizens. The state leader may give an interpretation. A government official may also act as the agent of the state leader to interpret that program. As public affairs are often managed by the government with a program, such a program is often interpreted by the personnel implementing this program. As those who manage public affairs are familiar with this program, they interpret those public affairs. They have the deep understanding of those affairs. So, the president of the United States may interpret the program of managing some public affairs. He may interpret why the government needs to implement a plan of scientific development. In the meantime, it may also be interpreted by other politicians, journalists, and scholars. In China, the government officials or the news media of the government also often interpret the programs of managing public affairs. They may interpret a program of reforming the administration of commerce or foreign trade. As long as the masses are concerned about a certain public affair, some government officials or news media often take initiative to make a comment on that public affair. They give an interpretation accordingly.

Second, the government interprets the management of public affairs with which ordinary people are not familiar. These public affairs may be in relation to social welfare and other public undertakings. Citizens may need to learn about these public affairs, yet they may not understand them. Ordinary people are very familiar with their own personal affairs. They usually know if the prices of consumer goods are high on the market because they often go shopping there. They know if the prices of some vegetables, meat and eggs are high. Yet they may not know if the cost of building a huge bridge in their city is reasonable. They may need to be advised by an engineer of public works. When a public affair needs to be dealt with, ordinary people may not know every detail of this public affair. In comparison with personal affairs, public affairs are strange. An interpretation may be given to let ordinary people understand them. Usually, the interpretation is given by an expert. It may be given by news media. But this interpretation is often given by the government. The reason is that those affairs often affect the distribution of interest among citizenry because all are taxpayers. People may argue if the way of managing a public affair is reasonable as long as this affair is a major one. Some citizens support the decision of the government, whereas some other people do not. The government sometimes has to come forward to interpret why it manages that public affair this way. For example, in the United States, citizens have been discussing the reform of medical care system. This reform will change the distribution of interest among the citizens because a great portion of the citizens may get medical care paid by some other taxpayers. Is a certain proposal for the reform of medical care system reasonable? If politicians debate this proposal in the congress, the government invariably has to interpret its idea. The government has to give its interpretation. Giving an interpretation means seeking consent from more people. Citizens often need to reach a consensus. If people cannot reach a consensus on managing a major public affair, the interpretation may fail to play a role in the organization of the state.

Third, the government interprets the management of public affairs citizens are often concerned about. Such public affairs, managed by the state, often need to be fully understood by ordinary people because such affairs have wide impact on the society. Such affairs may affect the building of the society and the living of the people in the state. They concern the interest of all. If the crime rate of a region goes up dramatically in a short period of time, local residents may be very concerned about this situation. The government has to act and may have to interpret how it will lower the crime rate. If a natural disaster occurs in a region, leaving many people dead and injured, the public will be very concerned about the rescue of that region. If an infectious disease spreads widely and seriously affects the health of the people across the country, local residents may be very concerned about this incident. The government has to act. The government has to take a measure to stop the spread of this infectious disease. The government has to use financial sources to eliminate the infectious disease. The public needs to know how the government acts to deal with this situation. The government often needs to interpret its work. If a war breaks out and the state is involved in this war, ordinary people may also be very concerned about what is going on. The government may need to interpret the warfare to win the understanding of the people and even to get active support from the people. All these affairs may have a bearing on the interest of the people. So the government interprets its management of public affairs from time to time. For example, according to Richard M. Weaver, during World War Two, the government of the United States established a vast office of war information to interpret the war from the point of view of the administration. Even separate departments of government had their public information services. The United States Navy had a high-powered publicity program. Its purpose was that photographs, radio programs and other public information about the navy were provided, so that the public support was captured.[18] The major task of the government in this regard was, in the main, to give an interpretation. People give an interpretation concerning the public affairs of the state. Such an interpretation concerns the interest of all.

In sum, people who form a tribe do not need such an interpretation, whereas people who form the state need such an interpretation. Such an interpretation is an approach for people to reach an agreement and to ensure the formation of the common interest. Such an interpretation also shows the following attributes.

First, the interpretation meets the expectation of those who accept the interpretation. The interpretation actually involves a dialogue. When an interpretation is given, it is usually given at the request of those who need the interpretation. As Hans-Georg Gadamer explains, hermeneutic phenomenon implies the primacy of dialogue and the structure of question and answer. Thus, according to him, "interpretation always involves a relation to the question that is asked of the interpreter."[19] Thus, giving an interpretation presupposes the existence of a question. If people do not ask that question, no answer will be given. Thus no interpretation will be given. Because of this the totality of an interpretation lies in the fact that the interpretation must satisfy those who need such an interpretation. This means that the interpretation must be given as expected. The interpretation should be accepted by those who face the interpretation. The acceptance of the interpretation means that people have reached an agreement in any form. Thus, this agreement reflects the common interest of all. To put it differently, if a portion of citizens do not accept the interpretation, the interpretation is not successful. Any interpretation may concern the distribution of the interest. Any scheme of distributing the interest may not always satisfy the expectation of all. But at least the basic expectation of all or the majority may be met. For example, if people interpret happiness, the interpretation may be accepted by all or the majority. Such an interpretation can become the interpretation for the collective. So Kelsen says that there can be no "just" order if one affords happiness to everyone as long as one defines the concept of happiness in its original narrow sense of individual happiness. This is because the happiness of one individual will, at some time, be directly in conflict with that of the other. Thus, according to him,

> The happiness that a social order can assure can be happiness in the collective sense only, that is, the satisfaction of certain needs, recognized by the social authority, the lawgiver, as needs worthy of being satisfied, such as the need to be fed, clothed, and housed.[20]

People have to give an interpretation widely acceptable. Thus, an interpretation should mean a due process of forming the common interest of all.

Second, the interpretation is in line with common sense or science or logic. As far as common sense is concerned, common sense comes into existence because people have proven experience. In the empiricist view, common sense is directly acquired by people in social practice and commonly considered true. If there is a disagreement between common sense and an interpretation even though common sense often does not need any interpretation, people will still rather believe common sense. Thus an interpretation which contradicts common sense will be self-defeating. For example, sometimes a political party claims in the election campaign that if it holds state power, it will realize the economic growth by twenty percent per year. If voters believe that that platform is unrealistic because according to common sense the economy of the state cannot grow as fast as that rate, the voters may not support it. This means that, objectively speaking, voters may think that that political party only aims to gain power instead of realizing the fast economic growth of the country because that platform cannot be realized. Only a realistic platform can realize the formation of the common interest. People make a judgment according to common sense. As far as science is concerned, unless a person rigidly adheres to a religious creed not in agreement with science, people usually believe science. People expect that a certain interpretation is given in the principle of science. If a person interprets a natural disaster in light of sorcery, the interpretation may not succeed because people do not believe sorcery in modern times. As far as logic is concerned, one may have a priori knowledge because he has the knowledge of logic. For example, sometimes anachronism, revealed in the government's interpretation of the management of a public affair, may frustrate the interpretation hermeneutically. What we find true today may become untrue tomorrow. If one interprets a historical event of the medieval times from the perspective of modern times, the interpretation may be anachronistic. As required by reason, citizens tend not to accept the anachronistic interpretation.

Third, the interpretation is accurate. The interpretation is not exaggerative. An accurate interpretation means the formation of the common interest of all. Such an interpretation is often given by the government when it can take into consideration the interest of all within the state. When it interprets a public affair, different groups of people or different communities of people may also interpret such a public affair. People from a certain part of the society may interpret the related public affair from their own perspective and in their own interest. For instance, sometimes we see that the leaders of the military industry of one country exaggerate the military threat from abroad in order to justify their request for an increase in funding appropriated by the state to national defense. The military threat to one country exists indeed when there is an armament race between one country and another. The military threat from abroad, however, is sometimes exaggerated particularly by the leaders of the military industry because they need more funding. Yet as the government needs to interpret the related public affair to all citizens in the state, its interpretation needs to meet the expectation of all. If people give different interpretations of the same public affair, it may often strike a balance between the inclination of one portion of people and the inclination of another portion of people. It is arguable that interpreting one certain public affair to all the citizens rather than a portion of people within the state enables the government to give an accurate interpretation. The accurate interpretation meets the formation of the common interest of all within the state.

Fourth, the interpretation is without prejudice. Prejudice means bias and partiality. Hans-Georg Gadamer believes that prejudice "means a judgment that is rendered before all the elements that determine a situation have been finally examined."[21] Prejudice may appear when people hold a traditional view that has already been out-of-date or obsolete. Prejudice may also appear because of the restricted vision of people or the inadequacy of the knowledge required for viewing a situation. Prejudice may also appear when people, viewing the situation, make the judgment under the influence of the interest of a portion of people. Like the abovementioned exaggerative interpretation, an interpretation, given under the influence of prejudice, does not presuppose the formation of the common interest of all but the formation of the common interest of a portion of people within the state. Prejudice reflects the view of a portion of people. While one gives an interpretation under the influence of prejudice, he gives this interpretation at the expense of the interest of another portion of people. The interpretation cannot succeed. Like exaggeration, prejudice is repugnant to any interpretation. Prejudice comes from one side. An interpretation needs to be accepted by all sides. The very act of an interpretation naturally tends to eliminate prejudice. A matter, or an issue, or a figure, must be viewed in all facets. The prejudice, the single faceted view, tends to be eliminated in an interpretation because the interpreter, intending to make such an interpretation successful, tends to prevent the formation of prejudice. Interpretation is the natural enemy of prejudice.

Fifth, the interpretation is not false. J. Dannhauer, a hermeneutic philosopher, holds that "hermeneutics is concerned with transmitting truth and combating falsehood."[22] My view is that the interpretation tends to be without any falsehood. Propaganda, a kind of interpretation in the nature of justification, is often required to be truthful though it is sometimes considered by some people falsifying something, or misleading, or distorting. Writing about the propaganda in the former Soviet Union and the United States in the last century, Jacques Ellul writes that:

> With regard to larger or more remote facts that cannot be the object of direct experience, one can say that accuracy is now generally respected in propaganda. One may concede, for example, that statistics given out by the Soviets or the Americans are accurate. There is little reason to falsify statistics. Similarly, there is no good reason to launch a propaganda campaign based on unbelievable or false facts.[23]

This is because falsification propaganda will be uncovered sooner or later and such falsification propaganda will backfire at the propagandist. Between the fact and the words, people, first of all, accept the fact. If the words contradict the fact, no one believes the words. The common sense of epistemology dictates that an interpretation must be identical with the fact.

Sixth, any interpretation is given by anyone freely. When Martin Luther so vehemently advocated the free interpretation of the Bible in the sixteenth century, he meant that monopolizing the interpretation of the Bible did not reflect what all thought of in terms of the interpretation of the Bible. As Hans-Georg Gadamer writes, Luther believed that they did not need tradition to achieve the proper understanding of the Scripture, nor did they need an art of interpretation in the style of the ancient doctrine of the four-fold meaning of Scripture. The allegorical method in particular, which had formerly seemed indispensable for the dogmatic unity of scriptural doctrine, was now legitimate only where the allegorical intention was given in Scripture itself. That is, the Old Testament should not acquire its specifically Christian relevance through an allegorical interpretation. People must take it literally.[24] Although Reformation theology was also dogmatic, this event indicated that the monopoly of the right to interpret might be based on the exercise of coercion according to the idea of a portion of people in any state in Europe in his times. That is, the conservative Catholic Church, which monopolized the interpretation of the Bible, prevented the interpretation of the Bible that correctly reflected what was thought of by a portion of religious believers. Through his act, Luther reinterpreted the ideas being formed in the religious community. That means that the interpretation should be given freely. An interpretation presupposes the existence of the common interest of the interpreter and others facing the interpretation. If no interpretation is freely given, no common interest of all exists.

People reach a consensus and hence unite through an interpretation. A process of linguistic communication, triggered by an interpretation, culminates in the formation of the common interest of all. Of course, people may give different interpretations about the related matter. People may propagate different ideas concurrently. Yet as long as people are free to give different interpretations, one interpretation tends to prevail over others. As Robin M. Williams writes,

> The nonobvious implications of sociological analysis of values are further illustrated by the proposition that opposition of interests and struggles among individuals and collectivities within a continuing polity and societal system actually can contribute to the establishment and elaboration of generalized values and symbols. In such contentions, each party will appeal to those values that are presumably accepted by third parties to legitimate its position and to attempt to recruit support or to disarm potential opposition. If successive contests and conflicts are then successfully resolved without repudiation of the values which legitimate the conflict-resolving process or mechanisms, the more highly generalized values will come more and more to be regarded as axiomatic or unchallengeable.[25]

Then people may reach a consensus on the interpretation of a public affair. Usually, the interpretation that spreads on the largest scale within the state is the most convincing one. Such an interpretation is most likely to be the one accepted by most of the people within the state. Thus as language allows people to extend the distance of communication step by step along with the functioning of media, the most convincing interpretation will finally become the dominant one across the state. The most widely-popularized idea is the one spreading on the largest scale. All finally embrace it. For example, in the first half of the nineteenth century the local southern milieu of the United States was hostile to black people and favorable to discrimination while American Society as a whole was hostile to racism. As the mainstream idea was interpreted on a larger and larger scale, the racism was finally overcome despite deep prejudices and local solidarities.[26] We can believe that as the right idea should be the only one, this right idea will finally triumph across the state. This is because an idea is always interpreted in the process of linguistic communication to which everyone will have access sooner or later. People will have a unified idea. The unified idea helps people to reach an agreement on the management of public affairs.

This case may also be illustrated by the interpretation in relation to the management of another specific public affair. Sometimes the government gives a related interpretation and all the citizens accept it. This case is indicative of the fact that the ideas, upheld by all, are unified. The common interest of all is formed. This situation can be clearly seen if we study the interpretations in relation to the management of public affairs in history. Specifically, the interpretations of the management of public affairs may change over time because of a change in the ideas upheld by people. Then ideas may be unified because reasonable ideas always prevail over those unreasonable ones. In Canada the federal government and the provincial government of British Columbia formally announced, in recent years, their formal apology of carrying out the policy of imposing head tax on Chinese immigrants in the nineteenth and early twentieth century. They announced that that policy was unfair toward the Chinese who immigrated to Canada in the nineteenth and early twentieth century. The said action, taken by the federal government and the government of the Province of British Columbia of Canada, shows a change in the idea upheld by the authorities of Canada. Such a change in policy and such an interpretation mean the unification of the ideas upheld by the mainstream society and the Chinese community and the enhancement of the common interest of all Canadian citizens.

Needless to say, an interpretation, given by one to the other, may be significant for the building of the society. But one may not always give an interpretation because no one is solely required to be in charge of building the society. The society is built in the process of the mutual interaction of passively existing people. The society does not officially entrust anyone to interpret itself. Yet since the formation of the state, interpretations, given by people, have been very significant for the organization of the state. So we see that whenever the state makes a decision on a public affair, common people will usually review it to see if this decision serves the interest of all fairly. The government may present a reason for the making of this decision. So humans do not give any interpretation of any decision in the tribe, but they give the interpretation of any decision in the state. Thus, the interpretations of public affairs become part of the operation of the state. This is because since the formation of the state a change has taken place in the structure of the community. In the operation of the state, people need to interpret the management of public affairs from time to time, so that it can be fully understood by all within the state. For example, whenever a policy, or a law, or a principle, or a plan, is made, the understanding of all within the state is often required. The government is often required to give an interpretation. Jean Grondin writes that "an interpretation can be criticized when it does not do justice to the object and its coherence."[27] People must give a fair or reasonable interpretation. This interpretation should be acceptable by those who face the interpretation. An interpretation is aimed at understanding. No understanding will be seen if there is no common interest. Giving an interpretation, the interpreter should consider the stance of those who accept the interpretation. Giving an interpretation, the interpreter should not act solely as one party to the dispute between this party and all others as another party. For example, interpreting the principle in the operation of the government, the government should not interpret it as the one reflecting the will of itself only. It should also reflect the will of the people. This is precisely because an interpretation should be given in consideration of the interest of the party that accepts the interpretation. Thus the interpretation should reflect the common interest of both the interpreter and all others accepting the interpretation. This is the nature of an interpretation. Conversely, if both parties do not have any common interest, no party will give an interpretation.

In the meantime, an interpretation may involve three parties. An interpretation may be given by one party to the other two parties. These two parties may be divided into the majority and the minority. How do people make these two parties reach an agreement on the interpretation given by another party? Reason is used. This reason may be included in the interpreted knowledge. This reason may also be included in the interpreted idea. Reason is used in the organization of the state. This is dictated by the nature of the state. That is, people form their tribe because of their own instinct. But when people form their state, reason is a basis for the formation of the state. Though in history the state is often formed through the use of force or because of conquest, the state cannot last long because of conquest. In other words, the state cannot last long because of coercion. If the state is expected to last long, people, forming the state, should be persuaded. Interpretations need to be given. This means that interpretations result in the formation of the common interest of all. The existence of the common interest is a reliable basis for the organization of the state. People within the state are required to understand the state. Interpretations are intended to realize this purpose. An interpretation is actually a way of organizing the state. To put it another way, the state is organized in the processes of interpretations. Interpretations are intended to persuade all to give support to the state.

First, since the formation of the state, both the public affair and the personal affair have been conceptualized. This is a step in the evolution of human society. When humans formed their tribes, there was no public affair or personal affair in each of the tribe. All affairs in the tribe were the affairs of all. People did not differentiate an affair of the tribe from any other affair. People were familiar with any affair of the tribe in the same degree. If people needed to have knowledge to understand this affair, knowledge, had by each, was almost the same as that had by another person unless a person was a child. Thus if knowledge was needed to understand a certain affair within the tribe, nobody needed an interpretation. Nobody needed another person to impart him additional knowledge. Yet a different situation occurs in the state. The state is a large community and people within the community may not keep in touch face-to-face. Each may be far from the other. In particular, ordinary people may be far from those who govern the state. The daily affairs of people vary. In particular, some affairs become public affairs in contrast to personal affairs. Thus there appears a demarcation between the public affair and the personal affair. Public affairs differ from personal affairs in character. Public affairs are normally or often managed by the government on behalf of the state. Public affairs may be far from ordinary people. Thus people may be very familiar with those personal affairs, but they may be unfamiliar with these public affairs, as mentioned earlier. Thus the state that makes a decision on a public affair is required to interpret its decision from time to time.

Second, in the tribe humans were quick to take joint action or to act in unison when a collective action was taken because they realized close mutual interaction in a small community. They lived together day and night. They performed face-to-face communication. They were always ready to act in unison if necessary. An affair of one was the affair of all. But since the formation of the state, a change has taken place. A person who deals with a personal affair may take action quickly. When a public affair is dealt with, some people may not be concerned with this public affair because a public affair is always dealt with by some other people. There may appear the "issue of a free rider." This is because people, as the members of the state, are dispersed or isolated. They may not often communicate with one another. They may not always stay in close contact with one another. They may not participate in the management of a public affair in the same degree. Thus the state seeks cooperation from the citizens. In particular, the state may need to mobilize the masses. Then the government needs to give an interpretation. It needs to interpret the reason for making a certain policy. It may interpret the significance of a public affair in detail. For example, if the state wages a war against another foreign state, the state may conduct propaganda. When it conducts propaganda, it gives the interpretations of the war. So Russell writes that:

> The part played by propaganda in national power has increased with the spread of education. A nation cannot succeed in modern war unless most people are willing to suffer hardship and many people are willing to die. In order to produce this willingness, the rulers have to persuade their subjects that the war is about something

important—so important, in fact, as to be worthy of martyrdom. Propaganda was a large part of the cause of the Allied victory in the War, and almost the sole cause of the Soviet victory in the years 1918 to 1920s.[28]

Third, in the tribe the tribal chief usually made a decision in the interest of all. Making a decision for the affair of the tribe, the tribal chief naturally considered the interest of all because he and all others belonged to the same family albeit a big one. The common interest of the tribe was very solid or monolithic. The instinct of mankind dictated that the person, in charge of management, took care of all others and all others also naturally obeyed the instructions of the person in charge of management. All obeyed the decisions made by the tribal chief without any objection. But the case for the state is different. In the state people do not have kinship ties. They may not always have the common interest. The state makes a series of policies. Each of these policies may be especially in favor of a group of people within the state. Thus the state may interpret that policy in order to placate another group of people opposing the related policy. When a law is to be made, the similar situation may also occur. As the interest of people varies, they may have a different view about a policy or a law. People may differ in view of a public policy or a law. In order to keep the solidarity of all within the state, the state, or the agents of the state, may be required to give an interpretation in order to persuade the people to accept the related policy or law. This means that the state usually advances a reason or a ground in its interpretation. If the interpretation is reasonable and the ground is convincing, all may accept the interpretation. If an interpretation is accepted, this can mean that an agreement is reached by all. So the related interpretation can buttress the unity of the state.

This situation also means that one takes initiative to give an interpretation, and he and others, accepting such an interpretation, have common interest. People may have different views about a policy or a law, but an interpretation may prompt people to reach a consensus. People witness the formation of their common interest when they reach a consensus on a public affair or a government's decision. Whether or not there is the formation of the common interest depends on whether or not people reach a consensus. Sometimes the common interest of the people has already existed, but people may not realize this fact. An interpretation may help people realize it. Thus a proper interpretation bolsters the unity of the state. This means that humans can think. Whenever they think in the same way, they may unite. Oration is a skill used by humans to let the masses accept an interpretation. If people do not have any common interest, no oration will be given. When an oration is given, there must be certain common interest. Language is a tool used by those who are especially capable of using language as long as an interpretation is needed. That means that a reasonable and convincing point of view can be propagated by someone and be accepted by all others. As people have the similar brains, the similar view can flow from one to the other. Thus people may unite because they hold the same view. One example that we can use is perhaps a piece of history about Cicero, a philosopher and orator in ancient Rome. He made the Romans feel how great a charming eloquence was and how invincible justice was. When he made a speech, he propagated an idea. He gave an interpretation. Ordinary people were persuaded by him. Then his idea was often accepted by the majority or all. Narrating the life of Cicero, Plutarch writes that:

> An incident occurred in the theatre, during his consulship, which showed what his speaking could do. For whereas formerly the knights of Rome were mingled in the theatre with the common people, and took their places among them as it happened, Marcus Otho, when he was a praetor, was first who distinguished them from the other citizens, and appointed them a proper seat, which they still enjoy as their special place in the theatre. This the common people took as an indignity done to them, and, therefore, when Otho appeared in the theatre they hissed him; the knights, on the contrary, received him with loud clapping. The people repeated and increased their hissing; the knights continued their clapping. Upon this, turning upon one another, they broke out into insulting words, so that the theatre was in great disorder. Cicero being informed of it, came himself to the theatre, and summoning the people into the temple of Bellona, he so effectually chid and chastised them for it, that again returning into the theatre they received Otho with

loud applause, contending with the knights who should give him the greatest demonstrations of honour and respect.[29]

It was a way used to govern the state.

If people, forming the state, do not have any common interest, no interpretation will be given. According to this logic, we can also believe that if a public affair, managed by the government, is interpreted and the related interpretation is accepted by all or the majority, it is very likely for people to perceive the formation of the common interest.

Some people may insist that interpretations are given by the authorities or news media or intellectuals in their own interest. They believe that interpretations are deliberately given by the authorities or news media or intellectuals. But such an interpretation is also needed by ordinary people. Unlike the primitive community, such as the tribe, the state is the community in which all public affairs require an interpretation. In ancient or medieval times people formed the agricultural society. The state was sparsely populated. People seldom communicated with one another across the state. The authorities hardly communicated with the masses and seldom interpreted a public affair. There were no mass media. Transportation was underdeveloped. The residents of different areas were isolated. There was hardly any interaction between the regime and ordinary people. The decision, made by the authorities on an affair of the court, was often unknown to the ordinary people residing in the far-flung corners of the state. If a war broke out, the scale of this war was usually small and the war was parochial. Only a few people were involved in the war. If the authorities appointed certain officials of the local government, no statement was made to the public. But since the formation of the mass society in modern times a change has taken place. Nation-state has emerged. When a war breaks out, the scale of this war may be large. Ordinary people begin to be concerned about the diplomacy and national defense of the state. Taxes, imposed on ordinary people, also increase substantially. People begin to be concerned about the financial policy of the state. People need the interpretation of the public affairs managed by the government. In the meantime, since the formation of the mass society, people, as individuals, have been mentally isolated because people do not stay in touch in all aspects. Though they cluster in the urban area, they feel psychologically empty. They feel lonely. They are concerned about the public affairs in relation to their own personal interest. They purchase newspapers, or magazines, or radios, or television sets in order to enter the society and seek interpretations. They are always susceptible to interpretations. They feel assured when a right interpretation is given to them. In some sense, the interpreters give interpretations on behalf of ordinary people. Interpretations are given as entrusted by ordinary people. Interpreters are, in fact, media. Those interpretations can also be deemed as the self-interpretations of the people. The result is that people interact with one another and reach an agreement through those interpretations, and those interpretations result in the formation of the common interest of all within the state. Those interpretations constitute part of the organization of the state.

Notes

1. Jean Grondin, *Introduction to Philosophical Hermeneutics*, translated by Joel Weinsheimer (New Haven: Yale University Press, 1991), 21.

2. Paul Ricoeur, *Interpretation Theory: Discourse and the Surplus of Meaning* (Forth Worth, Texas: The Texas Christian University Press, 1976), 72.

3. Plutarch, *The Lives of the Noble Grecians and Romans*, the Dryden Translation (Chicago: Encyclopaedia Britannica, Inc., 1952), 54.

4. Jean Grondin, *Introduction to Philosophical Hermeneutics*, 19.

5. Peter M. Blau, *Exchange and Power in Social Life* (New York: John Wiley & Sons, Inc., 1964), 263–264.

6. Alexis de Tocqueville, *Democracy in America*, translated by George Lawrence (New York: Harper Perennial, 1988), 550.

7. G. W. F. Hegel, *The Philosophy of Right,* translated by T.M. Knox (Chicago: Encyclopaedia Britannica, Inc., 1952), 106.

8. For the detailed description of the American Dream, please see: James Truslow Adams, *The Epic of America* (Boston: Little, Brown, 1930), 214-215.

9. See: Daniel Etounga-Manguelle, *Does Africa Need a Cultural Adjustment Program?* In Lawrence E. Harrison and Samuel P. Huntington (ed.), *Culture Matters: How Values Shape Human Progress,* (New York: Basic Books, 2000), 69.

10. Bertrand Russell, *Power* (W.W. Norton & Company, Inc, 1938), 145.

11. Aristotle, *The Nicomachean Ethics*, translated by Harris Rackham (Hertfordshire: Wordsworth Editions Limited, 1996), 11.

12. Benedict Spinoza, *The Ethics and Other Works*, translated by Edwin Curley (Princeton: Princeton University Press, 1994), 175.

13. Immanuel Kant, *Fundamental Principles of the Metaphysic of Morals*, translated by Thomas Kingsmill Abbott (Chicago: Encyclopaedia Britannica, Inc., 1952), 258.

14. Ibid., 270.

15. Ibid., 271.

16. Hans Kelsen, *Pure Theory of Law*, translated by Max Knight (Berkeley: University of California Press, 1967), 18.

17. Ibid., 18.

18. See: Richard M. Weaver, *Ideas Have Consequences* (Chicago: The University of Chicago Press, 1984), 99–100.

19. Hans-Georg Gadamer, *Truth and Method*, translated by Joel Weinsheimer and Donald G. Marshall (London: Continuum, 1975), 363.

20. Hans Kelsen, *General Theory of Law and State* (New Brunswick, U.S.A.: Transaction Publishers, 2006), 6.

21. Gadamer, *Truth and Method*, 273.

22. Jean Grondin, *Introduction to Philosophical Hermeneutics*, translated by Joel Weinsheimer (New Haven: Yale University Press, 1991), 49.

23. Jacques Ellul, *Propaganda: The Formation of Men's Attitude*, translated by Konrad Kellen and Jean Lerner (New York: Vintage Books, 1973), 54.

24. Gadamer, *Truth and Method*, 176.

25. Robin M. Williams, *Change and Stability in Values and Value Systems: A Sociological Perspective*, in Milton Rokeach (ed.), *Understanding Human Values* (New York: The Free Press, 1979), 30.

26. Please see: Ellul, *Propaganda: The Formation of Men's Attitude*, 42.

27. Jean Grondin, *Introduction to Philosophical Hermeneutics*, 129.

28. Russell, *Power*, 131–132.

29. Plutarch, *The Lives of the Noble Grecians and Romans*, 709.

Chapter Seven

Attitude

1. Honor

People not only interact with each other by giving an interpretation but also do so by displaying an attitude. To display an attitude means, in a fundamental sense, to show the possibility of cooperation. That attitude is sometimes considered or accepted. That attitude does not always denote a negative attitude. An attitude may be positive. Honor manifests such an attitude. Honor is, in essence, not what is attained by someone but what is conferred by someone. If this view can be accepted, I argue that an honor reflects a sort of attitude displayed by the one who confers that honor. This attitude is necessary in the state instead of the tribe.

That means that humans were not required to extend thanks to each other in the outset in the tribe because people took it for granted that each helped the other in the tribe that took form on the basis of kinship. Kinship means a very close blood relationship. People who associated together on the basis of kinship had a very close blood relationship, and they were geared by the awareness of this very close blood relationship to help proactively each other whenever a help was needed and they did not need any repayment for the related help. This phenomenon occurred because of the necessity of the reproduction of the species. As such, humans were not especially required to extend thanks to each other. If one received any assistance from the other and did not extend thanks thereafter, extending no thanks would not affect the relationship between one another. This means that some people may give more helps to others while some other people may give fewer helps to others, and this case will not affect the unity of the community. But this situation has changed since humans commenced to communicate using language. Since humans began to perform linguistic communication, they have extended the distance of communication. Then humans form a community larger than the one in which kinship was the essential element of the formation of the community. As now people are in a community called the state in which people are connected with each other by linguistic communication instead of kinship, the consciousness of kinship no longer plays an essential role in the formation of the community. Then people change their mode of mutual interaction. They are often no longer relatives. Then, given that people form their community of such a kind, we find that whenever one helps the other, this person usually needs a repayment. For example, when an employee works for the employer, the employer makes a payment to the employee. We can believe that as the employer needs a help from the employee, the employer makes the payment to the employee as the repayment. We can also believe that as the employee needs a help given by the employer, the employee offers to his employer his labor as the repayment. There are also some other cases showing that a person may not be required, or a person may not be able, to make a repayment for the help given by another person. Usually, a competent person gives a help to an incompetent person. Only thanks are extended. The first case is that an adult helps a child or the young helps the old or a man helps a woman. The second case is that a physically strong person helps a physically weak person or a healthy person helps a sick person or a rich person helps a poor person. The third case is that a person who holds power helps a person who does not have any power. In theses cases the person who gets the help may extend thanks to the person who gives the help. This means that after humans learn to use language, they can use language to adjust the relationship between each other. As the situation of each may often differs from that of all others, a help is often given when one needs it. Thanks are extended to encourage those able to give a help to others to give a help to others in need.

The abovementioned situation is the interaction between one another. There is also the interaction between a person and a collective being or the society or the state. For example, sometimes a person gives a help to a group of people or an organization or the state. As all form a collective being, a person who gives a help to all others within the collective being becomes a contributor. As so many people get benefits from the related contribution or as an organization or the state gets so great a benefit from the related contribution, extending thanks is often not enough. Thus, people give an honor to the contributor as a way of extending thanks to him. In other words, people, as a collective being, extend thanks to the contributor. An honor is a special form of extending thanks. As the organization of the state relies on the contribution made by some very competent people, an honor is conferred to express a positive attitude to encourage further contributions made by those very competent people. This is also due to the use of language. By using language, people extend thanks. Conferring an honor is also extending thanks because people usually indicate clearly why they confer an honor.

An honor actually means the due adjustment of the relationship between an individual person and the collective being. An honor, the privilege of pride, is needed by almost everyone. Everyone hopes to be recognized by his community. An honor is such recognition. Thus conferring an honor can show a very positive attitude. This is due to a change in the structure of the human community in the progress of civilization. Specifically, in a tribe the close blood relationship dictated that each member of the tribe tended to take care of the tribe as well as all other members of the tribe and their inclination to take care of the tribe and other members of the tribe stemmed from their natural instincts. Taking care of the tribe or all other members of the tribe, a member of the tribe would not weigh his own gain or loss because the tribe was his family and other members were the members of his family though his family was a big one. But in a state a change has taken place. Though the state is often formed by a nation and all the members of this nation are bound together by a special blood relationship, experiences indicate that, due to the existence of plentiful members of the community, the influence of blood relationship has attenuated to the extent that the blood relationship is unable to maintain the unity of the state, just like the situation in which one is unable to get any taste of wine after a small cup of wine is poured into a big water vat. Thus since the formation of the state, people have found themselves in two kinds of organizations, namely, the family and the state, concurrently. Though the state comprises plenty of families, a family does not constitute the state. Therefore, the interest of human beings splits up into two kinds of interest. One kind of interest is personal interest, or family interest, called the "private interest;" another is the interest of the state, or the interest of the public, called the "public interest." If one must choose one kind of interest between these two kinds of interest, his natural instinct guides him to choosing the private interest because choosing the private interest will enable him to obtain a portion of the interest as long as he knows nothing about if other people choose the private interest or the public interest when they have to choose between the two. If he chooses the public interest and others choose the private interest, he will incur a loss. So the private interest appears and egoism also appears. This is different from the situation of the tribe. The tribe was a simple organization. In this organization, the tribal people had no idea of the private interest or the public interest and they were not egoistic. Since the birth of the state, both the private interest and the public interest have made their appearance. And people have a natural inclination to seek the private interest at the expense of the public interest if they are unable to choose both of them. Thus, the state must adopt some means to safeguard and promote the public interest to maintain itself. Basically, there are two means at its disposal. One is to punish those who seek inappropriately the private interest at the expense of the public interest. The other is to reward those who sacrifice their private interest for the public interest, an act often committed by the state to encourage contribution made to the building of the state. Jean Bodin correctly points out that:

> If punishments and rewards are well and wisely distributed, the commonwealth will continue happy and flourishing. But if able and upright citizens do not receive the reward of their merits, or wicked ones the punishments which they deserve, there is no hope that the commonwealth can long endure.[1]

But in a state the difference between punishment and reward is not only that they push people to go in two opposite directions but also that punishment only results in the passive maintenance of status quo while reward is able to motivate individuals to make more contributions to the collective so as to change actively the status quo. Of course, if the public interest is damaged, the state must act to penalize the related person who has damaged the public interest and who should be held accountable. But to penalize him, the state must prepare a lot of resources, such as a law court, a jail and a police force. These resources are costly. Penalty may incur hatred and give rise to new issues, and penalty sometimes may even go against some of the most sublime humanistic values of all. If the state applies the death penalty to a criminal who has perpetrated every conceivable heinous crime and is unpardonable, this penalty may give rise to the consequence of doing harm to the life of humans objectively. If a state abolishes all laws applying to the death penalty, I believe that this state has considered this issue. So the state usually warns the citizens against damaging the public interest only. If the cases of damaging the public interest decrease in number, the application of penalty decreases accordingly. By contrast, the state keeps on rewarding those who make a great contribution to the state. The state encourages the citizens to make a contribution to the state in order to enhance the cohesion of the state. This is because a reward makes those rewarded feel happy so that a reward may further motivate them to make more contributions to the state. A reward will not sow the seed of hatred among people except giving rise to envy on a rare occasion, but will make those rewarded feel grateful. This is because a reward is an honor and an honor is a spiritual compensation which is given to the citizens who have made a great contribution to the state by those other citizens unable to make the equivalent contribution to the state in the related aspect.

On the other hand, if the state fails to confer a corresponding honor on a person who deserves it, the omission of the state may dampen the enthusiasm of those who are motivated to make their positive contributions to the state. That is, sometimes a person deserves being given an honor and the state fails to give the due honor to him. Then, the omission of the state sometimes dampens the enthusiasm of this person to make further contributions to the state. Sometimes a conflict arises because a person is not, as usual, given the honor which he deserves. Hegel writes, when discussing honor, that failure to give the honor that should be given will injure the principal. He mentions a story in *Iliad* that:

> Achilles feels himself injured only because the actual share of
> the booty which belongs to him and is his reward of honour,
> his γέρας, has been taken from him by Agamemnon. The
> injury occurs here in respect of something real, a gift which

of course implied a privilege, a recognition of fame and bravery, and Achilles is angry because Agamemnon treats him disgracefully and publicly deprives him of respect among the Greeks; but the injury does not pierce right to the very heart of personality as such, so that Achilles is now satisfied by the return of the share of which he had been deprived and by the addition of more gifts and goods, and Agamemnon finally does not deny him this reparation.[2]

Hegel believes that in romantic honor,

the injury affects not the positive real value infringed, i.e. property, position, duty, etc., but the personality as such and its idea of itself, the value which the individual ascribes to himself on his own account. This value at this stage is just as infinite as the individual is infinite in his own eyes.[3]

It is arguable that humans have the sense of honor because humans use language. Animals have no sense of honor because animals do not use language. People may punish the domestic animals controlled by them but they are unable to encourage the domestic animals to work for them more energetically by virtue of using the spiritual power of honor. Thus an honor, given by the state to an individual person, includes a process of linguistic communication essential for the vitality of the state. The honor, given by the state to an individual person, involves a process of linguistic communication which does not, in general, occur anywhere unless in a state or a civilized society organized by the state. An honor is like a product supplied by the state, and all the citizens need an honor. In other words, an honor is a product supplied by the state rather than being supplied by the family. This honor is not part of the society within the family but outside it. Within a family, each has the potential selfish mentality, but the motive of making a selfless contribution to the family, or the other members of the family, is also strong and perpetual. By contrast, in a state, a close blood relationship is no longer an important factor that influences the behavior of the citizens in the public life, and people's desire for the private interest is strong and uncontainable. People need to use other methods to recover the losses incurred under the circumstances that they are no longer able to take care of each other or the community, as guided by a close blood relationship. One solution is that people confer an honor on those who make a great contribution to the state and express thanks to them. This is because in a state the personal competence of each varies greatly and the citizens devoid of competence must gain benefits from the contribution made by the competent citizens. The citizens, devoid of competence, need to make a compensation to the citizens who make a great contribution to the state. What can the citizens, devoid of competence, give to the competent citizens as a compensation? My view is that those citizens confer an honor. We can also clarify this logic this way: Even though the competent citizens make a contribution to the state unwittingly, the citizens, devoid of competence, may also get a benefit from this contribution made by the competent citizens, giving rise to the so-called "free-rider problem" discussed by the public choice theory. For example, sometimes a competent man kills a beast which threatens the safety of the local people, and the local people, devoid of competence, gain some benefits from him. However, if the local people, devoid of competence, fail to extend thanks, their omission may dampen the enthusiasm of other competent people in their commitment to make a contribution. So after a competent man beats to death barehanded a beast such as a tiger that threatens the safety of the villagers, the villagers may consider him a hero and give him an honor to encourage him to continue making a contribution. Likewise, if a person makes a special contribution to the state, the state may give him an honor. Aristotle writes that in ancient Greece, Hippodamus of Miletus, as a legislator, "laid down a law that those who discover something of advantage to the city should be honored."[4] Each honor manifests a special exchange between material interest and spirit. Our experience tells us that in a family the parents of the family may make a great contribution to their children such as bringing up children without requiring to be given an honor because the selfless contribution made by them is often taken for granted. This situation should bear certain resemblance to the situation of a tribe. But in a state, for the abovementioned reasons, an important task of the state is to confer an honor on a person who deserves that honor. The value of the state lies in the fact that it is able to confer a sublime honor on a worthy person.

An honor is virtually a positive attitude expressed to a worthy member by the other members of the community surrounding him and presupposes various activities, social relations and marketable articles in favor of the recipient of the honor showing this positive attitude. The condition for the existence of an honor is the existence of various rewards that mean a kind of honor. The behavior of offering a reward is a linguistic behavior displayed to express a sort of attitude. People may use the words and sentences of praising a man and give him the honor orally only. However, they may give him the honor in another way as well. The behavior of rewarding a man may involve giving him a certificate of merit, a medal of honor or a job position of the higher level and paying respects to him as well. These types of behavior express an attitude. This behavioral communication is usually more significant than language itself on this occasion because such behavioral communication is more significant in the mutual interaction of all under certain circumstances. An oral praise may be forgotten shortly later, whereas a certificate of merit, a medal of honor, a prize or a title of honorary post may be an enduring incentive. Oral praises may be regarded as a lip service only and their effect may attenuate if they are given time and again, whereas a prize and the title of an honorary post may be deemed as a real benefit. However, any reward, given in the form of behavior or material or money, has to include an instruction or explanation given by using language. Then it is natural for people to confer an honor on a special contributor.

Conferring an honor is of the significance that after a person makes a contribution to the state, the state gives him an honor in a certain form. Then we see that this person acts first and the state gives him an honor later. But in many cases, these events happen in a reverse order. For example, in the event that people are aware that they will have an honor after committing an act or the state clearly announces that an honor will be given if a certain contribution is made, then the linguistic behavior of giving an honor set in advance occurs first and people make their contributions later. In the latter case, the behavior of making a contribution to the state may be the result of the behavior of linguistic communication performed for the purpose of giving an honor. When a military commander announces before a battle that if a fighter does not fear death in the fight, he will be given an honor, fighters may fight bravely and may not fear death though each fighter is always supposed to be brave. Under a promise of giving an honor, a very brave man may emerge.

So there are various forms of honor possibly given to a person who makes a great contribution to the state. In a tribe that tended to grow large, showing that kinship gradually failed to function in it, a man who demonstrated his wisdom and competence in production or showed bravery in a war might already win the esteem from others. This esteem was, in some sense, an honor. As there was no clear-defined property in a primitive society, a person, making a contribution, would give a benefit to all others who associated together not because of a very close blood relationship. The honor, gained by him, was purely a sort of linguistic form or the continuation of another form of the discourse that encouraged people to make a further contribution to the collective. This honor was given in various forms. And no matter whether this esteem was shown to an individual person by using language or by showing behavior or in some other forms, an honor would become an incentive encouraging people to act in the interest of the community. Then, a person, or even a group of people, might take action for the purpose of gaining an honor. For instance, in the primitive society, tribes often waged a war against each other. Men from a tribe might seize women from another tribe as trophies. The practice of seizing women from the enemy as trophies gave rise to a form of ownership-marriage, resulting in a household with a male head. This was followed by an extension of slavery to other captives and inferiors besides women. In this case, men often displayed their prowess to have a reputation for courage. And they emulated. As Thorstein Veblen writes, "The outcome of emulation under the circumstances of a predatory life, therefore, has been on the one hand a form of marriage resting on coercion, and on the other hand the custom of ownership." And "both arise from the desire of the successful men to put their prowess in evidence by exhibiting some durable result of their exploits. (And prowess) is a necessary condition of reputability."[5] That is, at that time, some people proved their prowess in front of others, and possessing a woman as well as other articles of a defeated tribe was an honor given by a victorious tribe. Then, because of adopting this incentive scheme which allowed people to keep trophies including women seized from the enemy to show their prowess, the tribe encouraged its male members to fight more bravely in an attempt to enhance the fighting capacity of the tribe.

In fact, the behavior that any authorities confer an honor on a person who makes a great contribution to the community is a sort of linguistic behavior or alternative linguistic behavior. Without language, there would be no phenomenon of spirit such as honor in a community. To give an honor, people will always explain why they give this honor. Without the explanation given by using language, nothing can be seen as an honor. The behavior of giving an honor to a person includes the evaluation, affirmation and interpretation of the related person and the related deed. The institution, giving an honor, may also leverage its influence and become an authority in the evaluation of a person or a deed in a certain aspect. The internationally prestigious Nobel Committees are organizations able to give evaluation by using language. They not only encourage the scientific discoveries of human beings, but also aim at promoting the peace and justice of the world. By giving Nobel Prizes, the nominators and the assessment committee disseminate their values across the world. In a state, the state also encourages people, or the groups of people, to make a contribution to the state by way of giving some honors to them and hence consolidates the cohesion of the state. An honor is a repayment given by the state to a person or a group of people who, or an organization which, makes a great contribution to the state. The state affirms the contribution made by the contributor in order to encourage the contributor to continue to make contributions to the state and to encourage others to follow the suit. All of these activities begin to occur mainly in the process of the dissolution of the tribe and the formation of the state.

In general, the state confers an honor on the contributors mainly in the four aspects described below.

First, the state gives an honor to those who make a great contribution in the defense of the state, including the war of resistance against foreign aggressors and even the war of aggression against another state because sometimes aggression is unilaterally interpreted as defense. As families constitute a state, giving an honor to the families or individual persons making a great contribution to the state is a compensation for their special contribution made to the state. The state is unable to mobilize and encourage the individual persons of many families to make a great contribution to the security of the state unless it gives the due honor to those who make a great contribution to the state. In ancient times, the state already gave some honors to the soldiers.

In Rome, the commanders and soldiers who beat back a large number of enemies would receive the honor of receiving a ceremony of triumphant return. Jean Bodin writes that:

> Anyone who had put to flight a legion of the enemy could demand a triumph, or at least some honourable distinction, and he could hardly fail to achieve one or the other…..The wisdom of the ancient Romans is to be much admired in this respect.[6]

Another form is also an honor. That is, soldiers receive certificates and medals according to the meritorious military service. Thomas Hobbes tells us that:

> Scuthions, and Coats of Armes haereditary, where they have any eminent Priviledges, are Honourable….This kind of Honour, commonly called Gentry, has been derived from the Ancient Germans….The Germans onely had that custome; from whom it has been derived into England, France, Spain and Italy, when in great numbers they either ayded the Romans, or made their own conquests in these Western parts of the world.[7]

He also tells us that the titles of honor, such as Duke, Count, Marquis and Baron, were honorable because they signified the value set upon them by the sovereign power of the Common-wealth. These titles were the titles of office in old time and command, derived some from the Romans, some from the Germans and French. Dukes, in Latin Duces, were generals in war. Counts, Comites, were left to govern and defend places conquered and pacified: Marquises, Marchiones, were Counts that governed the Marches or the bounds of the Empire. These titles of Duke, Count and Marquis came into the Empire about the time of Constantine the Great. In the process of time these offices of honor, by occasion of trouble and for the reasons of good and peaceable government, were turned into mere titles serving for the most part to distinguish the precedence, place and order of subjects in the Common-wealth.[8] In today's world, the state continues to give medals to, and promote the military ranks of, the soldiers who give the meritorious military service. The state confers honors on them. In Western states, veterans enjoy special honors. In the United States, the names of those who have fallen in the battle are engraved on the walls in memory of them. In China, there are the similar cases. Many soldiers who have died in the battle are proclaimed as fighting heroes. Monuments are built in memory of those soldiers who die for the defense of the nation-state.

Second, the state confers an honor on those who make a great contribution to the promotion of the cause of social justice. The concept of "justice" occurs after the dissolution of the tribe and the formation of the state. The existence of justice in the state is a prerequisite for the solidarity and long-term growth of the state. Justice can be divided into two concepts: judicial justice and social justice. The judicial justice normally means the justice of law for which the government is responsible. The social justice needs to be safeguarded by the society. Saint Thomas Aquinas insists that justice is the rectitude of will. He states that:

> There are two kinds of justice. The one consists in mutual giving and receiving, as in buying and selling, and other kinds of intercourse and exchange … The other consists in distribution, and is called distributive justice, whereby a ruler or a steward gives to each what his rank deserves.[9]

The following thinkers inherited this view this way or that way though their ideas may appear quite different. John Stuart Mill, insisting on the principle of the moral value of judging behavior in reference of the result, maintains that justice is done when personal freedom is guaranteed and the interest of the majority is realized. Karl Marx holds that the ultimate condition for realizing the justice is the elimination of private property and the realization of communism. Today, being influenced by the past thinkers more or less, a liberal thinker may view justice at the angle of personal freedom while a socialist may view the social improvement as the cause of justice. In short, justice is an ideal principle to be put into practice in the governance of the state. Though different people interpret justice in different ways, similar are the cases that people exalt, encourage and reward those who make a contribution to the enhancement of justice in different states. From ancient times onward, all the stories, tales and myths, about punishing wickedness and encouraging virtue or bringing peace to the good people and stopping bullies, have always reflected the human pursuit and desire for justice no matter whether these stories, tales and myths are told in the West or in the East. The protest and the fight of human beings against injustice indicate that the justice of the state is essential. In early modern times, those who waged the struggle against slavery, oppression and exploitation were exalted as heroes for justice. In modern times, the law enforcement officers such as police officers or lawyers who dare uphold justice and fight the wicked power and influence regardless of their own personal risks are exalted and given an honor by the state. Some journalists who bravely disclose the corruption scandals of the government officials are rewarded by the state. Some government officials who act in the principle of justice or handle a matter impartially are also praised by the people.

Third, the state confers an honor on those who make a great contribution to programs for public good. Programs for public good relate to the cause of justice. Charity means both a commitment to public good and the realization of justice because it helps people to alleviate the inequality and polarization between the rich and the poor and shows sympathy and gives social assistance. This is special in a state because there has often been apparent or sharp inequality between the rich and the poor in a state since extending the distance of linguistic communication led to the dissolution of the tribe and the formation of the state. However, a program for public good is not completely tantamount to the realization of justice. A program for public good means that an individual person sacrifices his time, energy and wealth or a group of people do the same thing to make a contribution to the state. If an individual or a group of people do not make a selfless and outstanding contribution to the state for various reasons, this situation does not necessarily mean injustice. Therefore, the state should first give an honor to those who make a special contribution to the safeguard of the justice before it gives an honor to those who make a contribution to a program for public good. However, the state also needs to give an honor to those who commit themselves to programs for public good because they make a selfless contribution to the state and the state should give an honor to them. In North America, volunteer organizations commit themselves to programs for public good and help those people in need such as those old, weak, sick, disabled and homeless. They make an outstanding contribution to public good, and the state rewards them and gives an honor to them. We often see that there are some successful entrepreneurs, bankers and other businessmen who repay the state by donating money or goods in kind to support various programs for public good such as donating money to charity foundations to support the causes of new technology development, education, public health, environmental protection, the elimination of poverty and other social developments. The state gives an honor to them by conferring the titles of honor and the certificates of merit to them. If they sponsor a program for public good, the state may name that program after them. Bill Gates, for instance, is the former leader of Microsoft Corporation, a well-known computer software company based in the United States. He has donated a large amount of money to programs for public good and he has been given certain honors from 1990s onwards. Warren Bufett, another investor, has also made contributions to some programs for public good by donating money for the undertakings of charity at the same time. He has also been given the corresponding honors. Literati and artists may also contribute their expertise and works for public good. When a war against the aggression of a foreign country breaks out, literati may donate money to support national defense. When a natural disaster happens, artists may give their performance to collect the money to be donated to the government or non-profit organizations to help those in need. They may also be praised by the people and given an honor. The state may also hold some events in memory of those who make a special contribution to the people after their death. The state actually gives them an honor.

Fourth, the state gives a personal honor to those individual persons who get another honor for the state. In today's world, all states co-exist. It is the interest of the state to obtain an honor for the state and to enhance the international status of the state. Therefore, the state gives an honor to those citizens who obtain another honor for the state through their own effort. The international sports competitions promote the undertakings of sports. Sports competitions are also held for entertainment. However, a sports competition is a show. It shows the quality of the physical bodies of the people of the related nation-states and hence indirectly demonstrates the mental attitude of those nation-states. As such, the winners of sports competitions are able to get an honor for their nation-states. They are often given an honor by the governments, or the peoples, of those nation-states for which they get an honor from abroad. That is, in an nation-state, excellent athletes not only receive the medals of honor from the international sports organizations during the Olympic Games or other sports games, but also are often given medals, prizes and other honors by the government of their own nation-state simultaneously because they win the honor for the nation-state. Similar cases also occur in the domain of scientific research and other domains. The award-giving activities of Nobel Prize Committee promote the causes of science, literature and peace of human beings. When the laureates of Nobel Prize win an honor given by this international organization, they also win the honor for their own nation-states because of their specific nationalities. Thus they also get the additional honor given by the peoples of their own nation-states. In an Asian nation-state where the laureates of Nobel Prize are usually fewer, it is particularly the case. If someone becomes a laureate of Nobel Prize, the state will probably give him a great honor because he brings in the honor greatly needed by the nation-state. In fact, even though a person who makes a great contribution to the cause of civilization and progress of human beings does not win any specific reward from abroad, if he is an outstanding figure, such as an outstanding scientist, a famous writer or poet or artist or thinker or even a well-known politician or social activist, he may be exalted by the people and be given an honor by the authorities because he gets some esteem for the nation-state or helps the state to enhance the international status of the state. In many nation-states, people are proud of the emergence of many great figures such as prestigious scientists and writers in their own nation-states and their contributions to the cause of the civilization of human beings. That is, proud thereof, they pay their due respects, and give an honor, to those who make a great contribution to the nation-state as well as the world.

Thus it follows that an honor involves a positive attitude expressed by the public or the authorities to the related person. To get an honor, a person usually needs to accomplish a certain achievement in a certain domain of the state and this achievement is the special contribution and service provided by him to the state. Thus the sense of honor motivates the citizens to make their greatest contribution to the prosperity and development of the state. A power holder may also be motivated to serve the people in good faith. For example, in the state a politician participates in the competition for power because power may bring an honor to him. Of course, a power holder has to do something for his state. Otherwise he may get into difficulties in holding power over the long term. Yet the honor brought in by power always comes from the contribution the power holder makes to his state. Power and honor associate with each other. In early times this phenomenon already occurred. In a primitive society, the head of a clan sometimes gained an honor because of his service provided to the clan such as the management service given by him as a person in charge of the clan. Even in a feudal kingdom or empire, the ruler sometimes had to do something in order to gain love and support from the people and hence to gain an honor. In ancient China, the so-called honest and upright officials of the feudal despotic regime were the officials who intended to serve the people and they received positive evaluation from historians. Some individual officials of such a type even stepped forward bravely to protect the interest of the state at the expense of the interest of their families regardless of their own life and death. Their heroic acts were exalted by the people as well as the following generations. On the other hand, the sense of honor motivated them. The circumstances remain unchanged today. In a state such as a modern nation-state, politicians' pursuit of power results to some extent from the people's act of giving them an honor. Because politicians obtain the special positions to serve the state, people pay respects to them and they have high social status. Then, politicians may make an extra effort in their work in order to get an honor. They compete for high-rank job positions because they compete for an honor. They enter the domain of politics because they want to get an extra honor. Sometimes a political leader whose activities are frequently covered by the news media suddenly appears on the street, talking with ordinary citizens, and citizens, seeing him with their own eyes, give warm applause to him; sometimes a political leader, whom ordinary people are very familiar with, suddenly visits, and extends greetings to, a family in poverty, and this family is excited by this unexpected favor. These behaviors mentioned indirectly indicate that the leader of the state is a special person. People pay respects to the leader of the state. The state also gives various special treatments to the leader. He has a nice office. He is protected by the bodyguards and he has secretaries and other service personnel. The personnel surrounding the leader may also demonstrate his special status. Behind his special status there is the honor given by the state. Of course, politicians have to make a contribution to the state or the people to get an honor. On the other hand, politicians accumulate the honor. If their honor is damaged, they also safeguard the honor. In order to accumulate the honor, they will not easily give up the power held by them.

Many other outstanding people in the state also grow up as spurred by the sense of honor. A typical case is that if a person is an entrepreneur, he may often have a sense of honor. An entrepreneur often endeavors to become a success in the business community because he loves the related honor. A successful entrepreneur not only brings in wealth but also receives an honor as long as he can make a contribution to the state. He gets the esteem of the society and gets an extraordinary social status. This situation may have already changed the original motive of an entrepreneur in his business commitment. That is, the original motive for human beings to do business is to ensure their own self-preservation, but since the development of market economy, an entrepreneur may no longer simply engage in production for his own material needs. He may begin to engage in production for market exchange and profits. Even though the wealth, produced by him, substantially exceeds his own need, he may desire to make more profits because he wants to have more wealth. He is neither merely engaging in production for the sake of production nor merely operating the enterprise for the sake of operating the enterprise. A certain entrepreneurship motivates him to engage in produc-tion and operation. This entrepreneurship includes some other complicated desires, such as the desire of seeking honor, esteem, social reputation and social status. In the last century, Veblen noticed this phenomenon. He writes that "the possession of wealth gains in relative importance and effectiveness as a customary basis of repute and esteem."[10] He believes that "In order to stand well in the eyes of the community, it is necessary to come up to a certain, somewhat indefinite.... standard of wealth."[11] Then he continues that:

> So soon as the possession of property becomes the basis of popular esteem, therefore, it becomes also a requisite to that complacency which we call self-respect. In any com-munity where goods are held in severalty it is necessary, in order to his own peace of mind, that an individual should possess as large a portion of goods as others with whom he is accustomed to class himself; and it is extremely gratify-ing to possess something more than others. But as fast as a

person makes new acquisitions, and becomes accustomed to the resulting new standard of wealth, the new standard forthwith ceases to afford appreciably greater satisfaction than the earlier standard did. The tendency in any case is constantly to make the present pecuniary standard the point of departure for a fresh increase of wealth; and this in turn gives rise to a new standard of sufficiency and a new pecuniary classification of one's self as compared with one's neighbours.[12]

Here we can also see that entrepreneurs seek an honor. Without an honor an entrepreneur may not continuously seek the higher standard of wealth.

The stars of the sports community, the celebrities of the art community and the renowned scientists of the science community also grow up as spurred by a sense of honor. They are by no means the inborn stars of the sports community, the inborn masters of the art community and the inborn scientists of the science community. They are common people in the outset, but they are a group of people who have an ideal and can be quickly motivated by a sense of honor. Famous athletes are personnel involved in sports activities. The original purpose of sports activities is to do exercise in order to improve the health of people. However, as gold medals also encourage people to do exercise and to improve health, people appear on arenas. They are motivated by the rewards set in advance to take part in the activities of a sports competition. These rewards keep on influencing and stimulating them and motivating them to make achievements and to get an honor. Those, taking part in the activities of giving a performance, may be indulged in the aesthetic appreciation of the environment of art and art is their interest, but a social honor also motivates them to make an extra effort in their professional career. An artist, well-known in a local area, may desire to become an artist well-known across the nation-state. After becoming an artist well-known across the nation-state, he may desire to become an artist well-known in the world. The title of honor impels him to grow and encourages him to create more works of art. The sense of honor, generated as a result of academic achievement, also inspires a scientist or a social scientist to work hard according to his research programs. The prizes of scientific research and the prizes of the research of social sciences encourage many to dedicate themselves to discoveries in the domains of science and social sciences. If a scientist receives a prize of the state, he may hope to receive Nobel Prize one day in future. When an outstanding person makes a special contribution in a certain domain, the state will give him the honor of the state. The effort, made by social celebrities, is also made under the influence of an honor. Even common people are also motivated by an honor. Because of this schools confer scholarship to encourage students to study hard. The human resources department of a company gives a bonus to the employees at the end of the year in order to raise productivity in the upcoming year. In a limited domain, an ordinary person may also become the winner of an honor. In a nutshell, without the functioning of an honor, each human community will be unable to stride the natural hurdle set by the private property mindset after the emergence of the state. Without the functioning of an honor, the state may lose its orientation in the development of human civilization, lose the motive of the state's progress from the lower level to the higher level and ultimately lose the basic conditions for its own construction. At least, without the functioning of an honor, there may not be a long-term positive contribution made by each to the state.

2. Loyalty

Humans, forming their tribe, were loyal to the tribe or to the tribal chief. This is out of the question because people were naturally motivated by kinship to cooperate with each other. Cooperation was the goal of loyalty. This is because people associated together because of kinship. They had common interest. They seldom had any personal interest. If there was any personal interest, it was often overwhelmed by the collective interest. In the community in which all had kinship ties with all, the collective interest was overwhelming. The mentality of kinship suppressed the consciousness of personal interest. But since the formation of the state, personal interest has begun to function widely and strongly due to the fact that kinship has failed to function as before. As such, the type of relationship between one another in the past has gradually vanished. Immediacy between one another has disappeared. There has been now uncertainty in the relationship between one another in the community. The result is that people, strongly motivated by their personal interest to act, may not always act as expected or required by others. The positive mutual interaction is no longer self-evident. People may not always cooperate with each other. Each of them may act at the expense of the interest of any other one. Then in order to ensure cooperation in economic, social and political activities in the building of the community, all expect others to be cooperative. They expect others to act according to their wishes and hopes. They expect others to commit any act as required. They require others to be loyal, so that they can obliterate the uncertainty in the relationship between one another. Thus along with the growth of the community, people more and more strongly feel the necessity of cooperation. They hope that everyone is loyal to the new community. Loyalty is particularly required by all those who play a role in the organization of this community. Specifically, anyone who organizes people in any social or political activity in the state may play a role in the organization of the state, and the organizer particularly expects loyalty shown by all others. For the organizer of any group of people or any organization, he needs the loyalty of all others. He calls on others to contribute to the organization of that group of people or the building of that organization. He needs cooperation and support from others when he promulgates a regulation. He hopes that all others are reliable. Organizing a group of people or setting up an organization, he hopes to see the expected responses given by all others just like the humans who were the members of a tribe. The loyalty of others is required. Among all those who do not directly participate in the organization of the state, each also needs the loyalty of all others in the mutual interaction between one another just like those in the tribe, but, first of all, they must be loyal to a group of people or an organization. Then people can build the state on a solid basis. The loyalty of all to the state is conducive to the establishment of people's subjective order in the organization of the state. Thus, with all being organized, the people of the lower level are loyal to the people of the higher level. People establish order with this arrangement. This is because loyalty often means submission to an organization. An organization establishes order. All organizations assist the state in establishing the order. Thus, all will feel assured because no subjective order can be established without loyalty. As Morton Grodzins writes,

> Loyalties are a part of every individual's life because they serve his basic needs. They function as a part of his

indispensable habit patterns. Loyalties provide him with a portion of the framework upon which he organizes his existence. In the absence of such a framework, he could establish no easy, habitual responses. He would be faced with the endless and hopelessly complicated task of making fresh decisions at each moment of life. He would soon degenerate into wild and random inconsistencies or into a brooding state of confusion and indecisiveness, conditions that merge into insanity.[13]

That means that loyalty is required in the relationship of people in the state because no kinship can now guarantee establishing the trust relationship between one another. In economic life, for example, an employer usually requires the employees to be loyal to him. Employees are engaged by the employer to realize the goal set by the employer. Employees are thus required to perform their duties. To perform their duties means to be loyal to the employer. Employees are required to work in good faith as well. All these mean that the employees are required to be loyal to the employer. In addition, some behaviors, shown by employees, may also be construed as being loyal to the employer. For example, employees take good care of the property of the company. Employees always come to the factory to work on time. Employees are willing to work overtime. Employees always work actively. Employees adapt themselves to the culture of their workplace proactively. In political life, we also see this typical phenomenon: A political party requires all members of the party to be loyal to the party. The members of the party are required to work under the command of the leader of the party. They are required to work wholeheartedly in order to realize the goal of the party. They are required to act under the command of the leader of the party absolutely. They are supposed to safeguard the interest of the party and support the work of realizing the goal of the party. They are sometimes required to donate a certain amount of money to the party. They must be loyal to the party. Besides, a nation-state also requires all the citizens to take part in the building of the state. All are supposed to safeguard the interest of the state. If the state is at war against another foreign state, citizens may be required to provide military service. All are required to be loyal to the state. Patriotism is propagated to encourage all to be loyal to the state.

In the past the relationship between one another was characteristic of immediacy. Now the relationship between one another is characteristic of intermediacy. Media play a role in this change. If people perform linguistic communication, they use, at least, a medium. The use of a medium extends the distance of linguistic communication. People extend the reach of linguistic communication. They form a large group or a large organization or a large community. This group, or organization, or community, may be a society. In this society, everyone is supposed by the social norm to be loyal to everyone in order to maintain the formation of this society. Then a person establishes a regime and governs this society. A state is born. Then people are supposed to be loyal to the person who governs the state. This means that people are supposed to be cooperative with each other. They cooperate with each other horizontally to form a society. People, governed by the state, are also supposed to cooperate with the person that governs the state. People cooperate vertically to form a state. The reason is that the loyalty of people to the tribe is shown on a small scale, whereas the loyalty of people to the state is shown on a large scale. The loyalty of people to the state is built in extending the distance of linguistic communication in contrast to the loyalty of people to the society. In the state, people are, first of all, loyal to some groups or organizations and then are loyal to the state. Such groups or organizations are media.

First, people are sometimes loyal to an ethnic group of people in the outset. Though people within this ethnic group have a blood relationship, they are no longer connected with each other by kinship. Thus people are no longer loyal to the original tribe, but they are loyal to their ethnic group. They are now grouped by ethnicity. They may not be strongly loyal to the state because they may not be completely governed by the state in the beginning. This ethnic group of people may be self-organized. They may be a group of nomads. If they farm land, they reside in a remote region. They may be self-sufficient in economic life. They have their own folk culture. They speak a different regional language. They form an ethnic group semi-organized by some leaders of the ethnic group. There may be a center of paternalist power. They worship ancestors. However, extending the distance of linguistic communication results in an increase in the size of the community and hence an increase in the population of this group of people. This ethnic group of people evolves to be a nation. Nationhood becomes a medium in support of the formation of a nation and a nation becomes a medium in support of the formation of a nation-state. Then people are required to be loyal to the state because now the people of the same nation form their state.

Second, people may be organized by a religious organization in the outset. As people need to hold a religious belief and a religious belief functions as a medium in support of the linguistic communication performed by all with all in early times, people are often under the influence of a religious organization. This religious organization organizes the social life of the local people. All local people are the believers of the related religion. This religious organization also proves powerful in the local affairs. It may have the real ability to mobilize the masses. Thus the local people may be loyal to this religious organization. For example, in medieval times churchgoers were loyal to the religious community. They might not necessarily be loyal to the state. Morton Grodzins writes that in the seventeenth century a Jesuit generally called patriotism "a plague and the most certain death of Christian love." And from the decline of Roman Empire to the times of Machiavelli, roughly a thousand years, there was no such a thing as national loyalty. The masses of people were generally regarded as scum, and generally regarded themselves as unrelated to larger secular institutions. The dominant ethic was a universal one which recognized no significant distinctions among Christian souls, wherever they resided. Nations did not exist.[14] The growth of nation, as a result of extending the distance of linguistic communication, changes this situation. The state gradually takes form on the basis of a nation, and religion becomes part of the state formed on the basis of that nation. It becomes a cultural resource in the building of the state. Religion is sometimes the peculiarity of the state. People may be loyal to the state because all of them are the believers of the religion upheld by the nationals. Religion becomes a medium in support of the formation of the state. Then the loyalty of people to the religious community is translated into the loyalty of people to the state.

Third, the administrative body of the state was sometimes not completely built and people were required to be loyal to the local potentates in the outset. This means that without a mature and monolithic administrative body, the local people were under the governance of the local potentates. The local potentates were required to be loyal to the sovereign because they were obligated to do so in accordance with an oath or a contract, but the local people might not be required to be loyal to the sovereign. In medieval Europe, for example, peasants were only required to be loyal to the local lords though there was a sovereign lord and all other lords guaranteed their loyalty to the sovereign lord through contracts into which they entered with the sovereign lord. Peasants, residing in separate manors, were only loyal to the lords of the manors in which they resided. Peasants were not required to be loyal to the kingdom. They were only obligated to be loyal to the lords. This means that the reach of administration of the state was limited and the governance of the state might not fully cover those local regions. There was hardly communication between those communities and the state. The villagers of a village did not often communicate with other people outside the village. The townspeople of a town did not communicate with other people outside the town. Villagers might be loyal to villages and townspeople might be loyal to towns. And different regions kept different customs and folk cultures and even used different regional languages or dialects. Besides, they were isolated due to the underdevelopment of transportation and communication throughout all regions and all were loyal to the local communities only. Yet since the development of transportation and communication extended the distance of linguistic communication later, people have consolidated the building of the state. A network of transportation and communication takes shape. A national market emerges. Local cultures start to merge. People have been required to be loyal to the state. As local authorities are now under the control of the central government, the loyalty of people to the local community means the loyalty to the state.

This process may also be illustrated by the development of economy due to extending the distance of linguistic communication. As now people can communicate by using language on a large scale, they develop commerce, transportation and communications. The mass society grows. In the meantime, the growth of capitalism underlies the growth of a national market, putting an end to the feudal system. People begin to interact with the state directly. The consciousness of the state spreads. As Grodzins opines, "Rousseau's argument in favor of a 'civil religion' as a substitute for Christianity was an argument for patriotism."[15] The French revolutionary leaders called on the French people to be loyal to the nation-state. Since then industrialization and urbanization has even led to the reorganization of the state. The circulation of workforce increases across the state. Public administration develops to meet the requirement of economic and social development. Then those groups, organizations, and communities turn to functioning as media in the building of loyalty to the state. The object of loyalty of people totally changes. As Joseph R. Sprayer says, there appears

> a shift in loyalty from family, local community, or religious organization to the state and the acquisition by the state of a moral authority to back up its institutional structure and its theoretical legal supremacy. At the end of the process, subjects accept the idea that the interests of the state must prevail, that the preservation of the state is the highest social good.[16]

This situation symbolizes the formation of a modern state. The modern state, in some sense, means the state in which people are universally loyal to the state. People may be loyal to some groups or organizations or communities within the state. But these groups, organizations and communities have become media in support of the construction of the loyalty of people to the state because all these groups, organizations and communities run according to the requirement of organizing the state.

The state becomes the largest political organization formed by each nation and such a political organization is also supported by some other political organizations functioning as media. People now have political consciousness. In the past, people might be grouped because they traditionally belonged to a region. They were the residents of a particular region. Now they may form a political party. In the past, people might be grouped as a social class. They were not necessarily organized at that time. Now people who belong to a social class may form a political party. Now they may form a political party because all of them uphold a social and political consciousness. In the meantime all political parties may be loyal or be required to be loyal to the state. Political parties function as media in support of the organization of the state. As loyalty is a phenomenon of social or political organization, people, loyal to a political party, are further required to be loyal to the state. As Grodzins writes,

The distinctive party function—indeed, the basic party function—is the attempt to gain control of the government through making appeals for the support of groups around which non-national loyalties cluster. Parties out of power make promises to these groups, and parties in power institute programs to preserve and widen group support. In both cases the effect is to align national loyalties with non-national ones.[17]

Therefore we find that the political parties in power are loyal to the state and the political parties out of power are also loyal to the state. The opposition party is the loyal opposition. In Great Britain the opposition in the parliament is "Her Majesty's Loyal Opposition."

Comparing the loyalty of people to the state with the loyalty of people to the tribe, we clearly see that the loyalty of people to the state is the result of the historical extension of the distance of linguistic communication. The loyalty of people to the tribe was inborn and natural. The loyalty of people to the state is constructed because of language. As people form their state because they construct the relationship of mutual interaction through language, loyalty is a result of the construction of a relationship of cooperation among ordinary people and between ordinary people and the organizers of the state. If the state were not to be organized, people would not be required to be loyal. The state is formed because people perform linguistic communication with each other, and the loyalty of people to the state is also built in linguistic communication. Thus, people, using language, request loyalty. People are loyal to a political party, or to the government, or to the nation, or to any object. This is precisely because they are required to be loyal. Loyalty said by us here is constructed by people. Loyalty is built in linguistic communication.

First, people are often required to affirm their loyalty to someone or an organization or the state as required by the organization of the state. There is the phenomenon that one party affirms loyalty and the other party feels assured. Language must be used. If loyalty is assumed to be cooperation, we find that people engage in cooperation by using language. In contrast, disloyalty does not require the use of language. This is because disloyalty means the relinquishment of cooperation. The relationship of loyalty should be established before the action of loyalty is taken. Linguistic presentation must go first. There is a gap of time between the affirmation of loyalty and an act committed to display loyalty. If loyalty must function well, it must be known beforehand. Therefore, in feudal times vassals affirmed their fealty to the lords who allocated land to the vassals. Otherwise the lords would not allocate land to the vassals. The social and political order of feudal times was crucially established this way. Obviously, language must be used to affirm fealty. Vassals were often required to take an oath to show their fealty. Taking an oath was a ceremony. The ceremony actually functioned as a medium in support of linguistic expression.

The feudal regime also relied on the loyalty of the officials to the ruler. The formation of a kingdom was due to the fact that the power holders of the lower level were loyal to the power holders of the higher level. The feudal state was formed in the principle of organizing the society, and personal loyalty was important for the subsistence of the feudal regime. This loyalty was also required to be affirmed by using language. Though action taken by people might bear testimony to their loyalty to the power holders of the higher level, verbal or written expression of loyalty was also often required because before any act was committed, assurance must be given by using language first. One case in point is that in a feudal society in medieval Europe, vassals swore oaths and affirmed fealty to the feudal lord. The feudal lord granted land to the vassals in return for the homage and fealty from the vassals. When granting land, the feudal lord required their vassals, receiving the land, to perform some carefully defined duties such as knight service and provide other aids for particular occasions. Swearing an oath was the behavior of expressing an attitude. A vassal received land from the lord first and then performed the duties for the lord later. The grant of land and the performance of the duties occurred at two separate times. Swearing an oath connected the two things that happened at different times. Only when a vassal solemnly expressed that he would be loyal to his lord would the lord comfortably grant land to him.

In modern times the states are usually nation-states. In a nation-state people are organized by various agents or organizations. In political life political parties participate in the organization of the state. The members of each political party are required to be loyal to the party. All may be required to swear an oath or make a statement in order to affirm their loyalty to the political party. For example, when a man becomes a member of a political party, this political party may require this man to make a statement in order to affirm his loyalty to the party. This means that this man may not be approved to be a member of this political party until this man affirms his loyalty to the party. This is because in each state the government is organized by at least a political party. All members must be loyal to the party. Following the establishment of representative democracy, the political party needs the loyalty of its members. Since this political party is preparing to form a government, it needs support from a large group of loyal citizens. It is prone to make sure that it wins support from its members first. Then it tries to win the loyalty from some other people outside it.

In the meantime we see that in modern times the main form of the human community is nation-state, and all within the nation-state are required to be finally loyal to the nation-state. When a person becomes a citizen of a nation-state, he may be required by the state to swear an oath to affirm his loyalty to this state. This person may not be approved as a citizen until he affirms his loyalty to the state. Particularly, if a person becomes a civil servant, he is especially required to be loyal to the state in all aspects. All civil servants may be required to take a special oath to affirm their loyalty to the state. If civil servants hold sensitive posts in the government, they may be subject to the investigation of loyalty to the state. Some evidence may be required to affirm the loyalty of those civil servants. Such evidence is usually or often in writing. Besides, if a person is elected as a representative sitting in the parliament, or as the president or the vice president, he may be required to be a natural born citizen. He is required to present a certificate of citizenship as a citizen. This means that his loyalty to the state is required to be verified by a document made by using language. Without language, his loyalty cannot be verified in this regard.

Second, loyalty is encouraged and cultivated. Loyalty is then exalted. Loyalty is described as a virtue or a duty. In all nation-states in the world, soldiers are often glorified. This indicates that as soldiers are especially required to venture their lives to show loyalty in combat, they are commended. As they are commended, they are encouraged to be loyal to the state in deeds. If a fighter is captured by the enemy in the battlefield and refuses to surrender, he may be deemed as being loyal to the state. Thus he may be commended and sometimes may be given an honor. He may be awarded a medal. Ordinary people may be taught to learn from him. If he dies, he may be confirmed as a martyr or a hero. People pay respects to him. His deeds may be propagandized. His family may also be glorified. Another case in point is that if a revolutionary, performing clandestine activities, is captured and tortured by the authorities and refuses to confess his comrades, he may be deemed as loyal to the revolutionary party. There may be a third case in point. That is, if a government official, controlling the secret of the state, refuses to be seduced by the intelligence personnel of a foreign state to sell the confidential information of the state, he may be deemed as loyal to the state. He may be praised and be given an honor. Citizens who happen to play a role in the defense of the motherland are also praised. Some of them become national heroes or heroines. They are praised because their spirit bolsters patriotism. Patriotism means loyalty to the motherland. As the state built by people is also the motherland, patriotism also plays a role in the building of the state. In addition, citizens who relinquish good living conditions in the big city to go to a backward rural area to help others in the social and economic development of that area as mobilized by the state may be regarded as being loyal to the state. Sometimes citizens, participating voluntarily in the activities of the celebration of the National Day, are deemed as loyal to the state. Conversely speaking, disloyalty is criticized and one, blamed for disloyalty, may be punished. If a man betrays his state, the state may penalize him. The state may even penalize him with a charge of treason. One specific case in point is that the state punishes its soldier who turns traitor and surrenders before a combat. In some states soldiers are not supposed to surrender in the battlefield. Thus the soldiers, surrendering in the battlefield and being sent back by the enemy, may be reproached and mistreated. Sometimes they are punished. Another case in point is that a traitor of the revolutionary cause may be punished by the revolutionary party. A government official who sells the confidential information of the state to a foreign state is normally punished. A person, showing patriotism, is praised while a person, betraying his motherland, is denounced and punished. Denouncing and punishing disloyalty compel people to be loyal to a certain political party or the state. Yet a person, determined to be loyal, is usually required to affirm loyalty. Conversely, a disloyal person usually does not affirm disloyalty. One does not need to affirm disloyalty in order to be disloyal, whereas one needs to affirm loyalty in order to be loyal. If one is disloyal, he may even conceal his act of disloyalty. This is because people, engaging in cooperation, need to use language. Being loyal is an attitude of cooperation though this cooperation is realized between the people of the lower level and the people of the higher level. This means that, cooperating with each other, people may use language to facilitate such cooperation. The people of the higher level often need to make sure that the people of the lower level are going to be cooperative in order to make a decision. Even though people are no longer connected with each other by kinship, they may still be cooperative, provided that language is used in communication between one another.

Third, loyalty is sometimes strengthened because it is idealized. Thus loyalty is described by using language. For example, citizens are often organized to pursue a cause. Then the discourse of loyalty may encourage people to be loyal to a cause. Thus, people idealize loyalty. As the cause is also the cause of the state, the loyalty to this cause is also the loyalty to the state. Thus people are often required to be loyal to a cause. This cause may be expounded as holy. It follows that people have a long-term plan, adhere to a principle, uphold a belief and devote themselves to an objective all their lives. As Josiah Royce writes, "loyalty is the will to believe in something eternal."[18] Thus, the idealization of loyalty primarily or thoroughly eliminates the uncertainty in the relationship between people and the state over the long term. Thus, unlike the case that kinship naturally determines the relationship between people and the tribe, loyalty in this context is a phenomenon occurring especially in the state. Loyalty to the state may be strongly cultivated when loyalty to a cause is cultivated. Loyalty should be constantly required. Constantly-required loyalty tends to be the loyalty to a state that devotes itself to a cause. Thus, people, committed to a cause, rely on a powerful spiritual power. The spiritual power is built up in the processes of linguistic communication. This means that loyalty to a cause can perpetuate people's loyalty to the state if the state is committed to this cause. For example, people are encouraged to be loyal to communism in China. Communism is an ideal promoted by the communist party. In some other Western states people are encouraged to be loyal to liberalism. Thus, the narrative of a related cause to which loyalty is required perpetuates the loyalty of people to the state. There is a discourse requiring the loyalty to this cause within the state. This discourse exists in the processes of linguistic communication that goes on throughout the state.

Fourth, loyalty is also often defined by using language because the object of loyalty may be changing. Loyalty is a discourse. In medieval times the object of loyalty of people might be a lord. In modern times the object of loyalty of people may be a political party, or the government, or the nation-state as the motherland. People tend to define the object of loyalty so that all know what they must be loyal to. People are often encouraged to be loyal to the nation-state or the motherland in modern times. The standard of evaluating loyalty varies. People discuss their loyalty to the nation-state or the motherland. They discuss the connotation of such loyalty. Then loyalty is especially cultivated as required or desired. For example, the exaltation of the motherland is particularly aimed at encouraging people to love their motherland so that they are loyal to the motherland. The definition of loyalty may also vary from time to time. In some countries formed mainly by immigrants such as Australia or Canada, a citizen in the heterogeneous cultural background might be sometimes regarded as being disloyal because of some specific situations. But since the adoption of the policy of multiculturalism, the state has modified the way of ascertaining disloyalty. The view of loyalty is also broadened. In some countries a citizen, holding political values different from the mainstream political values of the state, might be construed as being disloyal to the state. But as the state shows an inclination of more political toleration, the authorities may slacken the standard of evaluating loyalty. In some other cases the state defines loyalty under a policy. After the modification of that policy, the state may define the loyalty of the citizens again. Thus, people have to clarify the loyalty of the citizens by using language. For example, during Word War One, Australian citizens of German descent were denied their identity as Australians because their loyalty to Australia was doubted.[19] During World War Two the freedom of the residents of Japanese descent was restricted in the United States and Canada because their loyalty to the state in which they resided was doubted. After the end of World War Two the related special policy was terminated in those countries. Another example is that during the Cultural Revolution in China, the loyalty of those who had relatives living abroad was doubted by the regime of the Communist Party of China. They were sometimes especially investigated by the government.

They were mistreated simply because they were suspected of being disloyal to the state. Since the end of the Cultural Revolution and the start of carrying out the open door policy, having relatives living abroad has been no longer deemed as the act of disloyalty to the motherland. In other words, family loyalty may not need to be verified by the head of the family, but the loyalty to the state needs to be verified by the state, so that the state can be organized as required by the state. In other words, those who show their loyalty to the state need to be verified by the state to be the men and women loyal to the state. Their loyalty to the state is verified by the state, so that the state can confirm that citizens are really loyal to it. Thus, the authorities ensure the smooth organization of the state.

Fifth, the object of loyalty of people is also often imagined. People are required to be loyal to the state. This state may be imagined. This state may be imagined as a family. Thus, such imagination may strengthen the union of people. One example showing this case is that the original family loyalty may be imagined and be transplanted to the domain of the organization of the state. People imagine family loyalty in order to encourage people to be loyal to any object for the purpose of self-organization in the state. In other words, people need to be organized outside the family in the state. Then family nomenclature, such as the appellations of family members, are adopted to imitate the roles of family members in order to bolster the organization of people in the state. For example, people among a group of friends may sometimes call each other brothers or sisters. Soldiers within a military unit may informally call each other brothers. Churchgoers may sometimes call each other brothers or sisters. Even men among a gang of crime may call each other brothers. A country may sometimes be interpreted as a big family composed of brothers and sisters. The country in which one was born is always called the fatherland or the motherland. The founder of a certain nation-state is often called the founding father of the nation-state. The use of those terms which describe the family ties is aimed at making all feel close to each other. It is also aimed at cultivating the loyalty of a group of people or all to a certain object. This is the phenomenon of human organization in the civilized society. This phenomenon appears among people in the state instead of the tribe. In the family we are not aware of family loyalty because it is a default value. Yet in the state we strongly feel the necessity of loyalty because the loyalty of people in the state has to be deliberately cultivated. People need to use language to cultivate loyalty though they also have to take other measures. Then media can be used to help cultivate the loyalty of people to the state when loyalty to the state becomes essential.

This means that there is no adequate force ensuring the expected and required action of all within the state for the purpose of organizing all. If loyalty is not deliberately required, the organization of the state may not be smooth or realized. Thus people keep on requiring the loyalty of all within the state. Describing clashes in loyalty, A. Hirschman holds that clashes in loyalty seem to point to loyalty requiring an 'other' to define itself against.[20] James Connor believes that "loyalty needs competition, because one cannot be loyal to a cause if there is no other cause."[21] For example, a nation-state, at war against another nation-state, may require young men to join the army, and the loyalty to the family may be required to yield to the loyalty to the state. My view is that people are under the pressure in the organization of the state. This is the fundamental reason that people need and cultivate loyalty. If there is any clash or competition in loyalty, this phenomenon occurs in the organization of the state. The appearance of two or more choices of the object to which people are required or called on to be loyal is the phenomenon of organizing the state. Though different objects of loyalty sometimes clash or compete, this is not because each clashes with the other or competes against the other, but because people are required to be loyal in the state. But if we assert that loyalty in the family is not required to be articulated, the loyalty in the state needs to be articulated because the organization of the state is based on the functioning of linguistic communication.

As Morton Grodzins writes, "Loyalty is both attitude and act."[22] Loyalty is also an expected relationship between the two actors. The loyalty of people is constructed as required by the organization of the state. If the state, formed by people, does not need to be organized, people will not be required to be loyal. On the other hand, the state has to be accepted by people. Otherwise people may not be loyal to the state. The loyalty of people to the state is not blind or foolish loyalty. The loyalty of people to the state involves a relationship of exchange. People also establish such a relationship of exchange in the evolution of history. The evolution of history in this context pertains to the extension of the distance of linguistic communication among all. That is, without extending the distance of linguistic communication people may not establish such a relationship of exchange. Thus the construction of loyalty of people to the state may also reflect a process of building the state in history. In other words, the building of the state is aimed at satisfying the need of people. This goal is realized in the evolution of history. Thus the loyalty of people to the state is cultivated in the growth of the state. There are four aspects in need of explanation.

First, the state may not serve actively the people in the outset because the state is formed as a result of conquest. Thus people do not show their loyalty to the state. At least people do not have the strong sense of loyalty to the state. This is why in ancient or medieval times people were not universally loyal to the state. Since the early modern times, however, the distance of linguistic communication has been substantially extended due to the development of printing, transportation and communication. The mass society takes shape. People compel the ruler to provide public services. Then the state gradually evolves to be a special organization that provides material interest to people. People are loyal to the state. In this case the state is like an organization. When people join an organization, they intend to gain benefits. As a condition of exchange, they are also required to comply with the directives of the organization and to make a contribution to the organization. As Peter M. Blau writes, "The members recruited to the organization receive benefits, such as financial remuneration, in exchange for complying with the directives of superiors and making various contributions to the organization." [23] The services, given to the citizens of the state, may be considered benefits given by the state. Thus, like the tribe that provided primary services for the preservation and growth of all within the tribe, the state provides necessary services for the growth and development of all within the state in modern times. The difference only lies in the very fact that the services, provided by the state for the growth and development of all within the state, are provided through an invisible exchange. Those services are provided as public services because people have successfully realized that exchange. To put it another way, people are loyal to the state because the state is able to provide those public services especially needed by all within the state. In particular, in modern times the state is built in need of serving all within the state. So Morton Grodzins writes that:

The great state services—ranging from the supervision of
the newborn to the care of the aged, from the fixing of wages
to the allocation of scarce minerals —have made more and
more people dependent upon the state. The fostering of
dependency is one way of fostering loyalties. But if state
services are promised and then not produced, loyalties turn
sour. The state draws to itself strong allegiances by virtue
of its services; it also makes itself a universal scapegoat if
those services do not meet the expectations of the populations served. In the later event the state runs the risk that
its citizens will seek other sources of satisfaction and, in the
process, transfer their allegiance.[24]

That means that if the state fails to provide the required public services,
people may turn to being loyal to other objects. In this case people may
refrain from affirming loyalty to the state even though loyalty is exalted
and interpreted. People may refrain from using language to affirm loyalty.
They may show disloyalty to the state. They do not need to use language.
When they show disloyalty to the state, they demonstrate civil disobedience
or revolt against the state or the government representing the state. That is,
people, loyal to the state, need to use language. Conversely, people, disloyal
to the state, do not necessarily need to use language. This is inimical to the
building of the state.

Second, in pre-modern times the state was often built because of the
conquest of the conqueror. Though the state was formed, the formation of
the state did not necessarily mean that people were loyal to the ruler or the
state. People usually refrained from affirming their loyalty to the state. They
might affirm their loyalty to the local ruler, but they would not affirm their
loyalty to the state. The growth of nation has changed this situation. Though
a nation can be construed as a large ethnic group of people who may be
grouped because they have a blood relationship, a nation is no longer grouped
by kinship. As people, belonging to this nation, are no longer connected with
each other by kinship, they establish the system of private property. They
need to build a state to establish the order of the society. They may need the
state to defend the territory occupied by the nation. They may need the state
to manage the economy, so that everyone can make a living smoothly. They

may sometimes even need the state to support the development of national culture. They usually need the state to found a regime for the management of public affairs of the nation. Though I have mentioned earlier that nation functions as a medium in support of the formation of the state in modern times, the state, formed on the basis of a nation, is also required by the growth of the nation. In other words, in order to ensure the healthy growth of the nation, a state needs to be formed on the basis of the nation. Without the state, the nation may not be able to develop. This nation may be under the governance of some other nations. This nation may be dissolved because no state can protect the interest of this nation. In short, any nation that strives to survive and grow must build a state. In particular, after people extend the distance of linguistic communication, they disseminate national consciousness. Due to the dissemination of national consciousness, all strongly realize that they need to build a state. Then, in order to support the building of the state people show their loyalty to the state. This means that all need the state. People, forming a nation, cannot repose their hope on any other entity but a nation-state. Thus all are loyal to the state. People often think that people are loyal to the state because they are loyal to the nation. This is not fallacious. But we can also adduce another point of view here. That is, as the state can satisfy the demand of the nation, people are loyal to the state. In other words, as the state serves the nation, people are loyal to it. This is why people were not loyal to the state in pre-modern times, whereas people are usually loyal to the state in modern times. This means that the state is worthy to be an object of loyalty now. So patriotism is prevalent in modern times.

Third, in pre-modern times the state was built by using coercion mainly. People, coerced to submit to the organization of the state, might not be willing to affirm their loyalty to the state. In modern times, however, the state is often particularly built under the influence of an idea. As people extend the distance of linguistic communication because of the development of various media, they disseminate progressive or rational ideas. As these ideas are influential because many people embrace them, the state gradually adopts these ideas in formulating the principle of organizing the state. In other words, people gradually organize the state under the guidance of an idea rather than organizing it by using pure coercion. As such an idea is usually reasonable, people accept this idea widely. Thus people may be loyal to the state just because they agree to the idea adopted by this state. To put it differently, people, holding this idea, may believe that the state is just. Thus they are firmly loyal to the state over the long term. By contrast, if people hold the idea not upheld by the state, their loyalty to the state may be adversely affected. Here we may think of a man called Henry David Thoreau, an American living in the nineteenth century. He wrote an essay on civil disobedience because he was deeply disturbed by the twin evils of slavery and the U.S. war against Mexico in the late 1840s. Particularly, he opposed slavery. His point of view is that, as Stephen Nathanson writes, "Any government that sanctions and supports an institution as unjust as slavery is not a fit object of loyalty."[25] Thus Thoreau withdrew his loyalty given to the state. This means that an idea may be a medium in the cultivation of loyalty. If the loyalty required by the state differs from the loyalty people are willing to show, the loyalty to the state may become problematic. People may even commit sabotage or espionage or treason because they are no longer loyal to the state. In this case they may uphold an idea different from the one upheld by the state. Someone may give the secrets of the state to a foreigner or an agent of a foreign state because he embraces an idea that is not the idea of the state in which he resides. He is a traitor to the state, but he is loyal to his idea. One case in point is that Dr. Allan Nunn May, a physicist born in Kings Norton, Birmingham, supplied the official secrets of British and United States atomic research to Russian agents during World War Two because he embraced an idea different from that of the United Kingdom. He was sentenced to ten years hard labor on May 1, 1946. Yet he had no regrets about his spying activities. Grodzins comments that:

> The eminent physicist and British traitor, Dr. Allan Nunn May, declared that he gave official secrets about the atom bomb to Russian agents because he believed that both science and mankind were endangered if the results of Anglo-American nuclear research were not made available to all scientists throughout the world. These are not merely the extreme views of the traitor. They are commonplace among the scientific fraternity, and they have found their most explicit statement in novels by authors who are intimate with scientists. The theme of secrecy (and national

welfare) versus science (and international welfare) is central to Nigel Balchin's *A Sort of Traitors*.[26]

This case demonstrates that the formation of the state is different from that of the tribe in the aspect that people usually form the state on the basis of an idea. The idea that functions as a medium in support of cultivating the loyalty of people to the state bolsters the loyalty of people to the state. The loyalty of people to the tribe takes shape naturally while the loyalty of people to the state often takes shape because of an idea. People disseminate the idea in linguistic communication.

Fourth, the state gradually serves as a powerful identity of all. Whenever humans form a community, they may need an identity. But this identity is significant in the civilized society in general and in the nation-state in particular. In the primitive society, people formed a tribe. A tribe might have an identity such as a totem. But a totem merely played a role in the formation of the tribe among people who were kin to each other. They did not associate together because they had social or cultural characters in common. In the civilized society, people achieve development in culture and production technique. A group of people form a collective being such as a society because they have social and cultural characters in common. People organize themselves because they share a common identity. Then each regards himself as part of this large collective being because they have social or cultural characters in common. People realize their own development. They unite. This collective being becomes the state. Then, as the state develops socially or culturally, the success of this state is often deemed as the success of all. Thus the glory of the state becomes the glory of people. Then people are proud of the state in which they reside. Thus the glory of the state is a reason that people are loyal to the state. This means that people are loyal to the state because of its accomplishments. They tend to regard the accomplishments of the state as their own accomplishments. For example, the scientific discoveries and technological advancements made in the state are usually the pride of the state. People, belonging to this state, feel proud of these scientific discoveries and technological advancements. The state becomes attractive. People may feel happy to participate in the building of the state. They may think that the cause of the state is their own. Thus they are loyal. In the meantime people may also be loyal to the state because of its time-honored history. In the narratives of history, people mention the ancestors of the nation underlying the formation of the state, exalt national heroes and memorize the founding fathers of the state. People pay respects to all of them. They make special contributions to the building of the state. As a result, people are grateful to them. The state, built by them, thus becomes the very object to which people are loyal. People may also be loyal to the state because of the excellent culture flourishing in the state. This culture develops within the state. This culture may be construed as the very valuable spiritual assets of the state. These assets of the state may be deemed as the assets of people. For example, national talents create remarkable literature and art in the state. Many literary and artistic works, created by the talents in this state, are famous and highly evaluated. Likewise, people create a unique and great religion or philosophy in the state. Such religion or philosophy is widely recognized as the excellent religion or philosophy. The related religion or philosophy may be influential throughout the world. People are proud of having these very excellent cultural assets. As these cultural assets are created in the state, people are proud of being part of the state. Likewise, preeminent historians, writers, poets, artists, theologians, philosophers and others of the state may be famous throughout the world. They may be regarded as the representatives of people as these preeminent figures and other people are in the same state. The achievements, made by those preeminent figures, may be considered the achievements made for the state. Thus all are tempted to be always loyal to the state because they firmly believe that they belong to this state. They may also actively attend the rituals of the state to strengthen their own connection with the state. They keep strong emotional ties with the state. They are loyal citizens of the state.

As such, people affirm their loyalty to the state and the state exalts and highly evaluates their loyalty. The state also serves them. As they are satisfied with the service provided by the state, they are loyal to the state.

The loyalty of people in the tribe was natural, whereas the loyalty of people in the state must be especially built by using language. The state is built in the process of linguistic communication everywhere. As a result, people know that they are encouraged to work hard and they are supposed to protect the interest of the state whenever there appears an occasion that the interest of the state may be endangered. They know that they are sometimes obligated to join the army and if they join the army, they are sometimes required to venture their lives to go to the battlefield to defend their state. They know that they should be loyal to a political party, or the government, or the people, or the state. All communities know that they should be loyal to the state. All regions know that they should to be loyal to the state. All local governments know that they should be loyal to the central government. All civil servants know that they should be loyal to the state. All citizens know that they should be always loyal to the state or an agent of the state. In the meantime, loyalty is described as conscience and justice. Loyalty is also always affirmed. People may swear an oath to affirm their loyalty in a ceremony. They may also write a letter in their blood to affirm firmly their loyalty. As loyalty must be affirmed before the act of loyalty is committed, language must be used. Then those in charge of organizing the state can feel assured that their call can warrant an active response from all. They can then issue commands comfortably. All can be ready to act under their command. All can be of one heart and one mind. People organize the state this way.

This further means that linguistic communication, performed by people to affirm loyalty, to exalt loyalty and to interpret loyalty, culminates in the establishment of a wholesome relationship between the organizer of the state and all and among all. When all realize that they all are loyal to the state, they cooperate with each other and unite. This means that loyalty is the necessity of organizing the state. In the organization of the state, the loyalty of all is invariably required. When city-states were built by ancient Greeks, citizens were required to be loyal to the city-states. When Kingdoms were formed in medieval Europe, subjects were required to be loyal to their lords and their lords were further required to be loyal to the kings. When nation-states emerge in modern times, citizens are required to be loyal to the nations or the nation-states. Then patriotism prevails throughout the state. Loyalty actually denotes the construction of a myriad of social connections in which the vertical cooperation of all can be realized in the principle of organizing the state. On one hand, proactive submission to the organization of the state is loyalty, and on the other, satisfying the demand from all is also the cultivation of loyalty in the organization of the state. Loyalty is the cooperation of a special kind for the organization of the state.

3. Support or Opposition

As we assume that the state requires the loyalty of all and the state is also expected to meet the demand from people in order to win loyalty from people particularly in modern times, we also argue that such an interaction between the state and people is also characterized by the interaction realized by people to show their attitude of support or opposition. It is easy for the state to satisfy the demand from a portion of people. If the state is set to meet the demand from all, people should be able to express the attitude of support or opposition. That is, there is a scheme of distributing interest within the state, and the demand from all needs to be satisfied. People are supposed to be loyal to the state, but the expectations of all should also be met. For example, the state, making a policy or a law, may often need to get support from as many citizens as possible. The policy, or the law, of the state not only needs to be in the interest of people, but also needs to be in the interest of all. As the policy, or the law, of the state may concern the distribution of interest, it should be accepted by all. Citizens then show their attitude such as support or opposition because they desire the fair distribution of interest. This attitude is unlike the attitude shown by people when they confer an honor on someone or they confirm their loyalty. But this attitude is also essential in the organization of the state. The reason that such an attitude is essential is also that the state is a very special organization. Its structure is very much at variance with that of the tribe. For tribal people, any decision for the management of the tribe was accepted by all. There was no need for people to display any attitude. People had only one sort of interest in the tribe. If people were requested to display their attitudes in the tribe, their attitudes should be similar or the same. But in the state the interests of people vary greatly. A fundamental change has taken place in the state. That is, the interest of tribal people was unified and monolithic. It was meaningless for people to display their attitudes in the tribe because there was no problem of the fairness in the distribution of interest in the tribe. In the state, however, people vary in occupation due to the development of the division of labor. Some people are rich while some other people poor. Some people work in the sector of agriculture while some other people work in the sector of industry. Some people are only workers while others managers. Some people are laborers while others technicians and engineers. They may view the same policy or the same law from different perspectives simply because they vary in economic status. People may also vary in the structure of knowledge. Some people are well-educated while others are less-educated. Some people have the knowledge of science and social sciences while others only have common sense. They may view the same policy or the same law from different perspectives simply because they have different structures of knowledge. People may also vary in values upheld by them. Some people are conservative or liberal while others radical. They may also view the same policy or the same law from different perspectives simply because they hold different ideas or values. They are believed to show their different attitudes in the making of a policy or a law. The state cannot ignore any of these different attitudes. Now there is a dichotomy between the private interest and the public interest; there is a dichotomy between the parochial interest and the overall interest; and there is a dichotomy between the interest of the upper social class and the interest of the lower social class and so on and so forth. Thus, people need to display different attitudes, so that they can coordinate these different attitudes. Thus the management of public affairs not only needs to be interpreted so as to be accepted by all, but also needs the coordination of all different attitudes because an interpretation may not always result in reaching an agreement. Although an interpretation is expected to be accepted by all, the attitudes of all should also be taken care of by the authorities. If a group of people show a different attitude toward the management of a public affair, all should try to unify all attitudes through coordination.

This coordination is also feasible. If people display different attitudes lawfully, some people may coordinate these different attitudes and the authorities may consider them. If these different attitudes are considered, the interest of each will not be ignored. Thus attitudes are shown by people to coordinate their attitudes to reach a consensus on the organization of the state. These different attitudes are always shown by the people. These attitudes may be the most important ones that people intend to show. These attitudes may be in a form of action interpreted by using language, but articulation is indispensable. Each attitude directly or indirectly reflects one's inclination, or stance, likely to be different from the inclination, or the stance, of all others. This attitude may be in a crucial process of organizing the state. In other words, showing an attitude means displaying one's inclination or stance. There is an interaction. The state is also organized in the process of the mutual interaction among the citizens and between the citizens and the power holders. But this interaction is chiefly linguistic interaction instead of physical interaction. People normally interact with each other in the form of linguistic interaction instead of physical interaction because articulation can represent the direction of action. Articulation works on behalf of physical action in displaying an attitude because articulation can go before and in place of action and it is easier to articulate than to take action. Linguistic interaction is more efficient. This is significant for the organization of the state. Thus, aware of the possible or inevitable action, people interact with each other by way of articulation. The interaction of all within the state focused on by us should be the interaction of articulation because only such an interaction is constructive in the organization of the state. This articulation means displaying an attitude on the basis of using language. Although displaying an attitude may be in other forms such as the forms of displaying an attitude by demonstrating a special behavior in the course of action, displaying an attitude in the form of linguistic communication is the basic and essential form because displaying an attitude in the form of showing a special behavior can only be realized on a small scale and in a very limited number of ways. Without displaying an attitude in the form of linguistic communication, all other ways of displaying an attitude, including the way of displaying an attitude by showing a special behavior, will not be always meaningful for the formation of the state.

That is, the physical interaction of people on a small scale does not enable people to express their attitudes meaningfully. Attitudes, shown by using language, are significant in the organization of the state. This is a very particular way of organizing the state. This way of organizing the state differs from the way of organizing any tribe. A tribe was organized by people because of kinship. All members of the tribe were connected with each other by kinship. They formed their tribe for their own preservation. They usually submitted absolutely to the leadership of the tribal chief. They obeyed the will of the tribal chief without any condition. They did not worry about any decision made by the tribal chief because they fully trusted the tribal chief. As all were connected with one another by kinship, the tribal chief would not act against the interest of all. In addition, as any decision concerning organization, production and consumption was simple within the tribe, the tribe was governed according to experience. Such experience was rudimentary. Such experience never exceeded the level of common sense. All had the same common sense. If all were requested to express their attitudes toward the governance of the tribe, all should show the similar attitudes. This means that people did not need to display their attitudes in the organization of the tribe at all. But the case of the state is different. In the state the power holder of the state no longer always works as expected by people. People can no longer take it for granted that the power holder of the state always takes initiative to satisfy their needs. All within the state need to take care of their own interest from time to time. They have to express their attitudes in order to request the power holder of the state to respect their need of taking care of their own interest. Their own interest may include their own personal interest or family interest. In the meantime, due to the division of labor that arises from an increase in the size of the community as well as the development of technologies of production, the variation of the occupations of the citizens leads to the diversification of their interests. The community grows large, and the structure of the community becomes complex. Accordingly, only people who have certain knowledge can understand the public affairs of the state. People may receive different educations. They may view the same affair from different perspectives. Thus people may not always take action in unison or may not always cooperate with one another in the community larger than the tribe. People may not establish the order of the community smoothly. The organization of the state may encounter unexpected difficulties. As such, to enable people to view the same affair from the same perspective, to enable them to cooperate smoothly and to enable them to act in unison for the purpose of pursuing the common cause, for the purpose of establishing the order of the community, and for the purpose of organizing the state, people often show their different attitudes in order to coordinate with one another. Then people reach a consensus. They strengthen the solidarity of the state. If there are any tensions between different social classes, for example, the continuous process of expressing attitudes eases or unravels those tensions. People begin to see the formation of common interest. This occurs in the formation of the state. This is also a language solution used by people to support such an interaction in the organization of the state.

At least there are five basic forms adopted by people to show their attitudes in support of such an interaction in the organization of the state.

The first basic form is the meeting of the people. When people hold that meeting, they often express opinions. They often express their opinions to the authorities. In ancient Greece, for instance, people held the assembly called "ecclesia," meaning the meeting of the people. All qualified people were invited to attend that meeting. In 594BCE, Solon invited male Athenians over the age of 20 to take part. A certain group of people were even especially invited to participate. Aristotle noted that in ancient Greece mixed regimes favored aristocracy. As regards the assembly, they insisted that attendance at its meeting should be open to all, but a fine for non-attendance should be imposed only on the well-off, or the fine on them should be much heavier.[27] People were urged to participate. While the assembly elected some officials; the assembly legislated; and the assembly tried political crimes, attendants were especially allowed to give opinions freely. Though they merely gave their brief opinions because it was impossible for so many people to elaborate their opinions, giving opinions freely was conducive to the formation of common interest. The reason is that people, having given their opinions freely, tended to give different opinions. They showed their attitude of support or opposition. Narrating the life of Lycurgus (9th century B.C.), a lawgiver of Sparta of ancient Greece, Plutarch writes that "The people . . .being thus assembled in the open air, it was not allowed to any one of their order to give his advice, but only either to ratify or reject what should be propounded to them by the king or senate."[28] Showing their attitude this way resulted in the formation of common interest. In modern times, citizens adopt that method. They hold assemblies to give their opinions. Although they are no longer especially arranged for to express their attitudes, the law protects their right of holding an assembly. The First Amendment of the Constitution of the United States stipulates that Congress shall make no law respecting "the right of the people peacefully to assemble, and to petition the Government for a redress of grievances."[29] Women also participate, and nearly all can participate. The assembly is often a large-scale meeting. Different people may hold different assemblies. The authorities do not ignore their attitudes. The reason is that people express their opinions in the public. The authorities have to react. They often have to communicate with the masses through a dialogue. They have to take into consideration the broad interest of the people. Perhaps political scientists will argue that what is important is to find out the attitude of the majority. To me, what is important is that each side is allowed to express a different attitude. On the other hand, the governments of the states may impose reasonable time, place and manner restrictions on those assemblies to ensure that those assemblies are peaceful. As Jethro K. Lieberman writes, since 1930s the court has wrestled with the problem of balancing the right to assembly against the state's right to regulate time, place and manner of the assembly to further important public interests.[30] The government has to standardize the assemblies. The assembly held by the masses may not only serve as a form of communication among the masses but also serve as a form of communication between them and the authorities. Citizens need to express their attitudes lawfully.

The second basic form is the opinions expressed through various organizations. In ancient Rome a tribe might express an opinion on behalf of its members as it survived for a period of time. In medieval Europe a church might express an opinion on behalf of religious believers. In 1054 the Roman Catholic Church split into the Eastern and Western Christian Churches. In the sixteenth century the Protestant Church emerged. Different churches might express an opinion on behalf of different Christians. In England different religious organizations have been expressing the opinions of Anglicans, Catholics, Baptists and Quakers respectively since the 1600s. In modern times political parties emerge. They include liberal or conservative or socialist parties. As they express the opinions of their members, they are used by a portion of the citizens in displaying their attitude. These citizens may donate money to the political parties. They may work as volunteers for the political parties. They may attend the rallies held by the political parties to show their support to the political parties. Then those political parties can be construed as major media used by the citizens to show their attitudes toward the government or the policies of the government or the acts of the government. Through political parties, citizens not only interact with one another but also interact with the government that functions on behalf of the state. As a consensus must be reached for the governance of the state, the attitudes of all cannot be ignored or overlooked. Thus, all coordinate the demands of all and find a solution in the making of policies and laws. Likewise, citizens also form professional organizations such as a chamber of commerce, a trade union and a farmers' association. They help people to display their attitudes in the related professional domains. As laws and policies may concern a specific professional domain in the society or the state, those professional organizations help people to display their attitudes in a related professional domain. When businesses display their attitudes toward an industrial policy concerning their interest, they may display their attitudes through the chambers of commerce. When the workers of the factories display their attitudes toward an industrial policy or a social security policy concerning their interest, they may display their attitudes through the trade unions. Thus the trade unions help them to display their attitudes. When farmers display their attitudes toward an agricultural policy concerning their interest, they may do so through the association of farmers. Thus, the attitudes of all can be displayed. Particularly in those democratic states people display their attitudes. If people raise complaints or wage a protest through those organizations, they can also do so. Raising complaints or waging a protest is also a way of displaying an attitude. Thus, Morton Grodzins writes that:

> In the political sphere, democratic society allows for easy protest. The existence of political parties channels discontents into socially approved forms. Inside and outside the formal party structure, special-interest groups offer many opportunities for action within a wide spectrum of political beliefs. Politics within non-political institutions—business, labor union or club— attracts the energies of many. When local or national problems appear parochial, movements for world betterment challenge attention.[31]

When people display their attitudes to the state, they use the form of organization as a medium. Forming an organization, people are usually aimed at using such a form as a medium in linguistic communication on a large scale. Due to the operation of an organization, people communicate on a larger scale. They extend the distance of linguistic communication. Thus they display their attitudes effectively and powerfully across the state. People cannot realize such linguistic communication on individual basis. Those religious, political and professional organizations assist people in linguistic communication. Thus people realize their mutual interaction with themselves and with the government. All sides may reach the consensus on the governance of the state.

The third basic form is the attitude expressed by people by using ballots. Ballots are often used in election. Election has a long history. In ancient Greece people held election without ballots. Aristotle notes that citizens appointed officials by lot or election or by both means.[32] In medieval times, people expressed their opinions to the authorities in another way. As no political system allowed people to express their attitude, people refrained from communicating with the authorities unless they were in conflict with the authorities. When in conflict with the authorities, they revolted. They used their behavior to express their attitude. Yet such an attitude was usually expressed by a small portion of people. Such an attitude could not be displayed regularly and lawfully. In modern times the state grows due to extending the reach of linguistic communication, including the linguistic communication that uses paper as a medium and adopts printing, and people come to express their attitudes toward the governance of the state in every four or five or seven years through election. They can use ballots to express their opinions. Such opinions are their attitudes. As election enables voters to communicate across the state by using language, people express attitudes widely. Observers usually regard such attitudes as reasonable. This is because if a large number of people jointly express an attitude, this attitude must be accepted by the majority. If this attitude only reflects the narrow interest of a small portion of people, all others will not join them in expressing such an attitude. The attitude, expressed by the majority, must reflect the broad interest of the majority or even of all. Thus all or the majority will make sure that the opinion, given by displaying the attitude, is reasonable or fair. If each insists on expressing the attitude reflecting the narrow interest of his own, people will be unable to reach a consensus because the narrow interest of each is always in conflict with the interest of the other. Then each is urged to consider the interest of all others. As a result, attitudes, expressed by all or the majority, should be reasonable and fair. Thus we see that the public scheme of distributing interest was usually made by the power holder coming from the ruling class in medieval times. As this power holder represented a small portion of people, the public scheme of distributing interest was in favor of a small portion of people. There was no common interest of all. Yet since people commenced to hold election, the attitudes of ordinary people have had to be considered in the making of the public scheme of distributing interest. The influence of a small number of people from the ruling class declines. Then the common interest of all takes shape. Besides, we see that before the era of election in modern times, it was difficult for ordinary people to express their attitudes toward the governance of the state. They sometimes expressed their attitude by way of revolt when they suffered a lot from the oppression of the ruling class. Nevertheless, the ruler always tried his best to put down the revolt. He frightened the masses by using force in an attempt to prevent the revolt from arising. But since the beginning of the era of election in modern times, it has been easy for ordinary people to express their attitudes toward the governance of the state. They express their attitudes by using language and they never fear any violent conflict. They can express attitudes peacefully. And furthermore, before the beginning of the era of election in modern times, ordinary people only occasionally expressed their attitudes toward the governance of the state. They usually expressed no attitude unless they suffered a lot. Since the day when citizens commenced to hold election, people have been holding election regularly. Ordinary people can often express their attitudes. Thus their attitudes can be considered by the power holder at normal times. The common interest of all takes shape since all can express attitudes.

The fourth basic form is news coverage. When news media report news, they often make a comment. The comment shows the attitude of people. This phenomenon occurs in the civilized society. In the primitive society humans were not required to make any comment on any event occurring in the tribe. The tribe did not need such a comment in its organization because the tribal chief was fully trusted to govern the tribe. The tribal chief was believed to act in the interest of all. But since the formation of the state no one has ever acted as the tribal chief. The leader of the state may be selected or supported by people. But as the leader is often involved in the conflict of interest in exercising power, he is required to interact with those who are governed. The opinions of the citizens should be heard. Thus ordinary people may make a comment on any event in the state. They hope to give their opinions through a comment. This is a simple interaction between them and the authorities.

Of course, in ancient times there might not always be such a kind of form of interaction within the state because at that time the state was organized by the ruler using coercion except in ancient Greece and Rome. In medieval times news was spread through the gossips of townspeople and merchants. After people began to use paper, some people distributed flyers that reported news. In modern times, however, the masses need to be mobilized in support of the building of the state because now the state is built on the basis of a nation. Then the building of the state requires the interaction of all people. In the meantime people adopt the journalist form to facilitate the interaction of all with all within the state. Modern printing also figures prominently. Electronic media also develop. Then newspapers, magazines, radios and other means often function like the mouth of the people. They show their attitudes to the authorities. Such attitudes are often the attitudes of the people because they need to act on behalf of the people in order to increase their influence. They function as if they were entrusted by the people. They show their attitudes toward the authorities on behalf of the people. As they are media, they are used by ordinary people. They act as the agents of ordinary people. As ordinary people are their readers or audiences, they have to say what ordinary people intend to say. These attitudes should often be the attitudes of the masses unless these media are especially controlled by any organization or the authorities. In particular, in the states in which the freedom of speech is guaranteed by law, different news media show different attitudes on behalf of different portions of the people. As news media need as many readers and audiences as possible in order to augment their own influence in the state, what they think of should be what ordinary people think of. No unjust opinion can be expressed because when they reflect the attitude of the great majority of people as a form of collective linguistic communication, the unjust opinion of a small portion of the people cannot be expressed if news media are not controlled by the authorities. The opinion of the great majority should prevail and this opinion should reflect the common interest of all or the majority. Thus whenever an attitude is shown or expressed this way, it functions to help the coordination of people in order to express a general attitude toward a specific matter or issue. Though different news media show different attitudes, the expression of different attitudes cannot impede the expression of the unified attitude toward a matter or issue reflecting justice because people, enabled by the idea of justice to coordinate with each other, can finally reach a consensus. Only the just attitude prevails. Then people can act in unison.

The fifth basic form is a certain cultural form. As plenty of people in the state need to communicate with one another in order to share their views and express their wishes and expectations for the purpose of building the society and the state, they create the aesthetic forms of expression. These aesthetic forms of expression have evolved to be some cultural forms since ancient times. As these aesthetic forms of expression are attractive, they become media in support of the related linguistic communication. When those aesthetic forms of expression are adopted, people perform linguistic communication at the same time. Then people may use these forms to make comments on, or to express opinions about, the society or the state. People thus are enabled to exhibit their attitudes. Writers, poets and artists have been using these forms to display their attitudes on behalf of ordinary people since ancient times, for example. They are actually the media. This is because writers, poets and artists must create the works welcomed by ordinary people. Writers, poets and artists usually hope to become famous. Hoping to become famous, they create their works very welcomed by as many ordinary people as possible. We can believe that any work, welcomed by people, reflects the wishes of ordinary people. As this work makes a comment on the society or the state, we can believe that this work is a comment made on behalf of ordinary people on the society or the state. In other words, if this work expresses an opinion about the society or the state, it can mean that an opinion is expressed by ordinary people. And such a comment or opinion must be just or must tend to be just. If a writer, or a poet, or an artist, creates a work reflecting the opinion from plenty of ordinary people, it cannot be unjust. There is a process of collective linguistic communication that gives this opinion. If one ordinary person gives an opinion that is very selfish, this opinion must not be identical with the opinion given by another person under the condition that the other person also gives a very selfish opinion. If people give an opinion that can be accepted by all or the majority, these people should not be very selfish. They should consider the interest of the great majority of the people. Their attitude must be objective or reasonable. Thus their opinion tends to be just. Only the just opinion can be accepted by all or the majority. Thus, a writer or a poet or an artist creates his works in order to reflect the attitude of people of the largest number, and the opinion given by his works must advocate justice. Then it follows that people can always reach a consensus when a writer or a poet or an artist displays the attitude on behalf of them. Thus, people enhance the common interest of all. So in ancient times people had no other means to show their attitudes in the public within the state. People usually had no adequate means to perform linguistic communication across the state. People usually realized social intercourse in the local area by using language. An ordinary man could only perform linguistic communication on a very small scale. He usually communicated with his friends, neighbors, relatives, business partners and others. Therefore, since ancient times, people, performing linguistic communication across the state, have had to use a special medium. Then I argue that, from ancient to modern times, people create many cultural forms. So folk songs may express the attitude of ordinary people because folk songs may present a view or give an opinion about any matter such as a social custom in the state or even express an opinion concerning the state of the society or the governance of the state. People may also create poems to display their feelings. They may also give an opinion about any matter such as the origin of the nation at the same time. People may stage a play to make a comment on any matter such as a piece of history. People may also write novels to make a comment on any matter or express an opinion about any matter such as a social issue or a political event. They show their attitudes. Their attitudes may influence many other people.

In sum, people witness the formation of the common interest as a result of the fact that they display their attitude of support or the attitude of opposition. That people display their attitude of support undoubtedly bears testimony to the formation of the common interest. The fact that citizens display their attitude of opposition means that the government is willing to consider their attitude. In other words, the government is willing to take care of their concerns and hence their interest. Otherwise the display of the attitude of opposition will be prohibited. Thus people witness the formation of the common interest due to the display of an attitude. In history the state might be ruled by a despotic ruler. This ruler usually suppressed any act of displaying an attitude not welcomed by the ruler. In this case the display of support to the authorities might be fabricated. Only when people are able to display their attitude of opposition can they use language to show their genuine attitude. Needless to say, ordinary people are sometimes silent. Some people may interpret this silence by using language, and reveal a related attitude. For example, under the condition that a portion of people always oppose a certain policy of the government, their silence, in the face of another policy made by the government, may mean that they accept or support this policy. There may also be such a case: An opposition always opposes the ruling party. Its silence toward an act committed by the ruling party may mean that the opposition supports the ruling party on a certain matter. However, people cannot clearly see the exact attitudes of people until they display their attitudes by using language. The attitude, displayed by a portion of people by way of being silent in a certain case, is guessed by the public. People may not interpret that attitude accurately. Sometimes a portion of people are silent because the authorities suppress the opinion of the citizens. In the state in which the authorities do not ensure the freedom of speech, ordinary people refrain from expressing their attitudes because of fear. They may accept the rule of the ruler due to necessity. They may even succumb to the ruler in exchange for peace. This exchange is that they subject themselves to the rule of the ruler in exchange for the ruler not to harm them further. This is an extreme case. This case may occur or recur. But this attitude may not be sustainable. The so-called exchange may not be the normal social exchange. Peter M. Blau writes that:

> An individual may give another money because the other stands in front of him with a gun in a holdup. While this could be conceptualized as an exchange of his money for his life, it seems preferable to exclude the result of physical coercion from the range of social conduct encompassed by the term "exchange".[33]

The exchange between the masses and the government mentioned above is like the case described by Blau in nature. This is an abnormal social exchange. The man, holding a gun, should not be construed as engaging in a normal social exchange because people cannot see the formation of the common interest between the two sides. The exchange, discussed by people, usually does not mean that one should be forced to engage in an exchange since every exchange is supposed to ensure the formation of the common interest of the two sides. An exchange is usually the one in which people engage on voluntary basis. Likewise, if citizens are prohibited from displaying their attitude of opposition while being required to display their attitude of support, the display of their attitude of support is not genuine. People do not see the formation of the common interest between the people and the government. To put it another way, if the government of a state prohibits citizens from showing the attitude of opposition, the state is not built due to the formation of the common interest. Then there must be one side unwilling to enter the mutual interaction. The genuine attitude of support must be displayed on voluntary basis. That is, people will not witness the formation of the common interest until they are free to display their attitudes. As long as people are allowed to display their attitudes, the attitude of support and the attitude of opposition alike, on voluntary basis, it is hard for the government to ignore the attitudes of the people. Considering the attitudes of people means the formation of the common interest in some sense. The interest of all becomes homogeneous. That is, following the formation of the state, the formation of the common interest of all needs a process of linguistic communication that enables people to show both their attitude of support and their attitude of opposition. This situation is unlike the situation of a tribe.

There was only one kind of interest in the tribe. This interest was the interest of the tribe. There was no interest of a specific person. The tribal chief worked in the interest of the tribe. Thus, people can suppose that whichever decision was made by the tribal chief in the governance of the tribe was agreed to by all other members of the tribe. Yet people were not required to affirm their consent thereto. It was unnecessary because no one was skeptical about the commitment of the tribal chief. Yet since people began communicating using language, they have expanded their community. They form their state. Then following the formation of the state, kinship discontinues playing a role in the formation of the community. The interest of the tribe is replaced by the interest of the state. As people form the families of monogamy at the same time, there also appears the interest of family. Then a person may be involved in the conflict of interest if he holds a government post. This means that a person, holding a government post within the state and being supposed to work in the interest of the state, may seek the interest of the family. People also have different social backgrounds. There may be the ethnic groups of people. Then a power holder of the state may seek the interest of an ethnic group of people he belongs to when he works for the state. Social classes also emerge. Then a man who becomes a power holder of the state may seek the interest of the social class he belongs to. Political parties also emerge. Then, a power holder who is a member of a political party may seek the interest of that political party when he presumably exercises his power in the interest of the state. These are all examples. Thus the authorities need to consider the attitudes of ordinary people concerning the governance of the state. This means that in some sense all need to agree to the governance of the state if it must be guaranteed that the state is governed in the interest of all. Ordinary people need to communicate with the power holder. People need to confirm the agreement to the governance of the state in the process of linguistic communication, whereas people did not need such an agreement on the governance of the tribe.

In a greater part of human history a state was governed by the ruler by using force. The rule of violence means using force. But this does not mean that ordinary people do not need to express their attitudes. If the rule of the ruler is unbearable, ordinary people revolt against the ruler. In order to avoid the revolt, the ruler should consider the attitudes of the masses. The masses should actively show their attitudes toward the governance of the state, too. These attitudes should be known and considered. The power holder needs to pay attention to these attitudes. Thus the power holder and the masses may cooperate with each other. So, sometimes various arrangements are made to allow for people to express their attitudes, and ordinary people are indeed enabled, or arranged for, to show their attitudes. The attitudes are not the attitudes of a few people. Instead, they are the attitudes of many people. If the attitudes of many people are considered, the power holders may be guided to working in the interest of the state or the people. In the history of some European states, power holders used to design some forms of linguistic communication to allow for ordinary people to display their attitudes in order to engage in the political mobilization of the masses. Specifically, after the state ensured the freedom of speech, it further gave the freedom of press and suffrage to ordinary people. At the same time, the ruler enhanced the ruling legitimacy of the government. Then people established democracy.

This shows that when the attitudes of all people are considered by the power holder, he works in the interest of all instead of a portion of people.

The different attitudes of the citizens also need to be unified so that the citizens express the mainstream attitude and the government makes laws and policies in consideration of the unified attitude. This is also a condition for the formation of the common interest. But the common interest takes shape in the process of showing attitudes freely instead of forging a unanimous consent. In other words, the common interest is formed in the process in which all are enabled to express their attitudes freely and regularly. Some scholars may argue that if the attitudes of the citizens are not well unified, it is difficult for the government to make a sound law or policy reflecting the common interest of all. My view is that, confirming the formation of the attitude of the majority, those scholars often ignore the attitude of the minority. The reason is that the formation of the attitude of the majority is not a complete course of forming the common interest. The common interest is formed across time. After one election the minority may become part of the majority next time. Their interest will be taken care of. In this case we cannot claim that no common interest takes shape. The prevalence of the attitude of the majority at the moment only means that the citizens are allowed to become the minority. This is the freedom enjoyed by all. To put it differently, the minority is not unimportant. When all citizens are allowed to display their attitudes, no matter whether or not a unanimous attitude can be expressed, the common interest of all comes into existence since all can keep on showing their attitudes time and again. The interest of all will be taken care of. This is because when citizens show their attitudes, though their attitudes differ, the authorities actually consider all the attitudes as long as the authorities seek support from as many people as possible. The attitude of each is actually not ignored over the long term. Since no one discriminates against anyone, the common interest of all exists. If the attitude, displayed by one, seems not so important this time, it may become important next time. As citizens show their different attitudes, they realize their mutual interaction. This is the method of forming the common interest. Pluralism prevails as a result. In order to make their own attitudes coordinated to form the unified attitude of the majority, all may be required to adjust their attitudes. Thus citizens may display and coordinate their attitudes, so that their attitudes can be considered and accepted in the scheme of distributing the interest. They may manage to understand each other through the display of their different attitudes. They may adjust their attitudes in order to express a unified attitude toward the making of a law or a policy. Thus, in a state under democracy people express their attitudes lawfully and freely, and the process of expressing the unified attitude in the public means the formation of the common interest of all within the state.

It is not the temporary result but the continuous process or procedure that conditions the formation of the common interest of all. As only the unanimous opinion means the formation of the common interest of all, one prerequisite should be that each is allowed to express his attitude freely. Otherwise, the unanimous attitude may be fabricated. For example, sometimes a major policy is made by the government, and there is no major dispute about it in the public. This may mean the formation of the common interest of all or the majority, provided that all sides are allowed to express their attitudes freely. But in most cases the common interest of the citizens takes shape due to a dispute. If a policy or a law involves a dispute, or this policy or law is controversial, or there are two distinct extreme views about a policy or a law, or two large groups of people keep on upholding the two different ideas, or the ruling party and the opposition fail to coordinate their policies and hence a large batch of the citizens wage a long-term demonstration on the street to put pressure on the ruling party, people are likely to see the formation of the common interest of the citizens. This is because all agree that all should be allowed to express their attitudes freely. If we assume that the attitudes of the citizens are diverse, pluralism means the formation of the common interest. The common interest should be, first of all, reflected by the unanimous agreement on the establishment of a process of expressing attitudes freely and the possible continuity of expressing attitudes by all sides. If the government of a state tolerates the expression of the attitude of opposition particularly in the public, it creates a condition for the formation of the common interest of the state. If the state makes a law clearly defining that citizens can express the attitude of opposition, there is absolutely the common interest. Conversely, the common interest vanishes when this government prevents citizens from expressing their attitude of opposition. The common interest vanishes absolutely when this government imprisons the citizens that express the attitude of opposition, for example. In short, the common interest of all only exists due to the establishment of a process in which people can express different attitudes.

Needless to say, expressing different attitudes results in the formation of the majority and the minority. The majority that expresses an attitude represents the people and anyone may become part of the people in the expression of attitudes at any time since we hold that the people should have one will. But this can only be realized in the process in which all are allowed to express their attitudes freely. If a portion of the citizens are not allowed to express their attitude, the common interest of all certainly vanishes. Thus the value of the expression of attitudes by the citizens is that very process. Hobbes writes that:

> If the Representatives consist of many men, the voice of the greater number, must be considered as the voice of them all. For if the lesser number pronounce (for example) in the Affirmative, and the greater in the Negative, there will be Negatives more than enough to destroy the Affirmatives; and thereby the excess of Negatives, standing uncontradicted, are the onely voice the Representative hath.[34]

My view is that this is the mechanism of forming the will of the people. The value of the attitude shown by the minority does not mean nothing. The attitude of the minority and the attitude of the majority constitute the entire process. What is completed, in the process described by Hobbes, is actually not the outcome but the process itself. Without the attitude of the minority, no attitude of the majority exists. In some sense, the greater part of the contribution made for the sustainability of such a system is made by the minority. Citizens who are not part of the majority this time yield to the presentation of the will of the majority of which they are personally not in favor. This is a process. However, this is not the only one process. A new process will begin next time. Only under the condition that different attitudes are allowed to be expressed continuously can people express their attitudes freely. Only under this condition is it possible for the citizens to see the formation of their common interest. As a result, it is arguable that if citizens can express attitudes freely, widely and continuously, no government can halt the formation of the common interest of all. Expressing one's attitude freely is the basic condition for the formation of the common interest of all within the state. Giving support and expressing opposition are both the essential forms for the formation of the common interest of all.

Whenever people communicate using language, language works toward the formation of the common interest of all involved in linguistic communication. As the common interest may change due to a change in an objective situation, people tend to keep on performing such linguistic communication so that the formation of their common interest does not discontinue. Conversely, if people do not display their attitudes, the common interest may vanish. If language is abused, no common interest exists. For example, if one deceives the other, no common interest exists. If one grieves the other, no common interest exists. The abuse of language is a process of linguistic communication that is not sustainable. The abuse of language may lead to a conflict between one portion of the people and another portion of the people. If people keep on performing normal linguistic communication to display their attitudes, it is possible to realize the formation of their common interest. Usually, the authorities seek support from as many people as possible. Thus the authorities have to allow people to display attitudes freely. The abuse of language cannot occur in this case. The most reasonable attitude must win support from most of the citizens. Thus, people have their common interest as long as they complete the related process and then continue to go through this process again.

Whenever the authorities allow people to express both the attitude of support and the attitude of opposition, the authorities have to consider the attitude of each side this time or next time. If the government is going to make a decision, it must try to win support from as many citizens as possible. The attitude of either side can be considered albeit possibly at different times. Yet as this process runs continuously, the interaction between all sides in expressing the attitude of support or opposition functions to cultivate the common interest in a long process. The authorities will not ignore the attitude of any side finally. Particularly, permitting the expression of the attitude of support or opposition will inevitably lead to the formation of the common interest between the power holders and the ordinary citizens. The system, allowing for all to express their attitudes, creates a condition for the formation of the common interest of all. Any power holder is prevented from using coercion to bar those people from expressing their attitude of opposition or to support some others in expressing their attitude of support. In expressing different attitudes, citizens are compelled to join one another to show their common attitude in order to be considered by the power holder not because of the enforcement of violence but because of the necessity of organizing the state. In this case they also often have to make a compromise. If people's attitudes serve as a foundation for the selection of legislators, administrators and judges in a series of elections, the selection of some of them who are willing to consider the attitudes of all groups of people or the attitudes of both majority and minority may reflect a compromise made by people. As John C. Livingston and Robert G. Thompson write, "The stability of democratic politics requires overlapping membership in groups and the selection of legislators, administrators, and judges who will define their roles as mediators of group compromise."[35] Besides, if and when politicians and political parties that reflect the attitudes of the citizens refuse to make a compromise, they will also be compelled to make a compromise in the legislature in order to approve an act or a public policy. For example, if a certain number of votes are required to approve an act or a public policy, a compromise is sometimes required. As Livingston and Thompson comment,

> If every political philosophy that exists were represented by a political party, the process of compromise would simply be shifted from the political party to the legislature. In order for the legislature to reach agreement on any public policy, it would be necessary to form, through compromises among groups of parties, proposals on which to vote."[36]

Making compromises is considering the interests of all sides. Then I argue that, in an ultimate sense, people witness the formation of the common interest in this process because people are actually forced by themselves to join each other to show a common attitude instead of being forced by any external actor such as a power holder. Expressing the attitude of support or opposition by using language reflects this situation. In short, expressing the attitude of support or opposition is coordination leading to a compromise which means the formation of the common interest. This is the fundamental good of the state.

Notes

1. Jean Bodin, *Six Books of the Commonwealth*, abridged and translated by M.J. Tooley (Oxford: Basil Blackwell,1955), 162.
2. G.W.F. Hegel, *Aesthetics, Lectures on Fine Art*, Vol.1, translated by T.M. Knox (London: Oxford University Press,1975), 557–558.
3. Ibid., 558.
4. Aristotle, *The Politics of Aristotle*, translated by Peter L. Phillips Simpson (Chapel Hill: The University of North Carolina Press, 1997), 54.
5. See: Thorstein Veblen, *What Veblen Taught: Selected Writings of Thorstein Veblen* (New York: the Viking Press Inc.,1964), 216–217 and 224.
6. Bodin, *Six Books of the Commonwealth*, 164.
7. Thomas Hobbes, *Leviathan*, edited with an introduction by C.B. Macpherson (London: Penguin Books,1985), 157–158.
8. Ibid., 158–159.
9. Saint Thomas Aquinas, *The Summa Theological of Saint Thomas Aquinas* (Chicago: Encyclopaedia Britannica, Inc.,1952), Vol.1, 124–125.
10. Veblen, *What Veblen Taught: Selected Writings of Thorstein Veblen*, 222.
11. Ibid., 223–224.
12. Ibid., 224–225.
13. Morton Grodzins, *The Loyal and the Disloyal: Social Boundaries of Patriotism and Treason* (Chicago: The University of Chicago Press, 1956), 6.
14. Ibid., 10.
15. Ibid., 11.
16. Joseph R. Sprayer, *On the Medieval Origins of the Modern State* (Princeton, New Jersey: Princeton University Press, 1970), 9.
17. Grodzins, *The Loyal and the Disloyal: Social Boundaries of Patriotism and Treason*, 58.
18. Josiah Royce, *The Philosophy of Loyalty* (New York: The Macmillan Company, 1924), 357.

19. Please see: James Connor, *The Sociology of Loyalty* (New York: Springer Science & Business Media, LLC, 2007), 92.

20. A. Hirschman, *Exit, Voice, and Loyalty: Responses to Decline in Firms, Organizations, and States* (Cambridge: Harvard University Press, 1970), 82; cited from Connor, *The Sociology of Loyalty*, 48.

21. Connor, *The Sociology of Loyalty*, 48.

22. Grodzins, *The Loyal and the Disloyal: Social Boundaries of Patriotism and Treason*, 126.

23. Peter M. Blau, *Exchange and Power in Social Life* (New York: John Wiley & Sons, Inc. 1964), 29.

24. Grodzins, *The Loyal and the Disloyal: Social Boundaries of Patriotism and Treason*, 13.

25. Stephen Nathanson, *Patriotism, Morality, and Peace* (Lanham: Rowman & Littlefield Publishers, Inc., 1993), 119.

26. Grodzins, *The Loyal and the Disloyal: Social Boundaries of Patriotism and Treason*, 224.

27. Aristotle, *The Politics of Aristotle*, 195.

28. Plutarch, *The Lives of the Noble Grecians and Romans*, the Dryden Translation (Chicago: Encyclopaedia Britannica, Inc., 1952), 35.

29. See: Anthony Lews, *Make No Law: The Sullivan Case and the First Amendment* (New York: Vintage Books, 1991), 47.

30. Jethro K. Lieberman, *A Practical Companion to the Constitution: How the Supreme Court Has Ruled on Issues from Abortion to Zoning* (Berkeley: University of California Press, 1999), 196.

31. Grodzins, *The Loyal and the Disloyal: Social Boundaries of Patriotism and Treason*, 32.

32. Aristotle, *The Politics of Aristotle*, 203.

33. Blau, *Exchange and Power in Social Life*, 91.

34. Hobbes, *Leviathan*, 221.

35. John C. Livingston and Robert G. Thompson, *The Consent of the Governed* (New York: The Macmillan Company, 1963), 156.

36. Ibid., 168.

Chapter Eight

Promise

1. Contract

My argument always rests on this premise: Tribal people formed their tribe because they were kin to each other. They formed a small community. In this community, people relied on each other to survive and grow. Due to group marriage, children were jointly nursed and brought up by adults. Children were dependent on adults. Personal relationship was natural. There was no relationship of contract between one another. Kinship served as a basis for the formation of the natural relationship between one another. People built their mutual relationship naturally. The tribe also grew naturally.

Then a change takes place in the evolution of the human community. This evolution covers the period from the slave-owning society to the feudal society. Specifically, as humans formed a small-size society in the beginning, they always built a close relationship. Although kinship attenuated gradually along with an increase in the size of the community, close relationship between one another still conditioned personal bondage in production and living over a period of time. If some people were taken as slaves at that time, they and their owners might form personal bondage. For example, in the Celtic tribal society, the most ancient society on British soil, bondmen were taken as slaves. There was personal bondage between them and their owners. As Paul Vinogradoff says, in this tribal society, there were slaves (*caeths*) villains—*taeogs*, *aillts*, etc., and there were strangers, *alltuds*. There was "the element of personal bondage."[1] And in Ireland, the *cumal*, the female slave, appeared as a standard article of trade and a unit in reckoning. And *taeogs* appeared as *nativi*, as serfs, settled on the land bound to perform certain duties and pay certain rents though they held personal property and followed fixed customs in their relations to their lords.[2]

In the feudalist times, the society was also a small community. As George H. Sabine describes, in medieval times economic and political organizations were almost wholly local. There were limitations on the means of communication. Trade was mainly local. Local units had a large amount of independence. Trade was controlled by producers' guilds and the unit of medieval trade organization was city. A large political territory was not governable in the fourteenth century.[3] Thus, personal bondage might remain in the society though the feudal society was based on property rights while in slavery the slave owners often extorted the surplus from the slave by way of their ownership of both property (land) and people. For example, the serf was tied to the land. The serf, who did not own the means of production, or labor conditions, such as land, was tied to the lord. He had to provide to the landlord a certain amount of unpaid surplus labor in the form of farming, etc.[4] The serf had no independent personality. The reason is that land was the only important wealth. Every class, from king to fighting man, was dependent directly upon the products of the soil.[5] As Karl Marx concludes, in feudalism instead of the independent man, we find everyone dependent; serfs and lords, vassals, land suzerains, laymen and clergy. Personal dependence here characterizes the social relations of production just as much as it does the other spheres of life organized on the basis of that production.[6]

Yet, it is arguable that as people kept on communicating by using language, they created more and more media. They built markets and developed transportation. They extended the reach of communication. In the meantime, the rulers of the feudal society took initiative to build large communities because, by building large communities, the rulers could get more wealth and power. As Sabine opines, by the sixteenth century all the royal governments had adopted a conscious policy of exploiting national resources, of encouraging trade both at home and abroad, and of developing national power.[7] Large communities took shape in place of the small ones. Laborers began to migrate from one place to another. As noted by Marx and Engels, "The flight of serfs into the towns went on without interruption right through the Middle Ages."[8] The migration of laborers loosened, and finally broke, personal bondage. People gained independent personality.

They turned to making promises to each other and building the relationship of contract in transaction because as Charles Fried writes, "contract is grounded in promise."[9] The relationship of contract now served as a way of building a new type of relationship between one another. If we assume that personal bondage is a relationship of inequality, the relationship of contract is a relationship of equality. The key is the keeping of promise on part of each side in the era of contract. As Hobbes notes,

> [O]ne of the Contractors, may deliver the Thing contracted for on his part, and leave the other to perform his part at some determinate time after, and in the mean time be trusted; and then the Contract on his part, is called Pact, or Covenant: Or both parties may contract now, to perform hereafter: in which cases, he that is to perform in time to come, being trusted, his performance is called *Keeping of Promise*, or Faith; and the fayling of performance (if it be voluntary) *Violation of Faith*.[10]

Establishing the relationship of contract, people have begun to exchange goods and services since that time. Then we see that exchanging goods and services on the market gives large scope to the cooperation of people in production and circulation in the principle of the division of labor.

First, people make promises to each other, and they ensure the certainty of mutual cooperation in the exchange of goods and services. This means that the exchange of goods and services pushes forward the division of labor. The division of labor gives play to the expertise of each individual person. The division of labor bolsters the growth of the economy. To put it differently, each person on the market has a surplus competence. This surplus competence stems mainly from his expertise or working skill. He himself cannot use up his expertise or working skill. If his expertise or working skill can be used by another person, people will create a surplus value. The reason is that his expertise or working skill is often unique in the market though he has many competitors. Thus people engage in the division of labor. Then language plays a role. Therefore, sometimes a shoemaker gives a pair of shoes made by him in exchange for an iron hammer made by a smith, and they communicate using language. They negotiate a price for that pair of shoes and a price for that iron hammer in order to realize the fair exchange. Exchanging goods, people make a contract. They ensure the certainty of exchange. As W. H. Buckler writes, "Merchants and bankers must have what soldiers and farmers seldom need, the means of making and enforcing various agreements with ease and certainty."[11] A contract normally contains at least two promises. If humans did not use language, they would not be able to make any promises. Then they would not be able to realize such an exchange. Without such an exchange people might not witness the formation of the common interest of people and the lack of the common interest would hamper the formation of the society.

Second, people make contracts to ensure the certainty of mutual cooperation in order to utilize effectively social resources available on the market. Every one may have surplus resources. These resources may be idle. Then people make a contract in order to use those idle resources. For example, one may need a fund in a certain amount to start a business and another man has this fund. They make a contract, so that one can borrow this fund from the other. The contract, made by them, ensures that the borrower of the fund repays this fund to the lender of this fund on a certain date in the future plus interest. The two parties reap benefits by making this deal. Without a contract, this deal is usually impossible. What make it possible are both the promise made by the borrower and the promise made by the lender. Thus people can use a certain amount of social resources. Other similar cases may be that people make a contract, through which one party borrows a piece of land from another party, or one party rents premises from another party, or one party engages the other party to work. The result is that people can use social resources effectively. Thus we see that on the market someone founds a bank to lend money to a money borrower. The man who founds the bank becomes the creditor while the man who borrows money from the bank becomes the debtor. We also see that on the market someone operates land in order to lease the land to a land user. One becomes landlord while the other the land developer or the land user. We also see that someone operates a property in order to lease the property to a property user. The former becomes the property lessor while the latter the property lessee. We also see that many people sell their labor on the labor market. Everywhere we find that a man enters into a contract in order to work for his employer or an employer enters into a contract to engage an employee to work for him. They not only exchange goods or services but also use the social resources effectively. They create wealth.

Third, people, using language, can make a contract. They make a contract for themselves to implement it in the future. Thus people not only enable themselves to use social resources effectively but also enable themselves to ensure certainty, or to avoid uncertainty, in their cooperation in the future. They reduce risks in cooperation. Thus they minimize the risks they are exposed to, so that they can avoid any economic loss and enhance the level of profitability. This is because, by making promises, people make a contract to allow for one side to shift the risk onto the other side that can most efficiently evade the risk. A merchant, needing the supply of some products some day in future, can also enter into a contract with a manufacturer to avoid such a risk. As P.S. Atiyah writes,

> X may contract to buy from Y 100 tons of coffee at a fixed price, delivery to be in 12 months time. The purpose of this arrangement is to shift on to Y the possibility of future price increases in coffee above a certain figure. This is a kind of speculation, a bet, but it is likely to have a more useful social or economic purpose than a simple bet. For risk-allocation between business men may be designed to shift risks to those who are better able to evaluate and absorb risks or even prevent them. In contracts of this kind, the whole purpose of the arrangement requires that it be entered into in advance, and that the parties be held to it even prior to any reliance or receipt of benefits.[12]

Fourth, people, entering into a contract, may add to the contract a provision defining the liability of each party and the method of dealing with the breach of contract. For example, people may define the date of delivery of the products and the penalty for breach of contract. This means that a contract is also a method of linguistic communication that requires expressly all parties to the contract to undertake certain obligations in order to cooperate with each other in good faith. All parties have themselves obligated by making a promise. Whichever party fails to honor the promise is going to be penalized. The related law also defines the liability of making a contract. The consequence of failing to comply with the contract is very serious. Thus, people make a contract to ensure mutual cooperation. As early as the times of ancient Rome, the authorities already made laws to allow people to punish those who failed to honor their promises in the contract made by them. According to W. H. Buckler, in the Twelve Tables *pactum* appears as a compact. He writes that:

> If this compact was broken the offended party pursued his remedy. Similarly where a positive *pactum* was violated, the injured person must have the option of chastising the delinquent. His revenge might take the form of personal violence, seizure of the other's goods, or the retention of a pawn already in his possession.[13]

As Buckler further concludes, "the essence of Contract is that the breach of an agreement is punishable in a particular way."[14] This means that a promise is warranted. If a promise is warranted, the certainty of future cooperation is ensured. People arrange the language to be used as a means to effect reliable cooperation. If one party to the contract intends to break the contract, he intends to give up cooperation. He does not need to use language at this moment. Then punishment does not necessarily require the use of language either. Cooperation, however, depends on the use of language.

The role of a contract is that a contract enables strangers to cooperate and hence to realize the division of labor on a large scale. The division of labor conditions the development of modern economy. Thus people, with diverse skills and other resources, can give play to their expertise or resources in the development of the economy of the state. They make possible the circulation of human resources, material resources, capital and technologies. Making a contract paves a way for people to develop market economy on a large scale. People give circulation to those resources because they exchange goods and services in accordance with various contracts made by them. Therefore, they give large-scale circulation to those resources in the growth of economy because the exchange of goods and services means the handover of those resources from one person to another. Some people can especially engage in the exploitation and development of natural resources. They supply some raw materials for agricultural or industrial production. They sell their products to the farms and factories. The farms or factories produce their own products and sell them to the market. Likewise, some people especially engage in investment. They have a lot of financial resources. They create an important condition for the growth of the enterprises. On the other hand, other people can engage in the development of technologies. They provide up-to-date technologies in support of the development of agriculture and manufacturing industry, for example. All of them engage in exchange in order to realize the circulation of all resources and products. This situation makes possible the rational allocation of resources. They support the growth of market. Market also ensures the effective distribution of their products.

The relationship of contract also appears in some other aspects. In premodern times, peasants worked on the land leased by the lord. Peasants were protected by the lord. Peasants gave tribute to the lord on annual basis in return. This tribute was unpaid surplus labor. The relationship of the peasants and the lord at that time was characterized by personal bondage. Along with the development of commerce and industry in early modern times, personal bondage began to vanish because the development of commerce and industry gave circulation to workforce throughout the country. The past peasants became laborers or workers on the market. Factory owners and the owners of other businesses began to engage them. Since then people have recognized the relationship of employment between the two sides as the relationship of contract.

In the feudal times, a lord might be involved in a war against another lord occasionally. While a war broke out, the lord would often assemble peasants to combat for him in the war. These peasants farmed on his land. There was personal bondage between these peasants and the lord, as mentioned earlier. These peasants became combatants. If the ruler of a kingdom was involved in a war against another kingdom, the ruler who was the lord of various vassals would assemble those vassals to help him to combat in the war. There was personal bondage between this ruler and those vassals. Then each of those vassals would assemble his men to combat. These men were the peasants or the serfs of the vassal. There was personal bondage between this vassal and his men. During the period when a feudal kingdom came to be ruled by the absolutist ruler, the ruler sometimes engaged mercenary troops for the war. The relationship between the ruler and the mercenary troops was the relationship of contract. Since the establishment of the citizen army in early modern times, citizens who provide military service to the country have become soldiers. As they are citizens, their relationship with the state is the relationship of a contract. They provide military service to the state because they are obligated. While a citizen undertakes obligations to the state, he also has some rights. Obligations and rights constitute a contract. A relationship of contract exists between the state and a citizen.

In the past, particularly, in the feudal times, the government of the kingdom was often a small organization. This small organization was the court of the kingdom. Officials within the court were a small number of people. They used to be the retainers of the king. Some of them might also be the friends or relatives of the king. There existed personal bondage between them and the king. They were loyal to the king because they were actually the servants of the king. The king represented the state. Yet since the formation of the nation-state, and, particularly, since the formation of the mass society, the administrative system of the state has expanded dramatically. The sovereignty of the state no longer belongs to the power holder of the highest level or his government at least in actuality, but belongs to the people. The government recruits civil servants on behalf of the state. People keep no personal bondage between thousands of civil servants and the power holder of the highest level or his government. As the state recruits civil servants from the labor market, the relationship between civil servants and the state is emphatically the relationship of contract.

Besides, while people can make promises to each other using language, they can make a contract. Then people, able to make a contract, formulate a rule through which they interact with one another to establish and keep order. In doing so, they build a system of constructive interaction open to all. All become partners in establishing a social institution in which all interact with all. Then they play games or gamble, setting an equal condition for all participants. They exchange opportunities through a competition. As there will be an uncertainty upon the end of the game or gamble, people show their competence to get a right or a privilege or a job position or an economic benefit or an honor. A system of constructive interaction comes into being. By "constructive interaction," I mean the interaction that constructs the community such as a society or a state. People build the society or the state through such constructive interaction. Everyone has his own opportunity, capability and interest, but this system of constructive interaction makes the opportunity, capability and interest of each part of the opportunities, capabilities and interests of a community. All seek them through this system. All get a benefit from it from time to time.

First, people engage in the constructive interaction in economic life to use special social and economic resources in the building of the society or the state. For example, people played lottery games. Lottery games can be traced back to between 205 and 187 BC during the Han Dynasty in China. During the Roman Empire, occurred the first known European lottery. Lottery reappeared as a means to raise revenue for the state in Europe in the fifteenth century. Today lottery tickets are sold to help the government to get more financial resources. People also hold auctions. Records, handed down from ancient Greeks, show that auctions can be traced back to 500 BC. In Rome, people auctioned family estates and war plunder. People also auctioned crops, livestock, tools, and entire farms after the arrival of the Pilgrims in America in the 1600s. Today, auctions are still popular. Sometimes a company or a government body holds an auction to sell a certain product or a certain article. For example, some artistic works are sold through an auction. While an auction is held, certain articles are sold to the buyer who offers the highest price. Similarly, if a construction project needs to be sub-contracted, many companies may be invited to bid for this construction project. This construction project may be given to the company which offers the lowest price for the completion of this project. Sometimes businessmen bid for a government project. They also compete against each other. People contrive to use economic recourses as efficiently as possible because they can make a promise and obey a rule. People try to make sure that their business is as profitable as possible. Promising to obey a certain rule in the competition is often required because a competition always involves an uncertainty or both a risk and an opportunity. Yet, as people promise to obey the rule, such a competition generates positive incentives. It is a constructive interaction.

Second, the formulation of a rule for people's competition for a prize or an honor may encourage people to develop their personal potential or skill to be used by the society or the state through a constructive interaction. As all want to get a prize or love honor, all are led to offer their talents to the society or the state. The sports competition helps people build their bodies, for example. As people compete on the basis of equality, they are encouraged to show the strength and tenacity of their body. The good body of the people is needed by the state. As such, since ancient times humans have been holding sports competitions. For example, ancient Greeks held the Olympic Games dated back to 776 BC. The Games were held every four years in Olympia in the western Peloponnesian peninsula. The Olympic Games were banned by Emperor Theodosius in 393AD. But the Games revived in modern times when the first modern Olympics took place in 1896 in Athens. Various other sports games are also held in each country in modern times.

People also hold other competitions. These competitions are other forms of constructive interaction. They inspire themselves to study hard, to hasten their personal development and to bolster the cause of culture and science. In ancient Greece, people held singing competitions. Amoebaean singing is believed to have been held by Greek Shepherds to entertain themselves. Later, it evolved into a judged competition, consisting of the multiple rounds of singing between competitors. Ancient Greeks also held poetry competitions. In modern times similar competitions are widely held. Sometimes people hold a poetry recitation contest; sometimes people hold a speech contest or a debate contest or a composition contest or a knowledge competition; sometimes people hold a dance competition or a piano competition or a drawing competition or an Olympic mathematics competition; sometimes people hold a bodybuilding competition or a beauty contest; sometimes people hold a fashion design competition or an interior design competition or a building design competition. By granting a prize, people hold a contest, or a competition, under a rule all participants promise to obey. As the winner of the contest or the competition is certain that he will get a prize or an honor, he will exert his effort to cultivate his capability. Each competitor is subject to luck, but the most capable people usually stand a chance of winning the prize and getting the honor. Playing the game, under a rule made by the organizer of the competition or the contest and obeyed by all participants, plays a positive role in the development of culture of a society or a state.

Third, formulating a rule, as a contract, for competition may help people resolve some disputes in decision-making and avoid a conflict. Discussing the role of lottery, Neil Duxbury writes that:

> The lottery offers a fair way of dealing with many uncomfortable, or even inherently unfair, dilemmas. A non-weighted lottery will be blind and so above corruption. That decisions reached by lot lack an element of human agency (excepting the initial decision to resort to lot) means that responsibility for especially troublesome decisions can be removed from the shoulders of particular people or groups.[15]

For example, if people compete for state power, they may make a rule of competition. Therefore, in ancient times people resorted to lot to select an official of the government. People resorted to lot under a rule people promised to obey. As Duxbury indicated, Athenians were committed to the use of lottery for political purpose.[16] If two candidates had been elected and only one would be finally appointed as the magistrate, the two candidates might face the destiny of being selected by lot. As Aristotle notes, "Selection by lot from among those previously elected is indeed common to both oligarchy and democracy."[17]

In modern times, people rarely select government officials by resorting to lot, but by way of election. Resort to lot is an activity performed by a small number of people who vie for power. By contrast, election is held across the state. Yet, election is also held under a rule which all promise to obey. This rule guides the constructive interaction. Such a rule is a contract. This contract supports the standardized competition. Without a prior contract, people will be unable to hold a fair election. Specifically, election candidates promise to obey the rule of election in order to compete in election. They will recognize, for example, that the candidate who gets the most votes will be the elect.

While we discuss the role played by promises in the building of the society and the state, we discuss all kinds of promises made by all parties in their interaction. Those promises are normally short-term promises. As people use language, they can also make long-term promises. By making long-term promises, they can cooperate for a long time. They can pursue their common cause. They join each other. They form groups or associations. As Rousseau asserted, the tendency to form societies is a universal trait; wherever individuals have a common interest they form a society, permanent or transient, and every society has a general will which regulates the conduct of its members. Larger societies are composed not directly of individuals but of smaller societies, and each more inclusive society sets the duties of the smaller societies that compose it.[18] These groups or associations may include estates, classes and guilds. G. W. F. Hegel contends in another way that the individual is "mediated" by a series of communities from family at the bottom, through the estates and the associations in the middle, to the state at the top.[19]

People, then, establish their organizations whenever necessary. In these circumstances, all members agree to form these organizations and to fulfill their obligations. There should be a constitution for each organization. This constitution is an agreement or a contract. All members of the organization may sign an agreement in order to join this organization. They will not become the formal members of the organization until they sign the required agreement. For example, a worker signs an agreement in order to join a local trade union. A farmer who joins the association of farmers is usually also required to sign an agreement. He may remit membership fees and attend certain meetings. He may also participate in the activities organized by the organization. All promise to act as required by the organization and the organization functions as supported by all. It can also function on a large scale and even across the whole state. That means that people, able to use language, can make promises. Then people are enabled to arrange collective activities. As the activities of social groups are part of the activities of the society or the state, we can believe that the organization, established by a social group, is part of the organization of the society or the state. All need to interact with all within the society or the state. They interact meaningfully with each other through the organization established by a social group. The organization functions across the state. Thus in a certain domain people organize themselves within the state.

This principle also applies to a political party. In the era of nation-state, people often establish a political party and formulate a constitution of the party. They define the idea of the party. They set forth the principle of organizing the party. They elaborate the procedure of joining the party. All members of the party may remit membership fees, attend the meetings and submit to the leadership. All members promise to act as required. Because of this a political party can work as expected. The related background is that in early modern times nation-states emerged and people established democracy in many nation-states in Europe. In order to win an election, people were bound to establish political parties to help those election candidates to win votes of the voters. People set forth all the agreements which would be combined to make the constitution of the party. Then on the basis of this constitution, they established political parties. Then people organized activities and all might take part in them. This means that nearly all the activities of the political parties are planned. As these activities are the collective activities, all need to make an appointment with each other in advance. They make promises to each other. In order to engage in the related activities regularly and constantly, they formulate the constitution of the political party. Collective activities depend on the promises made by them. Promises are made because language is used. As language can be used to perform communication on a large scale, all, belonging to the party, can interact and act in unison across the state. Thus a contract plays a role in the organization of each of those political parties and those political parties play a role in the organization of the society or the state.

The application of contracts may also be extended to another larger domain. In medieval times feudal contracts, made by lords and vassals, were intended to distribute land to the lords of various levels in exchange for the allegiance of the lords of the lower level to the lords of the higher level as well as to the sovereign lord, namely, the king. In the thirteenth century the Magna Carta, made by King John and baronage in England, was a series of feudal contracts as at that time feudal contracts were prevalent.[20] In other words, people clarified rights and obligations in the distribution of land to the lords of various regions and for the guarantee of the allegiance of those who received land to the feudal ruler. The Magna Carta became a de facto constitution or quasi-constitution of England in medieval times. Likewise, in November 1620, the Pilgrim Fathers landed from the *Mayflower* to North America agreed that "We do solemnly and mutually, in the presence of God and of one another, covenant and combine ourselves together into a civil body politic."[21] Such a contract served as a foundation for the building of a state in future. This means that, by signing a contract, all parties gain rights wanted by them and bear obligations required by all others. People build the state on the basis of a consensus reached by all. Though in history turmoil often occurs due to the conquest of the conqueror, the possibility of making a contract by using language enables people to build their state on the basis of promises made by the ruler and the ruled. The ruler and ruled can cooperate.

Thus, political thinkers or philosophers imagine that the state takes form because of the making of a social contract, as mentioned earlier. For example, John Locke insists that men, coming out of a state of nature, unite into a political society they agree to form through a compact.[22] Jean-Jacques Rousseau also insists that "conventions form the basis of all legitimate authority among men," as mentioned earlier.[23] The reason is that a contract contains a set of promises even though we have a reason to believe that social contract theory is a fiction.[24] Then it is not accidental that the making of constitutions of modern states is sometimes construed by people as the making of contracts because a constitution contains a series of provisions defining the rights and obligations of the citizens and the rights and obligations of the power holders. The definition, or the explanation, of the rights and the obligations is usually the content of a contract or part of it. A contract has a series of promises. Thus I argue that without language people are unable to make any promise. If people are unable to make any promise, they will be unable to make any contract. Without the consciousness of contract people will not make any constitution. A constitution is also the phenomenon of making promises. As a constitution can be construed as a series of promises made by people in the organization of the state on a large scale, it is regarded as a general contract made by people across the state because there are usually various promises made in the constitution. In particular, the constitution defines the rights of the power holders to use power and the rights granted to the citizens as well as the freedoms enjoyed by the citizens. As the power holders are required to provide services to the citizens and the citizens are required to be subject to the directives of the power holders, all get prepared for the organization of the society or the state. The action is to be taken in future, but language can be used to reach an agreement in advance. Thus people establish the political order of the state first. Then they organize the state.

2. Oath

While people formed their tribe, all trusted all. While people form their state, all may not always trust all. Although making a contract is a way of building a relationship of cooperation between one person and another, or a way of establishing order in the civilized society or the state, or a way of organizing the society or the state, people need to build their trust relationship in their long-term interaction in the state. People have to use language to build mutual trust. Unlike tribal people who trusted each other naturally, humans have to make an extra effort to build their trust relationship in the state. Language is always a tool. One of the reasons is that the state is not formed due to kinship and people always seek their own private interest. As the society or the state is formed by strangers, people are not always trustworthy. Therefore, sometimes a specific person makes a special promise. This promise is usually important. This promise is so important that sometimes this promise is made in the presence of a witness or by a holy thing. This promise is usually an oath. This oath strengthens the memory of all. Strengthening the memory extends the time of communication. Taking an oath always reminds the person of the fact that he has made a promise. This is a method used by people to build a trust relationship between one another in the state. This is a particular method. Although people can also build a trust relationship by making a common contract from time to time, such a way of building a trust relationship may not always suffice. The reason is that people are going to build the society and the state. People are required to devote all their lives to the building of the society and the state. Making a promise in a contract, a person, as one party to the contract, often requires the other party to the contract to make another promise. They make a deal on the basis of equality. By contrast, taking an oath, a person is often required to make a special contribution or a great effort beneficial to the society or the state. The person who takes an oath and the person who requires the oath may play different roles. The reason is that the person who requires the oath may act as the agent of the society or the state and a person is often obligated to make a great effort conducive to the building of the society or the state. If a person is not always trustworthy, another person who represents the society or the state may require this person to take an oath. Though this oath is a contract, this is a special contract. This special contract more strongly requires a related person to be cooperative. If a person is required to tell a truth, he is especially urged to tell the truth. He may even be pressured to tell the truth. As James Endell Tyler writes,

> [T]he evil in which oaths take their rise is the prevalence of falsehood and wrong, and the subsequent prevalence of suspicion and distrust. It is because we do not place confidence in the veracity of men in general, when they confess to speak the truth; it is because we cannot rely upon their good faith, when they make a bare promise, that we are driven to seek for something satisfactory to ourselves, by imposing upon them a more binding responsibility than that of their mere word.[25]

The oath is a special arrangement for people to build a trust relationship among themselves in the society or the state in which a trust relationship between one another is not always certain. People need to make a great effort. The reason is that people always need to rebuild their trust relationship in the state. If people form a small community, they build a trust relationship between one another in a certain way. If people form a large community, they build a trust relationship between one another in another way. While people were tribal people, they trusted each other naturally. They were kin to each other. The consciousness of kinship guided them to trusting each other. All were basically trustworthy. While people are citizens in the state in the civilized society, they no longer trust each other naturally. They are not kin to each other. The consciousness of kinship no longer guides them in their mutual interaction in the building of the society or the state. Now people are guided by other types of consciousness. As we suppose that consciousness had by people is a medium in the formation of the society and the state, I also argue that in the tribe the consciousness of kinship was a medium in the organization of the tribe. By contrast, in the state some other types of consciousness function as media in the organization of the state. While people arrange for a person to take an oath to build a trust relationship in the building of the society or the state, they have to take advantage of those types of consciousness in building a trust relationship. The reason is that those types of consciousness play a part in the building of the society or the state. While people arrange for a ceremony of taking an oath, they use a medium. Using that medium, people highlight those types of consciousness. As those types of consciousness are shared by all, highlighting them is conducive to the building of a trust relationship.

First, religious consciousness functions in the building of the society. It may also play a part in the building of the state on some occasions. It is a medium in support of the building of the society or even the state. Then people sometimes take an oath highlighting religious consciousness. Then we see that in ancient times people began to make promises in the form of an oath by god or a holy thing including alter, tomb, church, spear, sword, fountain, copper coin, stone and torch. At that time people normally believed in religion everywhere. People particularly often swore an oath by or in the presence of god. According to some western scholars, after the times of Old Testament an oath which served as a formal guarantee of truthfulness or of informed intention to follow an agreed-upon course of action was, at earlier phase of cultural (and individual) development, essentially a self-fulfilling imprecation that drew its coercive power from the magic of words.[26] An oath is a promise made by someone and accepted by other people for the association of people, or for the organization of the society, or for the organization of the state. Yet when a promise, in the form of an oath, is made, it highlights religious consciousness. Therefore, people may often do so with god acting as a witness or a supervisor. They imply that if they break their oath, they will bear divine punishment because the power of god is formidable. In ancient times most contracts were sealed with an oath and god was called upon to witness the oath of the covenant and to help the covenanters to keep to their good intentions or to enforce the curses that were to befall the breaker of the covenant.[27] As David Junkin writes, "The obligation of an oath, as we have shown, does not depend upon the form thereof, but upon the immutable principles of the moral government of God."[28] In the period of time when the influence of religion is strong while the government is weak, people are particularly prone to take an oath in the presence of god because religious consciousness guides the organization of the state. They may use their hand to touch the foot or the knee of the statue of the deity. When the religious community plays a powerful role in support of the authority of the state or the organization of the society and the state, it requires those who interact with each other to take an oath to certify their trustworthiness. For example, sometimes a debtor swears an oath to the creditor to return the loan in future, and god in whose presence the oath is taken makes sure that the intention of the debtor to return the loan is truthful. The debtor is obligated or urged by god to repay the loan. The Book of Psalms even indicates God's distaste for all forms of debt that are not being paid timely. As all or nearly all believe in god, an oath taken this way gives extra effect to the promise made between the promisor and the promisee.

Second, the moral idea takes part in the building of the society and the state. The moral idea guides people in their social and political activities. An oath is often taken to underline the guidance of morality in the mutual interaction between one another. Then morality can help people to build a trust relationship in the building of the society and the state. As people become strangers in the civilized society, they need faithfulness and trustworthiness in social interaction, and particularly, in the exchange of goods and services. As the exchange of goods and services is the most frequent and important mutual interaction, people are especially in need of building a trust relationship. In this regard, an oath taken by people will buttress the strength of the moral idea. As people take an oath to obey morality, it is most likely to build a trust relationship because all agree to obey morality. For example, people carry out professional ethics in pursuing their career. Some occupations are very important. Pursuing a career may require a person to take an oath. Usually people, involved in some very important occupations, need to take an oath to proclaim the obedience of professional ethics. I have not investigated how many occupations require people to take an oath. But it is well-known that the undertaking of medical treatment concerns the life and death of humans and patients are always concerned about the quality and standard of medical service. Physicians and patients need to have a good trust relationship. Therefore, a physician may make a promise in the form of a Hippocratic Oath for providing his service and pursuing his career. He takes an oath to keep confidential all that he learns about his patient. He guarantees that professional service is given to his patients. He may also promise not to give deadly drug to the patients. He may promise to prevent his patients from injustice. This is because the society requires the faithful cooperation between physicians and patients. As Steven Miles writes,

> With the consent of the patient, a physician may inquire about virtually any aspect of a person's life and may touch any part of the body. Physician may cut on living persons and dissect human corpses. They may disclose an impending death, write prescriptions for drugs that can kill, and then certify the cause of the death of the same persons who have taken those drugs. They are permitted to have a personal financial stake in treatment decisions and in the outcome of the research that they conduct.[29]

Thus the patients will feel assured to seek his service, and believe that the physician can meet their expectations. The physician relies on such a promise to establish a good trust relationship with the patients. This promise is made as required by a moral idea. Thus, Hippocratic Oath that at least appeared first in the first century in Greece was rediscovered by the churches in medieval times. Since the eighteenth century various versions of the Oath have been widely used in medical school graduation ceremonies in Europe and the United States.[30]

Third, customary thinking, traditional idea and legal spirit play a role in the building of the society and the state. People sometimes take an oath to display them. By doing so, they propagate, and stress, them in the building of the society and the state. For example, sometimes a man takes an oath because this is required by custom or tradition or law. If a man takes an oath to act in cooperation with another man, he exposes himself to the potential punishment at the time when custom, tradition and law define the punishment for failure to keep the oath. In ancient times, the Jews were accustomed to swear an oath and laid their hand upon the book of the Law.[31] In medieval times vassals who took an oath might also be obligated to the king by morality or god. But they might also be obligated by custom, tradition or law when they took an oath. In medieval Europe swearing on one's sword implied the expectation that the sword itself would turn against the perjurer.[32] Such an oath was taken under the requirement of custom or tradition or law. In early modern times the case was similar. If a man was required to take an oath, he was usually required to do so by law. Sir Edward Coke, an Englishman, states that "Oaths that have no warrant by law, are rather *nova tormenta* than *sacramenta*; and it is a high contempt to minister an oath without warrant of law, to be punished by fine and imprisonment."[33] This situation has remained primarily unchanged ever since. One case in point is that in a state which admits immigrants, immigrants are eligible to apply for citizenship after they have resided there for a period of time, provided that other requirements are met. Swearing an oath is promising to be loyal to the country before the state approves the conferment of citizenship. Naturalization and swearing an oath seem to be a relation of exchange. Only after swearing an oath can one gain approval to become a citizen. The act of swearing an oath is separate in time from showing allegiance in action, but as a result of swearing an oath, one undertakes the obligation of fulfilling his oath and showing allegiance in action to the relevant state in future.

Fourth, ideology plays a role in the building of the society and the organization of the state in modern times. Then people sometimes take an oath to express their attitude to adhere to that ideology. They ensure that they dedicate their lives to a cause advocated by that ideology. In these circumstances people often take an oath as a special arrangement. At the time when or at the place where the influence of religion declines, people may take an oath to spread the related ideology. For example, youngsters are sometimes arranged for to take an oath in front of a monument of the revolutionary martyrs built by the revolutionary party. Youngsters are, thus, arranged for to proclaim their devotion to the revolutionary cause. As the building of the state is interpreted as part of revolutionary cause, youngsters make clear their determination to make their contributions to the building of the state. As nationalism is also an ideology, nationalism often bolsters the cultivation of patriotism. People may also be required to take an oath in order to ensure that they are committed to the rise or revival of the nation. Thus, the state may find it easy to mobilize the citizens. The authority of the state will be buttressed. Swearing an oath, as a special promise, is a kind of behavior of guarantee, but it is different from the ordinary behavior of guarantee. This guarantee is given solemnly and the action guaranteed to be taken is often the long-term, or even the lifelong, action. The guaranteed action may reflect the lofty ideal of each and his lifelong pursuit while an ordinary guarantee may include a temporary expedient. As a result, a person, swearing an oath, is making an important promise. When he makes such a promise, he lets the related ideology play a role. One case in point provided by history is that in France in the 1850s, democrats were organized into Montagnard societies to prepare a republican uprising. To become a member, the recruit was blindfolded. Then the recruit recited an oath: "I swear to arm myself against tyranny, to defend the Democratic and Social Republic; I swear to kill a traitor if fate chooses me; I swear to die the most infamous death if I become a traitor or turncoat; I swear to help a brother in need."[34] People, pursuing a cause through fight and under the guidance of an ideology, are often required by the organizers of the fight to take an oath to get those organizers to trust them and assign an important task to them.

The reason that an oath assists people in building a trust relationship is also that while people arrange for one to take an oath, they hold a ceremony. A ceremony is always holy. As that ceremony is holy, the oath becomes a medium in support of linguistic communication. First, sometimes a man is required to take an oath in order to urge him to tell the truth. In other words, such an oath prevents him from giving falsified information. Thus the oath facilitates the circulation of truthful information. Second, sometimes a person is required to take an oath in order to confirm his loyalty. Confirming his loyalty is expressing a cooperative attitude. This also includes the transmission of information from one person to another because the oath forces the person to tell what he thinks. Third, sometimes a person takes an oath to confirm his commitment to a cause. This oath emphasizes his long-term will. In all these cases, the oath strengthens the interaction between one person and another. As a result, an oath can build a trust relationship more effectively.

Of course, an oath usually assists people in building a trust relationship between one another. It builds a personal trust relationship. Therefore, a man and a woman can swear an oath for marriage, for example. People may find a multiplicity of occasions that require them to take an oath in the society or the state. They need someone to take an oath to build a trust relationship in personal interaction from time to time. But people also need someone to take the oath to assist them in building the society and in organizing the state for a few very important occasions when and where this person is requested to perform an important duty. I believe that people come across a multiplicity of such occasions in the building of the society and the organization of the state from time to time. These occasions may not always be important. But the following occasions are often extremely important and almost always require a principal to take an oath.

First, since ancient times it has been a practice for the state to require soldiers to make a promise as an oath before they go to combat in the battle-field because they may lose their lives. The bravery and loyalty of fighters are important for victory. Soldiers are usually required to affirm their determination to fight for the state. As Tyler writes, in ancient Greece the Athenian youth were compelled to take an oath that they would bear arms for their country whenever their services were needed; and that the oath, when they were enrolled, was to this effect—"That they would not disgrace their arms, nor desert their ranks, nor injure their country, but would defend it to their power, and would, whether alone or with their fellows, fight for their religion and the state."[35] In ancient Rome, the first military oath was voluntary, and bound men to obey their officers, and execute their commands to the utmost of their power; and when the camp was formed they swore not to appropriate to themselves any of the spoils, or any property belonging to the camp.[36] In medieval and modern times soldiers are often arranged for to swear an oath particularly before or just before the beginning of the battle.

Second, people are sometimes required to take the oath of allegiance as a lifelong promise. As this promise is life-long, the oath is essential. This is a way used to ensure that some people are loyal to the ruler. The background is that in ancient and medieval times the allocation of the land by the ruler was an essential means in establishing the social system. In this process vassals, receiving land, were required to swear an oath of allegiance prior to the allocation of land, as already noted earlier. So in ancient and medieval times a vassal took an oath before the lord feoffed land to him. Vassals might be required to swear an oath by God, and they might also do so as guided by morality, but they were often obligated to serve the ruler. This practice underlay the whole feudalist system. This system was also conducive to the organization of the state. As Mendenhall and Herbert Schlesinger write, the Old Testament Covenant may derive in its form from suzerainty treaties of the Hittite kings, with which they established a bond with their vassals. The text of these covenants make clear that they were made by the king, who conferred certain privileges on a vassal, not because they owed to the vassal or because of any merit the vassal might possess, but as a matter of favor or grace by the king. In exchange for the explicit protection of the king and the right to hold his vassaldom, the vassal was obligated to conform to certain stipulations, chief among which were various expressions of loyalty to the true king and a prohibition against engaging in any independent foreign relations, that is, against trafficking with other kings (or gods).[37]

Third, before a magistrate, or an administrator, or a power holder, takes office, he may be required to make a promise and confirm that he is trustworthy. This promise is an oath. This is because, granting the power of the state to someone, the state needs to ensure that the power holder can work in good faith for the state and be loyal to the state in the years to come. The background of the power holder may not be known clearly. But what is important is that the use of power is in relation to the well-being of thousands of the citizens. Thus, it is important that the power holder works always as expected. He is not supposed to seek his own private interest or unlawful interest. In ancient Greece kings were sworn in some states to be faithful in their high trust. Judges were also required to take an oath before they took office. Pollux recorded the oath of the judges of Athens that they would give judgment according to the laws in those cases on which laws existed, and in cases not determined by law, they would give the righteous judgment.[38] And according to James Endell Tyler, "In Rome, the consuls swore, when entering upon their office, to discharge it faithfully; and on retiring, they swore that they had discharged its duties with fidelity."[39] Livy says that there was no nation that had been longer uncorrupted than the Romans. Montesquieu commented on this phenomenon that those who took public office were under the strong influence of oath in Roman Times. They were bound by oath more than by law.[40] In medieval times kings might swear an oath to be enthroned or to be supported by the parliament. John Locke mentions that in England King James the first made a speech to the parliament in 1609 that:

> The King binds himself by a double oath, to the observation of the fundamental laws of his kingdom; tacitly, as by being a king, and so bound to protect as well the people, as the laws of his kingdom; and expressly, by his oath at his coronation; so as every just king, in a settled kingdom, is bound

to observe that paction made to his people, by his laws, in framing his government agreeable thereunto, according to that paction which God made with Noah after the deluge.[41]

In modern times it is often seen that state leaders, senior officials and all others, taking high level office in the government, swear an oath upon taking office. In the United States, the president, the vice president, the congressmen and the justices or judges of the courts all swear an oath before taking office. For example, the president may state that "I do solemnly swear that I will faithfully execute the office of President of the United States, and will, to the best of my ability, preserve, protect, and defend the constitution of the United States."[42]

Fourth, if a case is heard by a judge in the court, witnesses may be called on to give testimonies. Before testimonies are given, witnesses may be required to swear an oath and confirm that they are trustworthy. This oath is a promise. This means that the faithfulness of the witnesses is not clear in the state as people become strangers. Certain true information is needed and a person cannot have the information concerning all the events happening in the state. Certain information must be provided by other people. To ensure that true information is gained, witnesses are required to swear an oath. Witnesses must solemnly promise to give true information. The oath enhances the probability of giving true information. The penalty of perjury often partly results from the legal requirement of an oath taken to give testimonies. In ancient times this was the method of the law courts to make a judgment in the states formed by Egyptians, Jews, Greeks, Romans and Germans. James Endell Tyler writes that:

> There is, consequently, no department of life, neither public nor private, neither in forensic nor domestic affairs, in which the use of oaths is not most frequent; but no where more frequent than in the courts of law and trials. For whenever the judge cannot be directed in his decision by the evidence of witnesses, or documents, or other lawful proofs, the litigant parties either at the requisition of their opponents, or by the direction of the judge, throw themselves on an oath, as a kind of sacred sheet anchor.[43]

Requesting any litigant party to take an oath to corroborate the truthfulness of the testimony is also a method used by the court to make a decision for judgment in medieval and modern times.

Fifth, the establishment of social or political organizations is part of the organization of the state as those social or political organizations participate in the organization of the state. If a social or political organization requires that its members must be absolutely trustworthy, this organization may require its members to make a promise in the form of an oath. Thus before someone acquires the membership of an organization or a political party, he may be required to swear an oath. This is because the identity of each becomes unknown after the dissolution of the tribe and the formation of the state. People, proving their trustworthiness, have to guarantee that all pursue the same goal in good faith. They must guarantee that all intend to realize the same goal and the same ideal. All must be trusted by an organization or a political party which requires loyalty from all. In order to prove that all are trustworthy, all are required to make a promise in the form of an oath. So in China anyone who is prepared to join the Communist Party of China is required to swear an oath in a ritual before he joins that party. By the same token, the state may also require its citizens to swear an oath to confirm that they can be trusted by the state. In some immigration states, immigrants are required to swear an oath of loyalty to the head of the state in a ceremony in order to become the citizens, as already mentioned earlier. This oath is designed to show one's trustworthiness. If the trustworthiness of a certain citizen is doubted, he may also be required to swear an oath. For example, in 1947 the president of the United States Harry Truman established the Loyalty-Security Program to impose a loyalty test on all federal employees and screen out those who had or had previously had connections with subversive organizations. This order encouraged loyalty oaths.[44] That is, the oath is a promise made by the person who takes the oath. After this promise is accepted, the person who takes the oath is trusted.

All of these cases show that an oath is a reinforced promise. It is a holy promise. One, taking an oath, is very much obligated as a result. He undertakes a special obligation. As he undertakes a special obligation, he sometimes, in some sense, exposes himself to a threat and then he may make every effort to avert this threat. Particularly, swearing an oath is a kind of ritualized linguistic behavior of promise for future cooperation. A ritual is adopted to confirm the promise. This means that, in the state, the relationship between one person and another in some aspects is uncertain. A trust relationship between one another in some aspects may not be ensured. Consequently, people adopt the form of oath to ensure a trust relationship in the organization of the society or the state. Thus people design such a procedure in which the authorities or the agent of the authorities can force those who swear an oath to honor their promise. That is, people, taking an oath, are obligated to honor that oath. If the oath is broken, dire punishment will befall the breaker. In ancient times a part of the oath ceremony might be that of dividing an animal. The ceremony was bloody. This was a threat. In order to avoid this threat, a person, having taken an oath, made his best effort to keep the oath.

Herbert Schlesinger opines that "The oath, like other forms of promise . . . is an act begun, and suspended, and (conditionally) fulfilled in due course."[45] My view is that the oath is a process of linguistic communication which is extended so as to emphasize the importance of the related promise. As people are able to use language, they can use a promise to establish a trust relationship. The person who takes an oath as a promise tends to reckon with the cost of giving or not giving a truthful declaration or making or not making a promise when he considers both his private interest and the interest of the public because he lives in the state in which he often has to seek his private interest and to defend the interest of the state at the same time. It is unlike the situation in a tribe. The interest, sought by people in the tribe, was the interest of the tribe only. But since the formation of the state people have not only had to take care of the interest of the state but also had to take care of the interest of their families. They are often involved in the conflict of interest. Will a man make a promise and then wholeheartedly honor that promise? Will a man make a faithful declaration as required by another man or an organization or the law court or the constitution and later prove that the declaration is faithful? Language is skillfully used. That is, a person is required to make a promise and then gains the trust from others or the authorities. The person may give a false testimony or make a promise he never intends to honor. Yet the authorities can set a condition that failure to tell the truth or to honor a promise will lead to severe punishment. Falsehood and cheating tend to be discovered in future because it is highly probable to discover falsehood and cheating over the long term. Perjury or cheating can cover up the truth or the real intention of the promisor in the short run. However, it is difficult to cover up the truth or the real intention of the promisor over the long term. If punishment is very severe, the cost of covering up the truth or cheating will be very high. For example, in England, excommunication was recognized in the statute of Elizabeth, as a punishment to be visited on one who had been guilty of perjury in the ecclesiastical court.[46] And the statute of Elizabeth inflicted the penalty of perpetual infamy and a fine of forty pounds on the suborner. Perjury was thereby punished with six 'months' imprisonment, perpetual infamy, and a fine of twenty pounds, or to have both ears nailed to the pillory.[47] Being deterred by the possible severe punishment, one tends to act as guided by the authorities or a body in charge of organizing the state. Because of this, people make a promise sincerely and faithfully if they decide to make a promise.

That means that taking an oath is very solemn. It is ritualized. In ancient times, a man, required to take an oath, might be required to perform a certain religious rite. He might be required to cloth himself in a special way. He might be required to hold something in his hand such as a burning torch or a piece of straw or a sword or a stone. Since medieval times, a person to swear an oath may be especially required to do so in a church or in the law court or in front of a national flag or a monument. When a person swears an oath, he needs a setting. When he takes an oath, he does so solemnly, sincerely and faithfully. The oath involves a ritualized process of linguistic communication. Ritualizing the process of linguistic communication results in the creation of a medium in support of the related process of linguistic communication. A rite renders a strong impression on the person who takes the oath. The rite emphasizes the importance of the process of linguistic communication. The rite extends the process of linguistic communication. The process of linguistic communication will be remembered by the related person and the process of linguistic communication connects him with the person or the body that requires the oath. In the meantime, each of the authorities in the presence of which the oath is taken takes this chance to promote its consciousness or values or spirit. As people are required to take an oath everywhere from time to time, the authorities are enabled to promote their consciousness or values or spirit continuously and widely through the process of linguistic communication. The related authorities can also function as a medium as a result because people scattered in the state are unable to spread the related consciousness, values or spirit across the state easily and hence the authorities are better positioned to spread those consciousness, values and spirit. Each of those authorities is an organization. An organization is, in some sense, a medium that facilitates linguistic communication performed by those who act on behalf of the authorities, as already mentioned earlier. In terms of linguistic communication that goes on in taking an oath, I argue that a church is a medium in support of the linguistic communication that spreads the religious doctrine. I also argue that a law court is a medium that facilitates the spread of the spirit of law among people. Thus people bolster the status of those authorities in charge of organizing the state and disseminate the related consciousness, values and spirit. As the organization of the state relies on the support of the related consciousness, values and spirit, swearing an oath bolsters the authority of those people or organizations or the government in charge of organizing the state.

Swearing an oath, as a promise, requires the display of honesty indeed. An oath is a promise or a presentation of a promise, and people tend to establish a trust relationship through an oath. Though the juror is threatened or forced to carry out or keep the promise made by him, people can cooperate on the basis of honesty and faithfulness. Though sometimes those who fail to keep their promise are punished, people can realize cooperation based on honesty to the effect that they organize the state effectively. People establish and buttress the authority of those in charge of organizing the society or the state. All faithfully submit to the directives of those organizers. People establish, maintain and strengthen the authority of those organizing the society or the state on the basis of honesty. They enhance the level of morality. To put it differently, the requirement of taking an oath encourages people to be honest and trustworthy. Thus people enhance the authority of those in charge of organizing the society or the state on the basis of enhancing the level of morality among themselves. Conversely, if the authorities do not give people any chance to display their honesty, people will feel that it is useless to be honest. Swearing an oath is part of a traditional culture in many countries. In those countries people show the high level of morality. By contrast, there may be some other countries in which swearing an oath is not a traditional culture. As a result, the authorities fail to foster the morality of people in this important aspect. For example, in ancient China, though people might be required to take an oath between individual persons or among gangsters, people were seldom required by any religious organization or the government to swear an oath. When the suspect of a criminal case was arrested by the government, the magistrate usually tortured the suspect in an attempt to force the suspect to confess the truth and plead guilty. The magistrate would not believe whatever the suspect confessed until the suspect was tortured. Thus the magistrate would not let the suspect to swear an oath. Thus it was useless to be honest. Though people propagated the idea of morality in the mutual interaction of people as required by the formation of the society or the state, the low level of morality among Chinese in ancient times was, I believe, substantially due to the failure of the despotic state to encourage ordinary people to be honest and faithful. In early modern times Westerners were astonished to find that Chinese businessmen often cheated each other in business. As the authorities could not rely on the sincere cooperation of ordinary people in the organization of the state, the authorities further resorted to severe oppression. By contrast, people were often required to make a promise in the form of an oath when the authorities needed the cooperation of ordinary people in many countries in Europe. This case indicates this truth: The authorities trust ordinary people if they are honest. Enhancing the level of morality of people ensures the wholesome governance of the state. The oath, after all, is a form of promise. As a promise, in the form of an oath, is a process in which language can be especially exploited to build a relationship of mutual trust between the two sides with the presence of a third party as a witness, or by a holy object, seen or unseen, language plays a remarkable role in the formation of the society and the organization of the state in many countries because an oath can function as a special language solution that underpins the building of the society and the state.

3. Promises Made to and by the Masses

People make a promise so as to make a contract in cooperation or to make a rule in competition or to establish an organization in association. Sometimes a person also takes an oath to stress his promise in order to build a trust relationship; or a person takes an oath as required by the authorities in the building of a trust relationship in the formation of the society or the organization of the state. If people make such a kind of promise, certain action is expected. As Charles Fried writes, "When I speak I commit myself to the truth of my utterance, but when I promise I commit myself to act."[48] Certainty is ensured because someone promises to act as expected. All cooperate and unite with all and trust all. People organize the state. On the other hand, in organizing the state, the power holder also interacts with all throughout the state. He and all others as a collective being also interact on a scale as large as the whole state. He has to act as expected by the largest number of people to make a promise in the state and perhaps the power holder is also interested in requesting the largest number of people, as a collective being, to make a promise to him. The reason is that people form their state because of language. As people communicate using language, they form a large community. This large community needs a person to organize it on behalf of all who are dispersed. This person is the agent of those people and is in charge of organizing the state. As an agent, this person needs to get entrusted by those people as a whole. Those people constitute the people. Then, if we assume that this person needs to make a promise in order to get entrusted, he has to make a promise to the people. He promises to organize the state as expected by the people. In the meantime, the people may also promise to submit to his rule. Thus, he gets entrusted. He and the people make special promises. There are mutual promises between the organizer of the state and the masses. Discussing promise, Charles Fried comments that "The principle of expanding human liberty by recognizing the self-imposed obligation of promises also entails that a man be able to condition his promise on receiving a return from the promisee."[49] So a promise from the power holder may get another promise from the people. In ancient Greek history Socrates refused to escape from the prison because he had promised to obey the laws in his heart.[50] I argue that the reason that Socrates made a promise to obey the laws is that the authorities had made a promise to the people to carry out the laws. There must be mutual promises between the power holder and the masses. No unilateral promise exists in the human society. Therefore, Socrates promised to obey the laws. The state may be organized this way. So we need to discuss the promises made to and by the masses in depth. The reason is that the structure of the state differs from that of the tribe. In the tribe, the tribal chief, in charge of organizing the tribe, was naturally supported by all because all had the common interest ensured by kinship. The tribal chief was appointed in a traditional way and people would not debate the issue as to who should be the organizer. The organizer emerged naturally. But since the formation of the state, the organizer of the state can no longer emerge this way. If a man, from a family among thousands of families, intends to be the organizer of the state, he may be required to gain consent from all others. Needless to say, a strong man may be able to force all others to be subject to his governance. A usurper who seizes the power of the state unlawfully or by force may also appear. In human history there are many cases showing that sometimes a man who ruled the state in an ironhanded way became the sovereign of the state. However, his rule might not last long. As humans form their state because of language and language presupposes that all, using it, should have common interest, the sustainable government, or the sustainable state, should be the one that runs with clemency and justice. This means that using pure coercion to keep the state usually fails to create a condition for the formation of the common interest while clemency and justice means the formation of the common interest. Describing the life of Dion (408?-353 B.C.), a historical figure in ancient Greece, Plutarch writes that:

> For fear and force, a great navy and standing army of ten thousand hired barbarians are not, as his father had said, the adamantine chains which secure the regal power, but the love, zeal, and affection inspired by clemency and justice; which, though they seem more pliant than the stiff and hard bonds of severity, are nevertheless the strongest and most durable ties to sustain a lasting government.[51]

That means that a ruler, using coercion to keep his rule only, may not intend to seek support from the people. A ruler, needing voluntary submission from the people, has to make his effort to show clemency and justice. In this case he is aware of the necessity of ruling legitimacy. Thus any ruler who finds it necessary to gain or retain support from the masses may try to persuade the masses to be subject to his governance. A legitimate ruler may find it necessary to gain support from the masses. For example, he may find that it is desirable to gain ruling legitimacy when he needs support from ordinary people, and he may act in an attempt to meet the demand from ordinary people. He may make a promise. He may promise to bring happiness to ordinary people. He may promise to realize the prosperity of the state. Because of this he may think of the necessity of not oppressing or disturbing the masses. He may issue a decree promising not to disturb or harm the masses. One case in point here is perhaps that when Pompey (106-48 B.C.), a political figure in ancient Rome, competed against Caesar for the power of the Roman empire, he especially considered what the masses were concerned about. He made promises to the masses. At a conference, he caused the attendants to pass a resolution of not disturbing the masses. When narrating the life of Pompey, Plutarch pens the following that:

> Afterwards in a meeting of their senate they passed a decree, on the motion of Cato, that no Roman citizen should be put to death but in battle, and that they should not sack or plunder any city that was subject to the Roman empire, a resolution which gained Pompey's party still greater reputation.[52]

That is, Pompey sought the power of the Roman Empire, and he thought it fit to take care of what ordinary people were concerned about in order to rally support from the masses. Ordinary people, thus, may change their behavior because of the promise made in a statement or in a decree. They may also make a promise tacitly to the power holder to be subject to the directives of the power holder under the condition that the power holder makes a promise to them. In particular, in modern times a power holder often finds that he needs to engage in the political mobilization of the masses. He makes promises to the masses. The masses may also make a promise to him. Unlike the promise made under a contract or an oath, however, the promise, made by the power holder or the masses, may not be required by a code or a regulation. Mutual interactions between the power holder and the masses may define a de facto code in the acts of making and accepting a promise. For example, the power holder may announce a policy of protecting the interest of the masses when he takes power. The masses may be silent because it is difficult for them to gather to give a collective response to the power holder. Nevertheless, the silence of the masses on this occasion may be regarded as an act of accepting the promise made by that power holder. Otherwise, the masses may stand up against the rule of this power holder if they strongly feel that they cannot accept the rule of this power holder. The power holder can find out what the masses need. Then he makes a promise. If the masses do not stand up against his rule, it can be largely indicative of the fact that the masses have also made a promise in their heart to be subject to his rule. Thus, language invariably plays a special role. That is, without language, people are never able to make promises to each other. If they happen to act in unison or act in concert, they do so coincidentally. Since they started to use language, they can act in unison not because of their coincidental act but because of mutual consultation. Then language enables them to make promises to each other in order to help them to build the society or the state jointly. For example, a person may make a promise to another person and the promise is accepted. The working mechanism of a promise is that it presupposes the behavior of communication between the two parties in cooperation and the behavior of the present promise for future action. Then, in case of a promise made by the power holder, this promise is just an exchange for the building of ruling legitimacy. That is, it is arguable that both making and accepting a promise are intended to obliterate the uncertainty of the future which dictates the status of the power holder. Language and action are combined. In case of the promises made for the building of ruling legitimacy, I argue that the power holder successfully makes a promise first. Then the masses accept the promise. After the masses accept the promise, they change their behavior. They agree and promise to submit to the rule of the power holder. The result is that, people, accepting a promise, think of the action that should be taken in future as promised while hearing one side making the promise and accepting that promise. The condition under which they accept this promise is the fact that they firmly believe that there is a positive causality between the present words and future action. That deeds accord with words is expected. This is a behavior control process consisting of words and deeds. This is usually the promise made by one party unilaterally or unilaterally first. For example, during a famine an elder man in a village tells other villagers of the village that if they follow his leadership and yield to his persuasion, everyone will be rewarded by finding some food. Hungry people follow his leadership to find food. In this case, people change their behavior. People change their behavior before they find food. For this reason, that elder man can change other people's current behavior only by ensuring the coming of the related desirable prospect. In this process of behavior, the relation between words and deeds is similar to the relation between the signifier and the signified of a sign. What differs is that it is up to the people of the community to decide if they accept this promise. The promise is an open offer alluring others rather than forcing them to take action. In the face of a promise, the people of the community may refuse to accept it. A promise will not influence the behavior of the people in the community unless the people accept it. Of course, the people of the community, accepting the promise, must consider the promise in view of their own interest, but the nature of a promise also requires each party to satisfy the requirement of the other party. The final result of making and accepting a promise may be beneficial to both parties and the entire community as well. Certainly, a person in the community will be at risk if he relies on a promise made by another person because that person who makes a promise may not honor his promise in the end. However, later, people learn to punish the person who fails to honor his promise and hence reduce the related risks. Thus people gain more opportunities of a positive mutual inter- action in the organization of the state by making, accepting and honoring a promise. This is the typical behavior of a human being who has left his tribe. Henry Maine, a British jurist, writes when describing the ancient contract law that "the positive duty resulting from one man's reliance on the word of another is among the slowest conquests of advancing civilization."[53]

The result is that people organize their state according to their own will. Though the state may not always be organized according to the will of the people, sometimes the power holder of the state seeks the opinions of the people particularly at the time when the power holder seeks ruling legitimacy and the masses expect the power holder to take care of their interest or expec- tation despite that the power holder, as the ruler, keeps his rule by relying on coercion in some sense. Then people may insist that the ruler should rule the state as expected. The ruler may be expected to obey the law or respect the rights of the people. The subjects of King of Aragon in medieval times used to take an oath that "We, who are as good as you, swear to you, who are not better than we, to accept you as our King and sovereign lord, provided that you observe all our liberties and laws, but if not, then not."[54] Bertrand de Jouvenel writes that:

> The much-cited anecdote of Frederick the Great and the miller of Sans-Souci faithfully represents the ancient state of affairs. The King's rights have incomparably greater scope than those of the miller; but as far as the miller's right goes it is as good as the king's; on his own ground, the miller is entitled to hold off the king. Indeed, there was a deep-seated feeling that all positive rights stood or fell together; if the king disregarded the miller's title to his land, so might the king's title to his throne be disregarded.[55]

In about 1567, George Buchanan, a Scottish scholar, contended that on the one hand the people have taken an oath of loyalty to their kings, while on the other "our kings likewise have taken an oath in the presence of our leading men that they will administer the law with fairness and with justice."[56] The reason is that Roman law and Christian teaching even insisted that the king was no arbitrary or absolute ruler, but the allegiance owed to him by his subjects was dependent on his recognizing their rights, and that in his legislative capacity he could only make laws after getting the advice and consent of his wise men, and in some sense of his whole people.[57] If kings ruled too harshly, they were even assassinated because they had broken their promises to obey the laws or give them liberty.[58] As Michael Lessnoff comments that "A free people is entitled to choose its ruler; a ruler who abuses his authority becomes a tyrant, and should be deposed."[59] This means that promises must be honored. Otherwise the ruler will be punished. Under the rule of James II of England the people "promise him obedience and he promises them protection and good government."[60] But he was deposed in the Glorious Revolution of 1688 because he had broken his promises. There was an exchange of liberties or rights and obligations between the ruler and the ruled. If the ruler respected the liberties of the ruled and the laws or the rights of the ruled, the ruled would be subject to the rule of the ruler. Otherwise the ruled would not accept the rule of the ruler.

Thus, to honor the promise means to retain rights. To make a promise means to undertake obligations. From ancient to modern times, promises are sometimes or often made by the power holder to the masses and made by the masses to the power holder. Thus, as the power holder makes a promise to the people and the people can accept this promise and can make a promise to the power holder, there appears a positive interaction between the power holder and the people. Making, accepting and honoring promises constitutes a special interaction between the power holder and the people particularly in modern times.

First, while a power holder makes a promise to the people, he tends to make this promise as expected by the people. What he promises is usually what is expected by the people. In ancient times, the ruler might make a promise to obey the law or to respect the rights of the subjects. From ancient to medieval times in Europe, the ruler promised to obey the law or to respect the rights of the subjects from time to time, as mentioned earlier. The reason is that the law of the state was important in the organization of the state and the rights of the subjects were essential in the formation of a just society. In the same period of time, the ruler of a state in the East might also make a promise to the masses from time to time. In China, the ruler sometimes promised to bridge the widening gap of income between the rich and the poor as the disparity of income between the rich and the poor was always a striking social issue. Sometimes insurgents promised that they would bridge the gap of income between the rich and the poor if they took state power. If their bid for power failed, the existing ruler might also be forced to promise bridging the gap of income between the rich and the poor so as to alleviate social tensions. The system of land was very crucial in the development of the agricultural society. Sometimes the land was state-owned and sometimes the land was privatized. Sometimes insurgents advocated the system of land to the tillers, a program meaning that the cultivator had his field. The ruler might also be forced to promise to realize this goal through the reform of the land system. Sometimes insurgents promised that if they took power, they would implement the so-called equal-field system. If they seized state power, they would carry out their promise. Along with the formation of the mass society in modern times, the power holder of the state is more than ever prone to make a promise to the citizens in an attempt to win support from the citizens. He may promise to improve the working conditions of the workers or to raise their wages. He may promise to increase benefits given to those in need in the society. He may promise to provide more medical care services. He may promise to develop the undertaking of education. Those promises are often what the citizens expect. Then citizens will promise to support the power holder. In election, politicians whose promise is entertained by the majority of the voters are usually elected. Voters promise to be subject to his governance. Mutual promises constitute a mechanism of organizing the state.

Second, a promise, made by the power holder, has a term. This term is determined by both the power holder and the masses. In ancient Greece, magistrates had the limited term of office. Re-election was prohibited. Officials held office for a short term. In Sparta, five ephors, who were the most important state officials, held office for only one year. In Rome, two consuls who led the Roman Republic were elected only for one year and thereafter could not be re-elected for ten years. The term of office was set by the citizens or some other people on behalf of the citizens. Therefore, after a power holder made a promise to the citizens, such a promise would be valid for one year only. In modern times, power holders may often hold office for four or five or seven years in a state in Europe. In China, power holders or officials held office without a term of office clearly defined in advance in ancient times. If a power holder made a promise to the subjects, such a promise did not have a term. But the subjects might expect the ruler to honor this promise within a period of time. In modern times, a promise, made by the power holder, may have a term if democracy is put into practice. In some countries in the East in modern times, democracy may not be put into practice. If the power holder of the state makes a promise to the citizens, the citizens may set the term of this promise tacitly. The principle of the operation of this mechanism is that a person who makes a promise may claim that he will realize an objective in economic development in ten years, for example. If he realizes this objective in five years or in ten years, he will gain creditability and a new promise, made by him, can be easily accepted by the people next time. Otherwise, if he realizes the objective in fifteen years or fails to realize the objective, he will be regarded as failing to honor the promise. If he makes a new promise in future, his promise may not be easily entertained by the people. If a citizen who entertains a promise thinks that it actually requires fifteen years to realize this objective in the abovementioned case though the power holder, who makes the promise, fails to honor that promise in ten years, the power holder of making a promise may be forgiven by the citizen who entertains the promise because the term of validity of the promise is defined by the citizen who entertains the promise. In general, what validates the promise is the congruence between the timeline of honoring the promise made by one and the term of validity defined by the other accepting it. If the promisor promises to realize the objective in ten years and the promisee believes that realizing this objective only needs five years, the ten-year term promise may be turned down and this promise may fail to influence the behavior of the other. However, if the promisee thinks that it needs to take fifteen years to realize the objective, he may accept the promise of realizing the objective in ten years or may refuse to accept this promise because he thinks of this promise to be unrealistic. In the interaction between the power holder and the citizens, there is such a mechanism. Therefore, the term of honoring a promise may be short or long. In a Western nation-state, the promises, made by the political parties in the election, are, in general, effective for a small number of years because the term for them to hold power is a small number of years. The promises, made by them, may be regarded as short-term promises. In China where no democratic election is held at the moment, the Communist Party of China, the ruling party, argues that it is a long historical process to build an ideal society and it will lead the nation in building such a society over the long term. In this case, its promise to build an ideal society may be regarded by someone as a long-term promise. If the related promise is accepted by the Chinese people, this should mean that the power holder and the masses have agreed that the term of the promise should be long. Otherwise, the term of the promise should be short.

Third, if the power holder fails to honor his promise, the masses may retract or cancel their promise. Specifically, the promise, made by the power holder to the masses earlier, leads the masses to make a promise to him. That is, his promise gets the promise made by the masses. He promises to serve the people and the people promise to support him. If he fails to carry out his promise, the masses will retract or cancel their promise. Then we see many cases in point. In ancient China, the rulers sometimes made a promise to the people. They might promise not to disturb the people. They might promise to cut state tax. They might promise to carry out a policy allowing every cultivator to have his field. They usually made such a promise in the beginning of their reign. The masses revolted at the end of their reign because the masses decided to cancel their promise made earlier to be subject to their rule. The term of the reign of a dynasty was often about two or three hundred years. In Europe, some revolutions that broke out in early modern times denote, objectively, the term of office of the rulers, too. In modern times, the power holder of a state, democratic or despotic, is often held accountable by the citizens in the governance of the state albeit to a varying extent. If a state is democratic, the power holder should be, legally, responsible to the citizens. If a state is still despotic, the power holder may be, morally or ethically, responsible to the people. As such, we often see the following cases: Some public employees announce their resignation for their failure to honor their promise made when they were sworn into office; the man in power announces his resignation due to a big scandal disclosed to the public during his term of office; some leaders announce their decision to step down before the end of their term of office because they make a wrong policy and hence make the nation incur huge losses; a leader of a political party announces his resignation from the leading post of the party after the defeat of the party in an election. In a European state or the United States, the major duty of the leader of a political party is to lead the whole party to win the election and obtain the ruling power. If that party is defeated in the election, it is often difficult for the existing leader to act as the leader of the party in the next election. If a power holder commits a fault or violates law, he may also resign. For example, in the history of the United States, Richard Nixon, the thirty-seventh president, resigned during his term of office on August 9, 1974 because of Watergate Scandal. Bill Clinton, the forty-second president, used to face the pressure of resignation during his term of office when a scandal in relation to him was revealed and the House of Representatives voted to impeach him for the obstruction of justice and perjury in December 1998 though he did not resign. In China, a state in which people do not hold free election and do not put into practice Western-style democracy, a leader who has committed an error in the revolution or in the construction of the nation-state may also be forced to resign or give up his real power. In the early times of the military struggle of the Communist Party of China, what forced a supreme leader to step down each time was that a major mistake had been made in making and carrying out a policy or a strategy. After the founding of the new China, namely, the People's Republic of China, Mao Zedong was forced to give up his position as the state chairman because of Mao's commitment of a fault in a political movement called the Great Leap Forward in the late 1950s and early 1960s. Certainly, China in the past was totally different from the Western states. In then China, the power holders did not go through the procedure of being sworn into office. However, no matter whether a politician lives in a Western state or an Eastern state such as China, he has the obligation to honor his promise after making the promise if any. Failure to honor the promise will usually result in punishment sooner or later.

All of those cases indicate that the internal organization of the state requires the power holder to function as a leader or a manager because he is a medium. The power holder and the masses need to interact with each other effectively. The effective interaction usually requires the power holder to make a promise acceptable by the masses and requires the masses to promise to submit to the governance of the power holder. The effective interaction also requires the power holder to keep his promise and requires the masses to keep their promise as well. Once a person of the community becomes a power holder, he has the power to issue commands to all others in the community and to make a decision in the distribution of the interest of the community. As such, the power holder and the people interact constantly with each other. Needless to say, the power holder holds higher social status. He is the governor of the state. All others are governed by him. So what is important is that the power holder must serve the people in order to take power, and this is a condition for the positive interaction between him and the masses. In the meantime, the common interest of the community cannot take shape until the power holder serves the people. But the power holder has to take power first and then takes action because the act of taking power is the precondition of honoring the promise made before the act of taking power. In this case, the power holder makes a promise to the people and this promise may be accepted by the people before the power holder takes action.

Besides, if a promise is made by the power holder and accepted by the masses, and the masses promise to be subject to the governance of the power holder under the condition that the power holder makes a promise, the act of making and accepting a promise needs to be committed time and again because if a promise is made and accepted, it is made and accepted under specific circumstances. Along with the passage of time, the specific circumstances change. The promise needs to be updated. Thus, the power holder makes a promise regularly and the masses accept it regularly. Thus, the power holder and the masses keep on engaging in such an interaction. In other words, any promise has a time limit. If such a promise reaches the time limit, a new promise needs to be made. The masses do not accept the promise that has already expired. Unlike a promise made under a business contract, the promise, made by the power holder to the masses to provide public services to them, may be made verbally, whereas the promise, made by the masses to be subject to the rule of the power holder, may be made by them tacitly only. However, both sides may make promises albeit in different ways.

In early times in the West, politicians held power in turn under democracy in Greek city-states, and the politicians of the Roman Republic took power and acted as magistrates after being elected. Politicians must have made at least a promise before they were elected. The term of office was also defined as they were not permitted to hold lifelong power, as noted earlier. This must be based on a promise made because if people argue about who is to take power, one way out is that politicians hold power in turn. There must be a promise if a politician allows another politician to hold power first. The politician who holds power first must have made a promise to all other politicians who accept that promise and wait for their turns. The term of office of the power holder is certainly defined. The linguistic behavior of a promise is the key for the state to put democracy into practice. It helps power holders to get out of the impasse of scrambling for power and eases the pressure on various power holders seeking the interest of their political organizations and the public interest at the same time. It makes it possible for various factions or groups of people to co-exist in one state. Some historical data also indicate that in ancient Greece and Rome, the eloquence of politicians was an important skill for them to take power. Politicians must cater to the needs of the public so as to get their support when they made a public speech or debated public affairs. They must appear to stress reason, or morality, or the public interest, and prove that their way of service will be in the interest of the public. This means that the common interest of all takes shape in the process in which promises are made and accepted. If we postulate that a despotic ruler may also make a promise to the masses and seek ruling legitimacy occasionally, he is often forced to do so. He may not make a promise to the masses voluntarily. If we admit that all the rulers in history may make a promise to the masses although some rulers often make a promise while others do not, the transition, from a despotic society to a democratic society in human history, can be regarded as a process of institutionalizing the promises made by the power holder to the masses and the promises made by the masses to the power holder.

To put it differently, such promises are institutionalized under democracy, whereas they are not institutionalized under a despotic system. Human political history is, in some sense, the history of institutionalizing the promises made by the power holder verbally and the promises made by the masses verbally or tacitly. This history is tortuous. As such, in the later periods of Roman Times and in the Middle Ages in the absence of democracy, rulers established and maintained their rule through the use of violence. That is, they controlled the behavior of the ruled by using the tool of enforcement. The ruler never got support from the people by making a public speech or taking part in an open debate and hence seldom made a promise. Likewise, in ancient China, the ruler established the administrative system in early times, but the ruler seldom met with the rank and file and never performed balanced and two-way communication with the populace. Certainly, some leaders of peasant uprisings advocated entering into an agreement with the populace and proposed the reallocation of land in favor of poor peasants in order to win their support. But in general after they took power, they continued the way of despotic rule and had no knowledge of election and democracy. They seldom made a promise to the people so as to win support from the people. The rulers of ancient China never regularly made a face-to-face promise to the populace. Knowing that the people were like the water and the ruler the boat and the water could either carry the boat or capsize it, the enlightened rulers took some measures to ease the oppression on the populace, but they never or seldom used the skill of promise to seek support from the populace. A promise was not a basic tool for them to seek and maintain power in the state. China's feudal rulers ruled the populace in the despotic way for a long time and thus, the people often stood up against them. The masses launched rebellions and uprisings. The organization of the state was devoid of a dialogue conducted between the ruler and the ruled. The rise of democracy in modern times marks a new epoch. Though there is a difference between the representative democracy of modern Europe and North America on one hand and the democracy of ancient Greek city-states and the Roman Republic on the other hand, the representative system inherits the practice of using linguistic skill of making a promise used by ancient Greek and Roman politicians to take and maintain their power. Now representation and electoral system are more and more popular across the world. This modern democracy is still conditioned by the linguistic communication of making and accepting a promise. Any political party, hoping to rule the state, has to make a promise to the constituency and has to take power under the condition that its promise is acceptable by the majority of the constituency. They may be required to make an agreement through mutual consultation. When an election campaign is waged, people need mutual consultation between the potential power holder and the voters. As Locke writes, "all peaceful beginnings of government have been laid in the consent of the people."[61]

In the meantime, citizens should promise to be subject to the organization of a political party. And accordingly, the ruling party is always under the pressure of honoring the promise made during the election campaign. Otherwise it will be defeated in the next election. As a political party and its candidates make a promise to the voters, the voters may consider giving power to them and allowing them to hold the power in a certain period of time. The leader of the nation-state emerges. In the meantime, each voter is also required to promise to yield to the opinion of the majority if he or she belongs to the minority in election. This means that prior to the election all voters promise to obey the principle that the opinion of the majority prevails over the opinion of the minority, as noted earlier. As democracy is the governance of the state on the basis of the consent from the people, the people emerge in the process of linguistic communication through which the common will of the people takes shape. The people are formed by the majority formed in election each time. Those citizens who belong to the minority in election this time may not be part of the people until the next election. In other words, the people are a cluster of people who have formed a common will. This cannot be done but in election. The common will generated by people is the common will generated by the majority though those who belong to the minority in election are still the citizens. Thus, as all agree to support the opinion of the majority, the promise, made by the power holder, and the promise, made by the citizens, constitute an exchange for the purpose of organizing the state. Thus, these promises alleviate tensions between a person in power and all others out of power, and help people to establish the internal order, to enhance the solidarity of the nation-state and to generate the authority acceptable by all within the state. Thus, I argue that the linguistic phenomenon of making a promise makes a great contribution to the building of a civilized political order within the state because at this time the power holder making promises and the masses accepting promises jointly contribute to the formation and cultivation of the common interest of all forming the state. Then, the masses submit to the governance of the power holder. In the past the power holder of any state might not make any promise to the masses as the state was despotic. The power holder merely governed the state in a limited domain. But the government was despotic. The masses might not have any personal freedom. They might be massively oppressed by the ruling class or the ruler. By contrast, in modern times the power holder governs the state in a nearly limitless domain. Yet, the masses may not feel that they are oppressed by the state apparatus. They may have more personal freedoms. This is because the power holder makes a promise to the masses and the masses promise to be subject to the governance of the power holder voluntarily. When each side makes a promise to the other side and the other side accepts this promise, this can mean that they have reached a consensus. When they reach a consensus, the consensus highlights the formation of the common interest between the power holder and the masses. Then the interest of the power holder becomes consonant with that of the masses. Thus the state becomes harmonious.

The nature of a promise is also a decisive factor. People who make promises in an interaction put pressure on themselves. To make a promise is to undertake an obligation. People are always potentially forced to act after they undertake certain obligations defined by them when they make a promise. If one party makes a promise, this party gives related rights to the other party voluntarily. This party is required by morality or law to honor the promise. If this party changes its mind and decides not to honor the promise, it may be forced to honor the promise or to make any compensation. Otherwise the promise will not function. Hobbes writes that "Covenant, without the Sword, are but Words, and of no strength to secure a man at all."[62] He implied that people were forced by the sword to honor the promise. In modern times, a person, failing to honor a promise, may also be forced to honor the promise by law. In terms of the promises made between the power holder and the citizens, such promises are not codified. Such promises may be made by the power holder informally. If promises are made by the citizens, they may only make them tacitly. That is, they may even give no expression to what they conceive of and hence they make no formal promises to the power holder. Such promises may not constitute a contract. As legal scholars sometimes argue, not every promise amounts to a contract. [63] In particular, in ancient times, the ruler might not make any promise to the people and the people made no promise to the ruler if there was no democracy, not to mention the social contract. As David Hume argues, in early times people might not subscribe to a compact or agreement because they were much too uncultivated to conceive of such a thing.[64] However, along with the passage of time, promises are more often made by the power holder and the people as democracy spreads across the borders of the states. Making promises and accepting promises are institutionalized. Language plays an important role in the organization of the state. Then we see that when the power holder makes a promise or the citizens make a promise, all are obligated to honor the promises because both sides are obligated by the organization of the state. The power holder is required to provide public services to the citizens and the citizens are required to submit to the governance of the power holder who is in charge of organizing the state. People witness the formation of the related common interest between the power holder and the citizens. The formation of such common interest finally lays a bedrock foundation for the building of the state. Then the power holder can govern the state legitimately.

Notes

1. Paul Vinogradoff, *The Growth of the Manor* (London: George Allen & Unwin Ltd, 1951), 24.

2. See: Ibid., 25.

3. George H. Sabine, *A History of Political Theory* (London: George G Harrap & Co., Ltd, 1937), 332.

4. Jun Li, *Chinese Civilization in the Making, 1766-221BC* (London: MachMillan Press Ltd, 1996), 25.

5. George H. Sabine, *A History of Political Theory*, 214.

6. Karl Marx, *Capital: A Critical Analysis of Capitalist Production*, translated by Samuel Moore and Edward Aveling and edited by Frederick Engels (New York: Appleton & Co., 1889), 48.

7. George H. Sabine, *A History of Political Theory*, 332.

8. Karl Marx and Frederick Engels, *The Germany Ideology*, edited by C. J. Arthur (New York: International Publishers, 1970), 70.

9. Charles Fried, *Contract as Promise: A Theory of Contractual Obligation* (Cambridge: Harvard University Press, 1981), 18.

10. Thomas Hobbes, *Leviathan*, edited with an introduction by C.B. Macpherson (New York: Penguin Books, 1985), 193.

11. W. H. Buckler, *The Origin and History of Contract in Roman Law Down to the End of the Republican Period* (Littleton, Colorado: Fred. B. Rothman & Co., 1983),1.

12. P.S. Atiyah, *Promises, Morals, and Law* (Oxford: Clarendon Press, 1981), 208.

13. W. H. Buckler, *The Origin and History of Contract in Roman Law Down to the End of the Republican Period*, 5–6.

14. Ibid., 6.

15. Neil Duxbury, *Random Justice: On Lotteries and Legal Decision-Making* (Oxford: Oxford University Press, 1999),3.

16. Ibid., 28.

17. *The Politics of Aristotle*, translated by Peter L. Phillips Simpson (Chapel Hill: The University of North Carolina Press, 1997), 49.

18. George H. Sabine, *A History of Political Theory*, 585-586.

19. Ibid., 643.

20. One English scholar gave the same opinion. Please see: J.W. Gough, *The Social Contract: A Critical Study of Its Development* (Oxford: The Clarendon Press, 1957), 33.

21. J.W. Gough, *The Social Contract: A Critical Study of Its Development*, 2.

LANGUAGE AND STATE

22. John Locke, *Second Treatise of Government*, edited by C.B. Macpherson (Indianapolis, Indiana: Hackett Publishing Company, Inc., 1980), 53.

23. Jean Jacques Rousseau, *Social Contract* (Chicago: Encyclopaedia Britannica, Inc., 1952), 389.

24. As Michael Lessnoff stated that "the social contract is a fiction, and can at best be considered as a hypothetical concept from which to deduce political authority and its limits." See: Michael Lessnoff, *Social Contract* (Atlantic Highlands, NJ: Humanities Press International, Inc., 1986), 120.

25. James Endell Tyler, *Oaths: Their Origin, Nature and History* (London: John W. Parker, West Strand, 1834), 6.

26. Herbert J. Schlesinger, *Promises, Oaths, and Vows: On the Psychology of Promising*, 189; please also see: J. Hastings' article on covenants, oaths & vows. *Encyclopaedia of Religion and Ethics* (New York: Scribner & Sons), 1924.

27. Schlesinger, *Promises, Oaths, and Vows: On the Psychology of Promising*, 180.

28. David Xavier Junkin, *The Oath: An Divine Ordinance and an Element of the Social Constitution* (New York: Wiley And Putman, 1845), 153.

29. Steven H. Miles, *Hippocratic Oath and the Ethics of Medicine* (New York: Oxford University Press, 2004), 50.

30. Please see: Ibid., 4.

31. Tyler, *Oaths: Their Origin, Nature and History*, 151.

32. Schlesinger, *Promises, Oaths, and Vows: On the Psychology of Promising*, 187.

33. Tyler, *Oaths: Their Origin, Nature and History*, 69.

34. David I. Kertzer, *Ritual, Politics, and Power* (New Haven: Yale University Press, 1988), 17; Please also see: Ted Margadant, *French Peasants in Revolt: The Insurrection of 1851* (Princeton: Princeton University Press, 1979); Edward Berenson, *Populist Religion and Left-Wing Politics in France, 1830–1852* (Princeton: Princeton University Press, 1984).

35. Tyler, *Oaths: Their Origin, Nature and History* , 303.

36. Ibid.,303–304.

37. Schlesinger, *Promises, Oaths, and Vows: On the Psychology of Promising*, 183; please also see: G. Mendenhall: *Mari* in D.N. Freedman & E.F. Campbell ed.: *Biblical Archeologist Reader*, II. (Garden City, New York: Doubleday/Anchor (1964), 3–20.

38. Polux, lib. viii.e. 9 and 10; cited from Tyler, *Oaths: Their Origin, Nature and History*, 298.

39. Tyler, *Oaths: Their Origin, Nature and History* , 137.

40. Charles de Secondat, Baron de Montesquieu, *The Spirit of Laws*, translated by Thomas Nugent (Chicago: Encyclopaedia Britannica, Inc., 1952), 55.

41. John Locke, *Second Treatise of Government*, 102.

42. See: Junkin, *The Oath: A Divine Ordinance and An Element of the Social Constitution*, 127.

43. Tyler, *Oaths: Their Origin, Nature and History*, 236–237.

44. See: James Connor, *The Sociology of Loyalty* (New York: Springer Science & Business Media, LLC, 2007), 97.

45. Schlesinger, *Promises, Oaths, and Vows: On the Psychology of Promising*, 188.

46. Tyler, *Oaths: Their Origin, Nature and History*, 227.

47. Ibid., 229.

48. Charles Fried, *Contract as Promise: A Theory of Contractual Obligation* (Cambridge: Harvard University Press, 1981), 9.

49. Ibid., 46.

50. See: Patrick Riley, *Will and Political Legitimacy: A Critical Exposition of Social Contract Theory in Hobbes, Locke, Rousseau, Kant, and Hegel* (Cambridge: Harvard University Press, 1982),107.

51. Plutarch, *The Lives of the Noble Grecians and Romans*, 784–785.

52. Ibid., 530.

53. Henry Maine, *Ancient Law* (London: John Murray, 1866), 312.

54. Morton Grodzins, *The Loyal and the Disloyal: Social Boundaries of Patriotism and Treason* (Chicago: The University of Chicago Press, 1956), ii.

55. Bertrand de Jouvenel, *Sovereignty: An Inquiry into the Political Good*, translated by J. F. Huntington (Chicago: The University Press of Chicago, 1957), 189.

56. D. H. MacNeill, *The Art and Science of Government among the Scots* (Glasgow: William MacLellan, 1964), 95-6; cited from Michael Lessnoff, *Social Contract* (Atlantic Hills, NJ: Humanities Press International, Inc., 1986), 31.

57. Gough, *The Social Contract: A Critical Study of Its Development*, 24-25.

58. Ibid., 58.

59. Lessnoff, *Social Contract*, 18.

60. Gough, *The Social Contract: A Critical Study of Its Development*, 3.

61. Locke, *Second Treatise of Government*, 61.

62. Hobbes, *Leviathan*, 223.

63. See: Lessnoff, *Social Contract*, 3.

64. David Hume, *Theory of Politics*, edited by F. Watkins (Edinburgh: Nelson, 1951), 195-6; cited from Lessnoff, *Social Contract*, 85.

Chapter Nine

Command

1. Naked Command

Apart from the fact that humans can provide information to each other, can give an interpretation to each other, can express an attitude to each other and can make a promise to each other to the effect that they organize the state in the different types of mutual interaction, people can request each other to do a certain job. The reason is that people can use language. Then they can indicate their intention of requesting each other to do a job. Sometimes a person may even force another person to do a job. Consequently, that person, forced to do a job, is under pressure. Then we find that sometimes one puts pressure on the other in the mutual interaction between one another. In the mutual interaction between one another, people are objectively required to coordinate their actions. Sometimes one has to change his action particularly as required by the other. This means that one compels the other to act as expected or required by him. In this process language is used by one to indicate his expectation or requirement in order to compel the other to act as expected or required. This person uses language to indicate the existence of the pressure. The other person may feel that pressure. The pressure evolves to be a command. This is a linguistic phenomenon seen in the state. This is also a special interaction between one another in the state. By contrast, people did not engage in such an interaction in the tribe. To put it differently, people have always interacted with each other within the state since the formation of the state. They face some pressure. They face the related pressure because the state, in which they are, has to be organized in a particular way. In the organization of the state, all are emphatically compelled to submit to the organization of the state. The pressure always exists. Sometimes the pressure becomes a special command because this pressure is especially put on somebody to compel him to act as required. The reason is that the organization of the state cannot be without a command. A command is often issued due to the necessity of organizing the state. Since the formation of the state people have become a collective being. As this collective being is formed in linguistic communication, the pressure, faced by each, is also indicated in the process of linguistic communication. Though the pressure includes potential enforcement, linguistic expression is indispensable. Without the related linguistic expression that guides one, potential enforcement is meaningless. Such linguistic expression becomes a command. The command further becomes, objectively, an important linguistic behavior in the organization of the state. Thus some people issue commands and others obey them.

If we assume that primitives often teamed up to go hunting, to build dwellings or vessels and to defend their land, we can also assume that people in the civilized society team up to engage in production and to defend the land and the sea of their state. People rely on the collective strength both in the tribe and in the state. At the same time, they need a leader. They need a common will in their collective action. They will not have their common will until a leader emerges because people, taking collective action, need organization and organization means that people need a leader to take charge of organizing them. But there is a difference between the chief of a tribe and the leader of a state: The tribal chief might not use language to issue a command for the organization of the tribe because all the members of the tribe followed him naturally while the power holder of the state has to do so. If the tribal chief let others perform a task, he issued instructions instead of commands. This is because people obeyed his will naturally. People had the common interest because of kinship. Yet the reality is that since humans formed their state and dissolved their tribes, the power holder has been required to issue commands to govern the state. This is because the common interest of the state and the personal interest coexist in the state. The common interest of the state and personal interest may not always be consonant with each other. Thus it follows that sometimes one ordinary member of the state opposes the certain action to be taken by the collective being. In this case the power holder may force him to obey the collective will in the interest of the collective being. On the other hand, each member, as part of the community, does not abandon necessarily his interest and may seek his own interest by sacrificing or ignoring the interest of the community without being discovered by other members. However, as he displays this behavior many times, the collective being usually establishes a surveillance system to issue a command to the members pursuing unfairly their own interest at the expense of the interest of the state and requires them to comply with the disciplines or regulations. Sometimes punishment may be inflicted. In short, in order to take care of, and protect, the collective interest, the state requires the person, holding power in its name, to issue commands. At the same time, issuing commands is a behavior of linguistic communication. It involves a special mode of the mutual interaction of people in the organization of the state. It is significant for the organization of the state. It is a special linguistic phenomenon.

In view of the interaction of humans, we find that the circumstances, under which a person forces another person to do a job by way of communication and possibly by force, are similar to those circumstances under which humans force animals to do a job. Farmers force animals to work by giving a signal with whistling sound through the rounded lips or uttering a word through the mouth. This signal is a sign, but the behavior of a farmer in this context does not mean that the farmer is unable to use language, but the animal is unable to use language. Because an animal is unable to understand the farmer's language, the farmer has no alternative but to order the animal to do simple work by using a sign. For example, the farmer can make the animal till the field or carry things. Even if an animal does simple work, it cannot do anything but under the "guidance" of the farmer, such as being whipped. So a community in which a person requires another person to do some work by using language is different from the community in which all do not use language. At least since humans came into a civilized society and formed their state, the original basic behavior of seeking their own preservation in the natural world has evolved to be complicated working behavior, the behavior of building society and other behavior, including the behavior of social organization, innovation and entertainment. When a person forces another person to do a job, he has to clarify what kind of job it is and he has to use language. So since humans started using language they have gradually built their state. In the building of their state, some of them issue commands.

We can regard such a command as a naked command. As such a command is emphatically issued by one to the other, this command usually involves an interaction between one another. This interaction should, at least, have three attributes.

First, this interaction is a sense-experienced interaction or, at least, a potential sense-experienced interaction. By the "sense-experienced interaction," I mean the interaction realized through the experience of sense. Without such an interaction or such a potential interaction, no command can be effective. The success of such an interaction is dependent on pure force. The reason is that when humans formed the tribe, all cooperated with all because they had the common interest that took shape due to kinship. Since humans started using language, they have expanded their community to the extent that kinship fails to function in the formation of this community. Thus people often conflict with each other. The community falls in disorder. Then a governor emerges to restore the order. This governor issues commands. Carrying out each of these commands invariably relies on the use of force. In the use of force, one feels the existence of force on the basis of sense-experience. Consequently, if a person issues a command to another person, he always makes that person realize that refusal to obey the command will result in physical enforcement or punishment. The interaction between the person who issues a command and the person who receives that command is, in essence, a sense-experienced interaction. The theory of conditional reflexes, proposed by Ivan Pavlov, a Russian physiologist, has proved that if a dog hears you ring a bell, and you then feed the dog, the dog will become conditional to expect to receive food after hearing a bell; the dog has created a relationship between the sound of the bell and receiving food. In a human society, there exists not only this kind phenomenon of positive conditional reflexes, but also the phenomenon of negative conditional reflexes. For instance, a person is punished because of his refusal to obey the command. As a result, he creates a sign relation between the command and the fact of being punished. Next time when receiving a command, he is aware that refusal to obey the command will result in punishment. To avoid being punished, he chooses to obey the command. He has already established this solid sign relation in his mind during his childhood if he lives in one of some Asian states. That is, in some Asian states, a parent sometimes threatens to beat a child in order to discipline him, a way of family education molded by the native culture. Likewise, the police force of the state threatens to put culprits into jail in order to prevent some people from offending the law. This bears testimony to the fact that a naked command is dependent on a sense-experienced interaction.

Second, while a naked command is issued, there is a linguistic interaction between the person who issues that command and the person who receives that command. Without such a linguistic interaction, a command will not work. That is, the person who issues a command has to guide the person who receives the command. Language has to be used. Then language, used by people, reflects the complexity of linguistic communication. That is, language is a form of a group of signs and is a complex sign system that takes form on the basis of simple signs. Words are linguistic signs. Ferdinand de Saussure believes that the linguistic sign is, in principle, composed of two parts: the signifier and the signified. As he indicated, "The linguistic entity exists only through the associating of the signifier with the signified. Whenever only one element is retained, the entity vanishes."[1] This means that humans use these two parts to form words which are further used to form language in which different words, based on different shapes and phonemic structures, carry different meanings. Each of different shapes of words and phonemic structures is the signifier and each of the different meanings is the signified. Language is a differential system composed of the corresponding relations between the said signifier and the said signified.[2] The use of this system lays a foundation for humans to convey diversified and complex information from one to another. This is also a condition for the evolution of the human community from the tribe to the state. While humans remained the tribal people, they realized the simple interaction between one another. The tribe rarely required the chief to issue a command to all others. But since the formation of the state, the interaction between one another has become diversified. Then language enables people to issue commands. As a command is a will expressed by one to force the other to act as required, the behavior of one will be controlled by the other, but linguistic communication has to be always effective. In the meantime, one-way communication, performed by the person who issues the command with the person who receives the command, is decisive. The linguistic interaction is unilaterally controlled by the person who issues the command. Under these circumstances, language functions like a signal used by humans to control their own behavior in the interaction between one another or in the course of establishing the order of the society or the state.

Third, while a naked command is issued, the person who issues the command puts psychological pressure on the person who receives the command. They are simply involved in a psychological interaction. The reason is that as people live in a community in which all no longer associate together because of kinship, all may be in conflict with each other without order. In establishing order, a governor emerges and the governor must issue commands. However, people do not use force directly to establish such order. They issue commands. This means that the control of the behavior of others by issuing a command creates apparently a gap of time and space between language and the action of coercion. After a command is issued, the person who receives the command has time to choose to obey the command before being coerced to act or being punished. Robert C. North and Doris A. Graber, two American scholars, point out this phenomenon in their book that:

> [M]any potentially physical actions never move beyond the verbal stage; for example, a presidential warning that troops will be used to man railroads in case of a threatened railroad strike may avert that strike without moving a single soldier or even issuing orders to move troops.[3]

The order of the state is established under such a psychological interaction. The result is that a power holder governs his people by issuing commands rather than punishing his people all day. He is able to make his people obey his commands by way of issuing commands as long as he is a successful governor of the state because there is a psychological interaction between him and his people. This is very significant in the building of the state. This is a skill adopted by humans in using language.

Nevertheless, while a command is issued, all those interactions between one another rely on the operation of language. As a person is a selfish animal, it is difficult for people to cooperate with one another and hence to establish order without the use of language. In some cases people have to be subject to the law of nature. Thus Hobbes comments that " the Lawes of Nature (as Justice, Equity, Modesty, Mercy, and (in summe) doing to others, as wee would be done so) of themselves, without the terrour of some Power, to cause them to be observed, are contrary to our passions." [4] But the law of nature itself cannot be directly used to establish order. People often require themselves in their mutual interaction to cooperate with each other and establish order. They have to make a rule for themselves in their mutual interaction and then establish order. There must be a power holder making the rule. Thus language must be used when people are made to obey a certain rule, as noted earlier. This requires a certain person to issue commands, particularly, specific and effective commands. When a person issues a command, he has to use language. Then people establish the order of the community. Though some people issue commands to other people and order established by way of issuing commands may not be justified temporarily, commands enable people to co-exist and make it possible to form a fair or comparatively just community in future in view of the possible long-term development of the human community. It seems that people may undergo a historical process of development into a just state managed by them, but people cannot live peacefully without the order established by using language to issue commands.

As people use language, they issue commands to control their own behavior in an attempt to establish the order of the state. The experience of people indicates that in the very beginning of the social evolution of humans, they were sometimes motivated by their own selfish psychology to loot, defraud, steal and murder everywhere. At that time language might not be used. People did not cooperate with each other when they did not use language. Conversely, it is also true that people, using language, can cooperate with each other. Then people start using language to issue commands and establishing order. It is self-evident that in the world of nature humans are not the first species that resorts to violence. Even today the weak are still the prey to the strong in the world of animals. The act of looting and killing in the human community does not differ in nature from the act of violence in the world of animals. However, since the birth of language, humans have established a system of control over their own mutual interaction by using language instead of resorting directly to violence and hence established the order of their community. Language has changed the mode of human behavior. Since then humans have entered the state in which the behavior of humans is controlled by issuing commands. Once humans are able to issue commands to control the behavior of each person, the public power appears immediately within the community. It is due to the fact that in a community, formed by two people, there must be one who is able to issue commands to the other. If a third person joins the community, there must be one who is able to issue commands to the other two. Language helps that person to communicate with the other two or even more. Obeying commands results in the establishment of order within the community and order means the possibility of ensuring public security. If all rely on a public authority for their own security in the community, they stop relying on their own resources to protect themselves and their property. Though the sum of the resources, had by each person, must be more than the resources had by the public authority, people who disturb the public order are usually the minority. The public authority which has the resources fewer than the resources had by all of the community is in most cases in control of enough resources that enable it to subdue a person or a few insisting on disobeying any command. As such, the act of controlling the behavior of humans themselves by issuing commands results in the establishment of order. Of course, sometimes people find themselves in the state of anarchy when they enter the state of violent confrontation or war due to the conflict of interest, but this is a temporary phenomenon because people always learn a bitter lesson from the violent confrontation or the war and are forced to get back to the command-controlled state which they have to accept at least at the moment.

Then, what kind of linguistic behavior is the command issued by a human being in this case? The command, issued by a human being, is a signal of putting pressure by one, acting as the power holder of the community, on the others acting as the ordinary people of the community. The command not only tells the existence of pressure put by the power holder, but also tells how to release this pressure. The result is that people act according to the will of the power holder. A command establishes a kind of tight and non-optional relationship between ordinary people and the power holder. Ordinary people must accept the community governed by the power holder. If ordinary people refuse to accept the community governed by the power holder, they will be punished. A command implies that if people refuse to obey the command, their freedom may be restricted and they may be forced to act against their own will. On the other hand, the important condition of establishing the ruling order by issuing a command is that people are willing to obey the command. The absolute governance of the power holder and the absolute obedience of ordinary people reflect the most effective function of a command that ensures the most stable order of the community.

In view of the nature of human beings, a person is a selfish animal in most cases. He is guided by "self-awareness" and he is likely to be in conflict with others. Neither he himself nor any other person can eliminate this likeliness. Neither he himself nor any other person is able to prevent him from seeking his own interest or even ignoring or harming the interest of all others while he seeks his own interest. But humans are also the animals able to rationalize the behavior of their own by using reason in the consideration of their own preservation and development. They understand how to relinquish certain existing limited freedom and interest to gain more freedom and interest in future or how to give up the freedom and the interest of the shorter time for those of the longer time. Besides, as they use language, the intention of each can be learned by the other. Then they can exchange goods and services. Each can provide what the other needs. As noted earlier, Adam Smith stated that a dog cannot exchange goods while a human being is an animal capable of exchanging goods. He used to vividly narrate that nobody ever saw a dog make a fair and deliberate exchange of one bone for another with another dog. He pointed out that no dog could suggest the exchange. He meant that only humans are able to exchange goods. Why are humans able to exchange goods while other animals are unable to do so? My argument is that humans communicate by using language. As humans communicate by using language, they reveal their intention. Knowing the intention of each other, they realize the constructive interaction. They become far-sighted. They are, thus, able to see the potential interest of future, or the potential interest of the longer time, and hence willing to relinquish the existing interest in exchange for the interest of the future or the interest of the longer time. They realize the division of labor. Each gives an extra benefit to the other as a result. This is proved by the human act of trade and investment. A dog is unable to engage in trade or investment. Likewise, a human being is also able to sacrifice temporarily personal interest to promote the collective interest because he understands that the realization of his personal interest may be based on the realization of the common interest of the collective and sometimes the common interest of the collective should prevail. Thus humans are able to respect the common interest and devote themselves to the cultivation of the common interest. Though there are those who issue commands and those who obey commands and the people of the community have different interests, there exists the common interest of the community. The common interest requires each to relinquish temporarily part of personal interest so as to maintain and enhance the common interest. As a result, the people of the community are divided into power holders who issue commands according to the regulations of the community and the ordinary people of the community who obey the commands. This is the starting point of the development of the civilized community of human beings. That is the community in which a small portion of people issue commands and a large portion of people obey the commands, a fact that makes possible the establishment of the order and the governance of the community. As John Stuart Mill indicates, "a people in a state of savage independence, in which everyone lives for himself, exempt, unless by fits, from any external control, is practically incapable of making any progress in civilization until it has learnt to obey."[5] Plutarch notes that the Spartans were good subjects, but bad governors. When one said that Sparta held up so long because their kings could command so well, King Theopompus replied that "Nay, rather because the people know so well how to obey." They were trained to obey. Someone trained them. Thus, one can also say that people did not obey unless someone trained them to obey. The man who trained them to obey was the man who issued a command. Obedience was a lesson taught by commanders.[6] That is, people were trained to obey various kinds of commands. They were trained to obey military orders. They were trained to obey administrative decrees. They were trained to obey laws. They were simply trained to obey. Narrating the life of Agesilaus (485-401 B.C.), an ancient Greek, Plutarch writes that Simonides called Sparta "the tamer of men" and it trained men to make them tractable and patient of subjection as horses that were broken in while colts.[7]

Needless to say, people are required to learn both how to obey and how to command. If people are required to obey, some others are required to learn how to issue commands. Their mutual interaction should be the mutual interaction characterized by obedience and command. Thus, Plutarch continues to talk about this matter while narrating the legend of Agesilaus, and writes that "he kept with him Xenophon, the philosopher, and made much of him, and proposed to him to send for his children and educate them at Sparta, where they would be taught the best of all learning: how to obey, and how to command."[8] Likewise, describing the organization of the human society in the past, Mill opines that "It required centuries of time to discipline" a tribe of North American Indians or the barbarians of the time of the Roman Empire "into regular obedience even to their own leaders."[9] This is because if people do not know how to obey, order will not be established. Then the frightful state of anarchy will not end and the state of conflict of people will continue. Under these circumstances, the relationship between one another is the competition in which one cannot accept the existence of the other or there is no power holder to whom people submit. This situation is against the expectation of humans in the progress of civilization.

The historical progress of civilization is reflected by the following developmental process of human society. Prior to the rise of slave-owning society, the wars of tribes were waged for the control of territory and the commitment of revengeful murder. After the slave-owning society had come into existence, the prisoners of war became slaves rather than being physically wiped out. The victorious states started to establish their rule over slaves. Some people started to learn how to rule while others gained the experience of being ruled. The act of issuing commands became an act of ruling the state. When humans entered the times of feudalism, the ruler of the state was no longer able to mistreat the ruled freely by killing them or injuring them. The ruler, such as a lord, changed the way of ruling by making the ruled such as peasants depend on land. The lease of land was a way of communication for continuous ruling. Then, the capitalist society arose. Since then, laborers have been liberated physically and become the employees who deserve the respect from the employers. They may also have freedoms and rights protected by the law. But the relationship of employment requires management to some extent through which some manage enterprises while others subordinate themselves to this management. A labor contract is a legal form of communication between the employer and the employee. In short, since the advent of the civilized society, humans have been accumulating the experience of leading and being led, ruling and being ruled and managing and being managed. Since then, violent conflicts have occurred time and again and each event of violent conflict has represented a failure of establishing the order of the community by humans themselves. However, each event of violent conflict provides an additional experience to humans as to how to issue commands to rule and manage and how to subordinate themselves to the rule and the management as well. Thus people create a way of organizing the state when someone issues a naked command.

In ancient times some European rulers kept despotic rule and in medieval times they all maintained despotic rule. The basic way of their ruling was actually or largely based on the naked command. Machiavelli, who gave an advice to the prince of one state in Italy in late medieval times, writes that:

> A Prince ought to have no other aim or thought, nor select anything else for his study, than war and its rules and discipline; for this is the sole art that belongs to him who rules, and it is of such force that it not only upholds those who are born princes, but it often enables men to rise from a private station to that rank. And, on the contrary, it is seen that when princes have thought more of ease than of arms they have lost their states.[10]

This phenomenon can still be seen in some states today. There are some nation-states on earth that still maintain the polity in which a despotic government functions. The related despotic government may still come under the influence of the method of the traditional rule that took shape in the past. This despotic government may also be under the governance of a ruling party that never steps down. Sometimes some citizens disobey the command issued by the government because they want democracy. Then the government issues naked commands because only naked commands can function effectively. The government forces the masses to obey its commands. Even in the state under democracy, a naked command may also be issued by the government if the masses conflict with the government on the streets because the government cannot persuade the masses to retreat and give up their petition. For example, sometimes we see that the masses wage a demonstration on a public square in the United States. They conflict with the policemen. The policemen often order the demonstrators to leave the public square and the demonstrators refuse to leave. Then they are forced by the police to leave the public square. In this case the order, issued by the police, is the naked command because such a command is pure enforcement. If the government cannot persuade the citizens to obey its command, the command, issued by the government, becomes naked. Any government, in charge of governing the state, preserves this primary means to maintain the order of the public and keep the operation of the state.

2. Systematic Imperative

On the other hand, we should see that such a phenomenon usually recurred in the beginning in the course of state formation. After a while the ruler found that he was no longer always able to continue to govern his state this way. He would also find it necessary to justify his rule. He would find it necessary to claim to have the right to rule the state on certain grounds. Thus in later times, particularly in modern times, this phenomenon of issuing a naked command usually occurs occasionally in the organization of the state. This is mainly because the state is usually formed because of the formation of the common interest between the ordinary people and those who govern the state at least to some extent. Ordinary people tend to be unable to resist the rule of the power holder if there is a conflict between them and the power holder because the power holder is usually a strong man though there may be some common interest in the state. Yet, if ordinary people resist the rule occasionally because they suffer from the oppression of the ruler, the ruler will also feel that he is required to justify his rule in some way so as to persuade ordinary people to obey his rule. So in the state the real picture is that the power holder tends gradually to justify his rule and his commands on certain grounds. So in the study of the genesis of the state we see that if people need to have common interest in the community, the command, issued by the power holder, needs an interpretation. Even in the later period of the development of the tribe instructions, given by the tribal chief, may also rely on a certain interpretation. For example, the tribal chief may rely on the power of a god to rule the tribe because people stand in awe of that god. He interprets the authority of that god. He may claim that he rules the tribe on behalf of that god. As a result people are compelled to obey his command. But this case may not necessarily mean that the interest of the tribal chief is repugnant to the interest of all other people in the tribe. This is because the tribal chief and others are connected with each other by kinship. However, in the building of the state a command particularly needs support given by an interpretation as the interest of an individual and the interest of the state may be at variance with each other. So it follows that since the formation of the state, the power holder has been exercising his power. Exercising his power, he issues commands. Issuing commands, he normally has to give an interpretation. This is because on one hand people have different interests and on the other hand people also have the common interest. The reason that all have the common interest is that the state, formed by them, is actually an organization intended to realize a goal of all. As all belong to this organization, all the members of the organization constitute a collective being. A collective being runs on the basis of collectivity, which requires that all the members of the collective being coordinate. All will feel that they are required to obey the command issued as required by the collectivity. The command becomes a systematic imperative. An organization exists because of its entirety. As required by the entirety of the organization, all the members of the organization often find that coordination among all members is almost always necessary. Therefore, the power holder of this organization issues a command from time to time, and all other members feel obligated to obey this command notwithstanding the existence of the pressure of obeying the command at the same time. All the members of the organization may voluntarily obey the command as an imperative. In the meantime, obeying such a command is understood because people may give an interpretation. An interpretation makes possible the formation of the common interest, as mentioned earlier. The command, issued by the power holder, is finally justified. The command becomes legitimate because issuing a command on behalf of the state and obeying the same as required by the functioning of the state becomes a custom or tradition. Such an interaction between the power holder and the ordinary people may be institutionalized. Then people obey the administrative order not because of the individual person acting as the power holder but because of the office held by that individual person acting as the power holder. Thus, people may perpetuate the system of issuing and obeying commands. The power holder, issuing commands, becomes an authority and all others submit to this authority. Peter Blau writes that:

> [T]he distinctive feature of authority is that social norms accepted and enforced by the collectivity of subordinates constrain its individual members to comply with directives of a superior. Compliance is voluntary for the collectivity, but social constraints make it compelling for the individual. In contrast to other forms of influence and power, the pressure to follow suggestions and orders does not come from the superior who gives them but from the collectivity of subordinates. These normative constraints may be institutionalized and pervade the entire society, or they may emerge in a group in social interaction. The latter emergent norms define leadership, which, therefore, is considered a type of authority.[11]

The situation described by Blau also applies to the organization of the state. Or as Bertrand de Jouvenel opines, a command was at first an observable fact. It became institutionalized by a complicity between leaders and led, who combined to stabilize a state of things, in itself unstable, which had proven beneficial.[12] Thus, the command becomes legitimate. It becomes a systematic imperative. One case in point may be that in nearly all the states either in ancient or medieval times or in modern times the relationship between the ruler and the ruled is ritualized. In ancient times Egyptian rulers kept on legitimating their rule by performing rituals. They built temples. Rituals were held in the temples. They were Pharaohs. They were also gods. Rituals made them sacred. In medieval Europe the succession of kingship must involve a rite. The new ruler could not be legitimate until he was enthroned in a rite. Various rites were designed and performed in order to institutionalize the relationship between the ruler and the ruled. For example, some rites were designed to sacralize power. In modern times this situation remains unchanged. Discussing the role of rites in the building of the authority of the state, David I. Kertzer writes that:

> Where the gap between rulers and ruled is greatest, rites of rulers are most highly developed. The logical outcome of

the sacralization of power is the divinization of the ruler, who reigns not by force, still less by illusion, but by supernatural powers vested in him. Such an ideology cannot take hold without a powerful ritual through which the ruler's supernatural power is made visible to the population.[13]

To ritualize the relationship between the ruler and the ruled is to institutionalize the relationship between the ruler and the ruled. In modern times, we see that the state leader also takes office on a ceremony. The ceremony can mean the institutionalization of the relationship between him and his people. This can culminate in the fact that when a command is issued, the command is institutionalized. The command is issued in the way that is traditional or required by the system. So administrative orders, issued in the organization of the state, are issued in the way accepted or acceptable by all. People who issue commands by using language can also use language to interpret commands. They can design rites to bolster the related interpretation. Then all may obey the commands voluntarily.

The interpretation can also be given in various ways. Various interpretations can be given. People can also interpret those commands in various ways. The commands, issued with an interpretation, are understood. Then they become the administrative orders which are pervasive, albeit varying with different systems or different historical backgrounds. There appear various administrative orders.

First, an administrative order may be the one issued in the name of a god. In ancient times Moses issued commands to Hebrews and he founded the ancient state of Hebrews in the Middle East. He did so in the name of God. He explained that he had the divine right to issue commands to all Hebrews. After he gained the legitimacy of issuing commands, he built the state for Hebrews. Likewise, each consecrated king of the Middle Ages issued commands interpreted as the commands of God. The king was usually crowned by the Church. The King relied on the support from the Church because the Church was often very influential among the masses across the state. The Church kept a close relationship with ordinary people. People often kept emotional ties with the Church instead of the state. Thus the king, supported by the Church, could issue the administrative orders supported by an interpretation endorsed by the Church. Though the Church took care that the king was the true servant of God, the king often claimed successfully the right of ruling the state with the support from the Church. As people were, in some sense, obligated to obey the divine will, the king strengthened his command. Thus in European history, the king of a state normally sought the recognition of the Church. Then it follows that, while the king interpreted his administrative order, he got support from the Church. As long as the interpretation was accepted, the administrative order would be accepted. Thus the king might rule his kingdom smoothly. The king strengthened his authority substantially.

Second, an administrative order may be the one issued in the traditional society in which people disseminate the consciousness of superiority of the upper class. It is interpreted that a portion of people belong to the upper class while another portion of people belong to the lower class. Then it is likely for those who are inferior, namely, those from the lower class, to submit to the command issued by the one from the superior, namely, the one from the upper class. It follows that people maintain the social hierarchy that creates a condition for someone to issue, and for some other people to obey, administrative orders. For example, in the feudal society a noble was not encouraged to marry a woman from the family of common people. There was a hierarchy strictly kept by people, as mentioned earlier. People had the strong consciousness of social class. There was a demarcation between the different social classes of which the ruling class stressed its blood lineage. People were prevented from blurring this demarcation. If some people tried to blur such a demarcation, they might be punished. Social hierarchy was a foundation for the organization of the society or the state in which some issued commands while others obeyed them. So Léon Duguit writes that:

> Those who act in the name of the sovereign authority and express a sovereign will are set above the rest and act in regard to them by way of command, and by no other way. Those whom the sovereign addresses are bound to execute the order which he gives them, not because of what is in the order but because it comes to them from a will which is naturally superior to their own.[14]

So in ancient times the ruler might also justify his rule of the state by interpreting the blood lineage. He might rely on the tradition of hereditary kingship to rule his people. The related interpretation might be accepted as people might believe that a man within the ruling family was eligible to hold state power and hence to issue administrative orders. Conversely speaking, people might believe that that a man outside the ruling family took power was usurpation. Thus the legitimate ruler issued commands to ordinary people. So there is the "alliance" between the command and the interpretation of blood lineage. Needless to say, people may not easily be aware of the existence of this alliance. However, history sometimes shows that if the command loses the support of the related interpretation, the command may not be smoothly issued and carried out. The related social hierarchy may even collapse. One case in point is that this alliance collapsed when the ruler summoned common people to attend the meeting of the parliament. For example, in eighteenth century the king of France decided to open the parliament because of the necessity of seeking fiscal support from various social classes. This act weakened the authority based on blood lineage because ordinary people were enabled to have a say in the parliament. In addition, according to Bertrand de Jouvenel, the nobility of birth surrounded the king and acted as a screen which prevented the rise of the plebeian servants who had so ably served his ancestors. But as Louis XIV had strictly excluded the nobles from every political office, this crowd of courtiers started to wage a continuous war against the king's ministers. The result was that the monarchical government no longer offered that stability.[15] We can interpret this case as follows: Once the interpretation of blood lineage discontinued functioning in support of the command issued by the king, the state fell in turmoil. The king's rule did not last long after these events.

Third, an administrative order may be the one issued with an interpretation given to advocate a progressive idea such as a democratic idea or a liberal idea. That is, since early modern times liberalism has been prevalent in Europe and North America. Democracy has been established in many states. Election has been held. If democracy is not established in some states, people have been at least mobilized in those states. Then the power holder of the state, taking power through an election or getting support from the citizens, issues commands to ordinary people. As this way of holding power is justified by the theory of democracy or liberty, or as the power holder is supported by the masses, the power holder is enabled to issue commands to the citizens almost without any resistance. For example, after the American Revolution, the United States of America was founded. Since the founding of the United States, power holders have governed this country in the name of liberty and democracy. The power of the power holder is substantially consolidated due to the interpretations of liberty and democracy. The administrative orders are issued by the government armed with the interpretations of liberty and democracy. The administrative orders are issued because of the consent of the people. And we also see that since the beginning of modern times some states have become those in which the government is formed in the principle of single-party system. The ruling party claims to rule the state by interpreting their cause as a just one. They explain that they issue administrative orders because they carry out the proletariat dictatorship theorized by Karl Marx. Their rule is also consolidated.

Fourth, an administrative order may be the one issued by the authorities that gain the ruling legitimacy due to the spread of a nationalist idea. Along with the growth of a nation, people build a nation-state. A nation-state is usually a large state. The administrative orders, issued for the governance of the state, have to be strengthened. Nationalism proves to be a powerful idea that bolsters the administrative orders in the governance of the nation-state. This situation first occurred in France in early modern times though in France the power holder might also issue commands on other grounds, as noted just earlier. Specifically, when the Legislative Assembly had plunged France into a military operation which the monarchy would never have risked, it soon appeared that her power resources were insufficient for opposing the rest of Europe, and it became necessary to require the almost total participation of her people in the war. This was an unprecedented demand. In whose name to make it? It must be in the name of the nation. Patriotism arose quickly, leading to the enhancement of the power of the authorities.[16] This is because as nationalism was widely embraced by the Frenchmen and Frenchwomen, it became easy for the Legislative Assembly to issue commands. The administrative branch of the government also found it easy to issue administrative orders throughout France. The growth of nationalism also created a strong nationalist discourse in some other countries such as Germany and Italy later.

In those states the authorities issued administrative orders which were more effective than ever due to an interpretation in relation to nationalism.

This means that the authorities give an interpretation in support of their command, and the authorities, giving that interpretation, form a government. The command, issued by that government, also becomes an administrative order. The government may not use much coercion to carry out the administrative orders because people may voluntarily obey the administrative orders. One case in point is that an illegitimate government has to use much coercion to carry out its administrative orders while a legitimate government may not need to do so due to the fact that the interpretation, given by the illegitimate government, is not so convincing while the interpretation given by a legitimate government is convincing.

This means that if an interpretation is accepted by the masses, the common interest of all or the majority is largely formed. In this case, the people of the state may voluntarily accept and obey the commands though commands are enforceable in nature. If commands are issued by the ruler of the state in which the common interest of the community is not formed, they may be disobeyed by people. People's willingness of obeying commands constitutes a pre-condition for the power holder to issue commands successfully all the time as no command but the command satisfying this pre-condition will be comfortably obeyed by people. Thus the power holder does not simply resort to overwhelming force to make people obey his commands. He fully realizes the importance of the legitimacy of the regime. He takes advantage of the legitimacy of the regime to issue and carry out commands.

Sometimes in a state the hereditary rule of a person or a family used to be legitimate. In this case people only accepted the rule of a family. The consciousness of regarding blood relationship as the source of ruling legitimacy made the people recognize and accept the next generation of a ruler such as a king or a royal family to continue the rule of the preceding generation. Any act not in line with this practice would be regarded as an act of usurpation of power and more or less resisted by them. In a state the charisma of a person may also help him win the support of the masses so as to help him gain the leadership in a state. As a man is admired, exalted, supported and followed by the people of the state, he is able to issue and carry out commands successfully. Any one who opposes the charismatic leader will be blamed or opposed by the masses. In the history of human society, this phenomenon recurs many times in the slave-owning system state, the feudalist state, and the capitalist state. In a state, in which an ideology, or a religion, or a theory, or a thought is considered generally a sacred, correct, just and all-powerful guiding principle, any leader who claims to represent and carries out the same may gain support from plenty of people. Conversely speaking, a person in power who fails to cater to this mass consciousness may be resisted as he is regarded as being illegitimate. In a state, in which tradition is steadfastly adhered to by people such as the tradition inherited by people from their ancestors, the person in power, issuing commands in line with tradition, is supported and recognized by the people. In this case the person in power dare not issue administrative orders which violate the tradition because doing so may lead to self-destruction unless the state is in the process of transformation in which new ideas are accepted by the people and the original tradition is not regarded as being legitimate anymore. In a state in which the constitution defines the procedure through which a person can lawfully be appointed as the state leader, a person who appoints himself as the state leader without going through that procedure will be construed as illegitimate. Thus any power holder, appointed in accordance with the constitutional procedure, will be accepted by the citizens. Likewise, in a state in which election is regarded as a necessary path for a person to take power legitimately, any person in power who takes power without being elected may be challenged by some people. In this case only the person in power who is elected can be accepted by the people. His administrative orders are likely to be obeyed by the people.

If, in a state formed this way, the power holder finds that he can motivate the people to obey his rule not only by increasing the pressure of enforcement but also issuing administrative orders in the way accepted by the people, he will take some measures to enhance the effectiveness of the commands. He needs legitimacy. Even though he uses force in governing the state, he still needs it. A power holder without legitimacy may even be forced to seek cooperation from a titular power holder. We can find a few cases in history indicating that sometimes a man holds state power, but he lacks ruling legitimacy. He then uses a titular ruler. The legitimacy had by the titular ruler can be used by him to enhance the effectiveness of commands. This situation has recurred since ancient times. For example, Emperor Xian of Han (181-234) was the last emperor of the Eastern Han Dynasty in China. He used to be a puppet ruler under the control of the warlord Cao Cao. The latter used Emperor Xian to bolster his legitimacy when he eliminated rival warlords in his move to reunify the Han Empire. I believe that scholars can also find some other cases concerning the titular ruler in history in the West. Sometimes a man is a titular ruler and sometimes a man is a ruler in actuality. Legitimacy is used by the one who has legitimacy, but a man who does not have legitimacy may also use the legitimacy had by another man. This situation remains unchanged in modern times. Prior to, or during, World War Two, some countries invaded some other countries. There was such a case: The occupation army met with strenuous resistance. In order to weaken the resistance from the native people, the occupation army installed a puppet regime so as to help the invader rule the invaded country. There are two related cases in point. The first one is that in the years before and during World War Two, Aisin-Gioro Puyi, the deposed Emperor of China, became the puppet emperor of Manchuguo, a client state of the Empire of Japan on the Mainland China, in 1934. The second one is that following Japan's invasion of a larger area of China, some political figures surrendered and formed a national government headed by Wang Jingwei under the control of the Japanese occupation army in 1940. In the West, we also find some other similar cases. One case is the operation of the Vichy Regime of France, formed in the same year, headed by Henri Philip Pétain and supported by the occupation army of Nazi Germany. That the ruler uses a puppet to rule an occupied country is a political phenomenon which indicates that the ultimate ruler, devoid of legitimacy, is forced to use a puppet in communication with the native people. Though a puppet has to obey the commands of the actor actually holding power or actual ruler and failure to do so will result in punishment, it is still believed that the rule by way of a puppet is different from the direct rule of the actual ruler because a puppet is after all needed. The administrative orders are needed to be issued by a puppet regime. A puppet itself indicates that an actor is needed to act as a representative in line with the orthodoxy of the native people to the effect that the native people maintain the symbolic sovereignty. The actor, actually holding power, or the actual ruler, is, after all, unable to come forward naked to rule the occupied country. The ruler needs to put on a legitimate gown.

In a state, people may disagree on what kind of a ruler is legitimate for the ruling of the state. If a state is involved in a revolution, some people may be in favor of the revolution while others may be against it. People against the revolution may insist that the old regime is legitimate while those in support of the revolution may hold the opposite view. However, in a state involved in gradual transformation, the ruler may use different legitimacy resources to gain the support of more people and to enhance the effectiveness of the administrative orders even these legitimacy resources are repugnant to each other or in mutual conflict. The United Kingdom switched itself from a feudal kingdom under the despotic rule of the royal family to a democratic country in history. But the United Kingdom still preserves the legitimacy resources of the hereditary ruling power. Many British citizens hope that the king or the queen continues to hold the position of the head of the state. The constitution of the United Kingdom stipulates that many powers belong to the king. In fact, the power of the king means nothing in respect of the actual operation of power because many powers that nominally belong to the king are actually exercised by the prime minister. So the regime in the United Kingdom maintains at least two different ruling legitimacy resources. One is given by the voters who directly elect the members of the Parliament and indirectly elect the prime minister who leads the government and the other is given by the king. The constitution of the United Kingdom stipulates that many ruling powers, including the power of appointing and dismissing the prime minister, belong to the king, but in practice the principle of democracy prevails in the governance of the state. The United Kingdom thus becomes a typical state in which there is a constitution but the provisions of the constitution are not totally and strictly complied with in this respect and the government's refusal to comply with certain provisions of the constitution is accepted. This may give, to the maximum extent, effect to the administrative orders issued by the authorities because two legitimacy resources may help gain support from more citizens. Another case is in relation to China. In China, the academic community has been discussing the issue of the rule of law. The leadership of the Communist Party of China in power is sometimes in conflict with the authority of the constitution in its governance of the state. Some scholars propose that the party in power should also comply with the constitution. In a state under the rule of law this situation will not occur. However, in the country in which the ruling party maintains its supremacy in the course of the governance because of its ideology, this becomes a controversial issue because there are also at least two legitimacy resources of administrative orders. One legitimacy resource is the constitution and laws and the other is the leadership of the party in power defined by the communist dogma. Relinquishing any one will result in the opposition from part of the people. Thus China has become another typical state in which there is a constitution but its certain provisions are not strictly complied with and the ruling party's refusal to comply with it is sometimes accepted or tacitly permitted though China totally differs from the United Kingdom in the respect of the political system. In comparison with the above-mentioned two nation-states, the legitimacy of the authorities or the regime in the United States is totally based on the constitution and the election process authorized by the constitution. The United States has experienced neither the process of the transition from feudalism to capitalism nor any communist revolution. The constitution of the United States was composed without the influence of both the old regime and the communist revolution. In the United States the constitution and laws enjoy supremacy and political parties must comply with the constitution and laws absolutely. The United States demonstrates another kind of system in which human behavior is controlled by administrative orders totally in line with law. Thus it follows that in the states practicing constitutional monarchy such as the United Kingdom or the states ruled by only one party such as the People's Republic of China, the said two kinds of legitimacy resources co-exist, reflecting a historic compromise while in the United States the constitution and laws prevail in every respect.

The power holder may issue administrative orders in his own interest or totally in the interest of the state. But the objective result of this action is always coordination among all. In some cases the person in power issues administrative orders completely in the interest of the state. He may reach this goal either by putting the external pressure of enforcement on the people or by taking advantage of the influence of the legitimacy enjoyed by him to urge the people to obey his administrative orders. In case his leadership is devoid of legitimacy and some other people do not accept his leadership for some reasons, he has to increase the external pressure to force the people to obey his administrative orders. Sometimes he has enough legitimacy and therefore he can have the people of the state obey his administrative orders voluntarily. Thus he seldom forces them to obey his administrative orders. That being said, the effectiveness of administrative orders always stands in the middle of the two ends of the spectrum. There are two extreme cases showing the relationship between the power holder and the masses. One case is that the ruler has a tool of enforcement without legitimacy. He rules the state with naked violence. His commands are simply the signal of possible use of force in future. There is no common interest of the state. The people of the state obey the commands totally because of necessity. Another case is that he is regarded as being legitimate but he does not have any tool of enforcement. His administrative orders are regarded by the people as totally reasonable and natural. Commands in this case become instructions. An instruction is actually a command without any pressure, and it is a phenomenon of linguistic communication that gives an interpretation and conveys information at the same time. An instruction only indicates what needs to be done. Apart from this assumed case, the real situation stands in a certain place right or left to the middle or in the middle between these two polar ends. However, some states heavily rely on the tool of enforcement to implement administrative orders while others often rely on legitimacy to issue administrative orders. In history the rise and fall of a regime may reflect a process in which the power holder grasps the tool of enforcement at the beginning and loses it in the end, but it is the process without exception in which the power holder gains some legitimacy in the beginning and loses it in the end. So whether or not commands are effective over the long term lies in whether or not they are in line with the interest of the people forming the state and hence accepted by the people of the state. Without legitimacy, power becomes naked.

Russell writes that:

> Power is naked when its subjects respect it solely because it is power, and not for any other reason. Thus a form of power which has been traditional becomes naked as soon as the tradition ceases to be accepted. It follows that periods of free thought and vigorous criticism tend to develop into

periods of naked power. So it was in Greece, and so it was in Renaissance Italy.[17]

The power, mentioned by Russell, can be regarded as the ability to issue administrative orders. If a power becomes traditional, the regime is able to issue administrative orders effectively. Conversely speaking, if a power is no longer traditional, the regime is no longer able to issue administrative orders effectively.

On the other hand, if the government improves its work, the improvement of the work may also be interpreted to legitimize the administrative orders issued by the power holder. Even in pre-modern times such a situation might also occur. One case in point is that if common people got the enough food and good houses, they would have no reason to oppose the king. So in medieval times even the king of the state in Europe had to take care of the good of the subjects if he wanted to be widely supported by common people. As Jouvenel writes,

> The monarch is not in the least the creature of his people, set up to satisfy their wants. He is rather a parasitic and dominating growth which has detached itself from the dominating group of parasitic conquerors. But the need to establish his authority, to maintain it and keep it supplied, binds him to a course of conduct which profits the vast majority of his subjects.[18]

Then his service might be utilized to persuade common people to submit to his commands. He might be able to issue administrative orders. The political system might also become traditional.

In modern times the increase of public services, given to the citizens to the satisfaction of all, is also a basis for the government to keep its ruling legitimacy as an interpretation can work in support of the administrative order. This means that providing what is needed by the citizens will be helpful to the interpretation given in support of the administrative orders issued by the government. The effectiveness of the administrative orders issued by the government not only depends on the strength of coercion but also depends on the power of an interpretation. Providing good public services will augment the power of the said interpretation and hence enhance the legitimacy of an administrative order. For example, capitalism used to lead to the polarization of the society in Western Europe in the nineteenth century. The poverty of the working population used to weaken the effectiveness of the administrative orders issued by the government. Workers' movement figured prominently often in defiance of the authority of the government. Then various measures, taken to increase the social welfare designed to narrow the gap of income between the upper social class and the lower social class, alleviated the contradiction of the society and bolstered the authority of the government. The threat, posed by the class struggle to the government, was eliminated or eschewed. The government again enhanced its ability to issue administrative orders throughout the state.

3. Law Based on Common Interest

While we insist that people are more likely to obey the command issued with an interpretation rather than a naked command, we suppose that people's obedience to the command, issued with an interpretation, depends on the acceptability of the interpretation. Yet sometimes an interpretation, given in support of a certain command, may not always be accepted by all. For example, if a command is issued, people may give different interpretations. If different interpretations are given at the same time, the interpretation, given in support of the command, may not be so effective. In other words, if different interpretations are given at the same time, a certain interpretation may challenge the legitimacy of the command. Thus if a command needs to be absolutely effective and absolutely acceptable, people may need another kind of support. This situation lies in the structure of the state that takes form after the dissolution of the tribes. Specifically, before the dissolution of the tribe, the only interest, had by tribal people in the tribe, was the common interest of the tribe because every one was merely connected with all others by kinship. Since the formation of the state, people have gradually had their own interest such as the personal interest or the family interest called private interest though they still have their common interest called the public interest of the state. The interest of the state is divided because of the juxtaposition of the private and public interest. There appears the dichotomy between the private interest, mainly, the personal interest, or the family interest, or even the group interest and the public interest, mainly, the interest of the community, the society and the state. Though we insist that a power holder should issue commands acceptable by all due to the formation of the common interest of all and hence he must do so in a certain name accepted by all, or the majority, we also behold that a power holder, issuing commands, such as administrative orders, may be involved in a conflict of interest. As such, even though the power holder may interpret his rule in an attempt to gain the legitimate right to rule the state, his rule may not be always totally in line with the interest of all within the state. This is mainly because since extending the distance of linguistic communication pushed forward the formation of the state, people have witnessed that a person actually forms dual personality if he becomes the power holder of the state. To put it another way, a power holder of the state may seek the personal interest by using the state power or a power holder may seek the interest of a social group or a social class he belongs to by using the state power. Specifically, he may seek the interest of his family or the interest of the social group he represents when he is in power. He may seek the interest of the political party he serves when he is supposed to work in the interest of all the citizens on his post as the president of the state or the prime minister of the cabinet government. That is, there is the conflict of interest. Then a law, made in this respect, is significant.

That means that a law is made amid the situation that a power holder is potentially involved in the conflict of interest. If a power holder were not likely to be involved in the conflict of interest humans would not make any law in this regard. If some people issue commands, they issue commands for the organization of the community, particularly for the organization of the state. Sometimes they keep such commands effective over the long term, and the commands, effective over the long term, may prevent the power holder from being involved in the conflict of interest. This is because where there is a conflict of interest involving the power holder in the organization of the state, the state is organized according to the principle of organizing the society. In the organization of the society, the organizer of the society seeks his own interest, including his family interest or the narrow interest of the social group he represents. But in the organization of the state, the power holder should be prevented from being involved in the conflict of interest.

This is because the state is formed by all the citizens while the society may be formed by a portion of the citizens. This means that in the formation of a society, the process of linguistic communication that issues a command may be short. By contrast, in the formation of the state, the process of linguistic communication that issues a command is long. Thus a law is made. A law is applied time and again. As it is applied time and again, it should be the same over time. As the same command is applied time and again, it becomes the eternal principle. It is difficult for it to be especially used by a special person for a temporary purpose. In the meantime, it is like a public product used by many due to the fact that the state is a large community while the society may be a small one. In other words, to guard against the appearance of the conflict of interest in the organization of a community, the organization of the community must be in the interest of all forming the community. This means that a law, promulgated by the state, must be promulgated to all. Thus the distance of linguistic communication, performed to promulgate the law, must be extended. The extension of the distance of linguistic communication that promulgates this law highlights the generality of the command. It is usually issued by the sovereign. Then because of this, we find that if a command becomes general throughout the state, it is usually a law. Jeremy Bentham writes that:

> [W]here the sovereignty is in a single person and the party who is looked upon as principally affected by it is an individual, neither the word *law* nor any conjugate of it seems, in common speech at least, to be employed. When the King of France orders a man to quit the metropolis, or sends him to the Bastille, the power he exercises is not spoken of as a legislative power, nor the act he performs as an act of legislation. *Lettres de cachet* are not ordinarily termed laws. They are termed *ordres souverains*, sovereign orders, or by some such name.[19]

In other words, if the command issued is a law, it must be effective for a long time and issued to all at the same time. A law runs over the long term and on a large scale. A command, issued by the sovereign to an individual person only no matter whether this command authorizes this individual person to commit an act or prohibits him from committing an act, is not a law because this command runs in the short run and may run on a small scale only. In some sense, a law is a command that is issued to all without any different treatments given to anyone because it is effective for a long time and general. A law must be issued in the process of long-distance linguistic communication.

Because of this, the application of law stands aloof from the conflict of interest. For example, politicians, involved in politics, may be involved in the conflict of interest because politicians often seek the interest of a certain political party. Politicians, seeking the interest of a certain political party, may be involved in the conflict of interest. If they become the power holders, they serve the interest of all the citizens and the interest of their own political party concurrently. Thus when a law is applied, the application of this law is understood by all as a reasonable command. This law is made for the purpose of keeping the order of the state or for the purpose of organizing the state. This law does not seek the interest of any individual person or a portion of people. If a law also compels people to obey its will, its purpose is to maintain the public order in support of the organization of the state. But if politicians compete against each other, they may seek the interest of their own political parties. Politicians in power may make a policy in line with their own idea and politicians out of power may oppose this policy because they hold a different idea. But the law is not supposed to be used by politicians to seek their own interest. Law is used by all instead of being used by a special group of people.

As law is applied time and again, the process of linguistic communication involved by law is long indeed. In the meantime, law is issued on a large scale and it functions across the state. As a result, as law is also a long process of linguistic communication performed by the lawmaker with the citizens, the lawmaker may never meet the citizens. The lawmaker may be a man who has died. This means that law is a command that functions over the long term. For example, the constitution of the United States was made more than two hundred years ago. This constitution is still applied. As a result, the makers of this constitution have actually performed linguistic communication with American citizens for more than two hundred years. As each of the lawmakers may be a man who passed away many years ago, and as the law is not executed by each of the lawmakers in person, the lawmakers are usually not in the conflict of interest. It is impossible for the lawmakers to seek their own interest if they make the law. It is also impossible for them to seek the interest of the social group they may belong to because the social group they used to belong to means nothing to them after their death. So Montesquieu comments that "Law in general is human reason."[20] So Alexis de Tocqueville also comments that in America "a man never obeys another man, but justice, or the law."[21]

As the law is used over the long term and on a large scale covering the entire state, the value of such a command increases dramatically. Conversely, if a command is effective in the short run and on a small scale, its value is comparatively low. Then, in terms of a law as a command, we can believe that as the value of the law increases, people tend to spend a lot of time and resources on the formulation of a law. As a law, a command, can be effective over the long term and on a large scale, it becomes cost-effective for people to spend a lot of human resources, material resources and time formulating it. Besides, as a law is applicable over a long period of time and on a large scale, more specific circumstances of the governance of the state may need to be considered; more experiences may be needed; and more advices of experts may be required to draft the text of such a command. Thus, as I already mentioned in my previous book, when people make a law, which is a process of long-distance linguistic communication, the state may invite the first-class jurists of the society to give advices and may make some deep investigations in an attempt to make a very good law. In addition, the state may invite philosophers to give their opinions from the perspective of morality. The state may invite historians to give their opinions from the perspective of tradition and custom. The state may invite political scientists to give their opinions from the perspective of justice or fairness. Usually professionals tend to stand aloof from the conflict of interest in giving professional advices. Particularly, this law may be made by the legislature. The representatives of the electorate may have a say in the making of this law. Though many people are involved in this process, it is cost-effective and reasonable. The conflict of interest is basically prevented. Extending the distance of linguistic communication is the key. In other words, if the law were not a long process of linguistic communication, the command would invariably come under the influence of the conflict of interest.

Some philosophers hold that a law is a command. Hobbes writes that "the Law is a Command."[22] Bentham also believes that a law is a command. He writes that "Every primordial law that is efficient is a command."[23] He also insists that the language of law should be the language of command.[24] Their views are correct. The orientation of their speculation is correct. But if we suppose that a naked command, or a military command, or an administrative order, is also a command, their explanation does not suffice to explain the law quintessentially. It is not tenable to argue that a command is a law. A command may be a naked command, or a military command, or an administrative order. The law is a command issued and carried out in a long process in which the distance of linguistic communication that activates and boosts such a command is the key. A naked command, or a military command, may be in the process of short-distance linguistic communication. For example, a military command may be issued temporarily. A military command may be effective in one week or one month only. After the end of the combat, the military command may expire. An administrative order may be issued in the process of long-distance linguistic communication. It may be effective in one year or in a couple of years. Yet if the government that has issued it steps down, it may be revoked soon later. Bentham writes that:

> With equal propriety (according to the definition) would the word *law* be applicable to a temporary order issued by any magistrate who is spoken of as exercising thereby a branch of *executive* power, or as exercising the functions belonging to any department of *administration*. But the executive power is continually mentioned as distinct from the legislative; and the business of administration is as constantly opposed to that of legislation. Let the Board of Treasury order a sum of money to be paid or issued to such or such a person, let the Commander in chief order such or such a body of troops to march to such a place, let the Navy Board order such or such a ship to be fitted out, let the Board of Ordinance order such or such a train of artillery to be dispatched to such a destination—Who would ever speak of any of these orders as acts of legislative power, as acts of legislation?[25]

How do we interpret the situation mentioned by Bentham? My view is that a law is a command issued in the process of long-distance linguistic communication. It is effective over the long term. It may even be effective perpetually. It is invariably effective across the state. Thus a law, as a command, displays three particular characteristics.

The first characteristic is the clarity of the presentation of a command. If a command is issued in the short run and on a small scale, the process of linguistic communication that issues this command should be short. The command may be ambiguously and vaguely or roughly presented. This is because when this command is issued, the person who issues the command and the person who receives the command stay in touch in the short run and on a small scale. They may use other media to clarify the command. In addition, the background in which a command is issued may help people understand the command. However, in the application of a law, it is usually applied over the long term. It is usually applied across the state. It is applied on a large scale. As the distance of related linguistic communication is long, people can rely on no other media. Thus the description of the text of the law must be very explicit in order that the law is exactly presented and effectively applied over the long term and on a large scale. When making a comment on writing, Plato opined that the specific weakness of writing was that no one could come to the aid of the written word if it fell victim to misunderstanding, intentional or unintentional.[26] This interpretation also applies to law as law is often written. Of course, this interpretation does not apply to unwritten law. However, codified law is prevalent today. Thus people often debate the real meaning of a law in order to apply this law correctly. In the application of this law, people often make every effort to find out the real meaning of this law in the law court. The lawmaker intends to make an unambiguous law, so that people can apply this law effectively. There will also be a debate about the meaning of the law in order to understand the law clearly and accurately in the application of the law. Otherwise people cannot guarantee the correct application of the law.

The second characteristic is publicity. If a person issues a command in a process of long-distance linguistic communication, it is difficult or unlikely for such a command to be kept confidential. If people carry out a command in a process of long-distance linguistic communication, it is more likely to be known to all. Extending the process of linguistic communication increases the possibility of enabling all to have access to it. Thus, people, making a law, promulgate it in the public. By contrast, sometimes a person, issuing an administrative order, requires all others who carry it out to keep it confidential. If a military order is issued, it is normally kept confidential. If a law is made, it is officially promulgated to the public. In implementing a law, people usually announce the result of implementing such a law to the public. For example, sometimes a judge makes a judgment in the court to apply a law, and this judge announces the judgment to the public. By contrast, a person, carrying out an administrative order, may not always announce the result of carrying it out to the public. After a military order is carried out, such a military order may never be mentioned in the public. The result of the military action is mentioned only. There is usually no formal procedure of reporting the result of a military action to the citizens. It is usually reported by the news media. By contrast, the judgment, awarded by the law court, is usually formally announced to the public as required by a procedure. The public monitors the process of carrying out the law. If a judgment, made by the judge, is improper, the improperness of such a judgment may be soon known to the public. The public may criticize such a judgment. By contrast, if an administrative or military order is improper, this matter may not be known to the public particularly under the circumstances that citizens have no formal rights of being informed by the government of the public affairs of the state.

The third characteristic is finality. As the law is effective all the time and across the state, all other commands are supposed not to be effective all the time or across the state. Otherwise the authoritativeness of the law will be impaired. As the law is applied over the long term and across the state, the integrity of the state is especially guaranteed by the effectiveness of the law. For example, a discipline made by an organization, or a decree issued by a religious community, is a command. This command may be disobeyed. But disobedience may not affect the organization of the state. Such a command may be issued in the interest of a certain portion of people only. It cannot be excluded that such a command is issued under the condition that the interest of another portion of people is affected. Yet if a law is disobeyed, the integrity of the whole state will be affected. The reason is that a law, disobeyed by one, will be disobeyed by all. Thus the state makes every effort to implement that law. In applying a law, people consider the interest of the whole state. The interest of all forming the state is invariably considered. People achieve fairness in the organization of the state.

In other words, since the formation of the state, the state may be in external conflict with another state. This conflict, normally, does not affect the integrity of the state. Yet within the state the interest of everyone needs to be taken care of or to be protected. As the interest of everyone within the state should be, primarily, the protection of the right of property of all, or the fair distribution of the interest, or the avoidance of a conflict or war, this objective should be basically realized by way of law simply because law is the only tool used to hold the entire state together. When discussing law, Hans Kelsen regarded law as a coercive order. He believes that the prevalence of this coercive order ensures the organization of the state. In other words, the state is formed if every person of a community is prevented by law from infringing the interest of any other person or from using force on any other person. He writes that:

> If the validity of this coercive order is restricted to a certain territory and if it is effective within this territory in such a way that the validity of any other coercive order of this kind is excluded, then the coercive order may indeed be regarded as a legal order and the community constituted by it may be regarded as a "state"—even if its external activity is illegal according to positive international law. Thus, from the sixteenth to the beginning of the nineteenth century so-called pirate states existed along the northwest coast of Africa (Algiers, Tunis, Tripolis) whose ships preyed upon navigation in the Mediterranean. These communities were "pirates" only with respect to their exercise of force on ships of other states, in defiance of international law. Yet, their internal order presumably prohibited mutual employment of force, and this prohibition was by and large obeyed, so that the minimum of collective security existed which is the condition for the existence of a relatively lasting community constituted by a normative order.[27]

This is the guarantee of the basic interest of all within the community. A rule is obeyed as long as such a community exists. The state is organized in an analogous method. Otherwise the community will dissolve for the basic interest of each cannot be guaranteed. The basic guarantee of the interest of each leads to the formation of the common interest of all at least to a certain extent.

Thus, so far as a law is concerned, it is a command that ensures the formation of the common interest of all. Although a law is a command issued by someone to some other people, the law reflects and represents the interest of all forming the state. We sometimes say that the moral thought of humans is the mother of law. People come up with a moral idea in the civilized society. Morality is not the rule made by the authorities. A moral idea is accepted by people because it is fair. The reason that morality is fair is that people come up with the moral idea in a long process of linguistic communication. It cannot be created by an individual person. It does not reflect and represent the will of an individual person. It reflects and represents the will of all forming the community. It resembles a law in nature in a certain aspect. Morality is categorical imperative in Kantian term. A law is also, in some sense, a categorical imperative in the place where the rule of law is put into practice. Thus unlike a naked command, or a systematic command, a law is a command surely reflecting and representing the formation of the common interest of all just like the fact that morality reflects and represents the common interest of all. This is a general command particularly in the times of democracy. Thus a law acquires the full and absolute sovereignty. This is the rule of law. It is expected by all. Thus it reflects and represents the common interest of all and gains supremacy over other authorities under democracy. All, working for it, also gain a high status. Judges are in charge of carrying out law. The authority of judges derives certainly from the supremacy of law. In case that a judge and an administrator are in a conflict, the status of a judge is often higher than that of the administrator because the judgment of the judge must be binding on that administrator and such an administrator is supposed to be subject to the judgment of the judge unless people fail to build a state governed in the principle of the rule of law. This is because people believe that law represents the common interest of all while an administrative order may not. The code or constitution thus gains prominence and dignity because people are invariably under the influence of the spirit of laws. If the officials of the government take office, they are sometimes required to swear an oath of office. Swearing such an oath, they often stretch out their right hand and place their hand on the code or the constitution. They swear by the code or the constitution. They swear in the sight of law. They promise to perform their work in good faith in the sight of law. They imply that they will faithfully respect and carry out law. This is because law reflects and represents the common interest of the people. The common interest of the people determines the sacredness of law. The procedure of dealing with any matter in the organization of the state also becomes solemn if this procedure is of legal kind. The creditability of handling a matter in the organization of the state is enhanced due to the fact that people handle this matter in accordance with a legal procedure. Thus sometimes a political struggle, waged by politicians, is dealt with through a legal procedure. For example, we sometimes see that a politician is defeated in a political struggle. Then the authorities may accuse him of committing a crime against the interest of the state, or a crime of treason, in the law court. A legal decision is usually more authoritative than a political decision because law is often considered fair. This means that sometimes people use legal resources as political resources.

The authority of law becomes omnipresent as a result. Then we see that people have to guard against the conflict of interest in the exercise of power because sometimes some people seek the interest of a portion of the people rather than the interest of all, and whenever they highlight or bolster the supremacy of law, they enhance the justice of the state and facilitate the formation of the common interest of all. This can even simply mean that a law should be the longest process of linguistic communication among the processes of linguistic communication performed by all commands. Particularly, the process of linguistic communication performed by a law should be longer than the process of linguistic communication performed by an administrative order. So if a law is made in advance, the administrators will often be required to affirm their loyalty to the law prior to their appointments. People build the rule of law. So in England there has been the tradition of the rule of law. The common law has served the state since medieval times. The common law is unwritten. The common law is often older than the written law. Thus the tradition of the rule of law in England is stronger than that in the Continent in history. So Jouvenel writes that:

> Beyond all question, the supremacy of law should be the great and central theme of all political science. But, make no mistake about it, the necessary condition of this supremacy is the existence of a law older than the state, to which it is mentor. For if law is anything which Power elaborates, how can it ever be to it a hindrance, a guide, or a judge?[28]

Conversely speaking, shortening the process of linguistic communication performed by administrative order, people may buttress the authority of law because they can highlight the advantage of long-distance linguistic communication performed by law this way. So if we compare the political system of China with that of Japan, we can find that though the replacement of the governments in Japan is frequent due to the operation of parliamentary democracy, people bolster the spirit of the rule of law there just because of the frequent replacement of the governments. The frequent replacement of the governments in Japan can be construed as a sign indicating short-distance linguistic communication performed by each government to issue administrative orders. In contrast, the longevity of the Chinese government, organized by the Communist Party of China that has kept on ruling China for over sixty years, enfeebles or even jeopardizes the spirit of the rule of law though people usually believe that the stability of the government is conducive to the governance of the state. In other words, the Communist Party of China has been keeping on holding power for plenty of years in China, and it extends the process of linguistic communication performed by administrative order to reach the length of the process of linguistic communication performed by any law made by the ruling party itself. The eclipse of the process of linguistic communication performed by the law results unfortunately in the weakening of the spirit of the rule of law in China.

This also means that a law often exists before the formation of the government. People can deem this law as a promise. That is, after this law is made, all promise to obey it and the government promises to carry it out. The state is built on the basis of this promise. This means that this law, a long process of linguistic communication, is a practice obeyed by all over the long term. As it is a practice, everyone agrees to abide by it as if all have made an agreement to abide by it. All, forming the government, also have to abide by it. There must be a promise therein. As P.S. Atiyah writes,

Parliament passes laws in order to tell citizens how to behave in various respects; and that if the citizen complies with these instructions, and assumes that if he observes the law he will not be subject to penalties, it would be morally wrong for Parliament to punish him. If we think that that would be morally wrong, it is because we think that people are justified in relying on the law as from time to time enacted, and that such reliance should be protected. So Parliament may well come under a moral obligation to respect such reliance.[29]

This shows that a law contains a promise. If a promise is made and accepted, a contract is made. Making a contract, people see the formation of the common interest of all sides unless one side or more are forced to make that contract. So the nature of law tells us that all true laws are contracts. Making a law, people have enough time to display their attitude of supporting it or opposing it. The lawmakers and the citizens can communicate with each other. All understand what this law means. All can inspect this law. While analyzing the method of communication that publicizes a law, Bentham writes that:

The commands of a sovereign will like any other communications be liable to receive a tinge from the channel through which they are conveyed. The channel through which along the bulk of a sovereign's commands can be conveyed is that assemblage of conventional signs which taken collectively are called *language*. A legislator in uttering a law which shall be general must in as far as it is intended to be general make use of general terms or names. By these general terms or names, things and persons, acts, and so forth are brought to view in parcels; which parcels are the larger and the more comprehensive in proportion as the extent or logical amplitude (if so it may be called) of such names is the more considerable.[30]

Language used this way is for the purpose of making a public promise. If the legislature uses, in the making of a law, the terms that can be understood as easily as possible and can be understood by as many citizens as possible, it intends to make it public across the state. It intends to request the citizens to confirm that a law is made on behalf of them. That is, the law is a promise made by the citizens who promise to obey this law though the legislature makes this law on behalf of the citizens. Thus this promise is an agreement or a contract in which every citizen makes a promise to any other citizen and accepts the promise made by any other citizen. Everyone is obligated to give certain rights to all others and entitled to have certain rights given by all others. As Kelsen writes, " 'To be a person' or 'to have a legal personality' is identical with having legal obligations and subjective rights."[31] Under the circumstances that everyone acts under a certain law, his behavior is almost always the fulfillment certain obligations and enjoyment of certain rights. As everyone agrees to give certain rights to all others and gains certain rights given by all others, or as everyone fulfills certain obligations under the condition that all fulfill the same obligations, they make a contract. A contract of such a kind creates a condition for making and carrying out this law, and this law, intended to meet the interest of all parties to it, ensures the formation of the common interest of all.

This is not a process of linguistic communication that satisfies the interest of a portion of the people within the state only but the interest of the whole people within the state. Thus a law the citizens agree to abide by is a contract. A naked command is not a contract. A systemic imperative may not be a contract. But a law is always a contract under the condition that all agree to obey it in advance and the government agrees to carry it out in good faith. Long-distance linguistic communication is a key for us to understand the essence of law in this regard. Thus the study of the nature of language can shed light on understanding how language helps humans to make laws to build a perfect community for them. A law is a process of communication performed by humans by using language to organize their state in the principle of justice. A law is actually a special process of applying language to guard against the conflict of interest arising from the exercise of power in the building of the state because the state is a human community organized by using language.

Notes

1. See: Ferdinand de Saussure, *Courses in General Linguistics,* translated by Wade Baskin (New York: McGraw-Hill Book Company, 1966) 67;102–103.

2. Ferdinand de Saussure states that "A linguistic system is a series of differences of sound combined with a series of differences of ideas." See Ibid., 120; He also states that "Language is a system of interdependent terms in which the value of each term results solely from the simultaneous presence of the others." See Ibid.,114; He also adds that "Phonemes are characterized not, as one might think, by their own positive quality but simply by the fact that they are distinct." See Ibid.,119.

3. Please see: Robert C. North, "Research Pluralism and the International Elephant," *International Studies Quarterly*, 11(1967), 407, cited from Doris A. Graber, *Verbal Behavior and Politics* (Urbana: University of Illinois Press, 1976), 8.

4. See: Thomas Hobbes, *Leviathan,* with an introduction by C.B. Macpherson, (New York: Penguin Books, 1985), 223.

5. John Stuart Mill, *On Liberty, Representative Government and Utilitarianism*, (Chicago: Encyclopaedia Britannica, Inc., 1952), 339.

6. Plutarch, *The Lives of the Noble Grecians and Romans*, the Dryden Translation (Chicago: Encyclopaedia Britannica, Inc., 1952), 48.

7. Ibid., 480–481.

8. Ibid., 489.

9. Mill, *On Liberty, Representative Government and Utilitarianism*, 329.

10. Niccolò Machiavelli, *The Prince*, translated by W.K. Marriott (New York: Alfred A. Knopf, 1992), 66.

11. Peter M. Blau, *Exchange and Power in Social Life* (New York: John Wiley & Sons, Inc., 1964), 200.

12. Bertrand de Jouvenel, *Sovereignty: An Inquiry into the Political Good*, translated by J. F. Huntington (Chicago: The University of Chicago Press, 1957), 32.

13. Davd I. Kertzer, *Ritual, Politics, and Power* (New Haven: Yale University Press, 1988), 52.

14. Léon Duguit, Souveraineté et liberté (Paris: 1922), 78-79; cited from Bertrand de Jouvenel, *On Power: Its Nature and the History of Its Growth*, translated by J.F. Huntington (Boston: Beacon Press, 1967), 112.

15. De Jouvenel, *On Power: Its Nature and the History of Its Growth*, 223.

16. Ibid., 47.

17. Bertrand Russell, *Power* (W.W. Norton & Company, Inc, 1938),97.

18. De Jouvenel, *On Power: Its Nature and the History of Its Growth*,106.

19. Jeremy Bentham, *Of Laws in General*, edited by H. L. A. Hart (London: The Athlone Press, University of London, 1970), 6.

20. Charles de Secondat, Baron de Montesquieu, *The Spirit of Laws*, translated by Thomas Nugent (Chicago: Encyclopaedia Britannica, Inc., 1952), 3.

21. Alexis de Tocqueville, *Democracy in America*, translated by George Lawrence (New York: Harper Perennial, 1988), 95.

22. Thomas Hobbes, *Leviathan*, edited with an introduction by C.B Macpherson (New York: Penguin Books, 1985), 317; he also writes that "Law in generall, is not Counsell, but Command." See Ibid., 312.

23. Bentham, *Of Laws in General*, 58.

24. Ibid., 105.

25. Ibid., 4.

26. Plato, *Seventh Letter*, 341c, 344c, and Phaedrus, 275; cited from Hans-Georg Gadamer, *Truth and Method*, translated by Joel Weinsheimer and Donald G. Marshall (London: Continuum, 1975), 394.

27. Hans Kelsen, *Pure Theory of Law*, translated by Max Knight (Berkeley: University of California Press, 1967), 48.

28. De Jouvenel, *On Power: Its Nature and the History of Its Growth*, 302.

29. P.S. Atiyah, *Promises, Morals, and Law* (Oxford: Clarendon Press, 1981), 153.

30. Bentham, *Of Laws in General*, 82.

31. Kelsen, *Pure Theory of Law*, 172.

Part Three
Language and State Rationality

Introduction

While humans organize the state, the state requires the establishment of a positive relation between the power holder who controls the government on behalf of the state and the masses consisting of the multitude of people. The power holder of the state often uses coercion in the organization of the state. With coercion being used in the organization of the state, people cannot always guarantee that the power holder can rightly exercise power. The exercise of power may not be always rational. If the exercise of power is irrational, people may be oppressed by the power holder with coercion being used. Thinkers keep on designing the schemes of guarding against the oppression of the people by the power holder. Some of them even offer a variety of the schemes of utopia. They contribute plenty of the schemes of building an ideal state. In ancient times Plato contemplated the building of an ideal state. He speculated on the ideal state governed by a philosopher-king. Aristotle compared the forms of government. He identified some of the good government forms. He seemed to prefer aristocracy to democracy. To him, oligarchy was a bad form of government and tyranny the worst. In early modern times Hobbes, Locke and Rousseau imagined that the state should have been formed on the basis of a social contract. They asserted that the state should be the one organized on the basis of a social contract all entered into though their elaborations of that social contract might differ slightly from one another. Generally speaking, they held that the power holder was authorized by the people to govern the state and the power holder was obligated to be responsible to the people. Karl Marx, who insisted that the state was formed because of the rage of class struggle given rise to by the sharp contradictions between the social forces of production and the relations of production, designed a stateless community as the ideal one built following the end of the capitalist society because he believed that the state would wither away in future.

My view is that the state can be an ideal community formed by people. The state is formed by humans because of linguistic communication performed by them. The organization of the state can be rationalized. The state can be an ideal community built by humans. Rationality in organizing the state that we can imagine is the enhancement of the harmony between the power holder and the masses. People may not always be in chains. As the state is formed due to linguistic communication, performing linguistic communication must also be conducive to the enhancement of the harmony between the power holder and the masses. Specifically, thinkers conceive of the ideal state. Thinkers offer their schemes of organizing the state on behalf of all within the state. We can also view the relation between the power holder and the masses, or the relation between the governor and the governed, from the perspective of language because language is a being and the whole state is built because of the role played by language.

That is, the state is originally formed due to the use of language. The totality of the state relies on language. Language is the combination of the subjectivity and objectivity of humans. While language is applied to human communication, they create and utilize various media. With various media, humans perform linguistic communication of a certain structure. Such linguistic communication may become a language solution that rationalizes the state. If we believe that freedom, equality, peace, democracy and justice, sought by mankind in the great pageant of history, represent the rationality of the state, we can also postulate that the realization of freedom, equality, peace, democracy and justice relies on the adoption of various language solutions. Language helps humans realize freedom, equality, peace, democracy and justice and freedom, equality, peace, democracy and justice rationalize the state. Freedom, equality, peace, democracy and justice are actually the results of adopting various language solutions in the rationalization of the state. If we study freedom, equality, peace, democracy and justice, we may soon find out this truth. This is a secret of the progress of human civilization. It is time to uncover this secret. Please allow me to discuss freedom, equality, peace, democracy and justice one by one to elaborate my view as follows.

Chapter Ten

Freedom

1. Speech

I would like to discuss freedom first. Freedom is the opposite of the state in which humans are not free. If a human being is not free, his movement is impeded. If we assume that sometimes humans may be in a stateless society or in the state of anarchy, we may find that a person's movement may be really impeded in that case. That is, in that case freedom is only enjoyed by the one who is stronger. In other words, if the freedom of one is impeded by the other, the strength of one may overwhelm that of the other. Thus only the stronger one may have freedom. Under these circumstances the freedom had by humans is random, unpredictable and ungoverned. That is, people may have complete freedom, but they may also lose it. People may have freedom, but temporarily. Such freedom reflects the predominance of violence and the untamed natural impulse of humans. If people must interact with each other in order to form a society, such freedom is repugnant to the formation of the society. That is, random, unpredictable and ungoverned freedom is the one outside the normal mutual interaction between one person and another. If people enter the process of the related mutual interaction, such freedom vanishes immediately because such freedom of anyone will end immediately when he interacts with the other who also has such freedom. If people have such random, unpredictable and ungoverned freedom, they will feel pleasant indeed, but they usually soon feel displeased because it is very likely for one to be in conflict with the other. Thus, people, forming their society, yearn for freedom acceptable by all. This freedom is by no means random, unpredictable and ungoverned freedom. This freedom is first endorsed by morality in the society. For example, morality may require everyone to respect the freedom of every other person to act as they choose as long as their action is morally sound. Then, people form their society. As the society needs to be governed, people build their state. Then under these circumstances a law, made by the state, usually does not contradict morality. Morality needs support from law and law protects morality. Law and morality perform the same duty, but they function in different manners and in different domains. The result is that the freedom of people is ensured by both morality and law. Freedom is ensured by the alliance of morality and law. Thus, G. W. F. Hegel holds that to the ideal of freedom, morality and law "are indispensably requisite."[1] In the meantime, as morality is often protected by the law backed by coercion and the law is implemented by the government by using coercion when necessary in order that lawful freedom can be surely enjoyed by people, they are sometimes even required to cooperate with the law and the government. Thus, John Stuart Mill writes that "a people must be considered unfit for more than a limited and qualified freedom, who will not co-operate actively with the law and the public authorities in the repression of evil-doers."[2] Only under the guarantee of the government becomes the freedom had by people one of the right bases of the mutual interaction between one another. Then we see that as this freedom, had by people, is ensured by the government, it is recognized and respected by each other in their mutual interaction. Freedom becomes sustainable, civilized and wholesome. This means that after the end of the state of anarchy, the freedom of the individual person must be both approved and guaranteed by the government. If two people are in a conflict because the freedom of one side is impeded by the other, the stronger one may be just. If the stronger one is just, he may use his own strength to ensure justice. If two people are in the conflict and the weaker is just, justice must be ensured by the government. Suppose that there are two people in a conflict because the freedom of one is impeded, and the one who is weak is just, this one cannot realize justice because he is weak. He has no alternative but to repose his hope on the government. The government must be just in order that people have freedom acceptable by all others. Because of this, freedom, discussed by us here, should be the freedom ensured by the government.

In other words, without a government, any freedom enjoyed by one will be likely to be in conflict with the freedom of all others. Without a just government, any freedom, enjoyed by one, may not be real. As Hegel writes,

> The idea which people most commonly have of freedom is that it is arbitrariness—the mean, chosen by abstract reflection, between the will wholly determined by natural impulse, and the will free absolutely. If we hear it said that the definition of freedom is ability to do what we please, such an idea can only be taken to reveal an utter immaturity of thought, for it contains not even an inkling of the absolutely free will, of right, ethical life, and so forth. Reflection, the formal universality and unity of self-consciousness, is the will's abstract certainty of its freedom, but it is not yet the truth of freedom, because it has not yet got itself as its content and aim, and consequently the subjective side is still other than the objective.[3]

In other words, when we discuss freedom, we must ascertain what freedom denotes. Freedom in reality must be defined by people jointly in order that everyone enjoys freedom. People need to act in unison as an entity to define such freedom. An authority is needed to ensure that the freedom enjoyed by any individual person is the one agreed to by all other people. Freedom is not anarchy. Freedom in reality, or the objective, rather than subjective, freedom, must be ensured under the supervision of the government. The freedom we talk about here is freedom in reality. Thus I conclude that people are not free unless they submit to the authority of the state governed in the principle, or according to the scheme, formulated in the process in which they participate directly or indirectly. The method, adopted by them to participate in formulating the said principle or the scheme, is to make a speech. If a person, like any other person, is able to make freely a speech in order to express his opinion on how the state should be governed, his opinion is likely to be reflected in the process of formulating that principle or scheme in the governance of the state to a varying extent. People are unlikely to be free unless they are in a state in which the authorities protect the freedom of speech. Without a state protecting the freedom of speech, people are unlikely to be free. If people do not form the state, freedom cannot be guaranteed. If there is no state, freedom, enjoyed by a person because he is born free, may be in conflict with the freedom enjoyed by all others for the same reason. If the freedom, enjoyed by one, is encroached by the freedom enjoyed by the other, there will be no freedom for anyone because people are likely to be involved in a conflict and even in a war at anytime. In the state of conflict, though each enjoys his freedom because no one is supposed to restrict his freedom legitimately, such freedom is not sustainable. Such freedom is precarious, discontinuous, short-lived and violent. Such freedom is random, unpredictable and ungoverned. The conflict will result in the termination of the freedom of a certain side and the hegemony of the other side. This is the reason that people form the state. Then, as the state is built to prevent any conflict or war, the only way for people to seek their freedom is that they submit to the authority of the state governed in the principle, or according to the scheme, formulated in the process in which they participate directly or indirectly. In other words, if freedom is not defined by the authorities as agreed to by all, freedom is not real. The key is that the will of people should be known by the government. How can the will of people be known by the government? The will of people cannot be known by the government unless people can articulate their will. Thus, freedom is guaranteed by free articulation. Free articulation is just the freedom of speech.

Then the freedom of speech becomes crucial. This is because the only way for people to ensure that the state is organized in the principle, or according to the scheme, formulated in the process in which they participate directly or indirectly is that they enjoy the freedom of speech. This means that opinions, expressed by them freely in their speech, can be finally reflected in the process of formulating the principle or the scheme in the organization of the state. If some citizens keep on expressing their opinions, the government cannot ignore them. As those citizens can express their opinions freely, they are free. Conversely, if people do not enjoy the freedom of speech, it may not be likely for them to agree to the principle, or the scheme, formulated by others for the organization of the state. Thus they may not be free. In this sense, language is essential.

Specifically, freedom, enjoyed by people in the state, is in relation to the language used by them. This is precisely because people enjoy the freedom of speech by using language as their tool. Language is the totality they can technically depend on. The building of the state is contingent on the use of language, and language supports freedom enjoyed by people building the state. The freedom of speech is enjoyed by people using language. If people make a speech, they often express their views to the authorities. As all are able to express their views to the authorities, their views may be reflected in the policies or the laws made by the state. This is due to the balance of linguistic communication that goes on in the state. Language always supports balanced communication. By "balanced communication," I mean the linguistic communication through which each end of linguistic communication can take initiative to communicate with the other. Each end can function as both the sender of information and the receiver of information. Besides, using language is using a medium. Using a medium enables all to express their views. Language does not discriminate against anyone. We know that people advocate the freedom of speech. In doing so, they advocate the right used by all to speak. If the freedom of speech is not enjoyed by people in a state, this does not mean that all are unable to speak in the public. This situation only means that only a small portion of people have the right to speak in the public. People, advocating the freedom of speech, advocate that all have the right to speak in the public. The freedom of speech is significant of the fact that all are enabled to speak in the public. This means that anyone can speak in the public. Linguistic communication can be freely performed by one to present a view, or to express an opinion, to the other or to the authorities. Thus, it is possible for the interest of all to be considered by the authorities. Conversely, if all people are not allowed to speak in the public, reasonable opinions or views from the masses cannot be considered or accepted fully. If some people are disallowed to express their opinions or views, opinions or views cannot be compared with one another fully. Then reasonable opinions or views may not spread. Not all useful opinions or views can be drawn on as a result. Thus the state may not be organized according to the will of the people. Thus people may not be free. For example, sometimes we see in history that a state turns despotic and then people no longer enjoy the freedom of speech. Ordinary people are kept from expressing their opinions or views to the authorities. Opinions or views expressed to the authorities may be only those expressed by some influential social groups or the ruling class formed by the minority. Thus other people are often not free. For example, in a feudal state in medieval times opinions, expressed to the authorities, were more often the ones expressed by the nobles or clergymen because they kept close relationship with the power holder. In modern times mass media facilitate ordinary people to express their opinions to the authorities. Then the state tends to be democratic or at least tend to pay attention to public opinion. Another case in point is that in medieval times people held no regular election in European states. This does not mean that ordinary people did not express their opinions at all. Sometimes peasants revolted against the authorities. The revolts of the peasants might serve as a method of expressing an opinion to the authorities. But peasants seldom expressed their opinions. Normally, those who expressed opinions were nobles and clergymen. They expressed opinions different from those opinions expressed by the peasants. Thus peasants suffered under the feudal yoke. This situation has changed since voting rights were granted to ordinary citizens. Then election is regularly held in modern times. This is because election is, in some sense, a method used by ordinary people, forming the majority of the population, to express to the government their opinions about the affairs of the state. Similarly, if the state holds a referendum, all the citizens are invited to express to the authorities their opinions concerning an important affair of the state. If the state holds no referendum, a decision may be merely made by a few people holding the power of the state. They may reflect opinions from a small portion of people only. At least we cannot guarantee that they reflect opinions from the majority. Yet if the state holds a referendum, we can be sure that opinions from the majority can be known to the authorities. Perhaps opinions from the minority may also be known. Then the state can be governed in the principle, or according to the scheme, formulated by the people themselves or at least agreed to by them. Thus all are free though they submit to the governance of the state.

That means that the freedom of expressing an opinion belongs to all. That opinion is expressed freely. People may express different opinions. If there are the opinion of the majority and the opinion of the minority, these opinions take shape naturally. As noted earlier, there will be no majority without the minority. The opinion of the majority and the opinion of the minority appear in the free argument. People express different opinions simply because they need to give different opinions to display their inclinations. Some people give the opinion of the minority in order to assist other people in expressing the opinion of the majority. If certain opinions are deliberately suppressed and other opinions are deliberately allowed to be expressed, opinions, allowed to be expressed, tend to be the opinions of the authorities. These opinions are the ones of the minority because if the authorities intend to accept the opinions of the majority, it will often allow different opinions to compete against each other and the opinions of the majority will naturally prevail. So if the authorities adopt the opinions of the minority, theoretically speaking, the opinions of the minority must prevail due to the use of coercion. The freedom of speech is suppressed as a result. In this case, the opinion expressed by the citizens is always the opinion of the minority. The opinion of the majority and the opinion of the minority cannot coexist and the opinion of the majority is suppressed. If the opinion of the majority is suppressed, some cases often occur as follows. The first case is that the authorities may prevent those citizens, expressing their opinions against the authorities, from meeting the reporters of the mass media. The authorities may even detain those reporters. Consequently, their opinions are never known by the public. The second case is that the authorities may imprison those people. The authorities may even restrict their freedom permanently. The third case is that the authorities may prevent citizens from uniting in order to express their opinions against the government. For example, sometimes a mass demonstration is put down by the authorities. The fourth case is that public opinion is steered by the authorities. Though there is public opinion, this public opinion is the one relished by the authorities. The authorities suppress the public opinion that opposes them. In the meantime, their mouthpiece manipulates public opinion. The authorities actually permit no freedom of speech. The fifth case is that the authorities force the citizens to express the opinions of the authorities. The citizens are prevented from expressing their own independent opinions. For example, in some despotic states the delegates of the citizens are arranged for by the authorities to attend a mass rally to make a speech in support of the government. Those who oppose the government are not allowed to make a speech at that rally. If ordinary people hope to express their opinions, the authorities may use the tool of coercion of this kind or that kind to prevent them from expressing their own opinions. Ordinary people are even forced to express the opinions that are not their own. Linguistic communication is not performed in a balanced way. A speech is made to express the opinions of the minority only. In this case people often complain that they are not free. The state is governed in the principle, or according to a scheme, they do not agree to. Thus the state imposes its will on them. People may regard the governance of the state as oppression. Conversely, the freedom of speech means that all can express their opinions as a result of their own initiative. They are motivated by themselves to express their opinions.

All in all, the freedom of speech presupposes a system operated by language in the formation of a constructive interaction between the authorities and the citizens. Citizens are particularly allowed to speak in the public. The authorities are cooperative. They do not confront. Thus, the authorities are not the oppressors, and the citizens are not the insurgents. In this case people avoid a conflict between the citizens and the authorities. They build a system in which the citizens are particularly allowed to communicate. The result is that the authorities obey an invisible rule that allows for the citizens to express their opinions freely. Then we see the following circumstances.

First, people, enjoying the freedom of speech, often express different opinions. Since the principle of the freedom of speech requires that the freedom of speech be given to all, not a portion of people only, the opinions given by the citizens may be divided into the opinion of the majority and the opinion of the minority. Both the opinion of the majority and the opinion of the minority have their grounds. The authorities show the attitude of neutrality. The authorities do not suppress any opinion. The authorities do not give any support to any opinion in the public either. Conversely, if only a portion of people enjoy the freedom of speech, this is not the real meaning of the freedom of speech advocated by people. If people argue that whenever the opinion of the majority prevails, the voice of the minority should be silenced, the minority may also silence the voice of the majority whenever they are in power. As Mill warns,

> If all mankind minus one were of one opinion, and only one person were of the contrary opinion, mankind would be no more justified in silencing that one person, than he, if he had the power, would be justified in silencing mankind.[4]

This means that although sometimes an opinion is supported by the majority, this opinion may not absolutely correct or rational. Sometimes an opinion given by the minority is correct or rational. Although the society usually accepts the opinion of the majority as the legitimate one, the opinion of the minority may still be respected. At least, the authorities will not prohibit the minority from expressing their opinion. The authorities will not express their attitude on this issue. In this case, the authorities do not oppose any opinion expressed by the citizens. Then we find no reason to believe that the authorities support any side. Citizens will not enter into any conflict with the authorities. Each side will not prevail over the other side by using coercion. The freedom of speech tends to lead up to the diversification of the opinions and the authorities do not disagree thereto. That is, though the authorities may demonstrate their inclination in making their policies, they do not make any statement in support of any opinion expressed by the citizens and they do not argue with the citizens either. The government is not an ally of any opinion. It does not stand with any opinion expressed by a certain citizen in the public.

Second, since the citizens enjoy the freedom of speech, they often present their opinions. These opinions are often concerned with the management of public affairs or the governance of the state. While they express their opinions, they often put pressure on the authorities. Or even if they do not pressure the authorities, the society may pressure the authorities. The citizens, however, will not abuse language. They will present their constructive opinions using language because they, enjoying the freedom of speech, often present their opinions in the public. While they present their opinions in the public, their opinions have to meet the expectation from the public. The public will not support the opinion that advances the narrow interest of a small portion of people. As a result, the citizens, enjoying the freedom of speech, always put forward the constructive opinions. Then we see that if a person presents a petition, requesting the government to pay attention to the poverty of some people residing in a certain town and to grant subsidies to those townspeople, his petition may be reasonable. The government may accept his petition and decide to grant subsidies to those people because his petition meets the expectation from the public. Then, the related petition may actually function as a proposal for the management of a public affair.

That is, some constructive opinions can become the suggestions of public policies of the state because they are reasonable or valuable. In this case the related opinion is constructive. Any speech which is not constructive will not be protected by law. The speech that harms the public interest or the security of the state may be banned by law. The speech, intentionally made to slander an innocent person, may be prohibited by law. The speech, deliberately made and proved to be a rumor, may not be protected by law. The speech, made to humiliate or swear at an innocent person, may not be regarded as the speech to be protected by law. Some materials of pornography, regarded as a speech polluting public morals, are usually banned by law. As such, the freedom of speech usually encourages all constructive speeches. Making constructive speeches, people only put forward constructive opinions. They will become the proposals for the organization or governance of the state or the management of public affairs. Some of them may even become the policies of the government. In other words, while the government adopts the opinion of the citizens, the citizens will be free. As they are free, they are free to give their opinions.

Third, as long as the citizens enjoy the freedom of speech, any opinion expressed by the citizens will not pose a threat to the ruling status of the government because what the government does is usually identical with the opinions expressed by the citizens. Conversely, if the government is formed against public opinion, public opinion, given by people having the freedom of speech, must pose a threat to the authorities. This concerns the distribution of the interest within the state. Public opinion takes shape often because of the necessity of distributing interest fairly. This is often because the government, formed not on the basis of the support of public opinion, tends to implement a scheme of distributing the interest of the ruling class or the minority. Public opinion, given by people who have freedom of speech, tends to reflect the opinion of all the citizens or at least the majority and hence represents a call for the fair distribution of interest. The recognition of the freedom of speech actually leads to the formation of the government that pays attention to the fair distribution of the interest of all. Language allows all rather than a portion of people to speak. The freedom of speech guards against the tyranny of the authorities or the social tyranny. Then, guaranteeing the freedom of speech means that the government will no longer be oppressive. All are free.

The result is that as the citizens are allowed to advance their opinions freely, they will advance different opinions because they often have different views. The government will no longer ensure that only one opinion is expressed by the citizens. Then different opinions will compete. Reasonable, correct and valuable opinions will prevail through a discussion or a debate. As Mill argued, the best proposal will come from the discussion and debate that reinvigorate the views of people. The limit to the freedom of speech should be the point at which harm to the other is instigated. That is, according to Mill, "on every subject on which difference of opinion is possible, the truth depends on a balance to be struck between two sets of conflicting reasons."[5] Likewise, as Nigel Warburton interpreted, assuming that we possess the truth having gagged or avoided dissenting voices is very different from holding a view that has been contested openly and emerged unscathed or even strengthened. The process of subjecting a view to critical scrutiny is a necessary part of its validation.[6] In this case, an opinion upheld by people over the long term is also regularly challenged in order to prove that such an opinion is still valid or correct. Any act of suppressing a different opinion without a discussion or a debate will damage the interest of the public.

In sum, the freedom of speech means the freedom of speech for all. While the citizens enjoy the freedom of speech, all enjoy it no matter whether the opinion advanced by them is the one of the majority or that of the minority or no matter whether the opinion advanced by them is correct or incorrect. Even if a person presents an obviously incorrect opinion, he may also enjoy the freedom of speech because all know that if he is prevented from presenting his opinion by depriving him of his freedom of speech, the public may not know why he is wrong. He is then permitted to present his opinion and other people are also permitted to present their opinions so as to allow the public to compare these different opinions to the effect that the public gets to know why one opinion is wrong and why all other opinions are correct. Without a discussion or a debate, one cannot know whether an opinion is really incorrect or correct. When people have a dispute, all are allowed to express their own opinions freely. The authorities will not come forward to rule on this dispute. The authorities will not prohibit anyone from expressing his opinion in the public unless his opinion harms the other. All interact with all linguistically. No one is going to interact with any other one by using coercion. All opinions compete against each other freely. Though no one is going to guide or supervise the competition of different opinions, all opinions obey reason. Linguistic interaction is an essential guarantee for the prevalence of reason. No opinion obeys the command from the authorities. The reason is that if a citizen adheres to his freedom of speech and the authorities insist on using coercion, it is difficult for reason to take precedence. People, advocating the freedom of speech, concede that all sides enjoy the freedom of speech. If they are involved in a dispute or an argument, the exchange of words is subject to the ruling of reason. Reason is usually the idea or the principle all sides accept or embrace. Such an idea must be presented by someone or such a principle must be formulated by someone though we do not know who is such a person. If all sides agree to be subject to the judgment of reason, they agree to be subject to the ruling of a third party. When a dispute or an argument is ruled on by a third party, justice is realized just like the judgment made by a judge in court. A judge, making a judgment, fulfills his duty according to law. A law is often or usually made by the lawmaker who is absent. Reason is to that third party which rules on the arguments presented by those who argue because they enjoy the freedom of speech what law is to the judge who makes a judgment because he fulfills his duty. The freedom of speech means the realization of justice under the auspices of a third party. Without the ruling of a third party, the state will always be in the potential or actual state of injustice. As a result, it is tantamount to the fact that the authorities, suppressing the freedom of speech enjoyed by the citizens, refuse to be subject to the ruling of a third party, albeit an unseen one. The freedom of speech does not contradict the rule of law simply because both the freedom of speech and law mean the ruling of a third party. The freedom of speech is aimed at justice. So I argue that people have built a natural relationship between the freedom of speech and the rule of law. Wherever there is the freedom of speech in a state, there is the rule of law. Wherever there is the rule of law in a state, there is the freedom of speech. We never see a state in which the freedom of speech is given, but the rule of law is not established; or the rule of law is established, but the freedom of speech is not given. People, ensuring the freedom of speech, carry out the principle that any dispute among them is ruled on by a third party because reason can act as an unseen third party. When a case is heard by a judge, such a judge acts as a third party. When he acts as a third party to deliver a judgment, he also submits to reason. Thus the ruling, awarded by a third party, is actually the one awarded as required by reason. Thus the freedom of speech reflects human reason.

In other words, the freedom of speech allows for people to present a variety of different opinions on the governance of the state or the management of public affairs. The freedom of speech normally allows for all to communicate with all. Both the argument from the majority and the argument from the minority are allowed to be put forward. Even the argument from an individual person is also allowed to be put forward. As the government is prevented by the constitution from interfering with the arguments among different opinions, the opinion that prevails is usually embraced by the majority of the people and the people obey reason. Therefore, any argument put forward in a discussion or a debate is subject to the judgment of reason. Reason plays a part in the organization of the state as long as the freedom of speech is guaranteed. So if the government deprives a portion of the citizens of their freedom of speech, it acts to rule on any dispute without being subject to the judgment of reason. The freedom of speech allows for the competition of different opinions so as to allow for reason to play a role. While people insist on the freedom of speech, they actually struggle for the right to guide the formulation of a principle or the scheme in the organization of the state. In this regard, they are free if they succeed. Yet, in view of a role played by language, the freedom of speech means an approach of using language to present the proposals for the governance of the state or the management of public affairs, and people, enjoying the freedom of speech, rely on the strength of reason and insist on the supremacy of reason. Using coercion does not necessarily mean reason. By contract, using language always means reason. The freedom of speech proves this logic.

2. Thought

The state is built over the society. As people, forming the state, are the members of the society, the interaction between the society and the state is also characterized by the interaction between people on behalf of the society and the state. For example, people's freedom originates from the society, but it is essential for the state to respect and protect such freedom. This is because people's freedom needs support from the state. This freedom also includes the freedom of thought. The freedom of thought is also realized in linguistic communication. If human thought comes from the process of production, the governance of the society, the development of education, the activities of culture, the cultivation of morality and others in the society, people are free because they realize directly or indirectly every objective they desire without any impediment. The state ought to respect this kind of thought. The reason is that thought must be disseminated in the mutual interaction of people. People interact with each other in two ways. One way of interaction is linguistic communication. Another way of interaction is the use of coercion. Thought is spread in the process of linguistic communication. The use of coercion relies on physical force. But in an ultimate sense the use of coercion restricts human freedom, whereas language supports it. A person cannot use language to restrict the freedom of any other person in an ultimate sense. Therefore, people disseminate and propagate thought by using language and have freedom in contrast to the fact that people coerce each other by applying physical force and hence force themselves to give up freedom. Normally, one cannot coerce the other into embracing a thought. Each holds the inborn sovereignty of mind that cannot be alienated. This is because people are free to come up with their thoughts in their brains. External intervention finally fails. As a person's thought is his will, he cannot be coerced into accepting the will of another person unless he lets his will be coerced. As Hegel writes,

> As a living thing man may be coerced, i.e. his body or anything else external about him may be brought under the power of others; but the free will cannot be coerced at all, except in so far as it fails to withdraw itself out of the external object in which it is held fast, or rather out of its idea of that object. Only the will which allows itself to be coerced can in any way be coerced.[7]

As thought is a person's subjective will, this subjective will must be based on freedom. As this subjective will is actually a person's spirit, this spirit must also be based on freedom. As Hegel writes,

> All will readily assent to the doctrine that spirit, among other properties, is also endowed with freedom; but philosophy teaches that all the qualities of spirit exist only through freedom; that all are but means for attaining freedom; that all seek and produce this and this alone. It is a result of speculative philosophy, that freedom is the sole truth of spirit.[8]

To put it differently, if we look at the nature of thought or the nature of spirit, the continuity of thought in another form, we can find that, at least, thought itself spreads from one to the other whenever and wherever a person interacts with another person and no one is able to keep people from developing their own thoughts in their brains or embracing the thoughts from others that they think fit. Mentioning the freedom of thought, we actually consider it the freedom of spreading thought. People, discussing any subject matter freely, can realize the freedom of thought in a certain form. As early as the times of ancient Greece, Socrates, a sage, already vindicated the freedom of discussion in seeking truth.[9] I mean that the freedom of discussion can be regarded as a form of the freedom of thought because people, discussing any subject matter, exchange thoughts. In the meantime we see that whenever people discuss a subject matter, thought, like water, flows in a process of linguistic communication. People, building their community in which all can cooperate with all in production, are in a situation that creates a condition for their own preservation. They must have certain impressions given by the related objective environment. They must master certain common sense. They must create certain knowledge. Then they must come up with certain ideas. These ideas may develop into thoughts. Then people may share certain thoughts because they can use language at any time to spread a thought. Not all thoughts may be shared, of course. But certain thoughts must be shared precisely because people tend to embrace proactively thoughts in the process of linguistic communication. People are the animals of thinking. The competence of thinking varies from one to another. The competence of thinking of certain people cannot be completely used up by themselves. There may be some surplus competence of thinking among people. As people communicate by using language and some of them disseminate their thoughts, others may utilize such surplus competence of thinking later. Such surplus competence of thinking is a medium in support of linguistic communication.

People communicate because they need thought. A person's thought may then become the thought of the masses. The thought of the masses is usually very powerful. People build up the strength of the collective being in the domain of the subjective world of mankind. Describing the strength of the collective being, Aristotle writes that:

> For the many, each of whom is not a serious man, nevertheless could, when they have come together, be better than those few best—not, indeed, individually but as a whole, just as meals furnished collectively are better than meals furnished at one person's expense. For each of them, though many, could have a part of virtue and prudence, and just as they could, when joined together in a multitude, become one human being with many feet, hands, and senses, so also could they become one in character and thought. That is why the many are better judges of the works of music and the [poetry], for one of them judges one part and another another and all of them the whole.[10]

This argument should more or less point out the superiority of a collective being in the process of judgment. Judgment needs thought. The thought of the collective being takes shape in one or many processes of linguistic communication.

So I argue that people, using language, are free to communicate with each other. People, who are free to communicate with each other, are able to spread thoughts freely. Thoughts serve as a spiritual basis for them to build their society. Then they have a society designed and needed by them. If coercion is not used in this case, the society, built by them, is what they choose freely. Thus, they are free. Since people can communicate with one another using language, some thoughts are finally embraced by all or at least the majority. No one can use language to stop the process of linguistic communication that spreads thoughts. Whenever or wherever language is used by people, it tends to disseminate information. If a piece of information is a secret, it tends to be divulged to the public if no effort is made to keep it confidential. Therefore, thought is disseminated in linguistic communication. A thought attaches itself to linguistic communication. Thus, whenever or wherever a thought is offered by a person without any impediment, it will be embraced by many or even by all, provided that this thought is absolutely rational and applicable. People will judge if a certain thought is rational and applicable. If they consider that thought rational and applicable, they usually embrace, uphold and even propagate it. People are unable to impede the spread of a thought because in the civilized society people are the animals of reason and any thought may carry the power of reason. People, debating the correctness of a thought, show their reason. If different thoughts compete, the most reasonable thought will prevail as it is embraced, upheld and propagated. The only one method that can be used by people to stop or impede the dissemination of a thought is the use of coercion. Any thought that insists on the use of coercion to ban other different thoughts is usually not acceptable by all. As a result, we find that whenever or wherever a thought takes shape in the community, language, in the ultimate sense, always supports it. Thus, whenever or wherever the authorities, holding another thought, insist that coercion should be used to ban this thought, these authorities are usually unable to use language to suppress the spread of this thought. What can be used by the authorities under these circumstances is coercion. This tells us that, in some sense, whenever or wherever the authorities use coercion to stop the dissemination of a thought that insists on the free competition of thoughts on the market of ideas, this thought at least tends to be rational. This thought may also be applicable. This is because if this thought is irrational or is inapplicable, the authorities will be able to use a rational thought or an applicable thought to defeat it. That the authorities use coercion to stop the spread of this thought is indicative of the fact that the authorities, armed with no rational or applicable thought, are unable to defeat the related thought on the market of ideas. They have no choice but to adopt some other approaches. For example, in history the authorities of certain despotic states in Europe or Asia used to ban the publishing of, or even used to burn, certain books because those authorities deemed those books, spreading various thoughts, as a threat to their rule. In modern times the authorities of many despotic states are unable to impede effectively or thoroughly the spread of rational or applicable thoughts within the state. But they are sometimes able to use coercion to stop the application of those rational and applicable thoughts though those rational and applicable thoughts have been spread. For example, in the former Soviet Union the idea of democracy that originated from the West was spread at least in the academic circle, but democracy could not be immediately established because the authorities announced that they would not put into practice the democracy of Western model and the authorities used coercion to keep their despotic rule characterized by one single-party system. The authorities were largely unable to refute the idea of democracy by using language in the ultimate sense because the people of the Soviet Union were likely to embrace the idea of democracy. What could be used by them was, in the ultimate sense, coercion. On the other hand, the authorities usually propagated a thought gradually regarded by people as irrational or inapplicable. The authorities were unable to protect this thought without using coercion. So in history thinkers, advocating the freedom of thought, called on the authorities not to use coercion to suppress the competition of different thoughts. They believed that the competition of different thoughts would enable the society to embrace a correct one. The society would advance on a correct track. Likewise, I also argue that if people propagate freely a thought by using language across the society, different thoughts will compete against each other and a rational and applicable thought will prevail over other irrational and inapplicable thoughts. If some people propagate a thought, other people should be allowed to refute it by using another different thought. Then people will single out and embrace the rational and applicable thought. The rational and applicable thought will prevail. So, describing his idea about liberty, Mill writes that:

> There is the greatest difference between presuming an opinion to be true, because, with every opportunity for contesting it, it has not been refuted, and assuming its truth for the purpose of not permitting its refutation. Complete liberty of contradicting and disproving our opinion is the very condition which justifies us in assuming its truth for purposes of action; and on no other terms can a being with human faculties have any rational assurance of being right.[11]

This case should also apply to thoughts. If the authorities protect linguistic communication performed freely to let different thoughts compete, a rational and applicable thought will prevail. It is possible for the prevalence of a rational and applicable thought to be reflected in the process of building a society. As such, it is possible for people to be free in the society built by them.

This situation mentioned above actually confirms again that thought represents a force and power represents another one. The way thinkers think differs from the way coercion is used in the organization of the state. When thinkers think, they obey logic, or reason, or follow their intellect. As Mill writes, "No one can be a great thinker who does not recognize, that as a thinker it is his first duty to follow his intellect to whatever conclusions it may lead."[12] The logic, or reason, or their intellect is usually used for the public good because thinkers cannot use the logic, or reason, or their intellect, for their own good only. Thinkers will not be thinkers if they do not work for the public good. In contrast, the way the government organizes the state by using coercion is different. Coercion relies on physical strength. Physical strength cannot judge whether or not an act is reasonable. In the meantime, we find that thought is supported by language while power is supported by coercion. Sometimes a thought is protected by power. Sometimes power comes under the influence of a thought. Thought and power can cooperate with each other. However, thought cannot replace power, and power cannot replace thought. If a thought does not support power or power refuses to be left under the influence of the thought, the thought may become a weapon used by people in their struggle for freedom while power cannot be used to get freedom for people, supposing that power is merely used for the operation of the government in its governance of the state. This is precisely because thought is usually embraced by people on voluntary basis while power can impose its own will on people. Thought is spread through the use of language to which everyone has access. All have the freedom of using language. So people are able to choose to embrace a thought. In contrast, the will, imposed by power, cannot be easily resisted. The will of power may not be what is selected by people. This means that people, accepting a thought on voluntary basis, are free. In contrast, the rule of the ruler is often arbitrary. The rule is despotic. The ruler is also despotic. People build the state as a despotic state. The state is governed in a despotic way. If there is a thought prevailing in the state, this thought is usually propagated by the ruler unilaterally. Ordinary people may not accept this thought. If ordinary people accept it, it may not be in their own interest in an ultimate sense. But if people build the state on the basis of democracy because the democratic constitution is carried out indeed as indicated by modern history, different thoughts may compete against each other. All different thinkers become attractive. Now, as coercion is prevented from being used to curb the competition of thoughts, thinkers, reflecting the wishes of the masses, try their best to offer their particular thoughts. Then, the best thought, chosen by the majority of people, becomes the mainstream thought of the state. Then people become free. Of course, the state is governed with power. But power may be prevented from being used to suppress the competition of thoughts. Power, used in the governance of the state, may not step in to influence the competition of thoughts unless there is a thought advocating banning the dissemination of all other thoughts. In this case, the mainstream thought is selected by people freely. People are free if they submit to a thought embraced by them of their own wills in the governance of the state.

In other words, prohibiting the competition of thoughts will lead to the outbreak of a conflict between thought and power. Power is normally held by the authorities. The authorities usually propagate one thought and suppress all other thoughts if the authorities do not come under the influence of a reasonable thought. Thus coercion gains dominance. The authorities are unable to use a thought to oppress people. The authorities are almost unlikely to impose a thought on people over the long term if people consciously oppose, or refuse to accept, that thought. A thought is usually a weapon used by the people if the thought, upheld by the people, opposes the thought adhered to by the authorities. If two camps of thought coexist, the thought, had by the people, is usually powerful because a thought, protected by the ruler's coercion, is comparatively weak. In this case, the thought, advocated by the people, tends to reflect the trend of social progress while coercion may not. This is mainly because a human thought always precedes a human act. A thought may reflect reason while coercion may not. Thus in many cases a thought is progressive, whereas coercion represents the conservative force. When religion was not free in history, the development of science was impeded because any scientific thought repugnant to the dogma of the Church was suppressed. A scientific thought was disseminated by using language. If the regime banned the dissemination of the scientific thought, it used coercion. One case in point is that the Renaissance age witnessed the signs of the rise of modern science, yet the inquiry into nature did not unfold smoothly. The history of modern astronomy begins in 1543, with the publication of the work of Copernicus revealing the truth about the motions of the earth. The publication of his work, however, raised an issue between science and Scripture. The related theory was denounced by the Church. The discoveries of the Italian astronomer Galieo de' Galilei, who demonstrated the Copernican theory, were condemned. He was silenced by the Holy Office that announced that Copernican system was absurd and, in respect of Scripture, heretical. The publication of one of his treatises on the two systems (the Ptolemaic and the Copernican) in the form of *Dialogues* was disapproved by the Pope. He was summoned before the Inquisition and threatened with torture.[13]

As scientific thought is usually offered by scientists on individual basis, scientists are isolated individuals. They usually do not belong to any organization. They disseminate scientific thoughts in the process of linguistic communication only. They act on individual basis. They are independent as individuals. In contrast, the authorities act on the basis of an organization such as a religious establishment or an administrative organ. If unreasonable coercion is prevented from being used, human thoughts will flourish. Thus the phenomenon, that some scientists who disclosed the principle of science against the dogma of the Church were burned or persecuted, disappeared over the period of time between the sixteenth and the nineteenth century. In modern times, since people adopted the principle of religious freedom, the religious organization has been no longer the original one that suppressed the development of science.

That means that no tool of coercion is under the control of the isolated individuals in the civilized society unless those people are organized and unite. Normally, there is no competition between coercion under the control of the regime and coercion under the control of ordinary people. In peaceful times isolated individuals of the civilized society are not armed as a group. But those people may have a thought. The thought, had by those people, is potentially more powerful than the thought had by the authorities. This is because a thought is a medium. The authorities may not simply organize the state with a thought. It may sometimes simply depend on coercion placed at its disposal in organizing the state. But a thought, spread to ordinary people, may be used as a medium to organize ordinary people. By contrast, coercion is usually at the disposal of a few people. It is usually under the control of the regime. If it is under the control of the majority of people, the majority of people will be unable to use coercion because the majority of people are usually not organized to use coercion unless they stay under special circumstances. In other words, the use of coercion relies on the power of organization. Personnel, sent out by the regime to force ordinary people to obey the decree, are organized. They obey the order issued by their supervisor. The order may be issued level by level, involving human-chain linguistic communication. Officials of each level function as media. They are personnel used by the official of the upper level. The regime may be involved in the conflict of interest. By contrast, a thought, mastered by a single person or a few people, should not be powerful. A thought becomes powerful when it is mastered by the majority of people or all within the state. The spread of a thought may not rely on any organization. Although ordinary people are isolated individuals, a thought spread to them may be embraced by them. A thought is duplicated repetitively when it is spread. A thought is usually not involved in the conflict of interest because it cannot play a prominent role in the organization of the state unless it is embraced by many or the majority or all. To put it another way, a thought, embraced and upheld by many, or the majority, or all, tends not to be involved in any conflict of interest because now such a thought does not serve a small portion of people only but a large portion of people or the majority or all. Thought is antithetical to coercion or power backed by coercion. A despotic regime relies mainly on the use of coercion to keep its rule though sometimes this regime also tries to indoctrinate the masses with the thought promoted by it. By contrast, a thought is spread gradually and continuously. If such a thought spreads widely, the thought may become a medium through which ordinary people unite. A thought may become a force. Ordinary people may be temporarily organized. The organization of ordinary people enables them to have a tool of coercion. This tool of coercion may override the tool of coercion had by the regime if a revolt or revolution erupts. The old regime may rely chiefly on the use of coercion to resist the revolt or the revolution of the masses if the masses decide to revolt or initiate a revolution. The use of coercion largely denotes the use of an army or a police force. The army or the police force is well organized according to a code. The hierarchy of the army, or the police organization within the administrative branch, ensures that an order can be effectively issued from the upper level to the lower level. The military personnel or policemen are strictly disciplined. But the powerful thought belongs to the masses. Though people may be the crowds of the masses without any strict discipline and hence may not be well organized, they may be strongly motivated by a thought. They may be temporarily organized. They owe their victory to the power of the thought to a greater extent. This means that a thought can be used to mobilize the masses. The masses may revolt against the regime and even overthrow the regime in a revolution if the masses confront the regime. Then it follows that a thought becomes a weapon used by people for self-emancipation. If that thought is later kept as the guiding thought in the governance of the society, people can finally have freedom. Although power is used in the governance of the society all the time, a thought gives freedom to people. If a thought, embraced by people, prevails, the governance of the state must satisfy the condition that freedom is given to people. For example, in early modern times the traditional rule of many despotic countries collapsed because of the triumph of liberalism. Liberalism is a kind of thought. It is not the tool of coercion, but it triumphs over the tool of coercion in the evolution of history. The reason is that a thought cannot be defeated by the tool of coercion but another thought that proves more advanced. Ludwig von Mises, in describing how liberalism prevailed over the traditional rule of the ruling class in Europe, writes that:

> When liberal ideas began to spread to central and eastern Europe from their homeland in western Europe, the traditional powers—the monarchy, the nobility, and the clergy—trusting in the instruments of repression that were at their disposal, felt completely safe. They did not consider it necessary to combat liberalism and the mentality of the Enlightenment with intellectual weapons. Suppression, persecution, and imprisonment of the malcontents seemed to them to be more serviceable. They boasted of the violent and coercive machinery of the army and the police. Too late they realized with horror that new ideology snatched

these weapons from their hands by conquering the minds of officials and soldiers. It took the defeat suffered by the old regime in the battle against liberalism to teach its adherents the truth that there is nothing in the world more powerful than ideologies and ideologists and that only with ideas can one fight against ideas. They realized that it is foolish to rely on arms, since one can deploy armed men only if they are prepared to obey, and that the basis of all power and domination is, in the last analysis, ideological.[14]

Thus, it is arguable that if the power of a thought, embraced and upheld by people, prevails over the power of the tool of coercion in the governance of the state, people should be free.

In pre-modern times, such as medieval times, the regime relied mainly on the use of coercion in the governance of the state indeed. If a thought played a part in the governance of the state, that thought was unilaterally propagated by the regime. For example, the regime propagated the idea of divine right. That thought was not freely selected by the masses because there was scarcely the competition of different thoughts. In modern times a thought can play a significant role in the governance of the state due to the fact that different thoughts can be chosen by people and one thought can figure prominently. There appears a process in which linguistic communication is widely performed to disseminate one thought to the masses; the masses compel the regime to adopt this thought in the governance of the state; and the regime adopts this thought in the governance of the state finally. That is, the nature of language makes it possible that, in the interaction between action and thought, a thought almost always precedes the action because people always seek the improvement of their living or social conditions no matter whether certain necessary conditions are fulfilled or not. If a person takes action without any idea, he may be blamed by all others as without a second thought. This means that the most cases seen by people are that when a new thought is disseminated in the process of linguistic communication, the old social or political system is still adhered to. The new thought clashes with the old social or political system because the thought is advanced and wholesome while the existing social or political system seems backward or corrupt. Thus, the freedom of thought is always requested by those who keep on engaging in speculation. The freedom of thought has never been advocated by the power holder. The freedom of thought is usually requested by those without power. To put it another way, the flag of the freedom of thought is always hoisted by those who have no power either in ancient or medieval or modern times. To make a social progress, people have to accept the freedom of thought. All wholesome thoughts should be allowed to compete. As J. B. Bury writes,

> [I]n order to readjust social customs, institutions, and methods to new needs and circumstances, there must be unlimited freedom of canvassing and criticizing them, or expressing the most unpopular opinions, no matter how offensive to prevailing sentiment they may be. If the history of civilization has any lesson to teach it is this: there is one supreme condition of mental and moral progress which it is completely within the power of man himself to secure, and that is perfect liberty of thought and discussion. The establishment of this liberty may be considered the more valuable achievement of modern civilization, and as a condition of social progress it should be deemed fundamental. The considerations of permanent utility on which it rests must outweigh any calculations of present advantage which from time to time might be thought to demand its violation.[15]

Thus although people submit to the regime in the governance of the state, one of the rationalities of the state sought by people is the very fact that people have the freedom of thought and the objective of the freedom of thought is that the regime governs the state in the principle formulated on the basis of the thought embraced and upheld by them. The progress of civilization, made particularly in modern times in this aspect, bears testimony to this case. There are various cases supporting this argument.

First, many education institutions are established in modern times. They form an education system. These institutions include schools, colleges and universities and other similar institutions. They disseminate knowledge. They also spread thoughts. This means that the process of disseminating thoughts is accelerated, strengthened and supported as the teachers, those who are most capable of disseminating thoughts, are recruited and the students, those who are in the most urgent need of gaining knowledge and thoughts, cluster at one location for going through this process. The regime can no longer ignore the role played by a thought in the governance of the society or state. As now people have their thoughts because of education, the regime may adopt one thought embraced by most of people. Thus people become free. The teaching program may be determined by the regime. A thought may be propagated by the teachers to the students as required and entrusted by the regime. However, in the society or the state in which the guiding thought is chosen freely by people, that thought is expected to be embraced by people freely. As people are able to change the thought they embrace at anytime, they can embrace freely the thought disseminated by the teachers. Thus people are free. In the society or the state in which the guiding thought is not chosen by people freely, the regime needs to interpret the thought disseminated to ordinary people. Ordinary people can make their judgment. As a thought needs to be accepted and embraced by ordinary people, the regime needs to interpret successfully the guiding thought. The regime faces the pressure that it needs to adopt the thought that can be embraced by ordinary people. The regime cannot deprive ordinary people of their freedom of thought. The common interest of people within the state also takes shape when people insist on the freedom of thought because the freedom of thought results in the fact that all or the majority of people embrace the same thought and that all or the majority of people embrace the same thought means that all or the majority of people have reached a consensus. If people do not have common interest, they will not reach that consensus.

Second, the use of language over the long term creates a condition for extending the distance of linguistic communication. People gradually communicate on a large scale. Such a situation leads, in some sense, to the birth of a mass society. Mass media develop in support of linguistic communication on a large scale. Though mass media disseminate knowledge, they also spread thoughts. The operation of mass media accelerates and strengthens the process of disseminating thoughts to ordinary people. Thinkers offer many different thoughts to ordinary people. Ordinary people choose to embrace one thought and put it into practice. As now plenty of people are likely to embrace one thought, this thought will gradually become the mainstream thought of the society or the state. The society or the state will function in the way desired by all. Thus people may become free. This indicates that those mass media can propagate a thought to the masses in the public and that thought can prevail. It is impossible for the society or the state not to be influenced by any powerful thought. Thus, the society or the state adopts a mechanism through which the masses embrace a thought as the guiding thought in the building of the society or the state. This ensures that people can have their freedom. One can corroborate this situation in any process of transition in which a traditional society becomes a modern one. In a traditional society people are fettered by many thoughts that prove obsolete and no longer applicable. People may feel that they are oppressed by the old society. They usually believe that they are not free. Yet after a new thought is successfully propagated in the society, people embrace this thought. Then people reform the society. People rebuild the society according to the new thought embraced by them. A modern society is born. People become free as a result.

Third, people, communicating by using language, build a civil society. Language is a medium used to disseminate a thought to many people on a large scale and a thought can also be regarded as a medium used by language in communication on a large scale. Thus, that thought plays a part in the building of the society. Cultural development in ancient or modern times may illustrate this situation. In ancient Greece literature spread thought when writers engaged in the criticism of life. J. B. Bury, describing the civilization of ancient Greeks, writes that "Their literature . . .could not have been what it is if they had been debarred from free criticism of life."[16] They, engaging in the critique of life, must disseminate a thought. In modern times the prosperity of literature and art allows for many writers and artists to disseminate their humanistic thoughts to the great masses of the people. Writers and artists are more capable of communicating with the great masses of the people, and they actually function as media. They are the media used by the great masses of the people to communicate with themselves. In the meantime, as writers and artists are those who are more capable of disseminating thoughts and the success of disseminating their thoughts usually depends on how the great masses of the people select a thought, the thoughts that prevail in the society are usually upheld by the great masses of the people. These thoughts must be reflected in the governance of the society or the state to a varying extent. In this case, people are free. In other words, the society or the state is governed under the influence of a certain thought upheld and cherished by the great masses of the people. Thus the people are free. For example, writers and artists who emerged in Great Britain, France, Germany and Russia as well as other European countries, such as Voltaire (Francois-Marie Arouet), Victor Hugo, Johann Wolfgang von Gothe, Johann Christoph Friedrich von Shiller, and Fyodor Dostoyevsky, in early modern times almost invariably disseminated liberal or progressive thoughts. Later the peoples of those countries established democracy or called for the establishment of democracy in all those countries in succession. The governance of the society or the state came gradually under the influence of those writers and artists. The thoughts, propagated by those writers and artists, are now the thoughts upheld by ordinary people in those countries. Now there is the free society in each of those countries.

Thus, in fact, where there is the freedom of thought enjoyed by people, the government does not use coercion in the political domain except in the legal domain. Thus, the people enjoy the freedom of thought and maintain the legal order of the state. The legal order of the state does not impede the freedom of thought.

3. Religious Belief

The freedom of thought, discussed by us in the previous section, is the freedom of the spiritual activity of humans. Religious belief is also a spiritual activity of humans. Disseminating a thought, people enjoy the freedom of thought. Spreading a religious belief, people enjoy the freedom of religious belief. A thought exists in the process of linguistic communication. A religious belief also exists in the process of linguistic communication. While in the secular society the spread of a thought is the quest for reason, in the religious society people stick to faith. Although people in the religious community obey the categorical commandment from the church or temple and stick to faith insulated from evidence, people in the religious community submit to moral commandment and seek the mutual love of brothers and sisters. A religious society and a secular society may cooperate in the building of the state. Particularly, under the circumstances that some basic social values are suppressed by a despotic government, the religious society and the secular society may unite. The reason is that the religious community is capable of mobilizing religious believers, and its commitment may be salutary to the building of the state. This is because some values, upheld by religious believers, may be shared by laymen. For example, the moral idea of the religious community may be analogous to the secular moral idea in some aspects. The religious idea, embedded in the tradition and folk custom, may not be repugnant to the social idea shared by all. Thus Brian Leiter states that the combination of categorical demands on action and insulation from evidence seems a frightening one, but it has often been responsible for laudatory and courageous behavior, such as resistance to Nazism and to apartheid.[17]

That means that religious believers also seek freedom. There is a similar case in the interaction between them and the organizer of the state in relation to religion. This similar case is that in the interaction between religious believers and the organizer of the state, religious believers engage mainly in linguistic interaction. They seek their own development. They uphold their religious belief. They always need to manifest their belief. In this case, language plays a role. To put it differently, in any state in the world there is almost at least one kind of religion. In many states there are different religions. People spread religion chiefly in linguistic communication. Unlike the case that coercion is used in the governance of the state or the society, language supports freedom in the spiritual life of humans needed by religious believers. This is precisely because a religious belief is spread by using language mainly. The community always needs governance and coercion is often used. The use of coercion suppresses people's freedom. Then people may feel that they are oppressed. Language in nature does not support coercion. Language is a tool distinct from any tool of coercion. Language is used to disseminate an idea. That is, some people disseminate an idea and some other people embrace this idea. This idea may be reflected in the governance of the community. People, agreeing to this idea, will submit to the governance of the state on voluntary basis. Coercion is not needed to be used. Thus, people become free. This is a case for religion, too. That is, religion involves the religious activities of upholding, propagating and manifesting a religious belief, and people often hold different religious beliefs. They may believe that there is a supreme being.

In the meantime, the supporters of a certain religion are tempted to think of their own religion as being superior to other religions and may support the dominance of their own religious faith. Without the guarantee to the freedom of religion provided by the government, religions or religious sects cannot always guarantee the freedom of religion by themselves. In history some religious groups persecuted some other religious groups. One of the reasons that some religious groups persecuted other religious groups is that some of them were strong while others weak. Religious groups are not always equally strong. Sometimes a group of people, holding a particular religious faith, are intolerant of another group of people upholding another religious faith, and a religious conflict or persecution unfortunately breaks out. In this case, people resort to violence. Then some people may be coerced into relinquishing their own religious belief or embracing a religious belief they do not want to embrace. The role of language in the spread of religion is absent. By contrast, if language is used by people to play a role in the spread of religion, people may avoid using coercion. People may advocate and encourage the tolerance of different religions or religious sects. In this case a ruler or a power holder of the state may intend to win support from the masses that embrace a religion and he may promise to recognize religious freedom. As early as the times of ancient Rome, religions were tolerated. As J. B. Bury writes, "The general rule of Roman policy was to tolerate throughout the Empire all religions and all opinions."[18] In England, the ruler might also tolerate religion. Hobbes writes that William the Conqueror used to take an oath not to infringe the liberty of the Church.[19] In Germany, before the formation of the new Empire (1870), the freedom of religion was ensured because Frederick the Great meant that every one should be allowed to get to heaven in his own way. He guaranteed the unrestricted liberty of conscience in his policy and principles formulated in the Prussian Territorial Code of 1794 and placed the three chief religions, namely, the Lutheran, the Reformed, and the Catholic, on the same footing and let them enjoy the same privileges.[20] This means that coercion was prevented from being used by any religion to push aside any other religion. People supported the flourishing of the spiritual world only in the processes of linguistic communication.

Based on the abovementioned analysis, we find that any person, advocating religious freedom against the use of coercion in support, or for the protection, of any religion, almost always advocates the freedom of religious belief that directly or indirectly confirms the role of language in the spread of religion. Religion grows in the processes of linguistic communication rather than in the use of coercion. All religions grow in linguistic interaction. In contrast, supporting the growth of one religion by using force is no more justifiable than suppressing another religion. A religious sect, persecuted in the past, may even persecute another sect, for example. According to J. B. Bury, "The Puritans who fled from the intolerance of the English Church and State and founded colonies in New England, were themselves equally intolerant, not only to Anglicans and Catholics, but to Baptists and Quakers."[21] People, upholding the principle of the freedom of religion, insist that one should be free not to embrace the religion of another group of people in order to adhere to his own religion. Roger Williams, a clergyman advocating the freedom of religion in the United States in the seventeenth century, upholds that "Christ does not endorse violent defense of religion."[22] He continues that "Religious persecution is inconsistent with Christ's way and a desire for civil peace." [23] He insists that:

> To batter down idolatry, false worship, heresy, schism, blindness, or hardness, out of the soul and spirit, it is vain, improper, and unsuitable to bring those weapons which are used by prosecutors—stocks, whips, prisons, swords, gibbets, stakes.[24]

Then he concludes that:

> [I]t is not the will of the Father of Spirits that all the consciences and spirits of this nation should violently . . . be forced into one way of worship, or that any town or so-called parish in England, Scotland, or Ireland be disturbed in their worship by the civil sword ([whatever] worship [that might be]).[25]

In this case we also insist that preventing resorting to violence will create a condition for language to play a role. Conversely, using coercion often prevents language from playing a role. Religion cannot be prohibited by using language. If people are allowed to use freely language to propagate their religious faith, there should be no coercion. If people embrace and obey a religious doctrine because they have been convinced by a religious thought, language will play a part. In this case people are free. Religious freedom is linguistic freedom.

The freedom of religion is actually a state of the activities performed by people in their own brains for the purpose of maintaining a kind of belief without any external obstruction. These activities are performed in their brains. All perform the similar activities. All share the same belief because all communicate with all by using language. Coercion cannot be applied inside the brain. Thus a belief is upheld by people often as a result of a kind of the activities performed in linguistic communication. Language and religious freedom always go hand in hand while language and coercion may not. A person cannot be coerced into accepting a belief. John Locke explains this logic most directly. He writes that:

> The care of Souls cannot belong to the Civil Magistrate, because his Power consists only in outward force; but true and saving Religion consists in the inward perswasion of the Mind, without which nothing can be acceptable to God. And such is the nature of the Understanding, that it cannot be compell'd to the belief of any thing by outward force. Confiscation of Estate, Imprisonment, Torments, nothing of that nature can have any such Efficacy as to make Men change the inward Judgment that they have framed of things.[26]

It is true that in history some religious groups used coercion to prevent the development of other religious groups. This indicates that people try to end the process of linguistic communication that spreads religion. Whenever coercion is used by a religious group to stop the growth of another religious group, language will stop playing its essential role in support of religious freedom. Thus, to allow for language to play that role, people ought to resist the use of coercion by any religious group in an attempt to curb the growth of any other religious group. This is the requirement for the administration of religion in the state if the state should be a secular organization. The reason is that the organization of the society instead of the state sometimes relies on religion. The society can be fragmented. Different religious groups can co-exist. The state should be monolithic. If the state needs to differentiate itself from the society, the state should ensure religious toleration. The state should even tolerate different ideas as long as they are not against law. So, Locke writes that:

> The *Sum of all* we drive at is, *that every man may enjoy the same Rights that are granted to others.* Is it permitted to worship God in the *Roman* manner? Let it be permitted to do it in the *Geneva* Form also. Is it permitted to speak *Latin* in the Market-place? Let those that have a mind to it, be permitted to do it also in the Church. Is it lawfull for any man in his own House, to kneel, stand, sit, or use any other Posture; and to cloath himself in White or Black, in short or in long Garments? Let it not be made unlawful to eat Bread, drink Wine, or wash with Water, in the Church. In a Word: Whatsoever things are left free by Law in the common occasions of Life, let them remain free unto every Church in Divine Worship. Let no Man's Life, or Body, or House, or Estate, suffer any manner of Prejudice upon these Accounts. Can you allow of the *Presbyterian* Discipline? Why should not the *Episcopal* also have what they like? Ecclesiastical Authority, whether it be administered by the Hands of a Single Person, or many, is every where the same; and neither has any Jurisdiction in things Civil, nor any manner of Power of Compulsion, nor any thing at all to do with Riches and Revenues.[27]

This means that the governance of the state differs from the governance of the society. The governance of the society may not rely on the use of coercion. The governance of the society relies on morality. Morality is based on a moral idea and that idea guides the operation of the society. Likewise, the society may be guided by a thought. It may also be guided by a belief. Thus a belief in the society may be very influential and powerful. By contrast, the governance of the state relies on the use of coercion though the person, in control of the state, may also come under the guidance of a thought. It is difficult to control the spread of a thought in the society. Similarly, it is difficult to control the spread of a religious belief in the society. The reason is that people use language and language is used to spread a religious belief. People use language every day. The strength of religion derives from language. If a religion suppresses another religion, the religion that suppresses another religion functions as an authority in the governance of the state. This is because sometimes some people use coercion to suppress a religion. Coercion always fails over the long term. The reason is that people use language every day. But people cannot use coercion every day. It is easier to use language to spread a religious belief than to use coercion to suppress a religion. Over the long term religion grows though in history it is occasionally suppressed. The reason is that the use of language underlies the growth of the state. A religion cannot be easily suppressed by another religion or the authorities supported by another religion because the use of coercion is doomed to fail over the long term. So Mill writes that:

> [T]he Reformation broke out at least twenty times before Luther, and was put down. Arnold of Brescia was put down. Fra Dolcino was put down. Savonarola was put down. The Albigeois were put down. The Vaudois were put down. The Lollards were put down. The Hussites were put down. Even after the era of Luther, wherever persecution was persisted in, it was successful. In Spain, Italy, Flanders, the Austrian empire, Protestantism was rooted out; and most likely, would have been so in England, had Queen Mary lived, or Queen Elizabeth died. Persecution has always succeeded, save where the heretics were too strong a party to be effectually persecuted. No reasonable person can doubt that Christianity might have been extirpated in the Roman Empire. It spread, and became predominant, because the persecutions were only occasional, lasting but a short time, and separated by long intervals of almost undisturbed propagandism.[28]

The state should be governed under the guidance of a secular idea. In this case people can enjoy the freedom of religion. Religious freedom will thus be enjoyed by people if a secular idea guides the governance of the state rather than the society. One case in point is that people accentuated the value of mankind throughout the period of Renaissance in Europe. An increase in knowledge motivated people to embrace new ideas. The thought of science gained momentum in defiance of the authority of the conservative church. Religious believers adhered to the faith that did not change over time. Laymen sought knowledge that was increasing and changing. Along with the passage of time scientific knowledge increased while religious faith remained unchanged. As Owen Chadwick argues, "A revelation from God is absolute. It can brook no change, no modification, no improvement. But knowledge is always growing, always modifying opinion, always in movement. Faith is stationary, science progressive."[29] Along with the struggle for the spiritual emancipation of mankind, the development of capitalist economy and the growth of nation-state in early modern times, liberalism, a secular thought, began underpinning the building of the state in place of the original idea of divine right. The alliance between the church and the state ended. This piece of history leads to the separation of state and church.

Some trends indicate the separation of state and church. People make a great progress in this respect particularly in modern times.

First, there appeared the movement for the revocation of religious tax imposed in support of the established church, a tradition existing widely in Europe and North America in early times. For example, in North America dissenters had to pay mandatory tax to support the established church, namely, the Anglican Church and then had to contribute to the maintenance of their own parish. They did not use the church and they might think that they were not responsible for the development of the related religion. The non-religious people were also required to pay mandatory tax in support of the established church. Thus, this movement was a step toward religious freedom. For example, in Massachusetts mandatory religious taxation ended in 1832.[30] In other colonies mandatory religious tax if any were also revoked because of pressure put by the society on the established church. In the past the dominance of the established church restricted the liberty of all others that had the faith different from the faith of the established church. The end of mandatory religious taxation symbolized a decline of influence enjoyed by the established church. As the established church was usually supported by the government or the law, such a decline of influence, had by the established church, meant that the established church could no longer rely on the power of the government to push aside the other religions or other religious sects. The freedom of religion became possible.

Second, there appeared a trend that different religious denominations, or different religious sects, or different religions, were gradually tolerated. The Act of Toleration made in 1689 in Britain marked a significant step toward the gradual implementation of religious liberty.[31] Though religious life was traditionally characteristic of the dominance of the Church of England in history, from the nineteenth century onward the church establishment had been gradually declining. Religious pluralism developed. In 1829 came Catholic Emancipation. In 1858 Jews were admitted to Parliament. From the nineteenth to the early twentieth century religious dissenters gradually gained equal status in the respect of education as endowed grammar schools began to be open to dissenters.[32] In France, the Declaration of Rights (1789) also laid down that no one was to be vexed on account of his religious opinions, provided he did not thereby trouble public order.[33] Though Robespierre established a state religion that required the worship of the Supreme Being and atheism was regarded as a vice at that time, the policy was made to hinder the preponderance of any one religious group.[34] The Constitution of 1795 affirmed the liberty of all worship.[35] In North America the tradition of impartiality between Christian denominations had taken form in the New England colonies except Rhode Island by the time when the Declaration of Independence was signed. Religious organizations other than the Anglican Church, such as Catholic Church, were gradually tolerated.

Third, religious organizations were announced as private organizations. In the United States, everywhere ameliorative legislation was removing the most galling of the exclusive rights of the state churchmen after the Declaration of Independence was signed. Church gradually lost the direct support from the state in the nineteenth century. In this aspect Great Britain followed the United States. In the first half of the twentieth century the church establishment finally ended though the Sovereign was still obliged to be a member of the Church of England and the Church of Scotland and the bishops still sat in the House of Lords as spiritual peers and were still appointed by the Crown.[36] Then the Church of England or the Church of Scotland was distinguished from the state. According to Rex Ahdar and Ian Leigh, in *Aston*

Cantlow and Wilmcote with Billesley Parochial Church Council v. Wallbank, the House of Lord held that a Parochial Church Council of the Church of England was not a "public authority" under the Human Rights Act 1998. And Lord Hope of Craighead stated that such a parish council:

> plainly has nothing whatever to do with the process of either central or local government. It is not accountable to the general public for what it does. It receives no public funding, apart from occasional grants from English Heritage for the preservation of its historic buildings. In that respect it is in a position which is no different from that of any private individual.[37]

This situation implies that the church is distinguished from the state, and the tool of coercion, usually provided by the state, will not be used to curb or support the development of any religion as long as or even though such religion causes no harm to the other religion or the public good. Thus, religion cannot grow in any process but in the process of linguistic communication. People only gain their freedom in the process of linguistic communication.

The result is that today the method, adopted by people to ensure that people have freedom to spread and put into practice their faith, is that any religious group is prevented from using the power of the secular authorities to promote itself. As it is not enabled to use the coercion of the secular authorities to promote itself against any other religious group or as no religious group is supposed to use coercion to curb the development of any other religious group, the growth of any religious group merely relies on the interpretative power of their religious doctrine. The interpretative power of their religious doctrine may be enhanced in the process of linguistic communication. But it is never enhanced in the use of coercion. Therefore, the principle of the separation of state and church is usually the guarantee that people enjoy their freedom when they uphold and put into practice their religious faith. The reason that people enjoy their freedom when they uphold and put into practice their religious faith is that people are free to communicate to spread that religious faith. If any religious group uses the physical coercion of the authorities directly or indirectly, using that physical coercion will affect the communication performed by using language to spread the religious faith. Then religious freedom enjoyed by people vanishes. So it follows that, for example, in a modern state sometimes a strife between one religion and another arises. In the face of this strife, the best way to solve this strife is to let different religions to compete against each other in the process of linguistic communication or let them run separately without any possibility of using the coercion of the secular authorities, provided that no religion causes harm to the public good. Thus people, believing in any religious doctrine, may enjoy their freedom. For the role played by the government in the protection of religious freedom, I argue that people are not free unless they submit to the governance of the government that recognizes the principle of the freedom of religion they agree to on voluntary basis. Without a government that recognizes the principle of the freedom of religion agreed to by religious believers, the freedom of religious belief is unsustainable or impossible. That is, without a government that ensures the freedom of religion, religious groups may be in conflict with each other at any time. As a result, the freedom of religion cannot be sustainable. In this respect I argue that religious believers are free only if they submit to the governance of the government that ensures religious freedom in the principle agreed to by them.

In terms of the relationship between religion and the government, if there is any conflict between the religion and the state governed by the secular authorities, the controversial issue is often how to deal with the issue of religious freedom. The key to resolving this issue is actually to prevent religious practice from being affected by any coercion used by the secular authorities if religious practice, as a special case, can be exempted from being subject to the governance of a general law or administration. That is, under the precondition that the public security and public good is not affected, the secular authorities are required to try its best to refrain from intervening in the religious practice to the effect that no coercion can be used to hamper the growth of religion.

There are several cases showing this tendency.

First, one kind of religious activities is the manifestation of religious symbols. Some symbols of religion are used by religious believers and they need to manifest the religion or the belief in teaching, practice, worship and observance in public or private. These symbols are also media used in support of the underlying religious discourse. This religious discourse should involve a process of linguistic communication spreading the religious belief. For example, a 2006 Canadian Supreme Court case *Multani v. Commission scolaire Marguerite-Bourgeoys* affirmed the right of a Sikh child to carry his ceremonial knife, the *kirpan*, in the school in accordance with his religion. The dispute is that those who sought to bar the carrying of the kirpan argued that this religious practice posed too great a risk of harm, which was why there was a general ban of weapons in school while those who defended the exception for the Sikh child argued that the risk of harm was very slight and that a kirpan had never been used to attack anyone in a school previously. Although Canadian Supreme Court admitted that the kirpan undeniably has characteristics of a bladed weapon capable of wounding or killing a person, and that carrying kirpans is, probably, prohibited in courts and on airplanes, the court nevertheless held that the student in question could carry the most dangerous kind of kirpan as long as "his personal and subjective belief in the religious significance of the kirpan is sincere."[38]

Demonstrating those symbols of religions symbolizes the existence of a kind of freedom enjoyed by people in their spiritual life. So today in some countries that absorb immigrants with different religious backgrounds, the government often finds that it needs to deal with the issue that while the public authorities need to regulate the related religious practice in order to govern the state, the right of showing religious symbols also needs to be respected.

Second, in terms of religious practice, if religious observance conflicts with the state or the society governed by the secular authorities, the secular authorities may consider giving concession. Whether or not a citizen can enjoy weekend, such as Sunday, is a case in point. That is, there was the identification of the Christian Sunday with the Jewish Sabbath in the eighth century and an edict of Charlemagne in 789 forbade all Sunday labor. Church councils from this time onward, or the Catholic Church long after the Reformation, regulated Sunday behavior, especially in the matter of games and dancing.[39] In modern times the court obviously tends to consider protecting such religious observance as long as public safety and public good are not seriously affected.

For example, since the end of World War Two the courts of the United States have clearly paid attention to protecting such free religious exercise.

This situation is exemplified by a case shown in *Sherbert v. Verner* (S.CT.1963). That is, Mrs. Sherbert, a Seventh-Day Adventist, for whom it was religiously forbidden to work on Saturday, her Sabbath day, was required to work six days a week. She resigned and sought unemployment compensation. She was denied by the state of South Carolina on the grounds that she had refused "suitable work." She went to court, arguing that the state had impermissibly impeded her free exercise of religion. In a famous judgment in 1963, the U.S. Supreme Court agreed. They held that benefits could not be made conditional on a violation of a person's religious scruples: This was just like fining someone for Saturday worship.[40]

Third, sometimes the religious faith, held by religious believers, prohibits those religious believers from fighting or going to war. As a result, pacifism, adhered to by those religious believers, becomes grounds presented by some of the citizens that they should not be drafted to join the army even though their own nation-state may be soon involved in a war against another nation-state. If the law, made by the state, supports the religious cause or is in favor of religion and if the conscription is unlikely to be seriously affected, those citizens, holding the pacifist view for religious reason, may be exempted from providing military service to the state. Sometimes religious freedom is considered by the secular government to the greatest extent. In the United States, according to Stephen Nathanson, religiously based pacifism qualified a person for exemption from military service according to the selective service law made in history in the United States because of the generally favorable attitude toward religion in American law and the government's confidence that few people would qualify for this exemption as long as the objectors were opposed to all wars and their opposition was based on a religious belief. That is, the government believed that few people would qualify for this exemption and the supply of people available for military service would not be threatened.[41] This indicates that the American government considers the issue of religious freedom.

On the other hand, we find that religious freedom, enjoyed by religious believers, is also what is conducive to the development of the society and the building of the state for a long time. There are mainly three aspects needing an explanation.

First, as long as no tool of coercion may be used to suppress or support a religious group, people establish a market of religious faiths. Different religious groups may compete against each other peacefully. The prosperity of a religious group depends on the power of interpretation of the religious doctrine. If a religious doctrine shows the power of interpretation, this situation often means that it is accepted and embraced by people. The reason that people accept and embrace it is that it has utility. In other words, this is because such a religious doctrine satisfies their need. Perhaps such a religious doctrine may make them feel secure in the unsecured world. Perhaps they feel that they can repose their destiny on the protection of God. If a religion can win more believers, it may play a big role in the building of the society. As long as no coercion is used to interfere with any religious affair, the most promising religion may play a due role in the growth of the society. As the state is built on the basis of the existing society, this is conducive to the organization of the state. Competition using the tool of coercion in the religious community only supports the religious group that may not have the biggest power of interpretation. Since the prevalence of religious freedom, competition within the religious community has been guided to letting each religious group demonstrate their power of interpretation. This is needed by the society. This culminates in the fact that people can give the greatest play to religion in the development of the society or the building of the state. Each religious group relies on the power of interpretation, and the development of religion, as a whole, involves various processes of linguistic communication. This indicates that the wholesome development of religion lies in the process of linguistic communication. In contrast, the use of coercion prevents language from playing its due role in the construction of the society and the state. There is a correlation between language and religious freedom. By relying on linguistic communication, religion flourishes.

Second, the freedom of religious belief does not oppose free competition between religious thought and secular thought. Religious freedom includes the freedom of not believing in any religion. People respect atheism. This creates a favorable condition for the development of various thoughts conducive to the development of the society and the building of the state. A reasonable secular thought can thus develop without any impediment. This is beneficial to the social progress. This may even be beneficial to the economic development of the state. This case is particularly salient in modern times. There is such a related trend in our times: A religious dogma remains unchanged over time while a secular thought, particularly, a scientific thought, develops fast. As the cause of science underlies the development of economy and society in modern times and the state takes care of the development of economy and society, the government tends to support the development of science. If the state and the church build an alliance as sometimes seen in history, the development of the scientific cause may be affected. The development of physics, biology, medicine and other branches of learning may be retarded. If a secular thought is more useful, this thought will play an important role in the development of the society and the building of the state. Therefore, religion is prevented from impeding the spread of those useful thoughts including the scientific thought. The economy of the state grows. The society, on the basis of which people organize the state, also develops. Thus, in some sense, the prevalence of religious freedom liberates the productive forces. People realize this goal in the process of linguistic communication.

Third, the freedom of religion goes hand in hand with the work of establishing the principle of the separation of state and church. The state ensures a degree of autonomy of the religious community. The religious community is part of the state, but the government prevents it from directly taking part in the organization of the state. This is because historical experience proves that the religious community is not a reliable basis for the organization of the state with different religious groups co-existing in a state. The state is organized because all hold a series of values, and people are able to come up with mainstream values in support of the building of the state. All, insisting on such values, may unite. This is because the prevalence of secular values depends on their rationality. Their rationality can be understood by all because people may reach a consensus through an argument. In the course of an argument people obey reason. People can be persuaded to embrace secular values. This is why liberalism prevails in modern times. By contrast, religion requires religious believers to adhere to the religious faith. Different religious groups uphold different religious doctrines. They cannot make any compromise. It is difficult to persuade a religious believer to relinquish his religious doctrine and accept another religious doctrine. Thus, the principle of religious freedom enables the secular government to organize the state in a secular principle. Different religious groups take part in the organization of the society because the society can be fragmented. But the state is organized in another principle. The state should be monolithic. As people form no alliance between a religion and the government, the religious community gains a status of autonomy. The secular government also gains a status of autonomy. Then the state is often organized without any influence of religion. In this way people ensure the unity of the state.

In short, religious believers enjoy the freedom of religious belief under the condition that religion does not serve as a foundation for the building of the state. Religion only contributes to the building of the society. As such, religious believers are free under the governance of the government that respects their freedom of belief. Such freedom of belief is maintained in the linguistic interaction of people instead of their physical interaction. The result is that religious believers are free in the state governed by the government in the principle that respects religious freedom expected by them.

Notes

1. G. W. F. Hegel, *The Philosophy of History*, translated by J. Sibree (Chicago: Encyclopaedia Britannica, Inc., 1952), 172.

2. John Stuart Mill, *Representative Government* (Chicago: Encyclopaedia Britannica, Inc., 1952), 329.

3. G. W. F. Hegel, *The Philosophy of Right*, translated by T. M. Knox (Chicago: Encyclopaedia Britannica, Inc., 1952), 16.

4. John Stuart Mill, *On Liberty* (Chicago: Encyclopaedia Britannica, Inc., 1952), 274.

5. Ibid., 284.

6. See: Nigel Warburton, *Free Speech: A Very Short Introduction* (Oxford: Oxford University Press, 2009), 27.

7. Hegel, *The Philosophy of Right*, 35.

8. Hegel, *The Philosophy of History*, 160.

9. See: J.B. Bury, *A History of Freedom of Thought* (New York: Henry Holt And Company, 1913), 32.

10. Aristotle, *The Politics of Aristotle*, translated by Peter L. Phillips Simpson (Chapel Hill: The University of North Carolina Press, 1997), 95-96.

11. Mill, *On Liberty*, 276.

12. Ibid., 283.

13. See: Bury, *A History of Freedom of Thought*, 86–90.

14. Ludwig von Mises, *Free and Prosperous Commonwealth*, *An Exposition of the Ideas of Classical Liberalism*, translated by Ralph Raico and edited by Arthur Goddard (Princeton, New Jersey: D.Van Nostrand Company, Inc.), 179–180.

15. Bury, *A History of Freedom of Thought*, 240.

16. Ibid., 23.

17. Brian Leiter, *Why Tolerate Religion?* (Princeton: Princeton University Press, 2013), 59–60.

18. Bury, *A History of Freedom of Thought*, 40.

19. Thomas Hobbes, *Leviathan*, edited with an introduction by C.B Macpherson (New York: Penguin Books, 1985), 364.

20. Bury, *A History of Freedom of Thought*, 120–121.

21. Ibid., 96.

22. Roger Williams, *On Religious Liberty*, edited and with an Introduction by James Calvin Davis (Cambridge, Massachusetts: The Belknap Press of Harvard University Press, 2008), 79.

23. Ibid. 82.

24. Ibid.115.

25. Ibid. 257.

26. John Locke, *A Letter Concerning Toleration* (Indianapolis, Indiana: Hackett Publishing Company, 1983), 27.

27. Ibid., 53.

28. Mill, *On Liberty*, 280.

29. Owen Chadwick, *The Secularization of the European Mind in the Nineteenth Century* (Cambridge: Cambridge University Press, 1975), 161–162.

30. Anthony Gill, *The Political Origins of Religious Liberty* (New York: Cambridge University Press, 2008), 101.

31. Ibid., 3.

32. See: E. R. Norman, *The Conscience of the State in North America* (London: Cambridge University Press, 1968), 11–13.

33. Bury, *A History of Freedom of Thought*, 111.

34. See: Ibid., 113–114.

35. See: Ibid., 114.

36. E. R. Norman, *The Conscience of the State in North America*, 11–13.

37. ([2003]UKHL37;[2004]1 AC546. Cited from Rex Ahdar and Ian Leigh, *Religious Freedom in the Liberal State* (Oxford: Oxford University Press, 2005), 77.

38. Leiter, *Why Tolerate Religion?*, 25; 64–65.

39. Albert Victor Murray, *The State and the Church in a Free Society* (London: Cambridge University Press, 1958), 166.

40. See: Martha C. Nussbaum, *Liberty of Conscience: In Defense of America's Tradition of Religious Equality* (New York: Basic Books, 2008), 16–17.

41. Stephen Nathanson, *Patriotism, Morality, and Peace* (Lanham: Rowman & Littlefield Publishers, Inc., 1993), 135.

Chapter Eleven

Equality

1. Book

Like freedom, equality cannot be realized unless it is realized in people's mutual interaction in which language plays a pivotal role. Equality is usually construed as the equal treatment given to all because people are often given different kinds of treatment. The reason that people are often given different kinds of treatment is that people are different from each other. Some people are male while others female. Some are tall while others short. Some are strong while others weak. Some men are handsome and some women are beautiful while other men and women are not. Some are competent while others are not. Some are born into a rich family while others born into a poor family. Scholars may believe that a difference between one person and another results in social inequality. Ludwig von Mises writes that:

> Men are altogether unequal. Even between brothers there exist the most marked differences in physical and mental attributes. Nature never repeats itself in its creations; it produces nothing by the dozen, nor are its products standardized. Each man who leaves her workshop bears the imprint of the individual, the unique, the never-to-recur.[1]

My view is that it is possible to give equal treatment to all though people show different characteristics or have different social backgrounds, a fact likely to lead to social inequality under certain circumstances. This is because a person needs to be considered in all aspects. A person may show a different character and have a different background in different aspects. Though a person may be inferior to another person in a certain aspect, he may be superior to another person in another aspect. Thus, a person, considered inferior in a certain aspect, may be considered superior in another aspect. His inferiority in a certain aspect may be compensated by his superiority in another aspect. Thus, if one is treated unequal because of his inferiority in a certain aspect, he may change this situation by showing his superiority in another aspect. Though a person cannot change some of his own characteristics and backgrounds easily, comparatively speaking, he may change some of his other characteristics and backgrounds easily. In this regard, I argue that knowledge, gained by people, is a factor that may often enable a person to change one of his characteristics or backgrounds. That is, knowledge is often saved in books, and books may make people equal in a certain aspect because knowledge is valuable. Whether or not a person reads books can make a difference. Rousseau believes that social diversity results in part from education.[2] This means that people, receiving education, acquire knowledge. They often acquire knowledge through books which represent the processes of linguistic communication. As people often save much systematic knowledge in books and spread it through books, books become media that expedite the circulation of knowledge. If this view can be accepted, I argue that, unlike the natural or social conditions mentioned by us earlier, language may enable people to acquire the same knowledge. As books represent, in some sense, the form of the intensive use of language that enables people to make a difference, people may become equal because of books. People, acquiring the same knowledge, may become the same people. Then they may be equal in a certain aspect. Though a person with knowledge and another person without knowledge may be unequal in a certain aspect, people may also learn knowledge so as to realize equality between one another. In other words, though language may lead to inequality, language may also be a tool that helps people to realize equality, depending on many other conditions. Like the case that freedom is won by people through the use of language, people may realize certain equality due to the use of language, too. Notwithstanding wide inequality appearing in the process of the growth of the state, the related process of linguistic communication may also contribute to the formation of equality gradually in another way. At least, it is arguable that if people use language more effectively, widely, frequently and continuously, language may create a condition for people to realize social equality in the state to a varying extent. Inequality may appear in various forms due to the difference of natural character of humans, such as the difference of gender, or the difference of age, or the difference of physical ability, or due to any social condition, in the civilized society. However, language may be one of the tools that can be most easily used to realize the goal that all gain equal social status at least in some important aspects if people are willing to make an effort. I mean that since the birth of language, humans have been building their society by using it. It is unlike other factors causing social inequality. Every man or woman has one mouth, two ears, two eyes, two hands, two legs and one brain, and all of them are equal in this aspect. The intelligence of every man or woman is usually not very much different from the intelligence of any other men or women. Language, used by people, is the same everywhere. The competence of each is potentially similar. Thus every man or woman can communicate with all others freely by using language. They can almost always communicate, using language, to realize all kinds of mutual interaction. If a person speaks using his mouth, another person can listen to him using his ears. If a person writes using his hand, another person can use his eyes to read what he has written. Every person can learn language, and language does not discriminate against anyone. As everyone learns language during his childhood, everyone is naturally equal in this aspect due to the fact that humans are animals that use language. Thus, language can be easily learned by anyone. Using language more efficiently, widely and frequently realizes and enhances equality among all.

It is true that many factors cause social inequality. Family background, personal luck and opportunity, physical strength, gender and others are all those factors. Even the cost of making books may also be a cause in view of the history of book. In history, books were very expensive, and only a few social elites could read books. But this was a provisional phenomenon. As time goes on, cheap books can be supplied on the market as long as people can use cheap materials of writing, such as paper. Thus, I venture to argue that the competence of reading and writing is perhaps what can be most easily gained by a person by learning how to read and write and hence he is likely to change his own lower social status because of his competence of reading and writing if he originally has such lower social status. As language can be more easily learned and more efficiently, widely and frequently used by anyone who is willing to learn it, language may play a more significant role in realizing equality in the state. The inequality of people in one aspect may not be thoroughly eliminated, but language may enable people, suffering from this inequality, to obtain a new opportunity to gain a social status in some other aspects so that the lower status he has in an original aspect can be compensated by the higher social status he obtains in a new aspect. If a person has a lower status in the society or the state because he is poor, or if he has a humble family background because his parents belong to the lower social class, for example, he can make an effort to learn reading and writing and acquire knowledge provided by books and even create knowledge by writing so as to enhance his social status. Being able to write and hence able to give substantial play to the potential of language can help a person change his social status in a certain aspect in order to compensate his lower status in another aspect and hence to avoid the unequal treatment though sometimes the competence of reading and writing may also lead to social inequality in another case because some others do not read books and do not write anything.

At least, we should be aware of the importance of book for those who are hungry for knowledge. As we argued earlier, learning to use language enables people to create a medium. After the creation of a medium, all have access to it. Book is a medium of linguistic communication. Book means linguistic communication that goes on efficiently, widely and constantly. That is, after a book is written by its author to communicate with readers, the author conveys more detailed and systematic information. Plenty of people read this book. As a book performs a task of communicating with readers, it can be read time and again. As this book is written to communicate with readers over time, this book may be read over the long term. The author of the book communicates with plenty of readers over the long term. He spreads knowledge. Then knowledge may enable those who acquire knowledge to gain a higher social status in the state.

We sometimes see that in human history some strong, bold and resourceful people conquer the multitude of people who are weak, timid and incapable. There is no equality between the ruler and the ruled. There is no equality between the ruling class and the ruled class either. However, as the state grows, the society also develops. People need to build the society. They need to understand the society. They need knowledge. They also need to govern the society. Governing the society, people also need skills. People, governing the society, become professionals. Besides, as the society grows, people also need to engage in socialized production or large-scale production. Engaging in socialized production, people also need knowledge and skills. In addition, the state also provides social services. Providing social services, people also need knowledge and skills. So while it may be difficult for a person to enhance his social status because it is impossible for him to make a lot of money or change his family background, for example, it may be comparatively easy for him to read books and acquire knowledge. If books are available, some people may change their destiny because they can read books. Sometimes they master the art of writing and other skills. Then they may be recruited to do a professional job that enhances their social status. There are different cases.

First, knowledgeable people may be recruited by the government to draft letters, reports and even decrees and laws if the state comes to be governed by the officials who have professional knowledge. In the outset, the government may not need many officials who have professional knowledge. Experience and common sense are very important in the governance of the state. But as people increase the size of the government step by step, the state is usually governed by the officials who have professional knowledge. Then knowledgeable people are recruited. Then some people become officials enjoying high social status even though they may come from a humble family. For example, in ancient Egypt papyrus was used to make books. Scribes, copying books by hand, were usually knowledgeable people. They ascended to a higher status. Leo Deuel writes that:

> Only the scribe has a genteel trade with minimal risks to health and comfort. And, no matter how humble his origins, his calling raises him above his class and may even bring him to the threshold of the mighty. In short, the schoolboy carries in his satchel the seal of the vizier, the staff of the field marshal, perhaps even a scepter. And there is a record of such meteoric careers in Ancient Egypt. The way to power was not through the sword but through the pen.[3]

In Asia or Europe those who were able to write and read might work for the state to copy the decrees or the laws in the same period of time when the state was governed by officials who had professional knowledge. Though it was inconvenient to use a lot of bamboo slips to make a book in China due to the fact that each strip of bamboo could only be used to write a limited number of characters, or though parchment was dear in Europe due to the fact that the supply of parchment on the market was limited, it was still comparatively easier for a person to read books to acquire knowledge and hence find an opportunity to become an official. After paper came into use widely, it became even easier for a person to obtain or keep a book. Therefore, in ancient China the regime administered the imperial examination to recruit those who had knowledge along with the use of related writing materials. The related knowledge included the knowledge of history, language and society. The knowledge was mainly acquired by those who kept on reading books though they might also be taught by private tutors. Those officials were those who used books efficiently and constantly because they kept on reading books. They drafted documents because, drafting documents, they made use of knowledge from books. Describing the recruitment of administrators in ancient China, Amalia E. Gnanadesikan mentions that Han dynasty (206BC to 9 AD) under the emperor Wudi (141-87BC) pioneered the practice of administering civil service examination. During the Sui dynasty (589-618) under the emperor of Sui Wendi bureaucracy was staffed at least in part with officials who had passed a written examination. The system grew during following Tang dynasty (618-907) and became fully developed under the Northern Song dynasty (960-1127). Then he writes that:

> Education became a highly prized attainment, a powerful means of upward mobility. The successful candidate joined the bureaucratic class, while the emperor received into his service an official without pre-existing powerful connection. . . . In the period from 998 to 1126, during the Northern Song period, nearly 50 percent of prominent officials came from poor (non-aristocratic) families.[4]

Similarly, in medieval Europe the ruler of each kingdom recruited plenty of officials when the territory, administered by the ruler, expanded and administration came to be professionalized. He often appointed priests as the officials of the government because priests were well-educated. At that time schools and universities were also run by the church. When education became an undertaking committed by the secular organizations or the government in early modern times, nearly all needed to be educated in order to be recruited by the government. Officials were often recruited through the examination administered by the government. Those candidates must read books and be able to write. So in the middle of the nineteen century, the British government established the system of civil servants. Later it adopted some new methods of recruiting the officials of the government, including examination. Civil service system was also established in all other states later. In modern times well-educated people are widely recruited by the government as civil servants. They have modern knowledge and skills of administration needed by the state. They read books to acquire such knowledge and skills when they are trained in colleges and universities. They become professionals. If one civil servant masters the required knowledge and skills very well, he may even be promoted quickly. Though working as a civil servant needs having work experience, a civil servant who graduates from a prestigious college or university and masters systematic professional knowledge may be promoted more quickly.

Second, we see the analogous picture in economic life. All know that productive forces will not develop unless the government recognizes private property right. That is, the government protects what people gain in their work and hence motivates people to engage in production. In the meantime, the wealth, had by different people, may vary along with the accumulation of social wealth. The result is that the more the social wealth, the more salient the disparity between the rich and the poor. Yet there are many factors of production that determine the growth of economy that may lead to a change in the status of each person in the relationship of production. These factors include knowledge. As knowledge is often acquired by people by reading books and also created by writing books and a book is a form of intensive linguistic communication, language provides people, in a lower social status in economic life, with an opportunity to change their social status. Particularly, complex and systematic knowledge, needed in production, enables people, mastering it, to enhance their social status. If economy is on the initial stage of growth, the role, played by the knowledge of production, may not be so significant. That economy may especially depend on some natural conditions in its growth. Therefore, natural conditions may sometimes be considered a reason for the appearance of social inequality. For example, some people may accumulate more wealth because the land they cultivate is fertile, whereas other people may not be so lucky because the land they cultivate is barren. Or some people accumulate wealth because they reside in the coastal area and engage in trade, whereas other people are not so lucky because they live in the mountainous area and do not engage in trade. Besides, if the mode of production relies mainly on the use of labor, people may not adequately exploit the potential value of literacy. In the production mainly dependent on labor, people may not need to use advanced knowledge. Accordingly, those, able to read and write, may not be able to have a higher social status. Conversely, the mode of production, relying especially on the use of knowledge, highlights the value of literacy. Literate people tend to gain a higher social status. In addition, the approach of getting wealth is also critical. In pre-modern times, some people plundered wealth through a war in some regions. The value of literacy was also low because production and trade might not be a major occupation. For instance, in medieval Europe, some armed people plundered property including land and became lords. Literate people might not be able to have a high social status because the value of literacy was low. As Elisabeth L. Einstein observes, "it was more compatible with sedentary occupations than with the riding and hunting favored by many squires and lords."[5] Yet along with the rise of commerce, a change took place. As sophisticated literacy and numeracy became two basic tools in business, many sedentary occupations appeared. Then, those who were able to read and write began to find good sedentary occupations along with the growth of commerce. As noted by Einstein, for example, in fifteenth-century England scriveners were already catering to the needs of lowly bankers, merchants, lawyers, aldermen or knights.[6] All involved in commerce were literate in contrast to illiterate army commanders and their illiterate followers who plundered property such as land in the past. Judging by this situation, I argue that people who get wealth through plunder do not need literacy. Commerce needs literate people though all literate people may not always become social elites.

That is, the development of economy depends on the amelioration of the mode of operation. Some people become rich because they find a new method of operation while other people have no way to increase their income because they fail to adopt an up-to-date mode of operation. As wealth is gradually concentrated through the operation of the market, no one plunders. Then, some people become merchants while others remain traditional producers such as peasants. When industry grows, those who pioneer in the development of industry by investing in the production of industrial products may soon find a way to reap profit on the market and become entrepreneurs while other people may become employees hired by those entrepreneurs. Entrepreneurs form the capitalist class while employees constitute the working class. In this case knowledge becomes important in the growth of modern agriculture and industry. Businesses need plenty of technicians and engineers. Large companies also need many managerial personnel. Those who have no capital may choose to receive a good education to become technicians, engineers and managers of the enterprises. They may become a portion of people who have a command of modern technology or professional stills. They read more books than others do. They can draft documents. They can do paperwork. They use language more intensively. They become part of the middle class. Though they originally do not enjoy higher social status, knowledge, had by them, may help them get another sort of social status that is not lower. This situation may rectify, albeit to a certain extent, the related inequality between those who have capital and those who have no capital because the operation of modern enterprises very much depends on the use of technology and professional skills. Many well-educated people become senior managerial and technical personnel in modern enterprises.

Third, in the state or the society, some people may not be able to gain any preeminent social status because they have no appropriate channels for them to ascend on the social ladder. Yet if they keep on reading books, they may gain knowledge and skills needed in providing services to the society. They may play a role in the spread of knowledge for social progress. They may even play a role in constructing the culture of the society. As they have related knowledge and skills, they may also become professionals and have a corresponding social status when people come to need social services. In pre-modern times some social workers might already assist in the undertaking of limited social services, including education, medical treatment and legal advice services. Particularly, in medieval Europe, priests provided education service, medical service, and legal advice service. They engaged in the cause of charity. Priests were knowledgeable. They read Bible and the scripture. They also read historical, philosophical and other professional books. They mastered the knowledge of social construction. As the society gradually needed the related knowledge, they were not required to do a labor job. They obtained remunerations because religious believers contributed money to them. They gained a high social status. They gained social esteem. They belonged to the social elite. They participated in the building of the society, and they were sometimes even invited to enter the government to govern the state. For example, the rulers of feudal kingdoms recruited officials who had originally served the church in Europe. As officials gained knowledge from the schools or universities run by the church, the government came under the influence of the church. Some priests held a prominent political or social status because they held a prominent position in the government. In some sense, priests belonged to the ruling class in medieval times. Although not all were nobles who enjoyed their higher status due to their birth into a noble family, those who were educated and hence became priests might find a channel of upward social mobility because of learning how to read and write. As Albert Murray writes,

> [I]n the West the Church was for centuries the leading and sometimes the only educator. It did, moreover, ignore class distinctions and at times gave ability its opportunity. It is interesting to notice how many high-ranking officers in Church and State in the Middle Ages came from very humble homes. The old jingle about Cardinal Wolsey declared him to have been 'begot by butchers' but nevertheless allowed that he was 'by bishops bred'.[7]

We can also find an example in the East. In Tibet, China, priests get a higher social status. They are not required to work, but they get good remunerations. To read books is a way to become a priest. Thus, Bertrand Russell comments that "Twenty years of study are required in order to obtain a

Doctor's Degree at the University of Lhasa, which is necessary for all the higher posts except that of Dalai Lama."[8]

In medieval times social services might be merely provided by those who were affiliated with the religious organizations. Those who engaged in the undertaking of public welfare were chiefly priests or clergymen. In modern times, however, social services are provided by more secular professionals and the construction of public welfare is one of the preoccupations of many secular people. More people manage to enhance their social status if they are professionals mastering related knowledge. They include teachers and professors, doctors, lawyers and legal advisors, consultants, writers, musicians, sculptors, painters, actors and actresses, singers, athletes, reporters and editors, sociologists, economists, psychologists, senior accountants among others. As the society needs social services widely and as the development of public welfare becomes a major work of social construction, more people who master professional knowledge engage in this cause enhancing their social status. They constitute part of the so-called middle class.

All these cases show that language is not an element that leads to the inequality among people. Language is a tool likely to be used by people to stand more chances of changing their social status. Those who study hard to acquire knowledge and use knowledge intensively are those who use language to the greatest extent. If a person is not in the social status of equality because, for example, he has no adequate financial resources, knowledge, acquired by him through books, may give him a chance to change his lower social status. The inequality of people may thus be rectified to some extent. Thus, people may enhance the equality of the society. That is, knowledge changes people. Likewise, books change people because books are the sources of systematic knowledge. Thus, to read books is to have an opportunity for upward social mobility. As those who belong to the middle class are middle-level income earners and have a middle-level social status and as the population of the middle class gradually becomes a greater part of the population of the state, the emergence of the middle class, in some sense, symbolizes the tendency to the equalization of all within the society and the state. This tendency is at least in part in relation to the role played by books because the most prominent characteristic of the middle class is that they are a group of people having knowledge. It is also because the success of the middle class lies in the very fact that they acquire knowledge efficiently and is able to use knowledge. Books provide plenty of knowledge.

That means that humans, communicating by using language, develop certain media to help spread knowledge. Book is one of such media. It is especially designed to save and spread knowledge. It performs long-distance linguistic communication to impart knowledge to as many people as possible. Books are circulated on the market. Everyone may read books. Books may also be kept by a special institution and be lent by it to many people. Such a special institution later becomes a library. Some special institutions may also be established to search manuscripts and edit, print and publish them as books. These special institutions later become publishing houses. Books change the traditional way used by people to acquire and spread knowledge. Before books were produced by humans, people acquired knowledge, including the experience of production and living, through their mutual interaction characterized by face-to-face contact. People acquired knowledge from each other through spoken communication. They acquired related knowledge on a relatively small scale. The persons with whom each was able to stay in touch were a small number of people who surrounded him. The average level of knowledge, provided by these people, was, in some sense, lower. Since humans started producing books, people have been acquiring knowledge from each other through written communication. Then people often perform mutual communication without face-to-face contact. They communicate with more people on a large scale. The average level of knowledge, provided by people through books, is, in some sense, higher. Thus books enable those readers to enhance the level of their knowledge. As knowledge is often needed in the state either for the purpose of production or for the purpose of the governance of the state or the society, those who master certain knowledge may enhance their social status just because they have the knowledge needed by the state or the society. These people may also include the authors of books. This is because people extend the distance of linguistic communication. Extending the distance of linguistic communication means allowing people to search for knowledge on a large scale. Then people may acquire systematic and rich knowledge provided by a large community. They ascend to a higher status in the state, or the society, because of having knowledge needed by the state or the society.

Mass education that has been developing since early modern times also gives a significant role to language in the equalization of all within the society and the state. As long as more books are read by the masses, books will play a greater role in the equalization of all. The more the books there are in circulation, the more the readers there will be. If there are more readers in the society, more people will create a condition for themselves to ascend to a status that is largely equal to the status enjoyed by all others who succeed in other domains. In the past only a small portion of people had the chances of being educated. These people were usually the children of the rich families such as the families of nobles. They might be taught by private tutors engaged by the rich families. They might also be taught by the church or the temple. These people were a small number of people. Mass education enables the children of all kinds of families to receive necessary education. As the potential intelligence of each person is similar to that of any other person, mass education enables all to use their potential intelligence to acquire knowledge or working skills. The inequality of people, caused by varying social backgrounds had by people, is thus reduced to some extent because knowledge or skills play a role in determining the social status of each person in the society or the state.

First, the background of the family of each person may not decisively determine each person's social status. When the child of a noble family and the child of a common family have the same chance to go to school to receive the same kind of education, the influence of the noble family will soon decline. What becomes prominent is the role played by knowledge acquired by people in determining the social status of each. Books enable all to gain knowledge no matter whether a person comes from a noble family or another kind of family. Family background is no longer important in determining the fate of each.

Second, the variation of the wealth of different families no longer determines whether or not a person receives education. In the past private teachers were engaged by each family to teach its children. If a family could not afford to engage a teacher because this family was poor, the children of this family would lose the chance of receiving education. Then, funding, had by a family, might decide whether or not the children of that family gained a higher social status in future. Now, as education becomes compulsory and the state provides funding to support the children of all families going to school, the children, from the families without adequate funds, may ascend to a higher social status in future because they have knowledge needed by the state or the society.

Third, power, held by a small number of people, is no longer a factor preventing the children of those families without any power from receiving education. In the past traditional society the children of the families, holding state power, might be arranged for to receive education for them to take state power in future as ruling the state required knowledge. Yet since putting mass education into practice, the state has been engaging those people, born into the families having no access to state power, in the governance of the state because they have knowledge. Public servants, engaged by the state through an examination, may be those whose families have no power. Education enhances their status.

As mass education is aimed to train talents needed by the modern state, reading books to learn knowledge can enhance one's social status. Thus one's lower social status in an aspect may be compensated by his higher social status in another aspect. This means that some inequalities of people are caused by their differences. It is largely impossible for people to eliminate all inequalities faced by them. But the disadvantage of one aspect may be compensated by the advantage of another aspect. Thus, comprehensively speaking, a person, in the disadvantageous condition in a certain domain, may receive the equal treatment by attaining his advantageous condition in another domain. People, asserting that all are not born equal, believe that each has different inborn competence or background. People, insisting that all are equal in the state of nature, think that inequality is caused by the civilized society. Hobbes writes that "The question who is the better man, has no place in the condition of meer Nature; where all men are equall. The inequality that now is, has bin introduced by the Lawes civill." [9] Hobbes evidently insists that inequality is caused by the civil society. My view is that among tribal people a difference between one another meant nothing in the tribe as such a difference did not lead to inequality due to the fact that the division of labor had not developed yet and there had been no social stratification. However, an inborn difference between one another may lead to social inequality in the civilized society because the division of labor has unfolded and social stratification has been under way. People cannot change their inborn difference. If one wants to gain an equal status because he is in an unequal status, the only effective method of making a change is to receive education. Receiving education requires one to read books. In this case language is the most basic tool to be used by people to gain knowledge and skills in order to gain the status of equality in the state if they are in a status of inequality in some domains. A person whose social status is originally lower can also write books and then he may find a chance to change his social status. People, different because of a different personal character, may have different destinies. A person of extroversive character may have a very good network of friends. He may get help from his friends. For example, he may get a job in a factory run by one of his friends. Personal character cannot be easily changed. Yet a person of introversive character may make a greater effort to learn technologies via books. He may also be engaged by that factory because that factory needs a technician. A person, born into a poor family, may not be able to have a fund to start his business. But if he can acquire knowledge by going to school and college, knowledge, acquired by him, may qualify him to get a job as a manager in an enterprise. He may join the team of the management in an enterprise. He can also have a higher social status.

In the era of knowledge economy, the social status of an individual person is often determined by knowledge mastered by him. In a pre-modern society, a success in business might be less-educated. Yet in a modern society nearly all successes receive a good education. The society is now operated with knowledge. Thus books play a prominent role in the change of the social status of an individual person. An individual person, reading books and acquiring knowledge, will have a chance to gain a corresponding social status. This is the case for an industrialized society. An individual person, writing books to spread knowledge, may even gain a very prominent social status. Books are very powerful media that can quickly change the status of a person. Conversely, an individual person in a traditional society may not be able to change his social status so as to be equal with others in this aspect because he may not have access to books. Books are prevented from playing a role in the making of a dynamic society in which one can find a channel of upward social mobility. People maintain the status quo as a result. This situation still exists today in some countries. For example, in a traditional society in Africa, people are accustomed to keeping a traditional society in which the social status of each seldom changes. This may affect the economic development because it needs talents who emerge in the society. As Daniel Etounga-Manguelle writes,

> The African will not accept changes in social standing: Dominant and dominated remain eternally in the places allocated them, which is why change in social classifications is often condemned. We complain about the difficulties in promoting the private sector in our states.[10]

In this case people actually or objectively try to maintain the status quo by refraining from exploiting the competence of talents who are potentially able to ascend to a higher social status for various reasons. In this case books cannot help people equalize the society if the society is not equal. That is, the traditional custom plays a role in the society in which some people are prevented from giving play to their superb ability. The traditional custom is maintained in spoken communication instead of written communication. This is by no means a result of using written language. Knowledge is often spread by using written language. Systematic knowledge is chiefly saved by books. If the traditional society maintains inequality, the traditional custom curbs freedom. Books hardly play a role in the creation of a channel of upward social mobility. If the traditional society maintains equality, the traditional custom curbs freedom, too. The equality of all is negative because it restricts freedom. That is, freedom is a condition for invention. Invention is a motive power for social progress. If freedom is restricted, equality, existing in the society, is not wholesome. This also reminds us of the fact that if people deliberately use coercion to forge the equality of the society, books are absolutely prevented from playing a role in the formation of positive equality. In some socialist states built in the twentieth century, the social and economic system, aimed at creating equality by implementing the equalitarian income policy, has proved counter-productive. The rigid equalitarian policy restricts freedom. This is because more freedom means more opportunities. More opportunities mean more potentials of social development. Productive forces may be developed and the general happiness may be enjoyed by all due to the active market built in the principle of freedom. Market releases the potential of humans. If people restrict the level of consumption of a portion of people in order to seek the equality of the whole society, the related policy will dampen the enthusiasm of producers. One example, given by Amartya Sen, illustrates this case. That is, in a given society, given symmetric care, women tend to live longer than men with lower mortality rates in each age group. If one were concerned with the equality of the capability to live long, it would be possible to construct an argument for giving men relatively more medical attention than women to counteract the natural masculine handicap. But giving women less medical attention than men for the same health problems would flagrantly violate a significant requirement of process equity that treats different persons similarly in matters of life and death.[11] The positive equality should be that realized under the condition that freedom is not restricted accordingly. That is, realizing positive equality will not affect freedom. Rousseau used to point out that "all the inequality which now prevails owes its strength and growth to the development of our faculties and the advance of the human mind."[12] The progress of civilization results in more social inequality because of an increase of diversity. In order to realize equality under the condition that the progress of civilization is not bridled, this equality should not be anything but dynamic equality. This goal cannot be realized unless people receive education. Thus, such equality is realized because people read books. The positive equality must be realized due to the use of language. In short, people, using state power to impose equality, use coercion. In contrast, people, seeking equality with freedom, realize this goal by reading books. Books symbolize the possibility of realizing equality by using language rather than using coercion.

2. Code or Common Law

Now we are going to discuss equality realized in the form of law. I have already discussed law in Chapter Nine. Now I would like to stress that once the law has been codified or announced as the common law, the codification of law, or the formation of the common law, highlights the nature of law. Codification, or the formation of common law, particularly highlights the equality of everyone before the law. This means that the invariable application of law within the state results in the equality of all before the law. Law is abstract in some sense because, comparatively speaking, people, as individuals in the face of law, are concrete. People may be equal before the law, but without law made by using language people may be in the state of inequality. People may map out their different plans of personal development. People may have different competences. People may adopt different methods of personal pursuit. People may have different opportunities and destinies. Then each will have a different personal background. They tend to have different social statuses. They even tend to become unequal in more aspects as a result. Thus, Hegel writes that:

> Men are made unequal by nature, where inequality is in its element, and in civil society the right of particularity is so far from annulling this natural inequality that it produces it out of mind and raises it to an inequality of skill and resources, and even to one of moral and intellectual attainment.[13]

In view of this situation, I argue that this situation is not always the direct result of using language. It is true that people have different social statuses and they are not equal in many aspects, but we cannot blindly blame this situation for the reason that the same kind of language is used by all. If inequality caused thereby is kept by the regime or the state, this inequality is kept by using coercion rather than using language though inequality is also often caused by many objective causes, such as the difference of each person's physical fitness or the difference of each person's inherent competence.

Besides, the inequality of people in the social or political domain, given rise to by the fact that people are different in physical competence, psychological status, family or ethnic background and other aspects, is not always repugnant to the principle of the formation of the society or the state. For the formation of the society people need to establish order. For the formation of the state people need to establish a government that has power in administration. To maintain order and to have a government, there must be a hierarchy. If one desires to break this hierarchy, he will probably do so in vain. This hierarchy represents a structure. As Richard M. Weaver, a philosopher of the last century, writes, "If society is something which can be understood, it must have structure; if it has structure, it must have hierarchy; against this metaphysical truth the declamations of the Jacobins break in vain."[14] So in the great pageant of history there emerged even idealists desiring the elimination of all social inequalities. But they failed to realize their ideals. If the equality of all aspects were to be realized, people were not required to receive education because if they received education, some of them would win high grades while others low grades, a fact of inequality. In this case people were not required to engage in production because people would gain the income of different levels due to the fact that the competence of each varied, a fact of inequality. Similarly, in this case people should not be required to participate in market competition because such competition would result in social inequality. As Robin M. Williams writes, "Equality diminishes in attractiveness among the winners in competitive activities. Achievement is likely to be stressed among populations experiencing high levels of richly rewarded opportunities for individual attainment."[15] In this case people were not required to be organized either because if they were organized, somebody would issue a command while others would have to obey the command, a fact of inequality. This means that in the formation of the society or in the organization of the state, there must be a hierarchy. To encourage all to make every effort to make contributions to the society or the state, people should accept or tolerate the inequality of people in certain aspects. People usually accept some inequalities. As Weaver observes,

> It is a matter of common observation, too, that people meet most easily when they know their position. If their work and authority are defined, they can proceed on fixed assumptions and conduct themselves without embarrassment toward inferior and superior. When the rule of equality obtains, however, no one knows where he belongs. Because he has been assured that he is "just as good as anybody else," he is likely to suspect that he is getting less than his deserts.[16]

Language is unable to change this situation particularly in the state. This is chiefly because in the formation of a state people cannot use language for any other purpose except the organization of the state. But language can create a condition for the realization of social equality in a certain domain due to the nature of language. Language can be used to construct a mode of interaction between the governor and the governed so as to create equality in a certain domain. Law, made by using language, is an example. Specifically, law is a system consisting of coercion and a discourse, a special process of linguistic communication that issues a command for the civilized governance of the state. The evolution of this discourse reflects a change in the governance of the human community. Coercion was sometimes used even on the late stage of the evolution of the tribe. Yet along with the growth of the state, the use of coercion becomes civilized. A discourse is created to issue a command for the governance of the state in a civilized way. If the law is obeyed, coercion is not actually used. As the law is usually obeyed by the majority of the people, coercion is less often used. The state is governed though coercion is not actually used or not often used. Thus, people are able to avoid violence in the governance of the state to the greatest extent. Thus, avoiding the use of violence to some extent, or even to the greatest extent, is helpful to the realization of equality because inequality always occurs under the circumstances that coercion is used and coercion is backed by violence. A person, coerced, is required to succumb. Succumbing means an interaction that presupposes the inequality between one another. In contrast, linguistic presentation is given across the state. Linguistic presentation involves a process of linguistic communication involving all. Everyone is equal as this linguistic presentation is given to all without any difference. Because of this, people give or make any law by using language. Law takes form in linguistic communication. As everyone is equal in linguistic communication, law creates a condition for the realization of equality in the related aspects.

That means that, by using language, the governor communicates with all under his governance in one process of linguistic communication. Inequality, appearing in the society or the state, may be specific. Yet, by using language, people may give an abstract linguistic description. Language may be used to describe a principle in the governance of the society or the state as a regulation people are required to obey, and it may be used to give a presentation conceptualizing equality by ignoring the social background of each individual person that is often the reason for the appearance of social or political inequality. Thus, implementing this regulation time and again and applying this regulation to all regardless of the natural character and the social background of each individual person creates a condition for the realization of equality in some important facets. Language is a form of communication adopted to make a law. This is a special way of using language. This is also a way of using any medium. Law rests on extending the distance of linguistic communication. The evolution of law, particularly code or common law, also hinges on the extension of linguistic communication. In the primitive society, namely, in the tribe, custom was used to rule on a dispute. Custom is one of the origins of modern law. Those laws, derived from the evolvement of custom in early times, were usually unwritten and used in a local area. Equality before the unwritten law might not be discerned because the unwritten law often depended on the interpretation of the person functioning like a judge, such as an elder in the village, and that interpretation was likely to vary from time to time or from place to place. In addition, the judge was very likely to fulfill his duty according to his own judgment that might not be always guaranteed to be consistent over time or across the state. Then along with the development of written communication, such as the development of written communication based on the development of certain media created by using some proper materials, including stone, parchment and paper, unwritten laws are replaced by written laws along with codification, or in the states in which unwritten law is still preserved today, law becomes common law. Codification, or the formation of common law, means that the authorities now especially rely on the form of law supported by linguistic communication that goes on directly across the state in the governance of the state. As the state is a community that grows large as compared with those villages and towns, the authorities need to use the law in the form that extends the distance of linguistic communication to communicate with the masses on a large scale. The reason is that social inequality becomes evident along with the growth of the community and the state needs to strengthen the role played by the form of law across the state. To put it differently, along with the growth of the community such as the society or the state, social inequality becomes salient. The code or the common law that applies in a large community apparently reflects the spirit of equality against the trend toward social inequality. The reason is that a written presentation, or a form of linguistic expression common across the state, is able to realize communication on a large scale, and code or common law does not vary in a large community, even in a far-flung corner of the community. Implementing code or common law highlights the equality of all before the law. Comparing code or common law with the original case law or customary law, we may find that the case law or the customary law was usually applied in a local area in the past. This means that if a law is only implemented on a small scale, it is likely for the judge to make a judgment in view of specific circumstances only. The law may not be abstract. Thus the judge is likely to make a judgment flexibly. This will affect the principle of equality before the law. In other words, a law, implemented on a large scale, tends to be abstract. As a result, it is less likely for code or common law to change over time because to change a law, people require the state to act. The state, acting on a very large scale, is not very flexible. Thus, nobody can bend this law to discriminate against anybody. This means that one of the attributes of law is abstract. Codification or the formation of common law means the abstraction of law to a certain extent. The abstraction of law lays a foundation for realizing equality of all before the law. In other words, the principle of equality of all before the law stems from the evolution of the form of presenting the law to a greater extent.

First, law is normally made to realize justice. Though in history law is sometimes made to serve the interest of the ruling class at the expense of the interest of the ruled classes, this is not due to the technical characteristic of law but due to the social conditions of that time. Along with the progress of the society, law is more and more apparently made to realize justice. That is, law is made to serve the interest of everyone. Then it follows that law, made to serve the interest of everyone, is actually applied to protect the legitimate interest of everyone without any difference. Before the law is made, people are not protected by any law because there is no law. Presumably, people are independent in this case. They are in the state of anarchy. People may rely on the use of their own force to protect themselves. Law, or positive law, is unavailable. If two people argue about how to distribute the game captured by them in their hunting cooperation, a stronger or a more resourceful person may be able to decide on how to distribute the game. The two people are unequal in the distribution of what they have got. Likewise, if two people fight against each other for the occupation of a piece of land which is a favorable location for the building of residential premises, each person uses his own force to protect his own interest. The capacity of self-protection of all varies. So people are unequal in this aspect. Likewise, if two people are involved in a dispute over the use of water along the river or in the mountainous area and the power holder is required to rule on the dispute, the person, possessing more financial resources, may be more capable of protecting his interest. This also gives origin to the inequality of people in the society. Yet since the formation of the state people have made laws in the governance of the state. Then, the capacity of protecting the interest of each person will not vary. Under the law each person has the same capacity of protecting his interest. This capacity is provided by the state. The state treats each person equal. Therefore, if a strong person and a weak person, or a rich person and a poor person, or a person with a high social status and a person with a low social status, or a person with power and a person without power, are involved in a lawsuit, theoretically speaking, it is possible for the capacity of protecting any party to be equivalent to the capacity of protecting the other party. Now all parties have the equal status in this context.

Second, people, making a law, communicate with all by using language. This law is a command issued to all. Any command exists in a process of linguistic communication that reaches all. In the meantime, communicating by using language, people perform one-to-many communication. While they make a law, they promulgate it. They promulgate the same law to all. This law, made to prevent people from offending a certain regulation made for the governance of the state, is a general rule. Then, people, in one-to-many communication, are all equal. Then, as long as the lawmaker communicates with all through a law, all are also equal. The related law made for each is the same as the law made for all others. This means that if a person violates the law, the law will be applied to penalize him. This person is not supposed to bend the law because the way of applying the law made for him must be the same as the law made for all others. Otherwise the said law will not be the real law. In Chinese history, laws made by the ruler used to be applied to the selected people. In some Kingdoms existing before the emergence of the Chinese Empire legal punishments might not be applied to nobles or senior officials. Yet what is seen by people over the long term is that if a prince violated the law, he must be punished like an ordinary man. That is, all are equal before the law. So, if a person violates a related law, he will get penalized according to that law no matter whether he is rich or poor, or no matter whether his social status is high or low, or no matter whether he is strong or weak, or no matter whether he is well-educated or less-educated.

The case for the measurement of meting out the penalty is the same. A person who commits one kind of crime receives the penalty that is the same as the penalty received by another person who commits the same kind of crime, all other conditions being equal. In short, this phenomenon is in relation to the use of language in communication though people usually believe that the equality of all before the law also stems from an idea. That is, people, performing linguistic communication on a large scale, tend to decrease the cost of that linguistic communication. Otherwise the linguistic communication may not succeed. One-to-many linguistic communication is a method used by people to decrease the cost of linguistic communication. Thus, a law, functioning through one-to-many linguistic communication, treats everyone equal. If we regard a law as a public product made in the interest of the public, it is a complex public product. As it is used by all collectively, it treats each in the same way. The codification of law means that a code is presented. A code is usually in the shape of a book. Such a book can be printed by a press. As the press manufactures countless copies of this book, the press is a machine producing media. Manufacturing the same materials by the press is, in some sense, like handling the judicial cases of the same kind in the same way, laying a technical foundation for realizing the equality of all before the law. Common law also seeks the similar goal though it is an unwritten form. That it is common means that it treats all equal.

Third, when a law is applied to a case, the judge usually does not personally know the two principals involved in a civil case or the suspect of committing a crime in a criminal case. This is because a law is usually made in a large community. Before the emergence of the large community people live in the small community. They may live in a tribe or in a village. If two people are involved in a dispute, the person who rules on the dispute may know the two principals personally. In this case we cannot expect that the person, ruling on the dispute, always handles this case fairly. If this person is a good friend of one of the principals, the ruling may be in favor of that principal. But along with an increase in the size of the community, people largely become strangers. As language is often used by more and more people, people extend the distance of linguistic communication to the far reaches of the community. Immediacy between one another vanishes. In this case the judge who rules on a dispute is usually a stranger. In the meantime, the lawmaker treats all within the community as strangers. This background reflects a special situation occurring along with an increase in the size of the community. When people are in a community structured by a community of spoken language, this community is small because people in this community usually interact with each other face-to-face. The development of written communication decisively breaks immediacy between one another. Under these circumstances people do not need to communicate with each other face-to-face. As language allows for people to communicate with each other on a very large scale, people develop transportation to cooperate in production through the division of labor on a large scale. Thus people become strangers gradually. The society of acquaintances is replaced by the society of strangers. This is due to extending the distance of linguistic communication. Extending the distance of linguistic communication underlies the growth of the community and hence the evolution of the division of labor. The reason is that extending the distance of linguistic communication underlies the growth of market and market is a basis for the development of the division of labor. So, according to Smith, in a small community, it is difficult for the division of labor to develop because the extent of market is very limited. That is, "when the market is very small, no person can have any encouragement to dedicate himself entirely to one employment."[17] A male of each household living in a small village in Scotland had to work as a carpenter, a mason and a smith at the same time. If a male worked only as a porter, the demand for the service provided by him in the village might not be high enough so as to allow him to work as a porter either. Only when the extent of market becomes large due to the fact that people engage in trade in a large area will the demand for the service provided by him in a large area, such as in a city or in a country, be high enough for him to work especially as a porter. So he especially mentions that some sorts of industry can be carried on nowhere but in a great town. A porter can find employment in no other place. A village is too narrow a sphere for him. Even an ordinary market town is scarcely large enough to afford him constant occupation. In very small villages which are scattered about in so desert a country as the Highlands of Scotland, every farmer must be butcher, baker and brewer for his own family. In such a situation one can scarcely expect to find even a smith, a carpenter or a mason within less than twenty miles of another of the same trade. [18]

That means that the development of the division of labor is conditioned by the exchange of goods and services among many people. The fact that many people exchange goods and services means the development of a market. As the market must be given birth to by the exchange of goods and services among many people, the society, formed due to the development of the market, should be the society of strangers. This society is a big society. Conversely speaking, acquaintances that form a small society cannot build a market because a market exists in a big society. This means that people increase the size of the community until they form a big society. Then they change the mode of mutual interaction between one another. The mutual interaction between acquaintances conditions the formation of a small society. Now people form a big society. In this society, the typical mutual interaction occurs between strangers. So the result is that along with the growth of a community, villages form themselves into a city and regions form themselves into a country. Then, people, having been originally acquaintances, become strangers. Consequently, people make a new law. In other words, a regulation, carried out to govern the community composed of strangers, becomes a law. A law in this sense is a regulation carried out to rule on the dispute between the two strangers. Then people formulate and put into practice the principle that all are equal before the law. If we compare the nature of law with the nature of administrative order, we will see this truth. Before a law is made, the state may be simply governed by the magistrates or the administrative officials or the power holders. There may be a special relationship between a power holder and certain people. For example, some people and the power holder may belong to the same family or the same region. The power holder may also hold the view that is the same as the view held by those people. If the power holder rules on a dispute between a certain person and any other person, the power holder may come under the influence of that special relationship. Thus, the power holder may fail to treat everyone equal. This means that this power holder makes an administrative judgment. The administrative judgment is an administrative order. An administrative order is in a comparatively short process of linguistic communication. This means that the administrative order may change at anytime. An administrative order that may change at anytime may be issued under the influence of the said special relationship. As an administrative order is often issued in a local area, it may also be influenced by the related special relationship. A law is different. A law exists in a comparatively long process of linguistic communication. A law is supposed not to change over the long term and throughout the state. The lawmaker is at a good distance off the principals. There is a long distance between the lawmaker and the principals, and the lawmaker does not have any special relationship with any principal. The lawmaker, making the law, is unable to consider if he and certain people belong to the same family or the same region and so on and so forth. This means that there is no special relationship between the lawmaker and ordinary people in the state. Of course, some scholars may argue that in history a law is often made under the influence of the ruling class. But again I argue that this is due to the certain social conditions existing in history. The technical characteristic of language dictates that law, made by people, involves a process of long-distance linguistic communication between the lawmaker and ordinary people. People, seeking justice, will realize their goal due to this characteristic of law. Thus, as there is no special relationship between the lawmaker and ordinary people, there is also no special relationship between the judge on behalf of the lawmaker and the principals. When a case is heard by the judge, the judge is selected by the court randomly instead of being selected by any principal. If a principal happens to be one relative, or friend, or neighbor, of the judge, the court will activate the challenge system. If two parties are involved in a lawsuit, no party has the capacity of influencing the judge. In this respect all are equal. In the meantime, the lawmaker is not involved in any personal relationship with any principal of the case either. Although a lawmaker is in the dominant position because of the supremacy of the law made by him, he is supposed not to appear because he is far away or he has actually died. As such, the equality of all before the law is not affected either by a judge or a lawmaker. Thus, the equality of all in this respect results from the characteristic of long-distance linguistic communication. This means that people, communicating by using language, come to extend the distance of linguistic communication. Then they make laws. Then as a law prevents the lawmaker or the judge from having any special relationship with those who are governed by the law, all are treated equal in the application of a law. Though the civilized society, formed by people, may be a community in which various inequalities arise as claimed by Rousseau or any other philosophers, the state, formed by people, makes the laws that realize the equality of people. My reasoning is that language is widely used in the state. By using language, people set in motion a process of communication that reaches all without any influence of personal relationship. As all use language equally, language plays a role in realizing the equality of all.

In other words, a law is composed of two parts, of which one part is coercion likely to be used to carry out the law and the other part is linguistic presentation. Without coercion a law cannot be considered a law. Similarly, without linguistic presentation a law cannot be a real law. Though coercion might be used by the ruling group within the state to serve the interest of their own and to keep the inequality of people within the state in history, linguistic presentation itself is not the form naturally prone to cause inequality. This is because language is what used by all. The same language is used by all. The language is, in essence, used by all in the same way. Language is the medium used by any one to communicate with all others in the state. Language can be used to perform one-to-many linguistic communication. As such, it can be used to convey the same information to all. If a regulation is promulgated by the government, this regulation must be obeyed by all. Thus, all must be subject to the same regulation. Everyone is equal under this regulation. That is, as long as the power holder considers the governance of the state in the interest of all as the cases of democracies established by humans in ancient and modern times show, people can realize equal justice under the law. So in the funeral oration that he delivered in 431 BC, the Athenian leader Pericles encouraged belief in what we now call equal justice under law. So we today also behold that "equal justice under law" becomes a phrase engraved on the front of the United States Supreme Court building in Washington, D.C. As long as people build a democracy in the building of their state, the will of the people must be reflected in the governance of the state. Then language can play a role in establishing a system in which all are equal before the law. Due to the nature of language, a law, made by using language, must be a regulation applying to all in the same way. Thus the principle that all are equal before the law is universally carried out in nearly all the states throughout the world.

The reason that law functions to maintain or protect the equality of people in a certain aspect is also that long-distance linguistic communication, performed by law, behooves the law to meet the expectation of the multitude of people within the state. The law is a process of linguistic communication that reaches all across the state. It is known to so many people. Normally, the lawmaker is under the massive pressure to make a fair law. This law, applied in the environment of publicity, is bound to establish the principle of the equality of all before the law. Unless the state is formed under a certain system of unfair social hierarchy and the social inequality is deliberately maintained by the ruling class, inequality before the law can hardly be accepted by all. In other words, people seldom assert equality under the administrative order. When an administrative order is carried out, the result of carrying out this administrative order is parochial. Specific circumstances vary from time to time and from area to area. Thus it is difficult to fathom if equality under a certain administrative order is ensured. The different results of carrying out certain orders at different times and in different areas can hardly indicate the existence of social inequality caused by multifarious factors. Accordingly, it is difficult to maintain complete equality if a specific matter is dealt with by the government at a certain time and in a local area. But people may make a law that defines once for all the rule of ruling on the same or similar cases frequently occurring from time to time and in all areas within the state. The universal application of the same law all the time across the state symbolizes and in most cases means the equality of every one before the law. Only such a law can be considered fair and only such a law can be accepted. The attribute of the long process of linguistic communication performed by law can be deemed as a factor resulting in establishing the principle of the equality of every one before the law.

The equality of everyone before the law also indicates that people realize such equality in a special process of linguistic communication. A law, the most typical form of linguistic communication performed by using language in the organization of the state, symbolizes the fact that the role, played by language in the realization of equality, is rationally abstracted in the judicial procedure in which the state protects generally the lawful interest or the civil rights of each. Such a law cannot be concrete. If it is concrete, the equality of everyone before the law may cause some social inequalities in the domain in which people cannot eliminate those social inequalities unless by gaining knowledge, as mentioned earlier. In other words, any regulation, concerning the distribution of specific interest, may be controversial. It is impossible for people to make a regulation to force social equalization. Social equality can be largely realized in the method that one's disadvantage in an aspect is compensated by one's advantage in another aspect as long as people take advantage of knowledge. The society or the state needs to be operated with efficiency. It is impossible to expect a law to be able to realize social equality in all aspects of social equity. For example, if a policy, made by the administrative body, is made law, it may not be accepted by all unless this policy is in relation to foreign affairs. That is, if a policy, concerning an economic or social or political affair, is made a law, it may be opposed by many citizens because people are in different situations in this context. Conversely speaking, the matters, concerning the lawful interest or civil rights, are usually the same to all in the same aspect. The regulation in this aspect can be as abstract as possible. Thus it can be prescribed by law. Thus a law is a process of linguistic communication that goes on throughout the state. This law is invariable and monolithic across the state. Thus, as a public policy is like a product, comparatively speaking, it can be regarded as a retail sale product. By contrast, a law is like a product that can be used repetitively over the long term and across the state. It can be regarded as a public product. It is a wholesale product. It is presented and applied in the same way everywhere. The invariability of law technically conditions the equality of all before the law. As such, the related law, made of the original policy, may be tyrant. Weaver writes that:

> It is generally assumed that the erasing of all distinctions will usher in the reign of pure democracy. But the inability of pure democracy to stand for something intelligible leaves it merely a verbal deception. If it promises equality before the law, it does no more than empires and monarchies have done and cannot use this as a ground to assert superiority. If it promises equality of condition, it promises injustice, because one law for the ox and the lion is tyranny. Pressure from the consumer instinct usually compels it to promise the latter. When it was found that equality before the law has no effect on inequalities of ability and achievement, humanitarians concluded that they had been tricked into asking only part of their just claim. The claim to political

equality was then supplemented by the demand for economic democracy, which was to give substance to the ideal of the levelers. Nothing but a despotism could enforce anything so unrealistic, and this explains why modern governments dedicated to this program have become, under one guise and another, despotic.[19]

This means that the organization of the state reflects the nature of mutual interaction between one another in the society or the state. The inequalities of certain aspects are natural and needed by the organization of the society or the state. A law is unable to efface such inequalities. Thus a law is usually made as an abstract regulation protecting the lawful interest or the civil rights. A law usually protects the basic rights of each and ensures providing certain basic conditions for each. A law usually functions in a certain number of spheres. In these spheres the state makes and implements effectively an abstract regulation. This results in the appearance of the equality of everyone before the law. That is, by using language, people communicate with each other across the state in one single process. The content can be abstracted. Then, the equality of all before the law is realizable. In some sense, only law performs a task of linguistic communication to apply an abstract regulation. As such, it is difficult for people to disagree thereto. Then law lays a foundation for the unity of the state.

To put it more specifically, a law can be used by all and language can be used by all, too. A law invariably serves all within the state and language also serves all within the state. Both law and language serve all within the state without a difference. Law and language serve all within the state evenly in a philosophical view though law or language may be used by different people differently. I mean that a law may be especially used by a certain person because he is involved in a particular civil or criminal case and language may be especially used by a certain person in a special way. Theoretically, a law and language can be used by anyone if people need to apply a law or if people need to use language. But some other forms, or some other things, do not belong to all evenly in the society or the state. These forms or things include money, honor, power, privilege and prominent social status. This means that the allocation of money, honor, power, privilege and prominent social status is not even in the civilized society. The appearance of these forms or things pertains to the competence, endowment, luck, effort, and idea of a person. For example, luck may not befall all evenly. If two job applicants apply for the only one job position, only one can get that job even though both of them are equally qualified to do that job. An honor is only conferred on those who deserve it. But if we assume that some of these forms and things should be distributed evenly in the society, it may be very difficult for people to reach an agreement. This situation is unlike the situation of the primitive society. In the primitive society, people do not have their own property. In this case they are equal in almost all aspects. After humans enter the civilized society, social inequality appears. Social inequality appears because of the achievements accomplished by some people though sometimes social inequality may also stem from exploitation or oppression. I mean that some people may accomplish certain achievements because they make a special effort and they have their own endowments and others. Entering the civilized society, people use language. In the meantime, a law, made by the lawmaker, creates certain primary equal conditions for all, including the equal opportunities to get a job, equal rights to get certain social securities and perhaps an equal status in the political life of the state. It is easy for people to agree to these basic regulations. This means that a law can be potentially used by all equally and language can also be potentially used by all equally because, by using language, people can give an abstract presentation and hence make a law. This means that law treats everyone in the same way. The law does not require that all should accomplish the same achievements. The law does not require that all should be rewarded in the same way. Thus, law is like the rule of a game. If the law defines that all should be rewarded in the same way even though they do not accomplish the same achievements, the game cannot be played. But if a game is played, it is potentially beneficial to all participants because it spurs all to make an effort, as already noted earlier. This is beneficial to the development of the society. In this case, at least technically speaking, law is accepted by all like a game. This represents a way of forming the common interest of all. So does language. Since the birth of language, it has been used by all. Language represents the formation of the common interest of all. Otherwise people will not communicate with one another by using language. In this sense, the attribute of law pertains to the attribute of language. To put it differently, before people commenced to use language for their mutual communication, they were in the tribe or even in the herd. All were equal. They had nothing but their own naked bodies. After people commenced to use language for their mutual communication, they finally entered the civilized society, and in the meantime they became unequal in certain or many aspects. Yet since then law, made by them, has gradually become the abstract presentation almost only concerning the basic rights and conditions of people to which they can hardly disagree in the societal development. Accordingly, law is the regulation that people are most likely to agree to. Law lays a foundation for the building of the state.

3. Ballot

Where there is any inequality in the society as social classes exist, such inequality is usually maintained by using coercion or force unless people accept widely social inequality relating to those social classes. Such inequality is given rise to by a certain social system and such a social system is chiefly maintained by using coercion. Coercion is usually used on a group of people instead of all such as a group of people residing in a region or a social class or an ethnic group of people or a group of religious believers. The regime, using coercion, is usually unable to coerce all within the state. This is because the regime, coercing all within the state, coerces a large number of people. These people, coerced, may revolt against the regime. People who are in a large number may subvert the regime. Assuming that coercion, used by the regime, forces an interaction between the regime and the masses, these masses are only a portion of people. The regime cannot coerce the entire people. But language, used by people, can be used by all. As all can use it to perform communication, common people may play a role. As all use the same language, communicating with each other in one process, those who have certain advantages in the state are prevented from using their advantages to influence the process of decision-making or policy-making. People realize equality. That is, in election or referendum, in some sense, ordinary people, casting ballots, become equal. Each person has a brain, two hands, and two eyes, like any other person, and in this case a ballot, cast by each in this process, most typically demonstrates the equality enjoyed by each because each ballot is totally equivalent to any other ballot in the aspect of the capacity of making a decision. As Hans Kelsen writes,

> Democracy requires that the right of suffrage should be not only as nearly universal but also as nearly equal as possible. That means that the influence which each voter exercises on the result of the election should be the same, in other terms, the weight of vote of every voter should be equal to that of every other voter. Mathematically formulated, the weight of voter is a fraction whose denominator is the number of voters of one electoral body, and whose numerator is the number of delegates to be elected by this body.[20]

That means that each ballot has influence on the decision-making and the influence, had by this ballot, is equivalent to the influence had by another ballot. Everyone is equal in this aspect. In view of the situation that in the past people never cast ballots in the decision-making of the state, we can believe that a great change has taken place in modern times.

In the past ballots were not in use, and people were usually not equal in the process of decision-making in the governance of the state. Any important decision was not made by all in the state. Some people were able to take part in the making of a decision, whereas others were unable to do so. Then the people were divided into the ruling class and the ruled classes. The appearance of the ruling class and the ruled classes means that the power for the governance of the state merely belongs to a group of people that have certain similar social attribute and the same social status. At least in medieval Europe in the regions where there was the feudal system as the form of organizing the society or the state, those who exercised their influence on the governance of the state were always only a portion of people and often a very small portion of people. As nobles were dominant in the process of decision-making because nobles were close to state power, there was no equality between nobles and common people. Some nobles had a higher social status because they were lords. There was certain inequality between lords and servants. Lordship was usually hereditary. Therefore, there existed the inequality of birth in the society. Thus nobles were prone to keep the high social status because of their family background. There existed the inequality of social relationship between nobles and common people. In addition, priests were often influential in the process of decision-making in the governance of the state because they were invited to act as the officials of the government in the feudal kingdom from time to time. There existed the inequality between priests and common people in this aspect. At least common people had no say in the process of decision-making at that time. This is the reason that sometimes a portion of peasants revolted against the ruler. They tried to influence the process of decision-making. But as the state did not arrange for them to take part in the process of decision-making, they were prohibited from giving an opinion. There was no equality between different social classes. Since people began to cast ballots in election in early modern times, a change has taken place. As each ballot has the influence of the same degree, each person, holding one ballot, is equal with the other person holding another ballot. This happens in the capitalist times. Thus, we see that an election is usually held in each country, and people realize a sort of equality by casting ballots no matter whether a voter, holding one ballot, is a very prominent entrepreneur or an ordinary worker or no matter whether a voter, holding one ballot, is rich or poor or no matter whether a voter, holding one ballot, is well-educated or less-educated or no matter whether a voter, holding one ballot, believes in a certain religion or not. As Kelsen writes,

> According to the democratic idea of equality of all citizens, the single voter counts only as a member of the whole people or, where proportional representation exists, as a member of a political party. Hence purely democratic systems do not attach significance to the social class or profession of the voter.[21]

Ballots, cast by all qualified voters in the decision-making in the governance of the state, contribute to a fundamental change in the governance of the state. Ballots symbolize the realization of the equality of all citizens in the governance of the state and the abolition of the privileges enjoyed by a small portion of people in the past. All citizens become equal at least in the public life. As common people account for the majority of the citizenry, the government comes to make and carry out the public polices largely in favor of common people or in consideration of the request from common people. Some phenomena prove this case.

First, the government sets up a progressive tax system. Those who are high-income earners are usually required to pay taxes according to a higher rate, whereas those who are low-income earners are allowed to pay taxes according to a lower rate. Those who are high-income earners are usually entrepreneurs, businessmen and businesswomen, the senior managerial personnel of big companies, the professionals of financial sectors, senior engineers and technicians, professors, lawyers, doctors, artists and sport stars, etc. And those who are low-income earners are laborers, factory workers, the employees of catering service sector, family caregivers, shop customer attendants, cleaners, part-time shop helpers and others. Implementing a progressive tax system averages the incomes of different social classes. People reduce disparity between the rich and the poor to a certain extent as a result. There appears a tendency to the equalization of the society. Such a tendency bolsters the solidarity of the state.

Second, the government expands the scope of public services provided by it to cover more and more people. As common people account for the majority of the people in the state, expanding the scope of public services is especially beneficial to common people. Though in the society certain portions of people may still be more influential than others because they have more social resources, the government especially considers the interest of common people in making a decision. The reason is that now common people, holding ballots, have a say in the process of decision-making and in the process of making a law as well. Then the government is required to provide those public services. For example, the government may be required to provide free medical care to all citizens no matter whether they are poor or rich. The medical care, provided by the government to the citizens, uses the financial resources of the state, which are available mainly because citizens pay taxes. High-income earners pay a greater part of taxes to the state. As low-income earners account for the majority of the population, free medical care tends to benefit low-income earners to a greater extent. Other similar cases include free education service characterized by mass education, free family care service provided to those in need and free special care given to the disabled people, and so on and so forth. If these programs of social welfare are absent, all may seek those services by themselves. Some people are able to enjoy those services because they have adequate funds. By contrast, some other people are unable to enjoy those services. For example, a high-income household may have a fund to get medical treatment given by a hospital while a low-income household may not. Likewise, a high-income household may have a fund to send their children to a good school while a low-income household may not. An increase in public services, offered by the state to the citizens, equalizes the society or the state.

Third, the government protects the interest of common people. Though those who are powerful and resourceful and hence have an advantageous status in the society or the state are more capable of protecting the interest of their own, the government tends to especially protect those who are powerless and weak. If we assume that in modern times those who are powerful and resourceful usually represent the party of capital while those who are powerless and weak belong to the party of labor, then the government tends to protect the interest of the party of labor. For example, the government may promulgate the minimum wage standard in order to guarantee the minimum level of income for the employees. The state may make a law requiring enterprises to improve the working condition for the workers in order to protect the interest of the workers. The government may promulgate a statute stipulating that the employer has to meet some requirements if he dismisses an employee. The society develops and people also become different in the society. People cannot eliminate all social differences. People are not only different in gender, age and physical fitness, and so on and so forth, but also different in family background, education background, income, and social relationship, and so on and so forth. These differences often give rise to social inequality. Yet now public policies, made by the government, tend not to increase, but to decrease, the said social inequality due to the fact that the government is now under the influence of ballots, a progress that, theoretically speaking, symbolizes the equality of all citizens or at least all voters.

When Rousseau narrated his view about the origin of the inequality of people in the civilized society, he ascribed the establishment of private property right to be one main origin of the inequality of people in the society. He thought that people were equal in the primitive society. He dreamed of the formation of a small republic in which people could realize equality. When Karl Marx offered his view about the private property of the society, he basically agreed with Rousseau in this aspect as he believed that in the primitive society there was no private property and the future communist society would abolish private property right. He must have thought that the society without private property was better than the society with private property. As he thought that the primitive society was a classless society, he maintained that people were equal before the arrival of the civilized society. When communism was realized, he imagined, people would again be equal because at that time social classes would vanish and the state, as an apparatus of the oppression of the ruled classes by the ruling class, would wither away. My view is that private property is a result of the development of the civilized society. It is impossible to eliminate private property in the era of civilization. This is because private property is a basis for the formation of the market of exchanging goods and services, which underlies the growth of the civilized society. Without private property people may not be motivated to work. What can lead to equality is language rather than the revocation of private property albeit to a certain extent. Language may provide a tool to humans to restore equality because language is a fundamental form of social equality. As language is actually a medium in the mutual interaction of people forming a society, all can use language equally. The extensive use of language is instrumental in the realization of equality in many aspects we seldom conceive of.

That means that language is a medium usable by all on equal footing. Everyone has access to language because everyone is capable of learning to use language. Language is at the disposal of everyone. People can also use media created because of using language on equal footing. The said media are the extension of language. As far as ballots are concerned, printing, developed to manufacture books and then adopted to manufacture ballots in modern times, also functions to realize equality. Printing, invented by geniuses, such as Johannes Guttenberg, makes it possible for people to manufacture ballots and ballots standardize collective communication. Thus citizens are enabled to perform the same linguistic communication although they are in the different circumstances, reside at different locations, belong to the different groups of age or gender, and have different occupations, education backgrounds and family backgrounds. What is meaningful is only the statistic work of the ballots cast in the process of election. The standardized media remove all obstacles in collective linguistic communication performed by the voters because all voters are made to perform the same linguistic communication.

Coincidentally, the repetitive printing of the press to manufacture ballots creates an essential condition for the voters to perform the same linguistic communication. Then voters express opinions in the same way, highlighting the equality of all voters in a process so important for the voters to decide how the state or the society is to be governed. The result is that, in election, all voters are treated in the same way and all voters express the same opinion or two opinions only. The state usually seeks one opinion only and usually it is the majority that expresses that opinion. This opinion is the mainstream opinion of the voters. The computation of ballots becomes decisive. The personal characteristics of each voter disappear and all are the same people. If people are very poor, they are almost equal in all aspects in the society. For example, if people live from hand to mouth, they almost have nothing else. They may not have their own residential premises. What they have may only be several clothes and basic kitchenware. Thus all of them are almost equal as far as their social attributes are concerned. If people become rich, they own a lot of property. They have their own houses, savings and shares. They have their leisure time. They may even enjoy the living of the high society. Then they have their diversified social attributes. Social inequality becomes notable. The attribute of a person is the combination of natural attribute and social attribute. The social attribute particularly exposes the inequality of people. If people have nothing but their own bodies, they may be equal in some aspects because they have nothing to show their different social attributes. Primitives are equal because they have no property. Slaves were equal among themselves because they did not have their own property. If people are required to do simple labor, the ability of doing the simple labor, shown by each, may be similar. If each gets the produce according to his ability or contribution, each may get the equivalent quantity of the produce allocated to each. Thus they are equal in this aspect. Yet if people are required to do complicated work, the ability of doing the complicated work, shown by each, may vary because it is very likely that not all are capable of doing the same complicated work. If each gets the produce according to his ability or contribution, the quantity of the produce allocated to each may vary. Thus, people become unequal in this aspect. Similarly, if voters express their opinions, they are doing the simplest job. The totality of the abilities of doing this simplest job stems from the simple requirement for the expression of a simple opinion. Voters are required to walk to the polling stations, read the ballots and choose the candidates of election. What is shown is that everyone is equal. Such an attribute is in line with the attribute demonstrated by the technology of the printing factories. Every ballot is the same. The opinions of the individuals form the opinion of the collective being. The trait of each voter is not shown on each ballot. The same attribute of each ballot prevails over the social difference of people. Language functions in a special way, dictating that all are equal in collective linguistic communication.

In the evolution of history social stratification led to social inequality. Language itself is not the factor leading to the social inequality in a final sense. People, receiving different educations, may show different social attributes. Thus they may not be equal in social life. They may belong to different social classes. Yet this does not mean that the related social inequality results from the use of language. Likewise, if election is not held, particularly, if ballots are not cast for election, social inequality is caused by some other factors such as social stratification or the diversification of the social structure following the economic development instead of being caused by language. Yet when ballots are manufactured for election, they contribute to the realization of social equality. This means that if citizens do not have the voting rights, this does not mean that ballots are unavailable. There are some other reasons. For example, when people established democracy in a nation-state, such as Great Britain or the United States, in early times, the state did not grant voting rights to female citizens immediately. It only granted male suffrage. Some other circumstances rather than the unavailability of ballots caused social inequality between men and women. The traditional idea that looked down upon the role of women in social production and life and ignored the rights of women may be a reason. Some incorrect ideas may also be a reason. For example, some philosophers claimed that the interest of women would be taken care of by their fathers or husbands. Thus, according to them, male suffrage would not adversely affect the interest of women. Ballots, however, create objectively a condition for the realization of social equality. In the election that runs in modern times, female voters can also cast ballots. Thus the same kind of ballots, used by male and female voters alike, symbolizes equality between men and women in political life. Likewise, the only way to symbolize or to demonstrate equality between the upper social class and the lower social class in political life is perhaps to cast ballots. As so large a number of the voters are required to enter the same one process of linguistic communication to express their opinions on the governance of the state, people have no alternative but to allow the multitude of the voters to simplify the presentation of their opinions. They take joint action indeed. They are only required to express their simple or general opinions. This situation is not meaningless because the government makes laws and policies concerning the good of all in view of the opinions expressed this way. As so many people use the same language and express the same opinion by using this language, people manufacture votes that allow so many people to enter the same process of linguistic communication particularly in the times of industrialization. Thus, talking about the similar case in the United States, Robin M. Williams opines that:

> At the level of national law and administrative policy there has been substantial movement toward establishing equality of political and civil rights for segments of the population formerly subject to discrimination and disadvantage—women, the propertyless, blacks, aliens, unpopular religious sects, and so on.[22]

This also means that equality, realized by ballots, is the equality in a process of decision-making. If any equality can be realized in the society, this equality is realized through mutual consultation. Such equality is the equality agreed to by all. It is difficult for all to see the realization of equality of all aspects in the society. People may not agree to the realization of equality in all aspects. If the equality of one aspect is opposed by a portion of voters over the long term, such equality may not be maintained. This is because efficiency in the economy of the state needs to be taken care of when people seek equality. As some people are more competent and intelligent, people admit that different contributions are made by those who show different competence and intelligence. This means that under the precondition that people obey reason, only the equality recognized by all is the genuine equality. Conversely speaking, if the equality of an aspect is controversial, this equality is not genuine. Equality cannot be realized in any method but in the method of linguistic communication. That is, the inequalities, not caused by coercion, are not the inequalities opposed by people. For example, the hierarchy of administrative system leads inevitably to inequality in a certain aspect because of the necessity of organizing the state. If the hierarchy of the administrative system is objectively beneficial to all within the society or the state, all may accept it. For example, in the organization of the state, competent people are needed to be appointed as the officials of the state in order to govern the state. The hierarchy of bureaucracy occurs as a result. Yet people usually do not insist on abolishing the hierarchy of bureaucracy though they sometimes request the authorities to simplify the procedures of administration. If there is no one issuing a command and hence there is no hierarchy of officials, the state will soon dissolve. Weaver states that:

> It seems plain that the democrats are ignoring a contradiction. Had they the courage to be logical, they would do as their predecessors in ancient Greece and choose their governors by lot. An election, is after all, a highly undemocratic proceeding; the very term means discrimination. How is it possible to choose the best man when by definition there is no best? If a society wishes to be its *natural* self, that is to say, if it wishes to flourish wild, unshaped by anything superior to itself, it should make a perfectly random choice of administrators. Let youth and age, wisdom and folly, courage and cowardice, self-control and dissoluteness, sit together on the bench. This will be representative; this is a cross-section, and there seems no room to question that it would create that society "filled with wonderful variety and disorder" which Plato called democracy.[23]

I cannot completely concur with Weaver on this point of view. However, I argue that indeed the most capable people need to be appointed to manage the public affairs of which the state is definitely in charge. For example, in ancient Greece, the most capable men were elected as military commanders. As Weaver continues, "It was seen that since the very existence of the state depends on them and since a general must have skill, it is better here to take note of differences and admit that in time of emergency authority goes to knowledge."[24]

Equality on ballot is the political equality. This equality means that voters, making a decision on the organization of the state, are equal in expressing their opinions. Though their competence may vary, they can enjoy equality in expressing opinions. This is the real equality. Though there is an administrative hierarchy, voters can cast ballots to exercise their right of equality to request the policies to be made in their interest. If the administrative system serves their interest, the hierarchy of administrative system is also beneficial to them. But if they are prevented from casting ballots, equality on ballot vanishes. Political equality, enjoyed by them, vanishes. The administrative hierarchy may become a political hierarchy, a form of political inequality. For example, if people think of the possibility of realizing equality not by using language, they may not realize any meaningful equality. If people think of realizing the equality represented by the equality of the level of income as a principle implemented by force, a bureaucratic system is required to implement a very large social program. As a bureaucratic system is established to realize social equality, establishing the bureaucratic system must lead to the formation of political inequality. Such a political inequality may become an element of the formation of new social classes. This may give rise to new social inequality. The old social inequality is replaced by the new social inequality. The reason is that the related equality ends up being controversial. This equality is not genuine. For example, in some countries claiming that they reform social system, the power holders abolish private property right in order to ensure the equality of all in economic life. They stipulate that the equal pay is given to all workers no matter whether or not they can work in good faith and they can meet the requirement of the job duty. In particular, they announce that equal pay is given to all workers regardless of their actual contribution made in the process of work. Consequently, such a move affects efficiency in production. In the meantime as such social equalization has to be implemented under the supervision of a bureaucratic system and people do not hold free election by casting ballots, such a bureaucratic system ends up playing a role in the formation of the new political inequality among the citizens. If people carry out the plan of equalization by force, there is no equality between the one that uses force and the other that is forced. Economic equality may not be realized either because people who have equal pay may not demonstrate the work performance of the same level. Such an endeavor often becomes an irony of fate. In contrast, if the government makes the economic and social policies in view of the opinions expressed by the citizens casting ballots, it will ensure political equality because everyone is equal on ballot. Though the administrative hierarchy exists as mentioned by Weaver earlier, this may not affect the interest and rights of all within the state if the administrators are supervised by the citizens. That is, the state needs the administrative hierarchy in its own operation and citizens accept the existence of such an administrative hierarchy. Thus, voters, casting ballots to request the realization of social equality, enjoy political equality. Political equality may enable them to seek social equality to the greatest extent because a precondition for the realization of equality is that no one can coerce citizens into accepting a scheme of equalization. The equality, realized in this case, is genuine. Since all acknowledge that this is equality without any controversy, it should be genuine, provided that people obey reason. Thus we can conclude that the only possible equality that can be realized in political life in the state is the equality realized by using language. Casting ballots is such a way of using language.

Notes

1. Ludwig von Mises, *Free and Prosperous Commonwealth, An Exposition of the Ideas of Classical Liberalism*, translated by Ralph Raico and edited by Arthur Goddard (Princeton: D. Van Nostrand Company, Inc., 1962), 28.

2. Jean Jacques Rousseau, *A Dissertation on the Origin and Foundation of the Inequality of Mankind*, translated by G.D. H. Cole (Chicago: Encyclopaedia Britannica, Inc., 1952), 347.

3. Leo Deuel, *Testaments of Time: The Search for Lost Manuscripts and Records* (New York: Alfred A. Knopf, 1965), 211.

4. Amalia E. Gnanadesikan, *The Writing Revolution: Cuneiform to Internet* (Chichester, West Sussex, UK: Wiley-Blackwell, 2009), 68.

5. Elisabeth L. Einstein, *The Printing Revolution in Early Modern Europe* (Cambridge: Cambridge University Press, 1983), 31.

6. Ibid., 32.

7. Albert Murray, *The State and the Church in a Free Society* (Cambridge: Cambridge University Press, 1958), 146.

8. Bertrand Russell, *Power* (New York: W.W. Norton & Company, Inc., 1938), 43.

9. Thomas Hobbes, *Leviathan*, edited with an introduction by C. B. Macpherson (New York: Penguin Books, 1985), 211.

10. Daniel Etounga-Manguelle, *Does Africa Need a Cultural Adjustment Program?* in Lawrence E. Harrison and Samuel P. Huntington (ed.), *Culture Matters: How Values Shape Human Progress* (New York: Basic Books, 2000), 70.

11. Amartya Sen, *The Idea of Justice* (Cambridge, Massachusetts: The Belknap Press of Harvard University Press, 2009), 296.

12. Rousseau, *A Dissertation on the Origin and Foundation of the Inequality of Mankind*, 363.

13. G. W. F. Hegel, *The Philosophy of Right,* translated by T.M. Knox (Chicago: Encyclopaedia Britannica, Inc., 1952), 67.

14. Richard M. Weaver, *Ideas Have Consequences* (Chicago: The University of Chicago Press, 1984), 35.

15. Robin M. Williams, *Change and Stability in Values and Value Systems: A Sociological Perspective*, in Milton Rokeach (ed.) *Understanding Human Values* (New York: The Free Press, 1979), 34.

16. Weaver, *Ideas Have Consequences*, 35.

17. Adam Smith, *The Wealth of Nations,* with an Introduction by D.D. Rapheal (New York: Alfred A Knopf, 1991), 15.

18. Ibid.,15–16.

19. Weaver, *Ideas Have Consequences*, 44-45.

20. Hans Kelsen, *General Theory of Law and State* (New Brunswick: Transaction Publishers, 2006), 294.

21. Ibid., 297–298.

22. Robin M. Williams, *Change and Stability in Values and Value Systems: A Sociological Perspective*, in Milton Rokeach (ed.), *Understanding Human Values* (New York: The Free Press, 1979), 38.

23. Weaver, *Ideas Have Consequences*, 46.

24. Ibid., 47.

Chapter Twelve

Peace

1. Social Exchange

We are going to discuss peace in this section. We also need to pay attention to the role played by language in the making of peace. The making of peace had not been possible until human beings started to use language. As humans communicate using language, they can exchange information and ideas. Then they can further exchange goods and services because one can tell his intention of exchanging something to the other. As humans need, first of all, to engage in production for their survival and growth, the exchange of goods and services becomes one of the most important social activities performed by humans, and the exchange of goods and services means cooperation between one person and another. This lays a foundation for humans to make and keep peace. To put it differently, humans, using language, exchange information and ideas and then exchange goods and services. Then, exchanging goods and services requires humans to make and keep peace. The reason is that while humans exchange goods and services, they are enabled to engage in socialized production and socialized production generates wealth. As humans can get wealth from the exchange of goods and services and the exchange of goods and services conditions socialized production, people cooperate with one another. They cooperate in the state of peace. Thus, what can compel humans to make and keep peace in the civilized society is, in a certain sense, the exchange of goods and services. While humans exchange goods and services, they need each other. Under these circumstances, they will not wage any war against each other. Then they make and keep peace. This is a way for humans to associate together peacefully. The exchange of goods and services represents the nature of human society. Any growing society relies on the exchange of goods and services. The reason is that the exchange of goods and services conditions the division of labor and hence economic development, and the wealth of the society comes from the economic development. I present three viewpoints here, though these viewpoints will be presented from the perspective of philosophy rather than the perspective of linguistics.

First, every one can speak, think and work. He has his own competence. When he speaks, he has to use his mouth. He has to use energy. He displays certain competence. If a person comes up with an idea, this idea should be produced in his brain. He uses energy. He displays competence. Likewise, people, making products, use both an idea and energy. People use their own competence. Though each person's competence finally stems from the energy of the earth, he cannot use up such competence by himself, as noted earlier. He offers certain surplus competence. If another person can use such surplus competence, such surplus competence becomes a surplus value. Then I argue that people cooperate with each other because a surplus value, offered by each, can be used by any other person. Conversely speaking, if another person does not use such a surplus value, it will be wasted. Thus, people tend to associate together. People become social animals. This is the reason that people may cooperate whenever they interact with each other. Though scholars may argue that some animals in the natural world are also social animals, I believe that humans are unlike those social animals in one important aspect. That is, people use language. As people use language, a linguistic interaction can be realized between one person and another. Each person becomes socially useful. Then a surplus value, provided by each, can be used by the other. The reason is that while people use language in communication, each can indicate what he needs. As he can reveal his need, the other person can provide his surplus value if this person has such a surplus value. Thus one provides a specific surplus value just needed by the other. As this surplus value often exists in the form of a product or a service, a related person provides the related product or service. Besides, the person who provides a product or a service and the person who needs that product or service can negotiate a price for the product or the service to make a fair deal. As no one can accept an unfair deal, the negotiation of a price is essential. In addition, the two parties may have to make an agreement to ensure that the product or service is provided in good faith and the payment is made in good faith. Perhaps, the quality of the product or service is warranted. Perhaps, the term of payment also needs to be defined. Without language people cannot show their faithfulness effectively. The result is that the social animals that use language differentiate themselves from the social animals that do not use language. Humans are distinct from animals. Though the social animals that do not use language may also associate together from time to time, they are unable to exchange their surplus values if any. They cannot take initiative to exchange any thing so as to use the surplus value likely to be offered by one to the other. For example, some animals have an acute sense of smell or hearing or sight. Yet this special capability had by each cannot be offered in exchange for another special capability had by the other. They cannot give expression to their intention of exchanging anything. One of them may be aware of the special capability of the other, but that special capability cannot be utilized by it. No one can articulate that your capability is needed by me. By contrast, a human being can offer an article or an assistance in exchange for another article or assistance given by another human being. Each person can offer a surplus value. Therefore, though social animals tend to associate together, they are often in conflict. They fail to gain the consciousness of coopera-tion. They cannot take initiative to cooperate. Because of this, I argue that language plays a crucial role in the mutual interaction of humans. Language plays a role in building a relationship of cooperation between one person and another. People can make peace in cooperation.

Second, people produce goods and provide the services by using labor. They create more value. Then they exchange goods and services through market, and they realize the division of labor. As they always have differ-ent competences, many of them produce products or provide services. Since people keep on enhancing labor productivity, they produce more products and provide more services. Without the division of labor, people will not develop many different working skills and will not make many products and provide many services. The division of labor motivates people to take advantage of their working skills to produce more products and provide more services. In ancient or medieval times some people got products and services in some other way. They pillaged property. They even took possession of natural resources such as land because those resources were important part of the wealth. A war might break out. Yet a war only resulted in the transfer of land, houses and some other wealth from one side to the other without increasing the wealth of the whole society. A war might even lead to a loss to the social wealth. A war could not motivate people to make more products or to provide more services. In this regard, humans were like other animals. Yet if humans exchange goods and services, a change takes place. This case is initially explained by Adam Smith. He invents a view. That is, the different tribes of animals are scarcely of any use to one another though all are of the same species. He mentions, as an example, that the strength of the mastiff is not supported either by the swiftness of the greyhound or by the sagacity of the spaniel or by the docility of the shepherd's dog. The effects of those different geniuses and talents, for want of the power or disposition to barter and exchange, cannot be brought into a common stock and do not contribute to the better accommodation and convenience of the species. Each family is obligated to support and defend itself separately and independently, and derives no advantage from that of a variety of talents with which nature has distinguished its fellows. Among humans, on the contrary, the most dissimilar geniuses are of use to one another. The different produces of their respective talents are, by the general disposition to truck, barter and exchange, brought into a common stock where each may purchase any part of the produce of other man's talents he has occasion for, a fact that contributes to the better accommodation and convenience of all.[1] The reason is that in almost every other race of animals each individual is entirely independent when it is grown up to maturity, and in its natural state each has occasion for the assistance of no other living creature. However, a person has constant occasions for the help of his brethren, and it is in vain for him to expect it from their benevolence only. He will be more likely to prevail if he can interest their self-love in his favor and show them that it is for their own advantage to do for him what he requires of them. Whoever offers to another a bargain of any kind proposes to do this. Then the meaning of every such offer is that give me that which I want, and you shall have this which you want. And it is in this manner that we obtain from one another the far greater part of those offices which we stand in need of. He believes that it is not from the benevolence of the person such as the butcher, the brewer or the baker that we expect their dinner, but from their regard to their own interest. Thus he concludes that

"We address ourselves, not to their humanity but to their self-love, and never talk to them of our own necessity but of their advantages."[2]

Third, while people provide their goods and services on the market, they will inevitably compete against each other. As they compete against each other, each of them will contrive to offer his special competence so as to provide his unique surplus value. For example, they may show their special working skills for the making of a unique product needed by others. They may provide their special service to others. They try to work as professionals. They further increase their own surplus value. The result is that as many people compete against one another, each offers a surplus value and the other uses it. This is quite different from armament race. While people engage in armament race, they produce weapons and some other military equipment. If a war breaks out, using those weapons and equipment will invariably cause damage to the property and even many injuries and deaths. There will be a huge loss to the wealth of the society as well as workforce. In contrast, market competition differs from the competition of another kind such as armament race. If people compete to gain what they desire without market exchange, they are not required to cooperate. They even do not need to use language. Yet, people, engaging in market competition, abide by a rule of the exchange of goods and services. As two sides submit to the rule made by using language, they become two parts of a system. They contribute to the establishment of the order though they compete against each other. Such a competition is conducive to the establishment of this order. Then market competition spurs the producers of goods to produce high quality goods and spurs the providers of services to provide high quality services. Such a competition is also cooperation. As Mariano Grondona states, "competition is a form of cooperation in which both competitors benefit from being forced to do their best."[3] As a result, people contribute more surplus value to the market. Although they compete, goods and services provided by them are needed by all. The result is that people always seek their own interest. But exchanging goods and services to seek their own interest, they also allow for all others to gain their own interest. As Hegel observes,

> When men are thus dependent on one another and recip-
> rocally related to one another in their work and the satis-
> faction of their needs, subjective self-seeking turns into a

contribution to the satisfaction of the needs of everyone else. That is to say, by a dialectical advance, subjective self-seeking turns into the mediation of the particular through the universal, with the result that each man in earning, producing, and enjoying on his own account is *co ipso* producing and earning for the enjoyment of everyone else.[4]

This means that the geniuses and talents of each animal if any, largely, cannot be used by any other animal. Thus, animals are, in some sense, at war. In contrast, the geniuses and talents of humans can be used by one another. Thus they may make peace. This is mainly because people can use language.

That means that people make peace when they use language in their social exchange. The day humans start to use language is the day it is possible for them to exchange goods and services that have a surplus value, and the day humans exchange goods and services is the day it is possible for them to make or maintain peace. Peace is not an original state of human society. If humans are assumed to be in the state of nature in the outset, there is no peace in the state of nature. If humans are assumed to form a primitive society before the arrival of the civilized society, I argue that there is peace in the primitive society because all within that society form that society due to kinship. As all are kin to one another, it is unlikely for them to be in a serious conflict. After humans form their civilized society, kinship no longer plays the original role. Humans have to exchange surplus values had by them. If humans also love each other, this should be the case that family members love each other. Outside the family people may not love each other. Unless they make friends, the only way for them to cooperate is exchanging a surplus value. Though a surplus value may also be provided by one to the other because they are friends, the exchange of goods and services is the mainstay of the exchange of the surplus value in the society. People usually exchange goods and services for a fair deal. A fair deal serves as a basis for the exchange of nearly all goods and services. Therefore, when humans engage in social exchange like the exchange of goods and services, both parties are happy. They get a benefit from the division of labor. The development of the division of labor guides humans to mutual cooperation. The reason is that people, providing a product or a service, offer a special value. As a value is offered through the exchange of goods and services, the exchange of goods and services evolves to be a social institution for the formation of the society and even for the organization of the state.

Then I argue that under the abovementioned circumstances a war is unlikely to break out. Specifically, we can imagine the following situation: When two people encounter a situation in which there is limited food or water for both of them, or there is one dwelling that can only allow for one person to reside in it, they may compete against each other. They may become adversaries. In this case each offers no benefit to the other if they are unable to use language. As a result each intends to kill or wipe out the other in order to possess the food or the water or the dwelling. Thus they are at war. Yet if these two people can use language, one can tell the other that he can give one thing to the other under the condition that the other can give him another thing in return. In this case each offers a benefit to the other. If both of them think that exchanging things will enable them to gain a benefit, they will agree to do so. Then each may not kill or wipe out the other. Peace may be made. Here I remember that once upon a time Hans Kelsen stated that "peace is the absence of the use of physical force."[5] We can also argue that, when two people are in a conflict, it will be possible for them to stop using physical force if they use language. When people are at war, they do not necessarily use language. They simply fight each other. At least the greatest effort is made to fight each other. When people fight each other, they often do not use language. They only resort to violence. But when people make peace, they must use language to communicate with each other. They may make an agreement of any kind. Usually people sign a peace treaty. I mean that people, at war, do not need to make any agreement. Usually, one side of the war is forced to wage the war. Sometimes both sides of the war are forced to wage the war. But when people make peace, they often need to make an agreement. So we see that sometimes a state wages an undeclared war against another state. But the two states usually sign a peace treaty to confirm the end of the war. If no peace treaty is signed, both states cannot confirm the end of the war. Peace is not the state in which the two sides do nothing. Peace is the state in which the two sides cooperate. To cooperate, the two sides have to communicate by using language. Language is an essential condition for making and maintaining peace.

As each human being has one brain, two arms and two legs and he needs to seek all conditions required for self-preservation, each human being is responsible for his own preservation. For his self-preservation, he needs all kinds of living conditions, including food, water, dwelling, land, clothes, working tools and all others. If humans do not cooperate with each other, they are naturally in the potential state of war of every one against every one. Yet because humans can use language, it may become a tool they can use to seek cooperation so as to make peace. When describing the exchange of goods and services on the market, Adam Smith famously argues that humans are animals of exchange while dogs are not. As mentioned earlier, he states that a dog does not make a fair and deliberate exchange of one bone for another with another dog. His insight into this phenomenon is very thoughtful indeed. Then we cannot help asking this question: Why are humans able to exchange goods and services while dogs are unable to do so? Some scholars may argue that dogs are not as intelligent as humans. They may also advance some other reasons. My view is that humans can indicate clearly their intention of exchanging something because they use language while dogs are unable to do so. Animals cannot cooperate deliberately with each other because they are unable to give linguistic expression to their intention. They are unable to make a contract. Thus, Smith writes that sometimes two greyhounds have the appearance of acting in concert in running down the same hare and each turns her toward his companion or endeavors to intercept her when his companion turns her toward himself. This is not their cooperation realized on the basis of a contract. As he opines, this is not the effect of any contract, but of the accidental occurrence of their passions in the same object at that particular time.[6]

By contrast, a person can indicate his need, intention and future action to another person, try to understand the need, intention and future action of another person, and discuss a scheme of mutual cooperation with another person and then enter into a contract between them. A person and another person can cooperate. As humans use language, they can engage in social exchange. Engaging in social exchange, they cooperate with each other because now each party offers a certain benefit to the other and each can discern it. They can make a contract. Then people refrain from initiating the dreadful and bloody war in which one does not need the other. Thus in the primitive society tribes often waged a dreadful and bloody war against each other for land or water or game or wild fruits or any other thing. A group of people killed another group of people brutally. After humans entered their most wonderful civilized society, the number of the cases that a group of people waged a war against another group of people for land, or water, or game, or wild fruits, or any other thing, decreased gradually. Social exchange appeared. In early times some people captured in war became slaves of those who won the war. They were, fortunately, not killed. They were made to work for the people acting as slave masters. As slaves provided labor to the masters, the masters allowed the slaves to preserve their lives. On the side of masters, they allowed the slaves to preserve their lives in exchange for the labor provided by the slaves, and on the side of slaves they provided labor to slave masters in exchange for their lives simply because language used by both sides created a possible condition for their profitable cooperation, albeit a cooperation not resulting in the fair distribution of wealth. Because of this people in the primitive society used the captives of war as slaves and people in ancient Greece and Rome did the same thing and even established slave-owning system. In medieval Europe, people thought of social exchange more flexibly. Lords, those who owned land, allowed for peasants to farm their land and to live on their land in exchange for the tribute paid by the peasants to them. They also provided security to the peasants in exchange for that tribute. Thus, this social exchange, realizable by using language, is that on the side of lords they provided land and protection in exchange for tribute such as crops and on the side of peasants they provided labor in exchange for the certain conditions of raising themselves and their families. People established the feudal system. In Europe the feudal system existed widely at that time. Then it follows that in modern times people even think of social exchange more flexibly. They establish the market. On the market they exchange as many goods and services as possible. One supplies one kind of goods in exchange for another kind of goods he needs. Businessmen exchange goods everywhere. Various services are also supplied. Laborers also provide labor in exchange for wages. Social classes appear because of the division of labor, assuming that such exchange means the division of labor. Hegel writes that:

> The infinitely complex, criss-cross, movements of recip-
> rocal production and exchange, and the equally infinite

multiplicity of means therein employed, become crystal-
lized, owing to the universality inherent in their content,
and distinguished into general groups. As a result, the entire
complex is built up into particular systems of needs, means,
and types of work relative to these needs, modes of satisfaction and of theoretical and practical education, i.e. into
systems, to one or other of which individuals are assigned—
in other words, into class-divisions.[7]

Some thinkers believe that the appearance of social classes in the civilized
society leads to the war of social classes. This is not necessarily so. My view
is that if different social classes engage in social exchange, a war of social
classes will not necessarily break out. People, engaging in social exchange,
will cooperate. Different social classes may also cooperate with each other.
Language will allow for people to make an arrangement. This case depends
on the feasibility of the transfer of goods or property or wealth or the means
of production. In ancient or medieval times the agricultural society dictated
that land was the most important means of production. Crops grew on land.
Fortune largely came from land. As land was fixed to a locality, it was not easy
to swap land. In the meantime, as grains, produced each year, only sufficed to
feed the population of the local area, people had no adequate goods or services
to offer in exchange for land. Thus the underdevelopment of the exchange of
goods and services prevented social exchange from playing a prominent role
in maintaining peace. Thus the allocation of land, the distribution of the
most important means of production in the past, was often realized via a
war. Land had been even originally pillaged by the ruler and then allocated
to his family members or other retainers since ancient times. Montesquieu
states that Roman citizens regarded commerce as the occupation of slaves
and they only knew the art of war which was the sole path to magistracies
and honors.[8] But since the development of market-oriented economy in early
modern times following the emergence of the capitalist mode of production,
the exchange of goods and services has been playing a role in the making of
peace. When goods and services can be transferred easily by way of exchange,
people come to exchange goods and services widely in a peaceful way because
it is easier to get goods and services by way of exchange. Of course, class
struggle sometimes happened or often happened in a certain period of time

in history due to the failure of the functioning of exchange even though different social classes engaged in mutual linguistic communication. However, the attractiveness of social exchange is great under the condition that it is easier to communicate by using language than to wage a war. When the importance of land in economic life declines along with the emergence of modern industry, social exchange develops fast throughout the state. Then we see that a great deal of wealth is produced by the society in which market plays a pivotal role, and peace supersedes war. When people work and learn the skills of production diligently, they prepare for social exchange. Since industrialization people have worked more diligently than before and people have mastered more skills of production. Commerce grows swiftly and widely. Laws especially require the protection of the private property. A civil war is less likely to break out.

We can explain this phenomenon in depth in the following way. If we assume that in feudal times social exchange was not well developed because people, residing within the territory of each of the lords, were basically self-sufficient, we will also assume that the development of social exchange in capitalist times allows for people to cooperate with each other through the development of the market. With the development of the market, people get benefits provided by each other. They depend on each other. Thus they are not tempted to wage a war for pillage. As Ludwig von Mises writes,

> Self-sufficient farmers, who produce on their own farms everything that they and their families need, can make war on one another, But when a village divides into factions, with the smith on one side and shoemaker on the other, one faction will have to suffer from want of shoes, and the other from want of tools and weapons.[9]

At that time, people had not established a system of the division of labor yet. The defense of the local area was important. As Mises writes, "There were towns whose fortifications were, from the very beginning, so constructed that in case of need they could hold out for a while by keeping cattle and growing grain within the town walls."[10] Niccolo Machiavelli states that "It has been a custom with princes, in order to hold their states more securely, to build fortresses that may serve as a bridle and bit to those who might design to work against them, and as a place of refuge from a first attack."[11] But since the growth of the capitalist market towns had stopped constructing, or razed, their fortifications or fortresses. When market exchange developed, people made peace. Those fortifications or fortresses became defunct or unnecessary later.

Analyzing the interrelationship between the division of labor and peace, Mises indicates that "The progressive intensification of the division of labor is possible only in a society in which there is an assurance of lasting peace."[12] His view is basically right. He points out the correlation between the division of labor and peace. I concur with him on this point. But what I would like to argue is that he believes that peace is a condition for the development of the division of labor. My view is that the exchange of goods and services conditions the development of the division of labor and the development of the division of labor is a major condition for people to make peace. As Montesquieu observes, "Peace is the natural effect of trade."[13] Trade means the division of labor. The reason is that people, engaging in social exchange and hence the division of labor, have to use language. Then they make a contract. This is part of the picture that humans, using language, make contracts. They cooperate with each other. They build their civil society. They also build their state. The use of language is a basis for making and keeping peace because a contract, made by using language, makes all sides cooperators. All are no longer adversaries. People make peace.

Peace is made even across the borders when humans begin to love trade. So now we see another picture. This picture is that in the past different countries were often at war against each other in Europe. In our times a war is rarely seen in Europe, particularly in Western Europe. In order to avoid a war, European countries have established European Union. In the past certain countries were at war because they competed excessively for resources, markets and others. But as humans, using language, can make contracts and hence can engage in social exchange, they get benefits from the value provided by each. International trade develops. Then the probability of a war decreases except the case that the conflict over the division of territory is likely to escalate into a war because it is difficult for the related countries to exchange territories. This means that despite that people are in conflict with each other from time to time, engaging in social exchange is a way to avoid a war over the long term. People can engage in social exchange by entering into a contract. If two parties engage in such an exchange, each provides to the other a value that cannot be gained by each in any other way. A war is unnecessary as a result. People make peace.

When people are involved in a conflict that may soon escalate into a war, people are tempted to use force to conquer each other. Some greatest thinkers of our world argue that the formation of a government prevents a war from breaking out. Hobbes holds this view. Yet I argue that the reliance on the use of force for the making of peace is precarious. Through history a despotic government often meets with the resistance of the masses. A civil war may break out when people settle their dispute by resorting to violence. In a civil war each party conquers the other by force or even wipes out the other. If humans feel that they need perpetual peace, the fundamental way for them to realize this goal is engaging in as many social exchanges as possible. As Kant writes, "The spirit of trade cannot coexist with war."[14] People, engaging in trade, use language. People, communicating by using language, build their state. If they want peace in the state, they invariably rely on language though there may be some other factors luring them to make peace. Language is forever the ultimate tool used by humans to make peace. Language, used in the social exchange, is an example.

2. Constitutional Arrangement

Language not only allows for people to make a contract in order to engage in the exchange in the economic domain to the effect that people avoid a war but also allows for people to make a long-term contract instead of a temporary one to coordinate their actions and hence to establish a mode of the constructive mutual interaction over the long term. They can make such a long-term contract as a collective being. They can establish order. A constitution is such a contract. Such a contract is an arrangement made by them to allow for themselves to co-exist peacefully in the same community. The linchpin is that, as they can use language, each can learn about the intention, idea and commitment of all others. They can make a contract. They may keep on coordinating their action and cooperate in accordance with this contract. Thus they can possibly avoid any conflict. They may also avoid a war. They may realize peace. People can discern a correlation between language and peace. This means that the situation in which people use language in their interaction is distinct from the situation in which people do not use language in their interaction. By using language therein, both sides can jointly engage in this mutual interaction. They may make peace. If two sides make peace, they usually have the same intention. They are willing to engage in the mutual interaction. They build a trust relationship. Conversely, if two sides are at war, they normally do not communicate using language. If two sides interact with each other at war, such an interaction may be unilaterally forced by one side. This interaction may not be accepted by the other side. There is no mutual trust. Such an interaction between one another is not constructive. Both sides do not accept their co-existence. Thus we see that peace is the constructive interaction between one another. A war is usually waged by one side to wipe out the other side while peace means the co-existence of the two sides. The interaction between one another at war is not sustainable while the interaction between one another at peace sustainable. In the state of peace, the interaction between one another must be basically linguistic, whereas in the state of war the interaction between one another is usually physical. If people make a constitution, they merely encourage linguistic interaction. Language is crucial. If we postulate that before people agree to form their community, they are likely to be in the state of war, it is also arguable that a contract, made by them to form their community so as to put an end to the possible state of war, is a peace treaty. A constitution can be such a kind of peace treaty. Language is, ontologically, in relation to contract and hence constitution. Language is also, ontologically, in relation to peace and hence in relation to the building of the society. We can ascertain these complex relations in three aspects.

First, while people communicate using language, they are equal. Language does not discriminate against anyone. As long as language is not abused, all should be treated equally in linguistic communication. Then all are willing to join this society. Though sometimes a person who communicates is strong while another person who communicates is weak, both are indispensable. As a process of linguistic communication needs to go on between the two sides, we cannot argue that one of them is more important than the other. If they sign a contract, they do so on the basis of equality. Equality is the basic element of the formation of this society. Conversely, if people are not equal, they may not be willing to sign a contract. They may not form a society. If they do not form a society, they may be in the state of war. They may not use language because each tries to subjugate the other. Each may not treat the other equal. Then we have all the reasons to believe that each side will be the adversary of the other. As they do not join each other to make peace, each side builds up unilaterally its military strength to defend itself. Linguistic communication between the two sides is of no utmost importance. What is of utmost importance is military strength. When they are in conflict, what is decisive may also be military tactic instead of language. As each side tries to get the upper hand, they will never treat each other equal. Each side interacts with the other, merely viewing both the strength of its own and that of the adversary. Only the strength of each side is considered to determine whether or not and how to engage the adversary. That is, each side tries to use its own advantage and the disadvantage of the other side to defeat the other side. Sun Tzu, an ancient Chinese philosopher, says that "It is the rule of war: If our forces are ten to the enemy's one, to surround him; if five to one, to attack him; if twice as numerous, to divide our army into two, one to meet the enemy in front, and one to fall upon his rear."[15] By contrast, each side expects the other side to cooperate in the state of peace. People may not be organized because they are not always to be organized to build an army to defeat the other side. But they are going to form a society. They are likely to make a constitution.

Second, while people communicate using language, they build their community. They build their society. They often take initiative to inform each other that they hope to make and keep peace. They reveal their plans of building the society. What is important is that their intention of making and keeping peace and their intention of building the society are not misunderstood by each other. Each side depends on the other side in cooperation. Each side may have made an agreement with the other side tacitly. By contrast, if people are at war against each other, they will not give any information to each side in mutual interaction. As two sides confront each other, each side may try to get information about the other side while trying to prevent the other side from getting any information about itself. Each side tries to get prepared to fight and defeat the other side. That is, each side is unwilling to let the adversary know its own disposition while trying its best to learn about the disposition of its adversary. In this case language is not used normally or not used at all though information from the adversary is gathered. Thus spies are sent out. As Sun Tzu states,

> Knowledge of the spirit world is to be obtained by divination; information in natural science may be sought by inductive reasoning; the laws of the universe can be verified by mathematical calculation; but the dispositions of the enemy are ascertainable through spies and spies alone.[16]

By contrast, each side tells the other side what it thinks in the state of peace. Both sides do not conceal their ideas. While people make and keep peace, each side always lets the other side know that it wants to make and keep peace. While they want to make and keep peace, they recognize that all can co-exist. Peace means the co-existence of all. All are cooperators. All act in unison. If they make an agreement, this agreement can be regarded as a constitution. The constitution is a language solution.

Third, while people communicate using language, language compels all to be honest. Honesty is required in the formation of the society. Honesty is part of morality. This means that people form their community in linguistic communication and they also form their community with morality. As long as language is not abused, linguistic communication supports the spread of morality in the community and morality supports the formation of the society. In terms of the relationship between morality and constitution, my view is that while people make a constitution, this constitution should be moral. The reason is that the constitution is usually agreed to by all. As all agree to this constitution, this constitution should not be immoral. In other words, if this constitution is immoral, all will not reach an agreement. If a document is immoral, it will always be controversial. In the meantime I argue that if people choose not to use language to make a peace treaty, they will be likely to be in conflict. Sometimes they will go to war. While people go to war, they are not able to adhere to morality. They will not be honest. They will cheat each other. Each side uses every method, including immoral method, to defeat the other side. For example, one side may especially conduct a night combat to beat the other side that is not prepared for that combat in the night. This side will never notify the other side in advance. Even the method of deception is adopted as a military tactic. Thus sometimes one side is misled by the other in the battle. An evil plot is sometimes adopted to defeat the adversary. If language is used, it is abused. Therefore, Sun Tzu opines that "All warfare is based on deception."[17] He even further writes that "when able to attack, we must seem unable; when using our forces, we must seem inactive; when we are near, we must make the enemy believe we are far away; when far away, we must make him believe we are near."[18] There is no honesty between the two adversaries. Each side does not trust the other. Both adversaries are in the state of nature. By contrast, people who make a constitution often clarify their intention. They are open and aboveboard. They build their society.

That is, linguistic interaction differs from physical interaction. In linguistic interaction, people are likely to obey a rule. A war is natural while peace is man-made. A war means the state of nature while peace does not mean the state of nature. As Kant argues, "The state of peace among men living in close proximity is not the natural state (*status naturalis*); instead, the natural state is a one of war, which does not just consist in open hostilities, but also in the constant and enduring threat of them."[19] The reason is that while people use violence in their interaction, all deny the rationality of the co-existence of all. Violence often rages regardless of possible linguistic interaction. In this case, each side may think that the best defense is offense. Each does not notify the other side by using language that the other side should get prepared in defense. If a truce or peace is made, however, each side is obligated not to assail the other. Then they may formulate an agreement and agree to be obligated to recognize the right to survive had by each. Then the relation among them under these circumstances will be distinct from that relation in the state of war. That is, the relation between the two sides at war may be imposed on a certain side. In some sense this relation may also be imposed on both sides. The related interaction may be the one in which a certain side or the two sides are unwilling to engage. For example, when a war breaks out, this war may be unilaterally launched by one side only, and the other side has no alternative but to wage the war. When people are at peace, however, they make and keep peace on voluntary basis. No side forces the other side to make and keep peace. Making and keeping peace meets their own interest. Both sides want to make and keep peace. Both sides have common interest. Peace is their common will. Peace is their common undertaking. Then each side may send out a piece of information and advance an idea to the effect that they coordinate their action because they can coordinate the brains of all people under the guidance of an idea. Then, the suggestion of making peace from one side gets a positive response from the other side. Each side may encourage the other side to keep peace. Each side may trust the other side. Each side has confidence in the other side. Thus they may standardize the interaction between the two sides. They may define the rights had by each side and the obligations undertaken by each side. They make a long-term contract. Because of this, they further make a rule for the organization of the state on the basis of this long-term contract. Thus people prevent any conflict, including a war. They begin to organize the state on the basis of a constitution. Then this constitution defines the procedure of making any law, the form of the government and the powers and obligations of the power holders as well as the rights and obligations of the citizens. As a document made by using language, the constitution displays that it is always characterized by the fact that all have reached a consensus on the organization of the state under the guidance of an idea. The constitution is a document that allows for people to form a peaceful society. As people build the state over this society, the constitution is also a document for people to build their state. They realize the overall peace of the society and the state. I mean that though people may engage in social exchange, leading to the cooperation between one another that puts an end to the personal war, people may not always avoid war. The social exchange, such as the exchange of goods and services, may mean the making of a parochial contract. People, engaging in social exchange, make a deal in a certain aspect, but not in all aspects. Thus in all other aspects, people may have different expectations and intentions whenever they cope with various specific matters and interact with each other. They may have different desires. They may show different inclinations. They may insist on different principles. They may devote themselves to different causes. They may be in conflict. They may even be at war. They may be even in the state of war of every man against every man. Yet when they make a constitution by using language, they coordinate their action. They may reach a consensus across the state. They are tempted to act under the guidance of this consensus. They may standardize their mutual interaction. They may even conceptualize their rights and obligations in order to standardize their mutual interaction. They avoid a conflict or a war. Thus, Hobbes believes that peace is made when the contract, according to which one transfers to the other his rights conferred by the law of nature, is implemented. He writes that:

> From that law of Nature, by which we are obliged to trans-ferre to another, such Rights, as being retained, hinder the peace of Mankind, there followeth a Third; which is this, *That men perform their Covenants made*: without which, Covenants are in vain, and but Empty words; and the Right of all men to all things remaining, we are still in the condition of Warre.[20]

That is, people may lower or minimize the probability of the outbreak of a conflict between one another if rights can be transferred by each side to the other. People may also lower the probability of the outbreak of a war. Though the theory about the law of nature, expounded by Hobbes, is hypothetical, this theory tells us how people make peace. People share an idea in linguistic communication and an idea conceptualizes rights. After people conceptualize rights, they formulate a contract that evolves to be a constitution. Thus a constitution, defining rights, becomes an important tool to create and main-tain peace. This further indicates that the two sides in conflict do not neces-sarily need to use language. Intending to coordinate their action or to make peace, they have to use language. If they sign a peace treaty, that treaty is the constitution. This bears testimony to the fact that peace does not simply mean the situation in which no war breaks out. In the situation in which no war breaks out, people must engage in linguistic interaction and make a constitution to ensure their peaceful co-existence. People are animals though they are different from other animals in many respects. They move. They have their own consciousness. They are in the potential state of being in con-flict with each other. Without the use of language and a constitution, people may not be able to coordinate their interaction. A conflict or a war may break out. Thus using language to make a constitution to coordinate the action of all to ensure their peaceful co-existence is a way to prevent any conflict or war from breaking out. This is the reason why people draft a constitution. The constitution is a peace treaty.

The reason for me to hold that the constitution is a peace treaty is that constitution only allows for people to engage in linguistic interaction. Linguistic interaction means peace. Linguistic interaction is normally standardized. Standardized linguistic interaction avoids a physical conflict or a war. Then people have certain chances to eliminate misunderstanding and find a solution to solve their dispute when they are involved in a dispute. Then people naturally turn to cooperating with each other. A constitution should be such a document especially formulated to allow for all to co-exist under the guidance of an agreement made by all. People make and have peace. This is the constitutional order. This is a constitutional arrangement. Language underlies a process of formulating a contract and finally the organization of the state.

First, people, making a constitution, give a joint presentation. A constitution is a document in which the formulators of the constitution especially define the rights and obligations of all the citizens, and people usually have no misunderstanding of the related provisions. As the rights and obligations of the citizens are defined by the constitution, a document agreed to by all, all understand such rights and obligations in the same way. The presentation of the constitution means that all confirm that they understand the provisions of the constitution without any error. Since the constitution is a document for all to cooperate to build their state, all know the expectations of others. This is because all accept the constitution. The reason is that people present all the provisions and no one opposes them. This proves that all agree to these provisions and all understand them in the same way. People will no longer argue about the real meanings of those provisions. People will obey the constitution without any controversy. As all the provisions are noted down, people will not forget them along with the passage of time. All know that they have accepted the constitution. Normally, the constitution is made by the delegates sitting in the legislature. In some states, these delegates might be only elected by a small portion of the citizens in history because at that time not all citizens were able to meet the requirement of the ownership of property or some other requirements. Yet if such a constitution was accepted by all the citizens in later times, we can still believe that the constitution was made on behalf of all the citizens. Thus there is no misunderstanding of the intention of all for cooperation.

Second, if a war is waged by a group of people against another group of people, these two groups of people may not perform linguistic communication with each other. If a man conquers a group of people, he may not perform linguistic communication with that group of people. However, if a power holder intends to build a state, he is required to have ruling legitimacy. He seeks support from the masses. Particularly, he seeks support from his people when he wages a civil war or a war against another state. He has to perform linguistic communication with the masses. He seeks support from the masses and the masses request him to provide public services. He makes a promise to the masses and the masses may also make a promise to him. As a result, he, in some sense, gives rights to the masses and the masses undertake some obligations to him. The constitution is in line with this logic. The constitution may mean that the two sides have made an agreement. This means that after people make the constitution, there will be the certainty of cooperation of all with all in the future because the constitution is a contract all are supposed to obey. In ancient times the constitution, made by people, was sometimes just a custom. As the custom was taken for granted, it was usually complied with by all as if it were a contract obeyed by all. As a result, all were aware that all intended to cooperate with each other. Thus, it would not be easy for a war to break out. Therefore in ancient Greece or Rome some constitutions of the states were unwritten. Those constitutions might be composed of several different forms including a custom. As all or the majority of the citizens agreed to and carried out the custom, the custom might function to prevent some potential conflicts from arising. In other words, as all obeyed that custom, they would interact with each other as required. People were prevented from being easily involved in any conflict. Likewise, if people formulate a constitution in writing in modern times, all confirm that they have made a promise in writing. As all make a promise, they cooperate with one another. All know that all will cooperate with one another. People prevent a war from breaking out as a result.

Third, a constitution is a general rule. This is because people always discuss the draft of the constitution. When they discuss the draft of the constitution, it is easy for them to reach an agreement in principle. As the constitution is a rule made for millions of people, people can only make the general rule. A constitution lays a foundation for the making of peace because people can formulate a general rule just like a law by using language. In formulating a constitution, people only lay down general provisions which constitute a principle covering all aspects of organizing the state. As there are plenty of citizens, their specific interests vary greatly. They belong to different social classes. They may belong to various ethnic groups. They reside in different regions. They receive a varying education. They may believe in different religions. It is totally impossible for them to get together to make a very detailed constitution satisfying all their specific demands. Thus, people formulate a constitution that defines the organization of the state in principle only. It is feasible to reach an agreement this way. It is easy for millions of people to reach an agreement on a general principle because a general principle is usually made according to an abstract notion or is a generally-delineated proposal. People can organize the state on the basis of this constitution though they may disagree to various policies that are regarded as failing to satisfy certain specific interests of the citizens. The result is that even though citizens may disagree to specific policies made and carried out by the government from time to time, the constitutional system remains intact. Sometimes a portion of people oppose a policy carried out by the government. They express their attitude of opposition to the government. They may even request the resignation of the head of the government so as to hold the leader of the government accountable for a policy they oppose. But people seldom think of changing the constitutional system. They sometimes oppose the government, but they do not challenge the constitutional system. Thus people maintain peace. This is because, by using language, people can communicate with one another throughout the state. If they are in conflict with each other because the constitution fails to provide a specific framework for them to solve this dispute, such a conflict usually only concerns a dispute between the authorities and the citizens and people usually do not hold the constitution accountable. This means that all have reached a general agreement throughout the state. People organize the state as an ensemble. In contrast, any conflict is usually parochial.

Fourth, as noted earlier, people, at war, do not necessarily need to use language while people, at peace, are required to use language. Similarly, people, waging a war, seek to realize a scheme of the distribution of interest in favor of themselves only. They do not necessarily use language. For example, in medieval times a feudal lord waged a war to pillage land, leading to the re-distribution of land in a local area. He might not be required to use language to engage in a mutual consultation with others. In contrast, people, intending to distribute interest peacefully, have to use language. If people want to maintain peace, they have to distribute interest fairly. Though people may not be absolutely able to maintain peace if they distribute interest fairly because some people may intend to distribute interest unfairly through a war, no unfair distribution of the interest can prevent a war from breaking out. If that war does not break out at the moment, it will break out in future. But if people distribute interest fairly, this may make peace. When people formulate a constitution, they set up a committee of constitution. This committee may be established as required by the legislature. The legislature is formed by the delegates elected by the electorate. This means that the constitution is made as consented by the people. It is made by the people. The blueprint of organizing the state is no longer the blueprint made in the brain of the power holder but the blueprint jointly made by the people. As it is made by the people, it must be made under the scrutiny of the public. Various detailed and long procedures are set up in advance to ensure that the constitution is properly and cautiously made, amended and approved. Making, amending and approving the constitution by using language under the scrutiny of the public highlights the extension of linguistic communication because people have to communicate across the state. In other words, the process of linguistic communication has to be extended to allow for citizens to discuss, and on the occasion of holding a referendum, to approve, the making or the amendment of the constitution. The constitution is thus made to establish a long process of linguistic communication through which the makers of the constitution communicate with all within the state. It is a general contract made by all. To make or to amend or to approve the constitution is to initiate a long process of linguistic communication that reaches all. The common interest of all takes shape. People also formulate various procedures for themselves to go through this long process of linguistic communication. Thus, all are supposed to obey the procedures of making, amending and approving the constitution when people make, or amend, or approve, the constitution. Thus Kelsen writes that:

The original constitution of a State is the work of the founders of the State. If the State is created in a democratic way, the first constitution originates in a constituent assembly, what the French call *une constituante*. Sometimes any change in the constitution is outside the competence of the regular legislative organ instituted by the constitution, and reserved for such a *constituante*, a special organ competent only for constitution amendments. In this case it is customary to distinguish between a constituent power and a legislative power, each being exercised according to different procedures. The device most frequently resorted to in order to render constitutional amendments more difficult is to require a qualified majority (two-thirds or three-fourths) and a higher quorum (the number of the members of the legislative body competent to transact business) than usual. Sometimes, the change has to be decided upon several times before it acquires the force of law.[21]

Fifth, when people are at war, they destroy their community. When people are at peace, they build their community. People, building their community, are guided by an idea disseminated by using language. In contrast, people, at war, may not necessarily be guided by any idea. They may not use language. If people are guided by an idea when they are at war, it cannot be always guaranteed that that idea is just. If all seek peace and all are guided by an idea, that idea should be just and all interact in linguistic communication. Thus, people, at war, may simply seek material interest such as land. The strongest man is usually the victor. Violence is a decisive factor. When people are at peace, they engage in the linguistic interaction. They cooperate with each other. They build their community. As they build their community, they may share an idea. This idea should be just. As all embrace the same just idea, they may always see eye to eye on the management of public affairs. They do not have disagreements on major public affairs. It may not be easy for them to be in conflict with each other. They keep peace. So we see that people, formulating a constitution, may always propagate some valuable ideas such as the idea of humanism, the idea of freedom, and the idea of human rights among others. These ideas may be originally offered by some past philosophers and handed down to the following generations. The reason that these ideas are handed down is usually that they are correct and valuable. These ideas may be the results of an effort made by many generations of people. To hand down these ideas, people use language. The making of a constitution bears testimony to this fact. This fact is that, formulating a constitution, people advance an idea accepted by all at the same time. People may proclaim that they insist on a major idea in the preamble of the constitution. This idea is usually the general guidance of organizing the state. As this idea can be interpreted, the same idea is propagated to all citizens. All the citizens may embrace the same idea. All of them may view the constitution from the same perspective. If all the citizens hold the same idea, their chances of being in conflict with each other will become slim. This is because all, embracing the same idea, usually accept the same method in organizing the state. They will see eye to eye on many matters concerning the organization of the state. Thus a constitution written under the guidance of an idea can function to create peace within the state.

In short, when people formulate a constitution, they eliminate misunderstanding and establish a mutual trust relationship; they ascertain long-term cooperation between one another; they agree to a general principle in the organization of the state; they create a framework for the fair distribution of interest through mutual consultation; and they embrace the same idea. Their common interest takes shape. Then people consider the state legitimate. They differentiate the state from the government. Thus, people tend not to oppose the state but the government whenever they disagree with the government on a policy or a law. This is distinct from the case of a despotic state. In a despotic state, people make no constitution. If people make a constitution, this constitution may not be really carried out. In this case people regard the government as the state. If people confront the government, they confront the state. They tend to revolt. If a constitution exists, people usually gain the freedom of speech. If they confront the government, they may wage a demonstration. They tend not to revolt because they respect the constitutional system, as mentioned earlier. However, in a despotic state, people sometimes act in unison not because they can lawfully take collective action but because of the functioning of some other media. If the state is governed by a despotic ruler, some media may function to make the masses act in unison to revolt against the government. At least there are three media in this context. The first medium may be a serious situation that occurs suddenly such as a famine or a plague or an international war. Under the despotic rule, ordinary people have many complaints. They are, however, unable to coordinate with each other so as to act in unison because they are unable to keep in touch with thousands of people on a large scale. They may not be able to communicate with many other people across the state so as to mobilize many people in the similar situation. If a special situation occurs across the state, this situation may function to trigger a civil war, or an uprising, or a revolution because millions of people may suddenly find that they are in the same situation and have the same idea. In ancient China, some massive peasant uprisings broke out state-wide because of a widespread famine. In other words, without such a famine breaking out in a large area ordinary people, in the far-flung corners of the state, would neither unite nor act in unison to revolt. The second medium is thought. It is not easy for so many people to unite firmly and keep on pursuing a goal over the long term because the more people there are, the more different expectations and interests people have. Yet a thought usually meets the expectation of plenty of people. A thought may motivate the masses to act. A thought may be jointly accepted by millions of people. If many people embrace the same thought, they may hold the same idea and show the same inclination. They may pursue the same goal. Thus, they may unite. Because of this, we can also believe that a thought can function as a medium under certain circumstances. Thus, as under the condition of the despotic rule a thought against the despotic rule may be spread, a revolution may break out. The third medium may be an organization. A social or political organization may mobilize the masses. As a social or political organization is formed by those who are most active in social and political activities, the members of those organizations actually function as media in support of linguistic communication that reaches all who support or are sympathetic with that organization. This organization may gather dispersed ordinary people. Ordinary people may thus stand up against the despotic government because without a constitution the related organization may not recognize the legitimacy of the state.

After the constitution is made, however, people tend not to oppose or challenge the constitutional system or the entire system of the state. Usually, the political system is characteristic of the separation of powers. All political organizations recognize the existing legal system. No political organization upsets the political system of the state. Thus some media that may stimulate people to unite to enter into a civil war are prevented from functioning. Because of this, the conflict if any is parochial. For example, in history when no constitution was made or the constitutional system was unstable, a revolt, or a revolution, sometimes broke out. Since people made the constitution or a stable constitutional system, they have been waging no war against the state but occasionally waging a demonstration on the street to make a protest against a policy or an act of the government only. In early modern times in Europe there were radical political movements intending to overthrow the government. Later, such political movements disappeared. People now usually accept the existing constitutional system. Thus, if they are dissatisfied with any policy or any act of the government, they raise a protest or attempt to change the government peacefully in stead of requesting a change in the form of government or the building of a new state. In this case a civil war is unlikely to break out. People make and keep peace.

This indicates that the acts of power holders and citizens are strictly defined by a document made by using language. As long as people obey the provisions of the constitution, it is unlikely to encounter a conflict. If there is any dispute that may lead to the outbreak of any conflict, such a dispute will be resolved according to the law made under the constitution or the constitution itself. A civil war is unlikely to break out. As language can be used by people many times and in various ways, the power of language cannot be exhausted by any provision. People, making many provisions in the constitution and the attached files, find the best method to ensure harmony and cooperation of all no matter whether they govern the state or are subject to the governance of the state. This means that the power holders are aware of how to use power in the governance of the state and ordinary people are aware of how to submit to the governance of the state in which the power holders engage. All can anticipate how power is exercised. All agree to the method of using power. The will of the constitution is the will of the people. It is difficult to gain power by violence or in the way not defined by the constitution. All agree to comply with the constitution when they settle any dispute. People organize the state at peace.

3. Ruling in Turn

As noted earlier, people have to make peace first and then build their state. If they cannot make peace, they cannot build their state. Though in the beginning they were at peace in the tribe, we find that in the building of their state, people have to make peace. They rely on language to make peace. This is because original tribes become defunct gradually along with the formation of the state. Then tribes do not support crucially the formation of the community anymore though tribes may still exist in a period of time. Then it follows that an original tribal chief is no longer able to organize the community as the chief. Kinship no longer functions in the formation of the community. As a result, people organize the state in another way. This way of organizing the state is using coercion. If we assume that in a period of time the paternalist ruler may rule the state, it is arguable that the paternalist rule cannot avoid despotism. Despotism means that coercion is always used in the organization of the state. Specifically, the power holder, ruling the state, always has to use coercion to keep his rule. The power holder must be the strongest man. Otherwise he may lose power. At this time the consciousness of blood relationship no longer functions crucially in support of the formation of the state. The ruler has to use coercion to keep his power in the organization of the state. So if a ruler is weak, he will soon be deposed by another ambitious, strong man. This means that competition for power often occurs in any human community that grows after the dissolution of the tribes and the formation of the state. Tensions exist between the ruler and the ruled. If a man rules the state for a long time, other people may complain. The ruler, keeping the rule of the state for a long time, may coerce others to be subject to his rule in order to keep his rule. Thus he may be hated by others because it is very likely for many others to feel oppressed by him. Sometimes the solution is the replacement of the power holder of the state according to an agreement made by all. Describing the life of Numa Pompilius (8th-7th century B.C.), a man in ancient Rome, Plutarch tells us a piece of history in relation to this matter. He tells us that Romans were originally ruled by a king. When Sabines, a nation, and Romans were to form a state, they were not willing to be combined with the Romans as inferiors. They hoped that the king was chosen out of their own nation. There appeared a dispute that would occasion general confusion. People finally came up with a solution that was similar to the solution of ruling in turn. As Plutarch narrates, people agreed that the hundred and fifty senators should interchangeably execute the office of supreme magistrate and each in succession should offer the solemn sacrifices and dispatch public business for the space of six hours by day and six by night, which vicissitude and equal distribution of power would preclude all rivalry among the senators and envy from the people when they should behold one. This one would be elevated to the degree of a king and would be leveled within the space of a day to the condition of a private citizen. This form of government was termed by the Romans interregnum.[22]

Likewise, almost in the analogous period of time ancient Greeks invented some other methods of resolving the same problem under democracy. That is, ancient Greeks invented a political system of arranging for people to rule and to be ruled in turn. They established the system of election. They realized the goal that citizens cast lots, as a form of election, to decide who was to hold state power, as already noted earlier. They averted a conflict or war this way. Describing the election of ancient Greece, Innis writes, in particular, that:

> From each tribe, 50 were elected by lot to serve in rotation on a monthly basis as a standing committee in a council of 500. Election by lot maintained a respect for the belief in the divine will as the basis of laws, and was a safeguard of equality of civil rights and equality before the law. The council of 500 and the courts, with their large popularly-chosen juries, became the essential governing bodies. Divisive issues were transferred to a new forum and settled by reliance on public opinion rather than on force.[23]

This means that any competition for power within the state without any rule may evolve to be a conflict or a civil war. One approach to avoid a war is the exchange of the chances of ruling the state among different factions of the people. The exchange of the chances of ruling is a process in which language is used for communication. The exchange of the chances of ruling involves a rule used to rule on any dispute about ruling legitimacy. Any rule is made by humans by using language, as noted earlier. If humans were unable to use language, they would not be able to make any rule. Thus after a rule is made and accepted by all, people can rule on any dispute. Thus they make peace.

The reason is that when people turn to engaging in linguistic interaction, a conflict will soon become a competition. Olympic Games were held when ancient Greeks engaged in sports competition as a relaxation during a truce defined by the Holy Treaty made among King Iphitos of Elis, King Lykourgos of Sparta and King Kleosthenes of Pisa and later ratified by all other Greek city-states because Greeks were tired of long-time military training and wars. After a rule was made, a sort of behavior, displayed by people at war, was changed into a standardized competition, as noted earlier. Marathon, a long-distance running race stemming from an event during a war in ancient Greece, becomes part of Olympic Games. Some sports games stem from a combat committed in a war, including archery and shooting. Sports competitions are construed by some scholars as the ventilation of chauvinism. David I. Kertzer writes that:

> Brazilians, like many other people around the world, view international soccer contests as a battle between themselves and other nations, and in this way ritually ventilate their national chauvinism and their hostilities toward other nations. This use of national sports teams as a symbolic means of international combat is institutionalized in the quadrennial Olympics, where nations are pitted against one another in struggle.[24]

Here we cannot claim that a certain form of competition can always replace a war. However, I argue that people may, through a competition, strengthen their mutual understanding. Then people may reduce or eliminate their mutual misunderstanding and hence minimize the probability of the outbreak of a conflict or a war. What we should pay more attention to is, however, that people are able to make a rule for a competition because they can use language to make an agreement on the making of this rule and then they can reveal their character, capacity, strength and mental outlook, and then they can get honor. This creates a condition for people to make an arrangement for a peaceful competition. A peaceful competition motivates people to train and educate themselves so as to get prepared for the building of their society or the state. This is quite different from any war. If people wage a war against each other, it is costly and difficult to win the war. At war, many personnel are mobilized and many material resources are exhausted. In contrast, a competition is less costly and difficult. A competition can prove who is more competent. Those who are more competent are given an award in the competition. People give them an honor. Then those who are given an honor feel proud. They are encouraged to make a contribution to the building of the society and the state. In other words, obeying a rule in a fair competition enables people to reveal their own character, capacity, strength and mental outlook in order to get recognized by the society and the state. Then the state guides them to taking part in a competition. Then people may avoid the outbreak of a war. Therefore, any fair competition is part of the formation of the society and even the state. Language is significant in the making of peace.

I believe that this is also the reason for the invention of chess. To play chess is often to mimic a war. Chess functions in the context of language. There is a relation between chess and language. Ferdinand de Saussure probes the relation between chess and language. He states that:

> [A] state of the set of chessmen corresponds closely to a state of language. The respective value of the pieces depends on their position on the chessboard just as each linguistic term derives its value from its opposition to all the other terms.[25]

Explaining that something touched upon does not differ from what we have elsewhere called value in a certain context, he states that:

> A new comparison with the set of chessmen will bring out this point. Take a knight, for instance. By itself is it an element in the game? Certainly not, for by its material make-up—outside its square and the other conditions of the game —it means nothing to the player; it becomes a real, concrete element only when endowed with value and wedded to it. Suppose that the piece happens to be destroyed or lost during a game. Can it be replaced by an equivalent piece? Certainly. Not only another knight but even a figure

shorn of any resemblance to a knight can be declared identical provided the same value is attributed to it.[26]

We can view this matter from this perspective: Creating a language is making a rule. This rule is grammar. Anyone who learns this language must agree to abide by the rule in order to use it. Thus, people are enabled to use language to make a rule in any interaction between one person and another, as noted earlier. People establish order. Thus Weaver observes that language is the vehicle of order.[27] Thus language is a kind of social institution. People, inventing chess, provide a method of entertainment by using a rule formulated by using language. Thus even a war can be imitated by a game. With language used to formulate a rule, people change the combat in the battlefield into the game on the chessboard.

An election, held by raising hands or by casting ballots, is a similar great accomplishment. While humans use language, they make a rule. While they select officials for the governance of the state, they make a rule that turns a civil war for state power into a peaceful competition. A limitless competition becomes a limited one. A limitless competition means the exclusion of co-existence, the disorder of the society and the damages of human property and the loss of human lives, whereas a limited competition results in the co-existence of all, the establishment of order and the advancement of welfare for all though people often liken an election to a battle or a battle to an election.

The real significance of this phenomenon is that people, making a rule using language, allow themselves to compete against each other in a process. Competition tests which participant is more competent. People, playing a chess, make their greatest effort to show their intelligent competence. People, participating in an election, try their best to convince the electorate that they will meet their expectation in providing service to them. Election, a rule of limited, and hence peaceful, competition, totally changes the method of governing the state.

First, while people compete for state power through a war, the person who wins the war decides how to distribute the property of the society. As this person is always self-interested, he always distributes a greater part of the property of the society to himself. In feudalist times, land was part of the most valuable property. So a greater part of the land of the society was distributed to the man who won the war for plunder. While describing the distribution of the property in Old England, Paul Vinogradoff notes that "The king got to be and always remained a great landowner."[28] If the king had to distribute land to some nobles, or organizations, or common people, it was normally distributed to nobles, churches and townspeople. As Vinogradoff writes,

> All land in England is described in Domesday as belonging either immediately to the king, or to his vassals of different degree, or to churches which held it by direct grant from kings, or to burgesses whose tenure though peculiar, still appears as a tenure, a form of conditional ownership.[29]

Land was not distributed to peasants who accounted for a significant portion of the population. Since the war, launched by people for state power, was replaced by a peaceful competition, namely, an election, for state power, land usually has belonged to the state. People who compete for state power promise to provide the best public services to all citizens in order to hold power.

Second, while people hold a free election for the purpose of selecting the power holder who governs the state, there is a rule for the election. Any potential power holder is required to obey that rule. In this case, all people are citizens. They have the rights of citizens. Usually, the rights of property of the citizens are protected by the law and respected by the power holder to the greatest extent. Then, as no one is allowed to wage a war to decide how to distribute the wealth of the state, such as the land of the state, because people now compete for state power through an election rather than a war, market competition prevails. Now, people get wealth through market competition rather than through a war. Market competition encourages efficient production. Efficiency in production advances the social forces of production. The reason is that, as already mentioned earlier, plunder merely leads to the redistribution of the wealth of the state, but will not increase the wealth of the state. Particularly, plunder that disregards the right of property dampens people's enthusiasm of production. This is the main reason that economy stagnated in history. By contrast, market competition, based on the recognition of the right of property, encourages producers to provide many quality goods and services to the society. This is the reason that economy booms in modern times. Thus, people select election as a way of selecting the state leader for an economic reason. The reason is that a power holder who emerges from a war eyes plunder and dampens market competition, whereas a state leader who takes state power through an election respects market competition.

Third, while people make a rule for an election, the power holder is supposed to rule the state for a period of time only. The citizens select the power holder regularly. The power holder is expected to govern the state to the satisfaction of the citizens to the greatest extent. An election harmonizes the relationship between the power holder and the people. An election ensures that the election candidate supported by the citizens becomes the power holder. Yet, if the power holder is the one who emerges in the civil war and insists on holding the state power all his life, this power holder may not be the one who is supported by the people. If this power holder promises to bring happiness to the people, he may not always honor his promise. Along with the passage of time a change takes place. In this case this power holder may no longer meet the expectation of the people. The people may expect him to step down, but they cannot give expression to their will. The reason is that there is no election. This power holder, emerging from the civil war, tends not to give up his power. He usually controls the armed forces of the state. He is the dictator of the state. He may be capable of winning a civil war, but he may not be able to govern the state well. By contrast, while people hold an election for the selection of the state leader, the state leader and the citizens will reach an agreement in the governance of the state and the management of the national economy. He is usually the most capable man of governing the state as long as citizens do not err.

That means that with language used to make a rule, people compete against each other as guided by this rule. Though people compete against each other, they also cooperate with each other. They compete against each other, but they all obey this rule. As this rule requires that the competition should be peaceful, peace is made. An election is realized under these circumstances. This means that if there is a rule, people will be guided to competing in a certain way. They are no longer allowed to compete in other ways. This culminates in the very fact that people are prevented from waging a war. Thus, Joseph A. Schumpeter insists that democracy is the recognized method to conduct competitive struggle; electoral method is practically the only one available; and the competition of military insurrection is excluded.[30]

Thus, "the democratic method is that institutional arrangement for arriving at political decisions in which individuals acquire the power to decide by means of a competitive struggle for the people's vote."[31] This indicates that democracy means that language is used to make a rule that regulates a competition for power. The result is that a rule, made by using language, creates a condition for people to interact with each other in a constructive way. In this case, people will not go to war. `

In ancient Greece people held elections in some city-states. A civil war if any must have been averted. In medieval times politics showed the same logic. In medieval times the power of the state was often held by a ruling family. The change of the regime was often due to the outbreak of a civil war. The war of dynasties often broke out. For instance, in the history of European countries the outbreak of a civil war often posed a threat to the stable rule of a related dynasty. As each dynasty was determined to rule the state forever, it was always hopeless to change a dynasty peacefully. Therefore, a war was nearly the only possible method used by people to change the regime. When political camps agree to rule in turn in capitalist times, a change really takes place. As each political camp agrees to rule the state in a period of time instead of ruling the state perpetually because people have made the rule of election, a war is unnecessary. People, using language, make a contract to define a rule of games that each political camp gives a chance to rule the state in a period of time in exchange for another chance to rule the state in the future. The result is that a free election allows for political camps to realize such an exchange. That is, before the election is held, all parties that are going to participate in the election agree to comply with the rule of election that the party that has won the greatest or greater portion of the votes holds power until the next election. No party is allowed to use violence to change this rule. As an election is held regularly and the opinion of the public changes over time, each party may have a chance to rule the state. This is a rule. This is a rule of ruling and being ruled in turn. People are only supposed to compete for votes.

People make this rule in historical evolution. Such an evolution is a process of establishing a mutual trust relationship between different competitors in linguistic communication. If two political camps rule in turn, both sides are required to make a promise that if one side loses the election, it is obligated to give the chance to rule the state in a certain period of time to the side that wins the election. They must trust each other. It takes a historical period of time for all political camps to build a mutual trust relationship. If one side fears that if it gives up a chance to rule the state, the other side may refuse to give up another chance to rule the state, this side may refrain from giving up a chance to rule the state at a certain time. In the history of England the Long Parliament was formed due to the fact that the members of the Parliament feared that if they gave up the seats of the Parliament, they would be never able to come back again. Thus, they insisted on their own perpetuity. The Long Parliament decreed that it could not be dissolved without its own consent. As Russell explains, in the absence of a revolutionary situation, the members of the outgoing Parliament were assured of a pleasant life even if they belonged to the defeated party. Most of them would be re-elected, and if they lost the pleasures of government, they would gain the almost equal satisfactions to be obtained by publicly criticizing the mistakes of their rivals. And in due course they would return to power. If, on the other hand, they made it impossible for the electorate to get rid of them by the constitutional means, they would create a revolutionary situation, which would endanger their property and perhaps their lives.[32] At that time the British politics was at a crossroad. The later development shows that the politicians of Britain made a right decision. Today the members of the Parliament are regularly elected. No long parliament appears again. This means that language is a fundamental tool to help people get out of this deadlock. Though the method of a confrontation of humans remains largely unchanged and weapons, used by them for a combat, always pose a threat to human lives, people ameliorate steadily the method of linguistic communication performed by them. People gradually create a condition for holding an election nationwide. As the rule of election is carried out many times, proving the fact that people can take state power in a better method, people are gradually convinced that after they give up the chance of ruling the state in a certain period of time, no one will threaten the safety of their lives and property and they will have a chance of coming back. This is a rule represented by an election. As each side respects the rights of lives and property of the other side and each side can come back to hold power, they manage to establish a mutual trust relationship. Thus, people make a tacit agreement. That is, guaranteed in an agreement made by both sides that those who leave the Parliament can come back if they win the election next time, politicians find a solution not by using force but by using language. As they use language, they cooperate with each other. The result is that they make peace.

This means that language and violence are two distinct things. If one uses language in social or political intercourse, he will not use violence. If he uses violence in social or political intercourse, he will not use language, or the use of language is not essential even if he uses language. Sometimes the state happens to be caught up in a war either civil or international, and military officers are usually not accustomed to using language but violence. So sometimes they may even refuse to give up the power taken by them during the war when they are supposed to give back the power to civil officials in the state of peace. Human psychology may play a role in this case. As Russell opines, in the state of war people are affected by violent psychology. Fear makes people wish for a leader. They admire this leader. Then the successful general often persuades his country to entrust him with the supreme power. As long as the crisis continues, he is judged indispensable, and when it is over he may have become difficult to remove.[33] The psychology of violence differs from the psychology of using language. The use of language should be prevented from being affected by any form of violence. This is not only because the use of language creates a condition for the realization of peace through the making of a rule but also because violence should be prevented in order to let language play the role in keeping peace. This means that the military officers should be prevented by the rule from holding power after the end of the war or the conflict. The rule, made by using language, should be respected and obeyed.

Thus the handover of the regime can be peaceful. The significance of an election is that all parties compete for power according to a rule. The rule is made by using language. The competition is also committed through the use of language. Far-sighted people thus avoid the possible outbreak of a war as long as the state power may be taken by anyone supported by the voters. In ancient or medieval times the rulers of the states were usually males. Hobbes discusses this matter once upon a time. He states that a monarch's will was that the government remained monarchical. A child of his own, male or female, was preferred before any other man or woman because men were presumed to be more inclined by nature to advance their own children than the children of other men, and of their own, rather a male than a female because men were naturally fitter than women for action of labor and danger.[34] The rulers are often required to be, in some sense, warriors because they may be required to act as commanders for warfare. The rulers have to be physically fit because they are required to go to inspect the far-flung borders of the state or the frontier of the war. The rulers should be brave or bold because they should guard against any usurpation of power committed by some ambitious men. As there may be the outbreak of a civil war, the ruler of the state should be a male. If there is a female ruler, this ruler usually gains the power because of her husband or her family that gained state power in the past. For example, after the death of the emperor, the empress was enthroned to be the ruler. At that time, the ruler of the state was often the commander of an army. And usually the military commander was a male. In other words, a female was not qualified to be a military commander. By contrast, in modern times a female is often elected as the president of the state or the prime minister of the government in some nation-states because an election is held. An election obviates a civil war. This means that when an election is held, females, able to govern the state, can be the candidates of the head of the state or the government and may be elected to the office of the president of the state or the prime minister of the government. Even if a war breaks out, the female president or prime minister can rely on professional soldiers that are usually unlikely to seize power in violation of law because an election stresses ruling legitimacy. For example, when the Falklands War between the United Kingdom and Argentina broke out in 1982, the British Prime Minister Margaret Thatcher solidly controlled the government. The professional soldiers were responsible for the command of the combat. This was because the head of the government did not emerge in a civil war. Under these circumstances, this power holder might be a female. This is a phenomenon indicating that when an election is held to single out the state power holder, people keep peace. When comparing the newly established democratic system of the United States with the despotic system of some European states still existing at that time, Thomas Jefferson, the third president of the United States, said to his son-in-law John Wayles Eppes that "our campaign will be as hot as that of Europe. But happily we deal in ink only;

they blood."[35] His statement also confirms the role of language in the making of peace because an election is a process of linguistic communication.

If people are involved in any war or conflict, no common interest of the two sides exists. By contrast, communicating by using language, people create a condition for the formation of their common interest. Even if people hold different views for the governance of the state in election, there is still the essential common interest of all. I mean that if there are the opinion of the majority and the opinion of the minority in the election, there is still the common interest of all in seeking the order of the state and the unified will of the citizens. This is because people, holding an election, make a rule of games. People make an invisible contract. This contract is that voters agree to accept and recognize the result of election no matter whether any of them belongs to the minority acting as one party to this rule of games or the majority acting as another party to this rule of games and voters agree that if any side becomes the minority it will recognize that the majority has the right to hold state power in a certain period of time. The minority will recognize the invalidation of their votes. In this case only the votes of the majority are valid. This is because any state should be run according to a mainstream idea. This mainstream idea should be the idea held by the majority. This is also implied by the rule of election. This also means that as voters, belonging to the minority, may become those who belong to the majority next time as an election is held regularly and the opinions expressed by the voters may change over time, the tyranny of the majority will never occur. In other words, if one side does not intend to rule the state forever, its rule cannot be tyranny. If the voters who happen to be the minority are obligated to recognize that the delegates of the majority hold state power, they gain the right to require other voters to recognize that their delegates hold state power when they happen to be the majority. Any portion of the voters undertakes the obligations to recognize the other portion of the voters, winning the election, as the majority having the right to send their delegates to the government. Voters, agreeing to obey the rule of games, implement a contract. They avoid a war. The reason that a war is avoided is that the power holder is not a tyrant. As voters cooperate with each other to avoid a war by relying on the rule of election, this is the situation of two-wins over the long term. They avoid the possible war launched to seek state power. They play chess. If a war is waged to make a decision, both of the two sides will lose. If people hold an election, the chance of holding state power is only the chance of holding state power in a period of time. As this is only the chance of holding state power in a period of time, the chance of holding state power in this period of time can be given up in exchange for the chance of holding state power in another period of time. People make peace.

Thus we see that political parties are expected to enter into rivalry under a rule made by the people. As this rule contains a value, each political party agrees to be ruled in turn to offer this value. This value is that a political party, failing to win the votes of the majority in an election, will agree that the power of ruling the state is to be held, for a period of time, by the political party that wins the votes of the majority. As each party offers such a value to any other party, political parties can rule in turn. People activate the rule of election regularly. They make peace. The two-party system or multiparty system, put into practice by people, is set up according to this rule. This is quite different from the single-party system that people put into practice in some other states. The single-party system means that if the opposition appears in the state, the single ruling party does not offer such a value as this single ruling party is determined to rule the state perpetually. Because of this the opposition usually has no alternative but to use force to overthrow that single ruling party. A revolution is likely to break out. A bloody civil war may break out. So the difference between the two-party system or the multiparty system and the single-party system is, in essence, not a difference of the number of the political parties but a difference between the solution of making good use of language and the solution of relying on violence. Where people establish a two-party system or a multiparty system, there is a rule accepted by all. The common interest of all takes shape. People make peace. By contrast, where people establish a single-party system, such a rule does not exist. No common interest of all exists. Without such a rule people cannot be sure that they are at peace. A single-party system relies on coercion while a two-party system or a multiparty system depends on the operation of a rule, which is made by using language. A two-party system or a multiparty system is aimed at cooperation between two sides while a single-party system is intended to keep the dominance of one side. People have no legal system for cooperation.

The difference between a multiparty system or a two-party system and a single-party system is the difference in the organization of the state. In the single-party system, that single party is the one in control of an army. In the state of a single-party system, the army is always controlled by that single party instead of the state. If two armies compete for the power of ruling the state, they clash with each other. They do not need to carry out a rule. If there is any rule of war, such a rule may not be steadfastly adhered to by any side involved in the war. But if two or more political parties compete for the power of ruling the state under the rule of election, they discuss the affairs of the state by using language. They make compromises. They reach an agreement on the matter of making a law or a public policy. If two armies fight each other, the survival of each army is not guaranteed because there may not be a rule of war. A war usually results in the termination of the co-existence of the two sides involved in the war. They, in general, do not need to use language. When a war breaks out, each side may not need to notify the other side that the war has been launched. But two political parties, competing for the turn of ruling the state, use language because each party agrees to give a chance of ruling the state in a period of time to the other party if the other party wins the election. Thus people realize peace.

That means that as humans are animals using language, they are often ready to make an agreement wherever possible or necessary. They may formulate and carry out a rule by using language. They avoid some unnecessary wars. Language presupposes peace because language is a basic tool used by humans for cooperation. Language is a tool that can be used by people to seek peace. Violence, as a form, used by people to solve their problems, should never be encouraged if language can be used to solve the problems. People may not be always clearly aware of this nature of language. Those who stress the importance of violence in unraveling the contradictions of the society or the state usually overlook the role played by language in unraveling those contradictions. In history some radicals believed the impossibility of unraveling the contradiction between the government and the masses in a peaceful way. They stressed the role of violence. Likewise, in history some revolutionaries believed that people could not resolve the contradiction of social classes except resort to violence in the form of revolution to overthrow the rule of the propertied class and establish a classless society. They insisted that violence was the midwife of revolution. Thus they overlooked the role played by language. They disdained democracy. They criticized the two-party system or the multi-party system. They believed that all those parties served the ruling class. By contrast, liberalism has been advocating a system in which the social system guarantees and respects the freedoms of the citizens and free election. In this respect I argue that the operation of the state hinges on the role of law. A law is also made in the process of linguistic communication. A law is also a rule. When different political parties rule in turn, they realize a sort of separation of powers across time. They buttress the rule of law as a result. In the meantime, people may make a law in the context in which the political system prevents the conflict of interest of the power holders from arising and ensures the reasonable distribution of interest to all the citizens. Thus, as all those freedoms and rights of the citizens are inviolable, citizens participate in politics and engage in a negotiation for the purpose of formulating a scheme of governing the state. They fulfill this task in an election. Language, as a result, plays a role in the making of an agreement on ruling the state in turn. People avoid the violent conflict or civil war to the greatest extent. They make peace.

Notes

1. Adam Smith, *The Wealth of Nations*, with an Introduction by D.D. Rapheal (New York: Alfred A. Knopf, 1991),15.
2. Ibid., 13.
3. Mariano Grondona, *A Cultural Typology of Economic Development*, in Lawrence E. Harrison and Samuel P. Huntington (ed.), *Culture Matters: How Values Shape Human Progress* (New York: Basic Books, 2000), 49.
4. G. W. F. Hegel, *The Philosophy of Right*, translated by T. M. Knox (Chicago: Encyclopaedia Britannica, Inc., 1952), 67.
5. Hans Kelsen, *Pure Theory of Law*, translated by Max Knight (Berkeley: University of California Press, 1967), 37-38.
6. Smith, *The Wealth of Nations*,12.
7. Hegel, *The Philosophy of Right*, 68.

8. Montesquieu, *Considerations on the Causes of the Greatness of the Romans and Their Decline*, translated by David Lowenthal (Indianapolis: Hackett Publishing Company, Inc., 1999), 98-99.

9. Ludwig von Mises, *Free and Prosperous Commonwealth, an Exposition of the Ideas of Classical Liberalism*, translated by Ralph Raico and edited by Arthur Goddard (Princeton: D. Van Nostrand Company, Inc., 1962), 25.

10. Ibid., 26.

11. Niccolo Machiavelli, *The Prince*, translated by W.K. Marriott (New York: Alfred A Knopf, 1992), 99.

12. Von Mises, *Free and Prosperous Commonwealth, An Exposition of the Ideas of Classical Liberalism*, 26.

13. Charles de Secondat, baron de Montesquieu, *The Spirit of the Laws*, translated by Thomas Nugent and revised by J.V. Prichard (Chicago: Encyclopaedia Britannica, Inc., 1952), 146.

14. Immanuel Kant, *Perpetual Peace and Other Essays on Politics, History, and Morals* (Indianapolis: Hackett Publishing Company, 1983), 125.

15. Sun Tzu, *The Art of War*, edited by James Clavell (New York: Delacorte Press, 1983), 16.

16. Ibid.,78.

17. Ibid., 11.

18. Ibid., 11.

19. Kant, *Perpetual Peace and Other Essays on Politics, History, and Morals*, 111.

20. Thomas Hobbes, *Leviathan*, edited with an introduction by C. B. Macpherson (New York: Penguin Books, 1985), 201–202.

21. Hans Kelsen, *General Theory of Law and State* (New Brunswick, U.S.A.: Transactions Publishers, 2006), 259.

22. See: Plutarch, *The Lives of the Noble Grecians and Romans*, the Dryden Translation (Chicago: Encyclopaedia Britannica, Inc., 1952), 49–50.

23. Harold A. Innis, *Empire and Communications* (Victoria: Press Porcépic Limited, 1986),74–75.

24. David I. Kertzer, *Ritual, Politics, and Power* (New Haven: Yale University Press, 1988), 129.

25. Ferdinand de Saussure, *Course in General Linguistics* (New York: McGraw-Hill Book Company, 1966), 88.

26. Ibid., 110.

27. Richard M. Weaver, *Ideas Have Consequences* (Chicago: The University of Chicago Press, 1984), 148.

28. Paul Vinogradoof, *The Growth of the Manor* (London: George Allen & Unwin Ltd, 1951), 221.

29. Ibid. 293.

30. See: Joseph A. Schumpeter, *Capitalism, Socialism and Democracy* (London: Routledge, 1976), 271.

31. Ibid., 269.

32. Bertrand Russell, *Power* (New York: W.W. Norton & Company, Inc., 1938), 192.

33. Ibid., 200.

34. Hobbes, *Leviathan*, 250.

35. Sandra Moats, *Celebrating the Republic: Presidential Ceremony and Popular Sovereignty, from Washington to Monroe* (Dekalb: Northern Illinois University Press, 2010), 83.

Chapter Thirteen

Democracy

1. Demonstration

Human linguistic communication underlies the growth of the state. Likewise, their linguistic communication serves as a basis for mutual interaction between ordinary people and the power holder of the state. That is, in the state, the power holder actually communicates with the masses through the officials of various levels of the government. These officials function as media. As these media do not appear as required by ordinary people, the masses have to communicate with the power holder by using other media. The masses act normally as a collective being, and they perform collective linguistic communication with the power holder. The presence of a collective being serves as a medium. This medium appears in the long-term growth of the society. This medium also gives rise to a variety of other derivative media. They appear in the society that develops to a certain level. A demonstration, waged in a public place, can be considered a medium in support of collective linguistic communication. This medium develops in the long-term evolution of the society. Although a demonstration may be deemed as an activity of social movements and social scientists who study social movements focus on the relationship between the masses and the state, a demonstration can be regarded as a medium in support of collective linguistic communication performed by the masses with the authorities.

The reason is that, since people started using language, they have recognized the private property, learned to exchange goods and services and established the market. The market is an economic basis for the growth of the state. As the market requires peaceful cooperation between one another instead of plundering property, people speculate on the possibility of establishing the social order that can guarantee cooperation. They use language to make a rule for cooperation. This leads historically to the making of the constitution in modern times. The constitution rules out any unlawful physical interaction between the power holder and the masses. What prevails is the linguistic interaction between the power holder and the masses. One of the indications of this change is that the revolt, waged by the masses across the countryside in the past, is replaced by the demonstration waged by the citizens in the cities.

This change is a change of the mode of interaction between the power holder and the masses. A revolt is a physical interaction, whereas a demonstration is, basically, a linguistic interaction. People tend to claim that a demonstration, waged by the masses in a public place, is a form of the freedom of speech. For example, a cohort of people wage a mass demonstration on the street, and the public will believe that a demonstration is a speech. My view is that a demonstration is a course of collective linguistic communication. It is like an election in some sense. It is a form of democracy. This is because it is a real process of collective linguistic communication. Various media function in this course of collective linguistic communication. These media may be the ones of a new type. This situation differs from the past.

The past situation is that in an agrarian society, normally, peasants waged no demonstration. For example, in medieval times the peasants of European feudal kingdoms never waged a demonstration though they revolted from the ruler occasionally. This shows that the ruler and the masses performed unbalanced communication. The ruler could issue decrees to the masses, but the masses could hardly express their opinions on the governance of the society. The ruler had access to some media, such as officials. The ruler performed one-to-many communication. But many-to-one communication, performed by the masses with the ruler, did not exist. The reason is that in early times in agrarian society people resided in isolated and faraway areas not connected with each other by way of communication due to the underdevelopment of transportation and communication. People, isolated from each other, did not communicate with each other. They were usually unable to gather at one location to perform linguistic communication with the power holder. At that time each area might be under the rule of a local lord. People, such as the peasants of each area, faced a unique situation. People, from different areas, seldom united to take initiative to perform linguistic communication with the sovereign of the state. The sovereign issued decrees through the officials of various local government bodies or the lords if the administrative system of the state had not been well established. This means that the specific situation prevented peasants, as a collective being, from taking initiative to perform linguistic communication with the power holder. It was difficult for the masses to get together to perform many-to-one communication. Under these circumstances the main linguistic communication, performed by the authorities with the masses, was one way and was usually the decree issued by the authorities. The authorities needed to communicate with the masses. The authorities established the governments of various levels. The officials of the governments of various levels functioned as human chains passing on the decrees issued by the supreme power holder. But linguistic communication, performed by the masses with the authorities, was usually devoid of support from the bureaucratic system. The officials were appointed to pass chiefly on the decrees issued by the supreme power holder and they might not reflect the opinions or requests from the masses at the grassroots level.

The replacement of agrarian society by industrial society should be a watershed. Although scholars may argue that the ruler's despotic rule is due to the initial conquest, linguistic communication serves as a foundation for the formation of the state. Because of this, along with the growth of a new society, a change, in the structure of linguistic communication, leads to a change in linguistic communication that goes on between the masses and the ruler. Specifically, commercializing production accompanies the exchange of goods and services on the market. People build the market in the public. Then they often gather in the public place. In the meantime, the commercialization of production creates a condition for industrialization, and industrialization enhances living standard. People enhance their living standard in the urban area first. People move to the cities to enjoy a high standard of living. Population particularly increases in the urban area. A city becomes a densely-populated area. Cities also expand. People broaden old streets and even construct new streets. They improve communication. They publish and issue newspapers. It becomes easier for people to communicate with each other because they are no longer isolated. People become socially closer to each other. Therefore, the masses are enabled to gather on the streets to communicate with the authorities. Thus it is not accidental that Europeans began to wage demonstrations in the nineteenth century when industrialization began. For example, Europeans have been waging demonstrations at least since 1848. According to Vincent Robert, at least eight demonstrations crossed Lyon during the first month of the 1848 revolution.[1]

Then, on the basis of the above analysis, I argue that people, using language, create various media in support of linguistic communication. The industrial society is a medium. If people did not use language, they would still use their own behavior as the original medium in their mutual communication. As behavior only functions in support of short-distance communication, only a small number of people communicate with each other in a community. Thus people should still reside in tribes or villages only. Cities are built to facilitate communication in which people engage along with the rise of handicraft in ancient times and the rise of industry in modern times. Thus, cities are media. Accordingly, transportation, developed in the urban area, is a medium. Communication, developed in the urban area, is a medium. Newspapers and magazines are part of such communication. All are conditions for people to wage a demonstration.

In the meantime, if we suppose that people face the same situation in the urban area, they may act in unison across the city. As long as the workers of one large factory can communicate with each other, they may communicate with the workers of another factory, for example. Newspapers and magazines printed and sold can be media in spreading some information needed by the workers across the city. An event or an act of the government, not welcomed by the masses, may trigger a demonstration. The message of an event or an act of the government, not welcomed by the masses, may incite the masses to take joint action. Unlike media used by the power holder, mass media are often used by the masses in their own communication and then they are enabled to unite to perform collective communication with the power holder. The good condition of transportation may also facilitate the masses to gather. In the past linguistic communication between the power holder of the state and the masses was not balanced. The power holder was well positioned to communicate with the masses because he could communicate with the masses by relying on the assistance from the bureaucratic system. Now the masses can also use their own media to compensate their disadvantage in linguistic communication. A demonstration, as a form of democracy in modern times, is often waged by the masses.

This is due to the fact that a demonstration is a face-to-face collective communication that functions on a large scale. As people are now socially closer to each other, they are enabled to meet each other. Various media are available for waging a demonstration.

First, one of the hallmarks of such a situation is that people have access to good transportation. Good transportation enables people to meet each other and to perform face-to-face communication even on a large scale. Thus, transportation becomes a medium. Transportation is usually accessible in the urban area. As everyone can use the condition of convenient transportation in the urban area, people join each other to wage a demonstration. Thus demonstrators usually wage a demonstration in the city. Even farmers, the residents of the rural area, may travel a great distance to a big city to wage their demonstration. This means that the masses are enabled to use the condition of convenient transportation. Then they perform face-to-face linguistic communication on a large scale. They create and utilize various media. If we compare ancient democracy with modern democracy, we see that in ancient times Greeks also put into practice democracy in their city-states. They put into practice their democracy in the cities instead of the rural areas because it was easy for the citizens to get together in the cities. In modern times the states are usually nation-states. People who express their opinion or raise a request also usually perform the related collective linguistic communication in the urban area. They take initiative to perform such linguistic communication in the urban area only. They use the condition of convenient transportation in the urban area.

Second, a place with a big traffic is a medium. As such, people tend to choose a big city instead of a small city as the location of waging a demonstration. People may choose the capital city as the most favorable location for a demonstration. The reason is that people congregate in a big city. The capital city is often the largest city of the country or one of the largest cities of the country. There is often the largest traffic. It is easier for them to gather to communicate with the power holder face-to-face. All the areas within a city may not be the ideal place. Sometimes a demonstration is not successful unless it is waged in the central area of the city because everyone can go there and meet each other. People usually wage a demonstration on the biggest street. They are very active in the central area of the city. They need to communicate with the authorities face-to-face. If they do not perform such face-to-face communication in the place with a large traffic, they may not wage any demonstration.

Third, the concourse of people is a medium. When people gather in a public place, their activity is special. That is, unless a special goal is set, one seldom proactively goes to a public place for face-to-face communication with the other members of the community. As the strength of ordinary people is the strength of the collective, they gather in the public place to show the special purpose of such face-to-face linguistic communication. Thus the concourse of people who wage a demonstration serves as a medium. Then people perform linguistic communication on a large scale so as to communicate with the government if their demonstration targets the government. In this case, people can use the number of people, joining the demonstration, to send out an extra message because, in order to have an equal status in communication with the powerful authorities, people have to rely on the strength of the collective being. Without the strength of the collective being, common people are always weak. For example, in the countries where universal suffrage is not given or referendum is not held for various reasons, demonstrators often express their opinions by waging a demonstration. To show that they are supported by the people, they often call on more people to join their demonstration to show the number of their supporters. In the United States people hold free elections. A referendum may be held in some states. However, citizens may also select demonstration as a form of communication with the authorities from time to time and they often call on more people to join the demonstration. For example, people wage some demonstrations, demanding the modification of the immigration policy of the federal government. They hope that the federal government can grant permanent residence status to some undocumented immigrants. These demonstrations are joined not only by the legal immigrants but also by the illegal immigrants. The immigrants want to show the number of the demonstrators to highlight their opinion or request.

Fourth, people also enlarge the scale of a demonstration in order to perform the related communication on a large scale. Enlarging the scale of a demonstration leads to the creation of a medium that allows demonstrators to communicate with more people. For example, demonstrators usually prefer to march on the streets before or after a rally. Marching on the streets, they communicate with more people as a collective being. The masses are unable to communicate effectively with the authorities unless they are able to make good use of the scale of that demonstration. People also extend the time of that demonstration in order to perform effective linguistic communication with the government. Extending the time of the demonstration strengthens the effect of face-to-face linguistic communication performed by demonstrators. Demonstrators may march on the streets in a long period of time in order to communicate with more people and to communicate with the authorities. They sometimes wage a demonstration in the form of sit-ins or other types of civil disobedience that go on in a certain period of time in the public. They may wage a long-time demonstration on a public holiday because they have more time staying on the streets on a public holiday. Such a demonstration, pioneered by American author Henry David Thoreau, the founder of modern India Mohandas Karamchand Gandhi and the American civil rights movement activist Dr. Martin Luther King Jr., often breaks out in any state in modern times.

Fifth, in face-to-face collective linguistic communication, each demonstrator uses all other demonstrators as media. Thus, people strengthen linguistic communication during the demonstration. The typical example of this case is that demonstrators shout slogans. They have to speak loudly as a collective being in order to make their voice heard by the authorities. This is the collective linguistic communication in the type of spoken language. A person, speaking to a large number of people, has to speak louder in order to get heard. Because he has to exert more strength to speak louder and he has limited strength, he has no alternative but to shorten the sentences and simplify the "text" of the information transmitted in linguistic communication. That is, a slogan is a sentence especially made to maintain the efficacy of face-to-face communication in collective communication between two sides which are far from each other. Meanwhile, shouting a slogan needs to be joined by many in order to raise decibel and to make voice far-reaching. In general, no one shouts a slogan in a public activity that only expresses a personal opinion or requests the authorities to address one's personal problem. Since a slogan is to be shouted by many, it is usually shouted at a public place because the masses are usually only able to get together at a public place to communicate with the authorities. Sometimes we hear someone shouting a slogan on the street, and we know that the slogan must be related to a public or political affair. No one shouts slogans that address a personal matter. A person, shouting a slogan, is an information sender. There must be an information recipient. As the slogan is invariably related to a public or political affair, the information recipient is usually the government which governs the state. Though the government may not be able to hear the voice of the masses directly, the news media will often take initiative to transmit their messages to the government. The reason is that a slogan, shouted at a public place, draws the attention of the news media. The news media will cover this event and send a message to the public and the government. When the masses are dissatisfied with a public affair or a government policy or are shocked by an event affecting their interest, their most emotional reaction is to hold a demonstration and during the demonstration, one of their most emotional acts is to shout slogans in the centre of a big city where a lot of people cluster. Sometimes, without shouting slogans in a public place, the masses will be unable to communicate with either the government or the broad masses of the people.

Sixth, some materials are also used as media during a demonstration for face-to-face communication that reaches all on a large scale. For example, demonstrators display signs on the streets during a demonstration. They display signs on the public squares or streets where people have a broad vision field. Signs are normally made by many or on behalf of many. They are seldom the form of communication performed by an individual person. They cannot succeed in communication unless people place them in a public place. One example is that people select bold letters to make big signs. They are aimed at taking advantage of the publicity to perform many-to-one communication. We often see that in industrialized countries people wage a demonstration by holding high big signs. These big signs take advantage of being placed in the public place to perform many-to-one linguistic communication. They force targeted information recipients to enter the communicative course. When signs appear on the streets, anyone who passes by the streets will see them. The signs keep on communicating with those who are passing by the streets. The signs perform communication in the open. If the signs pose a protest against the government, they communicate not only with the government but also with a third party, namely, a group of other citizens who are not involved in this affair. But accurately speaking, it is not the signs which force everyone to enter the designed collective linguistic communication, but the publicity used by the signs. If a sign is placed in a public place, no one can evade the public place. In this way, people perform many-to-one linguistic communication in the public place. This is a form of democracy.

Seventh, the masses who want to communicate with the authorities in a demonstration to exercise their rights of democracy choose to communicate with the authorities in public rather than in private. They expect other people to know that they raise a request to or protest against the authorities. They want to put pressure on the government. To communicate with the broad masses of the people as well as the government, they sometimes even use the enlarged images of some figures or other forms in communication. If they make a protest against the government, they may display the big cartoon pictures or effigies of some government leaders to perform such communication. These cartoon pictures or effigies are usually larger than the real persons because they are used to communicate with many citizens as well as the government on behalf of the many protestors in public instead of being used in private. Why are cartoon pictures or effigies used in a demonstration? Because it is easy for the public to see these cartoon pictures or effigies and understand the related meanings. Displaying these cartoon pictures or effigies provides a way of direct observation to enhance the efficacy of communication in a public place. For example, the masses, who advocate protecting the rights of animals, may hold up the effigies of animals on a public square to disseminate their ideas. Sometimes people also use life-size puppets. This is communication that functions on a large scale.

Eighth, in order to realize collective linguistic communication with many people on a large scale, people simplify the "text" of information transmitted through a demonstration. The simplified text is a medium. A demonstration is usually a reaction against a certain policy or a certain decision made by the authorities or a certain event happening unexpectedly. Linguistic communication, performed through a demonstration, is aimed to express an opinion or to raise a demand. It is impossible for people to wage a demonstration to explain completely a detailed social or economic development plan or a political theory or a philosophy. If one writes a book or makes a speech, he may be able to introduce his theory, philosophy or proposal in detail, in depth and at length. If people perform many-to-one linguistic communication in a demonstration, what they can do is to use short sentences to show their demand or opinion briefly. Otherwise, people will be unable to perform communication on a large scale. That is, using short sentences to express their attitude, opinion and demand briefly will make many people easy to organize because people, performing collective linguistic communication, have difficulties in coordinating their actions. They need a simplified text in face-to-face communication in the public. Therefore, they can communicate with the public or the authorities on a large scale.

Ninth, the power holder may also function as a medium in face-to-face linguistic communication that functions on a large scale. That is, after people formulate a constitution in a state in which the masses are needed to be mobilized, the constitution lays a foundation for the establishment of legal order. Such legal order defines the relationship between the citizens and the power holder. The constitution requires the citizens to be obligated to fulfill certain duties and requires the state to grant civil rights to the citizens. A mutual interaction between the power holder and the masses becomes a linguistic interaction. Establishing the constitutional system prevents the masses from revolting against the power holder. The masses are prohibited from using force to overthrow the government. What the masses can do is to express their opinion if they disagree with the government on a public affair. They have to communicate with the power holder by using language. The power holder respects the rights of the citizens to express their opinion or to raise their request. If the masses and the power holder are in a conflict, the masses and the power holder alike respect the constitutional system. Thus, citizens may have a right to wage a demonstration. Accordingly, the power holder is often required to pay attention to the demand from the masses when the masses wage a demonstration. Thus, this power holder also, in some sense, functions as a medium because he may facilitate such linguistic communication. As mentioned earlier, people, at war, may not use language, but people, at peace, have to use language. Likewise, the ruler, committed to the despotic rule, and the ruled, suffering from the despotic rule, may wage a civil war. In this case people may not use language. By contrast, under the constitution, the power holder and the masses engage chiefly in linguistic interaction. They take advantage of various media. Even the power holder can function as a medium in face-to-face communication that functions on a large scale. For example, if the power holder takes initiative to send his delegate to meet the demonstrators, the delegate functions as a medium facilitating the masses to communicate with him.

Thus we see that people, performing mutual communication by using language, create and use various media. Media, except non-verbal behavior functioning as an original medium, do not appear until people begin to use language. Whenever people communicate using language, they use a medium. Without a medium people cannot communicate by using language. In the meantime, we find that a medium, used by language, gives a special role to language. Like the fact that language plays a crucial role in the growth of the state and the establishment of the order of the state, language also plays a role in the progress of the state. A demonstration, a form of collective linguistic communication that goes on between the masses and the authorities, symbolizes a method of the constructive mutual interaction between the masses and the power holder in the state in which it is usually easier for the power holder to communicate with the masses than for the masses to communicate with the power holder. Language is an open system of human communication. With it, people create a variety of media. Such media support a demonstration. The power holder may issue a decree to the public. However, the development of more media gives a special role to language in communication between the citizens and the power holder. As each citizen needs to express his opinion to the power holder in order to participate in the governance of the state as required by the formation of the common interest of the state, citizens cooperate with each other. One of the greatest results of such a cooperation is that the medium, used by one, is combined with the medium, used by the other, for the same purpose. A medium, commonly used by all, appears. Each of the citizens functions as a medium used by all others in their collective action. They realize many-to-one collective linguistic communication. Such type of linguistic communication conditions any form of democracy including demonstration.

That is, I regard a demonstration, waged by people in a protest against a government's act or any affair or event in the public, as a form of democracy in modern times. Some other scholars may construe a demonstration as a speech. But it differs from the speech made by any individual person enjoying the freedom of speech discussed earlier. A demonstration is usually a speech made by a collective being. This collective being may not be equated with the people because those who wage a demonstration in the public are usually a portion of the people. They may claim that they are the people, but observers may disagree with them. Yet, unlike the speech made by an individual person enjoying the freedom of speech, a demonstration is a speech made by a group of people. Democracy may mean a form of speech made by the citizenry to express their opinions on the governance of the state and the management of public affairs. A demonstration means a form of speech made by a portion of the citizens to express their opinions on the governance of the state and the management of public affairs. Sometimes a demonstration can help the citizens to express their opinions that may not be expressed in an election because an opinion, expressed in the election, is general, whereas an opinion, expressed during a demonstration, may be specific. This is also significant for the formation of the common interest of all. When the masses wage a demonstration in the public, the government is under the pressure to pay attention to what the demonstrators say. The government is often obligated not to ignore the opinion of demonstrators. The reason is that if citizens unite to express the same opinion, their act may indicate the inclination or the opinion of the whole people. At least, one cannot rule out such possibility. If the opinion of the demonstrators can be considered by the authorities, the common interest of the state may take shape.

In other words, people can create a variety of media to facilitate the process of linguistic communication as required by people entering this process of linguistic communication. Language enables people to create and apply a wide range of media. Thus language conditions the establishment of democracy. One case in point is just demonstration. A demonstration means a process of many-to-one face-to-face linguistic communication. Whenever people find it necessary to safeguard their interest, they may perform many-to-one face-to-face communication to request the government to accommodate their interest. Accommodating their interest is often part of the process of forming the common interest of the state. Needless to say, the masses may wage a demonstration in support of the government. Then, we further see that without the existence of the government people may not perform many-to-one communication in public life. If people find themselves in need of communicating with the government, people may not be able to perform any effective communication unless they perform many-to-one face-to-face communication to raise their request or express their opinion in regard to a public affair which concerns their interest. Therefore, they stage a parade, a demonstration, a protest and a sit-down strike, etc. In this many-to-one face-to-face communication, many mean the masses while one means the representative of the government. All of the forms of demonstration are the meetings held outdoors, open to all and aimed at inviting the officials of the government to send their delegates to get in touch and talk with the related masses. A demonstration is a moving outdoor meeting designed to catch the attention of as many people as possible. Of course, in a human community whose population is large and territory is vast, the entire people are unable to get together to express their opinions. No matter how many demonstrators perform collective communication with the government, the opinion, expressed by them, is the opinion of a portion of the people. Yet, in the meantime, one cannot deny that a demonstration, waged by a portion of the people, may represent the wishes of the people. A demonstration may reflect the desire of the people. The opinion, expressed by the demonstrators, may become the opinion expressed by the voters in the upcoming election.

That is, a demonstration does not necessarily mean the weakening or the subversion of the rule of the authorities. Though a demonstration may evolve to be a conflict between the masses and the authorities, if people obey the order of the constitution, it will become a process in which the state accommodates the different interests of the citizens. For example, citizens may form two basic factions within the state. They have different interests. They express two different opinions. They may be represented by the ruling party and the opposition. Yet as the citizens can be allowed to express their different opinions and to seek their own lawful interest, a demonstration can be a process of forming the common interest of the citizens. In other words, the co-existence of different opinions is often a sign that the common interest of people has taken shape. Thus, under the condition that the government respects the lawful rights of the opposition, allowing for the opposition to wage a demonstration means the formation of the common interest of all. This is because now we not only see that the interest of those holding power is taken care of, but also behold that the interest of those not holding power is also taken care of. The state comes to rest on the formation of the common interest of the citizens.

In brief, people usually do not express their opinion or raise their demand or protest unless their interest, or their demand, is ignored by the authorities or any other organization or they feel the necessity of showing their attitude or expressing their opinion. When people wage a demonstration, they have to adopt a simplified form of expression to unify their expressions and show clearly their demand and opinion. They use some special media. Then language plays a special role in the formation of the common interest of all because allowing the opposition to express its opinion means the formation of the common interest between the citizens and the government. In the meantime, by using language, people can constitute a process of collective linguistic communication to facilitate themselves to express an opinion to the government, namely, the organizer of the state. A demonstration is one of the forms of such linguistic communication.

2. Poll

If the state is despotic, the relationship between the power holder and ordinary people is chiefly characterized by the asymmetrical interaction of the two sides. The construction of such a relationship relies on coercion. In this case linguistic communication between the power holder and ordinary people is characterized by the fact that it is important or essential for the power holder to issue commands to the ordinary people, whereas it is unimportant or inessential for the ordinary people to give any feedback to the power holder. In the mutual interaction between the power holder and ordinary people governed by the power holder, the crucial feature of such a mutual interaction is that the power holder is enabled to use coercion to impose his will on ordinary people as the systematic imperative while it is difficult, or often impossible, for ordinary people to use coercion to impose their will on the power holder. It is very difficult for a large number of people, dispersed across the state, to get together at one location to use their united strength to force the power holder to obey their will. The power holder depends on the state apparatus. The bureaucratic system and the armed forces are organized while ordinary people are not. This means that the advantage, had by the power holder, is force, whereas the advantage, had by ordinary people, is their number. The advantage of the number of people, had by ordinary people, cannot be manifested easily unless a war of the people is waged or the opinion of the collective being is expressed. As people are not supposed to wage a war of the people under normal circumstances, the possible advantage, had by people in their interaction with the power holder, is often to perform linguistic communication with the power holder to express their collective opinion. At least, linguistic communication creates an objective condition for ordinary people to interact with the power holder to show the number of people who support or oppose a decision in the governance of the state. Then they can have some control on such a mutual interaction. At least, people can use language on an equal footing, and it is possible for ordinary people to show the strength of the collective being in a process of linguistic communication.

The specific situation is that in a despotic state the first business in which the ruler engages is to control the tool of coercion, whereas in a democratic state the most prominent characteristic of organizing the state is establishing a constructive relation of linguistic communication between the power holder and ordinary people. In particular, there is a dialogue between the public and the power holder under democracy. In all democratic states the people and the power holder interact in linguistic communication. The related linguistic communication should be long-distance linguistic communication. As immediacy between one another often disappears in the state, long-distance linguistic communication becomes so critical that without such long-distance linguistic communication, the people and the power holder will not be able to interact with each other symmetrically. That is, it is especially easy for the power holder to communicate with all within the state. Such linguistic communication is one-to-many collective linguistic communication. Such linguistic communication, in which each engages, may not run at the same time and in the same area. The separation of all processes of linguistic communication in which all engage gives more freedom to the power holder in linguistic communication that goes on between him and the people. Though media are also needed to be used, it is easy to create those media. This is because those media are able to reach each individual at any time or at any place separately. For example, in ancient times the regime issued decrees. These decrees might be inscribed on a stele in the public that functioned as a medium. People, passing by this stele, read the text of each decree. Likewise, after the power holder makes a speech in the public and promulgates a stipulation in modern times, newspapers may cover the related event. Books, newspapers and magazines, printed in a large number due to the development of printing in modern times, serve chiefly the linguistic communication performed by the power holder with the public. By contrast, a demonstration is a way of many-to-one communication. But a demonstration may not enable the entire people to express their opinion. A demonstration is a process of communication performed by a portion of people with the authorities. It is required for the entire people in a large number and in a large area to enter jointly the process of linguistic communication. In the small state in the past, each person might learn about the opinions of all other people about the governance of the state through a gossip, or a discussion, because the population of the state was small. For example, in a city-state in ancient Greece, each citizen might learn about other citizens' opinions about the governance of the state through a gossip on the street or a debate on a public square. At that time, people relied chiefly on face-o-face contact for mutual communication and they knew what others thought of. Yet along with the growth of the state in modern times, face-to-face communication no longer suffices to support the linguistic communication that allows for each to learn about the opinions of all others about the governance of the state though people wage a demonstration occasionally. This situation in the state differs from the situation in the society. In the formation of a society each person of the society gossips with any other person to learn about the opinion about societal governance from that person. He does not need to learn about the opinions of all others because the society is self-organized without any one in charge of governing the society. By contrast, in the formation of a state a person governs the state. If this person needs to learn about the opinions of all other people about the state and what they think of, he cannot realize this goal by gossiping with all other people on individual basis because the state is a community large in population and area. If the power holder needs to learn about the opinions about the governance of the state from all other people of the state and what they think of, he tends to arrange a process of collective linguistic communication able to cut the costs of such linguistic communication. The state creates a series of media to facilitate ordinary people to perform collective linguistic communication with the power holder. If we argue that a meeting is actually a medium that facilitates numerous people to express their opinions because by gathering themselves many people can express their opinions, a poll is like a meeting in some sense. Describing the functioning of polls, Frank Newport writes that:

> Polls, in fact, are in many ways an extension of a town hall, deliberative process. Polling simply distills the opinions of all of one's neighbors in an accurate fashion—an expanded version of what the voter would find out by asking neighbors in the community where they stand on the issues of the day. The idea of town meetings wherein people get together to discuss their opinions is essentially as old as America itself. The idea of polling as an expanded town meeting is much newer, but not categorically different.[2]

This means that, in linguistic communication between the power holder and the people, the state has to support the linguistic communication performed by the people with the power holder so as to allow for the people to express their opinions to the power holder.

Thus, we see that in a state, a person, an economic, social or political organization, a news medium or a government body may sometimes intend to learn about the views, opinions and attitudes of all the citizens concerning a public policy or a public affair or a public figure. Citizens are usually unable to take initiative to express their opinions or their attitudes. Thus a certain organization or a government body takes initiative to seek their opinions or to request them to express their attitudes. People create the forms of polling. Polls gradually become prevalent. Particularly, prior to an election, some people may arrange for a poll to find out the trend of public opinion. We can take as an example the development of polls in the United States described by Frank Newport. That is, polls used to develop fast in the United States in history because people intended to forecast the result of the upcoming election. The first poll conducted in 1824 was intended to forecast the result of the upcoming election. By the end of 1800s, straw polls had already been very common across the United States because Americans paid attention to the election. Particularly, by the 1924 and 1928 elections, the Hearst newspapers chain conducted presidential pre-election polls involving almost all states of the Union. In 1936, George Gallup proved the value of a scientific approach to polling when he made the daring prediction that President Franklin Roosevelt would win reelection. As FDR did win, George Gallup went on to be a polling hero.[3] People intentionally seek the opinions of the citizens. Their opinions are valuable.

Sometimes it is under the condition that the government requests the citizens to express opinions or attitudes that some people conduct a poll, a form of many-to-one linguistic communication. Those people facilitate the related linguistic communication. Then a poll is used as one method of allowing for the citizens to perform many-to-one linguistic communication with the authorities in charge of managing public affairs or governing the state though a poll may also be conducted by any social organization such as a non-government organization or a business for all other purposes. For example, as the citizens are plentiful in the state, a body of administration is unable to seek the opinion of everybody concerning the public affairs. The body of administration has to use an alternative method to learn about the opinion of the people that closely approximates the opinion directly expressed by all. It is extremely difficult to arrange for everyone of the state to enter the same and one process of expressing opinions in the state. For this reason, investigators, in charge of conducting the poll, are often only able to select a small number of people to express opinions on behalf of all within the state. A small number of people function as media. The method is that according to the design and arrangement of the investigation made by an investigator, the selected interviewees answer questions in the forms of verbal or written communication so as to express an opinion. As long as the interviewees are supposedly able to represent the entire population, the outcome of the investigation will approximately reflect the opinion of the entire people. For using this type of investigation, people establish a sign relation between the opinion of the selected samples and the supposed opinion of the entire people. As it is difficult for the investigator to gather opinions directly from all, samples are used to represent them. It is just like the fact that a doctor uses a clinical thermometer to test the body temperature of a patient. A sample opinion is a medium.

The birth of polls paves a way for people to perform many-to-one communication in which a portion of people express opinions on behalf of all. The feature of polls is that those, involved in linguistic communication, are not required to get together in person at the same one location and at the same time. They are not required to act as the demonstrators to get together on the streets to express their opinions or raise their demands or reflect what they think of. They are able to enter this process of communication at different times and at different locations so as to perform otherwise comparatively difficult communications. In the course of conducting a poll, the interviewees act on individual basis and are not required to coordinate with others in verbal or written expression. They are not required to learn if others hold the same views. As the interviewees, in some sense, represent all the citizens due to the fact that the interviewers seek the opinions of the interviewees through a program designed on the basis of the theory of probability, people create a process of especially-structured linguistic communication. That is, the investigator takes charge of presiding over and adjusting the poll. Due to the arrangement made by the investigator, the interviewees enter this process of many-to-one communication.

There are several types of such polls as follows. The first type of polls is the polls conducted by the government. The government often conducts polls concerning the problems encountered by it in the management of public affairs or the governance of the state. The government, managing public affairs or governing the state, needs to know the opinions of the people. That means that the authorities need the people to enter a process of many-to-one communication with it either regularly or irregularly. Sometimes the opinions of the people are crucial in the operation of the government. Even the most despotic regimes in history could not refrain from paying attention to the opinions of the people. There are some historical stories saying that the emperors of some ancient empires or the kings of some ancient kingdoms traveled disguised as a commoner to observe the social conditions in order to learn about the wishes and expectations of the populace. They sometimes talked with commoners incognito. In today's nation-states, one of the most important works of the government is to gather the opinions of the citizens. But the ways of gathering the opinions from the people may vary from one nation-state to another. In modern China, the leaders of the state, or the officials of the government, make regular investigations by traveling to local areas to conduct direct interviews. They gather the opinions of common people by talking to them in person. For example, they may meet the farmers in the field or the workers in a factory. Then they may make decisions in consideration of the opinions gathered by them. These opinions are often believed to be representative. The investigations, made by the leaders of the state, or the senior officials of the government, are special in China because there are no active and diligent members of the legislature (the People's Congress) who reflect frequently and regularly the people's opinions to an organ of power or an administrative department. In China, the administrative system is centralized and the opinions of the common people are usually transmitted level by level up to the supreme leader of the state or the official of the highest level of the local government. Officials in the middle may refrain from submitting true and accurate information to the upper level because they consider the interest of the specific bodies of the government or the local government. The opinions of common people may not be reflected to the officials of the upper level. So the leaders of the state, or the senior officials of the government, often travel over a great distance to conduct on-site interviews in person. In some sense this is a particular way to conduct a poll. In the United States or Canada, the leaders of the state also travel over a great distance to local areas to conduct inspections in person regularly. However, the members of the legislature are active in reporting the conditions of their constituency. In the United States and Canada the channels of communication, performed by ordinary citizens with the government, have been diversified while in China citizens particularly rely on the leader's, or the official's, investigations to communicate with the state or the government. In China, the person who happens to be chosen by the local government to talk directly to a state leader to give an opinion is supposed to communicate with the authorities on behalf of the local people, but he may not be a right one because he is chosen by the government instead of being chosen by the people themselves or a neutral social organization or a professional research institute.

The second type of polls is the polls conducted by independent research institutions. When professional investigation institutions conduct polls to gather the opinions about public affairs from common citizens, citizens stand a chance to perform many-to-one communication with the government. However, citizens may not be able to perform such many-to-one communication unless the research institutions seek their opinions. In a Western nation-state such as Canada, democracy particularly requires the government and the party in power to pay attention to the expression of the opinions from citizens and research institutions or investigation institutions help the state, the government and the party in power to learn about the citizens' demands by submitting to them a lot of research reports. Many of those research reports are published or disclosed to the public. In a single-party system nation-state in which one party rules the nation-state, the government and the ruling party restrict or control the investigations made by the research institutions. They need citizens to communicate with them, but they do not want to see the citizens voicing their opposition to them, particularly, in the public. In China, the results of the investigations, made by the research institutions, are very often kept confidential and only available to the leaders of the state or the senior officials of the government unless those materials do not affect the authority of the ruling party or the stability of the state or the society. The government allows for citizens to file complaints to the designated bodies of the government on individual basis. It, however, does not want the people to speak to the government by way of a demonstration on the streets. It makes every effort to avoid being in direct conflict with the people in the public. Because of this, the Chinese people are usually only permitted to perform many-to-one linguistic communication with the government through an internal channel, including being allowed to accept the investigations made by some research institutions mandated by the government on special occasions.

The third type of polls is the type of polls conducted by news media. News media may conduct polls when they cover the events which give rise to the heated debate among the masses. If the opinions of the masses become the mainstream public opinion, the opinions of the masses may influence the government and influence the process of the decision-making of the government. At this time, communication, performed as supported by media, is also a process of many-to-one linguistic communication performed by citizens. As long as the result of the poll is disclosed to the public, the poll is many-to-one linguistic communication performed in the public. In a Western nation-state in which people implement the principles of the freedom of speech and the freedom of press, the authorities are unable to prevent the news media from conducting such polls. They are unable to prevent the citizens from performing many-to-one linguistic communication likely to give an opinion not in favor of the government. Particularly, if people debate which opinion is the mainstream opinion expressed by citizens or which policy is welcomed by the majority of the citizens, the poll may give an answer. Generally speaking, conducting a poll is of great significance in respect of providing a channel for the people to communicate with the authorities as well as among themselves.

First, a poll functions as a form of the presence of public opinion. In the state an opinion, expressed by one person, is not the opinion expressed by the people. If citizens do not perform many-to-one communication, no citizen knows if many others agree with him on a certain public affair or on a certain public policy. Promulgating the result of a poll allows for each citizen, participating in the poll, to know if many other citizens agree with him. If a government makes an internal investigation, not making its result public, each participant will not be able to know whatever answer others give except his own. Communication, performed this way, must be the communication performed at the request of the government instead of being at the request of the people. This communication is aimed at the feedback from the people in which the people take no initiative. A normal poll helps to create the presence of the will of the people or public opinion. If a poll is conducted, the outcome of the poll must be disclosed to the public to let the people know what public opinion is. Citizens, aware of the formation of a certain public opinion, will compel the authorities to act in response to the public opinion. This means that a certain institution arranges for citizens to express their opinions. This is a way of giving expression to the opinions of the people. This way of expression requires the state to permit the institution, conducting a poll, to disclose the outcome of the poll to the public and requires the government to recognize the existence of a certain public opinion and to be open to, and consider, it as well. In a nutshell, a poll creates a recognized way for the common citizens or the people to perform many-to-one linguistic communication with the authorities as well as among themselves in a large state such as a nation-state.

Second, unlike the outcome of a demonstration, the result of a poll shows the number and the percentage of the citizens expressing an opinion. Though waging a demonstration is a special form of many-to-one communication, it is unable to show a specific or accurate number of the citizens who take part in this process of communication. The number and the percentage of the citizens, supporting or opposing a proposal, or a policy or a decision in the management of public affairs or the governance of the state, is crucial because the numbers and percentages of the citizens, expressing opinions on public affairs, are always disclosed and some citizens, supporting a proposal, or a policy, or a decision, and some other citizens, opposing the same, always form different groups. Which opinion prevails over the other should be determined according to the opinion of the majority. A poll indicates the number and the percentage of the citizens who express a certain opinion though with a permitted error, and thus it is easy for people to see which opinion is expressed by the majority and which opinion is expressed by the minority. The poll is often supposed to show clearly the number and percentage of the citizens who express a certain opinion. It is obvious that the opinion of each will not be significant unless there is public opinion. The government may claim that its policy reflects public opinion. But how do people know and verify that the government's statement is true? A democratic government should take a special step. This step is to conduct a poll, to release the outcome of the poll and even to make and carry out the policies in consideration of the outcome of the poll.

Third, a poll has the advantages that other methods of many-to-one linguistic communication may not have in respect of allowing for the people to express their opinions to the authorities. To express their opinions through a poll, citizens do not need to get together on the streets, and do not need to use a lot of energy to shout slogans. Citizens may join this many-to-one linguistic communication at any time and location. In addition, unlike many-to-one linguistic communication performed by demonstrators, a poll does not give rise to any confrontation between the masses and a police force on the streets or any violent conflict leading to bloodshed or social and political turmoil. Generally speaking, people perform this type of communication without any strong emotional reaction. Except verbal or written expression, no specific action is to be taken. A poll allows for citizens to express their opinions at lower costs. It is a civilized, effective and peaceful way for citizens to express their opinions to the authorities on public affairs, provided that the authorities respect the poll and its outcome. The common interest of the people takes shape in this course. A poll is a medium used by people to cultivate their common interest.

In short, without the governance of the society or the state, people do not need to conduct polls in this regard. To conduct a poll, people must do some statistic work. The word "statistics" and the word "state" share the same lexicological origin. The true sense of a poll is that the people perform many-to-one linguistic communication with the government to raise their requests, express their opinions and attitudes and the government makes policies and laws to govern the state and the society in consideration of their requests, opinions and attitudes. The common interest of the state takes shape. Today, in the era of the quick growth of mass media, a democratic state must pay more attention to public opinion. Even a non-democratic state also finds that it cannot ignore public opinion anymore. Unlike a demonstration, a poll is not many-to-one linguistic communication in which citizens take initiative, and a poll relies on the planning and arrangement of an investigator. Therefore, whether or not the investigator is free to conduct a poll means whether or not citizens are free to perform such many-to-one linguistic communication. As mentioned earlier, the freedom of speech is significant for the creation of a condition for all to perform linguistic communication with all freely and for the formation of the common interest of all. A poll constitutes another form of linguistic communication that needs to be guaranteed in the principle of the freedom of speech. If people do not enjoy the freedom of speech, citizens may not be able to give their opinions through polls because freely-conducted polls are likely to be banned by the authorities. On the other hand, unlike the freedom of speech enjoyable by individual persons, polls especially allow for citizens to perform many-to-one linguistic communication with the authorities. It is the communication performed by a collective being directly with the authorities, and a special attention must be paid to it by the authorities. It is a form of democracy. Democracy means a system in which the common interest of the state takes shape through linguistic communication between the citizens and the authorities, especially many-to-one linguistic communication performed by the citizens with the authorities or the government. A poll is a tool that facilitates the formation of the common interest of all within the state.

3. Election and Referendum

In view of the structure of linguistic communication between the masses and the power holder within the state, we find that what is unique is the structure of linguistic communication required by democracy. It is opposite to the structure of linguistic communication required by a dictatorial system. Democracy heavily relies on the linguistic communication performed by the masses with the power holder while a dictatorial system does not. The reason is that the formation of the state goes hand in hand with the organization of the state. The organizer of the state becomes the power holder. The power holder issues commands to ordinary people through the officials of various levels of the government. The tool of coercion is crucial in the organization of the state. Though officials function as media in the related linguistic communication, what ensures the success of organizing the state is, in an ultimate sense, the tool of coercion. In other words, coercion is the last resort of the power holder to maintain the unity and order of the state. In contrast, ordinary people are usually unable to entrust those officials to express their opinions on the organization of the state or to make any request. It is easier for the state to be dictatorial than to be democratic due to the asymmetry of linguistic communication between the power holder and the ordinary people in their mutual interaction. It is difficult for ordinary people to take initiative to communicate with the power holder and the power holder tends to rule the state in a dictatorial way. In this case it is difficult for ordinary people to communicate with the authorities.

In contrast, democracy is very unique. Democracy requires a different structure of linguistic communication between the power holder and the masses. Under democracy, linguistic communication, performed with the authorities, is essential. This means that linguistic communication between ordinary people and the authorities needs to be skewed toward ordinary people. The center of gravity of communication needs to tilt to many-to-one communication. It is easy for the power holder to perform linguistic communication, possibly leading to the dictatorial rule, and the state needs to design a procedure to facilitate ordinary people to communicate with the authorities so as to allow them to express their opinions to the authorities on the governance of the state. In the past thinkers conceived of the size of the state suitable for democracy. They imagined that democracy only fitted in with a small state while monarchy a medium-sized state and nobility a large state. Montesquieu writes that "It is natural for a republic to have only a small territory."[4] Then he writes that "A monarchical state ought to be of moderate extent. Were it small, it would form itself into a republic; were it very large, the nobility."[5] Why does Montesquieu contemplate the correlation between the form of government and the size of the state? My understanding is that at least the internal communication of the state was considered. This means that the related linguistic communication has to be especially structured and the distance of linguistic communication has to be extended whenever necessary. He did not think of the role of media in extending the distance of linguistic communication. The reason is that by his times humans had not invented the theory of media yet. But the situation is different in our times. We are aware of the role of media and hence the role of language. It is not difficult to dawn on us that language, together with media, plays a special role in the building of democracy in a large state. Violence or coercion is the essential element of the dictatorial system no matter whether it is the dictatorial system characterized by the totalitarian rule or an autocracy, whereas linguistic communication is the essential element of democracy. Considering this situation, humans design and hold elections and referenda in democratic states. Election and referendum of modern times are two forms of linguistic communication that relies on media. Election and referendum are two important forms of democracy, too.

Let us discuss election first. People design election to create a possible condition for the citizens to communicate regularly with the power holder as required by the law particularly in modern times. An election is a process especially set for the voters, as ordinary people, to perform linguistic communication directly with the power holder regularly and on a scale as large as the entire state. The designer of this election fully considers the difficulties encountered by ordinary people in their communication with the power holder across the state. This election is characteristic of a form of many-to-one linguistic communication performed by ordinary people with the authorities. Language and media function in the same process of communication. On one hand, using language creates a condition for the creation of various media. On the other hand, various media assist language in playing a role in the organization of the state in the principle of democracy. Language and media work jointly to support a process of many-to-one linguistic communication that underlies the building of democracy. Then, under democracy, the state takes into consideration the interest of all. The common interest of all takes shape. People establish democracy.

First, like all other many-to-one linguistic communication forms, communication, realized through an election, depends on introduction and organization. Otherwise, people are unable to perform such many-to-one linguistic communication. In the course of an election, many-to-one linguistic communication, performed in the form of election, is guided by candidates in the course of the election campaign. The election campaign of the candidates creates conditions for many-to-one linguistic communication performed by voters because an election campaign enables voters to know candidates and learn about the policy proposals of the candidates and hence make their own judgments. At the same time, candidates set the themes of the campaign and explain their policy proposals. They address the future public policies expected by the voters to meet the need and expectation of the voters. This means that candidates function as media used by voters in many-to-one linguistic communication because candidates facilitate such communication. To put it differently, without the policy proposals raised by the candidates, the expectations of the voters cannot be known to anyone or the voters themselves as a whole. This is because the expectations of the voters can only be indirectly expressed by the candidates rather than the voters themselves. As an individual, a voter is usually only able to communicate on a small scale. If he intends to enter the process of linguistic communication realized by an election, he must find a candidate to help him express his expectation concerning public affairs. This is because a candidate is a public figure and a public figure is a medium for communication. A candidate is a medium of the pilot linguistic communication process in which the voters speak. The candidate speaks on behalf of the voters. The speech, made by a candidate during the election campaign, is an alternative, or a "trial," or a "rehearsal," of the many-to-one linguistic communication of the voters. Candidates act as the organizers and guides in the collective linguistic communication of the voters. A competition among the candidates means a process of adjusting their linguistic expressions and hence their policy orientations in line with the expectations of the majority of the constituency. Candidates try to make their linguistic expressions the linguistic expression of the majority of the constituency. If candidates do not take initiative to help voters to articulate their expectations concerning the governance of the state, it is usually difficult, or simply impossible, for voters to perform such many-to-one linguistic communication. If voters do not know the platform and policy proposal of a candidate, they are unable to elect him. Thus the process of an election involves a process of making, at least, one medium. Thus such linguistic communication is skewed toward voters. In other words, an extra effort, made in linguistic communication, is helpful to reflecting the opinions of the voters. In contrast, people do not need to make such an effort to facilitate the power holder to issue any decree.

Second, during an election, voters cast ballots to express their opinions. The reason is that voters are large in number and are unable to gather in one location to express their opinions in the election. Then people design ballots to help them to express their opinions. Ballots are media. Ballots constitute the form of written communication that functions as the medium of spoken communication. In the process of such written communication the voters agree to the conversion of the personal will of each individual voter into the common will of all. People tend to consider the will of all to be the sum of the wills of all different voters. The crucial point is that a nation-state is large in population and area, and it is impossible for the people in a number as large as one million, or ten million, or even more, to perform many-to-one verbal communication in one process. It is impossible for that number of people to get together at one location and at one time to accomplish the task of many-to-one linguistic communication. Then, written communication comes to play a part. Voters perform many-to-one linguistic communication by using ballots. The organizer of the election distributes ballots for voters to cast them and then gets back the ballots. It is easier to transport all ballots to an election center to count the ballots than to request every voter to walk to get together to give their opinions orally. Ballots are the extension of the behavior of verbal communication of all voters. Ballots are the records of the opinions from the voters of this collective linguistic communication. Ballots are special media through which millions of voters perform communications almost on the largest scale in their state. That means that millions of people, using ballots as media, perform many-to-one linguistic communication in one general process. Ballots are the results of industrialization. The development of the presses that make ballots is a great social progress. As Weaver writes, "The press is the great scribe, possessed of that preponderance of means which technology always provides. The ease with which it multiplies stereotypes makes it the ideal servant of progress."[6] This social progress includes the creation of a condition for the establishment of modern democracy.

Third, an election is a kind of many-to-one linguistic communication that runs on several stages, as I mentioned in my previous manuscript. Voters are often required to enter the many-to-one linguistic communication of several stages in order to select the leader of the state on the final stage if the process of linguistic communication is too long. The reason is that one process of many-to-one linguistic communication may not be adequate and more than one stage of collective linguistic communication may be required in order to generalize the different opinions of different voters. This is because each voter has his own brain which allows for him to think of any matter independently, to view everything in his own method and to take care of his own interest. In order to coordinate the opinions of many voters, the election often needs the collective linguistic communication of several stages. This means that during an election an easy process of many-to-one linguistic communication may substitute for a difficult process of many-to-one linguistic communication if that difficult process of many-to-one linguistic communication fails to realize the final goal. To put it differently, people tend to be patient with many-to-one linguistic communication because such linguistic communication is required by democracy cherished by them. In this case, the easy process of many-to-one linguistic communication functions as a medium of that difficult process of many-to-one linguistic communication. The arrangement of several rounds of voting in an election may involve such different processes of many-to-one linguistic communication. The totality of such processes of many-to-one linguistic communication is characteristic of a trapezium structure. For example, as I mentioned in my previous manuscript, people design two rounds of voting for the election of the president of the republic in the Fifth Republic of France. If there is one candidate who gains the absolute majority of the votes in the first round of voting, this candidate will become the president. If no one gains the absolute majority of the votes in the first round of voting, the two candidates who survive the first round of voting by winning the most votes in it will enter the second round of voting. Between these two candidates, the one who gains the simple majority of the votes in the second round of voting will become the president. In reality, it is difficult for a candidate to win the absolute majority of votes in the first round of voting and the second round of voting is often activated to concentrate votes on one candidate. Therefore, many French presidents are elected after the completion of the second round of voting. In the United States, the orientation of votes, cast in the presidential election, is also decentralized. It is believed that it is difficult to generate the outcome of the election with the absolute majority of the votes in favor of one candidate in one round of voting. Apart from the preliminary elections within each major political party, people adopt the system of an electoral college. Though the electoral college composed of electors was designed at the time of founding the United States to allow for elites to vote in the election of the president, this system still functions to concentrate votes on one candidate or two. In addition, the winner-take-all system, adopted in most of the states, functions to concentrate votes on one candidate. Alexis de Tocqueville writes in describing the democracy of the United States that:

> In practice it seldom happens that one man can win a majority of the votes of a great nation at the first attempt. That is even more difficult in a republic of confederated states, where local influences are particularly well developed and strong. To get around this second trouble, the following method was devised: the electoral powers of the nation were delegated to a body representing it. This mode of election increased the chances of a majority for the fewer the

electors, the easier it is for them to come to an understanding. This method also made it more likely that their choice would be good.[7]

There are also several rounds of voting in the general election of the president of the United States.

Fourth, in the process of an election some voters may withdraw from the process of the election because they want to save their time and energy. Though they, as qualified voters, may be obligated to cast their ballots, their act of withdrawing from the process of the election, in some sense, means that they allow for those other voters, casting ballots, to represent them. This results in the fact that a portion of the voters represent all the voters in the process of voting. Even though this portion of the voters are usually the majority of the voters, there is still a relationship of representation since a certain percentage of the votes, cast in favor of a certain candidate, will be recognized as the valid votes. That is, a smaller number of the voters represent a larger number of the voters. Then we can also believe that, in this case, the presentation given by this smaller number of the voters is the medium of the presentation of that larger number of the voters. As an election is, in some sense, held like a general meeting held across the state, this phenomenon may occur in almost all kinds of the meetings. So Mancur Olson believes in his book *The Logic of Collective Action, Public Goods and the Theory of Groups* that the size of a group affects the costs of the collective action of the group and small groups are more capable than large groups in influencing the government's policy-making. In a large group, an individual's participation in decision-making makes almost no effect in the decision-making of the collective. Thus an individual believes that he is also able to receive the benefit from the group, namely, the public product, without participating in the decision-making of the collective because the decision made by the group benefits every member of the group. He writes that:

> [M]eetings that involve too many people, and accordingly cannot make decisions promptly or carefully. Everyone would like to have the meeting end quickly, but few if any will be willing to let their pet concern be dropped to make this possible. And though all of those participating

presumably have an interest in reaching sound decisions, this all too often fails to happen. When the number of participants is large, the typical participant will know that his own efforts will probably not make much difference to the outcome, and he will be affected by the meeting's decision in much the same way no matter how much or how little effort he puts into studying the issues. Accordingly, the typical participant may not take the trouble to study the issues as carefully as he would have if he had been able to make the decision by himself. The decisions of the meeting are thus public goods to the participants (and perhaps others), and the contribution that each participant will make toward achieving or improving these public goods will become smaller as the meeting becomes larger. It is for these reasons, among others, that organizations so often turn to the small group; committees, sub-committees, and small leadership groups are created, and once created they tend to play a crucial role.[8]

Some phenomena in an election show the similar logic. But my view is that it is due to the application of media. A smaller number of people can represent a larger number of people. People often use a variety of media in many-to-one linguistic communication. The presentation of a smaller number of people is used as a medium by the presentation of a larger number of people.

Fifth, following the end of an election, those elected representatives may be considered the extension of the related many-to-one linguistic communication. Representatives are the result of the process of an election, a process of many-to-one linguistic communication, but they may strengthen this process of linguistic communication. Many-to-one linguistic communication is one-way communication. Yet in view of the process of linguistic communication that expresses the opinions of the voters, the election also often needs two-way linguistic communication. The election may need a dialogue between the power holder and the citizens concerning the specific affairs in the governance of the state, and people can hardly ignore the importance of the specific opinions expressed by the citizens. This situation is like the case of making and implementing a law. In implementing a law after this law is made, one-way linguistic communication, performed by the lawmaker with the citizens, may not suffice to ensure the effective or correct implementation of the law. People may need a process of two-way linguistic communication. As the lawmaker is far away from the citizens and hence unable to perform two-way linguistic communication, the organizer of the state appoints judges. Judges conduct a dialogue between him and the principals of the case on behalf of the lawmaker when hearing such a case. So there is a certain resemblance between the establishment of the representation and the growth of the judicial body in Western states. That is, though the state establishes the judicial system first, the two systems follow the same logic. Thus the state also establishes the parliament this way. This is particularly so in England, a state in which the authorities carry out common law. The growth of a judicial system and the establishment of the parliament, in some sense, share the same origin. That is, common law is unwritten. In applying the law in early times, some old men were called to gather to give a true account of customs and events under the condition that there was no writing or writing was not prevalent. From this emerged the jury system. Judges were also appointed in later times. Then the representatives of boroughs and counties appeared in the parliament, which provided the knowledge of customs and opinions.[9]

In summary, in many-to-one linguistic communication many people jointly perform this linguistic communication. These people, performing this linguistic communication jointly, may perform the related linguistic communication on a large scale. Then people may design the process of linguistic communication in order to realize such linguistic communication. Such linguistic communication is designed in the way that election candidates guide or coordinate the action of the collective being; voters perform written communication; an easy process of linguistic communication substitutes for a difficult process of linguistic communication; and all recognize the validity of the process of linguistic communication even though some people, required to enter the process of linguistic communication, fail to enter it. In addition, in view of expressing opinions only, on an initial stage voters perform one-way written collective linguistic communication to express their general opinions and on the later stage elected representatives perform two-way linguistic communication to give specific opinions on the governance of the state. Representatives function as media. The collective linguistic communication, designed for representative democracy, is a system in which people use language in a special way.

Now let us discuss referendum. Referendum is one major collective linguistic communication that allows for the people to communicate directly with an entity, especially, the government, when necessary. When the government, or a group of citizens, requests the people to express opinions on a very important public affair of the state, referendum plays an important role. A referendum is a process of communication that enables the people to express directly their opinions to the government or any other authority or the people themselves when required. Sometimes the people of a nation-state also express their attitude to a foreign nation-state through a referendum. Unlike an election through which voters express their opinions on the selection of the representatives of the people or the state leaders and authorize the representatives and the state leaders to take charge of managing public affairs or governing the state, a referendum means that citizens directly express their opinions on the management of a public affair or on an affair in the governance of the state. If we use a term of political science to give a definition, an election is a form of indirect democracy in modern times, whereas a referendum is a form of direct democracy inherited by people from ancient times.

The feature of a referendum is that in the event of holding a referendum, citizens are invited to express their opinions. They express their opinions at the request of the authorities or a certain number of the citizens among them. The questions are asked in advance and the explanation of the questions is aimed at allowing for the citizens to make an informed decision. The referendum is held under the arrangement of the authorities. One-to-many communication, performed for the purpose of explaining the issue, is designed to gather the opinions from the citizens in the following many-to-one communication. It is impossible to hold a referendum without the interplay between one-to-many communication and many-to-one communication. A referendum is the only way in the human community that makes the authorities know the straightforward opinion of the citizens given by them on a certain issue faced by the nation-state. In other words, a nation-state sometimes comes across an extremely important issue as the solution of this issue may affect the destiny of the nation. The authorities have to seek the opinion from the people. They hold a referendum. The referendum is of the significance that the leader of the state may gain strong support from the people or may unravel a certain controversial issue faced by the nation. A referendum is one of the most democratic forms in the governance of a nation-state in modern times.

On the other hand, though the arrangement of a referendum gives democratic rights to the citizens, the process of holding a referendum is a process for the authorities to guide the citizens in this nationwide dialogue and the state leader may consolidate his power status by taking advantage of the outcome of the referendum. This is due to the unique structure of our human community. That is, in our human community ordinary people are many and the supreme bodies of the authorities are few. The related communication is asymmetrical in the structure of transmitting information. More information moves from the authorities to the citizens than vice versa. The authorities arrange for the citizens to express their opinions and hence control the expression of these opinions to some extent.

Specifically, in a nation-state today a large number of the citizens jointly form a nation-state. In this regard, it is objectively difficult to invite the citizens to express their opinions on a state affair as such collective linguistic communication requires the participation of a large number of the citizens and it is difficult to subjugate the personal freedom of action into the concerted action of the collective in a state large in population and area. For this reason, it is considered unrealistic to allow for the people to make their decision on a public affair unless this public affair is very important. A state is unable to gather the opinions of its people in a referendum at any time and at any place. The state is unable to arrange for the citizens to perform such collective linguistic communication unless for a limited number of crucial matters.

By the same token, collective linguistic communication, designed for a referendum, shows that more words, sentences and texts are used by the state in its description of the procedure of the referendum as well as the questions themselves than those used by citizens in their answers. For example, in the process of a referendum held by the Province of Quebec of Canada in 1995 for a decision of this province on whether or not this province should withdraw from the Confederation, citizens, qualified to cast their ballots in the referendum, were only required to say "yes" or "no" while the authorities of the Province of Quebec prepared lengthy materials clarifying the purpose of that referendum and stated questions in full sentences on the referendum ballots. Likewise, on September 18, 2014 the Scottish government held a referendum to let the citizens decide whether or not Scotland should be independent from the United Kingdom. The referendum question, recommended by the Electoral Commission, was only that "Should Scotland be an independent country?" Citizens were only required to answer "Yes" or "No." The question had actually been debated for quite a long time. The issue of independence was interpreted in detail. The detailed and specific text of the question was presented. The answer was quite simple and general. Like the communication of applauding, shouting slogans and holding up signs in a demonstration, answering questions in a poll and casting ballots in election, the communication of casting referendum ballots is the collective linguistic communication especially designed to realize the asymmetrical exchange of information in consideration of the obstacles of normal two-way communication in a large human community. In such a two-way communication, people transmit detailed and complex information in the course of one-to-many communication while people transmit general and simple information in the course of many-to-one communication. The many-to-one communication usually relies on the information already given in the course of one-to-many communication performed before that many-to-one communication. It is the process of linguistic communication similar to the process of linguistic communication realized by a disjunctive question. In the process of linguistic communication created by a disjunctive question, the questioner raises a question in a full sentence, requiring the answerer to give an answer in a short form. It is different from a special question. For example, someone asks that "it is hot today, isn't it?" The answerer is only required to say "Yes, it is." or "No, it isn't." In contrast, a special question requires the answerer to give more information or to use at least a full sentence. For example, some one asks you that "Where are you from?" You answer that "I am from Quebec, Canada." This shortest answering sentence, in this dialogue using the special question, is longer than the answering sentence in the dialogue using a disjunctive question, as mentioned above. A disjunctive question is characterized by the fact that the questioner raises a question by using a full sentence and giving a detailed or complete description while the answerer answers that question by using a simplified sentence and the related language environment created by the questioner. The answer "Yes" or "No" skillfully uses the condition of questioning and answering at the same time by taking the content of the question as its own explanation.

It follows that a person, performing linguistic communication, will adopt different syntaxes depending on whether the information structure of linguistic communication is simple or not. If a person expounds a theory, the form of presentation is a treatise or a book. If a person conducts a discussion or makes comments, articles, published to give an interpretation or explanation, may be the form of presentation we often see. If people express their attitude or opinions, they may make a statement or give a letter of opinion. If people convey information to others, the form of presentation may be only one sentence or one word such as "yes" or "no," or "agree" or "disagree." Though a referendum is the linguistic communication of expressing an opinion, its nature makes it function as the form of communication providing the information of the simplest structure. Though people may perform the linguistic communication of conveying the information of complex structure outside the linguistic communication process of the referendum, such as discussing the issue in detail before the holding of the referendum, the referendum realizes the linguistic communication of conveying the information of the simplest structure. People will not hold a referendum unless they have to make a decision on a fundamental or very important issue. People may cast their referendum ballots to make a decision on the affair of changing the territory of the state or changing of the name of the nation-state, or to make a decision on the issue of war and peace among others. With the exception of these important issues, people will not hold any referendum.

The simpler and the more explicit the linguistic expression people give and the shorter the sentences people use, the easier it will be for many to perform collective linguistic communication. Because sometimes people need such collective linguistic communication in political life, they often perform such communication that transmits information in an asymmetrical way. A referendum is such a kind of collective linguistic communication between the government and the people. In the course of this referendum, the government raises questions and the people give their answer. The people, in general, answer "yes" or "no." As the people are in a large number and it is difficult for them to utter the same sentences in a general process, the shortest sentence is the most preferable choice, provided that the meaning is complete. It is even okay for the citizens to mark the boxes of choices of "Yes" or "No" on the ballots printed in advance. This structure of linguistic communication reflects the method of organizing our human community at a certain angle. The people, as a collective being, are incapable in the management of their own public affairs. They must mandate their representatives, or other agents, to manage their public affairs. The larger the number of the people there are in a community, the heavier their dependence on the representatives or agents for the management of their public affairs will be. It is difficult for the people to take collective action. In most cases, the people, acting as an entity, do not exist. They have to select their own representatives, or agents, and to authorize them to manage their public affairs on their behalf. This is just the law of unity of opposites functioning between personal freedom and the common will of the community.

Conversely, a government, deciding to hold a referendum, returns to the people the power of making a decision on a specific public affair. At this time, the state needs to get prepared to allow for the people to make an appropriate decision. As the issue on which a decision should be made by the people in the referendum is usually at variance with the issue considered by the voters who select election candidates, citizens need to be very cautious. The government has to mobilize the people by giving plenty of interpretations. The people should also find time to think of the issue concerning the destiny of the state which they do not especially care about in their daily life. It may take months or even a couple of years to prepare this referendum. Though citizens cast their referendum ballots in their local districts, the whole process of casting ballots functions like a national conference held by all qualified citizens to make such a decision. Each polling station functions like a sub-conference room. That means that it often takes a lot of time for a large number of people to enter the many-to-one communication on a very large scale to transmit the information that has the seemingly simplest content.

The guidance of political parties, politicians, and the state is essential. Without the guidance of political parties or politicians or the state, citizens are unable to cast their ballots or unable to make wise and informed decision on the important issue of the nation-state. Citizens are unable to take initiative to take collective action though they are supposed to be the sovereign.

They move very slowly. They need some one to guide them in exercising their rights such as the right of casting their referendum ballots. They perform collective linguistic communication by casting referendum ballots. They rely on the assistance of print media and the advices of political parties, politicians and the state. They are extensively involved in written communication rather than being involved in verbal communication. They do not debate the issue to be addressed in the referendum. They do not well exchange their views among themselves. They cast their referendum ballots individually. Giovanni Sartori, an American scholar, writes that the referendum loses the directness of interactions. It is a direct democracy of isolated, discrete individuals, not of interacting participants. In the referendum, the referendum actor is like the electoral actor: He performs in solitude, by himself, without a debating participation. His deliberation is not preceded by a dialogue that goes to shape the deliberation. The "enlightenment of discussion" is ruled out. Certainly the issues submitted to referendum will be debated on the media, but the referendum-type decider remains, if he listens, a passive listener who does not contribute, not even minimally, in that debate.[10]

This type of linguistic behavior is similar to that of an election in which voters usually do not directly share information about their voting decisions with each other. But in other aspects, the linguistic behavior of the citizens in the referendum is different from that in the election. In the course of an election, voters cast their ballots in the ridings where they reside. Within a riding, voters may have some chances to exchange their views and opinions during the process of the election campaign. As voters are to elect their representatives in their own ridings, they are not necessarily required to exchange views and opinions nationwide. But in the course of a referendum, theoretically speaking, citizens need a nationwide discussion or a nationwide debate so as to make a wise and informed decision and it is more difficult for them to discuss and debate those important issues nationwide.

This situation is given rise to by the nature of written communication of today's referendum. In a state, a large community, the citizens of the state are sometimes required to express their opinions on an important matter of the state they come across. They rely mainly on the written communication form for this purpose because written communication allows for people to establish one communicative process on a large scale. It is difficult for the citizens to hold a general meeting to discuss this matter on a large scale. In other words, people can only perform verbal communication on a small scale. On the other hand, written communication is one-way communication, albeit the communication that may function on a large scale, and it is difficult for the citizens to exchange their views and opinions by way of written communication. That is, the state and the citizens should first exchange their views and opinions in two-way verbal communication, and then make a formal decision. But it is, in general, impossible to do so as there is only one written language community large enough to cover the whole state. The written language community normally conditions one-way communication, and there is no integral spoken language community in the state. The larger a state is built by the people, the more difficult it will be for the citizens of the state to perform such verbal communication, and the more seldom it will be for the citizens of the state to discuss and debate directly the issue they come across. There is no integral spoken language community in the state, but a written language community. Suppose that in a nation-state such as Canada that has a population of over 31 million, over 20 million qualified voters are going to cast their referendum ballots. How can they discuss and debate the issue they face and how do they make a decision thereon in a referendum in one big conference hall or in the open? They may be able to discuss and debate that issue in a group of over twenty people at a meeting, but they are unable to do so at a meeting which is attended by thousands of people. If millions of people are arranged for to enter one collective linguistic communication such as a referendum, citizens are only able to give their answers in the shortest written form carefully designed by the state or the authorities. Though the decision the citizens are going to make may concern a fundamental issue the nation-state faces such as the separation of one part of a nation-state from the rest and at the same time citizens are required to have historical, geographical, cultural and political knowledge so as to make this decision, they give their opinions in a simplest form such as that of simply saying "yes" or "no." Let us compare this linguistic behavior with the linguistic behavior we often see in our daily life. The linguistic behavior of adults and the linguistic behavior of children are different. If an adult communicates with a child, the child is very often only capable of using simple words in response. In the course of collective linguistic communication such as a referendum, citizens sometimes look like children.

These circumstances demonstrate that holding a referendum needs a special process of linguistic communication. Unlike the dictatorial rule which may not require the use of language because the will of the power holder may be imposed on ordinary people by force, a democratic system relies on various especially designed processes of linguistic communication. Each citizen needs to perform linguistic communication with the authorities. There is a correlation between language and democracy. This is also dictated by the nature of democracy. In short, democracy means the formation of common interest of all within the state. Language is also the basis for the formation of the common interest of all forming the state. Then we see that using language in a special way to facilitate citizens to express their opinions is the nature of democracy.

Notes

1. Vincent Robert, *Les chemins de la manifestation, 1848-1914* (Lyon: Presses Universitaires de Lyon, 1996), 94-100; cited from Charles Tilly, *Social Movements, 1768–2004* (Boulder: Paradigm Publishers, 2004), 40.

2. Frank Newport, *Polling Matters: Why Leaders Must Listen to the Wisdom of the People* (New York: Warner Books, 2004), 100.

3. Ibid., x.

4. Charles de Secondat, Baron de Montesquieu, *The Spirit of Laws*, translated by Thomas Nugent (Chicago: Encyclopaedia Britannica, Inc., 1952), 56.

5. Ibid.

6. Richard M. Weaver, *Ideas Have Consequences* (Chicago: The University of Chicago Press, 1984), 94.

7. Alexis De Tocqueville, *Democracy in America*, translated by George Lawrence (New York: Harper & Row Publishers, Inc.,1988), 132.

8. Mancur Olson, *The Logic of Collective Action, Public Goods and the Theory of Groups*, (Cambridge, Massachusetts: Harvard University Press, 1971) 53.

9. Please also see: Harold A. Innis, *Empire and Communications* (Victoria: Press Porcépic Limited, 1986), 132.

10. Giovanni Sartori, *The Theory of Democracy Revisited* (Chatham, New Jersey: Chatham House Publishers, Inc., 1987), 112.

Chapter Fourteen

Justice

1. Appointment

Now we study justice per se. To study justice per se, we need to discuss the correlation between language and justice. This is because justice is normally the justice in the distribution of interest within the state. In this regard, people realize justice in a certain process that requires long-distance linguistic communication. People cannot realize justice in short-distance linguistic communication. They realize justice in extending the distance of linguistic communication. This is precisely because extending the distance of linguistic communication enables people to communicate on a large scale. What conditions the realization of justice is that people communicate on a large scale because the distribution of interest, realized on a large scale, can prevent the conflict of interest involving a power holder from arising. The distribution of interest, realized in a process in which all have a say, tends to be just. This is because people will debate about the scheme of distributing interest. People often debate in the public. Debating in the public involves a process of linguistic communication to which all have access. This linguistic communication is of long distance. All may give their opinions and the state is expected to accommodate the interest of all. Thus, people extend the distance of linguistic communication to ensure justice in implementing the scheme of distributing interest. This leads to the formation of the common interest. Conversely, injustice is often given rise to by the absence of long-distance linguistic communication because the fair distribution of interest and hence the formation of the common interest relies on long-distance linguistic communication. Long-distance linguistic communication, covering the whole state, is essential for the formation of the common interest and hence the realization of justice.

In other words, humans who communicate using language create and use media. Media extend the distance of linguistic communication to the far reaches of the community. Those media enable them to communicate on a large scale. Then they form a large community. This community is a state. This community is no longer a tribe. In the meantime, extending the distance of linguistic communication also serves as a foundation for the realization of justice. Studying law, we find that law is the chief tool for the realization of justice. Yet the real reason that law can realize justice is that law is a process of long-distance linguistic communication. The lawmaker is far away from the masses. It is the extension of the distance of linguistic communication that makes it possible for people to realize justice. People proclaim any law they have made. Proclaiming a law normally means the acceptance of this law by all. Otherwise, people may revolt in order to force the power holder to revoke such a law. If a law has been implemented for a long time across the state, it is usually just. Thus, the formation of the common interest of all relies on the full development of linguistic communication within the state because all within the state need to communicate with one another for the formation of their common interest. The formation of the common interest means a certain kind of justice. Justice means the distribution of interest among all within the state. If the interest of the state is only distributed among those who constitute a portion of people within the state, the common interest of all will not take shape. Thus this is unjust. Although we sometimes argue that the judgment of justice may vary because people who hold different views may disagree on what justice is, the realization of justice invariably relies on the availability of certain physical conditions. Extending the distance of linguistic communication within the state is one of such physical conditions. Extending such a distance is a basis for the growth of the community. Then we see that extending the distance of linguistic communication paves a way for people to form their state. Then, extending the distance of linguistic communication creates a condition for humans to realize justice. Appointing the power holders of the government involves such a process of linguistic communication. We need to explain this proposition as follows.

First, if the power holders of the government are appointed in a process of short-distance communication, such appointment may be unjust. Conversely, if the power holders of the government are appointed in a process of long-distance communication, such appointments may be just. This case pertains to the origin of the state. Usually, initial conquest led to the formation of the state in early times. The conquered people were forced to form a state built by the ruler. They and the ruler might not communicate with each other by using language. They were subject to the rule of the ruler because of fear and necessity. People performed linguistic communication on a very small scale and the ruler and the ruled did not communicate with one another. The ruler was usually appointed by himself as the ruler of the state. The state belonged to the ruler. Linguistic communication usually went on within the ruling family. If this ruling family was supported by some other families, all the related families constituted a ruling group. Linguistic communication that went on within the ruling group functioned on a small scale. If the common interest of some people existed, such common interest only took shape within the ruling group. In the outset people built the regime in the principle of organizing the society instead of the principle of organizing the state. The power holder usually used coercion to rule the state. In the meantime, those who assisted him in ruling the state were his personal friends, relatives, retainers, and others. These people were administrators appointed by the ruler. These administrators were also power holders. Communication between them and the ruler went on in private. Normally, the power holders organized the state in the method of organizing the society. Linguistic communication, performed by power holders, was usually, or often, confined to the linguistic communication that went on among relatives or friends or between the master and retainers. This type of linguistic communication served as a foundation for the building of a feudal state in medieval times. This situation changed when written communication, supported by printing, substantially developed in early modern times. Written communication, supported by printing, apparently functioned on a large scale. So in early modern times written communication, supported by printing, extended the reach of linguistic communication. As Marshall T. Poe observes, in the era of manuscript in early modern Europe princes and priests monopolized writing and reading and were able to use text as an instrument of control in the beginning. In the following era of print, their monopoly was broken and the instrument based on it destroyed. Parties, confessions, regions, towns, classes, business interests, guilds and all others could now "speak."[1] The mass society took shape. The mass society meant the community in which the multitude of coexisting individuals of the same sort could directly communicate with one another. The masses formed a social entity. The mass society was able to raise a demand for public services. The power holders of the government faced pressure from the mass society. In this case the power holders of the ruling family were required to operate the state apparatus to serve the mass society. If they were unable to serve the mass society, they would face a new situation: They might be replaced by the power holders appointed by a revolutionary leader because the formation of a mass society often spawned a revolution if there were tensions between the ruler and the ruled. A change took place. In the past, the state belonged to the ruling family. All power holders served the ruling family. They governed the state because they served the ruling family. Now all power holders served the state. A change took place in the method of appointing the power holders. Some power holders were politicians. They might be appointed by a revolutionary leader. This revolutionary leader represented the great masses of the people. Thus, the related appointments involved a process of long-distance linguistic communication. Administrators of lower level were also appointed. The appointments of administrators also involved a process of long-distance linguistic communication. In the past administrators had been recruited from those who were friends, relatives and retainers of the supreme ruler or senior officials appointed by the supreme ruler. Those administrators served the ruler. Now the supreme power holder of the government was no longer the king, but a revolutionary leader. This revolutionary leader was later replaced by the first consul or the prime minister or the president. Then, the state recruited civil servants. The state recruited civil servants mainly from the members of a political party in the outset. For example, after the revolution the revolutionary government usually appointed administrators in any state in Europe in early modern times. Those who were appointed as the administrators were usually those who joined the revolution. They replaced those administrators who had been originally appointed by the monarch or the servants of the monarch. As now the government was expected to serve the need of the people, the state increased the size of the administrative system. The state appointed more administrators. Later, the state might recruit civil servants from the labor market. The state was organized in the principle of organizing the state.

This means that when administrators worked for the feudal ruler as their friends or relatives or retainers in the past, they and the ruler performed short-distance linguistic communication. They stayed in touch with each other in person. They might maintain personal relationship with each other. Those administrators might be appointed in consideration of their personal relationship with the ruler. The state might not be able to eliminate corruption because the competence of the administrators might not be of uttermost importance. Thus the service, provided by these administrators, might benefit the ruler instead of the public. This was mainly because no long-distance linguistic communication went on between these administrators and the people. Thus they were not appointed by the people. Yet when the state recruited administrators in view of the need of the cause of a revolution, they might be required to uphold the revolutionary belief and to be willing to serve the people. As they were large in number, the personal relationship between them and the supreme power holder might not exist. Thus, the administrators who upheld the required belief must work in the interest of the citizens who formed the state. They, required to work for the state, were also required to have working competence. It was likely for the state to prevent corruption. Thus, they could be considered to be appointed by the people at least indirectly because they would meet the expectation from the people. This finally paved a way to set up the modern system of civil servants in the nineteenth century. For example, Britain established the system of civil servants shortly after Sir Stafford Northcote and Sir Charles Trevelyan, at the request of William Ewart Gladstone, the then Minister of Finance, submitted a report on the recruitment of permanent civil servants in 1854. Then, since civil servants were recruited by the state, they have tended to be loyal to the state. The loyalty of civil servants to the state symbolizes the realization of justice in appointing the power holders of the state. As civil servants are now recruited from the labor market, long-distance linguistic communication goes on between the authorities and the citizens. The realization of justice in the appointment of the power holders relies on extending the distance of linguistic communication. This case satisfies the requirement of the mass society. In other words, the appearance of long-distance linguistic communication underlies the formation of a mass society. A mass society further requires the adoption of a new principle in the organization of the state. This new principle is that the state is organized in the principle of organizing the state instead of the society. The appointment of power holders is justified if they are required to organize the state in this principle. The common interest of the people takes shape as a result because power holders no longer serve a portion of people but all. In this case, the formation of common interest also means the realization of justice.

Second, extending the distance of linguistic communication to the far reaches of the community underlies a process of forming a public sphere and hence public opinion across the state. This evolution enables moral norms to enter the domain of politics. If the power holders abide by moral norms, their appointments tend to be just. This means that the process of linguistic communication, that reaches all without any conflict of interest involving any power holder in charge of governing the state, is a basis for the realization of justice. The reason is that morality exists among passively coexisting individuals forming the society. No morality spreads because of an effort made by the power holder. Morality germinates and spreads spontaneously. Thus the spread of morality means that all adhere to morality. Morality, adhered to by all, ought to be construed as just. Moral ideas may also enter the political domain. This is because the citizens, performing linguistic communication with each other across the state, may express their views or opinions. Moral ideas may spread in this process. The reason that people who do not perform linguistic communication across the state do not obey morality in politics is that people, realizing their mutual interactions by using coercion, prevent morality from playing a role. Morality is totally ignored by the man who uses coercion. For example, people, waging a war on each other, hardly obey moral commandments because each intends to kill the other in every possible method, including the method construed as immoral at the angle of pure ethics. But if the constitution or the law prevents people from using coercion in an illegal way due to the fact that the state protects the freedoms and rights of the citizens, including the freedom of speech, people spread moral ideas in the various processes of linguistic communication across the state. This is why in the past the ruler of the despotic state overlooked moral norms. At that time, people obeyed moral commandments in the society, but they did not obey any morality in the state. People competed for state power by virtue of violence. Resort to violence meant that people obeyed no morality. The ruler obeyed no morality in the state, but ordinary people normally obeyed morality in the society. That is, ambitious people seized the state by using force or maintained the state by using force after they had seized the state. Everything finally depended on the use of violence. They appointed themselves as officials. As violence dictated everything, moral authority was absent or very weak. Deception, conspiracy, assassination, faithlessness, and attaining one's end by hook or by crook and craft perplexed people. So Niccolo Machiavelli gave his advices to the prince of a European state that statesmen should not always comply with morality. He states that:

> [H]e who neglects what is done for what ought to be done, soon effects his ruin than his preservation; for a man who wishes to act entirely up to his professions of virtue soon meets with what destroys him among so much that is evil. Hence it is necessary for a prince wishing to hold his own to know how to do wrong, and to make use of it or not according to necessity.[2]

He continues that:

> Every one admits how praiseworthy it is in a prince to keep faith, and to live with integrity and not with craft. Nevertheless our experience has been that those princes who have done great things have held good faith of little account, and have known how to circumvent the intellect of men by craft, and in the end have overcome those who have relied on their word.[3]

He thus advises the prince that:

> Therefore it is unnecessary for a prince to have all the good qualities I have enumerated, but it is very necessary to appear to have them. And I shall dare to say this also, that to have them and always to observe them is injurious, and

that to appear to have them is useful; to appear merciful, faithful, humane, religious, upright, and to be so, but with a mind so framed that should you require not to be so, you may be able and know how to change to the opposite.[4]

Machiavelli's statements are tantamount to saying that the ruler should not absolutely obey morality in the state though it is always required to be obeyed in the society. This is mainly because social morality functions if each is able to exercise moral sanction in order to compel all other people to obey the moral imperative. In society each person functions on individual basis. Thus each person may directly, or indirectly, or effectively, compel any other person to obey the moral imperative because of moral sanction of the society. But in the sphere of the state, the state apparatus is usually under the control of a group of people, and the mechanism of moral sanction may fail to function. This results in the fact that the ruling group uses coercion regardless of morality. People who revolt also use force regardless of morality. Thus sometimes people wage a bloody civil war, and no one obeys pure morality. However, I argue that people restore the mechanism of moral sanction in performing linguistic communication across the state. If a discourse of morality prevails in the public because people are able to perform long-distance linguistic communication that covers the whole state and hence results in the formation of public opinion, politicians, acting as power holders, may be forced by public opinion to obey moral commandments. That is, a despotic ruler, ruling the state in a despotic way, relies on violence. When he uses violence, he will not use language. He who does not use language will not be subject to any moral sanction. Yet in modern times politicians are prevented by the constitution or the law from using violence in politics. Long-distance linguistic communication develops. Then politicians are subject to the moral sanction because they face the pressure to obey morality in the process of linguistic communication which is the only form adopted by them to interact with the people. The despotic rule of the ruler on the basis of naked violence in the past is actually corruption committed in broad daylight. Corruption is immoral. With the formation of the related public opinion, the public exalts or requires honesty, faithfulness, sincerity, integrity and clemency in the governance of the state because if all perform linguistic communication with all without any obstacle, the public opinion that does not further any particular interest will take side with no one. No one will thus oppose or disregard the act of obeying morality. The appointments of power holders should also meet the requirement of morality. Such appointments tend to be just. So I argue that if people have established the rule of law and have formed the related public opinion, the public tend to set a moral standard for the politicians who act as power holders. In this case political morality may be consonant with social morality in some crucial aspects. For example, honesty is the content of both political and social morality in the state in which people can express their opinions in the public due to the fact that the constitution or the law protects the freedom of speech. Humans make this progress due to the fact that politicians and citizens, as a collective being, perform linguistic communication. The prevalence of public opinion underlies the prevalence of political morality. So justice is represented by the morality that exists in the long process of linguistic communication that goes on in the pubic, and this justice is also realized in the linguistic communication performed lawfully by the citizens across the state. The prevalence of morality lies in the process of linguistic communication that goes on throughout the state. Then it can be just for the state to appoint power holders.

Morality also becomes categorical in the sphere of public affairs because no one can resist the dominance of linguistic communication performed by all with all throughout the state. Once morality gets a firm foothold in political life, no one can violate the common will of the people. In other words, the collectivity of the citizens takes form in the process of linguistic communication that goes on within the state. It is difficult to change the common will once it has taken form. As a result, the society often requires the politicians, holding state power, to obey the existing morality instead of the fact that morality is forged to meet the requirement of the politicians. As Kant writes,

> I can actually think of a *moral politician*, i.e., one who so interprets the principles of political prudence that they can be coherent with morality, but I cannot think of a *political moralist*, i.e., one who forges a morality to suit the statesman's advantage.[5]

In other words, it is possible for a politician to obey morality, but it is impossible for morality to obey the will of the politician. This is because morality is defined by public opinion that takes form in the process of linguistic communication performed by common people instead of the politician. As long as that public opinion prevails, morality prevails because of the dominance of the universality of linguistic communication that goes on throughout the state. Power holders are therefore appointed in a just way under the supervision of public opinion.

Third, in the state which was under the rule of the ruler who used to be a conqueror in the outset, linguistic communication, performed by the ruler with others, was often of short distance. The ruler, ruling the state by using coercion or violence, did not necessarily need to communicate with the ruled. The ruler usually performed linguistic communication with his retainers in the building of the regime. Linguistic communication only went on within the ruling group. The common interest of the ruling group took shape, but the common interest of all within the state failed to take shape. In the era when people hold an election, a change takes place. All political parties participate in the election. An election, held across the state, means a clearly and officially defined process of long-distance linguistic communication that goes on across the state. This election not only means the appointments of the power holders but also means the appointments of the power holders in a just way. This election realizes justice. When no election was held in the past, the power holders of the state were selected within the ruling group. The related linguistic communication was of short distance. But when people hold an election in modern times, the related linguistic communication, realized by an election, is of long distance. Long-distance linguistic communication is further characterized by the universality of linguistic communication that goes on within the state. The universality of linguistic communication means the realization of justice because the state cannot ignore the interest of each now.

Specifically speaking, the power holders of the government are now, in some sense, appointed by the citizens. The government must serve all the citizens. Without an election, the power holders of the state may be selected due to a deal made by a group of people with another group of people at the expense of the interest of the public. When an election is held, no one can bribe any others in selecting the power holders of the state at the expense of the interest of the public because now all participate in selecting the power holders of the state. Normally, the state appoints the power holders according to the opinion of the majority. The opinion of the majority is regarded as the one that represents the interest of the public because any particular interest, demanded or sought by any individual citizen, may not get support. Bentham argues that the voter's natural tendency would be to vote in a way that advanced his particular interest. However, the candidate for a political assembly who promised to advance particular interests would certainly not get electoral support. Only the candidate's promise to represent the common interest of the electorate would potentially attract electors.[6] I concur with Bentham on this point. However, I argue that we should also point out in detail why a proposal, representing the common interest of the electorate, may get support from the majority of the electorate. My understanding is that the particular interest, advanced by each individual citizen, varies substantially. The particular interest proves very much diverse. As the particular interest, advanced by each, is very likely to be different from the particular interest advanced by any other citizen, only general interests, advanced by the citizens, get support. Actually, voters advance varied proposals through representative candidates. Only a few proposals prevail throughout the state. Voters have to minimize the coverage of the proposals in order to reach an agreement. The voters, as a whole, accept the proposals representing the general interest. Each proposal may not dovetail the specific expectation of each voter. Yet the voter has no alternative but to accept it if it basically meets his expectation because the voter believes reason. Whenever voters are involved in a dispute, they tend to be subject to the arbitration of reason. Reason is powerful. Thus, voters are guided by reason to reaching an agreement. This agreement does not need to be based on the empirical experience. As such, they are illuminated by a light in the darkness in seeking a solution. If proposals are diverse, some of them may prevail over others. If a voter opposes a proposal, he may not oppose all the contents of that proposal. If a voter supports a proposal, he may not support all the contents of that proposal. As voters believe that they cannot reach an agreement on all matters for an objective reason, they reach an agreement in principle. The reason they rely on ensures that they can make an agreement. Then the common interest of all takes shape. They realize this goal by reaching an agreement through mutual consultation. This is because the result is not imposed on all voters by using coercion or violence but gained in a process of linguistic communication that goes on throughout the state. The universality of linguistic communication that goes on in realizing this goal ensures the realization of justice. Some great politicians, such as James Madison, and some great thinkers, such as Alex de Tocqueville, conceptualized the so-called phenomenon of the tyranny of the majority in history. They believed that when an issue was put to voting, the prevalence of the majority over the minority was tyranny. My view is that they conceptualized the tyranny of the majority incorrectly because the majority cannot commit tyranny. The majority cannot act in unison to use coercion unless people wage a civil war. Normally, the majority act in unison in the process of linguistic communication. Whenever people activate a process of linguistic communication, they hope that the common interest of all can take shape unless language is abused. Ruling on the result of voting is to form an agreement needed in the governance of the state. It is aimed at forming that common interest. When people advance various proposals, the authorities consider all proposals in order to seek support from all. Though the authorities only get support from the majority, the minority is not compelled by force to accept it but by reason. This is because the action is taken in the process of linguistic communication and reason prevails in the process of linguistic communication. If one particular interest, advanced by a certain voter, happens to be analogous to the particular interest advanced by another voter, the related interest may become part of the common interest that will take shape. In terms of the opinion of the majority prevailing due to the combination of various particular interests, the proposal, presented by the majority and accepted by the state, is not imposed on the minority by force but is raised by chance. Tyranny must include the use of violence. Voting is without any violence. Justice means the greatest happiness of the greatest number of people. Violence cannot realize this goal, but linguistic communication can. If one intends to fabricate a consensus of all, he cannot realize his goal unless he uses coercion. The reason is that people, expressing their opinions freely, express different opinions, whereas people, expressing a unanimous opinion, are often coerced.

In some despotic states today news media or the delegates of the representative body express a unanimous opinion. Under these circumstances this unanimous opinion may be indicative of tyranny. The appearance of both the opinion of the majority and the opinion of the minority just indicates that people can express their opinions freely. A voter happens to be part of the minority or the majority. No one forces him to be part of the minority or the majority. He advances his particular interest according to his own judgment, but he must be subject to the judgment of reason accepted by all. As we insist that the freedom enjoyed by one citizen should not harm the freedom enjoyed by any other citizen, a particular interest, advanced by a voter, should not harm the particular interest advanced by any other voter. The general interest, combining thousands or millions of different particular interests that do not or basically do not harm all other particular interests, is ascertained and the related proposal is accepted. This means that an election is designed to make a decision without being imposed by using coercion. Nobody is designated in advance to rule on the dispute. The decision, made by the majority, is neither the decision made by any individual voter nor the decision made by any portion of the voters. Nobody is involved in the conflict of interest. Thus, an election, held to appoint power holders, enhances justice. In the place where no election is held, injustice must prevail because the lack of election affects the distribution of the interest among the citizens. So I argue that people cannot realize justice in the appointment of the power holders without extending the distance of linguistic communication because all citizens, being the members of the state, must be able to enter the process of linguistic communication performed by all with all in order to ensure the formation, maintenance and enhancement of the common interest of all. Appointing the power holders in this method may be a case in point.

2. Procedure

If justice in appointing the power holders is assumed to be realizable in extending the distance of linguistic communication that goes on throughout the state, a procedure, formulated, or agreed to, by all within the state, can also realize justice in extending the distance of linguistic communication that goes on across the state in the governance of the state after the appointment of the power holders. The reason is that extending the distance of linguistic communication puts an end to the conflict of interest that often arises in the process of short-distance linguistic communication in the exercise of power. This procedure is a rule. People carry out this rule in a process of long-distance linguistic communication against the conflict of interest. This rule establishes order or guides the fair distribution of interest if any. Every procedure that serves as a rule realizes either procedural justice or distributive justice. There may be a correlation between procedural and distributive justice. In this case distributive justice depends on procedural justice. But procedural justice has an independent value because it can be separated from distributive justice. Thus, though distributive justice cannot be independent of procedural justice, procedural justice may be chosen first if procedural justice and distributive justice cannot be realized at the same time. In other words, distributive justice does not necessarily need to be directly realized in a process of long-distance linguistic communication, but procedural justice does. And the process of long-distance linguistic communication is the only one approach or condition for the realization of justice in an ultimate sense. If people choose distributive justice first, this distributive justice cannot be realized in an ultimate sense because the realization of distributive justice depends on procedural justice. A scheme of distributing interest in favor of a portion of people will always be opposed by another portion of people unless such a scheme has a reason. Such a scheme of distributing interest may not be perpetual or realistic. The perpetual or realistic scheme of distributing interest should be the one accepted by all sides. To realize this goal, people have to go through a fair procedure. Thus, going through a fair procedure leads to the realization of distributive justice. Justice is, however, a medium in support of the related linguistic communication in the formation of the state. That is, people, seeing the likelihood of realizing justice among them, unite. Thus, justice functions as a medium of linguistic communication in the mutual interactions of all. And all unite. As E. Allan Lind and Tom R. Tyler write,

> Procedural justice may be the key force that binds members
> of a political group together. Even those disadvantaged
> by a particular decision will maintain their allegiance to a

political system if they feel that the system's decision-making procedures are generally fair.[7]

If we suppose that this political group is a nation forming a state, we can also believe that a related procedure strengthens the allegiance of people to the state. If people get involved in a dispute, they may even go through a procedure to solve this dispute. They may realize procedural justice. One case showing this logic is voting. Though we have discussed election and referendum, I should also point out again that voting, required in an election or in a referendum, also involves a procedure. In order to explain the procedure, I would like to discuss voting here as an example again. This is because voting in the governance of the state at all levels is a very basic procedure for the realization of justice. Though voting is adopted to select a power holder or to make a collective decision, the most fundamental function of voting is not to select a power holder or to make a collective decision, but to go through a procedure. If there is no procedure, voting will not happen. My reasoning is that voting is a way adopted by the citizens to realize self-governance. In this process, the opinion of the majority is bound to prevail over the opinion of the minority. All accept this rule. A portion of voters or citizens who cast ballots and become the minority in voting accept the result of voting. Some thinkers assert that the rule of the majority tends to be the oppression of the minority by the majority. My view is that the so-called oppression is imaginary. The reason is that people, becoming the minority, accept the rule of the majority because they see the procedural justice as the first principle of justice. People need to seek procedural justice first. Only after the realization of procedural justice can they realize distributive justice later. The minority believe that accepting the rule of the randomly-formed majority is a condition for them to realize justice when they become the majority in the next voting. People who do not seek procedural justice cannot ensure the realization of distributive justice. To adhere to a fair procedure is to obey the ruling of an unseen third party. People, not subject to the ruling of a third party, cannot realize justice. In some states in which people have not established democracy yet, the ruling class claims that the good performance of the government in economic development legitimates its ruling status. The ruling class thus denies the necessity of a free election and the lawful competition of different political parties. Different political parties, however, may all claim that they can implement the best public policies in the management of public affairs within the state. Which political party is the better choice? A dispute is bound to arise. Thus, as a settlement, people need a fair procedure to test which political party can be accepted by the voters. An election is such a procedure. As far as a decision on a public affair is concerned, a referendum is also such a procedure.

In the meantime, I argue that people realize procedural justice in extending the distance of linguistic communication. The nature of any procedure can indicate the existence of a process of long-distance linguistic communication in such a procedure. That is, a procedure is, in fact, a rule obeyed by all sides. It is not obeyed by all sides at the same time or at the same place. It is obeyed by all sides at different times or at different places. In other words, it is obeyed by all on individual basis. This procedure is an extended process of linguistic communication. Therefore, we see the following four attributes of a typical procedure. First, a fair procedure is applied consistently across persons and across time. Consistency across persons generally takes the form of treating all equally under the procedure. In practice, the so-called consistency requires that all parties be convinced that they have the same rights under the procedure and are treated similarly. Consistency across time requires that the procedure follow the same rules and be enacted the same way each time it is used.[8] Thus, we can understand such a case from the perspective of the distance of linguistic communication. Consistency, required by a procedure, means implementing a rule over the long term. Conversely speaking, if inconsistency occurs, people stop the related process of linguistic communication. They shorten the distance of linguistic communication. Second, a fair procedure is gone through in the principle of impartiality. As people have to adhere to the principle of consistency across persons, as mentioned just earlier, such a procedure must be impartial. In other words, such a procedure must be accepted by all. As it is accepted by all, it must be impartial. Impartiality means fairness here. Fairness means justice. Yet as we suppose that such a procedure, accepted by all, must not be the one not accepted by all, we can believe that all have made a tacit contract. In other words, all have already reached a consensus on going through this procedure. All, having reached a consensus, must have communicated with all. Such communication must go on across the state as what we discuss is the procedure that runs across the state. So justice is in relation to extending the distance of linguistic communication. Third, this procedure, approved, or agreed to, by all, must be gone through under the surveillance of all. There must be a process of linguistic communication that informs all of going through this procedure. To go through this procedure in the method agreed to by all is also to ensure justice because failure to go through this procedure properly will not realize justice. The government engages in administration in the principle of publicity because publicity ensures that citizens, or their representatives, have the oversight of the procedure of administration supposed to be obeyed by the government. For example, in contemporary western countries, democracy ensures publicity after grievances are disclosed. Because of this, citizens are likely to expose the abuse of power committed by the officials and the representative body is able to impeach officials who exceed or abuse their powers. Under these circumstances, as Russell writes, the government will not be able to secure its own permanence by intimidation, the falsification of the register of electors or any similar method. The result is that the party government in democratic countries "causes politicians in power to be objects of hostile criticism by nearly half the nation. This makes it impossible for them to commit many crimes to which they might otherwise be prone."[9] Fourth, this procedure is not in the conflict with morality. Because this procedure is accepted by all and morality is also adhered to by all, such a procedure must be just. In other words, as morality denotes a principle of behavior in realizing justice in the society or the state, the procedure identical with morality must also be just. At least, this procedure is not against morality. Thus, as morality is actually a contract made by all with all throughout the society or the state, such a procedure is also a de facto contract. Such a procedure must also involve a process of linguistic communication that goes on among all throughout the state. The related linguistic communication underlying this procedure has the relevance to justice.

In other words, a procedure must be formulated and approved by at least one person and be gone through by another person and be overseen by a third person. As more people are involved, this process has to be extended. And as this process is extended and more people are involved in it, it becomes difficult for some people to get involved in the conflict of interest often occurring in the exercise of power. Thus, people realize justice in extending the distance of linguistic communication. In other words, going through a procedure in the exercise of power needs to satisfy the standards of consistency, impartiality, public surveillance and morality. The related act of administration tends to be just or fair as a result. This nature of procedure can be exemplified by some cases.

First, sometimes people make a law in governing the state. People, required to be authorized to make a law, have to go through a procedure. Usually, the legislature makes this law. The legislature, making this law, has to go through a procedure. If this procedure is altered temporarily as required by a supreme power holder such as a king in the medieval times, this alteration may lead to injustice because the alteration of the procedure may serve the interest of the power holder only instead of serving the interest of the people. As Locke once writes, "That when such a single person, or prince, sets up his own arbitrary will in place of the laws, which are the will of the society, declared by the legislative, then the legislative is changed."[10] Changing a procedure in the making of a law shortens the distance of related linguistic communication.

Second, the legislature usually holds regular meetings in order to make laws. It is fair and just for the legislature to hold meetings regularly because justice is realized when every legislature holds meetings regularly. If the legislature suddenly suspends holding the meetings regularly without any acceptable reason, this case may mean that an unusual decision is made in order to meet the requirement of the supreme power holder in his own interest. In this case, people shorten the distance of related linguistic communication. People change the nature of the legislature and even put an end to it. As Locke states that:

> When the prince hinders the legislative from assembling in its due time, or from acting freely, pursuant to those ends for which it was constituted, the *legislative is altered*; for it is not a certain number of men, no, nor their meeting, unless they have also freedom of debating, and leisure of perfecting, what is for the good of the society, wherein the legislative consists: when these are taken away or altered, so as to deprive the society of the due exercise of their power, the legislative is truly altered; for it is not names that constitute governments, but the use and exercise of those powers that

were intended to accompany them; so that he, who takes away the freedom, or hinders the acting of the legislative in its due seasons, in effect takes *away the legislative*, and *puts an end to the government*.[11]

Third, if the legislature is elected by the voters, an election is also a procedure. As all citizens agree to the holding of an election, the process of the election should be deemed as just and fair. In this case the legislature, formed as a result of the process of the election, should also be deemed as just and fair. Thus, changing the method of electing those entering the legislature without the consent from the citizens is likely to lead to injustice. Thus Locke further writes that:

> When, by the arbitrary power of the prince, the electors, or ways of election, are altered, without the consent, and contrary to the common interest of the people, there also the *legislative is altered*; for, if others than those whom the society hath authorized thereunto, do chuse, or in another way than what the society hath prescribed, those chosen are not the legislative appointed by the people.[12]

This again indicates that the violation of the rule of procedure shortens the process of related linguistic communication that underlies such a procedure. In sum, people realize justice in extending the process of linguistic communication. As the related process of linguistic communication is usually agreed to by the people throughout the state, justice is, in fact, realized in the process of linguistic communication that goes on throughout the state.

The administrative body is required to adhere to procedure, too. If the government is formed after an election is held according to a law made on behalf of all the citizens within the state, there is a formal procedure ensuring the realization of justice. Yet if this government is not formed after the election is held according to a law, the related procedure may not have been gone through. For example, if people form a government following a coup d'état or usurpation in the absence of a procedure, forming such a government may be unjust. In other words, the common interest takes shape if people form the government through a process of election held according to the law. Forming a government in an irregular way may mean that the common interest of a portion of the people takes shape within the state. In the absence of a process of linguistic communication that goes on among all across the state, the common interest of all will not take shape.

If the government starts to function, people may hold a formal ceremony to mark the beginning of the operation of the government in order to let the public know this matter. A ceremony in this regard often means a process of linguistic communication between the authorities and the representatives of the citizens because it is often held in the parliament. As long as such a process of linguistic communication is accepted and taken for granted, such a ceremony is also a procedure. Going through such a procedure ensures the legitimacy of the government. Yet if a government is not formed in a required process because some ambitious people seize or usurp the power, the breach of the procedure may mean injustice. In other words, sometimes some people seize or usurp the power of the government and they often cancel or change the original ceremony. In the absence of the consent from the citizens, no common interest of all will take shape. People will not be able to realize justice as a result.

The government that functions is subject to various procedures indeed. These procedures may be formulated by the legislature. The legislature formulates these procedures on behalf of the people. In some sense, these procedures are the indirect requirements of the citizens. They are not their direct requirements. The reason is that there is a long process of related linguistic communication between the citizens and various government bodies. As such, every act of the government is subject to these procedures, and every act of the government tends to be fair or just because these procedures make the conflict of interest impossible. In other words, every procedure presupposes the extension of a process. The extension of a process often means extending the distance of linguistic communication. An act, committed in administration, may be in a short process. Yet setting a procedure lengthens the process of linguistic communication behind this procedure. Conversely, violating a procedure shortens the process of the related linguistic communication.

Likewise, failure to obey the related rule for the dissolution of the government may mean the cancellation of a procedure. If the ruling party fails to win the next election, the government, organized by it, will be dissolved according to the law. The voters will the dissolution of the government. Thus, the dissolution undergoes a procedure defined by the law. Yet if the government is dissolved not because of an election but because of an unauthorized act, for example, a coup d'état, the replacement of the former procedure by a new one may not mean the realization of justice if such an act is against the will of the citizens. Usually one cannot be sure if such an act gets consent from the majority of the citizens. Thus, it may not be just because some people violate a procedure. This means that such an act violates the law. Thus, people cannot ensure the realization of justice. As such, a formal procedure, gone through for the dissolution of the government, means the realization of justice. A process of long-distance linguistic communication must go on among many people in this event. Thus, the so-called procedural justice must involve a process of long-distance linguistic communication.

In the activities performed by people in the governance of the state, people may further extend a procedure to ensure the realization of justice in long-distance linguistic communication. In the governance of the state, people formulate various administrative procedures. Another process of long-distance linguistic communication also appears in the formulation of a procedure. That is, people have to design a procedure in advance in formulating that procedure. The process of designing that procedure presupposes the existence of an idea. People come up with this idea in a process of long-distance linguistic communication if such an idea is scientific, rational, appropriate and acceptable. This means that whenever people make a procedure, two different processes of action appear. One process of action is engaging in administration. The other is the action defined by this procedure. The action, taken to engage in administration each time, must be identical with the action defined by this procedure. As the action defined by the procedure must be up to the standard, the procedure is formulated in advance. This procedure is the subjectivity of that standard. Before the procedure is gone through, such a procedure is subjective. After this procedure is gone through, it becomes objective. The procedure always exists in the process of long-distance linguistic communication. As such a procedure always lies in a process of long-distance linguistic communication, no one is able to bend this procedure because each acts in the process of short-distance linguistic communication when he seeks approval in this procedure. Thus, a procedure, made in advance and accepted by all on voluntary basis, must be just. In this case it is arguable that people realize justice on the basis of a process of long-distance linguistic communication.

This means that in the presence of a procedure the administrators of the state subject to such a procedure are required to gain approval from a certain authority. As such a procedure is formulated in advance, such a procedure exists in the process of long-distance linguistic communication. Those who make this procedure and those who obey this procedure may be far away from each other. For example, those who make this procedure do not engage in administration and they are not involved in the conflict of interest. Then we see that they do not exercise power in the specific work in governing the state, and they are not supposed to be able to seek any personal interest. These people, not involved, or not likely to be involved, in any conflict of interest, tend to formulate a fair procedure. In the meantime, administrators who govern the state are required to go through the fair procedure that realizes justice. A procedure may be aimed at maintaining a professional standard in the governance of the state. However, a procedure may also require the realization of justice in the governance of the state. The key is that the procedure involves a process of long-distance linguistic communication. In the activities of administration, the act of an administrator is in the process of short-distance linguistic communication because an administrative decision involves a process of short-distance linguistic communication. A procedure that extends the distance of the related linguistic communication creates a condition for the realization of justice because it is, in some sense, designed to prevent the conflict of interest from arising. For example, people keep on going through a procedure over the long term. Inasmuch as it is gone through over the long term, its value increases accordingly. The nature of procedure is like the nature of law. That is, as people apply a law over the long term, its value increases accordingly. After the formulation of a procedure, it will be gone through by many people for many times. Its utility increases substantially. People may draw on the experience of the past in order to make a fair and efficient procedure. The predecessors may be invited to give their advices. Some predecessors may have already died. Yet their advices can still be sought because they left over their books to us. As many people read these books, they must be beneficial to the following generations. If the contents of those books are not wholesome because they do not advocate fairness or justice, they will not be handed down to the following generations. For example, a book by a philosopher is usually intended to advocate justice if this book discusses law or politics. A philosopher is not motivated to propagate an evil thought in the public. He seeks as many readers as possible. Justice is sought by all. The reason is that the philosopher does not force the public to embrace his idea by using coercion. The method used by him is to persuade the public to accept his idea. He must disseminate a just idea. Thus, if people formulate a procedure in accordance with the advice of the predecessors including philosophers and the administrators of the following generations are required to obey it, it must contribute to the realization of justice. If an administrator governs the state without such a procedure, this situation may not necessarily mean the absence of any procedure in administration. Whenever an administrator acts to make a decision or to implement an administrative order, his act is actually a procedure, albeit the one that is not made in advance. Yet as this procedure is not made in advance, it is made by himself. As it is made by himself, it may be made in consideration of his own special interest. Such a procedure may not be the official or standard procedure. Such a procedure may not be approved by any authority as usual. So it may not be just.

An administrative procedure, made as required by a law, is actually a contract if we suppose that every administrator must go through the procedure in the same way when each of the administrators comes across the same situation and fulfills the same task. If all administrators go through the same procedure under the same circumstances, no one enjoys any privilege. Thus, such a procedure means fairness and justice. For example, sometimes people make a line in order to buy a bus ticket or to have his or her turn to get assistance provided by a teller in a bank or to enter the museum in sequence, and they follow a procedure. They take initiative to make a line so that each spends the time of the same or similar length, a procedure that represents the principle of equality of all. This is justice. If one customer jumps into the line in order to get service earlier than expected, he or she breaks the procedure. This is injustice. To put it another way, the procedure is a contract. The procedure under these circumstances is the contract made by the public. This contract is supposed to be obeyed by all. In political life we can see the similar phenomena. For example, if the same procedure is gone through no matter which political party is the ruling party, this procedure may mean justice.

As each political party acts under the requirement of this procedure, people realize the related justice in the process of long-distance linguistic communication. Likewise, an administrative procedure is also a de facto contract. This contract is carried out by all who are required to go through the procedure. Everyone is subject to this procedure. This procedure is not formulated for any specific person. Thus it means justice.

People may also extend an administrative procedure to avoid injustice. Under certain circumstances people may extend an administrative procedure to ensure the realization of justice. For example, sometimes the state needs to allocate the resources of policies and the interest that arises following the implementation of those policies. The state needs to solve the disputes in relation to the distribution of the resources of the policies and the interest that arises in the implementation of those policies. The state needs to gather information and to make a decision. The state needs to decide who is going to carry out the decision. The state is going to form a team of administrators. Thus, the state recruits administrators, rewards the administrators who show excellent performance and punishes the administrators who show poor performance. All such tasks are fulfilled in various procedures. In view of these procedures from the perspective of language, we find that to extend the administrative procedure is to extend the distance of linguistic communication that underlies such a procedure. There are some cases in point as follows.

First, an administrator, going through a procedure, needs to gain approval from his supervisor. His supervisor is the administrator of the higher level. The administrator of the higher level may also be required to gain approval from his supervisor until the approval is given by the supreme administrator. The supreme administrator is supposed to represent the government or the state with full mandate. Thus an administrator of a certain level seeks the approval from the administrator who is trusted to a greater extent. He enters the process of the linguistic communication over long distances. Administrators extend the related procedure and hence the distance of the related linguistic communication step by step. As the supreme administrator normally represents the interest of the whole state or all the public because he often interacts directly with the citizens on behalf of the state or the public, his approval implies the largest possibility of realizing the justice across the state. People often realize justice by extending the related procedure to the greatest extent within the administrative system.

Second, people, going through a procedure, may be required to get an approval from the parliament. There is a derivative procedure. For example, the ruling party, making an administrative decision, may be required to seek support from the parliament in which the opposition has the power to inspect this administrative decision. The ruling party is subject to the supervision of the opposition, as already mentioned earlier. The government is placed under the surveillance of the parliament. As the parliament is composed of the representatives elected by the voters, any administrative decision, required to be approved by the parliament, is absolutely expected to be just and proper. Such an administrative decision, subject to the approval of the parliament, is subject to the approval of the delegates of the electorate. Thus, this administrative decision must be just. This is a role played by a representative assembly. Mill states that:

> [I]nstead of the function of governing, for which it is radically unfit, the proper office of a representative assembly is to watch and control the government; to throw the light of publicity on its acts; to compel a full exposition and justification of all of them which any one considers questionable; to censure them if found condemnable, and, if the men who compose the government abuse their trust, or fulfil it in a manner which conflicts with the deliberate sense of the nation, to expel them from office, and either expressly or virtually appoint their successors.[13]

That is, the procedure involves a process of long-distance linguistic communication. As the procedure is valid and adhered to, the related process of linguistic communication continues. Thus, it ensures the realization of justice.

Third, sometimes administrators need to get another direct approval from the voters while they go through a procedure. They may need to make an important decision. Thus, this decision may be put to a referendum. Referendum has been discussed by us in the preceding chapter. Yet we have only discussed referendum from the perspective of democracy. If we look at referendum from another different perspective, we may find that it may also be the extension of a process of administrative decision. It may also be a procedure. The constitution or law may require that an issue, concerning the merger of the nation-state with another nation-state, or the change of the territory of the nation-state, or any other matter, be settled by putting the question to a referendum. Thus people extend the process of linguistic communication by putting the related issue to a referendum. Such an act of extending the distance of linguistic communication actually means that citizens participate in making a decision in a nation-state. All citizens are the participants of this process, and no corruption will occur. This prevents any deal made by any group of people with another group of people at the expense of the interest of all other citizens. This eradicates emphatically all kinds of injustice. As Rousseau writes, "the people is never corrupted."[14] Thus, extending the distance of linguistic communication to the greatest extent finally allows for the people make a decision by themselves. This is the most thorough way of realizing justice.

3. Trial

A trial is also a procedure. It is a legal procedure. People design such a legal procedure to settle disputes or conflicts between one person and another. They realize justice through this legal procedure. This legal procedure is usually exposed to the public for the purpose of public surveillance. Public surveillance also means justice. There must be a process of long-distance linguistic communication between the judge and the public. This process of linguistic communication is also as important as a procedure though the related process of linguistic communication is not a formal procedure. As a dispute, settled in the court, may be controversial, or as a case, dealt with in the court, may be sensitive, resulting in uncertainty in the realization of justice, the trial is usually overseen by the public. Thus, extending the distance of linguistic communication between the court and the public is also a particular aspect indicating that humans find a way to realize justice in the organization of the state in the process of long-distance linguistic communication in the public. In a trial there must be at least one judge and two parties as the principals. The judge discusses the dispute or the accusation with the two principals. The judge communicates with the principals on behalf of the lawmaker. The related linguistic communication is the extension of linguistic communication activated by the lawmaker in the outset. Montesquieu states that "the national judges are no more than the mouth that pronounces the words of the law."[15] That is, the judge finds out the truth of the case and acts to realize justice according to the law in a trial. A law presupposes a process of linguistic communication performed by a lawmaker with the citizens in the public. This is a process of long-distance linguistic communication. It is widely known to the public. In the meantime, the trial must be transparent. The result of the trial, namely, the judgment, ought to be announced to the public directly as required by the nature of the trial. If the result of a trial is not announced to the public, the trial will become less significant. The trial is a form allowing the public to inspect the process of realizing justice. Thus, the public is usually entitled to have the oversight of the trial unless the trial is conducted secretly on the grounds of the security of the state on rare occasions. Normally, a trial, conducted by the court of any civilized state, is conducted as overseen by the public. People normally insist on and carry out the principle of publicity. In comparison, an administrative procedure may not always be directly disclosed to the public. An administrative procedure may not directly concern the issue of justice. It may only concern the properness of an administrative decision. Thus, it is often overseen by the parliament or any other kind of representative body only. Thus, unlike the judge who goes through the judicial procedure in which the case heard by him is announced to the public, the administrator who makes or carries out an administrative decision or a policy may not always be announced to the public though he is perhaps required to follow a certain procedure. The process of carrying out an administrative order or a policy may not be placed under the direct scrutiny of the public. Thus, sometimes an administrative procedure may not be disclosed to the public, whereas a trial must be exposed to the public. An administrative procedure may not always be directly exposed to the public. In some sense, the process of making a law in the legislature is also like that of making an administrative decision or carrying it out. The trial, unlike the process of making or carrying out an administrative decision or even a law, is usually, or always, very transparent. A trial is especially arranged to ensure the realization of justice. Extending the distance of linguistic communication also serves as a basis for the realization of justice.

That is, the trial is especially conducted in the principle of publicity. Thus, the court, implementing the principle of publicity, announces the date of the trial to the public in advance and announces the outcome of the trial to the public after the end of the trial as well. As the public is composed of passively coexisting individuals who are dispersed in the state, the court needs to reach all of them through long-distance linguistic communication. News media then play a role in implementing the principle of publicity. Though we have already discussed public communication in the formation of the common interest of the state and the public surveillance of some administrative procedures earlier, I should especially point out in detail the development of media in support of the linguistic communication of reporting trials to the public. As we have already mentioned, extending the distance of linguistic communication is a basis for the growth of the state. Likewise, extending the distance of linguistic communication is also a basis for setting a process of linguistic communication that bolsters publicity for the realization of justice. This is also a case bearing testimony to the correlation between extending the distance of linguistic communication and justice. We need to explain three viewpoints as follows.

First, linguistic communication that can reach all lays a foundation for laying down the principle of publicity. In the outset, humans communicate with each other without using language. They display their behavior for communication. For example, they smile when they meet each other. Smiling is communication. Such communication relies on physical proximity. Such communication dictates the small size of the community. After humans commence to communicate by using spoken language, they gradually expand their community. After humans commence to communicate by using written language, they further expand their community until the formation of the civilized society. The evolution of our human community indicates that humans who use spoken language in mutual communication only build a residential community such as a neighborhood or a town or a city or a region. Such a residential community may be simply called the "community." Later, humans who communicate by using written language build society. Describing the development of such a human community, Ferdinand Tönnies differentiates a community (Gemainschaft) from a society (Gesellschaft). According to him, the difference between the community and the society is first and foremost constituted by writing.[16] Obviously, writing extends the distance of linguistic communication and hence plays a role in the expansion of the community. The society should be larger than the community envisioned by Tönnies. My view is that after humans enter the civilized society, they first build their residential community on the basis of the community of spoken language. Though written communication has already emerged, the community of spoken language may especially support the growth of a residential community such as a neighborhood or a town or a city. A residential community is a small society. Then human-chain spoken communication develops, leading to the formation of a region. A region is a medium-sized society larger than a residential community. Though written communication bolsters the growth of a region, a region may take form on the basis of a community of a dialect or regional language. In other words, people, speaking a dialect, perform frequent linguistic communication with one another and share the same local culture. These people form a larger community. Finally, written communication develops. In the outset written communication is only human-chain written communication. People, from different regions, may not communicate with one another effectively or frequently. People differentiate from one another because they belong to the different communities of language. Yet the development of printing extends the reach of direct written communication. A community of common language emerges. People build their largest society, on the basis of which they further form the state. Then the state takes form on the basis of the growth of the community of common language. This state is usually a nation-state. Extending the reach of linguistic communication underlies the growth of the state. One case in point is the appearance of newspapers in early modern times. The specific case is that extending the reach of linguistic communication enables people to perform intensive long-distance linguistic communication on a large scale. The so-called "intensive long-distance linguistic communication" means the communication of conveying a large amount of information over long distances. This type of linguistic communication gives birth to newspapers. Newspapers support the related linguistic communication across the state. Newspapers perform the communication that shows the characteristic of constancy, frequency, variety, cheapness, impartiality, candor, and others, as initially indicated by Bentham.[17] This paves a way for people to implement the principle of publicity.

Second, after newspaper becomes a medium, it is printed by an enterprise that runs in the principle of market operation. This means that a newspaper, read by the masses, cannot be printed and distributed by an individual person only. People need to incorporate an enterprise of a certain size. In the meantime, a person, able to exchange goods and services, may found an enterprise to print a large batch of newspapers to serve the masses. There is a market demand for newspapers and an enterprise may be profitable. Thus, enterprises are motivated by profit to print the newspapers to be read by the masses. Technological development also bolsters the growth of news media such as newspapers. As people are able to exchange goods and services, every link of exchange functions to support a process of long-distance linguistic communication at large. This is because news is not provided for free. Yet as an enterprise can provide a surplus value in printing newspapers and the public can also provide a surplus value in reading newspapers, commercializing printing in the principle of market operation is a scheme of two-wins. Thus, news media can report a trial to the public and realize the principle of publicity along with the emergence of newspapers. In some sense, the larger the population had by the state, the stronger the desire, had by the enterprise to operate business such as the business of printing newspapers because there is a bigger potential for making profits. On the other hand, the public will find that service, provided by an enterprise involved in printing, is more valuable because the public depends more heavily on that enterprise to get access to news reports. In this sense, an enterprise is also a medium because it facilitates the related linguistic communication. Some scholars may argue that the freedom of speech differs from the freedom of press because the process of the linguistic communication of the press may be controlled by the minority that has its own bias. Particularly, they argue that after an enterprise monopolizes the coverage of news, the so-called market of ideas will barely exist. For example, some scholars argue that the press not only becomes independent participant in the political process, but is also given more freedom and less responsibility than individual citizens are.[18] My view is that the expectation from the public should not be overlooked. Enterprises which serve the public in order to make profits have to meet the require-ment of the public. A news medium cannot cheat the masses. As there is an exchange between the enterprise and the public, they have to cooperate. As they cooperate, the common interest must exist. The ultimate goal of an enterprise, adhering to the principle of business operation, is to make profits. The most efficient way to make profits is to meet the expectation of the greatest number of people. Thus, commenting on the newspapers of the United States, Alexis de Tocqueville writes that "Newspapers do not multiply simply because they are cheap, but according to the more or less frequent need felt by a great number of people to communicate with one another and to act together."[19] If an enterprise undertakes a task to propagate a political idea and to suppress another political idea, this activity should be corruption viewed in accordance with the principle of business. Thus a news medium will not fail to cover the news needed by the public. The strength of a news medium lies in the high readership had by it. Though some reports may not completely reflect the truth, some other reports can reflect the truth. This suffices to realize the principle of publicity because under these circumstances no significant event can be concealed. The competition of the market forces those media into a disadvantageous position if they refrain from covering the news needed by the public.

Third, since written language began to play a prominent role in the build-ing of the state, ordinary people have been able to learn it. As we have already mentioned earlier, after the start of the process of industrialization, workforce needed to master industrial production skills. People needed to receive an education. Mass education flourished. The rate of literacy rose steadily. This means that people learn to use written language, the medium of spoken lan-guage. As ordinary people learn to use written language, they can then read newspapers. The readership of newspapers rises accordingly. As a result, there appears the linguistic communication performed by newspapers with a large number of people on a large scale. In some sense, without such a process of linguistic communication, the public may not take form. In ancient times people might discuss the public affairs on a public square because at that time people performed mainly spoken communication with one another. They kept a public tribune in the process of spoken communication. By contrast, in modern times people move such a public tribune to the newspapers. As Slavko Splichal writes,

> The first printed papers in the fifteenth century did not oust immediately the handwritten papers from the market since the latter were better able to evade censorship largely introduced after the invention of the printing press. With the rise of the daily press in the eighteenth century, newspapers paved the way for constitutional provisions of freedom of the press based on the Enlightenment principles of publicity and free speech. Papers of the sixteenth and seventeenth centuries mostly provided readership with news and were named appropriately: "Aviso" and "Relation" in Germany, "Examiner" and "Spectator" in England, "Messenger" in Italy, or just "News," "Novelties," or "Gazette" in different countries and languages. In contrast, newspapers during the Enlightenment often became a "tribune" (even taking on this name), where news intended for the public at large was followed by discussion and opinion was expressed to influence a large number of readers.[20]

Ordinary people, having learned to use written language, enter the process of linguistic communication created by newspapers. Though nation-state emerges, media also develop, enabling ordinary people to have access to the public communication that implements the principles of publicity. If a trial is conducted, the masses may get the news about it. The trial may be placed under the surveillance of the public.

As a result, newspapers realize the principle of publicity contemplated by some leading philosophers, including Immanuel Kant and Jeremy Bentham. Newspapers ensure the publicity of the process of governing the state as a prerequisite for the realization of justice. The related reason is initially illustrated by Kant as he believes that without the possibility of publicity, there will be no justice. When elaborating the principle of publicity, he writes that:

> This principle is to be considered not only *ethical* (as belonging to the doctrine of virtue), but also *juridical* (as pertaining to the rights of men). If my maxim cannot be

openly divulged without at the same time defeating my own intention, i.e., must be kept *secret* for it to succeed, or if I cannot *publicly acknowledge* it without thereby inevitably arousing everyone's opposition to my plan, then this necessary and universal, and thus *a priori* foreseeable, opposition of all to me could not have come from anything other than the injustice with which it threatens everyone.[21]

Bentham adds his comment that:

Fear is the expectation of eventual evil—evil at the hands of all those to whom publicity in relation to the event in question may come to be disagreeable. Against all such fear the most effectual of all securities is *concealment*: concealment of every person by whom any thing has been contributed to the publicity of the obnoxious state of things.[22]

He further points out that "publicity is the very soul of justice."[23]

Their views can help us to envision the publicity of the trial in question. Adhering to publicity requires extending the distance of linguistic communication between the governor of the state and the governed of the state. Extending the distance of linguistic communication between the governor and the governed allows the governor and the governed to communicate on a large scale and culminates in the coverage of the related linguistic communication throughout the state. Publicity means the universality of linguistic communication that goes on across the state. The universality of linguistic communication means that all are involved in the process of linguistic communication. This is especially so for a trial instead of an act of administration. It is especially so for a trial because a trial directly pertains to the realization of justice. As all have the oversight of the trial, the result of the trial, conducted by a judge in the court, must be acceptable by all. Thus, that all accept the result of the trial means the formation of the common interest of all. Then it is arguable that the formation of the common interest means the realization of justice. To put it differently, if the result of the trial is only accepted by a portion of the citizens, this only means the formation of the common interest of such a portion of people. Thus, the common interest of all fails to take shape. In this case we cannot confirm the formation of the common interest of all. Thus it follows that people cannot ascertain the realization of justice. Conversely, if the judge is aware that the trial, conducted by him in the court, is overseen by the public, he may think of making every effort to meet the expectation of the public because the result of the trial must be acceptable. As he exerts his greatest effort to meet the expectation of the public, he works toward the satisfaction of all. Thus the trial must be toward justice as long as the expectation of the citizens is not against the law. Though the expectation of all is transcendent because the public may not directly communicate with the judge in advance, this does not mean that such an expectation does not exist. The experience, had by the judge, guides him to working as expected by the public. When he conducts a trial in the court, he is also tried by the public. As Bentham asserts, publicity "keeps the judge himself, while trying, under trial . . . under the auspices of publicity, the original cause in the court of law and the appeal to the court of public opinion, are going on at the same time."[24] He further insists that there is a public opinion tribunal formed by people, a kind of informal tribunal or committee. Thus the public becomes a judicial body.[25]

The publicity of a trial means a process of long-distance linguistic communication between the judge and the public. If we suppose that the trial is conducted secretly, linguistic communication, performed by the judge, may be only restricted to a few principals appearing in the court. The result of the trial may not be disclosed to the public. The public may not be aware of such a trial. Thus, linguistic communication, that goes on within the court only, is of short distance. The result of the trial may not represent the formation of the common interest of all because the public has no oversight of the trial though a judge is always required to be loyal to the law. In other words, the interest of the public may be sacrificed. This means that as each trial, conducted formally in the court, directly concerns the justice because each trial ultimately pertains to the distribution of interest or the formation of the common interest, it is usually open to the public. So the judicial procedure is usually open to the public.

Free press is essential. If a trial is conducted by a judge in the court, the trial should be overseen by the public. Because of this, the task of the linguistic communication between the court and the public must be undertaken by the news media. In ancient times Germans, Greeks and Romans used to gather to form an assembly to deliver a verdict. As all the members of the community attended the assembly and all were entitled to have a say in the judgment, justice was realized. Yet in modern times as the community grows very large in population and area and the state grows to be a nation-state, the judge conducts the trial on behalf of all the citizens. In order to let the citizens know the trial and to collect the feedback from the citizens, mass media play an important role in the realization of justice. So Thomas Jefferson wrote in 1787 that the basis of the government being the opinion of the people, the very first object should be to keep that related right. He stated that "were it left to me to decide whether we should have a government without newspapers or newspapers without a government, I should not hesitate a moment to prefer that latter." So Bentham especially contemplates several functions of newspapers in the realization of justice in the principle of publicity, including the following functions:

1. Receiving claims and accusations.
2. Receiving oppositions and defenses.
3. Receiving, compelling, collecting and storing evidence.
4. Receiving and hearing or reading arguments of parties litigant or advocates.
5. Forming opinions or judgments on ditto: with correspondent will.
6. Giving expression to such judgments and will.
7. Giving impression to such expression.
8. Giving diffusion to such impression.
9. Giving execution and effect to such judgment[s] and will.[26]

Thus, we can conclude that what enhances justice is extending the distance of linguistic communication due to a role played by public media, including newspapers.

It is also arguable that long-distance linguistic communication in question especially goes on between the judge and the public. As the judge and the public may be far from each other because the public, mentioned by me, is the public of the entire state, news media invariably give support in the related linguistic communication. There is a process of long-distance linguistic communication. The existence of such long-distance linguistic communication can be proved by the fact that whenever such linguistic communication goes on, a certain medium is used. Using a medium usually presupposes the existence of a process of long-distance linguistic communication. Thus, if we can exemplify the existence of media in the process of related linguistic communication, we can prove the existence of such long-distance linguistic communication. There are at least three types of such media adopted by people in such a process of linguistic communication. The first type of such media is celebrity. If a celebrity is involved in a case, the public will pay a special attention to the trial of the case. Why does the public pay a special attention to this case? My understanding is that a celebrity is actually a medium. Ordinary people are often familiar with that celebrity because he or she is often covered by news media. Whenever there is an event involving that celebrity, news media may cover that event. Ordinary people are interested in hearing the news about that celebrity. That celebrity may be a famous actor or actress or a prestigious writer or a musician or a singer or a sports star or a poet or a philosopher or a thinker or a critic or a scientist or a politician. Ordinary people are interested in knowing them. Thus whenever a news medium covers a case involving one of them, people will pay a special attention. For example, O.J. Simpson's trial caught the attention of the citizens widely in 1994 in the United States. The Simpson trial was the most heavily covered legal case of all time. He was acquitted.[27] The related linguistic communication was intensive because more people entered the process of linguistic communication. The second type of such media is the importance of the case heard by the judge. If a case involves homicide, people may pay a special attention to the trial of this case. Montesquieu writes that in ancient Rome the law of Twelve Tables ordained that none but the great assemblies of the people should try a citizen in capital cases.[28] What is the most valuable is human life. The case for a modern state is analogous. If a person dies because of murder, the public is usually concerned with the outcome of the trial. They hope that justice is done for this case. Though it is impossible for the people to assemble in modern times, there are other arrangements. A jury may be organized to give an opinion. Several judges instead of only one judge may be assigned to hear this trial and many ordinary people hope to go to the court to observe the trial in person. We can also believe that if a case involves a dispute about the high amount of compensation requested by one principal in the case, people may also pay a special attention to this case. For example, if a billionaire is involved in a dispute of divorce, he may be required to make compensation in a very high amount to his original spouse. We may also argue that if the trial of a case involves a social issue that the public is very much concerned with across the state, people may pay a special attention. For example, many people may watch the trial of a case concerning the issue of the society given rise to by the wide use of gun in the United States. The third type of such media may be the controversy of a social or political issue involved in a case. If a social or political issue is highly controversial, many people will be very much tempted to join the debate. If a case involving such controversy is heard in a trial, people may closely watch the trial. Comments may be made on many news media. People may put a special pressure on the judges and juries. For example, if the issue of same sex marriage is debated, many people pay attention to this debate. The views of people are very much diversified. Different views are so much in the sharp opposite. If a case involves the controversy about the same sex marriage, the public pays a close attention to the trial of the related case. Thus, the nature of the controversy in the case becomes a medium because it is attractive to many people. Many people are led to enter the process of linguistic communication. Thus, news media are active in covering the progress of the trial of the case. As the publicity of the trial is enhanced, people lay down a high requirement for the judge to ensure the realization of justice.

The universality of linguistic communication that ensures the realization of justice should also be pointed out here again. The relationship between a trial and a law should be mentioned. That is, conducting a trial activates a process of linguistic communication in the public. This process of linguistic communication is actually connected with the law, which further underpins the process of linguistic communication that goes on throughout the state. There is a philosophical correlation between a trial and a law. Without a trial, a law cannot be proved. That is, a law is abstract. When this law is applied, it must be specified because the specific case is dealt with. Before a law is applied, one cannot prove the applicability of this law by using other means. Thus, a law is transcendent or subjective in this sense. A law becomes empirical or objective when a trial is conducted. So a trial is the medium of the law. People cannot directly experience the law until a trial is conducted. This means that the trial is a dynamic process of the law. A law is static. As a trial is conducted in a process of linguistic communication to which relevant people have access, it is the extension of the process of linguistic communication given rise to by that law. Thus whenever a trial is conducted, a law is proclaimed once. As one trial after another is conducted within the state, the same law is proclaimed time and again. The judge performs effective linguistic communication with ordinary people across the state. Thus, if the universality of linguistic communication within the state is assumed to be a necessary condition for the formation of the common interest of all, such linguistic communication must be just because justice means the formation of the common interest of all. The formation of the common interest of a portion of people will not lead to the realization of justice within the state. The formation of the common interest of all depends on the universality of linguistic communication that goes on across the state. When a trial is conducted, the judge and the lawyers may interpret the law from different angles. The understanding of a specific law must be deepened this way or that way. In the meantime, people try to achieve consistency in interpreting the law. They confirm the creditability of the law. They keep and consolidate effectiveness in the linguistic communication given rise to by the law. This means that an abstract law may not be an effective form of linguistic communication performed by the lawmaker with the masses particularly under the condition that a great portion of people may be unable to fully understand the law. The specification of a law in a trial may popularize a law. Popularizing a law is conducive to enhancing justice. For example, a fair judgment may gain support from more people. This strengthens communication between the judge and the masses. This reflects the nature of law. This is because a law means the universality of linguistic communication that reaches all across the state. Any justice lies in the universality of linguistic communication that reaches all across the state. A trial ensures the universality of such linguistic communication.

The final result is that if an aggregate of individuals who are far from each other beyond physical proximity form a virtual tribunal or committee throughout the state, it is more unlikely for them to get involved in the conflict of interest because they are normally exposed to the public and it is impossible for them to get corrupt by making a deal with each other at the expense of all others due to implementing the principle of publicity and hence they are more likely to concur in expressing their opinions because without the influence of the conflict of interest people tend to be guided by reason. Thus, such a public opinion tribunal or committee will enhance justice. Thus, the more the people who take part in the oversight of a trial, the more the people who concur, the greater the strength of justice. Therefore, Bentham writes that:

> The greater the suffering produced by any act of oppression, the greater, provided it has been made known to them, is the number of the individuals who, in the character of members of this Committee, are likely to take cognizance of the affair in the first instance. The greater the number of these members of this Committee who, having joined in the cognizance thus taken, pass condemnation on the deed, the greater the number of those other members who on the authority of their report take cognizance not of the affair at large but of the conduct of the actors, whoever they may be, in the act of oppression, so far forth as to concur in the opinion, the judgment, the sentence of condemnation, passed upon those oppressive agents in consideration of such their oppressive acts. . . . The greater the number of those who concur and join in the provisional sentence, the greater the number of those who are likely to concur and join in the definitive sentence.[29]

In a fundamental sense, realizing justice depends on the universality of the process of linguistic communication within the state. The universality of the process of linguistic communication is an indispensable foundation for the realization of justice in the state. In this sense I argue that using language creates a real condition for the final realization of justice in the state. The question is that the state should be willing to use this condition. People should not ignore the role of language in this regard.

Notes

1. Marshall T. Poe, *A History of Communications: Media and Society from the Evolution of Speech to the Internet* (Cambridge: Cambridge University Press, 2011), 119.
2. Niccolo Machiavelli, *The Prince*, translated by W. K. Marriott (New York: Alfred A. Knopf, 1992), 70.
3. Ibid., 79.
4. Ibid., 80–81.
5. Immanuel Kant, *Perpetual Peace and Other Essays on Politics, History, and Morals,* translated by Ted Humphrey (Annapolis: Hackett Publishing Company, 1983), 128.
6. See: Slavko Splichal, *Principles of Publicity and Free Press* (Lanham: Rowman & Littlefield Publishers, Inc., 2002), 49.
7. E. Allan Lind and Tom R. Tyler, *The Social Psychology of Procedural Justice* (New York: Plenum Press, 1988), 169.
8. The consistency required by a procedure is well defined by E. Allan Lind and Tom R. Tyler. So I cited their related description. Please see: Lind and Tyler, *The Social Psychology of Procedural Justice*, 131.
9. Bertrand Russell, *Power* (New York: W.W. Norton & Company, Inc., 1938), 292.
10. John Locke, *Second Treatise of Government*, edited by C.B. Macpherson (Indianapolis, Indiana: Hackett Publishing Company, Inc., 1980), 108.
11. Ibid., 109.
12. Ibid.
13. John Stuart Mill, *Representative Government* (Chicago: Encyclopaedia Britannica, Inc., 1952), 361.
14. Jean Jacques Rousseau, *Social Contract* (Chicago: Encyclopaedia Britannica, Inc., 1952), 396.
15. Charles de Secondat, Baron de Montesquieu, *The Spirit of Laws*, translated by Thomas Nugent (Chicago: Encyclopaedia Britannica, Inc., 1952), 73.

16. Ferdinand Tönnies, *Kritik der öffentlichen Meinung* (Berlin: Julius springer, 1922), 220, cited from Splichal, *Principles of Publicity and Press Freedom*,10.

17. Please see: Jeremy Bentham, *Securities against Misrule and Other Constitutional Writings for Tripoli and Greece*, edited by Philip Schofield (Oxford: Clarendon Press, 1990), 46.

18. See: Splichal, *Principles of Publicity and Press Freedom*,15.

19. Alexis de Tocqueville, *Democracy in America*, translated by George Lawrence (New York: Harper Perennial, 1988), 519.

20. Splichal, *Principles of Publicity and Press Freedom*,15.

21. Kant, *Perpetual Peace and Other Essays on Politics, History, and Morals*, 135.

22. Bentham, *Securities against Misrule and Other Constitutional Writings for Tripoli and Greece*, 41–42.

23. Jeremy Bentham, *The Works of Jeremy Bentham*, Vol. IV, published under the superintendence of John Bowring (London: Simpkin, Marshall, & Co., 1843), 316.

24. Jeremy Bentham, *The Works of Jeremy Bentham*, Vol. VI, published under the superintendence of John Bowring (London: Simpkin, Marshall, & Co., 1843), 355.

25. See: Bentham, *Securities against Misrule and Other Constitutional Writings for Tripoli and Greece*, 121.

26. Please see: Ibid., 60–61.

27. Jon Bruschke and William E. Loges, *Free Press vs. Fair Trials: Examining Publicity's Role in Trial Outcomes* (Mahwah, New Jersey: Lawrence Erlbaum Associates, Publishers, 2004), 2.

28. Baron de Montesquieu, *The Spirit of Laws*, 81.

29. Please see: Bentham, *Securities against Misrule and Other Constitutional Writings for Tripoli and Greece*, 121–122.

Conclusion

To conclude, I present ten arguments.

First, this monograph offers a view about the genesis of the state. This view is unlike those adduced by the forerunning thinkers or philosophers, who argued that the state is given origin to by natural growth, or social contract, or initial conquest, or self-defense, or class struggle or others. I believe that those views merely interpret the genesis of the state from a single perspective. Some of those views may not be sufficient or correct in shedding light on the truth. People often overlook the role of language. This means that the making of the state is impossible without language. Using language means using media. Using media extends the distance of linguistic communication. Then people communicate on a large scale and form a large community. Thus, without language, people would not build any large community. They would still stay within the tribe. The community, formed by them, would still be a small one. As it were a small one, kinship would be the essential element of its formation. Thus we might not see the growth of any state. In this regard I argue that only the slow evolution of tribes is natural. Likewise, we might not see people making a social contract to build a state without language. Without language, people would not conceptualize their rights and obligations within the society. Without language people would not see the initial conquest and the building of the state. If there were any conquest, this conquest should be the conquest of one tribe by the other. The genesis of the state should be due to the use of language though initial conquest may function as a medium in the beginning. And without language, we might not see either that people would unite to strengthen their self-defense. If language did not come into use, people could hardly cooperate with each other except that they did so because of kinship. If they formed the community in which kinship was an essential element of the formation of the community, they would not found the state. If a community invaded another community, this phenomenon should be the fact that a tribe invaded another tribe. If language did not come into use, we might not see the emergence of any social class. Then we shall see that in the tribe the difference of people only lies in the fact that some people belong to the old generation while others the young generation and the gender of a portion of people is male while the gender of another portion of people female. People are unlikely to be divided along the line of rich people versus poor people. That is, there will be no disparity between the poor and the rich. This means that all are connected with each other by kinship, and all are the members of a communal family. People tend not to divide the property they have. Thus there should be no phenomenon of the formation of the state in the method mentioned by those thinkers or philosophers who insist that the formation of the state results from the rule of one social class by the other. In contrast, I argue that people, using language, extend the distance of linguistic communication and hence expand their community. Then kinship is no longer the basis for the formation of the community. Instead, language begins to play a role. Language plays a role in almost all aspects of the genesis and growth of the state. Then people, using the same language, establish government, set up the system of property rights and hence build a market to exchange goods and services to realize the division of labor and create history, religion, law, literature and art as well as philosophy, and so on and so forth. The state emerges.

Second, humans, using language, create a variety of media in support of linguistic communication. Whenever or wherever they communicate using language, they use, at least, a medium. Without a medium, they are unable to perform linguistic communication. Thus, philosophically speaking, a medium, used in the process of linguistic communication, is an intrinsic part of linguistic communication though it takes the form of an exterior being. Originally, spoken communication alone only functions to support the formation of the society rather than the state. It is difficult to extend the distance of human-chain spoken communication over long distances. Human-chain spoken communication often only reaches a small number of people on a small scale. Such communication is only significant for the formation of the society. Linguistic communication is often for social intercourse. People communicate with one another for personal affairs. Thus each individual is not known across the state. He is only known by others in the community in which people usually keep in touch face-to-face. For example, he is known in his neighborhood. Linguistic communication is significant for the operation of the society, and information, sent through such linguistic communication, may not be controlled by a single person because of the fragmentation of society. The content, conveyed through human-chain spoken communication, is likely to vary if people perform such communication on a large scale. Thus written communication, able to realize long-distance communication without the variation of the content conveyed on a large scale, especially supports the formation of the monolithic state though it also strengthens linguistic communication within a society. That is, written communication, that uses a material medium that exists or moves between the two ends of the process of linguistic communication without affecting the conveyance of the content, represents the communication likely to reach all on a large scale, laying a foundation for the formation of the state. The reason that people, having created script, build the civilized society and hence the state is that written communication enables them to communicate more effectively on a large scale. Thus Paul Ricoeur writes that:

> Writing is much more than mere material fixation. We need only remind ourselves of some of these tremendous achievements. To the possibility of transferring orders over long distances without serious distortions may be connected the birth of political rule exercised by a distant state. This political implication of writing is just one of its consequences. To the fixation of rules for reckoning may be referred the birth of market relationships, therefore the birth of economics. To the constitution of archives, history. To the fixation of law as a standard of decisions, independent from the opinion of the concrete judge, the birth of the justice and juridical codes, etc. Such an immense range of effects suggests that human discourse is not merely preserved from destruction by being fixed in writing, but that it is deeply affected in its communicative function.[1]

Yet, spoken or written communication does not function independently after the appearance of written communication. People often perform written and spoken communication at the same time. Spoken and written communication may support each other. People, performing written communication, may perform spoken communication several times to remind someone of the fact that the related written communication is going on to send a message. People, performing spoken communication, may also perform written communication to corroborate the fact that the related spoken communication is going on to send a message or to prevent any distortion of the text conveyed in the process of spoken communication. For example, a law, promulgated in writing, may also be memorized by people in spoken communication or an unwritten law may be memorized by people in writing. Besides, behavior, displayed by people in communication, may function as a medium in support of linguistic communication. Consciousness may also play the similar role. Thus language presupposes a process of linguistic communication. Language always functions in conjunction with a medium. Language in use presupposes a process of linguistic communication in which a certain medium plays a part. Armed with a medium, language supports the growth of the state. Thus, we see that a medium in use is part of the process of linguistic communication in support of the formation of the state. Human being, material, behavior and consciousness are all media. All those media contribute to the formation and the building of the state. The state is a complex of media.

Third, philosophers think that language is a creature of human society. They believe that humans are social animals and language is created to meet the requirement of their association and collaboration and hence to meet the requirement of forming their community either in the form of the society or in the form of the state. They may even hold that language reflects the spirit of the society or the state built by a nation. Karl Vossler writes that:

> If a language, or a coherent group of languages, is examined as a relatively closed community, the student will find that all the other factors that are capable of founding and keeping together a human community, such as the landscape with its mountains, valleys, streams, roads, cities and deserts, politics, commerce, industry, the arts and sciences,

the churches and religions, *eo ipos* will contribute to the stream of language.[2]

He further writes that:

> Although language furthers and acts for the social intercourse and the communities of man, it has not got the power of founding a community by itself, nor of maintaining one. Language societies arise late, are impure, and unstable. Men first come together under the pressure of their natural needs, and only after these primitive, animal-like communities have been formed can language arise as an attempt at a spiritual transfusion and elevation of social existence. Language is neither root nor trunk, but flower and fruit of social life.[3]

My view is that environment and condition on one side and language on the other side interact. I stress the role of language in the formation and the growth of the state. Though human society comes into existence before the appearance of language, there is a difference between the primitive society and the civilized society. As far as the primitive society is concerned, language is indeed created in any way after the formation of the community in the primitive society. But language appeared before the formation of the community in the civilized society. Thus, in view of the formation of the state, language plays a pivotal role in the civilized society. Studying this role played by language is of philosophical significance. Studying this role is throwing a light on how humans form the state. Unlike the formation of a tribe, forming a state depends on language. Thus I argue that it is not because all factors, such as mountains, rivers, valleys, roads, cities, politics, commerce, industry, arts and science, contribute to the stream of language, but because all such factors appear due to the fact that humans use language significant for the formation of a state. Stones, clay tablets, woods, metals, paper and other media have been discussed by us in this manuscript. At least, the discussion of them in this manuscript can bear testimony to the very fact that they would not be processed or produced and used so that they could play a role in the formation of the state or any civilized community if humans do not communicate using language. This means that those materials would not play any role in the formation of the state if language did not come into use. Similarly, a behavior, demonstrated by people in communication in the state, is significant for the formation of the human community and even the building of the state because people use language. Behavioral communication in the tribe differs from the behavioral communication in the state. The former is primitive, whereas the latter civilized. A behavior, demonstrated by people in communication in the state, is a medium used by language. Such a behavior functions in support of the state when it serves as a medium used by language. Consciousness is another medium. As a medium, consciousness plays a role in the formation of the state, too. Though various consciousnesses initially result from linguistic communication, consciousness is also a medium used by language in the formation of the state. Thus the spirits of the state arise because humans use language. The spirits of the state stem from language rather than the fact that language reflects the spirits of the state. To put it differently, using language in communication is a reason for humans to depart from the tribes to advance toward the state. While humans keep on communicating using language, they create various media. These media transmit various kinds of information that help humans to understand the outside world as well as themselves. These media manifest their experience, intention, hope, desire, idea and belief. Then people build various spirits. All these further become the media for people to strengthen their mutual communication. Then people see the formation of the common interest, the formation of common values and the reinforcement of the solidarity of all. Language is the key to interpreting the dissolution of tribes and the formation of the state. Language appears first and spirits appear later. Language is the secret that humans advance from the primitive society to the civilized society and hence dissolve their tribes and build their states. Language is the mother of human civilization.

Fourth, language functions to extend the distance of communication. Then people dissolve their tribes and form their state. Extending the distance of communication is also extending the distance between one another within the community. But language only extends the physical distance between one another. Language does not extend the psychological distance between one another. Though language functions to help humans to form a large community, the psychological distance between one another can remain basically unchanged. Broadly speaking, people within the tribe feel close to each other. Likewise, people within the state can also feel close to each other if they perform linguistic communication that goes on across the state. In the process of linguistic communication people always avail themselves of all media. Certain organs of human bodies are naturally designed to perform communication. One organ tends to support the other if possible. For example, if one hears a real story and has a deep impression of the hero of the story, he may be tempted to go to see that hero with his own eyes. It is also arguable that after one reads a novel or watches a film about a real person, he will be interested in going to pay a visit to the hero of that novel or that film if that hero is still alive. One sort of perception needs to be supported by another sort. Indirect perception needs to be supported by direct perception. Even though a person obtains a piece of information indirectly and over long distances, he is not at a good psychological distance from the hero of the novel or the film. Otherwise this person will not be tempted to perceive the object both directly and indirectly. That is, after one obtains the related information in linguistic communication performed by using a certain medium, he is tempted to verify that information in the process without the support of that medium. The former is long-distance communication, whereas the latter short-distance communication. There is another case in point, too. This case is that after ordinary people read the novels of a famous novelist, they are strongly tempted to go to the hometown of that famous novelist in an attempt to meet that famous novelist. If that famous novelist has already passed away, they will be tempted to see the former residence of that famous novelist. The former residence of that famous novelist may become a tourist resort. Similarly, we can also argue that after ordinary people read the works of a renowned philosopher, they are strongly tempted to go to the hometown of that renowned philosopher in an attempt to meet that renowned philosopher. If that renowned philosopher has already passed away, they will be tempted to see the former residence of that renowned philosopher. For example, after a German gentleman reads the works of Karl Marx in Munich, he may be tempted to go to Trier to visit Karl Marx House. Likewise, I also argue that believers, reading the Bible, are strongly tempted to go on a pilgrimage to see God. As God has already died, they are tempted to see the birth place or the death place of God instead. So the birth place or the death place of

God is often visited by believers. It is the same for a prophet. For example, the believers of Islam may feel obligatory to go on a pilgrimage to Mecca to visit the birthplace of Muhammad. These examples show that people who are far from each other and hence have to perform written communication to communicate with each other over long distances are tempted to use another way to get closer to each other and hence to communicate with each other face-to-face. This means that even though people often perform long-distance communication and they are far from each other, the psychological distance between people may remain unchanged. This means that as long as people are able to perform effective linguistic communication in the state, they are still able to unite. Humans, using language, are able to build a large community such as a nation-state. Though people may not interact with each other face-to-face, they are still able to build one community.

Fifth, since humans commenced to use language, their relationship with the community built by them has been defined by language. The progress from the primitive society to the civilized society culminates in the fact that human relationship with the community is defined by language as a medium. Immediacy between one another has often disappeared because the interaction between one another now rests on language. The truthfulness of information conveyed by one to the other means, in some sense, the elimination of the obstacle of distance between one another. When humans stayed tribal people, they might acquire all information through visualization or a course of perception only. Such information was true because no falsification was possible. The conveyance of truthful information by using language has often replaced the original course of perception ever since. Knowing everything about the community is, however, no longer self-evident along with the extension of the distance of linguistic communication due to the fact that increasing the size of the community to make it a state results in the complexity of the community. Sometimes learning about the surrounding world becomes difficult, leading to the fact that people learn about their surrounding world in a dialogue between one another. Learning about the community is no longer learning about a small community, but a large one. People not only get first-hand information, but also seek second-hand information. People may also search for third-hand information. This is the reason that people provide information to each other. People also give interpretations. Then they disseminate knowledge and values. As they can gain the same knowledge and embrace the same values, they unite to build the state. Interpreting the management of public affairs also enhances people's understanding of public affairs in the state. This is a basis for the organization of the state. In addition, the attitude of people needs always to be expressed because their inclination, or disposition, or intention, or plan, needs to be revealed in realizing the positive interaction between one another. The original direct interaction between one another in the tribe is now replaced by the interaction realized by way of using language. People, realizing positive interaction, have to use language. Linguistic communication also serves as a condition for people to confer honor, to confirm loyalty and to voice support or opposition. In some sense people may not be able to reveal or clearly reveal their attitude without using language. But in the state people have to reveal such attitude clearly. People need to take collective action. They have to use language. Thus they unite though they are now in a large number and dispersed in a large area. As they are enabled to express attitude, they realize their own internal mutual interaction as meaningfully as before. Extending the distance of linguistic communication to the far reaches of the community does not affect people's mutual interaction as long as they can use media. So the increase in the number of them will not affect the mutual interaction of all either. The unity of the state may be as strong as that of the tribe. For example, people can expect the loyalty of one to the other. People then make promises to each other to ensure the certainty of their cooperation. Everything can be orderly. Everyone is aware of the action to be taken by all others if a promise is made. Speech always precedes action. Speech predicts the action and action confirms the speech. Speech and action cooperate with each other. An interaction cannot fail even though people are estranged from each other in so large a community like a state. If we argue that the state is organized under a command, such a command works because everyone knows the consequence to be borne if he fails to obey it. Such a command can be issued to all on a large scale. Between the organizer of the state and the organized, there is a process of powerful linguistic communication. Language is a proto-medium in the relationship between one person and another. Language is the mother of all other media. Language extends distance between one another, resulting in the fact that a change of quantity leads to a change of quality. Language is omnipresent and omnipotent. Language supersedes behavior as a chief medium in the mutual communication between one another. People create a wide variety of media in support of language. Thus language becomes decisive in the mutual interaction of people and the organization of the state. Language connects all because all use it. So language underpins the formation and the growth of the state.

Sixth, linguistic communication, performed by all with all, results in the formation of the common interest of all. It is true that the close blood relationship, or kinship, served as a basis for the formation of the common interest of all in the tribe. It is also true that using the same language serves as a basis for the formation of the common interest of all in the state. While people perform linguistic communication, they need each other. They interact with each other. Then considering and taking good care of the interest of each warrants the sustainability of such an interaction. Such a sustainable interaction leads to the formation of the common interest of all sooner or later. Linguistic communication proves that mutual need underlies the operation of linguistic communication between the two sides. Otherwise such linguistic communication can neither start nor continue if it has started. As both sides are needed, such linguistic communication must satisfy the expectation of each. Common interest takes shape between the two sides. If a public affair or a significant event is reported by news media to the citizens, it is supposed to be known by all within the state. Why is such a public affair or a significant event reported to all? This is because all need to know it. A public affair or a major event may affect the interest of each. The management of public affairs is interpreted or justified to all because it needs to be accepted by all. Interpreting the management of public affairs involves a process of linguistic communication needed by all. In the process of linguistic communication people give an interpretation. When an interpretation is given, it is done as if a question were asked in advance. In this case, one gives an interpretation at the request of those accepting the interpretation. The two sides cooperate with each other. If they do not cooperate with each other, no one will give an interpretation. This phenomenon is very significant particularly in the process of the mutual interaction between the government and the citizens. Besides, the attitude, such as support or opposition, needs to be fully demonstrated because the opinions of all need to be considered.

Promise is also a linguistic phenomenon pertaining to the formation of the common interest of all particularly in the interaction between a power holder and the masses. The fact that a crucial promise is made by the government and a crucial promise is also made by the citizens indicates the formation of the common interest. A law is invariably promulgated after it has been made. Its promulgation means the notification given to all within the state. The law is usually the rule accepted by all. The law is, in some sense, a contract made by all in advance and obeyed by all in the aftermath. All types of abovementioned linguistic communication display the fact that the side, inviting the other side to perform linguistic communication, and the side, accepting the invitation of performing linguistic communication, are equal in this process of linguistic communication. No side is unilaterally forced into this process of linguistic communication. Such a process is needed by both sides. If one side initiates a process of linguistic communication, the other side must, in reality, be invited to enter this process. In the interaction between the two sides the process of linguistic communication must be symmetrical. In history linguistic communication between the power holder and the masses might not be symmetrical. In medieval times the feudal ruler might also communicate with the peasants. But it was comparatively easy for the regime or the sovereign to issue a decree or to promulgate a law. In contrast, peasants found it difficult to express their opinions on the governance of the state. This is because it was difficult for plenty of peasants to gather to perform collective linguistic communication. In modern times a change takes place. In modern times citizens are enabled to express their opinions via news media or a demonstration or an election or a referendum. The power holder, elected by the voters, usually takes initiative to seek the opinions of the voters as he always needs support from the voters. Thus the law, or the government, protects various ways of displaying support or opposition. People see the formation of the common interest of all. The promise, made by the government to the masses or the promise, made by the masses to the government, shows the similar logic. People also make laws on the basis of the formation of the common interest of all.

Seventh, while we discuss the formation of the common interest of all that serves as a foundation for the building of the state, we also have to pay attention to the reason why linguistic communication can lead to the formation of common interest. The reason that linguistic communication can lead to the formation of common interest is that each person, as an individual, always offers a surplus value. He cannot use it up by himself. This value is usually in the form of competence. That is, a person is a biological entity that transforms energy from the earth. A person absorbs nutrition given by other biological entities on the earth. This means that he absorbs energy. He also provides energy to be consumed by him. For example, he gives off energy when he runs or walks. Then such energy is transformed to be competence. As a man absorbs energy, he is able to work. He has competence. Such competence cannot be used up by himself. Some competence, had by him, may be wasted if such competence is not used by others. Such competence is the surplus competence that has the surplus value. Since humans commenced to use language, it has become possible for people to cooperate with each other because a person can use the surplus value offered by another person. For example, when a man is in danger, he asks another man to help him. The man, providing the help, can do a special job. This man may save the life of the man asking for help. The surplus value of the man asked for help is used this time. Otherwise the surplus value is useless. We can also explain this principle by discussing other types of mutual interaction of people. The reason that people can engage in the division of labor, namely, cooperation, is that the surplus value provided by each can be used. The division of labor generates wealth as elaborated by Smith. The reason that the division of labor generates wealth is that one can use the surplus value offered by another person. The division of labor means exchanging the skills of production. Exchanging the skills of production is the continuity of exchanging values in another form because the competence of people can be diversified and the surplus value, offered by each on the labor market, can be used by any other person needing it. In addition, people offer their surplus value in the form of products. They may also offer the surplus value in another form. The exchange of surplus value may be in the form of exchanging ideas and knowledge. That is why people disseminate ideas, concepts, thoughts, discoveries, knowledge and beliefs among themselves. All such exchanges depend on the use of language. This is why the common interest of all takes shape in the process of linguistic communication. So I insist that linguistic communication leads to the formation of the common interest of all and the formation of the common interest of all leads to the formation of the state. If people did not have any common interest, they would not build their state. In addition, I should point out that the surplus value, discussed by me, is different from the surplus value discussed by Karl Marx in his work *Das Kapital*. The surplus value, discussed by Marx, is the surplus value created by the worker employed by an entrepreneur. Marx believed that only the worker creates a surplus value and the entrepreneur does not create any surplus value. My view is that both the worker and the entrepreneur create a surplus value. But this surplus value is not necessarily created in the relation of production but in the mutual interaction of two people. As long as two people interact with each other, they are likely to offer a surplus value to each other. Otherwise the mutual interaction between one another will not be sustainable. Thus, I argue that two sides create and offer the surplus value, and humans build their society or state on the basis of their mutual interaction. Their mutual interaction leads to the formation of the common interest of all instead of the formation of the common interest of a portion of people only. Thus the state is the community of all instead of the tool of the oppression of a portion of people by another portion of people. If people cannot realize the distributive justice in the society or the state, they can make an improvement. There is no need to change a state in order to change the scheme of distributing interest. The state is, basically speaking, a community due to the formation of the common interest of all.

Eighth, along with the formation of the common interest of the citizens, the citizens are often going to reach a consensus on the governance of the state or the management of a public affair. Mutual linguistic communication is essential. If any dispute arises between the majority and the minority in their expression of attitudes such as the attitude of support or opposition, or if there is any disagreement between the majority and the minority in their expression of opinions in a poll or during an election or a referendum or even in the public, they finally depend on the ruling of a third party, invisible or visible. The ruling of a third party always involves a process of linguistic communication. A dialogue goes on among three parties, namely, two parties involved in the dispute and the third party that rules on the dispute. This third party may be an invisible one. As there is a process of linguistic communication in which each side is willing to enter, all are cooperative. Thus we cannot simply claim that one side oppresses the other. Thus, discussing the nature of language, I also present a view about this issue because the formation of common interest often involves such a process. That is, as ruling on a dispute or disagreement between the majority and the minority often takes place under democracy, scholars are often puzzled and perplexed by the issue concerning the prevalence of the will of the majority over the will of the minority. For example, following any general election the minority may have to live under the presidency or premiership of someone they did not vote for or following any referendum the minority may have to live under a law or a policy or a decision endorsed by the outcome of the referendum in which their opinion has been turned down. Some scholars and thinkers used to question the rule by the majority. James Madison, a thinker and one of the famous politicians of the United States in early times, points out the adverse effect of factions in American Politics and writes that "When a majority is included in a faction, the form of popular government, on the other hand, enables it to sacrifice to its ruling passion or interest both the public good and the rights of other citizens."[4] Concerned with the omnipotence of the majority, Alexis de Tocqueville writes that:

> What is a majority, in its collective capacity, if not an individual with opinions, and usually with interests, contrary to those of another individual, called the minority? Now, if you admit that a man vested with omnipotence can abuse it against its adversaries, why not admit the same concerning a majority?[5]

He also states that:

> I regard it as an impious and detestable maxim that in matters of government the majority of a people has the right to do everything, and nevertheless I place the origin of all powers in the will of the majority. Am I in contradiction with myself?[6]

The issue, discussed by them, is sometimes called the issue of the "tyranny of the majority." In order to prove that the effect of the so-called tyranny of the majority is exaggerated because the building of the political system ensures the rights of the minority in democratic states such as the United States, Frank Newport writes that:

> As a result of the possibility that majorities might make decisions that oppress minorities, most democratic societies have built-in safeguards to avoid blatant legalized tyranny. In the United States, these include most notably the Bill of Rights and the power of the third branch of government, the judicial, to interpret the Constitution and to overrule laws that might oppress the minority or deprive citizens of basic rights.[7]

Albeit not completely concurring with Newport, Amartya Sen also fears that "a ruthless majority that has no compunction in eliminating minority rights would tend to make the society face a hard choice between honouring majority rule and guaranteeing minority rights."[8] My view is that although the freedom of speech and other freedoms as well as the judicial independence can be regarded as designed to protect the minority in this regard, the rule by the majority is hypothetical. When we mention the word "tyranny," we mean that one side uses coercion to impose its will on the other side. Interpreting the tyranny of the minority can be plausible because the tyranny of the minority often refers to the despotic rule by one man on behalf of a small group of people. When the minority imposes their rule on the majority, they have to use force. This means that though language may also be used, linguistic communication is not essential. Yet as far as the rule by the majority is concerned, it is displayed in a process of linguistic communication. Linguistic communication is essential in this case. As linguistic communication means the formation of the common interest of all involved in the linguistic communication, interpreting the tyranny of the majority this way is untenable. This situation actually indicates that prior to the realization of the rule by the majority, all make an agreement. Since people make such an agreement, the rule by the majority should be accepted by the minority. In other words, if there is a disagreement between the two sides both of which do not know which side will be the majority, each side decides to relinquish the right to decide on whether or not the opinion of its own should prevail. What prevails in such a decision is not the specific opinion of either side but the larger number of the votes cast by a randomly-formed side. If the will of the majority should be accepted as the will of the people, it is due to the requirement of the totality of the state. Tyranny denotes the cruel governance of the state. The majority actually do not act to govern. As Rousseau stated, "It is against the natural order for the many to govern and the few to be governed."[9] To express an opinion is not to govern. If governance becomes tyranny, the specific power holder should be responsible. Tyranny means that the tyrant imposes his own will on the people unilaterally and in his own interest only. That is, as the opinion of the larger number of the votes is supposed to reflect the public interest while the opinion of the smaller number of the votes is supposed to reflect the particular interest of each only, the rule by the majority is actually the ruling of a third party for the purpose of finding out the opinion that represents the largest number of the voters at a certain time. The reason that an election divides the voters into the majority and the minority is that the inclination of the voters needs to be found out. Without the opinion of the minority, there will be no opinion of the majority. As at least two political parties compete for state power, people realize the separation of powers between these two political parties across time. Then people need the ruling of a third party. In this regard, the rule of election functions as a third party ruling on the dispute. As we insist that the freedom of speech actually involves the ruling of a third party and the rule of law is also the ruling of a third party, as mentioned earlier, we also assert that the rule by the majority is analogous in nature to the freedom of speech and the rule of law. Conversely speaking, if people cannot realize such separation of powers across time between the two parties, they cannot realize the separation of powers between the ruling party and the opposition in the parliament. In other words, the opinion of the minority does not vanish after the election. The opposition, representing the opinion of the minority, checks the power of the ruling party. If a referendum is held, two camps compete against each other. These two camps are also often supported by two political parties respectively. As people may hold an election regularly and may hold different referenda from time to time, citizens, belonging to the minority, may have the equal chance or many chances to become part of the majority in future. Thus both the interest of the majority and that of the minority will always be taken care of since the power holders need to seek support from as many voters as possible. Party competition creates a mechanism of the checks and balances of powers between the majority and the minority. This represents truly the checks and balances of powers among the people. The rule by the majority is a way to allow for each voter of each side to have an equal chance to influence a decision. What determines the method of solving the dispute is not violence but language. Thus scholars should not regard the rule by the majority as the tyranny of the majority. On the contrary, it should be a procedure gone through for the realization of justice if the majority and the minority cannot totally agree. This justice is the procedural justice, which is a foundation for the establishment of political order. This political order is based on the checks and balances between the two political parties, or the majority and the minority supporting different political parties, across time. Tyranny is the rule of the state in which a portion of people, holding power, makes every effort to ensure their own perpetuity. That people change the power holder regularly and each voter has the equal chance to elect a person as the power holder at a certain period of time is not tyranny. That is, without a procedure to rule on a dispute, the people can never give expression to their will, and the nominal rule of the majority is rather the only major procedure to guard against tyranny. It is part of a procedure of checks and balances between two political camps designed to guard against the political incursion of any political camp. In the past some great philosophers held that democracy is not the best form of government or that democracy is the least bad form of government. They all believed that democracy has some shortcomings. Among them, the so-called tyranny of the majority is one. To me, this shortcoming does not exist. That is, voting resulting in the formation of the majority and the minority is a design to establish a system of the separation of powers between two or among more than two political parties. This design culminates in the fact that the ruling of an invisible third party takes shape.

Ninth, historically speaking, people rationalize the state step by step. Discussing the rationality of the state, we take it for granted that the rationalization of the state is beneficial to all within the state. All expect to rationalize the state. The key is rationalizing the state for all. This means that people rationalize the state for the good of all regardless of the particular background of each. In human history freedom, equality, peace, democracy and justice are sometimes only enjoyed by a portion of people within a state. In ancient times, freedom, equality, peace, democracy and justice, enjoyed by a portion of people, were conditioned by the slavery of another portion of people. For example, Athens was a city-state in which about ten thousand citizens, forming the city-state, were free and equal among themselves. They enjoyed peace and justice. When this state was under the despotic rule, it did not violate the interest of the citizens because citizens had privileges. But this city-state ruled over thirty thousand slaves including serfs called Helots. Aristotle, the greatest thinker of ancient times, did not think that there should be the equality between citizens and slaves. Jouvenel also writes that at Athens there were fifteen to twenty thousand citizens, as against four hundred thousand slaves. And the slavery was, even in the eyes of the philosophers, the condition of freedom. As they argued, a section of humanity had to be tools.[10] In some sense citizens enjoyed freedom at the expense of forcing those slaves to lose freedom. In the city-states citizens were equal politically among themselves. Among slaves there was also equality because they had nothing by themselves. Between citizens and slaves there was, however, no social equality at all. Citizens enjoyed democracy because they were not required to work all day. They let slaves work for them. Thus, people maintained ancient democracy because of a slave economy. Citizens enjoyed peace because they did not have to wage a war in order to decide who controlled the state. But there was no peace between the slave-owners and the slaves. Peace means cooperation between the two sides. At normal times slaves were prevented from revolting against the exploitation and oppression of the slave-owners because of fear and inability. But this does not mean the existence of peace between the slaves and the slave-owners because such "peace" does not mean the voluntary cooperation between the two sides. In other words, both sides must engage in cooperation on voluntary basis. The "peace" existing between the slaves and the slave-owners at certain time does not fulfill this condition. In medieval times only the ruling class enjoyed freedom. The state restricted the freedom of the ruled class, mostly composed of peasants, and they suffered under the feudal yoke. They were exploited and oppressed by nobility and clergy. Social inequality between different classes was evident. The state could not always guarantee peace because the masses sometimes revolted from the rule of the lords. The despotic rule of the monarch prevailed. No democracy existed. The state might realize limited justice because it began to set up law courts, but it did not fully realize justice because it had not completely established the rule of law. Along with the rise of capitalism in early modern times nation-states began to implement the principles of freedom, equality and democracy after the success of a series of revolutions in Europe and North America. Citizens began to enjoy freedom and democracy, but in a period of time only a portion of the citizens had voting rights. Universal suffrage was not granted to all eligible citizens until the twentieth century. Since then, people have largely realized peace in those states, but a civil conflict may break out between the upper class and the lower class. Those states have ameliorated social equality with the establishment of a social welfare system, but they have not realized complete social equality yet. People may not expect the realization of complete equality, but there is the room for the enhancement of social equality as market capitalism is prone to lead to the polarization of the society if the state does not take a special measure. This shows that the complete realization of justice relies on the final realization of social equality ideated by people.

Tenth, freedom, equality, peace, democracy and justice are five goals that, philosophically speaking, depend on and underpin each other. All of them have the relevance to one another. The interrelationship between one another is very complex. Basically speaking, freedom can be taken first and foremost as a standard whereby people measure if they can realize equality, peace, democracy and justice. Justice should be used finally as a standard whereby people measure if they have realized freedom, equality, peace and democracy. First, freedom and equality should go hand in hand. In history, Montesquieu opines that "In republican governments, men are all equal; equal they are also in despotic governments: in the former, because they are everything; in the latter, because they are nothing."[11] A despotic government deprives people of their freedom, but a republican government is supposed not to do so. This means that realizing freedom or equality rather than both is still far from the rationalization of state building. In today's liberal states freedom is stressed by people on the basis of a series of values upheld by people. The freedoms of various kinds are protected by the constitution. Social inequality still exists. Thus socialist states sometimes criticize the social inequality of the liberal states. Some even believe that freedom only allows for the bourgeoisie to gain upper hand in the governance of the state as the ruling class manipulates election. By contrast, realizing social equality is the aim of the policies of the socialist states. But these states restrict the freedom of the citizens because they are placed under the strict economic and social control of the government. In the meantime, freedom and peace should go hand in hand. In history making peace means restricting freedom in the state ideated by Hobbes. Thus, in order to establish order, the state sometimes keeps the despotic rule. In this regard the state ignores the freedom of the citizens. Thus, liberal ideology insists on realizing both peace and freedom. Coercion and violence are counter-productive. Freedom and democracy should also go hand in hand. If people realize freedom, but fails to realize democracy, such a situation may not last over the long term. And freedom should also go hand in hand with justice. If people cannot realize freedom, they cannot realize justice completely. Second, equality and peace should go hand in hand. If people fail to realize social equality, they may be dissatisfied with this situation. Class struggle may still rage. During the French Revolution, those who hoped to realize social equality resorted to violence. The scheme of distribution should ensure that people realize equality or nobody ends up worse off. If distribution does not display the spirit of equality, some people must be forced to obey the decision. Thus as Johan Galtung writes, "if enforcement becomes a major way of obtaining normative compliance, by using direct violence, then we are certainly not creating peace."[12] Equality and democracy should go hand in hand. For example, the state implements the principle of one man one vote. This symbolizes equality. If people fail to implement this principle, democracy should be flawed. Equality and justice should also go hand in hand. Usually, realizing equality means realizing justice if the state does not restrict freedom at the same time. Third, peace and democracy should go hand in hand. If people realize peace, they should also realize democracy. If they fail to realize democracy, peace is not genuine, or is not stable or sustainable. People should realize peace and justice at the same time. Sometimes making peace means realizing justice because under the circumstances of peace, we suppose that plunder, robbery, theft and others do not exist. People realize limited justice when they make peace. Fourth, democracy and justice should also go hand in hand. If democracy is absent, justice may not be realized by the despotic rule because despotic rule means the conflict of interest in relation to the power holder. Usually people cannot realize justice unless the state implements the rule of law. The state, putting into practice the rule of law, needs democracy. The historical process of realizing these five goals in succession may throw light on this case. That is, in the great pageant of history people usually tried to realize peace and limited justice in the outset. The despotic state in the ancient times belongs to such a case. Later states first realized freedom and then realized democracy. Some states realized freedom and democracy simultaneously. The historical transition from the rule of absolutist monarchy to the polity of freedom and democracy in Great Britain in early modern times may belong to such a case. Some states witnessed the process in which people realized equality at the expense of losing freedom. In the years immediately following the French Revolution the state stressed equality, yet it could not ensure freedom because the government insisted on its despotic rule albeit with a revolutionary ideal. As de Tocqueville writes, "They had sought to be free in order to make themselves equal. But in proportion as equality was established by the era of freedom, freedom itself was thereby rendered more difficult to attain."[13] In the former Soviet Union people realized equality of some kind through the establishment of a communist system that emphasized the fair distribution of income. However, the planned economy that kept this system restricted the freedom of citizens. History seems to indicate that the sequence of realizing these five goals should be that peace and limited justice should be realized first. Then freedom and democracy should be realized. Equality should be realized last. If humans intend to change this sequence or historical procedure, they will encounter man-made calamity. If people seek freedom and democracy first without peace and justice, the society will be in disorder or in the state of anarchy. This is the situation that philosophers make every effort to avoid. Such freedom and democracy become meaningless as a result. If people seek equality first without freedom and democracy, they will be subject to the rule of despotism or totalitarianism. If they seek equality first without the maintenance of peace, they ensure no procedural justice. Under these circumstances, people cannot realize genuine justice. In other words, if people forge equality by way of violence, there is no procedural justice. In this case people may not guarantee distributive justice. De Tocqueville once complains that:

I do not think there is a single country in Europe where the progress of equality has not been preceded or followed by some violent changes in the status of property and of persons, and almost all these changes have been accompanied by much anarchy and license, because they have been brought about by the least self-controlled part of the nation in opposition to its most orderly members.[14]

The result of the communist practice of some East European or Asian states in the twentieth century also exemplifies this case. One cannot skip any stage of this historical procedure. In advanced states it is still difficult to realize complete equality. Freedom and equality are sometimes in conflict with each other. Discussing the relationship between freedom and equality in the British House of Commons, Donald D. Searing writes that:

During the age of democratic revolutions equality and freedom were allies in a struggle for political rights. More recently, issues have shifted to social and economic ground where Socialists push hard for equality while freedom becomes increasingly identified with defending the status quo; contemporary conflicts often pit the one against the other. Many Socialists still have a high regard for Freedom, particularly as it applies to conscience issues of censorship and morality. But, when forced to choose, they opt for Social Equality as relatively more desirable.[15]

If people realize equality without affecting the realization of peace, freedom, democracy and justice, observers may admit that people have completely realized justice. That is the ideal state of rationalizing state-building. In sum, the ideal state is the one in which people have realized all these five goals. But they have to realize these goals one by one rather than realizing all of them at the same time and at one fell swoop.

Notes

1. Paul Ricoeur, *Interpretation Theory: Discourse and the Surplus of Meaning* (Fort Worth, Texas: The Texas Christian University Press, 1976), 28.

2. Karl Vossler, *The Spirit of Language in Civilization*, translated by Oscar Oeser (London: Routledge & Kegan Paul, Ltd, 1951), 186.

3. Ibid., 187.

4. Please see: *American State Papers* (Chicago: Encyclopaedia Britannica, Inc., 1952), 51.

5. Alexis de Tocqueville, *Democracy in America*, translated by George Lawrence (New York: Harper Perennial, 1988), 251.

6. Ibid., 250.

7. Frank Newport, *Polling Matters: Why Leaders Must Listen to the Wisdom of the People* (New York: Warner Books, 2004), 82.

8. Amartya Sen, *The Idea of Justice* (Cambridge, Massachusetts: The Belknap Press of Harvard University Press, 2009), 352.

9. Jean Jacques Rousseau, *Social Contract* (Chicago: Encyclopaedia Britannica, Inc., 1952), 411.

10. Bertrand de Jouvenel, *On Power: Its Nature and the History of Its Growth*, translated by J. F. Huntington (Boston: Beacon Press, 1967), 323.

11. Charles de Secondat, Baron de Montesquieu, *The Spirit of Laws*, translated by Thomas Nugent (Chicago: Encyclopaedia Britannica, Inc., 1952), 34.

12. Johan Galtung, *Peace by Peaceful Means: Peace and Conflict, Development and Civilization* (London: Sage Publications, 1996), 63.

13. De Tocqueville, *Democracy in America*, 689.

14. Ibid.

15. Donald D. Searing, *A study of Values in the British House of Commons*, in Milton Rokeach (ed.), *Understanding Human Values* (New York: The Free Press, 1979), 173.

Epilogue

The approach, adopted by me in the study of the genesis and growth of the state in this monograph, differs from the methods used by the forerunning scholars studying the origin of the state. I accentuate the role of language. My basic view is that language itself is a proto-medium in human communication. Language extends the distance of human communication. Language makes possible the creation of various media. Language, supported by those media, plays a role in an increase in the size of every human community. This evolution leads to the dissolution of the tribes and the formation of the state. In a nutshell, extending the distance of linguistic communication is a process in which a qualitative change takes place along with a quantitative change. This qualitative change is the very fact that the state is no longer dependent on the functioning of kinship that is a basic element of the formation of the tribe. As now kinship discontinues playing a role in the formation of the community large in population and area, language plays a crucial role in the growth of the state. On the basis of this thinking, I have presented a proposition of language about the birth and growth of the state. If we feel interested in probing the role of language in the growth of the state further, I think that we can consider the following three aspects. To me, these three aspects will unfold a promising prospect for working on this proposition further.

First, humans extend the distance of communication by using language. Extending the distance of communication underpins the development of the division of labor. Unlike the fact that there was no formal division of labor in any tribe that might keep on enhancing productive forces of the tribe and supporting the development of the tribe, the development of the division of labor serves as a basis for the enhancement of productive forces within the state and the development of the state. The division of labor is usually realized on a scale large enough. This division of labor relies on a community that takes form due to extending the distance of linguistic communication. Discussing the division of labor in economic domain, Adam Smith writes that "As it is the power of exchanging that gives occasion to the division of labour, so the extent of this division must always be limited by the extent of that power or, in other words, by the extent of the market."[1] As noted earlier in this book, he exemplifies this case by pointing out that some industries can be carried on nowhere but in a great town. A porter, or a butcher, or a baker, or a brewer, or a carpenter, or a mason, in the countryside like the Highlands of Scotland can scarcely afford him a constant occupation. As the village is small, the market demand is low. This situation hampers the development of the division of labor.[2] According to this theory, we can believe that along with the growth of the market, the division of labor will develop. Various occupations, mentioned by Smith, will certainly appear due to the expansion of the economy on a large scale.

Similarly, building a human community always gives importance to its security because people need to protect the wealth they have created in production. The defense of the community is dependent on the development of the division of labor, too. In pre-modern times the defense of the community might depend on those who routinely engaged in agricultural production. The soldiers, called upon by the ruler of the state to combat in the battlefield, were also peasants or farmers. Yet if the community grows to be large enough, the division of labor in this domain may develop. Though I have mentioned in my previous book that in some European countries in early modern times extending suffrage to the ordinary citizens proved, in some sense, to be a method utilized by the authorities to mobilize the citizens to join the army, to build a standing army and to establish modern national defense because the grant of voting right to the citizens led to the formation of the common interest of all in the state, the growth of a large community, allowing for the development of the division of labor, should also be a reason for the emergence of professional military personnel and the building of a standing army of the state. As Jack Goody writes, "The specialization in war leads to the emergence of the military in the shape of the standing army."[3]

The development of the division of labor also occurs in the governance of the state. Specifically, the personnel, in charge of the administration of the community, are not many in a small community. The earliest personnel, in charge of governing a small state, might not be professionals. The earliest rulers in human history might include the head of a group of nomads or the head of a group of farmers. They had certain basic skills of governing the state, but they learned these skills in practice. They governed the state according to their own direct experience. The administrators, engaged by the ruler, were not professional in the outset either. The team of administrators was formed very often by those who stayed in touch with the ruler face-to-face. For example, in ancient times the administrators of a feudal state were often the personal retainers of the ruler. The administrators of the state were sometimes just the court servants of the ruler. The team of the administrators took form in the principle of forming a society. The ruler appointed administrators because the ruler knew them personally. The ruler and these people might be friends or relatives. However, along with an increase in the size of the state in modern times, the government needs many personnel of administration in governing the state. The government is unable to find and recruit these personnel through the limited social intercourse of the power holder. They have to be found by recruiting talents from the labor market. Those talents may be required to pass an examination. In its growth, the government also needs to enhance the standard of governing the state and it needs especially trained personnel to govern the state. The government sets up a civil service system. Establishing a civil service system is a process of professionalizing administration. This is part of the development of the division of labor in modern times.

Lawmakers are also assumed to be the governors of the state in a certain context. In early times, the law was made by some unknown people on behalf of the society. This society was a small community. Those who made the law were not professional jurists. They might be the elders of the local community or the folk society. They might be involved in governing the community, but they might not be professionals. As the community was very small in size and hence the output of production was low, the community could not especially afford to engage a professional to draft a law. In some cases ordinary people were invited to participate in the making of a law. For example, in ancient Rome some ordinary people were chosen by the ruler to participate in the making of a law. But these people were not professional lawmakers. Yet along with an increase in the size of the state, increasing the size of the state over the long term needs people to govern the state in a professional way. Thus the state employs jurists to draft the law. For example, in nowadays the parliament takes charge of making laws. However, the parliament which is about to make a law usually invites jurists to draft the law for it.

Judges become professional, too. In a traditional folk society in the past a law was unwritten. This law was the customary law or case law. The judges were the elders of the community. After a verdict was awarded, there was no organ to enforce the law. The law was enforced by the society, usually a group of people who were the relatives and friends of the party that won the lawsuit. Since the growth of the state, people have begun to govern the state in a professional way. The state appoints professional judges and sets up law courts enforcing laws. This is because along with the growth of the state, the cases, needing to be dealt with and heard, increase in number. Then the state engages professional judges to hear those cases and sets up courts to enforce laws. Financial sources are also available in support of the operation of the judicial branch.

If we assume that in the outset the human society was self-organized, the establishment of various other government bodies in modern times also means the development of the division of labor. Some people are those who especially govern the state. Hans Kelsen once writes that "Legal independence of parliament from the people means that the principle of democracy is, to a certain extent, replaced by that of division of labor."[4] I think that his comment can apply to all branches of the government.

If we look into the development of culture in any human community, we may also find the similar situation. There is also the division of labor in the development of culture. As early as the times of the primitive society, people already created certain forms of art to manifest their feelings and to disseminate their ideas. For example, Europeans who arrived at the New Continent after the Great Discovery of Columbus found that Indians, or Indigenous peoples of Central America, or South America, had created their own cultures. For example, the humans of the primitive society in those regions created murals and stone sculptures. When Europeans stepped on the Continent of North America, Australia and Africa for their overseas adventure, they also found that peoples in those continents could create some artistic works such as wooden sculptures. But people usually create very good artistic forms, demonstrating clearly a humanistic spirit, in the civilized society. This is because people usually organize the civilized society as a state, a large community, that creates a condition for people to realize the division of labor on a large scale. Then, along with the growth of the community, there appears a condition for some people to get trained to become professional artists to serve many people as a career. For example, only professional painters create masterpieces. The state may also establish art academies to cultivate professional artists. Some people may even engage in teaching art in an art academy as a career.

There is a similar case in the development of literature. When humans remained tribal people, it was very difficult to create literary works. The number of the members of a tribe was comparatively small, and a professional, especially trained to create literary works such as poems as a career, could hardly emerge. Homeric poems are said to have been created by Homer, a blind poet of ancient Greece. However, as script did not come into use, or did not come into use widely, by that time among Greeks, literary works were rare. There was no wide array of literary works. Ushering in the era of civilization, people increase the size of the community and there emerge some geniuses creating literary works. If people reside in an isolated region such as a mountainous region, they may form a folk society. They create folk literature. Yet they may not be professional writers. Though they create some literary works, they also engage in some other careers to make a living. Only those professional writers who create their works as a career in a nation-state in modern times create the literary works that show professional level and perhaps a humanistic spirit. These professional writers usually emerge in the state, particularly in the nation-state, a large community.

Likewise, it is also arguable that people can hardly see a professional historian, chronicling history, in a small community. A small community hampers the development of the division of labor because there is hardly a market for the exchange of goods and services. This small community cannot afford to engage a professional historian. Therefore, few people learn about history in a community small in population. This community does not give high value to history. Conversely speaking, the growth of a community will give high value to history because plenty of people need to learn about history. In the meantime the community, growing large, can also afford to employ a good historian to write history. This is the reason that people create their history.

Similarly, a small community does not need someone to create philosophy. Though people need ideas, they may not need systematic ideas. This is mainly because people, forming a small community, are not many. If they genuinely need philosophy, the value of philosophy should be low because the philosophy can only serve a small number of people. Along with an increase in the size of this community, however, people, forming the community, increase in number. Many people now need philosophy. Then philosophy increases its value due to the fact that it is now needed by plenty of people. Market demand surges. Then the community can afford to engage a philosopher to create philosophy as a professional.

So we come into conclusion that humans extend the distance of linguistic communication and increase the size of the community. The community, growing large, gives larger scope to the development of the division of labor. Then, professionals emerge. Then it follows that culture flourishes.

Second, people extend the distance of linguistic communication, laying a foundation for increasing the size of the government. Extending the distance of linguistic communication not only leads to the steady growth of the state but also necessitates the expansion of the government. As now people from all areas are able to communicate with one another directly or indirectly, they submit to the government that controls a vast territory and a large population. This trend forces the government to undergo a change. The government in the outset organized the state on the basis of social intercourse. The government was organized by acquaintances. It served mainly the interest of the ruler because the regime was usually set up by the ruler in the beginning. This is why in the beginning the ruler ruled the state by way of conquest. The regime was, in the main, organized according to the need of the ruler. The regime was organized like a social organization under the rule of the ruler. But everything has two sides. As far as the organization of the regime is concerned, the regime needed to serve the interest of the ruler indeed. But at the same time the regime was also required to serve the interest of ordinary people across the state because the regime, governing a very large community, was also required to serve the interest of ordinary people to a varying extent in order to gain ruling legitimacy. Language has dictated this trend ever since.

Specifically, people, having created language, naturally extend the distance of linguistic communication step by step. Then people begin to communicate across the frontiers of different regions. They need to engage in economic cooperation or to disseminate a religious belief, for example. People may develop transportation and communication. It becomes easier for the government to govern the state than before. Thus the masses naturally require the government to take more responsibilities of public administration and to expand the scope of public administration as well. So E.N. Gladden tells us that after Industrial Revolution during which steamed engine was invented railways were constructed in England. Then he writes that:

> This revolutionary extension of the basic communications network of modern societies greatly widened the effective scope of administrative activity, at the same time increasing the responsibilities of public administration and causing it to reach out for new means of fulfilling its new duties.[5]

In the meantime people form the mass society. Then public opinion takes form, pressing for the provision of public services. In ancient times public opinion might take the form of folk song or ballad. In modern times public opinion may be formed due to reports given by mass media including newspaper. Then the regime tends to increase public services. The regime turns to be the government. Particularly, the ruler who rules a large country has gained huge wealth. This wealth can never be consumed up by the ruler himself all his life. Then the ruler may allocate certain wealth to ordinary people. This time he may do something for his people. He may provide certain public services to the masses. This is because by serving the masses, the power holder can get some honor. An honor is sought by the ruler. This is due to the nature of the ruler. The ruler usually has some basic desires. The ruler has the desire for wealth. The ruler has the desire for power. The ruler also has the desire for honor. No ruler does not seek honor in human history. Bertrand Russell once writes that "Of the infinite desires of man, the chief are the desires for power and glory."[6] The "glory" said by him can be construed as the honor discussed by us here. Yet, as I mentioned earlier, if we study the origin of honor, we may also find that the origin of honor in human society is due to extending the distance of linguistic communication. In the beginning tribal people formed the tribe due to kinship. Kinship functioned to adjust and harmonize the relationship between one member and another. There was, in general, no honor. But since humans extended the distance of linguistic communication, they have built a large community. Kinship becomes defunct. Some people give honor and some other people get honor in this community. The reason is that tribal people did not require repayment if one person did some work for the other. If a father took care of his son, he did not request repayment. If his son helped him, his son did not request repayment. But a change takes place when people become the citizens of a state. As a person usually does not link with any other person because of kinship, a person usually requests repayment if he works for, or provides service to, another person. But there is also such a situation in which a person or a few are unable to give repayment after another person does some work or provides certain service. This is because humans vary in competence in human society. Some people are very competent, whereas others are not. Some competent people are very clever. Some other competent people are physically strong. If a competent person does some work for an incompetent person, the latter may be unable to give any repayment. Then an honor may be given instead. The honor is sometimes like thanks given by one person or a collective being. Thus, as an honor is so dear and it is loved by people, that honor encourages those competent people to continue making contributions to the society or the state. Similarly, if a ruler is positioned to govern the state well, the masses may give an honor to the ruler in exchange for the contributions made by the ruler. The larger the population, the more the honor that may be given to this ruler. When describing the monarchical government, Montesquieu points out the role of honor. He states that "Honour sets all the parts of the body politic in motion, and by its very action connects them; thus each individual advances the public good, while he only thinks of promoting his own interest."[7] This means that an honor plays a special role in the domain of organizing the state. For this phenomenon, I should say that the extension of linguistic communication in support of the formation of the state underpins a change in the method of organizing the human community. The appearance of honor goes hand in hand with the formation of the state larger than a tribe because both the genesis of honor and the formation of the state are based on extending the distance of linguistic communication.

Though people, usually, or often, form the state because of the conquest of the conqueror in the outset, after the conqueror becomes the ruler, he is also required to serve the masses. So in history Napoleon not only made every effort to keep the power of ruling France but also sought the grandeur of France. He codified civil law for the French people. He made several attempts to expand the territory of France by launching wars against other neighboring countries on European Continent. Although he wanted to increase his power, he also hoped to gain an honor. If he demonstrated the grandeur of France, he might gain some personal honor given by the French people. So as told by Bertrand de Jouvenel, when talking with Caulaincourt, Napoleon sincerely articulated that "People are wrong in thinking me ambitious—I am touched by the misfortunes of peoples; I want them to be happy and, if I live ten years, the French will be happy."[8] If the French people felt happy, they would certainly give an honor to their leader. Likewise there were some other well-known rulers like Napoleon in this certain aspect or in that certain aspect in history who committed the same or similar act for their countries in order to gain an honor. Peter the Great of Russia in history may also be such a historical figure. They hoped to do something that could finalize their historical position. Their act was aimed at gaining a certain honor at the same time. Thus de Tocqueville comments that:

> When the world was under the control of a few rich and powerful men, they liked to entertain a sublime conception of the duties of man. It gratified them to make out that it is a glorious thing to forget oneself and that one should do good without self-interest, as God himself does.[9]

Accordingly, it is arguable that the ruler, having built the state, may consider giving or increasing public services in order to gain an honor. Thus the regime may give more public services to the masses. The government is established or the government is expanded to realize this goal instead of satisfying the need of the ruler only. In the meantime, following the formation of the mass society, the masses demand more public services from the government and even pressure the government to engage in the political reform for the modernization of the government. Then there appear many changes to the shape of the government. These changes are mainly as follows.

The first change is that the ruler usually has a team governing the state. This team is organized by the ruler himself in the outset. This team is small in size. As Wolfram Fischer and Peter Lundgreen write that:

> At the beginning of the seventeenth century, English central government agencies employed between 1,400 and 2,000 officials. Some hundred customs officials, administrators of Crown lands and local administrators, e.g., Clerks of Justices of Peace, have to be added. At the same time there were about 650 senior officials in the central French government and 3,000 to 4,000 provincial administrators alone in Normandy. The government of Castile had about 530 *major* posts, and it is said to have employed 60,000 subordinates of its Exchequer and 20,000 in the Inquisition.[10]

The members of this team were usually those retainers or the friends of the ruler. They were actually the court servants of the ruler. They might also include the servants of the servants of the ruler. For example, in medieval England, public officials were "servants of the crown and not of a particular minister."[11] As Jos C.N. Raadschelders writes, "At first the civil servant was a *personal servant* of a lord. They were small in number and provided strictly personal and clerical services."[12] As these servants were not large in number, they might not be professional. This is because the team of governing the state was small and what was important was the personal relationship between the ruler and the servants as well as the personal relationship between the servants and the servants of the servants. Thus the ruler might not stress professional standard. Servants or the servants of the servants might be semiprofessional. This means that the original purpose of the conqueror is to hold as much property, including territory, as possible. Yet since the establishment of the regime, the ruler has also needed to meet the basic requirements in governing the state. The ruler needs ruling legitimacy. The ruler even contrives to get honor by being committed to excellence in governing the state. If a ruler rules the state without ruling legitimacy, the ruler will need to use coercion to suppress the masses who are dissatisfied. Suppressing the masses will not bring any honor to the ruler. The regime needs to provide certain basic services to the ruled. A change takes place in the nature of the state. That is, in the outset the state was almost the possessions of the ruler. But later the state belonged seemingly to both the ruler and the ordinary people. So Raadschelders opines that "Even during the heyday of absolutist rule in the seventeenth and eighteenth centuries, wherein the king embodied sovereignty, the king could no longer say that the territory he ruled was his possession."[13] Then the regime recruits a large number of public employees to work for the government that now turns to paying attention to the necessity of serving the people in modern times. Then it follows that public employees, very large in number, are recruited through the labor market. They have to meet the requirement of professional standard. They may be required to pass an examination. Because of this we further see that as they are large in number, it gradually becomes difficult for them to establish any personal relationship with the ruler or the supreme power holder. If there is any relationship between a public employee and an employer, such relationship gradually much more looks like the relationship between the public employee and the state. Public employees are gradually required to be ultimately loyal to the state. As a result, the emergence of civil service becomes part of the reform of the government.

The second change is that the government expands. In the outset the influence of kinship existed in the organization of the state, but this influence faded along with an increase in the size of the state. In the period of Warring States in ancient China, the king of each kingdom feoffed lands to his relatives. After the First Empire unified all lands conquered into one empire, he revoked the practice of feoffing lands after a heated debate in the ruling group, believing that that way of organizing the state by feoffing lands to the ruler's relatives endangered the unity of the state because princes or their offspring often revolted against the ruler. He set up provinces and counties. An administrative system took shape. The ruling power was no longer granted to those who had kinship ties. Kinship no longer functioned in support of the organization of the state. The unity of the state was going to be underpinned by an administrative system set up across the state due to extending the distance of communication. Then the government bodies of the higher level issued orders and the government bodies of the lower level submitted reports. The common interest took shape among the ruling group not due to kinship but due to the cooperation between the ruler and the officials as well as among the officials of all levels. In the West, in ancient times or medieval times except the times of ancient Rome, the state never had its territory larger than the area in which the ruler exercised control by means of his own household. The territory was subdivided into smaller units governed by the representatives of the sovereign. The task of operating the state was also assigned to the representatives of local areas. For example, Charlemagne divided his empire into counties and markcounties at the regional level and built upon the existing local communities for the construction of a local government. This territorial division was not matched with a functional division. Administration was the business of the ruler's household.[14] The specific situation is that in medieval times the state often took the form of kingdom if it was not an empire or a principality. People did not set up adequate organs for the governance of the state in all aspects. The king was usually the largest lord among many lords who ruled their lands by themselves. The king kept the relationship of contract with other lords. If the society needed any public services, these public services might even be subcontracted by lords or some other people. For example, some tasks of security were subcontracted to local knights. At that time the ruler was aided by a royal council, a collegial advisory body, consisting of members of clergy and aristocracy. But later this situation changed. As the government was expected to increase public services provided to the masses in late medieval times or early modern times, the government needed to establish certain departments in charge of providing certain public services. In England or France field administration developed. In the twelfths and thirteenth centuries bailiffs were created in England and France. The authorities needed to strengthen their control across the state in the derogation of the power of feudal lords. In early modern times government was further centralized in Britain, France and Prussia. As the government took more and more tasks of managing public affairs, functional differentiation appeared. The departmentalization of the government commenced, meeting the necessity of building a network of administrative units implementing laws and delivering policies and programs. Thus the government has been growing in size since early modern times.

A case in point is the growth of the government departments of Great Britain. More or less like any other regime established in Europe in medieval times, the central administration of Britain in medieval times was composed of the committees of the medieval king's councils which were directly responsible to the ruling monarch. For example, after the restoration of Charles II in 1660 boards and committees used to administer key functions such as revenue collection and the Navy. Yet as the government needed to function widely along with the passage of time, departmentalization began. By the eighteenth century some committees had become the boards and committees functioning like departments because the tasks of the government increased. In the late eighteenth century and early nineteenth century some boards further acquired the characteristics of ministries because power and responsibility became concentrated in the hands of a minister responsible to Parliament.[15] In medieval times there were only two departments, namely, the Northern Department and the Southern Department. But from late eighteenth century onward after the dissolution of the aforementioned departments more new offices and departments had emerged. Apart from the fact that the Treasury undertook more tasks in the nineteenth century and the twentieth century, the Ministry of Labour was created in 1916. Department of Agriculture and Fisheries, Department of Transport and Department of Health were established in 1919. Department of Education and Science was formed in 1964. Department of Trade and Industry was created in 1970. In the meantime, Prime Minister's Office grew in the twentieth century after the post of Prime Minister came into being in the eighteenth century. Foreign Office was formed on the basis of the original Northern Department in 1782. This organ and other organs merged later and the Foreign and Commonwealth Office, a department in charge of foreign and overseas affairs, was formed in 1968. War Office was set up in 1854. This organ became the Ministry of Defence in 1964.[16]

Though the United States was founded on the basis of the making of a constitution and this state was not initially organized in the principle of social organization but in the principle of organizing the state, the growth of the government in size also clearly indicates that as the nature of the state dictates that the state ultimately needs to serve all forming the state, the state gradually expands the scope of public services provided by it. The departmentalization of the executive branch of the federal government of the United States is also a case in point. The specific situation is that after the constitution of the United States went into operation in 1789, three departments, namely, Department of State, Department of Treasury and Department of War, were established. The Department of Navy was established in 1798. The work of the executive branch of the federal government was mainly focused on diplomacy, finance and national security then. Later the scope of governing the state needed to expand. The administration of the federal government gradually took the responsibilities of domestic security, economic management and various social services. More departments, having the Cabinet status, were set up one after another. So the Department of Interior was established in 1849 and Department of Justice was established in 1870. The Department of Agriculture was established in 1862 and Department of Commerce and Labor was established in 1903. When Department of Labor was established, the responsibility of labor service originally given to the Department of Commerce and Labor was transferred to this new department. In 1953, Department of Health, Education and Welfare was established. Department of Housing and Urban Development, Department of Transportation and Department of Energy were established in 1965, 1966 and 1977 respectively. Then Department of Education was set up to assume the responsibility of education that was originally belonged to the Department of Health, Education and Welfare established in 1953. In 1989 Department of Veterans Affairs was set up to assume the responsibility of veterans administration.

The third change is that in early times in history the finance of the state was actually the finance of the ruling family. The main responsibility of the authorities at that time was to manage the family. The primary function of the authorities was to maintain the living of the ruler's family and dependents. The budget of the state was made mainly for the operation of the ruling family. If taxes were levied, the levy of the taxes was often exceptional. For example, taxes were especially levied because of the outbreak of a war. The kinds of taxes were not many either. This is mainly because the state was organized in the principle of organizing the society at that time. The influence of kinship had not faded totally. The ruler did not perform many duties in the operation of the state. This case can be shown by the history of public administration of Sumer, Egypt, Babylon, Persia, Rome, Byzantium and China. Yet as the ruler ruled the state, the tasks, needed to be taken by the authorities in governing the state, also, objectively, increased steadily. As the ruler was also motivated by the sense of honor to govern the state and an increase in the wealth owned or possessed by the ruler also depended on the growth and the prosperity of the state, the ruler gradually turned to governing the state in the principle of organizing the state. The influence of kinship in the organization of the state commenced to fade. Then the ruler not only needed to maintain the ruling status of the ruling family in the state, but also needed to build the state that provided public services to the masses. It follows that the state, taking charge of managing the public affairs of the state, expanded the budget. The authorities formulated the budget gradually in need of the operation of the state to a greater extent. The levy of taxes became frequent. The levy of taxes was gradually aimed at the building of the state to a greater extent. Then taxation became a normal operation of the government. Parliament was established to help the authorities to levy taxes. Parliament could also be used by the king to seek support from ordinary people in the derogation of the power of nobility. In England like some other European countries the sovereign sought support from the burghs. So Smith writes that as the sovereign could impose no tax on cities, the sovereign called upon them to send deputies to the general assembly of the state, where they could join with the clergy and the barons in granting, upon urgent occasions, some extraordinary aid to the king. These deputies were employed by the sovereign as a counterbalance in the assembly to the authority of the great lords. This is the origin of the representation of burghs in all great monarchies in Europe.[17] This indicates that the state's taxation gradually developed and came to serve as a foundation for the formation of public finance because this time levied taxes were usually not used for the ruling family but for the state. So in England Henry VII (1485-1509) improved financial administration. Public affairs of the king, different from the private affairs of the king, appeared. Then it follows that under the Tudor rule, the central government took shape. The government was absolutist. "Under the Tudor rule the government was firmly in the hands of the King; royal authority and popular consent had been successfully combined."[18] Later in the sixteenth century Parliament took the initiative to impose taxes. As Rudolf Braun writes,

> The Crown had neither sufficient sources of income nor borrowing power to support an adequate military force. It was the Parliament which imposed contributions and a variety of taxes, collected customs, and sequestered property

of the royalists and the Crown in order to maintain a navy
and organize a standing army.[19]

The origin of state taxation shows a process in which public finance gradually took shape. In the past the state belonged to the ruling family. Later the
ruling family belonged to the state.

In sum, extending the distance of linguistic communication served as a
foundation for the growth of a large human community such as a nation-
state. A nation-state, as a large community, needed public finance and public
finance called for democracy. That is, since the extension of the distance of
linguistic communication, the state has been organized in the principle of
organizing the state instead of the principle of organizing the society. As a
result, public finance comes into being. Then people organize the state in the
principle of democracy.

Third, if we look into the role played by language in the growth of the
state, we can also find that language augments the power of ideas. This is
because humans, using language, extend the distance of communication.
Extending the distance of communication bolsters the dissemination of ideas
in the interest of all instead of a few power holders or the upper social classes.
This is unlike the case of using coercion. If a ruler rules a state, he is in
control of the tool of coercion so as to use coercion to keep his rule. If the
masses revolt against him, he may send out policemen or troops to suppress
the revolt of the masses. By contrast, ideas, embraced by the masses, may not
be controlled or easily controlled by him. If he uses coercion to keep his rule,
he may refrain from discussing the issue of justice. He may be able to ignore
the realization of justice in a certain period of time though over the long
term justice must be realized at least to some extent in order to keep his rule.
But on the other hand ideas spread fast and afar. Many people may embrace
an idea. It is not easy for the ruler to prohibit the masses from embracing
a certain idea. If the tool of coercion is available for use, it is usually used
by the ruler. But sometimes the tool of coercion is also used by the masses.
For example, when peasants launched an armed uprising in medieval times,
the peasant uprising army might also use the tool of coercion. The tool of
coercion, used by the ruler, was usually superior to the tool of coercion used
by the revolting peasants. But this case may not always remain unchanged
in history. If thinkers disseminate ideas, these ideas have to be reasonable or

fair for them to be accepted by many ordinary people. As thinkers communicate with the masses over long distances, they always persuade the masses to embrace their ideas. They are unable to force the masses to embrace their ideas. Thus due to the nature of long-distance linguistic communication, those who embrace those ideas should be the majority of the population as long as those ideas are rational. The power of an idea lies in the fact that it has reason. It can be embraced by many people or even all, and thus it can influence many people or even all. In contrast, the tool of coercion may be controlled by a small number of people. Thus, throughout history the ruler always keeps the tool of coercion. But the ruler may not have a reasonable idea to support himself. By contrast, ordinary people usually do not have the tool of coercion, but they often embrace a reasonable idea. Thus the tool of coercion and a reasonable idea become adversaries when the ruler and the masses enter into a confrontation. Sometimes the ruler is very powerful because he keeps a tool of coercion. But over the long term the masses will get the upper hand. This is mainly because the relevant power of the tool of coercion, controlled by the ruler, largely remains unchanged over time. The ruler is capable of organizing the regime and commanding an army. The opposition may also organize itself and build an army to confront the army of the authorities. The army, controlled by the authorities, may use advanced weapons. The opposition may also use advanced weapons. But the ideas keep on changing. As humans are able to communicate using language, they are able to perform long-distance communication. Then they can accumulate and ameliorate their ideas. As their ideas become more and more rational and convincing, those ideas become more and more powerful. Then the masses may be effectively mobilized by those ideas. Thus those regimes in control of the tool of coercion but not armed with rational and convincing ideas tend to decline over time. Some ideas are especially powerful particularly in those states in which many thinkers emerge in history. One case in point is that in early modern times in Europe the rulers of feudal and despotic states, facing the pressure from the society, were forced to embark on reform and their regimes were later overthrown by the masses in a series of revolutions because the masses embraced the ideas of Enlightenment.

That the society hastens the dissemination of reasonable ideas along with the passage of time can also interpret the historical triumph of reasonable ideas over the violence used in the governance of the state. This is because humans communicate using language and they create various media in support of linguistic communication. Linguistic communication, supported by various media, is instrumental in the dissemination of reasonable ideas. Thus reasonable ideas will spread to every corner of the state quickly. Then reasonable ideas may become very powerful because these ideas motivate thousands of people to act.

That industrialization in early modern times in Europe created many media in support of linguistic communication may prove that the creation of media sooner or later bolsters the dissemination of reasonable ideas. One case in point is that in early modern times industrialization led to urbanization in Europe. Urbanization in turn resulted in the increase of the density of population of each city. People came to reside closer to one another. Then people more often performed linguistic communication with one another. Cities functioned, as media, in support of linguistic communication that reached all. Reasonable political ideas spread quickly. Then a large portion of the population came under the influence of some political ideas, and the power holders of all the states in Europe could no longer govern their states in the original way. They had to be more attentive than ever to the demand from common people in governing the state.

Industrialization also led to the development of printing. Modern printing relies on the industry of machine building. The development of printing enables people to perform linguistic communication directly across the state. That is, before the development of printing, people usually performed linguistic communication in the local area. People were unable to perform direct linguistic communication across the state easily. Political ideas did not spread fast. Then a change took place. Written communication developed across the state due to the development of printing. People also developed some new media. These media enhanced efficiency in communication. For example, the development of printing enhanced efficiency in communication performed by books in the process of disseminating political ideas. Due to the wide reach of printed media, all literate men and women came under the influence of some political ideas. More people expected that the state was governed according to those political ideas.

Industrialization has also been facilitating the growth of certain urban social classes. Industrialization was a social process leading to the emergence of a large working class. Industrialization also contributes to the emergence of a large middle class. As people, belonging to each of such social classes, are in the same or similar situation, or as they have the same or similar social status, it becomes easier for them to unite. They are all dissatisfied with malpractice in the management of modern society from time to time. Industrialization functions to organize a great portion of the population of the state. For example, a large number of the workers work in the factory owned by one employer or a large number of the workers work in the same one industry. The factory or the industry may actually function as a medium in support of the related process of linguistic communication. This situation differs from the situation faced by the class of peasants in rural area in medieval times. In medieval times peasants were under the rule of lords of different regions. The circumstances, faced by them, varied from region to region. The circumstances, faced by people in the city, differ in modern times. Thus if one political idea is disseminated to each of those urban social classes, this political idea may be embraced by all belonging to that urban social class. Then someone may launch a political movement. As a result, people cannot ignore the role played by political ideas in the governance of the state under whatsoever circumstances in modern times.

Because of this, an idea, disseminated by thinkers or philosophers, may be used as a medium. The idea, disseminated by them, may objectively become a medium used by them to communicate with the masses. In the mass society thousands of people, forming the society, are actually organized due to the use of media. The mass society takes form partly due to the development of mass media. Thus, although people vary in age, occupation, the level of income, ethnicity, education background, personal character and hobby, they may embrace the same idea if such an idea is convincing and applicable. Thus political parties may mobilize and organize their supporters in the mass society by disseminating an idea. A conservative party may gain support from a large group of the citizens who hold conservative values. Likewise, a liberal party may also gain support from a large group of the citizens who hold liberal values. Language is actually a powerful medium. An idea can use it to reach the masses. Then a political party can mobilize and organize the masses.

Then thinkers, or philosophers, can use their ideas to influence the masses. Thinkers, or philosophers, in some sense, participate in the governance of the state. The ruler, or the power holder, of the state also often comes under the influence of a related idea. This phenomenon particularly occurs in modern times because more and more valuable, reasonable and applicable ideas, or thoughts, are created and disseminated in modern times. By contrast, coercion, had by the power holder, fails to augment accordingly. If weapons become sophisticated, it is difficult to use them to deal with civilians. The power of ideas augments due to the fact that ideas can develop and spread among civilians.

In the meantime, as thinkers must offer their ideas acceptable by as many people as possible in order to maximize their influence in the state built by people as their largest possible community due to the extension of the distance of linguistic communication, thinkers offer their ideas in favor of love, kindness, liberty, equality, and democracy among others because the related ideas can be embraced by the vast majority of people or even by all. So as long-distance linguistic communication allows for people to come up with more reasonable ideas step by step, civilization gradually substitutes for savagery; and liberty and democracy gradually substitutes for despotism and dictatorship. So after his death Jesus soon became very powerful throughout the world because some great theologians disseminated his idea and millions of people embraced that idea. Similarly, after Martin Luther stuck his thesis to the door of the church of Wittenberg, his idea became very powerful in a great part of Europe. The case is the same so far as a secular idea is concerned. For example, after John Locke expounded his liberal idea and advocated the establishment of the government that respected the freedom of people, he influenced the political progress in England and perhaps many other European states. Likewise, after Jean Jacque Rousseau disseminated his idea of democracy, his idea attracted many ordinary people and many states were built as republics in Europe according to the idea he advocated. A series of changes, taking place in various European states, are ascribed by the scholars to the role played by the thoughts stemming from the thinkers, including abovementioned great thinkers. These thinkers are great because their ideas pushed forward the progress of human civilization. In fact, each ruler of the state rules the state on individual basis. If a ruler rules the state against a progressive idea because the ruling method is irrational while the related progressive idea is rational, each ruler fights against a group of thinkers. The idea, promoted by a thinker, is actually the idea offered by one thinker on the basis of his own speculation in reference of all the reasonable ideas propagated by the predecessors. The ruling method largely remains unchanged, whereas the idea has been evolving. The power of the ruler remains largely unchanged, whereas the power of the idea keeps on augmenting. As a result the philosophical ideas, disseminated by thinkers, become more and more powerful.

That means that in pre-modern times ordinary people were not inspired by thinkers as they were not encouraged to seek any solution of their problems. They were supposed to subject themselves to the rule of the ruler blindly. Politics was reserved for the ruler. In modern times, however, political leaders have begun to mobilize them in the growth of the nation-states since the fall of feudal states because political ideas are disseminated to them. This great change takes place due to many factors. But one fundamental factor should be the fact that the accumulation, amelioration and dissemination of human thoughts are realized in a long process in which the distance of linguistic communication extends step by step. Some scholars may argue that the historical process of democratization, occurring in many states, is due to the economic development. They believe that after the income, had by people, reaches a certain level, the middle class will emerge. The middle class, growing large and powerful, will usually demand democracy. My view is that the state realizes democratization due to the dissemination of those very powerful ideas and those ideas appear in a long historical process established in the process of long -distance linguistic communication. Without extending the distance of linguistic communication, convincing and powerful political ideas might not appear, and hence a wide wave of democratization in modern times might not occur.

This situation further bears testimony to the fact that the formation of the common interest of the state has been impossible unless in the process of linguistic communication since the dissolution of the tribe. Though in the state the interest of the power holder and the interest of the masses may be in conflict from time to time, linguistic communication will work its way in the formation of the common interest of all. The reason is that language not only enables humans to communicate over a long stretch of time and on a large scale, but also facilitates them to build the civilized society. All have common interest since they form the same society. Linguistic communication is significant for the building of the society. Linguistic communication is also the sum of all their social relations. Then, linguistic communication further buttresses the building of the state. This is the grandiose proposition of language. This is also a basic proposition of civilization.

In short, humans, communicating using language, extend the distance of linguistic communication. Extending the distance of linguistic communication results in the expansion of their community. Expanding their community further results in the fact that this community is no longer formed because of kinship. Then people build their community on a new basis. Language plays an essential part in the formation of this community. This community finally becomes the state and the state is finally built in the principle that benefits all forming the state. On one hand, people enhance efficiency in production or in the governance of the community, and on the other hand, people are increasingly enabled to realize justice because more and more people come under the influence of an idea. That is, if an idea is not aimed at realizing justice, it will not be accepted by all or the majority and it will soon lose influence. As a result, language and the application of language in communication in conjunction with media function to make the progress of civilization over the long term. Many years ago Karl Marx asserted that class struggle pushed ahead with the development of human society. He believed that class struggle led to a change in the relation of social production and such a change liberated productive forces. Liberating productive forces resulted in a change in the superstructure. My view is that humans are animals using language. Using language, people create media. They use media. Using media extends the distance of linguistic communication and extending the distance of linguistic communication allows people to build a big market. A big market deepens the division of labor and deepening the division of labor enhances productive forces. Media give a role to language in changing the relation of social production. Then people enhance productive forces with the new relations of social production. They build the corresponding state. People realize the progress of their society and their civilization because they use language in conjunction with media rather than waging any class struggle. In the meantime, extending the distance of communication leads to the flourishing of culture which generates ideas for the progress of society.

Based on the above judgment, I argue that the proposition of language may help us study the proposition of civilization. Language enables humans to exploit their potential in producing goods and providing services because language plays a role in the building of a large community in which they build a market or a society for the development of division of labor. Language plays a part in the building of a large community which necessitates the development of an administrative system that provides public services to the masses. Language also enables humans to communicate effectively on a large scale so as to disseminate a variety of knowledge and ideas. Such knowledge and ideas drive the society to make steady progress. Language has already preset the whole process of human civilization. If we intend to probe how humans create civilization, we should pay attention to the interrelationship between humans and language. Humans create their civilization because they use language. Using language, humans even create media. Media give a role to language in changing the society and the state. If we believe that we can build a theoretical edifice of the interrelationship between humans and language, it is arguable that we can found a new branch of learning about civilization called the "science of civilization." In doing so, we may further explore systematically how human society makes its progress and how human civilization makes its progress as well. I hope that scholars, interested in this regard, can join each other to build this new branch of learning one day. I expect that day to come in future.

Notes

1. Adam Smith, *The Wealth of Nations* with an Introduction by D.D. Raphael (New York: Alfred A. Knopf, 1991), 15.
2. Please see: Ibid., 15–16.
3. Jack Goody, *The Logic of Writing and the Organization of Society* (Cambridge: Cambridge University Press, 1986), 90.
4. Hans Kelsen, *General Theory of Law and State* (New Brunswick: Transaction Publisher, 2006), 292.

5. E.N. Gladden, *A History of Public Administration, Vol.2: From the Eleventh Century to the Present Day* (London: Frank Cass and Company Limited, 1972), 366.

6. Bertrand Russell, *Power* (New York: W.W. Norton & Company, Inc., 1938), 11.

7. Charles de Secondat, Baron de Montesquieu, *The Spirit of Laws*, translated by Thomas Nugent (Chicago: Encyclopaedia Britannica, Inc., 1952), 12.

8. Mémoires de Caulaincourt; cited from Bertrand de Jouvenel, *On Power: Its Nature and the History of Its Growth*, translated by J.F. Huntington (Boston: Beacon Press, 1967), 117.

9. Alexis de Tocqueville, *Democracy in America*, translated by George Lawrence (New York: Harper Perennial, 1988), 525.

10. See: G.E. Aylmer, *The King's Servants: The Civil Service of Charles I, 1625–1642* (New York: Columbia University Press, 1961), 440; cited from Wolfram Fischer and Peter Lundgreen, *The Recruitment and Training of Administrative and Technical Personnel*, in Charles Tilly (ed.), *The Formation of National States in Western Europe* (Princeton, New Jersey: Princeton University Press, 1975), 461.

11. Wolfram Fischer and Peter Lundgreen, *The Recruitment and Training of Administrative and Technical Personnel,* in Tilly (ed.), *The Formation of National States in Western Europe* , 459.

12. Jos C.N. Raadschelders, *Handbook of Administrative History* (New Brunswick, U.S.A.: Transaction Publishers, 1998), 151.

13. Ibid.

14. Ibid., 109.

15. The Government of UK, *History and Functions of Government Departments* (London: HMS O Publications Centre, 1993), 4-5.

16. Please see: Ibid., 32, 36, 40, 49, 53, 82, 98, 101, 106.

17. Smith, *The Wealth of Nations*, 356-357.

18. Rudolf Braun, *Taxation, Sociopolitical Structure, and State-Building: Great Britain and Brandenburg-Prussia*, in Tilly (ed.), *The Formation of National States in Western Europe*, 264–265.

19. Ibid., 281–282.

Acknowledgements

In writing out this book, I got a benefit from the speculation of some great predecessors who explored the objective world in their academic domains. In order to extend my thanks to them and to clarify to what extent I got a benefit from the academic achievements made by those predecessors in my research, I would like to set forth them one by one in the following and explain exactly which of their writings were used in reference in writing out my monograph.

The first predecessor among them is Adam Smith, whose famous book *The Wealth of Nations* was a favorable book read by me in writing my manuscript. This book is the one in the purview of classical economics. But some of the arguments presented in this book are worth engaging in philosophical speculation further. For example, Smith stated that humans can exchange goods while animals cannot. His idea reminded me of the feasibility of analyzing the relationship between the use of language and exchange as well as the relationship between language and peace. The role of language in the making and maintenance of peace is particularly stressed by me in this book due to the fact that animals cannot make peace while humans can because humans can speak.

The second predecessor is Harold A. Innis, a Canadian historian. Although Innis was a historian, he showed strong interest in the exploration of the role of media in the growth of civilization. He is, in some sense, remembered by Canadian scholars and even the scholars from across the world because of two books by him, namely, *The Bias of Communication* and *Empire and Communications*. As his writings focused on media, my writing about the role of language in state growth in Part One of this book in the beginning gets some benefits from some of his ideas.

The third predecessor is Thomas Hobbes. His book *Leviathan* was often read by me when I wrote this manuscript. When I wrote certain contents about law or government, I felt the need to consult his book. His insightful writing often sharpened my view about the formation of the state. He did not view the law or the government or the state from the perspective of language. Yet, his description was indeed useful when I wrote about the role of language in state organization. He focused on the action of humans. Language, however, is always used in the mutual interaction between one and another because language and action always interact with each other. Thus his book was one of the most useful books consulted by me.

The fourth predecessor is Immanuel Kant. His book *Fundamental Principles of the Metaphysic of Morals* translated by Thomas Kingsmill Abbott and another book *Perpetual Peace and Other Essays on Politics, History, and Morals* translated by Ted Humphrey are the main books read by me. Particularly, some of his invented views supported my observation of freedom and the principle of publicity.

The fifth predecessor is G. W. F. Hegel. His book *The Philosophy of Right* translated by T.M. Knox and *The Philosophy of History* translated by J. Sibree were two main books read by me. His writing is not in direct relation to the role of language in the building or organization of the state. However, his writing was often referred to when I wrote my manuscript because with his idea something could always be written to adduce my argument about the role of language.

The sixth predecessor is John Stuart Mill. His book *Representative Government* and *On Liberty* are well-known. His analysis has no relevance to the role of language. But whenever the role of language was mentioned, his observation and idea could often be used to write out the chapters that focused on language. For example, his idea about freedom of speech was absorbed by me to enrich my argument when I studied the correlation between language and freedom. Drawing his idea, I highlighted the role of language particularly in the description of state rationalization.

The seventh predecessor is Jeremy Bentham. His book *Of Laws in General* and book *Securities against Misrule and Other Constitutional Writings for Tripoli and Greece* edited by Philip Schofield were read by me. His imaginations about the social effect of law and the principle of publicity were unique.

Some of his ideas inspired me when I wrote about law and justice. I am grateful to him.

The eighth predecessor is Hans Kelsen, whose book *General Theory of Law and State* and book *Pure Theory of Law* translated by Max Knight were read by me when I wrote about quite a few chapters of this book. Though he focused mainly on the issue of law, his writing covered a wide range. His writings about politics and ideology beside law were helpful to my writing indeed.

The ninth predecessor is Peter Blau. His book *Exchange and Power in Social Life* was read by me. I am indebted to his idea in writing about the role of consciousness as a medium in state formation, about promise and others. His book focuses mainly on social interaction. As language is also used for social interaction, I studied social interaction from the perspective of language in reference of his book. Reading his book resulted in the invention of some new ideas presented in my monograph.

The tenth predecessor is Bertrand Russell. He wrote many books. The book *On Power* is the only one read by me when I wrote this manuscript. His vision was very broad. His insights displayed in this book reminded me of some aspects needing further description. Social or political life observed by him was a rich raw material for political analysis. In the meantime, some of his ideas shed light on my way to build an inventive theory of the state at the angle of language.

The eleventh predecessor is Hans-Georg Gadamer, a German philosopher. His book *Truth and Method* translated by Joel Weinsheimer and Donald G. Marshall was the main reference book read by me. Without his description the writing of Chapter Six about interpretation would not have been so smooth. Though I viewed interpretation from the perspective of language only, Hermeneutics created by those predecessors, particularly Gadamer, became a philosophical basis for me to write that chapter.

The twelfth predecessor is Ferdinand de Saussure. His book *Course in General Linguistics* was read several times when I wrote my manuscript. He especially studied linguistics. But language is related to social interaction. His linguistics was sometimes a basis for me to probe state formation and state rationality from the perspective of language because there is a close relationship between language and the mutual interaction of humans. In some sense, the structure of language is the structure of society. As a result, his book mentioned by me here is very helpful.

In addition, I should extend my thanks to Richmond Public Library (particularly Interlibrary Loan Division) of British Columbia for their support. Without the books borrowed through the warm service of this public library, this manuscript cannot be written out. I should thank Paul Fish, who operates U.S. Certified Translation Service, for giving me a part-time translation job for me to survive in a long period of time and for giving me some advices on how to write idiomatic English. I am very grateful to him for giving me his support.

Lastly, I would like to extend my thanks to all other scholars who helped me in my writing out this manuscript. Without their help, it would have been impossible to write out this treatise indeed. Due to the length limitation of the presentation, however, I am unable to set forth these scholars one by one. Please refer to the bibliography for details about the books of all scholars read by me in writing out this manuscript. I extend my heartfelt thanks to them all indeed.

Xing Yu
British Columbia, Canada
Date: March 24, 2021

Bibliography

Adams, James Truslow, *The Epic of America*. Boston: Little, Brown, 1930.

Ahdar, Rex and Ian Leigh, *Religious Freedom in the Liberal State*. Oxford: Oxford University Press, 2005.

Aquinas, Saint Thomas. *The Summa Theological of Saint Thomas Aquinas*. Chicago: Encyclopaedia Britannica, Inc.,,1952.Vol. 1.

Aristotle, *The Nicomachean Ethics*, translated by Harris Rackham. Hertfordshire:Wordsworth Editions Limited, 1996.

The Politics of Aristotle, translated by Peter L. Phillips Simpson. Chapel Hill: The University of North Carolina Press, 1997.

Atiyah, P.S. *Promises, Morals, and Law.* Oxford: Clarendon Press, 1981.

Bentham, Jeremy. *Of Laws in General*, edited by H. L. A. Hart. London: The Athlone Press, University of London, 1970.

Securities against Misrule and Other Constitutional Writings for Tripoli and Greece, edited by Philip Schofield. Oxford: Clarendon Press, 1990.

The Works of Jeremy Bentham, Vol. IV and Vol. VI, published under the superintendence of John Bowring. London: Simpkin, Marshall, & Co., 1843.

Berkhofer, Robert F. Jr. *Beyond the Great Story: History as Text and Discourse*. Cambridge, Massachusetts: The Belknap Press of Harvard University Press, 1995.

Blanning, Tim. *The Culture of Power and the Power of Culture:Old Regime Europe 1660—1789.* Oxford: Oxford University Press, 2002.

Blau, Peter M. *Exchange and Power in Social Life*. New York: John Wiley & Sons, Inc., 1964.

Bodin, Jean. *Six Books of the Commonwealth*, abridged and translated by M.J. Tooley. Oxford: Basil Blackwell,1955.

Bowman, Alan K. and Greg Woolf (ed.). *Literacy and Power in the Ancient World*. Cambridge: Cambridge University Press, 1994.

Buckler, W. H. *The Origin and History of Contract in Roman Law Down to the End of the Republican Period*. Littleton, Colorado: Fred. B. Rothman & Co., 1983.

Burke, Peter. *Languages and Communities in Early Modern Europe*. Cambridge: Cambridge University Press, 2004.

Bury, J.B. *A History of Freedom of Thought*. New York: Henry Holt And Company, 1913.

Chadwick, Owen. *The Secularization of the European Mind in the Nineteenth Century*. Cambridge: Cambridge University Press, 1975.

Cipolla, Carlo M. *Literacy and Development in the West*. Baltimore, Maryland: Penguin Books, 1969.

Connor, James. *The Sociology of Loyalty*. New York: Springer Science & Business Media, LLC, 2007.

Croce, Benedetto. *History, Its Theory and Practice*, translated by Douglas Ainslie. New York: Russell & Russell, 1960.

Deuel, Leo. *Testaments of Time: The Search for Lost Manuscripts & Records*. New York: Alfred A. Knopf, 1965.

Deutsch, Karl W. *Nationalism and Alternatives*. New York: Alfred A. Knopf, Inc., 1969.

Dietrich, Richard F. *British Drama 1890 to 1950: A Critical History*. Boston: Twayne Publishers, 1989.

Diringer, David. *The Book Before Printing: Ancient, Medieval and Oriental*. New York: Dover Publications, Inc., 1982.

Disraeli, Isaac. *Curiosities of Literature*, Vol. II. Boston: William Veazie, 1858.

Duxbury, Neil. *Random Justice: On Lotteries and Legal Decision-Making.* Oxford: Oxford University Press, 1999.

Eisenstein, Elisabeth. *The Printing Revolution in Early Modern Europe.* Cambridge: Cambridge University Press, 1983.

Eliot, Simon and Jonathan Rose (ed.). *A Companion to the History of the Book.* Malden, MA, USA: Blackwell Publishing, 2007.

Ellul, Jacques. *Propaganda: The Formation of Men's Attitude*, translated by Konrad Kellen and Jean Lerner. New York: Vintage Books, 1973.

Engels, Frederick. *The Origin of the Family, Private Property and the State.* New York: International Publishers, 1972.

Fischer, Steven Roger. *A History of Writing.* London: Reaktion Books Ltd, 2001.

Fried, Charles. *Contract as Promise: a Theory of Contractual Obligation.* Cambridge: Harvard University Press, 1981.

Friedrich, Carl Choachim. *Man and His Government: An Empirical Theory of Politics.* New York: McGraw-Hill Book Company, Inc.,1963.

Gadamer, Hans-Georg. *Truth and Method*, translated by Joel Weinsheimer and Donald G. Marshall. London: Continuum, 1975.

Galtung, Johan, *Peace by Peaceful Means: Peace and Conflict, Development and Civilization.* London: Sage Publications, 1996.

Gill, Anthony. *The Political Origins of Religious Liberty.* New York: Cambridge University Press, 2008.

Gladden, E. N. *A History of Public Administration, Vol.1: From Earliest Times to the Eleventh Century ; Vol.2: From the Eleventh Century to the Present Day.* London: Frank Cass and Company Limited, 1972.

Gnanadesikan, Amalia E. *The Writing Revolution: Cuneiform to Internet.* Chichester, West Sussex, UK: Wiley-Blackwell, 2009.

Goody, Jack. *The Interface between the Written and the Oral.* Cambridge: Cambridge University Press, 1987.

The Logic of Writing and Organization of Society. Cambridge: Cambridge University Press, 1986.

The Power of the Written Tradition. Washington: Smithsonian Institution Press, 2000.

Gough, J. W. *The Social Contract: a Critical Study of Its Development*, Oxford: The Clarendon Press, 1957

Graber, Doris A. *Verbal Behavior and Politics*. Urbana: University of Illinois Press, 1976.

Grodzins, Morton. *The Loyal and the Disloyal: Social Boundaries of Patriotism and Treason*. Chicago: The University of Chicago Press, 1956.

Grondin, Jean. *Introduction to Philosophical Hermeneutics*, translated by Joel Weinsheimer. New Haven: Yale University Press, 1991.

Habermas, Jürgen. *The Structural Transformation of the Public Sphere: an Inquiry into a Category of Bourgeois Society*, translated by Thomas Burger. Cambridge, Massachusetts, The MIT Press, 1991.

Harris, Roy. *The Language-Makers*. Ithaca, New York: Cornell University Press,1980.

Harrison, Lawrence E. and Samuel P. Huntington (ed.). *Culture Matters: How Values Shape Human Progress*. New York: Basic Books, 2000.

Hayes, Kevin J. *The Road to Monticello: the Life and Mind of Thomas Jefferson* (Oxford: Oxford University Press, 2007.

Hegel, G.W.F. *Aesthetics, Lectures on Fine Art*, Vol.1, translated by T.M. Knox. London: Oxford University Press,1975.

The Philosophy of History, translated by J. Sibree. Chicago: Encyclopaedia Britannica, Inc., 1952.

The Philosophy of Right, translated by T.M. Knox. Chicago: Encyclopaedia Britannica, Inc., 1952.

Herbst, Susan. *Numbered Voices: How Opinion Polling Has Shaped American Politics*. Chicago: The University of Chicago Press, 1993.

Hirst, John. *The Shortest History of Europe*. Collingwood, Victoria: Black Inc., 2009.

Hobbes, Thomas. *Leviathan*, edited with an introduction by C. B. Macpherson. New York: Penguin Books, 1985.

Hui, Victoria Tin-bor. *War and State Formation in Ancient China and Early Modern Europe*. Cambridge: Cambridge University Press, 2005.

Humboldt, Wilhelm von. *On Language: The Diversity of Human Language-Structure and its Influence on the Mental Development of Mankind*, translated by Peter Heath. Cambridge: Cambridge University Press, 1988.

Innis, Harold A. *Empire and Communications*. Victoria: Press Porcépic Limited, 1986.

Johnson, Paul. *The Birth of the Modern: World Society 1815–1830*. New York: Harper Collins Publishers, 1991.

The Renaissance: A Short History. New York: Random House Inc., 2000.

Joseph, John E. *Language and Identity: National, Ethnic, Religious*. New York: Palgrave Macmillan, 2004.

Jouvenel, Bertrand de. *Sovereignty: an Inquiry into the Political Good*, translated by J. F. Huntington. Chicago: The University Press of Chicago, 1957.

On Power: Its Nature and the History of Its Growth, translated by J. F. Huntington. Boston: Beacon Press, 1967.

Junkin, David Xavier. *The Oath: a Divine Ordinance and an Element of the Social Constitution*. New York: Wiley And Putman, 161 Broadway, 1845.

Kant, Immanuel. *Fundamental Principles of the Metaphysic of Morals*, translated by Thomas Kingsmill Abbott. Chicago: Encyclopaedia Britannica, Inc., 1952.

Perpetual Peace and Other Essays on Politics, History, and Morals. Annapolis: Hackett Publishing Company, 1983.

Keightley, David N. *Sources of Shang History: the Oracle-Bone Inscriptions of Bronze Age China*. Berkeley: University of California Press, 1978.

Kelsen, Hans. *General Theory of Law and State*. New Brunswick, U.S.A.: Transaction Publishers, 2006.

Pure Theory of Law, translated by Max Knight. Berkeley: University of California Press, 1967.

Kertzer, David I. *Ritual, Politics and Power*. New Haven: Yale University Press, 1988.

Leiter, Brian. *Why Tolerate Religion?*. Princeton: Princeton University Press, 2013.

Lessnoff, Michael. *Social Contract*. Atlantic Highlands, NJ: Humanities Press International, Inc, 1986.

Lind, E. Allan and Tom R. Tyler. *The Social Psychology of Procedural Justice*. New York: Plenum Press, 1988.

Locke, John. *A Letter Concerning Toleration*. Indianapolis, Indiana: Hackett Publishing Company, 1983.

Second Treatise of Government, edited by C.B. Macpherson. Indianapolis, Indiana: Hackett Publishing Company, Inc.,1980.

Lyons, Martyn. *Books: A Living History*. Los Angeles: The J. Paul Getty Museum, 2011.

Machiavelli, Niccolò. *The Prince*, translated by W.K. Marriott. New York: Alfred A. Knopf, 1992.

Maine, Henry. *Ancient Law*. London: John Murray,1866.

Martin, Henri-Jean. *The History and Power of Writing*, translated by Lydia G. Gochrane. Chicago: The University of Chicago Press, 1994.

Marx, Karl. *Capital: A Critical Analysis of Capitalist Production*, translated by Samuel Moore and Edward Aveling and edited by Frederick Engels. New York: Appleton & Co., 1889.

Miles, Steven H. *Hippocratic Oath and the Ethics of Medicine*. New York: Oxford University Press, 2004.

Mill, John Stuart. *On Liberty, Representative Government and Utilitarianism*. Chicago: Encyclopaedia Britannica, Inc.,1952.

Mises, Ludwig von. *Free and Prosperous Commonwealth, an Exposition of the Ideas of Classical Liberalism*, translated by Ralph Raico and edited by Arthur Goddard. Princeton: D. Van Nostrand Company, Inc., 1962.

Moats, Sandra. *Celebrating the Republic: Presidential Ceremony and Popular Sovereignty, from Washington to Monroe.* DeKalb: Northern Illinois University Press, 2010.

Montesquieu, Charles de Secondat, Baron de. *The Spirit of Laws*, translated by Thomas Nugent. Chicago: William Benton, 1952.

Morris, Desmond. *The Human Zoo.* New York: McGraw-Hill Book Company,1969.

Muller, Jerry Z. (ed.). *Conservatism: an Anthology of Social and Political Thought from David Hume to the Present.* Princeton: Princeton University Press, 1997.

Murray, Albert Victor. *The State and the Church in a Free Society.* Cambridge: Cambridge University Press, 1958.

Mutschler, Fritz-Heiner and Achim Mittag (ed.). *Conceiving the Empire China and Rome Compared.* Oxford: Oxford University Press, 2008.

Nathanson, Stephen. *Patriotism, Morality, and Peace.* Lanham: Rowman & Littlefield Publishers, Inc., 1993.

Newport, Frank. *Polling Matters: Why Leaders Must Listen to the Wisdom of the People.* New York: Warner Books, 2004.

Norman, E. R. *The Conscience of the State in North America.* London: Cambridge University Press, 1968.

Nussbaum, Martha C. *Liberty of Conscience: in Defense of America's Tradition of Religious Equality.* New York: Basic Books, 2008.

Olson, Mancur. *The Logic of Collective Action, Public Goods and the Theory of Groups.* Cambridge, Massachusetts: Harvard University Press, 1971.

Oppenheimer, Franz. *The State.* Montréal, Canada: Black Rose Books, 2007.

Peyrefitte, Alain. *Le Mal français.* Paris: Librairie Plon, 1976.

Plutarch. *The Lives of the Noble Grecians and Romans*, the Dryden Translation. Chicago: Encyclopaedia Britannica, Inc., 1952.

Poe, Marshall T. *A History of Communications: Media and Society from the Evolution of Speech to the Internet*. Cambridge: Cambridge University Press, 2011.

Raadschelders, Jos C.N. *Handbook of Administrative History*. New Brunswick, U.S.A.: Transaction Publishers, 1998.

Ricoeur, Paul. *Interpretation Theory: Discourse and the Surplus of Meaning*. Fort Worth, Texas: The Texas Christian University Press, 1976.

Robert, Vincent. *Les chemins de la manifestation, 1848–1914*. Lyon: Presses Universitaires de Lyon, 1996.

Rokeach, Milton (ed.). *Understanding Human Values*. New York: The Free Press, 1979.

Rousseau, Jean Jacques. *A Dissertation on the Origin and Foundation of the Inequality of Mankind*. Chicago: Encyclopaedia Britannica, Inc., 1952.

On the Origin of Language translated by John H. Moran and Alexander Gode. New York: Frederick Ungar Publishing Co., Ltd, 1966.

Social Contract. Chicago: Encyclopaedia Britannica, Inc., 1952.

Royce, Josiah. *The Philosophy of Loyalty*. New York: The Macmillan Company, 1924.

Russell, Bertrand. *Power*. New York: W.W. Norton & Company, Inc., 1938.

Sabine, George H. *A History of Political Theory*. (London: George G Harrap & Co., Ltd, 1937.

Sartori, Giovanni. *The Theory of Democracy Revisited*. Chatham, New Jersey: Chatham House Publishers, Inc.,1987.

Saussure, Ferdinand de. *Courses in General Linguistics,* translated. by Wade Baskin. New York: McGraw-Hill Book Company, 1966.

Schlesinger, Herbert J. *Promises, Oaths, and Vows: on the Psychology of Promising*. New York: The Analytic Press, 2009.

Schumpeter, Joseph A. *Capitalism, Socialism and Democracy*. London: Routledge, 1976.

Sen, Amartya. *The Idea of Justice*. Cambridge, Massachusetts: The Belknap Press of Harvard University Press, 2009.

Shklar, Judith N. *Political Thought and Political Thinkers*, edited by Stanley Hoffmann. Chicago: The University of Chicago Press, 1998.

Smith, Adams. *The Wealth of Nations*, with an Introduction by D.D. Raphael. New York: Alfred A. Knopf, 1991.

Spinoza, Baruch. *Theological Political Treatise*, translated by Samuel Shirley. Indianapolis: Hackett Publishing Company, 1998.

Spinoza, Benedict. *The Ethics and Other Works*, translated by Edwin Curley. Princeton: Princeton University Press, 1994.

Splichal, Slavko. *Principles of Publicity and Free Press*. Lanham: Rowman & Littlefield Publishers, Inc., 2002.

Sprayer, Joseph R. *On the Medieval Origins of the Modern State*. Princeton, New Jersey: Princeton University Press, 1970.

Starr, Paul. *The Creation of the Media: Political Origins of Modern Communications*. New York: Basic Books, 2004.

Thompson, Daniel V. *The Materials and Techniques of Medieval Painting* (New York: Dover Publications, Inc., 1956.

Tilly, Charles. ed.: *The Formation of National States in Western Europe*. Princeton, New Jersey: Princeton University Press, 1975.

Social Movements, 1768–2004. Boulder: Paradigm Publishers, 2004.

Tocqueville, Alexis de. *Democracy in America*, translated by George Lawrence. New York: Harper Perennial, 1988.

Tyler, James Endell. *Oaths: Their Origin, Nature and History*. London: John W. Parker, West Strand, 1834.

Tzu, Sun. *The Art of War*, edited by James Clavell. New York: Delacorte Press, 1983.

Veblen, Thorstein. *What Veblen Taught: Selected Writings of Thorstein Veblen.* New York: the Viking Press Inc., 1964.

Vinogradoff, Paul. *The Growth of the Manor.* London: George Allen & Unwin Ltd, 1951.

Vossler, Karl. *The Spirit of Language in Civilization,* translated by Oscar Oeser. London: Routledge & Kegan Paul, Ltd, 1951.

Waquet, Françoise. *Latin or the Empire of a Sign: From the Sixteenth to the Twentieth Centuries,* translated by John Howe. London: Verso, 2001.

Warburton, Nigel. *Free Speech: a Very Short Introduction.* Oxford: Oxford University Press, 2009.

Weaver, Richard M. *Ideas Have Consequences.* Chicago: The University of Chicago Press, 1984.

Williams, Roger. *On Religious Liberty,* edited and with an Introduction by James Calvin Davis. Cambridge, Massachusetts: The Belknap Press of Harvard University Press, 2008.

Index

SUBJECTS

AUTHORS

About the Author

Xing Yu, a political scientist, was born in 1955 in Nanjing, China. He worked in two universities successively in China from 1980s to 1990s. He obtained a Bachelor of Arts degree after his four-year study in the major English in the Department of English, Sichuan Foreign Languages Institute in Chongqing, China from 1978 to 1982 and he further obtained a Master of Laws degree after his three-year study in the major international politics in the Department of International Politics of Fudan University in Shanghai, China from 1982 to 1985. This manuscript is the result of his over 20-year effort in academic research. He now lives in the Province of British Columbia, Canada.

CPSIA information can be obtained
at www.ICGtesting.com
Printed in the USA
BVHW011514300422
635743BV00014B/349/J

9 781039 125179